COMMERCIAL DIVER TRAINING MANUAL

CW00544241

COMMERCIAL DIVER TRAINING MANUAL

Hal Lomax

BEST PUBLISHING COMPANY

The opinions expressed in this work are those of the author and do not reflect the opinions of Best Publishing Company or its editors.

Information contained in this work has been obtained by Best Publishing Company from sources believed to be reliable. However, neither Best Publishing Company nor its author guarantees the accuracy or completeness of any information published herein, and neither Best Publishing Company nor its author shall be responsible for any errors, omissions, or claims for damages, including exemplary damages, arising out of use, inability to use, or with regard to the accuracy or sufficiency of the information contained in this publication.

The editor, author, publisher, or any other party associated with the production of this diving manual does not accept responsibility for any accident or injury resulting from the use of materials contained herein. Diving is an activity that has inherent risks. An individual may experience injury that can result in disability or death. All persons who wish to engage in diving activities must receive professional instructions. This diving manual does not constitute legal, medical, or other professional advice. Information in this publication is current as of the date of the printing.

All rights reserved. No part of this book may be reproduced, stored in a retrieval system, or transmitted in any form or by any means, electronic, mechanical, photocopying, recording, or otherwise, without written permission from the publisher.

Copyright 2016 by Best Publishing Company

Front cover photo courtesy of Cygnus Instruments

Back cover photo courtesy of Stanley Hydraulics

All interior photos/diagrams/tables are from the author unless otherwise indicated.

ISBN: 978-1-930536-95-1

Library of Congress Control Number: 2016945093

Best Publishing Company
631 US Highway 1, Suite 307
North Palm Beach, FL 33408

TABLE OF CONTENTS

INTRODUCTION

The 6th Edition of the *Commercial Diver Training Manual* represents an almost total rewrite. Where previous editions were designed to be utilized in conjunction either with the *NOAA Diving Manual* or the *U.S. Navy Diving Manual*, the 6th Edition has been written as a stand-alone work that covers history, physics, physiology, diving medicine, and first aid in addition to those chapters devoted to diving technique, diving equipment, and working underwater.

This manual is presented with the understanding that fully qualified instructors experienced in underwater work will provide any further explanation required by the reader. At the same time, the intent was to provide a manual to enhance both the theoretical and the practical training of the diver, with a vision of producing graduates that are more knowledgeable and well-informed in their chosen trade, performing their assigned tasks in a safe and productive manner. To that end, this manual strives to present the following: diving physics in a clear, concise manner; the latest theory and procedure in physiology and diving medicine; the latest in practice and procedure both inland and offshore; and the most commonly used diving and support equipment accepted for use in today's industry.

While it is understood it would require several volumes to address every conceivable task performed on every type of underwater project employing commercial divers, this manual endeavors to cover the most commonly performed tasks and the most common underwater operations. By presenting these more common projects and tasks in detail, it is hoped the reader will be better informed and better prepared for a career underwater. In addition, by further illustrating both technique and safety concerns with case studies and personal accounts from the author's career, the manual shows the reader these are more than just words being presented: suggestions help the reader become more proficient and safety guidelines keep the reader from injury or death. That is the real intent of this manual.

PREFACE

Most of my extended family were and are commercial fishermen. But, like most families, we had one uncle who was different. My great-uncle Snooks was a commercial hard-hat diver. Once, when I was about five, Snooks set his copper MKV helmet on my head. I still remember looking through the faceplate and thinking, "Yup, I want to do this." I asked that man a lot of questions, and he answered every last one of them. I kept that dream and became a commercial diver.

Back when I started out, there were no commercial diving schools; divers were either trained by the navy or they were trained on the job. As for me, I got really lucky: Most of the divers I worked with starting out were ex-military, and I was their "pet project." Those men taught me everything they had learned in their training, and everything they had learned the hard way after their training had finished. I spent just as much time as I possibly could under the water, and when I absolutely had to be on surface, I usually had my head stuck in the *U.S. Navy Diving Manual*, trying to learn as much as possible about the job.

As a diver, I ended up working on every type of underwater project imaginable, with some very interesting people, in a lot of different places. I never forgot the people who answered all the questions I had; the people who helped me learn to be a diver and a seaman. I met a few people who considered knowledge to be "trade secrets" that you keep all to yourself, as if sharing knowledge would somehow harm you. As for me, I always enjoyed teaching the younger divers the "tricks of the trade" and sharing what was passed on to me. That is the whole reason behind the books I have written; I am a diver, not an author, but the books allow me to pass things on to more people.

There are quite a few people who helped out with this manual, all of whom I owe a debt of gratitude. My friend CPO1 Charles Trombley, MMM, CD, RCN (Retired), provided the initial technical editing on the physics, physiology, and hyperbaric emergency chapters. Charley is the guy who ran the manned testing of the DCIEM Diving Tables a few years back when he was still with the Experimental Diving Unit. He then went on to be Chief Diver, Fleet Diving Unit Atlantic until he hung up the helmet. Then there is Don Barthelmess, Professor of Marine Diving Technology at Santa Barbara City College (the oldest commercial diving school in North America). Don provided the overall technical editing on the entire manual. Another old friend, Darin Baumann, saturation supervisor, provided technical editing on the saturation chapter along with photos, and my friend Nick Gill, a saturation diver, provided some excellent photos as well. And then there is my old buddy Barry Humphrey: Barry and I spent an awful lot of time together on diving projects before he "retired" to run ROVs. Barry provided technical editing on the ROV chapter. There is one other friend who provided constructive input and editing on the salvage chapter, but he wishes to remain anonymous; you know who you are, and you know that I appreciate the help. As always, my wife, Myra, tolerated me having my mind on the manuscript for so long and gave me a ton of good ideas to use in the book. I am not going to forget the folks at Best Publishing Company – always there for me. Thanks so much, every one of you.

I sincerely hope the young divers who use this manual have a great career; I also hope this book has helped you understand your job and keeps you safe. This book is dedicated to all of you young divers and to the old diver, my Uncle Snooks. I wish he had lived to see this.

Hal Lomax

1.0 COMMERCIAL DIVING HISTORY

1.1 ANCIENT DIVING METHODS

Humans have been on earth for a very long time, at least several thousand years. Archeological evidence may not prove exactly how long men have been here, but it does prove one thing: From the earliest times, man has operated on the seas. Whether it was fishing for food, moving cargo, moving armies, or fighting battles, they were constantly on the water. Writings, drawings, and archeological evidence from some of the earliest civilizations show this to be a fact. Written records and drawings have also been found that show for as long as humans have worked on the water, they have tried to work under the water as well.

1.1.1 Breath-Hold Diving

It is common knowledge the Japanese and Koreans had pearl divers, but many are not aware the Arabs did also. The city of Dubai on the Persian Gulf was originally founded over one thousand years ago as a center for trade and pearl diving; today it is the central location for oil-field diving in the Persian Gulf.

The earliest references to commercial diving have been found in ancient Greek and Roman documents. The Greeks had both military and sponge divers, and ports in the Roman Empire employed divers to retrieve cargo lost overboard over two thousand years ago. Attempting to perform work underwater was not a phenomenon exclusive to any one civilization or country. All of these early divers, however, had one common problem— their bottom time was limited to the length of time they could hold one breath.

Arab pearl diver (Persian Gulf area)
Photo courtesy of wain.yamsafer.me

Traditional Japanese pearl diver
Photo courtesy of Wikipedia

1.1.2 Bladders, Bells, and Armored Diving Suits

To extend the underwater working time, there were many inventions over the centuries: bladders full of air, bells full of air, and armored diving suits. The Greeks had primitive diving bells, and a British astronomer, Dr. Edmund Halley, designed a wooden diving bell in 1691 which was used for salvage until diving helmets were invented over a century later. An armored suit built by John Lethbridge was used to salvage silver ingots in 1718 from a shipwreck off the Cape Verde Islands. This contraption was a forerunner of today's one atmosphere diving suits (ADS), but it had no way of renewing the operator's air supply as today's suits do. It was not until the diving helmets of the Deane brothers (1829) and Augustus Siebe (1830), however, that the time a diver could work underwater was no longer severely restricted.

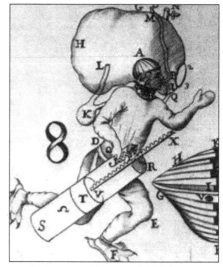

Early drawing of diving with bladder
Photo courtesy of divingheritage.org

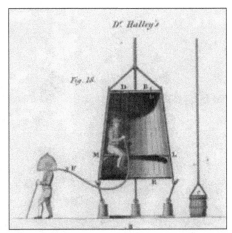

Drawing of Haley's wood stave diving bell
Photo courtesy of divingheritage.org

John Lethbridge's armored diving suit
Photo courtesy of U.S. Navy

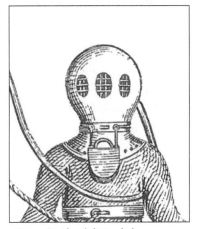

Deane Brothers' diving helmet
Photo courtesy of *Magazine of Science* 1842

Augustus Siebe's diving helmet
Photo courtesy of divingheritage.org

Siebe's suit and helmet
Photo courtesy of divingheritage.org

1.2 MODERN DIVING METHODS

1.2.1 Surface-Supplied Air Diving

The Deanes and Siebe created helmets that allowed the diver to breathe air from the surface, and they ushered in a new era of working underwater. The Deane's design was prone to flooding, so Siebe's helmet was used by the Royal Navy on the salvage of the HMS *Royal George* and became the accepted design. The MKV diving helmet was based directly on Siebe's design and became the primary helmet for the U.S. Navy diver until 1984, when it was replaced by a modern fiberglass and brass helmet, the MK12.

U.S. Navy diver, dressed in MKV gear and in the stage ready to descend
Photo courtesy of U.S. Navy

The MKV (or similar designs based on it) was the workhorse of virtually every navy in the world for 150 years.

The navy divers, however, were not the only ones using the MKV. Commercial divers worldwide began using various versions of the hat, which became known as "Standard Heavy Gear." In the United States, the MKV was built by Morse, Schrader, and DESCO, and in later years, a lighter version by Kirby-Morgan. In Canada, it was built by John Date & Co; in the UK it was built by

Siebe Gorman; and the Japanese, Italians, and Russians each built their own versions. These MKV hats were a breast plate mounted free-flow helmet. They were worn with standard divers dress, which consisted of a constant volume dry suit of rubberized canvas, a harness belt, and lead-soled boots. The commercial versions of the hats varied somewhat from the navy. The navy version had a hinged faceplate, where the commercial version (shown in right photo) had a screw-on faceplate. Then there were other versions, such as the "Abalone" helmet, which did not have protective bars over the faceplate, top, and side viewports. In later years, there were mixed-gas versions of the helmet for deeper work, but they all retained the same basic design.

The Author in a Schrader MKV (commercial version)

Although the MKV (standard heavy gear) appeared to be very awkward, it was comfortable to wear in the water, as long as the diver was on bottom or on a midwater stage. Only when you exited the water or attempted to climb a down-line or a ladder did the weight actually become apparent. It took great effort to climb on board and walk to the dress-down area. In addition to the copper helmet and breastplate, the harness belt was 60 to 70 pounds, and the lead-soled brass boots were usually 70 pounds—35 pounds on each foot. However, because of the weight the diver wore, the diver was able to work in stronger currents quite easily.

1.2.2 Development of Decompression Tables

Shortly after the MKV was developed, work began on a new bridge to link the boroughs of Brooklyn and Manhattan in New York City. The bridge was to be a suspension bridge, and the piers had to be built on bedrock, which required having men work underwater. To allow a very large crew of men to work at the same time, wooden caissons were used. These caissons were huge boxes, open on the bottom to allow the crew to work, and they were pressurized with air to the point that the inside pressure was equal to or slightly above the water pressure, thereby keeping the water out of the caisson and keeping the work site dry. When construction was started, the caissons proved to work perfectly, but with one

Drawing of the new Brooklyn Bridge, viewed from Governor's Island, circa 1870
Photo courtesy of historicbridges.com

minor flaw: the crews working inside the caissons complained of pain in their limbs after work each day. It got to be so bad that some of the workers could no longer stand up straight. The condition came to be known as "caisson's disease" or "the bends" after a dance style "the Grecian Bend," popular at that time in New York City.

Dr. Andrew Smith was the physician in charge on the project, and he documented 110 cases of this mystery illness; approximately 25 of these became paralyzed at some point. Although he was not entirely sure what caused the symptoms, he discovered a gradual reduction of pressure would make the symptoms less likely to appear. Unfortunately, his findings were not published for a few years.

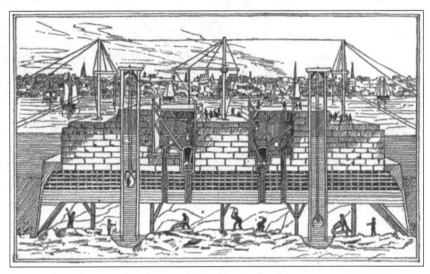

Cross section drawing of workers inside Brooklyn Bridge Caisson, circa 1870
Photo courtesy of historicbridges.com

Caisson's Disease had also been a serious problem on the EADS Bridge in St. Louis, Missouri, a year or two earlier. There were 30 workers seriously injured and 12 men died from the condition. In 1904, during the construction of the New York harbor tunnels, 30 men (sandhogs) died from Compressed Air Disease, as it was called on that project. These and other incidents led to JS Haldane's work "The Prevention of Compressed Air Illness" which recommended a revolutionary idea: staged decompression.

The U.S. Navy published their first manual, *Manual for Divers* in 1905. In 1916, it was renamed *U.S. Navy Diving Manual*. This manual has been the accepted diving manual worldwide since 1924, when the new *U.S. Navy Diving Manual* came out with standardized decompression tables, partially based on the theories of JS Haldane. These tables were validated through manned testing by the U.S. Navy Experimental Diving Unit, located at that time in the Washington Navy Yard.

The U.S. Navy's contribution does not end there. It has consistently led the way in the development and acceptance of new procedures and equipment up to the present day. Just two examples of this are as follows:

1) Helium/oxygen diving tables developed by the Navy EDU in 1939 and used the same year on the salvage of the submarine USS *Squalus*. This, along with Dan Wilson's mixed-gas dives, led to the widespread usage of "mixed-gas" worldwide in commercial diving

2) Saturation diving performed at SEALAB I for the first time in 1962. This led to the Smith Mountain Dam project in 1965, the first commercial use of saturation diving.

There have been many more contributions made to the diving industry by the U.S. Navy over the years, far too many to be listed here.

1.2.3 Atmospheric Diving Systems (ADS)

At the same time these advances were taking place in the diving industry, various individuals kept up with their work on armored (one atmosphere) suits. Joseph Peress, a British engineer, built the Tritonia in 1930. This suit used modern submarine technology by using soda lime to "scrub" carbon dioxide out of the air in the suit as the operator breathed. It also had oil-filled rotary joints that allowed the arms

of the suit to move as the man inside moved. The Tritonia made dives as deep as 404 fsw (feet of seawater) in Loch Ness, 1930, and it was used to explore the wreck of the RMS *Lusitania*, sunk by a German U-boat during World War I. While still a long way from today's ADS, this suit was still truly remarkable. Unfortunately, the Tritonia was the last of the ADS suits to be built until the late 1960s.

"Tritonia" ADS and Siebe Gorman standard dress on RMS *Lusitania* (1935)
Photo courtesy of divingheritage.org

1.2.4 Development of Modern Diving Helmets

By the early 1960s, manufacturers were coming out with new lightweight free-flow helmets. These included the Imperial Aquadyne (UK) and the Swindell, Savoie, and Miller (US). The new lightweight free-flow hats were available with a breastplate or with a neoprene neck-dam and jocking harness. These lightweight hats were not a lot lighter than the MKV because of the fiberglass, brass, and stainless steel required to build them.

Some divers in the late 1960s and early 1970s modified their hats to reflect the changing times. Scuba bottles were now readily available, and they would provide a supply of gas the diver could use in emergencies. Savoie and Swindell helmets were both modified to allow for bailout capability. Those of us that modified our hats were often the subject of ridicule, until the use of bailouts became more accepted in the industry, and the safety of the diver started to become something people actually thought about.

The author in Swindell with bailout (1970s)

JC Roat's bailout-equipped Savoie helmet
Photo courtesy of John Carl Roat

During that same time period, another revolution was taking place in diving helmets. Bob Kirby and Bev Morgan, two commercial divers in Santa Barbara, California, started building their own diving helmets. After several prototypes, they licensed U.S. Divers to produce the KMB-8 band mask (1969), which was the first commercially produced "demand" diving helmet. In 1975, U.S. Divers released the KMB-10 (another Kirby Morgan mask), which was identical (except for the side block) to the current KMB-28 from Kirby Morgan Dive Systems. In 1975, Kirby and Morgan formed Diving Systems International (DSI) and brought out the Superlite 17, which went on to become the most used diving helmet in the world and is still used and very popular today. In 1976, DSI started production of the Heliox 18 band mask, now known as the KMB-18. While Kirby and Morgan were producing demand hats in the United States, Comex was producing them in France. But the Kirby Morgan designs were a much better helmet and band mask and far more popular.

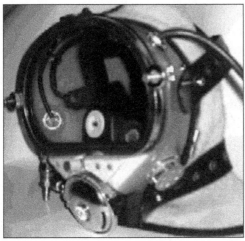

Comex Mark 3 band mask (1970s)
Photo courtesy of frogmanmuseum.free.fr

Kirby Morgan's KMB-10 (1970s)
Photo courtesy of Kirby Morgan

Even though commercial diving occurred elsewhere in the world (the Soviets were producing oil in the Caspian Sea, American contractors were in Saudi Arabia, British and American contractors were in the North Sea), the vast majority of the improvements to diving helmets and equipment were happening in the United States. The reason was this: Not only was the Gulf of Mexico the busiest place of all, but many of the same large U.S.-based diving companies were the ones performing most of the diving elsewhere in the world as well (in the Persian Gulf, the North Sea, and later in West Africa and Asia).

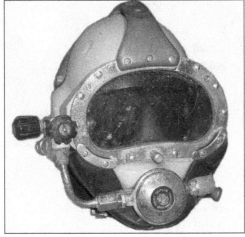

Superlite 17B, most popular helmet ever built

Superlite 17C with gas reclaim unit

1.2.5 Mixed Gas and Saturation Diving

Meanwhile, other advances were being made in the industry. Since mixed-gas theory had been proven to work by Swede Momsen and his divers on the USS *Squalus* salvage, a group of former abalone divers started using HeO2 in the Santa Barbara Channel in the early 1960s. In 1962, Dan Wilson proved that HeO2 could be safely used to 400 fsw. This allowed oil patch work to be performed as deep as 400 fsw. Wilson then went on to develop the first lockout diving bell in 1964. It was the search for (and production of) oil off California and in the Gulf of Mexico that was the driving force behind many of the changes and improvements in diving procedures. In 1965, Allen Krasberg's saturation diving system was successfully used at the Smith Mountain Dam. Subsequent saturation dives in the Santa Barbara Channel and the Gulf of Mexico brought saturation into the mainstream of commercial diving. The diving industry changed more in the years between 1960 and 1980 than it had at any time previously or has at any time since then.

1.2.6 Development of Underwater Photography and Video

In the early 1960s, underwater still cameras appeared on the scene, the most popular being Nikon's Nikonus line. These 35mm film cameras were used for inspection work worldwide and were basically a standard surface camera built with a waterproof body and O-ring seals. Though they were a great camera, you never knew how your photos had turned out until the film was developed. The 35mms film cameras have given way to the modern digital underwater cameras, where the photos can be uploaded to a computer and either be viewed or printed immediately.

The underwater video camera first appeared in the early 1970s. The first video cameras were handheld, the size of a large coffee thermos, produced a black-and-white image, and recorded on a reel-to-reel video tape recorder. The modern cameras are the size of a butane cigarette lighter, small enough to be helmet mounted, and they produce a digital signal recorded onto a computer hard drive.

1.2.7 Development of Modern Atmospheric Diving Systems

In the late 1960s, work began on the Jim Suit, an atmospheric diving suit named after Jim Jarret, the pilot of the Tritonia suit in the 1930s. These new suits were made of titanium, an extremely strong alloy, had onboard battery power, and had a very advanced scrubber system that, in an emergency, could last for up to 72 hours. Completed in 1971, the Jim Suit broke all depth records, performing a dive to 905 fsw.

  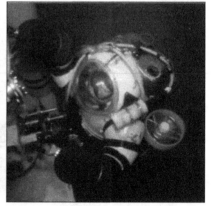

Jim Suit entering water
Photo courtesy of NOAA

Oceaneering's WASP Suit
Photo courtesy of Oceaneering International

Newtsuit performing underwater work
Photo courtesy of Hardsuits, Inc.

In the mid-to-late 1970s, the Jim Suit was modified to have a clear acrylic bubble top and battery-powered thrusters instead of legs. This modified suit was named the WASP. An American diving company,

Oceaneering International, kept a fleet of several of these suits operating in the Gulf of Mexico and worldwide until recently. In 1987, Canadian Phil Nuyten (one of the original founders of Oceaneering) developed the Newtsuit, which had the lightest weight, the most thrust, and the deepest operational depth rating of any ADS until that time. Work continues today on atmospheric diving systems in several countries.

1.2.8 Remotely Operated Vehicles
Between 1978 and 1980, several manufacturers worked on and tested the latest "big thing" for underwater work: the remotely operated vehicle or ROV. Initially viewed as a video inspection tool only, these ROVs quickly evolved into a machine that could perform small repairs, recover small objects, perform NDT on structures, and many other tasks, depending on the machine involved.

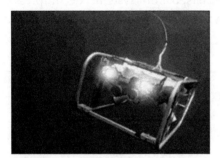
Small inspection class ROV
Photo courtesy of oilandenergydaily.com

Medium work class ROV
Photo courtesy of rov.org

Today's large work class ROVs typically are outfitted with a hydraulic power system that allows the use of hydraulic thrusters, manipulator arms, and tools so the ROV can actually perform work. For example, valve manifolds in some oil fields offshore are now being designed and built ROV friendly to allow ROVs to open and close the valves and to save bringing a diving support vessel in for a 10-minute job. Large, tracked work class units are also being used for trenching and burial of both pipelines and cables

1.2.9 Evolutions in Diving Equipment and Procedures
In the 1970s, the introduction of drysuit zippers (an idea borrowed from exposure suits in the NASA space program) and variable volume drysuits, spelled the end of belly entry and neck entry constant volume drysuits, as were used with the standard heavy gear. Transistorized radio-telephones were also introduced at this time. These new radios were half the size of the old vacuum tube units; the communications were much louder and clearer; and they did not have to warm up for several minutes before being used.

Other diving equipment saw a lot of changes. Hand lights went from the size of a garbage can cover (1960s) down to coffee can size (70s), and down to the size of a soda can (80s). High pressure bottles, originally made of steel, started to be made from aluminum in the 70s, which drastically reduced the weight. Climbing helium prices brought reclaim technology (1979) to reuse the diver's breathing gas.

In the late 1970s, surface decompression using oxygen was introduced, drastically reducing the time a diver had to spend in the chamber and dramatically reducing the incidence of decompression sickness seen when using surface decompression using air.

Also during the mid-to-late 70s, the search for oil began in the North Sea. Because of the very high numbers of diving personnel killed on the job there and the public outcry over it, safety became a priority. In the early 1980s, many changes were made to improve diver safety, including the mandatory use of bailouts, the requirement for standby divers, better communications, and overboard dump built in breathing system (BIBS) to reduce the fire danger in deck decompression chambers.

1.3 CURRENT AND FUTURE DIVING METHODS

At one time, when you chose diving as your occupation, you knew you eventually would suffer decompression sickness (the bends). You just hoped you were one of the lucky ones and could limp away after the fact. With the newer decompression tables in use today (U.S. Navy and Canadian Navy), it is highly unlikely that a diver will be bent. Until the past few years, the diving supervisor always chose the brightest person on the crew (and the one who read the *U.S. Navy Diving Manual* regularly) to perform any treatments required. Now we have paramedics trained to help us, known as diver medics, and we have diving doctors (hyperbaric physicians) on call or on the job when we are working. Diving medicine has seen its share of changes over the years as well, and it continues to see changes every year.

The equipment has been evolving continually. What would have been acceptable a few years ago from a safety standpoint is no longer acceptable. This applies to helmets, bailout systems, decompression chambers, saturation systems, hot water systems, cranes, stages, and diving support vessels. All have seen many dramatic changes over the years.

2-man saturation bell from 1970s

3-man saturation bell from 2013

These advances continue even today. Underwater cameras and lights get smaller by the day; lights now use LED technology; and underwater video can now be recorded, stored, and edited on just about any laptop computer. Handheld lights are seldom seen on the job today, as the lights are small enough to mount on the helmet. Hat communications are modular on most of the newer helmets to save maintenance time on the job. Diving hoses, or umbilicals, used to sink, and three people were required to carry a 600-foot coil. Now there is "floating" diving hose, and two people can easily carry a coil. Deck chambers and saturation systems are now equipped with video cameras, so the supervisor or life support personnel can constantly monitor the occupants. Gas flow rates and percentages are monitored and displayed digitally, while actual gas samples had to be taken before. Pingers are available to display the exact position of the diver on the seafloor in relation to the vessel position on the vessel's survey computer screen. Vessels can "park" on location with Dynamic Positioning, a computerized multi-point thruster system that enables diving support vessels to work in the same spot (in almost all weather) for long periods, without ever dropping an anchor.

Every one of these advances has made life easier for the working diver, made the diver more efficient, and has transformed the underwater workplace into a much safer environment. It would be foolish to try to predict what changes the industry will see in the future. If you had told Augustus Siebe, Swede Momsen, or even a 1960s commercial diver that diving crews would be wearing temperature-controlled suits with television cameras mounted on their helmets, living under pressure for up to 28 days, and working in depths up to 1,000 feet of seawater, they would have thought you were crazy. This author received an e-mail from a friend in 2008, sent from a saturation living chamber pressurized to 750 fsw. A few short years ago, that would have been impossible. It will be interesting and exciting to see the changes new technology brings to this industry in the years to come.

The future is not to be feared. We were told in the early 1980s that remote controlled miniature submarines were in the design stage and within 10 years, the working diver would be obsolete. Well, the miniature submarines have been around for a while (some not so miniature), and ROVs create more work for the divers than they take away from us. We love the things!

As stated earlier, there are changes occurring regularly in diving medicine, and there are changes occurring in how divers decompress. In the mid 1980s, the Canadian Navy Experimental Diving Unit began work on validating the new Canadian Navy Diving Tables and performing manned testing using Doppler ultra-sound to track inert gas bubbles in the test subjects after they performed dives. Released to the public in 1992 as the DCIEM Diving Tables, these tables are considered by most in the industry to be the safest decompression tables ever developed. In April 2008, the United States Navy released *the U.S. Navy Diving Manual, Revision 6,* which represents the greatest change to the *U.S. Navy Diving Manual* since it was first published in 1905. A few of the many changes in the manual include: surface decompression using air is no longer used, the method of timing surface decompression has totally changed, ascent rates have changed, no-decompression limits have changed, and the practice of in-water oxygen decompression has been introduced. Each of these changes in procedure represents a safer way to perform our job.

At the rate underwater technology and procedure are advancing today, it's likely this generation of divers will see twice as many changes in the industry as we all saw in the previous generation. These next few years promise to be exciting times for the working diver, and you will definitely want to be a part of that.

2.0 UNDERWATER PHYSICS

The intent of this chapter is not to make a detailed study of physics but to examine the physical properties of matter and energy as they relate to the diver and working underwater.

2.1 MATTER

Matter is defined as anything that occupies space and has mass. Matter may consist of an element or a compound of two or more elements. An element is the simplest form of matter that displays the distinct physical and chemical properties of that matter. It cannot be further broken down by chemical means. More than 100 of these elements have been identified. Each element is made up of atoms. Atoms can be further broken down, but when they are, they do not display the properties of the matter. For our study, we will stop at the atom.

Atoms are so small that more than a million of them placed side by side would be required to equal the thickness of a single sheet of paper. When atoms group together, they form molecules, which may display different properties than the individual atoms. An example of this is when two hydrogen atoms combine with one oxygen atom, a molecule of water is formed (H_2O). Molecules may be active or inert. Active molecules try to combine with other molecules moving around them; inert molecules do not combine with others. The presence of inert elements in breathing gas will be discussed later in this chapter.

2.1.1 States of Matter

All matter, whether elements or compounds, may exist in one of three states: solid, liquid, or gas. Solids have a definite shape, weight, and volume. Liquids have a definite volume and weight but take the shape of their container. Gases have a definite weight but do not have a definite shape or volume on their own. A gas will expand to fill any container, or if uncontained, will spread continuously throughout the earth's atmosphere. Gases and liquids, because of their properties, are known as fluids.

Whether any given substance exists as a solid, liquid, or gas depends on temperature and to some extent, pressure. In the solid state, molecules move slightly, in a fixed pattern, and they tend to bond together. As the temperature is increased, molecules move around more, separate from each other, and the solid becomes a liquid. As the temperature climbs, some molecules will leave the surface of the liquid and become a gas. As the boiling point of the given substance is reached, the molecules move in all directions at a speed of over 1,000 mph. At this point, the liquid rapidly becomes a gas. When the temperature is lowered, the sequence is reversed. As the gas cools, the molecules move slower and the gas condenses and becomes a liquid. Further cooling slows the molecules more, and the liquid freezes to become solid.

2.2 PRESSURE

Pressure is defined as a force or weight acting on a particular area of matter, or **pressure is force acting on a unit area.** Expressed as a mathematical formula it is:

Pressure = Force/Area or P = F/A

In diving operations in North America, pressure is typically measured in pounds per square inch (psi). It can also be measured in kilograms per square centimeter or in bar. For the purposes of this text we will deal primarily in psi.

Underwater, the diver is affected by two different kinds of pressure: the weight of the water surrounding and above the diver and also the weight of the earth's atmosphere. One thing must be remembered at all times regarding pressure and diving operations: **any diver, regardless of depth, must be in pressure balance with the water surrounding him/her.** The human body can only function normally when the pressure differential between the inside of the body and the outside environment is very small. **Ambient pressure** is the term we use for the pressure of the surrounding environment, regardless of whether that environment is on the moon, at sea level, or 1,000 feet below water.

2.2.1 Atmospheric Pressure

Atmospheric pressure is **the pressure exerted by the earth's atmosphere**, from the outer edges far above the planet, to the earth's surface. When you travel high above the earth's surface, there is less of the atmosphere above you, and the pressure is lower. If you were to measure the pressure at 10,000 ft., for example, you would find that it is 4.6 psi lower than the pressure at sea level. Sea level pressure is the pressure used as the baseline in all underwater calculations and is reckoned to be 14.7 psi. Even though atmospheric pressure fluctuates with changing weather conditions, and these fluctuations cause reactions in the human body (arthritis flare-ups, migraine headaches), these fluctuations are considered to be too small to affect the baseline in underwater calculations.

2.2.2 Hydrostatic Pressure

Hydrostatic pressure (**the pressure exerted by the water**) is a direct result of the weight of the water; the deeper one dives, the more water above the diver and the greater the pressure exerted on the diver. Weight (or pressure) is exerted equally from all sides and increases by 0.445 psi for every foot of seawater. This change is great enough that a six-foot tall person standing in seawater has 3 psi greater pressure on his/her feet than on his/her head. At a depth of 33 ft. seawater (fsw), the diver has 14.7 psi exerted on the body or the equivalent of one atmosphere. Freshwater weighs less than seawater, so the diver would have to descend to 34 ft. freshwater (ffw) to have the equivalent of one atmosphere of pressure. Since 33 fsw and 34 ffw are both equal to one atmosphere, to determine how many atmospheres of pressure a diver is under, we divide depth (seawater) by 33, and depth (freshwater) by 34.

2.2.3 Absolute Pressure

When making gas law calculations for underwater operations, one must use absolute pressure. Absolute pressure is **the sum of the atmospheric pressure plus hydrostatic pressure**. Absolute pressure can be expressed as pounds per square inch absolute (psia) or in atmospheres absolute (ATA). To convert a pressure in psi to psia, we add 14.7. To convert atmospheres to ATA, we add 1. So a diver in 33 fsw is at 1 atmosphere, or 2 atmospheres absolute (2 ATA). The pressure exerted on the body would read 14.7 psi on a gauge, but the absolute pressure would be 29.4 psia.

2.2.4 Ambient Pressure

Ambient pressure is the term used for **the pressure of the surrounding environment**. When a diver is at 33 fsw, the ambient pressure is 2 ATA or 29.4 psia. It is important for a diver to maintain the pressure inside the body (and helmet) equal to the ambient pressure. The one exception is when using an atmospheric diving system (ADS).

2.2.5 Gauge Pressure

Pressure is measured by gauges. Some gauges have a digital readout, some have analog readout, some read in psi, and some read in bar, but all have one thing in common: they read **zero at sea level.** So, when you measure the pressure in a scuba bottle, you are measuring the difference between the atmosphere (zero on the gauge), and the actual pressure of air in the bottle. To avoid any mix-ups, always state gauge pressure as psig, to differentiate between it and absolute pressure (psia).

2.3 DENSITY

Each substance, whether it is a solid, liquid, or gas, has its own density. Density is defined as **weight per unit volume.** Stated in a mathematical formula it is:

$$\text{Density} = \text{Weight/Volume} \text{ or } D = W/V$$

Some differences in density are obvious, some are not. Steel is obviously much denser than wood, which is obviously denser than Styrofoam. In other cases, differences are not so obvious. Seawater has a density of 64 lb./cubic foot (cu. ft.); freshwater has a density of 62.4 lb./cu. ft., but they both look and feel very much alike. Because of its greater density, however, seawater is much easier for a swimmer to float in, and a diver requires more weight than in freshwater. Gas density is directly related to absolute pressure. As depth below water increases, gas density increases. Breathing gas mixtures respond the same, and as the depth increases, the effort required to breathe increases as well.

2.3.1 Specific Gravity

Specific gravity is **the ratio of density of one substance to the density of a control**. The control for solids and liquids is freshwater, which is said to have a specific gravity of 1.0 at 39.2°F. Substances more dense than freshwater have a specific gravity higher than 1. The specific gravity of seawater, which is heavier than freshwater, is 1.026. Air is the control used to measure the specific gravity of gases.

2.4 BUOYANCY (Archimedes Principle)

The ancient Greek mathematician Archimedes studied how some objects sink while others float and why this occurred. Archimedes Principle states: "**Any object wholly or partly immersed in a liquid is buoyed up by a force equal to the weight of the liquid displaced by the object**." This applies to all objects and all liquids.

There are, of course, variables. The buoyant force of the liquid depends on the density of the liquid. Saltwater, for example, has a density of 64 lb./cu. ft., and freshwater has a density of 62.4 lb./cu.ft. So an object floating in seawater would have 1.6 pounds additional buoyancy for every cubic foot of water displaced than the same object would have if in freshwater. The buoyancy of any substance depends on the specific gravity of that substance. Any substance with a specific gravity less than that of water will float in water. If the specific gravity is greater than water, it will sink in water. The average human body has a specific gravity very close to 1.0, and because of this, the average person has little difficulty in floating. Humans with more fat on their body float more easily, and those with thinner leaner bodies tend to sink more easily. Any object that floats is said to have **positive buoyancy.** Objects that sink are said to have **negative buoyancy.** If the object has the same specific gravity as the water, it is said to have **neutral buoyancy.** A swimmer can increase buoyancy by taking a deep breath. A diver can increase buoyancy by adding air to the drysuit. The swimmer and the diver have both done the same thing – they have increased their size, displacing more water without increasing their weight, which causes them to float.

Objects immersed in water, even if they do not float, weigh less in water because of the water they displace. Steel, for example, weighs 490 lb./ft^3 in air and 426 lb./ft^3 in seawater. In the case of a steel ship, the displacement is great enough to overcome the weight of the steel in the ship and the ship's cargo. However, as more cargo is loaded, the ship sinks farther into the water.

> **Example 1:** A square tank 10 × 10 × 10 feet and weighing 40 tons is lowered into the water. What will the tank weigh, if it is seawater?
>
> The volume of the tank is 1000 ft^3, so it displaces 64,000 lb. of seawater. The tank weighs 40 tons or 80,000 lbs. The tank would weigh 16,000 lb. when immersed in seawater.

Example 2: Another square tank 10 × 10 × 10 feet and weighing 10 tons is lowered into the water. What will the buoyancy of the tank be, if it is seawater?

The volume of the tank is 1000 ft³, so it displaces 64,000 lb. of seawater. The tank weighs 10 tons or 20,000 lbs. The tank would have 44,000 lbs of buoyancy when in seawater.

2.5 pH OF LIQUIDS AND GASES

All matter when in the liquid or gaseous state contains alkalis or acids. The pH of a liquid or gas expresses the level of alkalis or acids in that liquid. You have probably had water "burn" your eyes when swimming in a pool. You may have assumed the chlorine level was too high. It usually is because the pH level is off, either on the high or low side, and your eyes, like the rest of your body, are comfortable at a neutral pH level, between 6.5 and 7.5. (So don't reduce the chlorine, adjust the pH.)

ACIDIC	NEUTRAL	ALKALINE
< pH 0.0	pH 7.0	pH 14.0>

The pH balance of human blood is what triggers a sensor in the brain stem, which causes the urge to breathe. Carbon dioxide is acidic. When the carbon dioxide levels in the blood are high, the blood actually becomes acidic. When the body needs to reduce the acidity of the blood, it increases the rate of ventilation (breathing).

2.6 UNITS OF MEASUREMENT

There are two systems used for measuring weight, length, and time: the English System and the Metric System, also known as the International System (SI). The English System is the system commonly used in the United States, some West African countries, and in Canada until the 1980s. This system is based on the pound, foot, and second. The Metric System (SI), used in much of the rest of the world, is based on the kilogram, meter, and second. The following tables will help with conversions and comparisons.

Metric to English Conversion Factors

Metric Unit	To English Units	Factor (Multiply By)
Pressure		
1 kPa (kilopascal)	pounds per square inch (psi)	0.145037738
1 kg/cm²	pounds per square inch (psi)	14.22
1 bar	pounds per square inch (psi)	14.51
Volume		
1 m³	cubic feet	35.31
1 liter	cubic feet	0.035
1 liter	fluid ounces	33.81
1 liter	quarts	1.057
Weight		
1 gram	ounce	0.035
1 kg	ounces	35.27
1 kg	pounds	2.205
1 tonne (metric ton)	pounds	2,200
Length		
1 cm	inch	0.394
1 meter	inches	39.37
1 meter	feet	3.28
1 km	miles	0.621
Area		
1 cm²	square inch	0.155
1 m²	square feet	10.76
1 km²	square mile	0.386

Pressure Equivalencies

	atmospheres (atm)	bar	psi
(atm)	1	1.013	14.7
bar	0.9869	1	14.51
psi	.06804	.06895	1

2.7 TEMPERATURE

Temperature is a measurement of heat retained, whether in a solid, liquid, or gas. Heat is determined by the movement of molecules. The faster the molecules move, the higher the temperature reading, the slower the molecules move, the lower the temperature.

Every country in the world uses one of two temperature scales. The countries that use the English System of measurement (pound, foot, second) use the Fahrenheit (°F) scale. The countries that use the Metric System (SI) (kilogram, meter, second) use the Celsius (C) scale.

In order to perform Gas Law calculations, **absolute temperature** must be used. The absolute temperature scales are based on the lowest possible temperature that could be reached, where all molecular motion would cease. On the Fahrenheit scale, this would be – 460°F degrees. On the Celsius scale, this would be -273 C. Absolute temperature, used with Fahrenheit is the Rankin scale, so 0 R = -460°F. In order to convert to Rankin, add 460 to the Fahrenheit temperature. Absolute temperature, used with Celsius, is the Kelvin scale, so 0 K = -273 C. In order to convert to Kelvin, add 273 to the Celsius temperature.

Temperature Comparisons Notice only the Fahrenheit scale uses the degree symbol (°); none of the other scales use this symbol. Graduations are referred to as degrees, but no symbol is used to designate degrees.

State of H2O	Celsius	Fahrenheit	Kelvin	Rankin
Boiling point	100	212°	373	672
Freezing point	0	32°	273	492

2.8 GASES ENCOUNTERED IN DIVING

It is very important that the diver have a good working knowledge of the properties and behavior of gases, particularly the breathing gases used.

2.8.1 Atmospheric Air
The most commonly used breathing gas in diving operations worldwide is atmospheric air. The following chart shows the composition of unfiltered atmospheric air, as it is found in the natural state. Any gases not listed here or any gases found in concentrations different from those shown are considered to be contaminants. It is vitally important that diver's air be filtered to remove any contaminants.

Components of Dry Atmospheric Air

Component	Percent by volume	Parts per million
Nitrogen	78.084	
Oxygen	20.946	
Carbon Dioxide	0.033	
Argon	0.0934	
Neon		18.18
Helium		5.24

Components of Dry Atmospheric Air - cont'd

Component	Percent by volume	Parts per million
Krypton		1.14
Xenon		0.08
Hydrogen		0.5
Methane		2.0
Nitrous Oxide		0.5

Source: *NOAA Diving Manual*, ©Best Publishing Company

For the purposes of gas law calculations, we assume the percentages of breathing air by volume to be the following: Nitrogen 79%, Oxygen 21%

Air supply contamination can be caused by industrial pollutants or by naturally occurring phenomena. Areas that have an extreme tidal range often have decaying marine growth deposited on the tidal mud flats. These organisms give off gases including both hydrogen sulfide and methane (hence the rotten egg smell). The most common industrial pollutant is carbon monoxide, followed closely by sulfur dioxide. The importance of either filtering out these contaminants or moving breathing air compressors to a contaminant-free location cannot be over stressed. In even small concentrations these contaminants are both deadly to divers.

Water vapor is found in compressed air. Small amounts of water vapor are important to avoid drying out the mouth, throat, and sinuses of the diver, but there must be control over the amount. This is accomplished by moisture drains on compressor filters and volume tanks. Excessive amounts of water vapor can cause faceplate fogging or ice build-up in valves, fittings, and hoses when diving operations are performed in colder climates or when large volumes of air are being used.

2.8.2 Oxygen
One of the most abundant elements found on the earth, oxygen is the most important of all of the gases. Life, as we know it, cannot exist without oxygen, and fire cannot burn without oxygen. Atmospheric air contains approximately 21% oxygen, which exists in a diatomic state: This means that two oxygen atoms combine to make up one molecule. This gas is colorless, odorless, tasteless, and active – it readily combines with other elements. In fact, when elements burn, or corrode, they are combining with oxygen. Rust, which is formed when steel corrodes, is iron oxide (FeO_2). Oxygen by itself will not explode or burn, but the presence of oxygen is necessary to allow other elements to explode or burn. Water is made up of 89% oxygen by weight. Oxygen is the only gas in breathing air that is used by the human body. The other gases simply dilute and carry the oxygen. Oxygen is breathed in its pure form (100%) in space flight, aircraft, medical, and also hyperbaric treatments. High percentages of oxygen are toxic under pressure, and this issue will be expanded on in Chapter 3: Underwater Physiology.

2.8.3 Nitrogen
Another of the more abundant elements found on earth, nitrogen is found in the make-up of every living organism. Unlike oxygen, nitrogen by itself will not support life, nor will fire burn in a pure nitrogen environment. Nitrogen is, like oxygen, a diatomic element. It is also colorless, odorless, and tasteless. Nitrogen is an inert gas: It does not combine itself easily or readily with other elements. In diver's breathing air, the nitrogen is a carrier for the oxygen, and it serves to dilute the oxygen so it is not toxic under pressure. Nitrogen has one enormous disadvantage: It has, at higher partial pressures, an anesthetic or narcotic effect. This leads to disorientation and a lack of judgment in divers. Because of this problem, for deeper dives special mixtures are used to replace the nitrogen in atmospheric air.

2.8.4 Helium

A colorless, odorless, tasteless gas, helium is monatomic: The element can exist as a single atom. Helium is an inert gas: It does not combine with other elements. Helium is seven times lighter than air and has been used for inflating airships and weather balloons. It is an extremely rare (therefore very expensive) element found with natural gas in a very few wells in the United States, Canada, and Russia. The entire world's supply of helium comes from these wells, and the separation process is costly. Because of the cost, diving operations using helium today usually employ a reclaim system that recaptures the exhaled gas and reuses it after removing contaminants and adding more oxygen. Helium is used in deep-diving operations to replace nitrogen because it does not have the narcotic effects found in nitrogen. Helium, however, has its own problems. Speech is distorted in a helium atmosphere because helium has different acoustic properties. Divers breathing helium have the "Donald Duck Effect," and special helium unscrambler radios are used. The other problem with helium is high thermal conductivity. In a helium environment, the diver loses body heat more rapidly (roughly six times faster) than in an air environment. When breathing helium mixes, even in an air environment, the diver loses body heat at a tremendous rate. Because of this, helium, when used as a breathing gas, is often heated.

2.8.5 Hydrogen

Another colorless, odorless, tasteless gas, hydrogen is diatomic: The element always exists as two atoms. Hydrogen is an extremely active element – it is rare to find it in its free state (not combined with another element) on earth. This is not the case in the rest of the universe, however. It is the most abundant element in the universe; the sun and the stars consist of almost pure hydrogen. Hydrogen is the lightest element, and for many years it was used to inflate airships. This ended with the *Hindenburg* crash in New Jersey in 1937. Pure hydrogen is violently explosive and has claimed the lives of many divers involved in underwater cutting operations. Hydrogen has been used in the past in diving operations to replace nitrogen, but because of the explosion hazard and the availability of helium, it is rarely used for anything short of experimental work.

2.8.6 Neon

Yet another colorless, odorless, tasteless gas, neon is a monatomic inert gas found in very small quantities in the earth's atmosphere. Most people know neon because it is a good conductor of electricity at low pressure and glows with a distinct orange-red color when energized. Neon signs are found all over the planet. Neon does not have the narcotic properties of nitrogen, and the U.S. Navy Experimental Diving Unit has experimented with it as a nitrogen replacement in breathing gas. Because it is heavy, neon does not distort speech as helium does, and it has very low thermal conductivity. In all areas where helium has problems as a breathing medium, neon shows promise. The only drawback: Due to density, breathing resistance is elevated.

2.8.7 Carbon Dioxide

Carbon dioxide has no color, odor, or taste when it is found in small percentages in air, but when the percentages get greater, it has an acidic taste and smell. Carbon dioxide is a chemically active gas, which can be seen as bubbles in carbonated drinks. It causes bread dough to rise, is used to power pellet guns, paintball guns, and to extinguish fires. CO_2 is nature's by-product. It is given off by animals and plants as they oxidize the carbon in their food. Although carbon dioxide is exhaled by every human being, divers must be concerned with it because in high concentrations, it is extremely toxic. It is considered by many to be the most dangerous gas encountered in diving.

2.8.8 Carbon Monoxide

Carbon monoxide does not occur naturally in air. It is the result of the incomplete burning of fuels, particularly carbon fossil fuels (petroleum products). It is found in the exhaust of internal combustion engines (gas and diesel) in high concentrations and also occurs when lubricating oil in breathing air compressors becomes overheated. This gas is very poisonous to humans, and because it is colorless, odorless, and tasteless, it is difficult to detect. It is dangerous for divers because often there are no symptoms before the victim lapses into unconsciousness. In addition, CO effectively stops the human body from being able to take and utilize oxygen from the air it breathes. The danger of CO **cannot** be overstressed **nor** can the need to keep the diver from breathing CO at depth.

2.9 BEHAVIOR OF GASES

The molecules in any given gas are constantly in motion, moving at very high speed, bouncing off of each other in all directions. Our word "gas" is derived from the Greek word "chaos" because it so accurately describes the motion of gas molecules.

Changes in temperature have an effect on gases. The higher the temperature, the faster the molecules move, the faster they move, the greater their impact force (or pressure) on what contains them. Conversely, if the temperature is lowered, the movement of the gas molecules is slowed down, reducing the impact force. The molecules in heavier gases, such as argon, move much slower than those of the lighter gases, such as helium, but because they are heavier, they hit harder, and so they have the same impact force as if they moved faster. If the number of, or the force of these impacts are changed, the pressure will change.

Changes in the volume of a gas will also cause changes in pressure. If you compress a given quantity of gas into a smaller volume, the number of molecule impacts per square inch on the wall of the container (pressure) will increase. If a fixed volume container has more gas squeezed into it, the same thing happens: more gas molecules, more impacts per square inch (greater pressure).

2.10 GAS LAWS

As you have just read above, every gas is subject to (and influenced by) three interrelated factors: pressure, volume, and temperature, and a change in one of these factors results in a change in the others. All gases and mixtures of gases behave the same. Since all gases do behave the same, we can use the gas laws to predict how gases will change as conditions change. The diver needs to have a grasp of the gas laws to understand the effects the depth has on the body and equipment; to calculate the pressure and volume required to deliver breathing gas to a given depth; or to understand why an air tank filled to capacity should not be left out in the summer sunlight. The gas laws the diver must learn are:

- **Boyle's Law (pressure and volume)**
- **Charles' Law (temperature and volume)**
- **Gay Lussac's Law (temperature and pressure)**
- **General Gas Law (combination of Boyle's and Charles')**
- **Dalton's Law (partial pressures)**
- **Henry's Law (gases dissolving in solutions)**

IMPORTANT NOTE

When working with these gas laws, all pressures must be converted to absolute pressure, all temperatures must be converted to absolute temperature, and all measurements must use the same system (English or SI) from start to finish.

2.10.1 Boyle's Law
"For any gas at a constant temperature, the volume of the gas will vary inversely with the pressure, while the density of the gas will vary directly."

If you were to take a balloon, fill it with air at the surface, then take it down to 33 fsw, the balloon would be half the size it was on the surface. Return the balloon to the surface, and it will return to the size you had originally filled it to. Any space that contains a gas and is compressible will change volume on descent and ascent. This may be the diver's ears, wetsuit, or a lift bag. Expressed as a formula, Boyle's Law is:

$$P1 \times V1 = P2 \times V2$$

Where:
P1 = initial pressure absolute
V1 = initial volume
P2 = final pressure absolute
V2 = final volume

> **Example:** An open bottom diving bell is lowered into the water from a surface support vessel. The volume of air in the diving bell is 36 cubic feet. No air is added to or taken from the bell. Calculate the volume of air in the diving bell at 33, 66, and 99 fsw.

First, we calculate for 33 fsw:
P1 = 1 ATA, P2 = 2 ATA, V1 = 36 ft³, and V2 is unknown

$$V2 = \frac{P1\,V1}{P2} \qquad V2 = \frac{1\,ATA \times 36\,ft^3}{2\,ATA} \qquad \mathbf{V2 = 18ft^3}$$

Next, we calculate for 66 fsw:
P1 = 1 ATA, P3 = 3 ATA, V1 = 36 ft³, and V3 is unknown

$$V3 = \frac{P1\,V1}{P3} \qquad V3 = \frac{1\,ATA \times 36\,ft^3}{3\,ATA} \qquad \mathbf{V3 = 12ft^3}$$

Finally, we calculate for 99 fsw:
P1 = 1 ATA, P4 = 4 ATA, V1 = 36 ft³, and V4 is unknown

$$V4 = \frac{P1\,V1}{P4} \qquad V4 = \frac{1\,ATA \times 36\,ft^3}{4\,ATA} \qquad \mathbf{V4 = 9ft^3}$$

Boyle's Law calculations may be performed using the pressure stated as force/area, or in atmospheres, but regardless of the method of choice, the pressure used must be absolute.

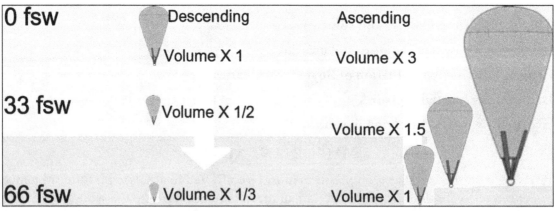

Boyle's Law Illustrated

2.10.2 Charles' Law

"For any gas at a constant pressure, the volume of the gas will vary directly with the absolute temperature."

If you were to take a balloon, fill it with air at the surface, and take it down to 33 fsw where the temperature is lower than the surface temperature, the volume of air would change due to the pressure change and would further change due to the change in temperature. Expressed as a formula, Charles' Law is:

$$\frac{V1}{V2} = \frac{T1}{T2}$$

Where:
V1 = initial volume
T1 = initial temperature absolute
V2 = final volume
T2 = final temperature absolute

> **Example:** An open diving bell is lowered by the surface support ship to 66 fsw. The water temperature at the surface is 80°F, and the temperature at 66 fsw is 44°F. The volume of air in the bell is 36 ft³. What is the volume of gas at 66 fsw?

$$V2 = \frac{V1\ T2}{T1} \qquad V2 = \frac{12\ ft^3 \times 504R}{540R} \qquad V2 = 11.2\ ft^3$$

2.10.3 Gay-Lussac's Law

"For any gas at a constant volume, the pressure of the gas will vary directly with the absolute temperature."

If you have a rigid container of any gas and change the temperature, the pressure of the gas inside the container will change. Gay-Lussac's Law stated as a formula is:

$$\frac{P1}{P2} = \frac{T1}{T2}$$

Where:
P1 = initial pressure absolute
T1 = initial temperature absolute
P2 = final pressure absolute
T2 = final temperature absolute

> **Example:** A decompression chamber is pressurized to 44 psia, when the temperature is 50°F . The sun comes up, and the temperature climbs to 78°F . What then is the pressure in the chamber?

$$P2 = \frac{P1 \times T2}{T1} \qquad P2 = \frac{44 \times 538R}{510R} \qquad P2 = 46.42\ psia$$

2.10.4 Dalton's Law

"The total pressure exerted by a mixture of gases is equal to the sum of the pressures of each of the gases making up the mixture, with each gas acting as if it alone was present and occupying the total volume."

According to Dalton's Law, the total pressure of a gas mixture is the sum of the partial pressures of the component gases in that mixture. So, a 50/50 nitrogen/oxygen mixture that has a total pressure of 1500 psi would have an oxygen partial pressure of 750 psi, and a nitrogen partial pressure of 750 psi.

Dalton's Law stated as a formula:

Pt = PP1 + PP2, etc.

Where:
Pt = total pressure of the mixture
PP1 = partial pressure of the first gas
PP2 = partial pressure of the second gas, etc.

Also, according to Dalton's Law, the pressure exerted by any gas in a mixture is directly proportional to the percentage of that gas within the mixture. Stated as a formula:

Px = Gas % × Pt

Where:
Px = partial pressure of the gas
Gas % = gas percentage in the mixture (stated as a decimal)
Pt = total pressure of the gas mixture

Example 1: Determine the partial pressure of oxygen in a scuba bottle that is filled to 2,500 psi.

Px = Gas % × Pt   Px = 0.21 × 2,514.7   Px = 528.1 psia

Example 2: If the air at the surface contains point 4% carbon monoxide, what is the partial pressure of carbon monoxide at 140 fsw?

Px = Gas % × Pt   Px = 0.04 ATA × 5.24   Px = 0.209 ATA

Another way of expressing Dalton's Law as a formula is the "Tee Formula," as shown below:

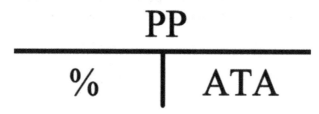

The Tee Formula requires there be two known values in order to find the third value. This formula is used in diving to answer the following three questions:

1. What is the partial pressure of a given gas at depth?
   (PP gas = Decimal % of gas × Depth in ATA)

2. What is the best gas mixture to use at a given depth?
   (Decimal % of gas = Partial Pressure Limitation / by Maximum Depth in ATA)

3. What is the cut-off depth for a gas mix?
   (Cut-off depth in ATA = PP limit divided by decimal % of gas)

In order to use the Tee Formula, depths must always be expressed in ATA, and therefore once the calculation is completed, values in ATA will want to be converted back to feet of seawater for easy usage.

Example 1: A diver is breathing surface-supplied air at 165 fsw. What is the partial pressure of oxygen (PPO_2) at that depth?

PP = Gas % × ATA PP = .21 × 6 PP = 1.26 The partial pressure of oxygen at 165 fsw is 1.26

Example 2: There is a riser clamp that must be released by a diver a 240 fsw. The IMCA limit for PPO$_2$ is 1.4 percent. What is the best HeO2 mix to use for this dive?

Gas % = PP/ATAGas % = 1.4 /8.27 Gas % = .169 The answer is 83/17 HeO$_2$.

Example 3: You have 4 quads of 60/40 nitrox onboard the vessel. Your company has a PPO$_2$ limit of 1.4 and you want to perform as built inspections on a pipeline in 85 fsw. Can you do the dive with this gas?

ATA = PP/Gas % ATA = 1.4/.40 ATA = 3.5 or 82.5fsw. The answer is no.

2.10.5 Henry's Law
"The amount of a gas that will dissolve in a liquid at a given temperature is almost directly proportional to the partial pressure of that gas."

According to Henry's Law, if one unit of gas is dissolved at one atmosphere, than two units will be dissolved at two atmospheres; three will be dissolved at three atmospheres; etc. Henry's Law is stated:

$$\frac{VG}{VL} = oc\ P1$$

Where:
VG = volume of gas
VL = volume of the liquid
oc = solubility coefficient
P1 = partial pressure of the gas

When a gas-free liquid is exposed to a gas, gas molecules will enter the liquid, moved by the partial pressure of the gas. As molecules enter the liquid, they add to the **gas tension**, which is the term used to describe the partial pressure of that particular gas in the liquid. The difference between the gas tension (inside the liquid) and the partial pressure of the gas (outside the liquid) is called the **pressure gradient.** If the gradient is high, with high partial pressure and low gas tension, there will be a high rate of absorption of gas into the liquid. Once enough gas enters the liquid so that the partial pressure becomes equal to the gas tension, the pressure gradient is zero, and the liquid is **saturated** with gas. Unless the temperature changes or the pressure changes, no more gas transfer will occur. Solubility of gases is directly affected by temperature: the lower the temperature, the higher the solubility. As the temperature of a liquid is increased, any gases dissolved in the liquid will start to leave the solution. If you place a pan of water over heat, bubbles will rise to the surface long before the water boils. These bubbles are dissolved gas leaving solution as the liquid temperature rises.

Each gas in a diver's breathing mixture will be dissolved into the diver's body in direct proportion to the partial pressure of the gas. Because different gases vary in solubility, the amount of a particular gas dissolved depends on the length of time the diver breathes the gas at that pressure. If a diver breathes the gas long enough, the body will reach the point of saturation. Saturation takes between 30 minutes and 72 hours, depending on the gas used and the body tissue involved. No matter how much gas has been dissolved and no matter at what pressure, the gas will stay in solution for as long as the pressure and temperature are maintained. Any reduction in pressure (ascent from depth) must be at a carefully controlled rate. Ascent at a rate that does not allow the body to properly dispose of the gas as it leaves solution will result in serious injury or death to the diver.

2.10.6 The General Gas Law

We have already seen that in gases, pressure, volume, and temperature are interrelated. If one factor changes, one or both of the others must also change. The General Gas Law is a combination of Charles' and Boyle's laws and is stated as follows:

$$\frac{P1\ V1}{T1} = \frac{P2\ V2}{T2}$$

Where:
P1 = initial pressure (absolute)
V1 = initial volume
T1 = initial temperature (absolute)

and
P2 = final pressure (absolute)
V2 = final volume
T2 = final temperature (absolute)

Example: An open bottom diving bell has a capacity of 24 cubic feet. The bell is lowered to 99 fsw. The surface temperature is 80°F , and temperature at depth is 45°F . Find the volume of gas in the bell at depth.

P1 = 14.7 psia
V1 = 24 cu. ft.
T1 = 540 R (80F + 460)
P2 = 58.8 psia
T2 = 505 R (45F + 460)
V2 = Unknown

Transposing:

$$V2 = \frac{P1\ V1\ T2}{T1\ P2}$$

$$V2 = \frac{(14.7\ \text{psia})(24\ \text{cu.ft.})(505\ \text{R})}{(540\ \text{R})(58.8\ \text{psia})}$$

V2 = 5.61 cu. ft. of gas are in the bell at depth.

2.11 ENERGY IN DIVING

Three forms of energy typically affect the diver. These are light, sound, and heat. An often overlooked fourth form of energy, known as stored energy, affects divers in certain operations. Each of these forms of energy will be discussed only as it relates to underwater work.

2.11.1 Light

Light allows the human eye to see. What the eye actually sees are images created by light reflecting off of various surfaces, objects, and shapes, or light given off by a luminescent object. Light energy is actually electromagnetic energy, traveling in waves. The different colored lights in the visible spectrum, from red to violet, have different wavelengths. If an object absorbs all of the light except green, it will appear green to the human eye because the green light waves are reflected back.

As light travels from air to water, the speed at which it travels is slowed considerably. As it enters or leaves water, the change in speed causes light rays to actually bend. When you hold a pencil in a glass of clear water, it appears to be bent. This "bending" of the pencil is caused by **refraction** or the bending of light rays. Underwater, objects closer than four feet appear closer than they are; those farther than four feet appear farther away than they are. This is also caused by refraction. Another effect is that objects appear 25% larger than they actually are when viewed underwater through a faceplate.

The straw at left appears to be bent. Actually, it is the rays of light that are bent while traveling from the air to the water, reflecting off of the straw, then traveling from the water back to the air. This bending or "refraction" of light rays affects the diver every day in his work. It makes the tools lying on the bottom appear closer than they really are, causing the diver to misjudge when reaching for a tool. Certain operations, such as using a hammer to drive in concrete anchors, are more difficult due to refraction, so watch your fingers.

The deeper a diver goes underwater, the more natural light is absorbed and colors are blocked, eventually leaving a world of blacks and grays. At 15 ft., red is largely blocked, orange at 30, yellow at 60, green at 70. Artificial lights, such as a helmet light or video camera light, when directed at objects, will cause them to be seen in original color. This is because surface light that cannot reach depth is being replaced by the artificial light, and the objects are again reflecting light as they would on surface.

Crystal clear water (which you will probably never work in), allows enough natural light to remain for a diver to see at almost 300 ft. What reduces light's ability to penetrate water is turbidity (suspended particles). In very turbid water, even with a helmet light, the diver cannot see. All the diver will see is the light reflecting off of the suspended particles. The same particles cause problems with underwater video and photography, a condition that is known by the technical term "backscatter."

2.11.2 Sound
Water has an effect on sound, as it does on light. Sound travels in waves, but sound waves are pressure waves, whereas light are electromagnetic. The vibration of an object produces pressure waves in the gas or liquid surrounding that object. The pressure waves then cause a similar vibration in the eardrum (or the diaphragm of a microphone).

The denser the medium, the more closely packed the molecules; the more closely packed the molecules, the better they transmit sound waves. Since water is denser than air, sound travels about four times faster than it does in air. In air, as sound travels, the difference in time when it arrives at each ear allows a human (or an animal) to be able to determine the direction that the sound is originating from. In water, since the speed of sound is faster, a diver cannot determine the direction a sound is coming from. Not only does sound travel faster, but it travels much farther, with far less loss of intensity of the sound waves. The U.S. Navy recorded the sounds of the submarine USS *Thresher* breaking up and sinking on underwater microphones located in Newfoundland, Canada. The *Thresher* sank off the Azores, a group of islands closer to West Africa than Canada. No sound could possibly carry that far through the air.

Because sound carries so quickly and easily through water, sounds that would not bother a diver on surface can do hearing damage underwater. Divers should restrict their time of exposure to tools such as jackhammers, to avoid ear damage. Drop hammer pile drivers, when used on steel piling, can cause hearing damage in divers. Low frequency sonars and search fathometers should always be turned off

Underwater Blast – 30 cases of Tovex (HE) detonated 50 feet below the surface. The U.S. Navy states "there is no safe distance underwater from an explosion."

when diving operations are in progress. Sound waves are not, however, the only pressure wave that can affect the diver.

The hydraulic shock waves from explosions are very similar to sound waves, and they, too, move with more efficiency in the water. Hydrogen explosions caused by cutting or welding underwater kill divers every year. These same explosions, if they occurred on the surface, would be loud, but would likely not cause injury. In surface blasting, you can crouch down behind a boulder and fire off a charge close to yourself without injury. Underwater, there is **no safe distance** from an explosion of any size. Recently, an attempt was made to break the Guinness World Record by a scuba club in South Africa by having 200 scuba divers in the water at one time. Once all of the divers were in the water and the record was broken, a Thunder Flash (a non-lethal stun grenade used by military and police) was used to recall the divers. One diver in the group was killed, and several more had serious injuries.

2.11.3 Heat

Temperature and heat are closely related, but they are not the same. Two different substances may be the same temperature but have very different levels of heat. Heat is a form of energy proportional to the molecular motion of a substance. Temperature is measured in degrees Fahrenheit or in Celsius. Heat is measured using British thermal units (BTUs) or calories. One BTU is the heat required to raise the temperature of 1 lb. of water 1°F. One calorie is the amount of heat required to raise the temperature of one gram of water one Celsius unit. Specific heat is the ratio of the amount of heat required to raise the temperature of a given substance by 1 degree to the amount of heat required to raise the temperature of the same amount of water by 1 degree. As with specific gravity, water is the baseline, and has a value of 1.0. The specific heat of air is 0.24, which means that 0.24 calories will raise the temperature of 1 gram of air by 1 Celsius. If you look at the same comparison by volume, rather than by weight, you will see that it takes 3,600 times as much heat to raise a given volume of water by 1 degree than it does the same volume of air. Heat can be generated by burning fuel, chemical or nuclear reactions, friction, and also through metabolism (cellular activity in living beings). Heat is moved from one place to another by conduction, convection, and radiation. These methods of heat transmission are explained below:

- Conduction is transmitting heat through direct contact. An example of this is when you are chilled and get into a hot bath. Your body temperature rises from direct contact with the warm water.

- Convection is transmitting heat through the movement of liquids or gases. An example of this is a hot air heating system in a home. Hot air rises, cold air drops, and airflow is used to warm the house by the heat in the air passing through.
- Radiation is transmitting heat through electromagnetic energy waves. Examples of this are the sun and radiant heaters (the type without fans).

The method of heat transmission that affects divers the most is conduction. Water is an excellent conductor of heat. Air is a very poor conductor of heat. Wetsuit neoprene works to insulate a diver because of the tiny air bubbles within the neoprene. Drysuits use an air space between the diver and the suit as insulation. Helium is also an excellent conductor of heat. Actually, helium is seven times more efficient as a heat conductor than is air. For this reason, during dives using helium and oxygen mixtures, maintaining the diver's core temperature is a matter of grave importance, and when done properly, it requires hot water suits and heated gas for breathing by the divers.

2.11.4 Stored Energy
One additional form of energy that affects the diver is stored energy. Stored energy is the term used when an object has been bent, stretched, or otherwise deformed, and held in that position, sometimes for many years. Divers are injured or killed every year by objects containing stored energy. The object containing stored energy may be a rope, cable or chain under strain, or a steel piling under strain.

Many materials, once stretched or bent will return to their original shape, even after many years. Often, this return to the original shape is sudden and violent. Although the density of water does "dampen" the effect somewhat, there is often sufficient energy release to cause injury or death to a diver as the object returns to the original shape. Before cutting any rope, cable, chain, or structural member, measures must be taken to protect the diver against the release of stored energy in the item to be cut. This will involve investigation of the properties of the materials involved, since not all materials react the same. For example, in Chapter 19: Rigging, we are told that rope and cable that breaks or is cut under strain will whip violently to either side, while a chain that breaks or is cut under strain will go straight back on itself. It is imperative that the distinctive properties of the material to be cut be investigated prior to cutting.

2.12 PHYSICS FORMULAS YOU WILL WANT TO KEEP:

1. Volume of a cylinder under pressure: $$V = \frac{Pa}{SP \times FV}$$

Where:
V = volume of the cylinder
Pa = pressure of the cylinder (absolute)
SP = surface pressure
FV = floodable volume

2. Gas volume requirements using an LP compressor: SCFM = ATA × ACFM × N

Where:
SCFM = standard cubic feet per minute
ATA = atmospheres absolute
ACFM = actual cubic feet per minute
N = number of divers

3. Gas volume requirements using an HP gas bank: $SCF = ATA \times ACFM \times N \times T$

Where:

SCF = standard cubic feet

ATA = atmospheres absolute

ACFM = actual cubic feet per minute

N = number of divers

T = time (in minutes)

GAS CONSUMPTIONS FOR ABOVE VOLUME CALCULATIONS

Free-Flow Hat (MK V, Desco, Swindell, MK 12, Rat Hat)	4.5 ACFM
Demand Hat (Kirby Morgan, Miller, Gorsky, Beat Engel)	1.4 ACFM
BIBS Masks (Scott Pressure-Vac II, Divex)	0.3 ACFM

4. Bailout Calculations:

$$\text{Time Available} = \frac{\text{Gas Available}}{\text{Gas Consumption}}$$

$$\text{Gas Available} = \frac{\text{Volume} \times \text{Available Pressure}}{\text{Pressure When Full}}$$

$$\text{Gas Consumption} = \text{Absolute Pressure} \times \text{Helmet Requirements (stated in ACFM)}$$

5. Convert Depth (fsw) to PSIG : Depth × .445 = PSIG.

6. Convert PSIG to Depth (fsw) : PSIG / by .445 = fsw.

3.0 UNDERWATER PHYSIOLOGY

3.1 THE SYSTEMS OF THE HUMAN BODY

It is necessary for the diver to have a basic understanding of the human body systems to know how they operate and how the body will react when in a hyperbaric environment. This will help the diver to avoid pressure related illness and/or injury, and also help describe pressure related symptoms to medical personnel if and when they do arise.

3.1.1 The Musculoskeletal System

The human skeleton provides a framework for the body, giving it strength, allowing it to stand erect, and providing protection for the internal organs. The skeleton is made up of many individual bones, jointed to allow movement. The bones are the densest tissue in the body, and they have the least blood flow through them. This is the reason why they are the last tissues to become saturated with inert gas and the last tissues to off-gas during decompression.

The skeletal system is a problem area in decompression. Type I (pain only) decompression sickness usually (but not always) involves an inert gas bubble that occurs in a joint. Type I can also have different symptoms, but when pain is involved, it most often is in a skeletal joint. Another skeletal problem that is quite rare is dysbaric osteonecrosis, also called diver's bone rot. It was long thought a bubble of inert gas trapped in the tissue caused nearby bone to die. Now, however, it is believed this condition is most likely caused instead by exposure to high partial pressures of oxygen over long periods of time.

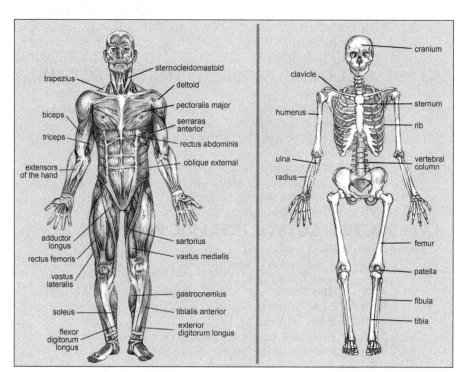

Diagrams courtesy of ©Chris Dean

Type II decompression sickness occurs primarily in the central nervous system or in the inner ear (soft tissue). The area of the central nervous system that usually is involved is the spinal cord and the brain stem; these are found inside the vertebra and the base of the skull, respectively. Perhaps it is coincidence, but both areas mentioned are surrounded by bone tissue.

The separate bones of the skeleton are joined with ligaments, a flexible connective tissue. Joints that see constant motion, such as the knee, shoulder, hip, and elbow, have a solid lubricating material known as cartilage between the bone ends. Osteoarthritis destroys this cartilage, as do trapped nitrogen bubbles from untreated decompression sickness.

There are two types of muscle response in the human body – voluntary and involuntary. Involuntary muscle responses are the ones we don't have to consciously think about, such as the heart muscle, the diaphragm and external intercostals (which are the breathing muscles), and the eyelid muscles we use for blinking. The voluntary muscle responses are the ones we do think about – legs and arms for walking, jaw for eating, etc. The muscles attached to the bones are what provide the body's movement. Technically, it all starts with an electrical impulse sent from the brain. This causes a given muscle to contract or expand, providing movement. The muscles are attached to the bones by semi-rigid tissue called tendons. Muscles also serve to provide additional protection to the internal organs.

3.1.2 The Nervous System

The command and control system for the human body is the nervous system. It consists of the brain, a mass of tissue that weighs roughly 3.5 pounds and is housed within the skull, the brain stem, the spinal cord, and a very complex network of nerves that course throughout the entire body. The nervous system is considered to consist of three systems: the central nervous system (CNS), the peripheral nervous system (PNS), and the autonomous nervous system (ANS).

The central nervous system consists of the brain, brain stem, and the spinal cord. The peripheral nervous system is the vast network of nerves that travel from the brain and spinal cord to the peripheral regions of the body, controlling muscle movement, vascular responses, and sweat glands. This same system also carries impulses associated with sight, hearing, smell, balance, taste, temperature, pain,

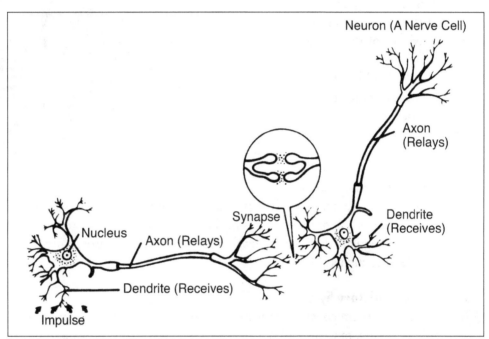

Source: *NOAA Diving Manual* ©Best Publishing Company

and touch sensation from peripheral sensors back to the brain where the information is processed (control center).

The autonomous nervous system consists of the nerves that lead from the brain and the spinal cord to control the activity of the body's internal organs including the heart, lungs, and kidneys.

The brain activates neurons, which are cells with the ability to transmit electro-chemical impulses, and these neurons transmit signals at speeds of up to 350 feet per second. It is estimated there may be as many as ten billion of these neurons in the human body.

3.1.3 The Digestive System

When a human eats food, that food has to be broken down to a form that can be used by the cells making up the body. In order to be used by the cells, the food must be reduced to amino acids, fatty acids, sugar, and water. Food, broken down mechanically by the teeth, travels to the stomach, where stomach acids break it down chemically. When the food leaves the stomach, it travels through the large and small intestines, where it is broken down biologically, and the nutrients are picked up and distributed by the blood stream. The unused portions of the food are voided through the rectum and urinary system.

3.1.4 The Excretory System

Waste must be removed from the body's cells in order for the body to properly function. This waste is removed by the excretory system. The system consists of the kidneys, the ureters, and the bladder. As the blood flows past the body's cells, solid and liquid waste is dissolved and carried to the kidneys. In the kidneys, these waste products are filtered out of the blood and then passed through the ureters to the bladder, where it is stored as urine, to be expelled periodically from the body.

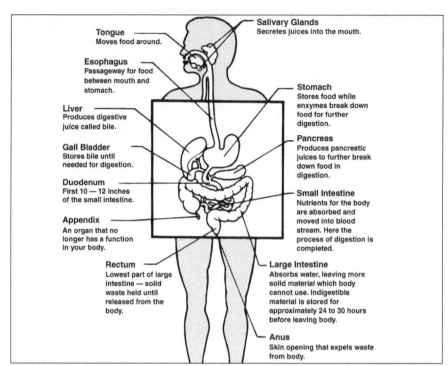

Source: *NOAA Diving Manual*, ©Best Publishing Company

3.1.5 The Endocrine System

The endocrine system consists of the pituitary, thyroid, parathyroid, adrenal glands, the pancreas, and the testes or ovaries. All of these glands in the endocrine system secrete the chemical messengers called hormones that regulate the body's growth, metabolism rate, temperature control, blood vessel size, and blood properties, such as blood sugar.

3.1.6 The Circulatory System

The circulatory system consists of the heart, arteries, veins, and capillaries. The mission of this system is to deliver nutrients, oxygen, and hormones to each cell in the body, and to carry away waste products, carbon dioxide, and heat generated through metabolism. The heart is the pump, the arteries and veins are the pipelines. Arterial blood is oxygenated, and bright red, venous blood is de-oxygenated, and blue.

It is a closed system with large arteries that branch out smaller, reducing down to the tiny capillary arterioles. These arterioles then become venules and get progressively larger in size, becoming veins which get larger as they get closer to the heart. The arterioles and venules in the capillaries are so small that human blood cells can only go through in single file. The capillaries of the blood system are where the transfer of nutrients, oxygen, waste products, and carbon dioxide take place. The tubing of the capillaries is constructed to allow the transfer of these products but still contain the blood and maintain the blood pressure. Capillaries are found in every square inch of tissue in the body and allow the body's cells access to the blood stream.

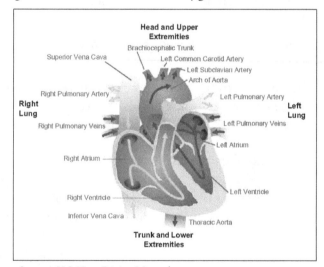

Source: *U.S. Navy Diving Manual*

The circulatory system is made up of two circuits: the pulmonary (lung) circuit and the systemic circuit. The heart is also two pumps in one, with the right and left halves having no direct relationship with each other. The right half of the heart handles the blue de-oxygenated blood sent to the lungs to dispose of the carbon dioxide and pick up oxygen. The left half handles the red oxygenated blood sent to all of the other body tissues from the brain to the skin on the soles of the feet.

3.1.7 The Respiratory System

The lungs and the various air passages make up the respiratory system. The whole purpose of this system is to bring oxygen into the body and to get rid of the carbon dioxide. To make this happen, the ribs are elevated and the diaphragm drops down, creating a larger volume (lower pressure) in the lungs (Boyle's Law). Air then enters the lungs until the pressure is equalized. The primary stimulus for the human body to breathe is the level of CO_2 produced by the body. This triggers the respiratory center in the brain stem, causing electrical impulses to be sent out, making the rib cage rise and the diaphragm drop, filling the lungs. There is a secondary stimulus as well – the oxygen level in the blood, which is picked up by sensors located in two different areas of the heart.

The close proximity of the heart and lungs is illustrated in these drawings. The heart is situated directly between the lungs. The right lung has three lobes, and the left has only two to make room for the heart. The physical proximity reflects just how closely these systems work together.

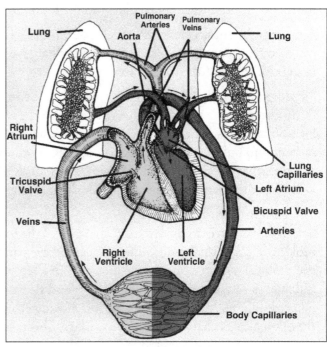

Source: *NOAA Diving Manual* ©Best Publishing Company

Air is brought in through the nose and the mouth, moves down the trachea into the bronchial tubes, and ends up in the alveoli. Alveoli are tiny air sacs covered with capillaries. As these sacs fill with air, the oxygen from the air is transferred through the capillary walls into the blood stream. Carbon dioxide already in the blood then transfers into the air sacs and is exhaled from the body. This gas transfer happens by pressure gradient and by a chemical process known as the Haldane Effect or diffusion.

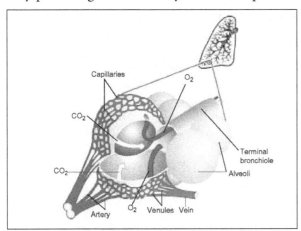

Source: *U.S.Navy Diving Manual*

When the lungs have expanded and are filled, the partial pressure of oxygen in the lungs is much higher than in the blood stream. Oxygen molecules travel rapidly down this pressure gradient, until there is equilibrium. When the blood first reaches the lungs, it has a much higher partial pressure of carbon dioxide than the interior of the lung. The CO_2 also travels the pressure gradient from high to low. Once the blood reaches the body tissues, the reverse happens. The blood has a high ppO_2, the tissues do not. The tissues have a high $ppCO_2$, the blood does not. So gas transfer is initiated by pressure gradient.

3.2 BODY PROCESSES AS THEY RELATE TO DIVING

3.2.1 Gas Transportation in the Blood Stream

The average human body contains about five quarts of blood. Blood is made up mostly of water (plasma). Warm water is not an efficient carrier of oxygen or other gases. In blood, there are also red and white blood cells. The white cells fight infection; the red specialize in transportation. In the red cells are red proteins called hemoglobin. The hemoglobin is a very efficient carrier of gases. Up to four oxygen molecules bond to each molecule of hemoglobin, forming a compound known as oxyhemoglobin.

A hemoglobin molecule with oxygen bound to it has a bright red color, and without the oxygen it is so dark red that it actually looks blue. This is what gives the arterial blood (oxygenated) the red color, and the venous blood (de-oxygenated) the blue color.

Hemoglobin carries some of the carbon dioxide in the blood stream, but up to 70% of the CO_2 is transported by the plasma. CO_2, reacting with the water, forms carbonic acid (H_2CO_3), then becomes bicarbonate ions, which diffuse into the plasma. Bicarbonate ions are the same ingredient that causes soda pop to bubble up when opened, releasing carbon dioxide gas. They work the same way when the blood reaches the capillaries in the lungs. The CO_2 is released from the blood, passes through the capillary walls into the alveoli, and is exhaled. The lungs contain enzymes that speed the process up considerably.

The carbon dioxide carried by the hemoglobin from the body's cells to the lungs is acidic. As the hemoglobin arrives in the alveolar capillaries of the lungs, it first picks up oxygen molecules. The oxygen molecules cause the hemoglobin to become even more acidic. This causes the hemoglobin to release the molecules of carbon dioxide, in order to keep its pH levels correct. The hemoglobin, now with a full load of oxygen, moves through the blood stream to body cells that require oxygen. On arrival, the hemoglobin first picks up acidic carbon dioxide. To keep the pH level correct, the hemoglobin releases the oxygen that it has carried from the lungs. This process, mentioned earlier, is called the Haldane Effect after the man who discovered it. J. S. Haldane was a physiologist who co-developed the first formulas to estimate the amounts of inert gas absorbed and released by the body. Every decompression table used by divers is at least partially based on work performed by this man.

3.2.2 The Respiratory Process

To fully discuss the process of breathing and respiration, it is necessary to know the definition of the terms used. The following definitions are important in diving:

Respiratory Cycle – One complete breath, including inspiration and expiration.

Respiratory Rate – The number of complete respiratory cycles that occur in one minute. At rest, the normal adult will have a rate of between 10 and 20 breaths per minute.

Total Lung Capacity – The total volume of air the lungs will hold when completely filled. Normally, this figure is five to six liters.

Vital Capacity – The volume of air expelled from the lungs after a full inspiration. The average is four to five liters.

Tidal Volume – The volume of air moved in and out during a single, normal cycle. At rest, tidal volume averages one half liter. This increases greatly during exertion.

Inspiratory Reserve Volume – The amount of air brought in by continuing to inhale after a normal inspiration. It averages 2.5 liters at rest.

Expiratory Reserve Volume – The amount of air that can be expelled by continuing to exhale after a normal expiration. The normal amount is one liter at rest.

Residual Volume – The amount of air that remains in the lungs, even after forcefully expiring. It averages one to 1 to 1.5 liters.

Respiratory Minute Volume (RMV) – The total amount of air that moves into and out of the lungs in one minute. By multiplying the tidal volume by the respiratory rate, you get the respiratory minute volume. RMV averages 6 liters per minute (l/m) at complete rest and may be 100 l/m or more when performing severe work.

Maximum Breathing Capacity (MBC) – The greatest respiratory minute volume a person can produce during a short period of forceful breathing.

Respiratory Dead Space – The parts of the respiratory system that have no alveoli and in which no gas exchange takes place (trachea, bronchial tubes, bronchi). This dead space normally averages less than one quarter of a liter, but increases with shallower breathing.

OXYGEN CONSUMPTION AND RMV AT VARIOUS WORK RATES

Activity	Oxygen consumption l/m	RMV l/m	Oxygen consumption cfm	RMV cfm
Rest				
Bed rest	0.25	6	0.00875	0.21
Sitting	0.30	7	0.0105	0.25
Standing	0.40	9	0.014	0.32
Light Work				
Slow walking, hard bottom	0.6	13	0.021	0.455
Walking 2 mph	0.7	16	0.025	0.56
Swimming 0.5 knot	0.8	18	0.028	0.63
Moderate Work				
Slow walking, mud bottom	1.1	23	0.039	0.805
Brisk walking 4 mph	1.2	27	0.042	0.945
Swimming 0.85 knot	1.4	30	0.049	1.05
Fast walking, hard bottom	1.5	34	0.053	1.19
Heavy Work				
Swimming 1.0 knot (hard)	1.8	40	0.063	1.4
Fast walking, mud bottom	1.8	40	0.063	1.4
Running 8 mph	2.0	50	0.07	1.75
Severe Work				
Swimming 1.2 knots (severe)	.5	60	0.0875	2.1
Uphill running	4.0	95	0.14	3.325

Rates are averaged; individual rates vary. Oxygen values reflect medical standard temperature and pressure, using dry gas. RMV values reflect a body temperature of 98.6°F, ambient barometric pressure, and gas saturated with water vapor.

The level of work performed determines the amount of oxygen the body consumes. The table above compares oxygen consumption and respiratory minute volume at various levels of work. Each individual has an upper limit to their ability to work, since the heart and lungs can only supply so much oxygen to the body's cells. Anything that restricts the ability to breathe or increases the work of breathing will limit the ability to work even more.

In emergency situations, the human body will operate on an oxygen debt, with the muscles working for a short time without oxygen. This is a very limited time, and the oxygen must be consumed a short time later, but it can save a life. The better physical condition a person is in, the greater the available oxygen debt, and the greater the physical work that can be performed with an oxygen debt.

The human body produces almost exactly the same amount of carbon dioxide as the amount of oxygen it consumes. The ratio between the carbon dioxide produced and the oxygen consumed is known as the respiratory quotient. This respiratory quotient can vary from 0.7 to 1.0, depending on diet and level of work.

The carbon dioxide produced by humans on the surface is not usually a consideration, unless in a very confined, sealed area. Underwater, however, carbon dioxide must be constantly ventilated from the diver's helmet, as it poses a considerable threat to life.

3.2.3 Thermoregulation

A huge issue in diving operations is exposure to cold water, and increasingly more in recent years, exposure to hot water. The human body is designed to operate at 98.6°F (37 C). There is a narrow range in which body temperature can fluctuate, and outside of this range, the body cannot function normally. The human body generates enough heat every hour to warm two liters of cold water up to body temperature; while performing heavy work, up to ten times that amount of heat may be generated. If the heat generated was not transferred and allowed to build up within the body, in a short time the temperature would pass 105°F (41 C), the point at which damage is being done to the body's cells.

The heat generated within the body is transferred by the blood and cooled using two organs: the lungs and the skin. Some of the heat is carried by the bloodstream to the lungs and discharged with exhaled breath, but the majority of the heat transferred is carried to the capillaries beneath the surface of the skin. The sweat glands release moisture, and with the evaporation of this moisture, the skin is cooled, which in turn cools the blood. This explains why, on hot, humid days (when less sweat evaporates) a human is unable to perform as much work. Water has far greater thermal conductivity than air does, and because of this, heat transfer occurs at a much higher rate when the body is immersed in water, than when surrounded by air.

3.3 PHYSIOLOGICAL PROBLEMS THAT AFFECT THE DIVER

3.3.1 Thermal Stress

An air temperature of 72°F is comfortable for a person at rest, but in order not to have significant heat loss, water temperature must be at 91°F (unless some sort of suit is worn). Conversely, if the water temperature is above 93°F, the core body temperature will rise. Lower water temperatures will cause hypothermia, higher temperatures cause hyperthermia. Either one of these conditions in extreme cases will result in death; less extreme cases will affect gas transfer and likely will lead to pressure related illness.

3.3.1.1 Hypothermia

When the core temperature of the human body drops below the normal range, the condition is known as hypothermia. Hypothermia is a threat to any human exposed to colder temperatures, but much more so to those immersed in water. This includes shipwreck survivors, those who fall overboard, and of course, the working diver. As the body temperature drops, the metabolism increases as the body attempts to bring the temperature back to the normal range. This increased metabolism multiplies the effect on the hypothermic diver exponentially, as it changes the rate at which the diver takes on a gas load, and the rate the gas load eliminates through decompression. Worse still, the onset of hypothermia is typically late in the dive, when the diver's tissue is already saturated with inert gas, and the metabolic changes prevent off-gassing during the decompression phase of the dive.

SYMPTOMS OF HYPOTHERMIA IN ORDER OF APPEARANCE

Initial onset	Chills, slight shivering
Mild hypothermia	Metabolism increases, uncontrolled shivering
Moderate hypothermia	Impaired mental function, slurred speech, enunciation problems
Serious hypothermia	Decreased shivering, muscle and joint rigidity, jerky movements

PATIENTS WITH SYMPTOMS BELOW MUST BE HANDLED WITH CARE TO AVOID DAMAGE TO INTERNAL ORGANS

Severe hypothermia	Irrational behavior, confusion, stupor, joint and muscular rigidity, decreased pulse and respiration
Critical hypothermia	Unconsciousness, lack of response to pain stimuli, loss of reflex, pupils fixed and dilated, ventricular fibrillation, cardiac and respiratory failure, death

Source: *The Commercial Diver's Handbook* ©Best Publishing Company

The diving supervisor or radio operator should be aware of any changes in the speech patterns of the diver, as well as inability to perform simple tasks. Shivering does not occur in all cases of hypothermia. The diving supervisor must be made aware when the first symptoms of hypothermia present. The dive should be aborted as soon as hypothermia symptoms are noted.

Thermal Protection for Divers

Water Temp (°F)	Type of Suit
80 - 75	3 – 5 mil wetsuit
75 - 65	5 – 7 mil wetsuit
65 - 35	variable volume drysuit (thinsulate underwear for colder temps)
below 40	hot water suit

Source: *The Commercial Diver's Handbook* ©Best Publishing Company

The above chart is only intended for a guideline; divers can work below 40°F in a drysuit but extended bottom times at temperatures below this will require a hot water suit to keep the diver's core temperature up sufficiently. Even a slight drop in the core temperature is an issue in deep diving, since metabolic rates change, affecting the rate the body will take on a gas load and the rate that it off-gasses. A chilled diver, particularly when decompressing, is more susceptible to decompression sickness. The task the diver is performing seems to have some bearing on the onset of symptoms of hypothermia. Tasks such as welding, where the diver has to remain very still, seem to be worse than tasks involving heavy work.

Treatment of Hypothermia:

Patients with mild, moderate, or serious hypothermia must not be rewarmed quickly, as blood circulation through cold tissue may cause **after drop**, a condition in which the core temperature drops further after rewarming begins. Do not use direct heat to rewarm the casualty. Use blankets or sleeping bags and direct body contact. Do not rub the casualty's skin; give warm drinks, not hot, and heat breathing gas if possible. Continue to monitor pulse, respiration, and blood pressure until core temperature is in the normal range.

Patients with severe or critical hypothermia should be re-warmed only on the advice of a physician, or in the absence of a physician, a diving medical technician. If there is no pulse or respiration present, do not assume death. Hypothermia victims with no detectable vital signs have been rewarmed and made full recoveries, even after hours with no apparent vital signs. It is believed after the initial rise in the metabolic rate, the metabolism slows (when the core temperature drops to a certain level), and the body goes into a near hibernation state. There is an old saying regarding hypothermia patients: "They are not dead until they are warm and dead." Do not start CPR unless it can be continued throughout the rewarming process under the advice of a physician or a diving medical technician.

3.3.1.2 Hyperthermia

Typically, when divers think of thermoregulation, they think of hypothermia issues arising from cold water. In the past few years, however, hot water and hyperthermia have become more common. Industrial facilities have divers work on heat exchangers. They want the divers in before it has even cooled down because they want to minimize downtime. Any water above 80°F poses a risk of hyperthermia to divers. Shortening bottom times will help, but if the water is warmer than 95°F, a hot water suit with cool water running through the system is the only safe solution. Hyperthermia is a threat to surface crew as well as divers. A supply of cold drinking water or high electrolyte drink should be readily available to the crew. If the temperature exceeds 90° F, the crew should operate in short shifts to minimize individual exposures. Depending on the temperature and the work involved, salt tablets may also be required by the crew.

Hyperthermia is also an issue to decompression chamber occupants. Internal temperature of deck decompression chambers should never exceed 85°F. If there is no interior chiller on the chamber, or if it is not in an air-conditioned room, blankets or burlap with water running over them will keep the temperature down considerably. Shielding the chamber from the sun with a tarpaulin helps as well.

SYMPTOMS OF HYPERTHERMIA IN ORDER OF APPEARANCE

Initial onset	Excessive sweating, excessive thirst
Mild hyperthermia	Unquenchable thirst, fatigue, lethargy, elevated pulse rate
Severe hyperthermia	Shock, rapid shallow breathing, unconsciousness, cardiac arrest

Source: *The Commercial Diver's Handbook* ©Best Publishing Company

Diving supervisors and personnel should be aware that hyperthermia can occur both underwater in warm water and on surface. Symptoms must not be ignored as initial onset symptoms will rapidly progress to severe in some individuals, depending on the individual's metabolism.

Treatment of Hyperthermia:

Patients with initial onset symptoms should be removed to a cooler area and hydrated with high electrolyte drinks such as Gatorade. Patients with mild symptoms should be removed to a cooler area and may be cooled by immersion in a cool bath or shower. They should also be hydrated with high electrolyte drinks. Patients with severe symptoms must be cooled as quickly as possible, while monitoring vital signs. Resuscitation may be required. Medical attention will be necessary for severe patients.

Over the past few years, with the thinning of the ozone layer, UV rays have become a safety issue on the job site. When working in the sun, particularly on the water, polarized UV-rated safety glasses or sunglasses should be worn, as well as sunblock on exposed skin. A little protection today will save having the parts surgically removed tomorrow.

3.3.2 Respiratory Problems in Diving

Respiratory problems can occur on the surface, but these problems are increased in both severity and also in consequence because of the environment the diver works in. If a person were to lose consciousness on the surface, the most serious consequence may be falling to the ground. In the underwater environment, losing consciousness can lead to death or serious pressure related injury.

Normal breathing is more difficult at depth, due to the increased density of the breathing gas. As depth increases, gas density increases as well. Air is 4 times as dense at 100 fsw as it is on the surface. This difficulty in breathing, known as increased breathing resistance, or increased work of breathing, dramatically reduces the ability to perform heavy work. On modern demand diving helmets, there is a knob that allows the second stage regulator to be adjusted to overcome the increased breathing resistance, but the diver still has to make the adjustments.

Increased pressure at depth also means higher partial pressures of the gases making up the breathing gas mixtures. These higher partial pressures increase the severity of various respiratory problems. Percentages of various gases and contaminants that would not be a concern at surface pressure can be lethal at depth.

3.3.2.1 Hypoxia

Although the term hypoxia may apply to any situation where the body's cells are not able to receive sufficient oxygen to function normally, in diving operations, hypoxia is taken to mean **insufficient oxygen available in the diver's breathing gas**. Hypoxia may occur due to using improper gas mixtures (bottom mix used at surface), equipment problems (rust in HP cylinders), medical problems (near drowning, CO poisoning), or by entering a confined space with poor air quality. Regardless of the reason, hypoxia is deadly serious. The brain uses 20% of the oxygen the body takes in, and the brain will only survive between 4 and 6 minutes without oxygen before it dies.

Signs and Symptoms:
- Frequently none (the diver may suddenly lose consciousness)
- Mental changes similar to alcohol intoxication (lethargy and sleepiness)
- Confusion, clumsiness, slowed responses
- Inappropriate or foolish behavior
- Cyanosis (blue lips, nail beds, skin)
- No breathing

Treatment:
- Get casualty to surface or into fresh air
- If casualty is conscious, administer 100% oxygen
- If casualty is unconscious, treat as for gas embolism
- Monitor ABC (airway, breathing, circulation), and administer CPR if necessary

EFFECTS OF VARIOUS PARTIAL PRESSURES OF OXYGEN

ppO$_2$ (atm)	Effect and Where Encountered
<0.08	Coma, death
<0.08 – 0.10	Unconsciousness in most humans
0.09 – 0.10	Serious signs and symptoms of hypoxia
0.14 – 0.16	Initial signs and symptoms of hypoxia
0.21	Normal oxygen level in sea level air
0.35 – 0.40	Oxygen level in normal saturation diving operation
0.50	Threshold for whole body effects, maximum saturation diving exposure
1.4	IMCA limit for maximum ppO$_2$ for a working diver's breathing gas
1.6	Oxygen level on 100% at 20 sw (in-water O$_2$ decompression, USN Rev.6)
1.9	Oxygen level on 100% at 30 fsw (in-water O$_2$ decompression, USN Rev.6)
2.2	Oxygen level on 100% in chamber at 40 fsw (surface decompression)
2.4	60/40 nitrox treatment gas at 6 ATA (165 fsw)
2.8	100% oxygen at 2.8 ATA (60 fsw) as in USN TT5, TT6, and TT6A
3.0	50/50 nitrox treatment gas at 6 ATA (165 fsw)

Source: *The Commercial Diver's Handbook* ©Best Publishing Company

3.3.2.2 Hypercapnia

The most common respiratory problem encountered in diving operations is hypercapnia. Hypercapnia is defined as **excessive carbon dioxide in the body tissues**. This buildup of carbon dioxide can be caused by the following: inadequate ventilation of the helmet, a failure of a carbon dioxide scrubber, excessive carbon dioxide in the breathing gas, and also by "skip breathing." Diving equipment always has dead air space, and dead air space will trap exhaled carbon dioxide, leading to hypercapnia. It is imperative to ventilate the diving helmet on a regular basis. Skip breathing is a dangerous practice. Carbon dioxide poisoning occasionally produces no symptoms until after the diver has resurfaced. The most common symptom, thankfully, is a headache and slight dizziness.

Signs and Symptoms:
- Overwhelming urge to breathe (air starvation)
- Headache (usually after surfacing), confusion
- Dizziness, nausea, perspiration, flushed skin
- Muscle weakness, clumsiness, slowed responses
- Muscle twitching, convulsions, unconsciousness (severe cases)

Treatment:
- Ventilate helmet immediately.
- If headache or other symptoms occur in water, surface as soon as possible.
- Administer fresh air or 100% oxygen, depending on severity of symptoms.
- Do not physically restrain a convulsing casualty.
- Place unconscious casualties in the recovery position and monitor ABCs.

3.3.2.3 Carbon Monoxide Poisoning

The most dangerous respiratory problem encountered by a diver is carbon monoxide poisoning. Carbon monoxide is produced by the incomplete combustion of hydro-carbon fuels in internal combustion engines and also by burned lubricating oils, such as those used in compressors. Diesel engines produce less carbon monoxide than gasoline engines, but diesels still produce it in high enough concentrations that exhaust fumes picked up by an intake and delivered to the diver can have dire consequences.

Since carbon monoxide (CO) has no odor, taste, smell, and it can't be seen in the air, its presence is difficult to detect. Often there are not any symptoms of poisoning prior to the casualty losing consciousness.

In addition, the hemoglobin in the blood (the red protein that bonds to oxygen) bonds with carbon monoxide about 300 times more readily than it does with oxygen. This stops the hemoglobin from bonding to both the oxygen and the carbon dioxide. CO bonds with myoglobin (the protein in muscle that stores oxygen and transports it) and also with the respiratory enzymes. (They permit oxygen use in the cells.) This basically stops all of the cellular functions in the body. Oxygen uptake, transport, and utilization is disrupted. Carbon monoxide poisoning is, in effect, hypoxia caused by carbon monoxide – the body starves for oxygen.

Carboxyhemoglobin(HbCO) Relative to CO Exposure

Continuous Exposure Level of CO in PPM (Parts Per Million)	HbCO in Blood
50ppm	8.4%
40ppm	6.7%
30ppm	5.0%
20ppm	3.3%
10ppm	1.7%

Source: *NOAA Diving Manual* ©Best Publishing Company

The toxic effects of carbon monoxide exposure increase as the depth increases. Once the CO has bonded with the hemoglobin (creating carboxyhemoglobin), it then is very difficult to eliminate it from the body, often requiring hyperbaric oxygen treatment. CO elimination is in half-times, in the same way that nitrogen elimination occurs. Breathing sea level air, it takes 5.5 hours for the first half of the CO to leave, 5.5 hours for half of the remainder to leave, 5.5 hours for half of that to leave, and so on. By breathing 100% oxygen at the surface, the half-time is cut to 1.5 hours. At 3 ATA in the chamber on O_2, the half-time is reduced to about 23 minutes. For this reason, CO poisoning is best treated with hyperbaric oxygen.

Signs and Symptoms:

- Often no symptoms before unconsciousness
- Headache, nausea, dizziness, muscle weakness, numbness in lips
- Cherry red lips (Once considered the classic symptom, it typically occurs only when the casualty is deceased or near death.)

Treatment:

- Provide fresh air immediately and oxygen if available.
- Unconscious casualties require treatment with hyperbaric oxygen.
- Monitor casualty closely.

3.3.2.4 Excessive Breathing Resistance

The human body, because of its construction, requires a certain amount of effort in order to breathe. Effort is required to lift the rib cage and expand the intercostals, (the muscles of the chest) when inhaling. This effort is known as "work of breathing." When the work of breathing becomes too great due to excessive breathing resistance, the body does not get the breathing gas exchange required to exhale enough carbon dioxide or to inhale enough breathing gas. The carbon dioxide levels build to the point of hypercapnia. This has been established as the probable cause in past diving accidents.

Causes of Excessive Breathing Resistance:
- Regulator not adjusted for depth (increased gas density)
- Insufficient delivery pressure of breathing gas to the diver
- Poorly tuned regulator in helmet (bent horseshoe yoke)
- Diving hose with too small bore
- Diving hose with dirt or debris inside bore
- Partially closed main supply valve on the air supply system
- Tight-fitting suit that constricts chest

Prevention:
- Use free-flow adjustment (dial-a-breath) as you descend.
- Ensure proper delivery pressure on gas supply.
- Tune up helmet regulators on a regular basis.
- Use the proper umbilical, and tape ends when not in use.
- Ensure that supply valves are properly opened during operations.
- Wear only proper fitting suits and equipment.

3.3.2.5 Lipoid Pneumonia

If a diver breathes air or breathing gas with suspended particles of petroleum vapor, lipoid pneumonia will be contracted. When petroleum particles reach the lung, they prevent the lung from properly exchanging gases, in the same way that bacterial and viral pneumonia do. The difference is, with the proper medication, the other pneumonias are often cured. Lipoid pneumonia remains as long as the petroleum particles remain, which is usually a period of many years. This condition has often been called "black lung."

Prevention:
- Use only approved breathable compressor oil.
- Use clean filters on the downstream end of the system.
- Do not allow petroleum products around life-support gear.

3.4 DIRECT EFFECTS OF DISBARIC PRESSURE

3.4.1 Barotrauma

Barotrauma is a term that means *pressure injury*. As the diver descends, the pressure on the outside of the body increases. Body tissues that are solid, or cavities that are liquid filled, are not compressed. Any cavity in the body that is gas filled, however, compresses, and must be equalized. Failure to equalize, either on descent or ascent, causes the tissue in and around these cavities to be injured (suffer barotrauma). The most common areas to suffer barotrauma are the ear and the sinus cavities. The body areas most often affected are the ear, sinus cavities, teeth, lungs, stomach, and intestines.

3.4.1.1 The Ear

The human ear serves two main purposes: hearing and balance. The ear is divided into three sections: outer ear, middle ear, and inner ear. The outer ear consists of the external ear and the ear canal. The middle ear consists of the eardrum, the small bones connecting the eardrum to the inner ear, and the eustachian tube. The inner ear consists of the cochlea and the vestibular apparatus.

Sound waves are captured by the external ear and travel through the ear canal to the eardrum. The eardrum vibrates, causing the linkage of small bones between it and the cochlea to vibrate. The cochlea is filled with fluid and contains hair cells. The hair cells pick up the vibration and transmit electrical impulses through the cochlear nerve to the brain. Different impulses are sent for different sounds. The vestibular part of the inner ear is the part that senses movement and controls our balance.

As the diver descends, pressure increases on the outside of the eardrum. To avoid injury, this pressure must be equalized. This may be done by swallowing, moving the jaw, or by the Valsalva maneuver. The Valsalva involves pressurizing the nose and mouth with the nostrils blocked. This forces gas into the eustachian tube and equalizes the pressure on the outside of the eardrum. Divers should always clear their ears as they descend and avoid excessive pressure on the eardrum. Failure to clear the ears will result in barotraumas (ear squeeze), which can cause various conditions including tinnitus (ringing in the ears), vertigo, and ruptured eardrum.

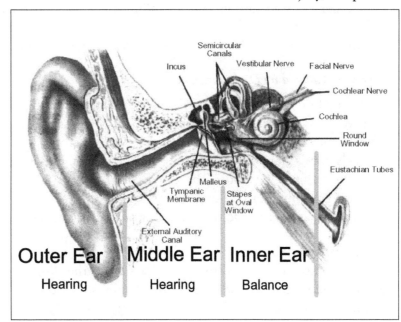

Source: *U.S. Navy Diving Manual*

Divers may encounter problems clearing the ears due to inflammation and swelling of the eustachian tube. This inflammation may be caused by cold or flu virus, allergies, or smoking. Decongestants and antihistamines will often reduce the swelling, allowing the eustachian tube to open. Divers should not use these drugs prior to diving, however, for two reasons: They alter other body functions (heart rhythm and temperature control), and they can wear off during the dive, resulting in a reverse squeeze.

Inner Ear Problems (Vertigo)

The inner ear performs two separate functions. The cochlea is the hearing sense organ, and the vestibular apparatus (including the semicircular canals) is the organ that senses motion and regulates the body's balance. If the balance mechanism is disrupted, the result is vertigo. Vertigo is not the same as dizziness. When experiencing vertigo, often the diver will see the horizon shift abruptly, then the environment will spin fast. If walking, the victim may stumble and fall. Loss of balance, nausea, and vomiting are the typical symptoms. There are three different types of vertigo that commonly affect divers: alternobaric vertigo, caloric vertigo, and vertigo caused by disbaric illness, such as Type II decompression sickness or arterial gas embolism. All three types involve either the inner ear or the vestibular nerve that runs from the inner ear to the brain.

Alternobaric Vertigo

This condition results from over pressuring the middle ear, due to repeated attempts to clear the ears when the diver is having difficulty clearing. It also results when, during ascent, a reverse squeeze occurs, causing the middle ear to be over pressurized. Vertigo is often preceded by pain in the involved ear. Usually the vertigo does not last long, but it is often intense while it lasts and may be incapacitating to the diver. If the pressure causes damage to the round or oval window, or other structures of the inner ear, ear surgery may be required.

Caloric Vertigo

This condition results from having cold water stimulating the balance center (vestibular apparatus) in the inner ear. It may be caused by cold water entering one ear canal and not the other or by a ruptured eardrum allowing cold water to enter one of the middle ears. Caloric vertigo is incapacitating to the diver, but the symptoms typically will pass as soon as the water in the middle ear warms up to body temperature.

Vertigo Caused by Disbaric Illness

This condition typically does not involve the inner ear or the vestibular apparatus, it involves the vestibular nerve. This condition is a result of inert gas being released too quickly by body tissue and forming bubbles. The bubbles place pressure on the nerve, causing improper signals to be sent to the brain. Bubbles can also form in the inner ear itself, putting pressure on the vestibular apparatus. This can occur in Type II (CNS) decompression sickness or in arterial gas embolism. The only way to correct this type of vertigo is through recompression treatment, appropriate to the condition causing the vertigo.

3.4.1.2 The Sinus Cavities

The nasal sinuses are located in hollow cavities in the skull bones. They are lined with mucus membranes identical to those in the nose. The sinuses have air pockets in them joined to the nasal cavity by small passages.

The sinuses must be equalized as the diver descends and ascends, or a painful sinus squeeze will result. The sinus passages are susceptible to inflammation and swelling in the same way the eustachian tube is. The sinuses will often hemorrhage, leading to a bloody discharge out of the nose after a dive.

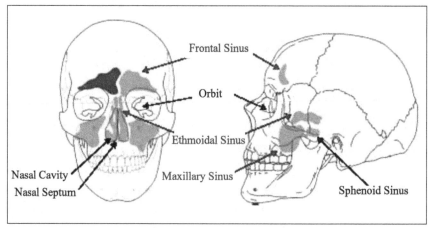

Source: *U.S. Navy Diving Manual*

Sinus squeezes can be extremely painful, and a diver that pushes past the initial pain can find a descending and ascending causes extreme sinus pain. Head colds, allergies, and air pollution can cause the sinus passages to become inflamed. Divers must not dive with a head cold or allergic symptoms.

3.4.1.3 The Teeth

When a tooth is decaying, it gives off gas. A small pocket of this gas in a tooth, when compressed, will often suck the surrounding pulp into the cavity, creating pain.

Poorly fitting or cracked dental fillings also may allow gas to leak in, around, and under them. If the gas exits the tooth as easily as it enters, there is no problem. If it does not, the tooth can crack, or in extreme cases, explode.

Wet welding and burning involve the diver being exposed to electrical current while immersed. This current usually will cause electrolysis in metals exposed to it. Fillings in teeth that are metallic will corrode and disappear when this happens. If this process allows gas to enter a tooth under pressure, it may not vent out of the tooth on ascent quickly enough to avoid an exploded tooth. Divers should have metallic fillings replaced with epoxy fillings whenever possible. Good dental health for divers is always a good idea.

3.4.1.4 Lung Squeeze

This condition is the result of diving to depth without adding any air to the lungs, a practice normally carried out by breath-hold or free divers. When air is not added to the lungs as the diver descends, blood and tissue fill the areas normally filled with air, and eventually the chest collapses, bringing death. For this to happen to a working diver would have to be heavily weighted and fall rapidly to bottom.

3.4.1.5 Body Squeeze

If a diver does not adjust the air in a variable volume drysuit during descent, the suit will collapse and folds in the suit will pinch the diver's body, creating purple welts and bruises. This is known as suit squeeze. Although a severe case looks bad, it is only painful for a short while, if at all. With surface-supplied diving gear, if the umbilical is cut off at the surface, the only thing preventing the diver from being squeezed up into the helmet is the presence of the non-return valve. For this reason, these non-return valves must be checked for proper function every time the helmets are installed online.

3.4.1.6 Reverse Squeeze of the Stomach and Intestines

Gas produced in the gastrointestinal tract during digestion can cause problems for divers. If this gas is generated while the diver is under pressure, it will expand on ascent, causing pain in the abdomen. Each diver should know what foods cause gas and avoid eating them prior to pressurization.

3.4.2 Pulmonary Overinflation Syndromes

According to Boyle's Law, gas in the diver's lungs will expand during ascent. If the lung is full, and air is not exhaled, the result will be a pulmonary overinflation. This condition is sometimes called "ruptured lung" or "burst lung syndrome," but this is misleading. In overinflation incidents, the lungs do not have to rupture or burst in order for an arterial gas embolism to occur. Breathing gas may be forced through the alveolar membrane and into the capillary, causing an embolism without any "rupture" of the lung.

Excessive internal pressure on the lungs can be caused by deliberately holding the breath in a rapid ascent (panic), blocked airway (unconscious diver) in an uncontrolled ascent, a medical problem (diver with pneumonia or chest cold), or by a regulator failure occurring while the diver is inhaling. A pressure differential between 1.5 and 2.0 psi is sufficient to lead to pulmonary overinflation syndrome. The possible consequences of pulmonary overinflation include the following: mediastinal emphysema, subcutaneous emphysema, simple pneumothorax, tension pneumothorax, and arterial gas embolism. In each of these, gas escapes from the lung and causes various problems in other parts of the body.

3.4.2.1 Mediastinal Emphysema

In mediastinal emphysema, gas from the lung escapes into the tissues around the heart, the major blood vessels, and the trachea.

Signs and Symptoms:

- Pain under breastbone, in neck, shoulder
- Shortness of breath, difficulty breathing
- Shock, cyanosis of skin or nail beds
- Deviated Adam's apple, swollen neck
- Cough, voice changes

Treatment:

- Monitor ABCs; monitor for shock.
- Administer 100% oxygen.
- Watch for signs of other pulmonary barotraumas.
- Transport to the nearest medical facility.

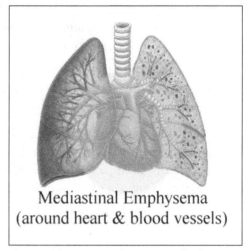

Mediastinal Emphysema
(around heart & blood vessels)

Source: *The Commercial Diver's Handbook*
©Best Publishing Company

3.4.2.2 Subcutaneous Emphysema

In subcutaneous emphysema, gas from the lung is forced under the skin of the neck. It sometimes occurs along with mediastinal emphysema.

Signs and Symptoms:

- Full feeling in neck, change in voice
- Swelling around neck and upper chest
- Crackling under skin (rice crispy neck)
- Cough

Treatment:

- Give oxygen if breathing is impaired. See a doctor.
- Watch for signs of other pulmonary barotraumas.
- Recompression only necessary if symptoms of embolism are present.

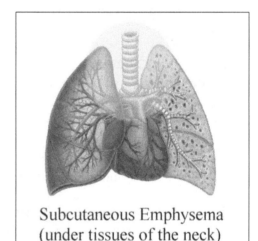

Subcutaneous Emphysema
(under tissues of the neck)

Source: *The Commercial Diver's Handbook*
©Best Publishing Company

3.4.2.3 Simple Pneumothorax

A simple pneumothorax is a one-time introduction of gas into the pleural space; gas from a torn alveoli gets between the lung and the chest wall. This area has a two-layered membrane called the pleura. The gas between the layers forms a bubble that expands on ascent, causing the lung to partially collapse. Symptoms clear up over time.

Signs and Symptoms:

- Chest pain (on deep breathing)
- Leaning toward the affected side
- Hypotension, rapid shallow breathing
- Decreased lung sounds on affected side

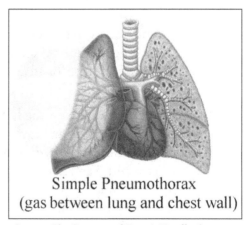

Simple Pneumothorax
(gas between lung and chest wall)

Source: *The Commercial Diver's Handbook*
©Best Publishing Company

Treatment:
- Monitor closely for signs of tension pneumothorax.
- Monitor ABCs; administer 100% oxygen.
- Transport to nearest hospital.

3.4.2.4 Tension Pneumothorax

The difference between tension and simple pneumothorax is that tension gets worse with every breath. Each breath allows more gas to escape, collapsing the lung, and even pushing the heart out of place in some cases.

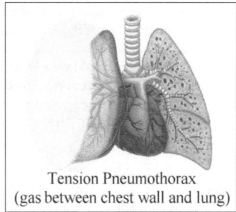

Tension Pneumothorax
(gas between chest wall and lung)

Source: *The Commercial Diver's Handbook*
©Best Publishing Company

Signs and Symptoms:
- Severe chest pain (during breathing)
- Leaning toward affected side
- Absence of lung sounds on affected side
- Dyspnea, hypotension, cyanosis, shock

Treatment:
- Place casualty injured side down, monitoring ABCs.
- Treat casualty for shock and administer 100% oxygen.
- Transport immediately to hospital (air must be vented from chest cavity).

3.4.2.5 Arterial Gas Embolism

The most serious of the pulmonary over-inflation consequences is the arterial gas embolism. In the past, it was thought that an embolism occurred only with torn alveoli. It has been proven that gas pressure, if too high inside the alveoli, can force the gas through the membrane into the capillaries. The abbreviation AGE is commonly used; if there is brain involvement, it is referred to as a cerebral arterial gas embolism, or CAGE. The bubbles in the arteries expand on ascent, blocking blood flow, resulting in the death of the affected tissues or organs. Any or all of the signs or symptoms below may be present.

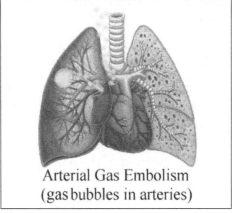

Arterial Gas Embolism
(gas bubbles in arteries)

Source: *The Commercial Diver's Handbook*
©Best Publishing Company

Signs and Symptoms:
- Chest pain, severe headache, cough, shortness of breath
- Bloody sputum, bloody froth around nose and /or mouth
- Impaired or distorted vision, blindness (partial or complete)
- Numbness, tingling, weakness or paralysis, dizziness, confusion
- Sudden unconsciousness (usually immediately after surfacing)
- Respiratory arrest, death

Treatment:
- Closely monitor ABCs, start CPR if necessary.
- Administer 100% oxygen with the casualty in the recovery position.
- Immediate recompression on 100% oxygen to depth of relief (not less than 60 fsw).
- Perform neurological examination on the casualty as soon as possible.

IMPORTANT NOTE

Type II Decompression Sickness and AGE often present the same or similar signs and symptoms. Typically, Type II symptoms are displayed after the casualty has been on the surface for 10 minutes, and symptoms of AGE or CAGE often are presented immediately upon surfacing; certainly in less than 10 minutes. **Casualties presenting any neurological symptoms less than 5 minutes after surfacing must be treated for arterial gas embolism**. If there is a medical facility in the immediate area with hyperbaric treatment capability, the casualty should be transported immediately to the facility. If not, recompress on site, and get a physician to the chamber ASAP. Any delay in recompression will dramatically reduce the casualty's chances of recovery.

Prevention: Never hold your breath underwater, do not dive with a chest cold, and always ascend at the prescribed ascent rate for the table. On uncontrolled ascent – EXHALE.

3.5 INDIRECT EFFECTS OF INCREASED PRESSURE

The injuries and conditions explained so far have been caused by unequal pressure causing damage to portions of the body (direct effects of pressure). The indirect effects of pressure are those resulting from elevated partial pressures of the individual gases in the diver's breathing gas mixture. They include changes in the body function caused by the high partial pressures and also saturation of the tissues by the gas.

3.5.1 Inert Gas Narcosis

Inert gas narcosis occurs when the high partial pressure of inert gas dissolved in the body tissues causes the diver to display symptoms similar to intoxication. The most common inert gas narcosis encountered is nitrogen narcosis. Although it was named the "Rapture of the Deep" by Cousteau, there often is nothing particularly "rapturous" about nitrogen narcosis, especially when it occurs in fast-moving, dark, or very cold water.

Nitrogen narcosis is dangerous to the diver because it increases the risk of getting into trouble, while reducing the ability to get out of trouble.

The inert gases that cause narcosis, unless breathed at elevated partial pressures, have no narcotic effect. High pressure causes the gas to dissolve in the protein coverings of the nerve cells, and this, in turn, interferes with the ability of the nerve cells to respond to stimulus and to transmit the proper signals to the brain. The higher the partial pressure, the more inert gas is dissolved, and the more it affects the normal function of the nervous system. The chart below illustrates the effects of nitrogen narcosis at different depths.

Narcotic Effects of Nitrogen in Air Diving

Depth in fsw	Effect on diver
0 - 100	Mild impairment of performance, mild euphoria.
100	Reasoning and memory affected. Delayed response to visual and auditory stimuli.
100 - 165	Inappropriate laughter (may be overcome by self-control). Idea fixation and overconfidence. Errors in calculation.
165	Sleepiness, hallucinations, impaired judgment.
165 - 230	Party atmosphere. Terror reaction in some. Talkative, dizziness, uncontrollable laughter approaching hysteria in some divers.
230 - 300	Exaggerated delay in response to stimuli. Lack of concentration, mental confusion. Increased auditory sensitivity (sounds seem louder).
300	Stupefaction. Severe impairment of practical activity and judgment. Mental abnormalities and memory loss. Euphoria and hyperexcitability. Hallucinations similar to those caused by hallucinogenic drugs.

Source: *U.S. Navy Diving Manual*

The chart was developed through testing performed by the U.S. Navy Experimental Diving Unit. The effects of narcosis increase as the depth increases. Nitrogen is not the only inert gas that causes narcosis. Helium does not appear to have any narcotic effects, nor does neon, but argon is narcotic, although at far deeper depths than nitrogen.

It appears that divers can, to a point, become acclimatized to the effects. With repeated dives to deeper depths on air, many divers are less susceptible to nitrogen narcosis. It is thought that narcosis plays a large part in diving related hypothermia, as the ability to perceive cold is reduced. Susceptibility to nitrogen narcosis is affected by the diver's diet, alcohol consumption, and by the partial pressure of carbon dioxide. Controlling the fat level in the diet appears to help in susceptibility, as does avoiding coffee and other diluents. Proper hydration prior to the dive appears to help. Having the diver vent the helmet when reaching the bottom often will dramatically reduce the effects. In many cases, the divers may not recall any of the effects of nitrogen narcosis after surfacing.

Signs and Symptoms:
- Lack of judgment, loss of practical skills
- A false sense of well-being, regardless of circumstances
- Lack of concern for the job at hand or for personal safety
- Inappropriate laughter, euphoria
- Inability to remember or carry out instructions

Prevention and Treatment:
- Have divers eat healthy and cut fat intake.
- Have divers refrain from alcohol if diving the following day.
- Have divers ventilate the helmet well as they near bottom.
- Reduce the diver's depth until symptoms subside.
- Gradually work the diver to deeper depths, over a period of time.

3.5.2 High Pressure Nervous Syndrome (HPNS)

When it was originally noticed in the mid-1960s, this condition was known as "helium tremors," since it was thought to be caused by breathing a helium mixture. Since then, other inert gases have shown to produce the same "tremors," and it has become evident it is increasing pressure and a high rate of compression that bring on HPNS.

HPNS occurs at depths greater than 400 fsw, and can be reduced by adding small amounts of nitrogen (5 – 10%) into the mixture, since nitrogen is a natural depressant. Slower compression rates or stage compression, with long intervals, can reduce the effects of HPNS. Some divers appear to be more susceptible than others to the effects of HPNS.

Symptoms include: dizziness, nausea, vomiting, postural tremors, fatigue, muscle twitching, abdominal cramps, decreased intellectual performance, insomnia, and poor sleep with terrible nightmares.

3.5.3 Oxygen Toxicity

Oxygen is the one gas we cannot survive without, yet at high partial pressures it becomes toxic. Divers are affected by two different types of oxygen toxicity: CNS (toxicity involving the central nervous system) and lung (toxicity involving the rest of the body, particularly the lungs).

3.5.3.1 CNS O$_2$ Toxicity

CNS oxygen toxicity can occur on the high end of the partial pressure levels with even a very short exposure. With a partial pressure above 1.6 atm, it can occur in as little as 5 minutes. CNS oxygen toxicity can lead to sudden unconsciousness, with no warning, and seizures. The most common signs and symptoms can be remembered by using the acronym CON-VENTID: CONvulsions, Vision, Ears ringing, Nausea, Tingling and twitching of face and lips, Irritability and restlessness, Dypsnea and dizziness. These can present in any order. The most common is the twitching of lips and facial muscles often seen during surface decompression and hyperbaric oxygen treatments.

3.5.3.2 Lung and "Whole Body" Toxicity

Lower partial pressures of oxygen over longer periods of time will cause oxygen toxicity to develop, affecting other parts of the body, particularly the lungs. Symptoms of lung and whole body toxicity include: chest pain, pain or coughing on deep breaths, fluid in the lungs, skin numbness, itching, headache, dizziness, nausea, vision problems, and reduction of aerobic capacity.

Individual Tolerance

Different individuals show different susceptibility to oxygen toxicity. Any one individual may be more susceptible at one time than at another. The exact reason for these variations is not presently known, but it is suspected temperature, physical exertion, immersion, and breathing gas density increase susceptibility to O$_2$ toxicity. Also, UHMS states CO$_2$ retention as well as some antibiotics will reduce the seizure threshold in O$_2$ toxicity. In the past, divers were required to have an "oxygen tolerance test" prior to employment as a diver. Due to the variations in susceptibility mentioned above, the test is seldom used today, as it has little, if any, predictive value.

Prevention of Oxygen Toxicity

Decompression and treatment tables that use 100% oxygen administered in the chamber have "air breaks" built in to help prevent oxygen toxicity from affecting the occupant. By having a five-minute air break between each of the specified oxygen breathing periods, the risk of oxygen toxicity is reduced, and the body's cells can repair damage caused by the oxygen radicals during these oxygen breathing periods. CNS oxygen toxicity is a significant threat to divers and individuals undergoing hyperbaric oxygen treatments. Even with air breaks, chamber operators must be constantly watching for signs of oxygen toxicity. CNS oxygen toxicity is most often seen later in oxygen breathing periods.

3.5.4 Decompression Sickness

By weight, ⅘ of the human body is liquid. Also, at high partial pressures, gases are absorbed into liquids until there is no longer a pressure gradient. Because of this, the deeper a diver descends, the more inert gas the body absorbs, up to the point of total saturation. This inert gas takes the same amount of time to go into solution, regardless of the depth, but less goes into solution at shallower depths, more at deeper depths. There are several different terms used for the process of the body taking on inert gas: gas uptake, taking on a gas load, and on-gassing. The terms used for the elimination of inert gas are: decompression, de-saturation, gas elimination, and off-gassing. Different tissues in the body take on a gas load and off-gas at different rates. Tissue with greater blood flow will absorb inert gas quicker and decompress quicker. Denser tissues will take more time to absorb and off-gas. Some tissue will absorb more inert gas and will require more to get it to the point of saturation. Body fat will absorb five times as much inert gas as will water. To reduce chances of decompression sickness, the diver must keep the percentage of fat in his/her body to a minimum.

For this inert gas to safely come out of solution, it has to happen at a precisely controlled rate. If inert gas is allowed to come out of solution too quickly, bubbles are formed in the tissues and bloodstream. These bubbles, when in tissue, put pressure on the surrounding tissues, whether nerves or organs, causing pain and damage. This condition, regardless of the inert gas used, is known as decompression sickness, or "the bends." When the bubbles (emboli) occur in the bloodstream, they reduce, restrict, and even block the flow of blood, causing damage and tissue death. This condition is known as an arterial gas embolism. Only one method can be used to treat either of these conditions – hyperbaric oxygen treatment.

Decompression sickness (DCS) is usually categorized as Type I or Type II by symptoms. When treating decompression sickness, we always treat according to the symptoms presented – never the history.

3.5.4.1 Type I Symptoms:
- Joint or muscle pain – a dull ache that does not move and is present at rest
- Lymph nodes – swelling and pain in the lymph nodes and surrounding tissue
- Skin symptoms – welts (resembling purple hives), itching with a mild reddish rash

3.5.4.2 Type II Symptoms:
- Skin symptoms – marbling or mottling (starts as itching, redness, then becomes bluish rash)
- Unusual extreme fatigue, numbness, tingling, muscle weakness, paralysis
- Vertigo, dizziness, hearing loss, ringing in the ears, vision problems, blindness
- Disrupted motor performance, lack of coordination, disrupted mental status
- Difficulty walking, balance problems, difficulty in urination
- Cardio-respiratory symptoms (chokes) – chest pain, cough, rapid shallow breaths

The percentage of cases in which various symptoms of decompression sickness occur:

Decompression Sickness Symptom	Percentage
Localized joint pain (30% in arm, 70% in leg)	58%
Motor or sensory impairment	10%
Skin bends (marbling, welts, rash, or itching)	10%
Dizziness, balance problems	9%
Lymph node swelling and/or pain	6%
Extreme fatigue, altered mental state, collapse	5%
Cardiopulmonary involvement (chokes)	2%

Source: *U.S. Navy Diving Manual*

Symptoms of decompression sickness usually occur shortly after the diver surfaces. Type I symptoms often occur between 30 minutes and 12 hours of surfacing, while Type II symptoms often are seen within 10 minutes of surfacing. The following figures are provided by the U.S. Navy:

- 60% of cases of DCS occurred within 1 hour
- 75% of cases of DCS occurred within 3 hours
- 95% of cases of DCS occurred within 6 hours
- 1% occurred after 12 hours

Divers presenting Type I symptoms initially, when not given immediate treatment, have progressed to Type II symptoms suggesting that a pain-only incident, when not treated immediately, may progress to a CNS incident. The frequency of this happening is not known, but several cases have been recorded to date. It is important to treat symptoms of either type of DCS as soon as possible. The chance of complete recovery diminishes as the length of time before treatment increases.

In the past, all cutaneous (skin) symptoms were considered to be Type I symptoms. However, marbling or mottling of the skin on the torso often precedes serious Type II symptoms. It typically starts as intense itching, progresses to redness, then to a dark bluish discoloration resembling marble. This is always treated now as a Type II symptom.

Pain from a sprain, strained muscle, or bruise may occasionally be mistaken for Type I DCS pain. Make notes if the diver mentions a soft tissue injury while in water and watch the diver walk and move as soon as he/she comes out of the water. If a diver limps, a painful ankle later on will not necessarily be considered an issue. Type I pain is always localized. It does not move around, and it does not radiate. Type I pain feels like someone has a crowbar in your joint and is trying to pry it apart. Type I pain may be felt in a muscle as well, but not nearly as often as in the joints. If there is any question as to whether pain is a DCS symptom or the result of a soft tissue injury, always treat for DCS.

Girdling pain, abdominal or thorax pain (not associated with breathing), pain that shoots down an arm or leg, or pain that moves from one location to another is considered to be a symptom of Type II, indicating spinal cord involvement. Any pain in the back which can not be linked to pain in a hip or shoulder should be considered a Type II symptom.

Any neurological symptom occurring after a dive should be considered a symptom of Type II DCS or arterial gas embolism. If there is any question whether it is AGE or DCS, always treat for AGE. Typically, neurosymptoms presenting within 5 minutes of surfacing are treated as embolism, and more than 5 minutes after surfacing are treated as a Type II bend. Symptoms of AGE are always sudden and dramatic. Fatigue is listed as a symptom of Type II DCS. Normal fatigue as occurring after a strenuous dive should not be considered a symptom, but if the diver is unusually fatigued after a dive that was not strenuous, perform a complete neurological examination and an extremity strength test to eliminate the possibility of Type II DCS. It is more common to notice problems in the extremity strength tests than it is in the neuroexamination, but a deficit in either should be considered a Type II symptom. The other area to watch for neurosymptoms is the diver's balance. Balance problems or vertigo may indicate inner ear barotrauma, but they also can indicate vestibular nerve problems, or a bubble in the inner ear, which are symptoms of Type II DCS.

An easy way to see if there are extremity strength or balance problems is to have the diver walk. The gait will seem awkward and unsteady. The diver's eyes will often tell you a lot as well. Unequal sized pupils are very noticeable, as is a squint indicating a vision problem. Talk to the diver and watch for indications of memory problems or other mental deficit.

3.6 TREATMENT OF ARTERIAL GAS EMBOLISM AND DECOMPRESSION SICKNESS

Hyperbaric treatment is always performed in a decompression chamber and is always based on treatment tables that specify the treatment depth, breathing gas used, travel time between stops, and time spent at each stop. Occasionally the Royal Navy treatment tables (British Royal Navy) are used since they have some deeper treatment options. The most commonly used tables worldwide are the U.S. Navy treatment tables. The diving supervisor is in charge of hyperbaric treatment; the diver medic consults with the hyperbaric physician on call, advises the diving supervisor, and takes care of the stricken diver during treatment. The decompression chamber is usually operated by divers during treatments. It is imperative to closely follow the treatment tables used in all respects every time and get the casualty breathing 100% oxygen (even before pressurization) with a tight sealing mask. Neurological assessment (including extremity strength testing) is the method used to determine neurological involvement, and baseline information is necessary to determine whether relief has been achieved. As soon as possible, perform a neurological exam on the casualty. (See Chapter 10: Hyperbaric Emergencies for the USN Neurological Examination and the RCN Rapid Neuro.).

3.6.1 Two Schools of Thought on Treatment of Decompression Sickness

There are currently two schools of thought in the industry on the treatment of decompression sickness: The first holds to the U.S. Navy method of differentiating between Type I (pain only) and Type II (central nervous system involvement), and uses the U.S. Navy Treatment Table 5 for Type I incidents; the second group tends to consider that "a bend is a bend" and treats every incident as if it is a Type II and uses the U.S. Navy Treatment Table 6 as a minimum for all incidents, even those that could be considered Type I. Both positions are acceptable; the second prefers to "err on the side of caution." The determining factor is typically the diving company's emergency procedures manual or corporate diving manual.

3.6.2 How Hyperbaric Treatment Works

The only way to treat decompression sickness or arterial gas embolism is through recompression. When the diver is recompressed in the chamber, the bubbles of inert gas are compressed back down and return into solution in the tissues and blood. By using various "treatment gases" as the diver's breathing media, the inert gas partial pressure is kept low while the pressure gradient (from tissue to bloodstream and bloodstream to lungs) is elevated. While this is happening, the pressure exerted on the diver's body is kept high enough to keep the gas in tissues and blood from bubbling during off-gassing and exhaling the inert gas. This is the same technique used in surface decompression using oxygen. There are several different treatment gases used: medical oxygen, oxygen enriched air (nitrox), and various helium/oxygen mixes. The most common and by far the best of theses treatment gases is medical oxygen.

4.0 DIVING AND SUPPORT EQUIPMENT

Commercial divers must work in a **hostile environment** that **will not support human life**. The human body, though it is primarily made up of water, cannot breathe a liquid. It must have a breathable gas for respiration. Gas must be delivered at a pressure acceptable to the human body, or serious problems will arise. All of the systems involved in the delivery of breathable gas to the diver are known as "life support" systems. For surface-oriented dives (air and mixed gas), these include the gas supply, the bailout, the umbilical, and the diver's helmet. In this chapter, we look at 1) life support equipment, 2) diver support equipment and 3) diver worn equipment. On most offshore projects, commercial diving equipment is inspected and function tested every six months as part of the IMCA D023 Air Diving System Audit.

4.1 LIFE SUPPORT EQUIPMENT

4.1.1 LP Gas Supply

There are two types of gas supply: low pressure (LP) and high pressure (HP). LP gas is supplied from either a low pressure compressor or from a portable volume tank filled by a compressor. The only gases used in the LP form are air and sometimes nitrox. LP gas is supplied by a breathing air compressor with a maximum output of 175–250 psi. These LP compressors differ from industrial compressors. They use food grade oil for lubrication, and they have a filtration system on the output end. Volume tanks are used on these LP compressors for two reasons: to minimize pressure fluctuations downstream at the diver's end and to allow moisture to settle out of the air and be bled off either manually or automatically.

Quincy 350 compressor

Quincy 5120–most popular compressor used worldwide

4.1.1.1 Care and Maintenance of LP Compressors

LP compressors **must not** be used in any environment where there is smoke (exhaust or otherwise), dust, chemical fumes, or any condition that causes poor air quality. The crew should be constantly aware of air quality when using LP compressors. Compressor oil and diesel oil must be checked prior to starting the compressor (every time). Filters should be checked on a regular basis. The frequency of filter changes will depend on both air quality and humidity. Drive belts should be checked for tension daily. Compressors outfitted with a manual moisture drain should be bled at least twice per hour. (See Chapter 25: Diesel Engines and Compressors.)

4.1.2 HP Gas Supply

High-pressure (HP) gas is supplied in cylinders that vary in size from the diver's bailout bottle, to the large semi-trailer-size cylinders used to supply helium and oxygen for deep saturation work. HP gas is supplied in the 2,000–3,000 psi range, and must be then regulated down to the delivery pressure required by the diver (at depth). From the storage cylinders, it is routed to the gas panel, where HP air or breathing gas is regulated down to the final required delivery pressure, which for the helmets used today is in the range of 100–120 psi over bottom pressure. For dives in the air range, the most common HP cylinder used is the "K" bottle, which is the same size as an industrial oxygen bottle. These are supplied in racks (also called quads) of between 4 and 54 cylinders. The cylinders are linked together by a manifold (made of either HP tubing or HP hose) and a king valve, and may be regulated at the gas rack or at the gas panel with a high-volume pressure regulator. If the regulator is at the rack, a low-pressure hose (whip) is used to connect to the panel. When the gas is regulated at the panel, a high-pressure whip is used. Whether HP or LP, all gas transfer whips must be restrained to keep them from whipping around in the event of a broken whip. HP breathing gas cylinders and quads must always be clearly marked as to content. Even when color coded, breathing gas must also be clearly labeled in English letters.

54-cylinder HP rack (quad)

King valve

High volume regulator

4.1.3 Bailout Gas Supply

Several different sizes of cylinder are used for bailout bottles—one size does not fit all. It is extremely important that the diver has sufficient bailout gas to return to surface or the bell. If there is not a large enough bailout bottle to allow for returning safely, then the answer is a set of doubles. Doubles tanks are often used for a bailout supply when performing long pipeline penetrations. (See Chapter 2: Underwater Physics to determine the duration of a bailout bottle.) Having the proper size bottle will not help, if the bottle is not full. Therefore, bailout cylinders must be checked with a gauge prior to and at the end of every dive. Safety conscious contractors have areas on the dive sheet to fill in the bailout pressures. The bailout, sometimes called the emergency gas supply, is to be worn on every dive, regardless of depth or duration. The only exception is on older free-flow units, such as the MKV, which do not have bailout capability. That is the primary reason this heavy gear is not used very often today. Bailouts, or emergency gas supply bottles (EGS), may be fitted with a standard scuba backpack, an integrated bailout vest, or attached directly to a harness style weight belt. The integrated bailout vests are the best and safest to use, as they have pockets for lead weights, a secure system to hold the bailout, and a tested 5-point diver recovery harness built into the unit.

Bailout bottles, whether air or mixed gas, use a standard scuba first stage regulator. The only difference in air and mixed-gas usage is that if the gas has high oxygen content (as in nitrox), both the regulator and cylinder must be oxygen cleaned prior to use. The bailout regulator should only have

Aqualung Legend bailout regulator
Photo courtesy of Aqualung

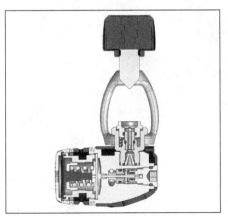

Cutaway drawing of Legend bailout regulator
Graphics courtesy of Aqualung

the required hoses. All other ports should be plugged off. In most cases, this is one hose – the LP whip to the helmet side-block at the bailout valve inlet port. Additional hoses increase the chances of the diver getting fouled. The bailout regulator is inspected and tested prior to each dive as part of the predive checklist, but they should be well cleaned and serviced on a regular basis.

80-cubic-foot bailout with standard backpack

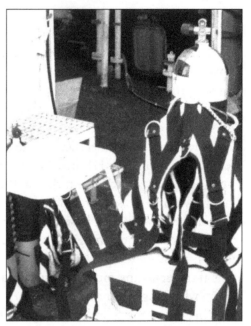

Integrated bailout harness vest (recovery vest)

4.1.3.1 Care and Maintenance of HP Gas Cylinders

HP gas cylinders must always be secured while being transported, whether on a truck or a vessel. Loose (single) cylinders should never be transported without being lashed down securely and never without the protective caps over the valves. Every high pressure cylinder, regardless of size, is required to be hydrostatically tested every five years and visually inspected every year. When the cylinders are hydro tested, they are stamped on the top of the cylinder, near the neck. Always look over HP cylinders to ensure the tests are up-to-date. If you fill or use an out-of-date cylinder, you are liabile for injury or damage.

Never use a damaged HP cylinder. HP cylinders should never be run completely empty. Always keep at least 150 pounds of gas in the cylinders. It is important to use caution when using HP gas. Prior to installing a regulator or gland for a manifold on a cylinder valve or king valve, crack open

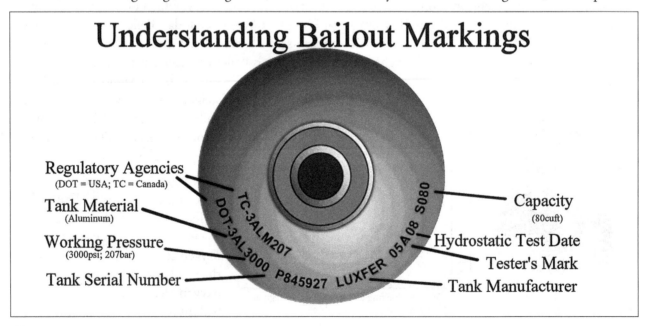

Understanding Bailout Markings

Regulatory Agencies
(DOT = USA; TC = Canada)

Tank Material
(Aluminum)

Working Pressure
(3000psi; 207bar)

Tank Serial Number

Capacity
(80cuft)

Hydrostatic Test Date

Tester's Mark

Tank Manufacturer

TC-3ALM207
DOT-3AL3000 P845927 LUXFER 05A08 S080

the valve briefly to ensure no debris is in the valve. When you open the valve on any HP cylinder, open it slowly, fully open, and then close it one quarter turn. When the temperature is below the freezing point, it is very important to be cautious with HP regulators. Bailout regulators freeze, and O-rings tend to become more like wood than rubber. First stage bailout regulators have suffered sudden and catastrophic failure, exploding in pieces at extremely cold temperatures; O-rings have failed as well. It was an O-ring failure due to extreme cold that brought down the space shuttle *Challenger* in January 1986. When working in cold climates, store bailout bottles and regulators in a warm (not hot) spot on the job until needed. On the opposite end of the scale, extreme heat will cause the gas in bottles to increase in pressure (remember your gas laws), blowing the overpressure relief disc. Never store HP cylinders in a hot area or in direct sunlight. If it cannot be avoided, keep the sun off them with a tarp and keep pressures lower than normal to avoid overpressure.

4.1.4 Umbilicals

The diver's hose, or umbilical, serves several purposes. It delivers breathing gas, is a safety line, is a means of communication to the surface, and allows the surface support crew to accurately gauge the diver's depth, allowing for safe decompression. The basic surface diving umbilical, therefore, requires four parts: the gas hose, the safety line, the communication (comms) wire, and the pneumofathometer (pneumo) hose. There are additional parts required for the umbilical in some cases. These include but are not limited to: hot water hose, breathing gas return (for hazmat or HeO_2 reclaim), helmet mounted lights, and helmet mounted cameras. The diver's umbilical is tended (hands-on) by at least one member of the diving crew **at all times**, both while the diver is dressed in on deck and while in the water. Some divers prefer a short leash, some like more room to move; each diver requests more or less slack (loose hose) from the supervisor, who passes the information on to the surface crew.

Until a very few years ago, the diver's umbilical remained unchanged from the ones used in the 1800s. Traditionally, the individual parts of the umbilical were joined together by seizing them with tarred marlin twine. Since the 1970s, seized umbilicals are rarely seen. Today they are constructed with duct tape joining the members, or they are the newer type of umbilical: the twisted umbilical. The various parts of a twisted umbilical are wound like the strands of a rope. The ends of the umbilicals (terminations) have seen a few changes over the years. A properly constructed umbilical still uses the telephone line clamp, unless it is a twisted umbilical. This clamp is a cast bronze two-piece clamp that bolts over the gas line and has eyes to accept the safety line and the snap shackle. Until the 1970s, umbilicals always used brass submarine fittings, but today they use long barbed O_2B or JIC fittings to match the non-return valves on the modern helmets. The biggest changes in umbilicals were the introduction of the lightweight hose in the early1990s and the change from ½" to ⅜" diameter.

Application	Type of Umbilical Used Versus Performance Rating	
	Standard Umbilical	**Lightweight Umbilical**
Working in a debris field	*Poor* – fouls in debris	*Excellent* – floats above debris
Mid-water working	*Poor* – pulls down on diver	*Good* – no downward pull
Strong current	*Good* – no additional drag	*Poor* – creates drag
Abrasion (chafing) threat	*Good* – stands up well	*Poor* – chafes very easily
Long penetrations	*Poor* – lays on bottom	*Excellent* – floats on top
Surface crew handling	*Poor* – very heavy	*Good* – much lighter

4.1.4.1 Care and Maintenance of the Umbilical

The importance of taking proper care of the diver's umbilical cannot be overstressed. If the umbilical is being used in an area where there is a severe abrasion threat, such as on corroded steel pilings, use a protective shroud to cover it. An easy method of constructing a shroud is to take a canvas fire hose, split it, wrap it around the umbilical, and secure it with tape. When laying out the diving gear on any given site, care must be taken not to have the umbilical in a traffic area where people will step or walk on it. It must **never** be in an area where there is a risk of being severed by falling objects or moving machinery. Never let the hose lay in petroleum or chemicals while in use or in storage. Never store diving hose in direct sunlight or in high heat. A cool, dry place is best. Always cover the ends of the gas hose when not in use. At least once per year, clean the interior of the hose. Add a drop of non-ionic dish soap to a half-quart of water. Blow all of this water through the hose and chase it with 2 quarts of potable water. Make sure all of the water is blown out. Inspect each umbilical often, looking for cuts, abrasions, bubbles in the wall of the hose, frayed safety lines, tape missing, and any other sources of potential problems.

Standard umbilical hanging on dive control van

Twisted lightweight umbilical outside dive control
Photo courtesy of Darin Baumann

Each year, the umbilical requires testing. It is pressurized to 1½ times the normal working pressure, and a heavy strain is put on the termination fittings. The umbilical is kept in this manner for several hours (24) to ensure it will not fail in use.

4.1.5 Helmets

The diver's helmet must accomplish at least three things: deliver breathing gas to the diver, offer head protection against cold temperature and injury, and contain earphones and a microphone to allow communications with the surface support. The first helmets developed were free-flow helmets. There was a constant flow of air into, and through, these helmets. Free-flow hats are still used, often preferred for heavy work on bottom. The most common helmets used today, however, are demand helmets. They are equipped with a demand regulator, much the same as a scuba regulator. The demand hats are much quieter, allowing the diver and radio-telephone operator to hear one another much better. Demand hats require less air to operate than free-flow helmets do. Also, the demand hats are a lower volume hat, which reduces dead space (CO_2 buildup). Both types of hat come standard with a non-return valve. This valve must be tested regularly, and if it sticks, the helmet must not be used until the valve has been serviced. If the helmets are taken off daily, check the non-return valve before that hat goes back on. If the hats stay on the hoses, remove them and test the non-returns weekly.

In the United States, most commercial divers own their own helmets, but in every other country in the world, the diving companies own the helmets. In almost all jurisdictions, however, diver's helmets are required to be inspected on a regular basis by an inspector certified by the helmet manufacturer. Offshore, the helmets are serviced by a diving systems technician (dive tech) or a life support technician (LST), but on inland jobs, there usually are no technicians. If you are diving the hat, make sure the person servicing it is certified and trained to service life-support equipment. If you have not been certified and trained, leave them alone.

Performing helmet regulator service and adjustment

4.1.5.1 Care and Maintenance of Helmets

Always remember the helmet is **life support**. Store and transport helmets carefully. Do not use a damaged helmet. Always keep diving helmets clean, including the regulator and valves. If the helmet does not remain attached to the umbilical, keep caps (or tape) over the non-return and bailout nipple. If you are qualified to service helmets, always follow the manufacturer's instructions when making adjustments or servicing diving helmets. Always use a checklist to perform daily inspections on helmets. This checklist should include the following:

- Test non-return valve.
- Test bailout valve.
- Test free-flow valve.
- Test dial-a-breath.
- Test communications.
- Inspect the neck dam or yoke and all securing hinges, pins, latches, and locks.
- Clean the oral nasal pouch between divers and after every dive. (This prevents head colds, viruses, etc. from being passed through the crew.)
- Remove the helmet liner when it is wet, and replace it with a dry one.

Diver in below freezing water with a Superlite 17B

Some manufacturers require major service and inspections be performed by factory-trained personnel. Some jurisdictions require this of all diving helmets, regardless of the brand. If you have your own helmet, have it serviced and inspected regularly. If you use a company hat, have the LST or the systems technician service and inspect the hat you use regularly. Check the serial number, and look your hat up in the maintenance logs. Remember – it is **life support**, so treat it with the utmost of respect.

4.2 DIVER SUPPORT EQUIPMENT

4.2.1 Radio-Telephone

The diver's radio-telephone (radio) has had some major changes over the past 30 years. Today's radios are more powerful, smaller in size, and are wired to be used in either press-to-talk or in open-mike (round-robin) mode. Press-to-talk is most often used since background noise is a problem when using the open mike. Available in single, two, and three diver units, the most common units seen are the two diver units. Most of these allow cross talk between the divers. In mixed-gas operations, radios with a helium speech un-scrambler are used. These units allow the pitch to be adjusted, so the diver can be understood while he/she breathes helium oxygen mixtures, which seriously affect the diver's voice. In many cases, the supervisor (or timekeeper) uses a headset and microphone to block out all background noise.

4.2.2 Pneumofathometer

The pneumofathometer (pneumo for short) is a gauge that reads in feet or meters of seawater and attaches to an open-ended hose on the umbilical. This gauge is always mounted at the panel and allows the diving supervisor, at any given time, to accurately check the diver's depth. Gas is taken from the panel by a needle valve and used to evacuate water from the pneumo hose. The hydrostatic pressure of the water pushes the gas back up the pneumo hose when the valve is closed, causing the pneumo gauge to register the diver's depth. Used properly, the pneumo not only gives an accurate reading of the diver's depth while working but is also used for the in-water portion of decompression and to control the diver's ascent rate. These pneumos are calibrated at least twice annually, with accuracy of ¼ of 1%. Pneumos are required on every offshore job, but some smaller inshore contractors try to get by without them. Smart divers won't ever work without a pneumo; they know it is not safe.

4.2.3 Dive Control Panel (Gas Rack)

Control panels require valves to control gas from the main gas supply, the secondary gas supply, and the backup gas supply. They direct the gas from each of these sources to the primary diver, the standby diver, and to each diver's pneumo. Each of the supplies must be isolated from the others, allowing each diver to have access to more than one supply without tapping into the other diver's supply. Anything more than this serves to confuse the operator and is unnecessary. The pneumo gauge may be mounted on a bulkhead near the dive radio or be part of an integrated panel. The radio may be installed in the control panel or may sit on a table or shelf. The panel is usually located in a van (sea container) or a shack. This allows the supervisor and/or timekeeper to control the dive while protected from the elements and protected from most of the background noise (compressors, etc.) typically found on the inland or offshore job site. The dive control van or shack must be well-lit, heated when in colder climates, and air-conditioned when in tropical climates. There should also be a window facing the area of the deck where the divers are tended from, and a closed-circuit television camera system and intercom system should be provided to allow the supervisor to communicate easily with the surface crew out on deck. The flat screen and hard drive for the diver's helmet camera may be located above or below the actual panel. For operator comfort, below the panel is the most common location.

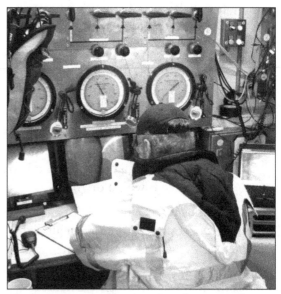

Supervisor running a dive on 3-diver deep air panel

4.2.3.1 Portable Panels

On smaller vessels and on many inland diving operations, the pneumo and radio are often mounted in a portable dive control box or "rack box." There are different manufacturers of these boxes, but a properly constructed unit will have the following features: separate main and backup supply for two divers, valves to control theses supplies, and a separate pneumo for each diver. Not all of these units come with a radio.

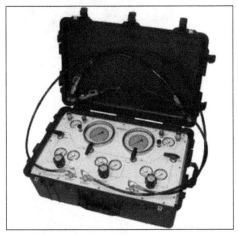

Portable panel without radio

Portable panel with radio

4.2.4 Diver Egress

Every job site or vessel requires a safe means of diver egress. If the air gap (distance from the deck to the water's surface) does not exceed six feet, a ladder may be used if there is a safe method to recover an injured or unconscious diver. This can be a dedicated crane and man-basket or a purpose-built diver recovery winch. In cases where the air gap exceeds six feet, a launch and recovery system (LARS) or a man-riding certified man-basket and crane are used. Most diving support vessels (DSV) use twin LARS to allow both the primary and standby diver clear and ready access. The LARS A-frames, winches, wires, and stages (baskets) are all built to man-riding

Twin LARS on an American construction barge in the Persian Gulf

specifications. Each basket will hold two divers (in emergency) and if there is a basket winch failure, the basket may be brought up with the clump-weight winch.

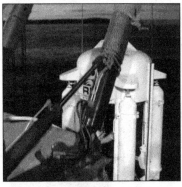

Wetbell with onboard gas supply on an offshore project in Canada

In the photo above, "K" cylinders are in the LARS baskets. These are kept there (with submergible regulators) as an additional backup gas supply for the divers. What you cannot see are strobe lights on the top of each basket for night operations. This allows the diver to locate the basket if helmet light is lost. On some jobs, particularly mixed gas, you will see a wet-bell used instead of a basket. The wetbell offers a refuge for the diver. There is a gas pocket maintained in the dome at the top of the bell. To utilize the gas pocket, the diver would have to remove his/her helmet. There is also the option of slipping a pneumo-sized tube (provided in the bell) up under the neck dam of the helmet. The LARS are available in either air or hydraulic powered, but hydraulic is recommended and the best.

4.2.5 Deck Decompression Chamber

On every offshore vessel or platform where surface-oriented diving is performed, there is at least one deck decompression chamber. If surface decompression operations are planned, there will be two of these chambers, one designated as a spare. In either very hot or cold climates, the chambers will be mounted in a climate controlled chamber van (sea container). Each chamber has its own primary and backup air and medical oxygen supplies. This chamber is considered a piece of emergency equipment and is kept in a constant state of readiness. Cleaning, maintaining, and operating the chambers is the responsibility of the divers. (See Chapter 11: Hyperbaric Chambers.)

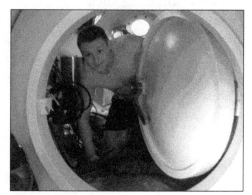

Diver leaving inner lock after surface decompression

4.2.6 HP Compressor

Almost all job sites will have at least one HP compressor. These units are powered by diesel or electric motors. Most contractors avoid gasoline engines as the fuel is more volatile than diesel. Usually on inland jobs it will be a small portable unit for topping up bailout bottles. On an offshore vessel or platform it will be a larger unit, used to top up HP gas supplies as well as the bailouts. As a diver, you will be required to use the HP compressor on a regular basis. These units are very loud when running, so hearing protection is a must when you work with or near them. Like the LP compressors, the compressor oil level needs to be checked before each use, and the filter system requires monitoring. (See Chapter 25: Diesel Engines and Compressors.)

Electric-powered HP breathing air compressor

4.2.7 Hot-water Unit

Most offshore platforms and vessels have hot water units for the diving operation. These units use either diesel fuel or electricity to heat seawater, and then they pump it down through the umbilical to help maintain the diver's core temperature. On larger crews, the LST looks after the hot water, but on many jobs, the task falls to the divers. Two important things to remember: Do not let the unit run dry of fuel (if it is a diesel unit), and do not let it lose its water supply. The water is maintained at a constant temperature by using a mixing tank with an internal thermometer. The temperature used depends on the water temperature at depth, the length of umbilical used, and whether the diver is using a wetsuit or a hot water suit. Quite often, divers will use an ordinary wetsuit and just stick the hot water hose down the neck when they feel a chill. While not as comfortable as a real hot water suit, it still works well in cool (not cold) water.

There are several different manufacturers of hot water units, and each has several models, ranging from small portable units to large, skid-mounted units. Often the hot water system will be housed in a mini container along with the HP compressor and the bailout fill station. The diver should take the time to read the manufacturers operating instructions prior to use. There will also be instructions for care and maintenance. If there is not one available, take the time to make up a daily and weekly maintenance checklist for every piece of diver support equipment.

Skid-mounted diesel hot water unit

4.2.8 Hydraulic Power Unit

A Hydraulic Power Unit (HPU) will be found on many inland construction projects and every offshore platform and vessel. They are used to power the LARS and operate underwater tools. Sometimes the LSTs will look after the HPU, sometimes the vessel's engineers will, but most times it will be the diving crew who operates and maintains the HPU. These units may be electric or diesel powered. There are three things that must be watched: fuel level in the diesel, oil level in the diesel, and hydraulic fluid level. The unit used to power the LARS is never used to operate tools. On occasion, the backup unit is. Like all other machines, they differ by manufacturer, so the diver should read the operators manual before using and go over it with a crew member who is familiar with the unit.

Skid-mounted HPU

4.3 DIVER WORN EQUIPMENT

4.3.1 Diver's Dress

The diver's dress (suit) serves four purposes: thermal protection, isolation from contaminants, protection from abrasion, and buoyancy control. The common types of diver's dress used by divers offshore today are below: .

- Wetsuit – Minimal thermal protection (to 55°F), poor isolation from contaminants, reasonable protection from abrasion, no buoyancy control without vest
- Neoprene Drysuit – Good thermal protection (to 40°F), good isolation from contaminants, reasonable protection from abrasion, good buoyancy control
- Vulcanized Rubber Drysuit – Good thermal protection (to 40°F), excellent isolation from contaminants (used for hazmat), good protection from abrasion, good buoyancy control
- Trilaminate Drysuit – Good thermal protection (to 40°F), good isolation from contaminants reasonable protection from abrasion, good buoyancy control
- Hot-water Suit – Excellent thermal protection (below 30°F), poor isolation from contaminants, reasonable abrasion protection, poor buoyancy control (Hot water suits require a hot water system which requires more surface support.)

Location, conditions, water depth, and time of year determine the suit needed. For example, in New York Harbor, wear a vulcanized or trilaminate suit year-round due to temperature and contaminants. In the Gulf of Mexico, wear a 5 or 7 mm wetsuit. In the Persian Gulf, wear coveralls and rubber boots in summer with a thin lycra bodysuit underneath in winter. In Alaska, wear a neoprene drysuit in summer and a hot water suit in winter. In most locations, hot water suits are worn on deeper dives, regardless of the time of year.

Some projects require the diver to work in contaminated water, such as radioactive water in nuclear plants or untreated water at sewage treatment plants. In these cases, hazmat equipment is used, which requires a vulcanized rubber suit with a mating flange to match the helmet being used, and gloves sealed directly to the suit with hard rings.

Wetsuit and coveralls   Vulcanized rubber suit   Hot-water suit

4.3.2 Harnesses

The umbilical requires a secure attachment to the diver. To facilitate this, a harness is worn over the diver's dress. The harness must be constructed of nylon, Kevlar, or poly webbing and triple stitched at intersecting joints. It must be fastened with a double D ring and not with a "quick release" buckle. The umbilical must attach to a tested D ring with a tested snap shackle or carabiner. The harness may have an integrated weight belt and/or bailout, but the umbilical should never be attached to a standard scuba backpack or non-harness weight belt. Harnesses should be protected from direct sunlight and should be inspected on a regular basis.

5-point recovery vest

5-point harness (with bailout)

5-point H-3 Harness
Photo courtesy of Aqualung

Any harness used in commercial work must be a 5-point harness. This means a strap comes over each shoulder, two come up around the crotch, and one passes around the waist. Harnesses should also be tested and certified to lift no less than 3 times the weight of a fully dressed diver.

4.3.3 Gloves or Mitts

Like suits, the water temperature and operation performed determine what is worn on the hands of a diver. In colder water, 3-finger mitts are the warmest choice, as they keep most of the fingers together, thereby maintaining some heat. When diving with a hot water suit, both the mitts and the boots must have bleed holes punched in them, or they will be blown off by water pressure. In cold areas such as Alaska, Canada, and the North Sea, 3-finger mitts are worn most often, with 5-finger being worn in summer. Moderately warm areas like the mid-Atlantic states and the Gulf of Mexico in winter will see the 5-finger gloves in winter. Warmer climates tend to use a latex palmed nylon 5-finger glove year –round.

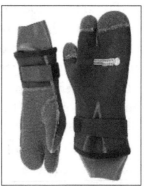

3-finger neoprene mitts

5-finger neoprene gloves

Special operations require special equipment. When working on severely corroded H beams, large leather mitts over neoprene mitts are recommended. For hazmat work, special gloves are worn that attach directly to the suit using hard plastic rings, sealing out the contaminated water.

5-finger nylon gloves

Hazmat glove with ring
Photo courtesy of Aqualung

4.3.4 Boots and Fins

A commercial diver will wear fins, but if working in marine construction, industrial work, or the oil patch, boots will be worn 90% of the time. Fins permit easy swimming, but the commercial diver walks and climbs more than swims. The exceptions to this are inspection divers and support divers on pipe-lay barges. On inspections, the diver wants to cover a lot of ground, so usually fins are worn. Support divers on pipe-lay barges perform stinger inspections and touch-down inspections, so a lot of swimming is involved. On certain inspections (offshore platforms, pilings), the diver will want to have a shorter blade on the fins to allow the feet to get into tighter areas with less trouble. Although they give propulsion, fins provide little protection for the diver's foot. The most common boot worn is a rubber boot, usually called wellingtons or gum-rubbers. The boots are several sizes larger than the diver's foot, to allow for a wetsuit or drysuit boot inside. Usually, at least one hole is punched on the side of the arch to allow the boot to be pulled on and off more easily. Depending on the job, steel toes and steel shank are used on occasion.

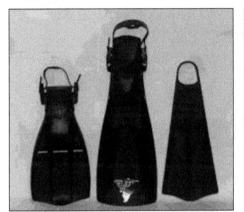

Short- and long-bladed fins

Rubber boots (Wellingtons)

Steel toe, steel shank boots

4.3.5 Light Sources

The three most common light sources used underwater are handheld, helmet mounted, and tethered. Hand lights are available from several manufacturers, in different sizes and different intensities. Halogen lights replaced incandescent lights in the 1980s, with krypton and zircon lights in the market in the 1990s. Now there are mainly LED underwater lights. Commercial divers usually require both hands to work, so anything other than hand lights is preferred. Handheld lights can be used as helmet lights, and many divers carry one on a lanyard "just in case." Helmet lights are usually hard wired to the surface. When using hard-wired helmet lights, it is best to turn the light off once the diver reaches the surface. These units tend to get very hot and may overheat and burn out. As well, tenders have been known to get severe burns when helping to remove the diver's helmet.

Handheld diving lights

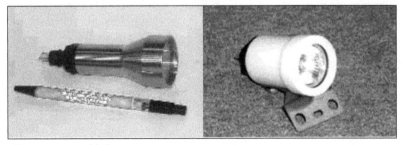

Helmet-mounted lights

4.3.6 Knives

Back in the 1970s, when this author first went offshore on a diving job, an old hand pulled me aside and said, "Kid, two things will keep you safe from shark attack – a good knife and a buddy." When I asked him to explain, he said, "When a shark attacks, stab your buddy and swim hard for the surface!"

Since then, this author has learned the knife is indeed the most important tool in the toolbox. It will be used on almost every dive. Cutting ropes, and prying and scraping marine growth are only some of the many uses for a knife. A diver's ingenuity and imagination is the only limit. All knives, however, are not created equal. A serrated (toothed) edge is often necessary, and the blade must be strong enough for prying. The knives used with MKV gear had a wood handle and screwed into a brass sheath. The most popular knives used by divers offshore today are the Green River Knife and the Spiderco Knife. Most divers use the Green River knives on their harness, and most carry a Spiderco on their harness for a spare since it folds up flat. Another popular knife is the Mora Companion with the serrated blade. These knifes cost less than half of what the others do, but are exceptional quality Swedish steel, with a hard plastic sheath that can be easily duct-taped to the chest strap of a harness. If a knife is dull, it is useless. Knives must be kept sharp and should be checked for sharpness before every dive.

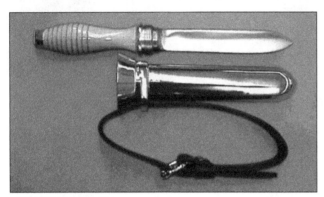

DESCO MKV knife
Products of DESCO Corp

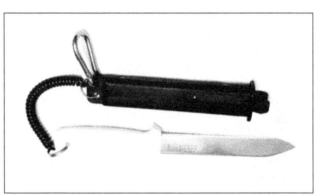

Green River knife
Products of Submarine Products

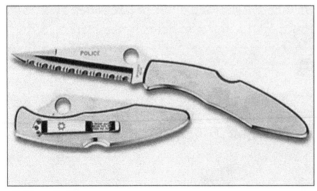

Spiderco knife
Products of Spiderco

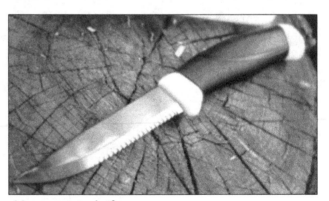

Mora companion knife
Photo courtesy of Mora of Sweden

5.0 AIR DIVING AND DECOMPRESSION

Underwater physiology has taught us whenever the human body is placed under pressure, inert gas from the breathing mixture is absorbed into the tissues of the body up to the point of total saturation, and as the pressure on the body is reduced again, the rate must be carefully controlled. By knowing the amount of inert gas absorbed and controlling the rate at which we reduce the pressure, we allow the inert gas (in air diving the inert gas is nitrogen) to safely come out of solution without forming bubbles.

There are methods and formulas to compute the levels of gas absorbed by the body and the safe rate of ascent to allow for off-gassing. These were developed by various physiologists (Haldane and Buhlmann being the most notable), but to simplify the process and avoid painful or deadly mistakes, we utilize standardized decompression tables. The first known standardized decompression tables were published by the British Royal Navy in 1906. The U.S. Navy did more extensive research and published their first standardized tables in 1924, and as stated in Chapter 1: Commercial Diving History, these tables and the subsequent revisions to them have gone on to become the accepted standard for this industry worldwide.

5.1 DIVING TABLES USED TODAY

Several decompression tables (diving tables) are used in the industry today, including: U.S. Navy Rev. 6, Modified U.S. Navy, DCIEM, Royal Navy, and the Comex Tables. The ones most commonly used are the U.S. Navy Rev. 6, followed by the Modified U.S. Navy and the DCIEM Tables.

5.1.1 How Diving Tables Were Developed

To better understand the differences in the three most commonly used tables in the diving industry, we will examine how each one of these sets of tables was developed.

5.1.2 USN Rev. 6

The U.S. Navy Diving Tables are the result of many years of testing by the U.S. Navy Experimental Diving Unit. The air diving tables were first developed in the early 1900s, and the earliest mixed-gas tables were developed in the mid-to-late 1930s, just prior to the salvage of the submarine USS Squalus off Portsmouth, NH. The USN tables were developed by manual testing. The subjects used in the testing were all navy divers who were young, fit individuals. Divers dived at a given depth for successively longer bottom times and ascended to the surface, until DCS incidents occurred. In this way, the no-decompression limits were established. Then they dived beyond these limits and stopped at various depths to allow for decompression. This was done at intervals of 10 feet, until workable decompression schedules were developed. Each time there was an incident of DCS, it was noted and further testing was done. For treatment of decompression sickness, the treatment tables were developed in the same way. The U.S. Navy tables have an acceptable incident rate of 5 in 100. Many people in our industry do not realize that the USN tables were designed as "one-time exposure" tables. This means they were not intended to be used for diving to the indicated depths and times on consecutive days. In order to use these tables every day, they had to be "padded" well in both time and depth. The Revision 6 tables are considerably better than the previous edition (Revision 4), but they still do require padding in time and depth, particularly when used on many dives over many consecutive days.

5.1.3 Modified USN

The Modified USN (also known as Oceaneering or Gulf of Mexico Tables) are, as the name suggests, U.S. Navy tables that have been modified – with the padding already done. They are based on the *U.S. Navy Diving Manual Rev. 3*. There has not been a careful evaluation of the rate of incidents when using these tables, so the rate is unknown. But taking into consideration the bottom times and the decompression required closely resembles Revision 6, they should be relatively incident free. Treatment for incidents with these tables is referred to the current U.S. Navy treatment tables.

5.1.4 DCIEM

The DCIEM (Defense and Civil Institue for Environmental Medicine), or Canadian Navy Diving Tables, were developed over a period of time between 1962 and 1983 by the Experimental Diving Unit of the Canadian Navy at the DCIEM, now known as Defense Research and Development Canada (DRDC). Divers from the Navy EDU and students from commercial diving schools were used as test subjects. During the testing, the subjects were monitored during the decompression phase for inert gas bubbles using Doppler ultrasound. The DCIEM tables appear to be a very safe table, and there are no known incident cases. The DCIEM tables refer treatment to the current U.S. Navy treatment tables.

5.2 DIFFERENCES IN USAGE

Each individual table has its own characteristics; the no-decompression limits, the ascent rates, the allowed surface interval, the decompression stop depths, and the decompression times. For example, the U.S. Navy Diving Tables Rev. 6 have a standard ascent rate of 30 feet per minute (fpm) from the bottom to surface, unless performing surface decompression. In the DCIEM Tables, we see an ascent rate of 60 fpm for all dives. When you look at the 60-foot table in *U.S. Navy Diving Manual Rev. 6*, you will see that the no-decompression (no-D) limit is 60 minutes, whereas in the DCIEM Manual, the 60-foot table has a no-D limit of just 50 minutes. On surface decompression dives, the USN tables have a 5-minute surface interval allowed, while DCIEM has a 7 minute interval. On no-D dives, there is still a gas load on the diver, and all of these tables have been developed so that the ascent on no-D dives is the required decompression for the dive. But even with the timed ascent rate, the diver has residual nitrogen in his/her body after no-D dives. This is the reason any dive following another within a 12-hour period (18 hours for DCIEM) is considered a repetitive dive and requires calculation of the residual nitrogen to establish the bottom time of the second dive and any consecutive dives. Due to all of these differences in the various tables, it is absolutely imperative divers and supervisors choose a table and stick with it. The required ascent rates, stop times, etc. cannot be substituted between various diving tables.

NEVER UTILIZE THE ELEMENTS OF MORE THAN ONE TYPE OF DECOMPRESSION TABLE ON ANY GIVEN DIVE

5.3 *U.S. NAVY DIVING MANUAL REVISION 6*

Although the other decompression tables mentioned above are used and accepted on many commercial diving operations, this training manual concentrates only on the tables from the *U.S. Navy Diving Manual Rev. 6*. The reader is strongly advised to become familiar with the table-specific usage instructions, terms, and definitions of any diving and decompression tables prior to use on the job.

5.3.1 Terms and Definitions

The following table provides terms and definitions used for no-decompression dives, repetitive dives, and in-water decompression dives utilizing USN Revision 6.

Term	Definition
Ascent Rate	From bottom to surface = 30 fpm ($\pm$ 10 fpm allowable)
Bottom Time	Time (in minutes) from when diver leaves surface until leaving bottom
Depth of Dive	Deepest depth of the dive with the pneumofathometer correction factor added
Table Used	The next deeper depth designation beyond depth of dive (above)
Travel Time	Time (min:sec) from leaving bottom to surface or stop; time between stops

Term	Definition
Stop Time (1st stop air)	Time (min:sec) from diver's arrival at decompression stop until leaving stop
Stop Time (other stop)	Time (min:sec) as above, but including travel time from previous stop
Stop Time (oxygen)	Time (min:sec) begins when the diver is confirmed breathing oxygen
Stop Depth (oxygen)	The deepest in-water oxygen stop is at 30 fsw
Stop Depth (final)	The final in-water stop (air or oxygen) is at 20 fsw
Surface Interval	Time (hr:min) from arrive surface (this dive) to leave surface (next dive)

5.3.2 Conditions for Usage of the USN Rev. 6 Tables

There are several conditions that must be met in order for the USN Rev. 6 tables to be utilized with minimal risk of decompression sickness. These are as follows:

- The diver's depth is always determined by a calibrated pneumofathometer (pneumo) gauge.
- The pneumofathometer correction factor is applied to all readings.
- The deepest depth (with correction factor added) is utilized to determine the proper table.
- For depth of dive, the pneumo reading is taken at or below the diver's ankle (when standing).
- For decompression stops, the pneumo reading is taken at the diver's mid-chest level.
- The table selected is always at least the next greater depth than the maximum depth of the dive.
- Bottom time runs from leaving surface to leaving bottom, rounded up to the next full minute.
- The table selected is always at least the next longer time than the actual bottom time.
- The next longer table again is used if the diver is exceptionally cold or performing strenuous work.

5.3.3 Pneumofathometer Correction Factor

Pneumofathometers are constructed and calibrated to read in feet of seawater with an accuracy of ¼ of 1% over the range of the gauge. Because of this, the pneumofathometer correction factor is always used when determining the diver's depth, as illustrated by the following table:

Table 9-1 Pneumofathometer Correction Factors

Pneumofathometer Reading	Correction Factor
0 fsw – 100 fsw	+ 1 fsw
101 fsw – 200 fsw	+ 2 fsw
201 fsw – 300 fsw	+ 4 fsw
301 fsw – 400 fsw	+ 7 fsw

Source: *U.S. Navy Diving Manual*

5.3.4 Choosing the Proper Table and Using It Correctly

Once the diver is on bottom, we take the initial pneumo reading and apply the appropriate correction factor to establish the maximum depth. We use the next greater table than the maximum depth. For example, a pneumo reading of 72 fsw is taken. With the correction factor applied, the maximum depth is 73 fsw, so choose the 80 fsw table or greater, depending on what your company's procedure states. Most diving contractors offshore use the +5 rule or the +10 rule. You take the maximum depth +5 or +10 feet, and then select the table to be used. This is what is known as "padding for depth." The +5 or +10 rule is also used on time and most offshore outfits add either 5 or 10 minutes to the actual bottom time when selecting the decompression schedule on the table.

To illustrate the need to "pad" tables when running consecutive dives, we will examine two case studies:

1) On a salvage project in 2012, 36 surface decompression dives were run per day (6 separate crews), 7 days per week, for well over 4 months. Tables (Rev 6) were padded properly (+5+5) and each diver had 2 days out of the water in each 7-day work period. There was not one incident of decompression sickness on this project.

2) In 2013 on an oil field project in West Africa, there were 2 crews running 10 dives per day with in-water decompression. One day in week two, 3 divers on one crew presented Type I symptoms and had to be treated. At the oil company's request, the author investigated and it was found a supervisor had taken pneumo readings of 117 fsw and ran the bottom times to 28 min. He then selected the USN 120/30 Table from USN Rev. 6. After 8 consecutive days, three young divers suffered decompression sickness. The contractor had a +5+5 policy that was not implemented and the divers had no days out of rotation. This was the first job for the supervisor, and he was subsequently terminated.

5.4 SINGLE NO-DECOMPRESSION DIVES

Any dive made more than 12 hours after a previous pressurization (either in water or in a chamber) is considered a single dive, and any dive within the no-decompression limits is a no-decompression dive. The no-decompression limits for any given depth are found in three places in the Revision 6 tables:

1. In the second column of the No-Decompression Limits and Repetitive Group Designation Table,
2. On the top selection line of each individual decompression table, or
3. In the Shallow Water Tables 2A-1 and 2A-2.

Problem:

The company you work for uses the +5+5 rule for depth and time. You sent a diver in to recover tools from a pipe flange. The diver has just arrived on bottom, and you took a pneumo reading of 74 fsw. How much bottom time can your diver have with no decompression, using the No-Decompression Limits Table?

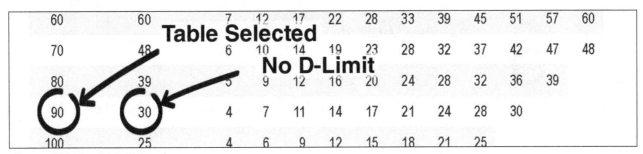

Source: *U.S. Navy Diving Manual*

Solution:

The pneumo reading is 74 fsw and the correction factor is +1 fsw, so the depth of dive is 75 fsw. Using the +5 rule, it becomes 80 fsw, so you go to Table 9-7, follow the "Depth" column on the far left down to the next greatest depth, which is 90 fsw. Looking straight across to the right in the "No-Stop Limit" column, you see the figure 30, which represents a maximum of 30 minutes bottom time. You know that your company requires +5 padding on the bottom time, so you must then subtract 5 minutes from the figure shown in order to stay within your company's rules. Therefore, the maximum actual bottom time you can give your diver is 25 minutes without decompression.

The problem above was solved by using Table 9-7 (No Decompression Limits and Repetitive Group Designations), so we will present one more problem utilizing Table 2A-1 (Shallow Water Table).

Problem:

You are on a diving crew sent to a power plant to inspect and repair a travelling trash screen on their sea water intake. Your company has strict rules on padding: they require +5+5 on every dive. The new safety guidelines for the power plant state that unless you have a chamber on site, you cannot perform decompression dives. There is no chamber on site. You have been here several times for your company, and the bottom pneumo reading is always the same – 38 fsw. Using the USN Shallow Water Table, how much bottom time can your diver have if you stay within your company's rules, and the power plant's safety guidelines?

Table 2A-1. *No-Decompression Limits and Repetitive Group Designators for Shallow Water Air No-Decompression Dives.*

Depth (fsw)	No-Stop Limit (min)	A	B	C	D	E	F	G	H	I	J	K	L	M	N	O	Z
30	371	17	27	38	50	62	76	91	107	125	145	167	193	223	260	307	371
31	334	16	26	37	48	60	73	87	102	119	138	158	182	209	242	282	334
32	304	15	25	35	46	58	70	83	98	114	131	150	172	197	226	261	304
33	281	15	24	34	45	56	67	80	94	109	125	143	163	186	212	243	281
34	256	14	23	33	43	54	65	77	90	104	120	137	155	176	200	228	256
35	232	14	23	32	42	52	63	74	87	100	115	131	148	168	190	215	232
36	212	14	22	31	40	50	61	72	84	97	110	125	142	160	180	204	212
37	197	13	21	30	39	49	59	69	81	93	106	120	136	153	172	193	197
38	184	13	21	29	38	47	57	67	78	90	102	116	131	147	164	184	
39	173	12	20	28	37	46	55	65	76	87	99	112	126	141	157	173	
40	163	12	20	27	36	44	53	63	73	84	95	108	121	135	151	163	
41	155	12	19	27	35	43	52	61	71	81	92	104	117	130	145	155	
42	147	11	19	26	34	42	50	59	69	79	89	101	113	126	140	147	
43	140	11	18	25	33	41	49	58	67	76	87	98	109	122	135	140	
44	134	11	18	25	32	40	48	56	65	74	84	95	106	118	130	134	
45	125	11	17	24	31	39	46	55	63	72	82	92	102	114	125		
46	116	10	17	23	30	38	45	53	61	70	79	89	99	110	116		
47	109	10	16	23	30	37	44	52	60	68	77	87	97	107	109		
48	102	10	16	22	29	36	43	51	58	67	75	84	94	102			
49	97	10	16	22	28	35	42	49	57	65	73	82	91	97			
50	92	9	15	21	28	34	41	48	56	63	71	80	89	92			

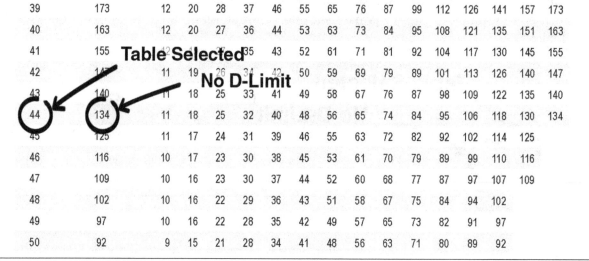

Table Selected
No D-Limit

Source: *U.S. Navy Diving Manual*

Solution:

Assuming the pneumo reading is 38 fsw again, with the pneumo correction factor, the depth of dive becomes 39 fsw. Padding the depth according to your company's rules (+5), that becomes 44 fsw. In Table 2A-1, when you look down the far left column (Depth fsw) to 44 fsw, we see that the no-D limit is listed as 134 minutes. Your company requires padding of +5 on time as well, so you subtract 5 minutes from the no-D limit on the table. To stay within your company's rules, you can allow the diver 129 minutes.

5.5 REPETITIVE DIVES

Any time a second dive is performed less than 12 hours after the first dive, the second dive is then considered to be a repetitive dive. Diving contractors today do not allow repetitive dives to be performed after any dive that required decompression. Most offshore diving contractors do not allow repetitive dives under any circumstances, regardless of depth or nature of dive. Some still allow repetitive dives following no-decompression dives, (particularly inland contractors) and some allow repetitive dives on shallow dives only. Even with no-decompression dives, the diver still carries a gas load and any gas load carried is added to the gas taken on while performing these repetitive dives and must be accounted for in subsequent decompression. The gas load the diver carries following a dive and any subsequent surface interval is known as "residual nitrogen" (RN). The depth and bottom time of the first dive obviously determine the RN, and the longer

Table 9-7. *No-Decompression Limits and Repetitive Group Designators for No-Decompression Air Dives.*

Depth (fsw)	No-Stop Limit	A	B	C	D	E	F	G	H	I	J	K	L	M	N	O	Z
10	Unlimited	57	101	158	245	426	*										
15	Unlimited	36	60	88	121	163	217	297	449	*							
20	Unlimited	26	43	61	82	106	133	165	205	256	330	461	*				
25	595	20	33	47	62	78	97	117	140	166	198	236	285	354	469	595	
30	371	17	27	38	50	62	76	91	107	125	145	167	193	223	260	307	371
35	232	14	23	32	42	52	63	74	87	100	115	131	148	168	190	215	232
40	163	12	20	27	36	44	53	63	73	84	95	108	121	135	151	163	
45	125	11	17	24	31	39	46	55	63	72	82	92	102	114	125		
50	92	9	15	21	28	34	41	48	56	63	71	80	89	92			
55	74	8	14	19	25	31	37	43	50	56	63	71	74				
60	60	7	12	17	22	28	33	39	45	51	57	60					
70	48	6	10	14	19	23	28	32	37	42	47	48					
80	39	5	9	12	16	20	24	28	32	36	39						
90	30	4	7	11	14	17	21	24	28	30							
100	25	4	6	9	12	15	18	21	25								
110	20	3	6	8	11	14	16	19	20								
120	15	3	5	7	10	12	15										
130	10	2	4	6	9	10											
140	10	2	4	6	8	10											
150	5	2	3	5													
160	5		3	5													
170	5			4	5												
180	5			4	5												
190	5			3	5												

* Highest repetitive group that can be achieved at this depth regardless of bottom time.

Source: *U.S. Navy Diving Manual*

Table 9-8. *Residual Nitrogen Time Table for Repetitive Air Dives.*

Locate the diver's repetitive group designation from his previous dive along the diagonal line above the table. Read horizontally to the interval in which the diver's surface interval lies.

Next, read vertically downward to the new repetitive group designation. Continue downward in this same column to the row that represents the depth of the repetitive dive. The time given at the intersection is residual nitrogen time, in minutes, to be applied to the repetitive dive.

* Dives following surface intervals longer than this are not repetitive dives. Use actual bottom times in the Air Decompression Tables to compute decompression for such dives.

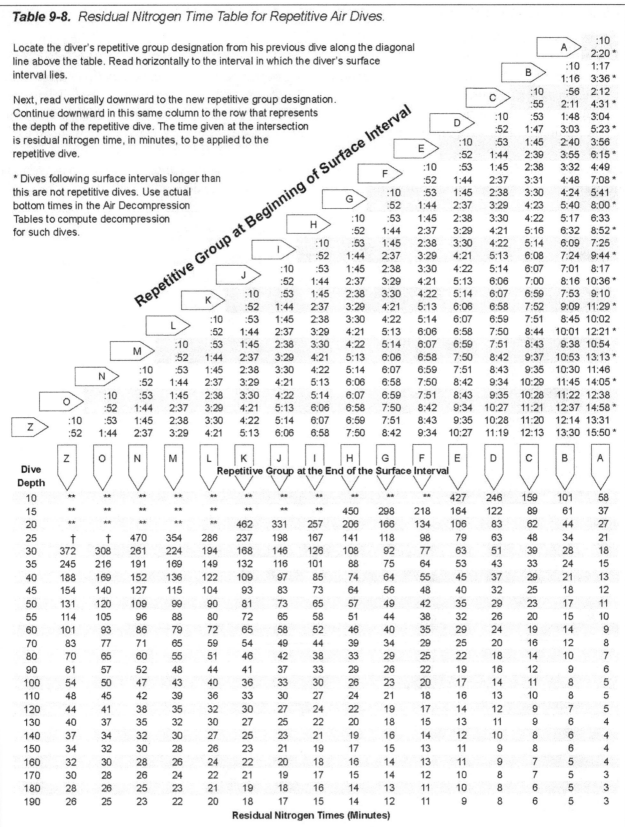

Repetitive Group at Beginning of Surface Interval

Group	Surface interval ranges
A	:10 / 2:20 *
B	:10 1:17 / 1:16 3:36 *
C	:10 :56 2:12 / :55 2:11 4:31 *
D	:10 :53 1:48 3:04 / :52 1:47 3:03 5:23 *
E	:10 :53 1:45 2:40 3:56 / :52 1:44 2:39 3:55 6:15 *
F	:10 :53 1:45 2:38 3:32 4:49 / :52 1:44 2:37 3:31 4:48 7:08 *
G	:10 :53 1:45 2:38 3:30 4:24 5:41 / :52 1:44 2:37 3:29 4:23 5:40 8:00 *
H	:10 :53 1:45 2:38 3:30 4:22 5:17 6:33 / :52 1:44 2:37 3:29 4:21 5:16 6:32 8:52 *
I	:10 :53 1:45 2:38 3:30 4:22 5:14 6:09 7:25 / :52 1:44 2:37 3:29 4:21 5:13 6:08 7:24 9:44 *
J	:10 :53 1:45 2:38 3:30 4:22 5:14 6:07 7:01 8:17 / :52 1:44 2:37 3:29 4:21 5:13 6:06 7:00 8:16 10:36 *
K	:10 :53 1:45 2:38 3:30 4:22 5:14 6:07 6:59 7:53 9:10 / :52 1:44 2:37 3:29 4:21 5:13 6:06 6:58 7:52 9:09 11:29 *
L	:10 :53 1:45 2:38 3:30 4:22 5:14 6:07 6:59 7:51 8:45 10:02 / :52 1:44 2:37 3:29 4:21 5:13 6:06 6:58 7:50 8:44 10:01 12:21 *
M	:10 :53 1:45 2:38 3:30 4:22 5:14 6:07 6:59 7:51 8:43 9:38 10:54 / :52 1:44 2:37 3:29 4:21 5:13 6:06 6:58 7:50 8:42 9:37 10:53 13:13 *
N	:10 :53 1:45 2:38 3:30 4:22 5:14 6:07 6:59 7:51 8:43 9:35 10:30 11:46 / :52 1:44 2:37 3:29 4:21 5:13 6:06 6:58 7:50 8:42 9:34 10:29 11:45 14:05 *
O	:10 :53 1:45 2:38 3:30 4:22 5:14 6:07 6:59 7:51 8:43 9:35 10:28 11:22 12:38 / :52 1:44 2:37 3:29 4:21 5:13 6:06 6:58 7:50 8:42 9:34 10:27 11:21 12:37 14:58 *
Z	:10 :53 1:45 2:38 3:30 4:22 5:14 6:07 6:59 7:51 8:43 9:35 10:28 11:20 12:14 13:31 / :52 1:44 2:37 3:29 4:21 5:13 6:06 6:58 7:50 8:42 9:34 10:27 11:19 12:13 13:30 15:50 *

Repetitive Group at the End of the Surface Interval

Dive Depth	Z	O	N	M	L	K	J	I	H	G	F	E	D	C	B	A
10	**	**	**	**	**	**	**	**	**	**	**	427	246	159	101	58
15	**	**	**	**	**	**	**	**	450	298	218	164	122	89	61	37
20	**	**	**	**	**	462	331	257	206	166	134	106	83	62	44	27
25	†	†	470	354	286	237	198	167	141	118	98	79	63	48	34	21
30	372	308	261	224	194	168	146	126	108	92	77	63	51	39	28	18
35	245	216	191	169	149	132	116	101	88	75	64	53	43	33	24	15
40	188	169	152	136	122	109	97	85	74	64	55	45	37	29	21	13
45	154	140	127	115	104	93	83	73	64	56	48	40	32	25	18	12
50	131	120	109	99	90	81	73	65	57	49	42	35	29	23	17	11
55	114	105	96	88	80	72	65	58	51	44	38	32	26	20	15	10
60	101	93	86	79	72	65	58	52	46	40	35	29	24	19	14	9
70	83	77	71	65	59	54	49	44	39	34	29	25	20	16	12	8
80	70	65	60	55	51	46	42	38	33	29	25	22	18	14	10	7
90	61	57	52	48	44	41	37	33	29	26	22	19	16	12	9	6
100	54	50	47	43	40	36	33	30	26	23	20	17	14	11	8	5
110	48	45	42	39	36	33	30	27	24	21	18	16	13	10	8	5
120	44	41	38	35	32	30	27	24	22	19	17	14	12	9	7	5
130	40	37	35	32	30	27	25	22	20	18	15	13	11	9	6	4
140	37	34	32	30	27	25	23	21	19	16	14	12	10	8	6	4
150	34	32	30	28	26	23	21	19	17	15	13	11	9	8	6	4
160	32	30	28	26	24	22	20	18	16	14	13	11	9	7	5	4
170	30	28	26	24	22	21	19	17	15	14	12	10	8	7	5	3
180	28	26	25	23	21	19	18	16	14	13	11	10	8	6	5	3
190	26	25	23	22	20	18	17	15	14	12	11	9	8	6	5	3

Residual Nitrogen Times (Minutes)

** Residual Nitrogen Time cannot be determined using this table (see paragraph 9-9.1 subparagraph 8 for instructions).

† Read vertically downward to the 30 fsw repetitive dive depth. Use the corresponding residual nitrogen times to compute the equivalent single dive time. Decompress using the 30 fsw air decompression table.

Source: *U.S. Navy Diving Manual*

the surface interval, the more the RN diminishes. When calculated after the surface interval, the RN, now known as "residual nitrogen time" (RNT) is expressed in minutes. This RNT is added to the bottom time of the second dive, becoming the Equivalent Single Dive Time (ESDT) of the second dive and is used to calculate any decompression requirement. The tables on the preceding pages from the *U.S. Navy Diving Manual* are provided to determine RNT and thereby calculate the ESDT of the repetitive dive. Before performing repetitive dives, first ensure repetitive dives are allowed by the contractor and the client. It is **strongly recommended** that repetitive dives not be performed following any dive requiring decompression.

5.5.1 Shallow Water Tables

At first glance, there does not appear to be any difference between Table 9-7 and Table 2A-1. When we look more closely at the column on the far left—Depth fsw—we notice two vast differences: Table 9-7 has 5 fsw increments up to 60 fsw, then 10 fsw increments to the depth limit for the table, 190 fsw. Table 2A-1 has 1 fsw increments from 30 fsw up to the depth limit for the table, 50 fsw. Also, when we look at Table 9-8, we see that again, the depth increments are 5 fsw up to 60 fsw, then 10 fsw up to 190 fsw. But Table 2A-2 has 1 fsw increments from 30 fsw up to the maximum depth, which is 50 fsw.

These tables are designed to be used when the depth of the dives are fixed, known prior to the dives, and will not fluctuate during the dive. Examples of this would be when the diver performs ship husbandry while working on a fixed stage, when the diver works in a potable water or sewage tank, or when the diver is inside a power-plant chamber. These tables allow the maximizing of available bottom time for the diver and are used exactly as Table 9-7 and 9-8 are used.

Depth (fsw)	No-Stop Limit (min)	Repetitive Group Designation															
		A	B	C	D	E	F	G	H	I	J	K	L	M	N	O	Z
30	371	17	27	38	50	62	76	91	107	125	145	167	193	223	260	307	371
31	334	16	26	37	48	60	73	87	102	119	138	158	182	209	242	282	334
32	304	15	25	35	46	58	70	83	98	114	131	150	172	197	226	261	304
33	281	15	24	34	45	56	67	80	94	109	125	143	163	186	212	243	281
34	256	14	23	33	43	54	65	77	90	104	120	137	155	176	200	228	256
35	232	14	23	32	42	52	63	74	87	100	115	131	148	168	190	215	232
36	212	14	22	31	40	50	61	72	84	97	110	125	142	160	180	204	212
37	197	13	21	30	39	49	59	69	81	93	106	120	136	153	172	193	197
38	184	13	21	29	38	47	57	67	78	90	102	116	131	147	164	184	
39	173	12	20	28	37	46	55	65	76	87	99	112	126	141	157	173	
40	163	12	20	27	36	44	53	63	73	84	95	108	121	135	151	163	
41	155	12	19	27	35	43	52	61	71	81	92	104	117	130	145	155	
42	147	11	19	26	34	42	50	59	69	79	89	101	113	126	140	147	
43	140	11	18	25	33	41	49	58	67	76	87	98	109	122	135	140	
44	134	11	18	25	32	40	48	56	65	74	84	95	106	118	130	134	
45	125	11	17	24	31	39	46	55	63	72	82	92	102	114	125		
46	116	10	17	23	30	38	45	53	61	70	79	89	99	110	116		
47	109	10	16	23	30	37	44	52	60	68	77	87	97	107	109		
48	102	10	16	22	29	36	43	51	58	67	75	84	94	102			
49	97	10	16	22	28	35	42	49	57	65	73	82	91	97			
50	92	9	15	21	28	34	41	48	56	63	71	80	89	92			

Source: *U.S. Navy Diving Manual*

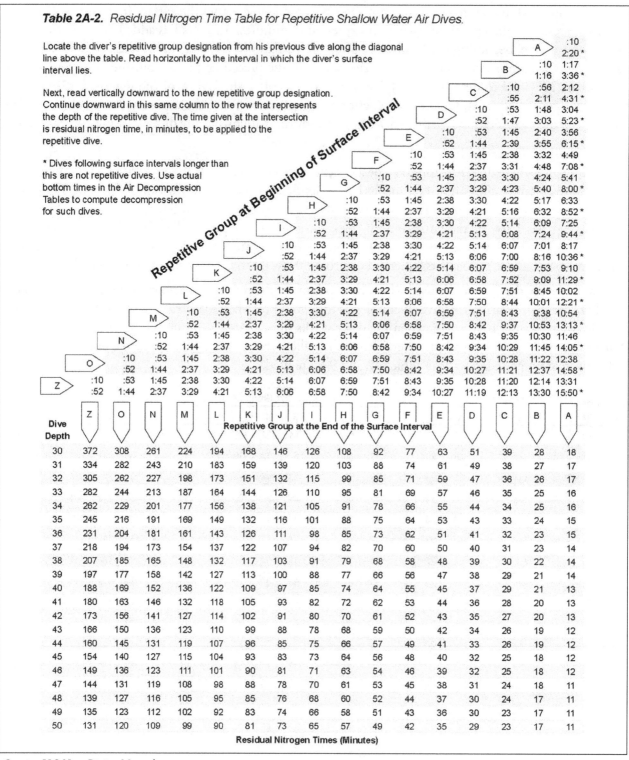

Table 2A-2. *Residual Nitrogen Time Table for Repetitive Shallow Water Air Dives.*

Locate the diver's repetitive group designation from his previous dive along the diagonal line above the table. Read horizontally to the interval in which the diver's surface interval lies.

Next, read vertically downward to the new repetitive group designation. Continue downward in this same column to the row that represents the depth of the repetitive dive. The time given at the intersection is residual nitrogen time, in minutes, to be applied to the repetitive dive.

* Dives following surface intervals longer than this are not repetitive dives. Use actual bottom times in the Air Decompression Tables to compute decompression for such dives.

Repetitive Group at Beginning of Surface Interval

Dive Depth	Z	O	N	M	L	K	J	I	H	G	F	E	D	C	B	A
30	372	308	261	224	194	168	146	126	108	92	77	63	51	39	28	18
31	334	282	243	210	183	159	139	120	103	88	74	61	49	38	27	17
32	305	262	227	198	173	151	132	115	99	85	71	59	47	36	26	17
33	282	244	213	187	164	144	126	110	95	81	69	57	46	35	25	16
34	262	229	201	177	156	138	121	105	91	78	66	55	44	34	25	16
35	245	216	191	169	149	132	116	101	88	75	64	53	43	33	24	15
36	231	204	181	161	143	126	111	98	85	73	62	51	41	32	23	15
37	218	194	173	154	137	122	107	94	82	70	60	50	40	31	23	14
38	207	185	165	148	132	117	103	91	79	68	58	48	39	30	22	14
39	197	177	158	142	127	113	100	88	77	66	56	47	38	29	21	14
40	188	169	152	136	122	109	97	85	74	64	55	45	37	29	21	13
41	180	163	146	132	118	105	93	82	72	62	53	44	36	28	20	13
42	173	156	141	127	114	102	91	80	70	61	52	43	35	27	20	13
43	166	150	136	123	110	99	88	78	68	59	50	42	34	26	19	12
44	160	145	131	119	107	96	85	75	66	57	49	41	33	26	19	12
45	154	140	127	115	104	93	83	73	64	56	48	40	32	25	18	12
46	149	136	123	111	101	90	81	71	63	54	46	39	32	25	18	12
47	144	131	119	108	98	88	78	70	61	53	45	38	31	24	18	11
48	139	127	116	105	95	85	76	68	60	52	44	37	30	24	17	11
49	135	123	112	102	92	83	74	66	58	51	43	36	30	23	17	11
50	131	120	109	99	90	81	73	65	57	49	42	35	29	23	17	11

Repetitive Group at the End of the Surface Interval

Residual Nitrogen Times (Minutes)

Source: *U.S. Navy Diving Manual*

Problem:

You send a diver in to inspect a trash rack on a power plant water intake. His pneumo reading was 61 fsw and his bottom time was 34 minutes. You send him in again to the same depth to take measurements. His surface interval was 2 minutes over 4 hours. The bottom time of the second dive is 34 minutes. Will the diver require decompression?

Solution:

The depth of dive (Dive 1) is 62 fsw (the correction factor is +1 fsw), so you follow the far left column on Table 9-7 down to 70. Because his bottom time (Dive 1) was 34 minutes, you go across to 37 minutes, go up, and the Group Letter is H at the start of the surface interval. On Table 9-8, you locate Group Letter H on the diagonal side, follow it across to where the surface interval (4:02) fits in. You then follow this column down to find the New Group Letter, D. Then you follow the Group D column down to where it intersects with the depth line (70 fsw) and you see that the RNT is 20 minutes. The bottom time (Dive 2) is 34 minutes, and added to the RNT, the ESDT is 54 minutes. We see in Table 9-7 that the No-Decompression Limit for 70 fsw is 48 minutes, so the answer is: yes, this diver will require decompression.

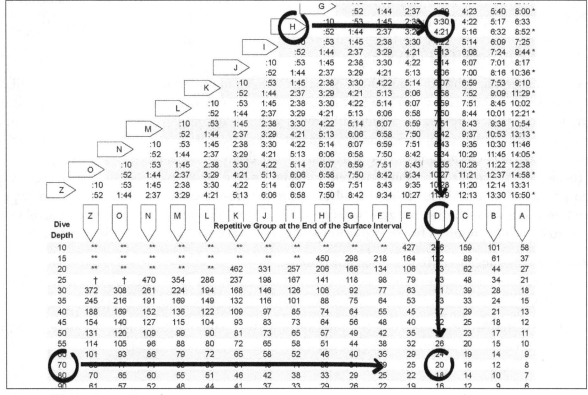

Depth (fsw)	No-Stop Limit	Repetitive Group Designation															
		A	B	C	D	E	F	G	H	I	J	K	L	M	N	O	Z
10	Unlimited	57	101	158	245	426	*										
15	Unlimited	36	60	88	121	163	217	297	449	*							
20	Unlimited	26	43	61	82	106	133	165	205	256	330	461	*				
25	595	20	33	47	62	78	97	117	140	166	198	236	285	354	469	595	
30	371	17	27	38	50	62	76	91	107	125	145	167	193	223	260	307	371
35	232	14	23	32	42	52	63	74	87	100	115	131	148	168	190	215	232
40	163	12	20	27	36	44	53	63	73	84	95	108	121	135	151	163	
45	125	11	17	24	31	39	46	55	63	72	82	92	102	114	125		
50	92	9	15	21	28	34	41	48	56	63	71	80	89	92			
55	74	8	14	19	25	31	37	43	50	56	63	71	74				
60	60	7	12	17	22	28	33	39	45	51	57	60					
70	48	6	10	14	19	25	26	32	37	42	47	48					
80	39	5	9	12	16	20	24	28	32	36	39						

Source: *U.S.Navy Diving Manual*

Source: *U.S.Navy Diving Manual*

5.5.2 RNT Exception Rule

Occasionally, the RNT figure provided in Table 9-8 is a little greater than required, particularly when the surface interval between dives is very short. After following the procedure outlined on the previous page, the diver (or supervisor) may recalculate the decompression requirement by adding the bottom times of both dives and using the deeper of the two depths to select a table and schedule. If the result shows a longer no-decompression time, or less required decompression, then the shorter table and schedule may be used. This procedure is known as the RNT Exception Rule.

Problem:

On a harbor dredging project, a diver is sent in to stem the holes with crushed stone in a pattern of explosives that have been set in a rock ledge. The deepest pneumo reading is 54 fsw, which, once corrected gives a depth of dive of 55 fsw. The bottom time to stem the holes is 39:44, which, rounded up, is 40 min. Ten minutes after the diver has reached surface, the dredging supervisor tells the diving supervisor the detonator cord is ready to attach. It always takes exactly 15 minutes to wire the det-cord and bring the lead back to the surface. Can the diver wire the charges without decompression?

Solution:

With a depth of dive of 55 fsw, we go to 60 fsw in the "Depth" column of Table 9-7 and follow it across horizontally to 45 min, which is the next greater bottom time beyond the actual BT of 40 min. We follow this column up and see the diver's Group Letter for Dive 1 is H. Next, we go to Table 9-8 and enter the table on the diagonal side at H. We know the surface interval fell between :10 and :52, so we follow that column down and see the New Group Letter for Dive 2 is also H. Knowing the diver will be again at 55 fsw, we follow the H column down to 60 fsw, and see the RNT is 46 min. Adding the RNT of Dive 1 to the expected BT of 15 min. for Dive 2, we conclude the diver cannot do both dives without having decompression stops. If we decide to use the RNT Exception Rule, we add the Dive 1 bottom time to the Dive 2 bottom time, giving us a total of 55min. Knowing the depth of dive is unchanged at 55 fsw, we then conclude the diver can perform both dives without decompression.

5.6 DECOMPRESSION DIVES

The air decompression tables found in the *U.S. Navy Diving Manual Rev. 6* represent the most significant change in the U.S. Navy tables seen in a new revision of the manual since the first edition was published. Where formerly there were separate sets of tables for in-water air decompression (standard air) and surface decompression (surface decompression using air and surface decompression using oxygen), all of the tables are now combined in one document. The practice of surface decompression using air is no longer accepted, and this is reflected in the new tables. As well, these tables give the user the option of in-water oxygen decompression. **Users of these tables should be aware that in-water oxygen decompression requires special precautions, including oxygen cleaning of the diving equipment and the dive control panel. Failure to do so may result in fire or explosion and may have serious or fatal consequences.**

5.6.1 Selecting the Safest Mode of Decompression

The easiest mode of decompression is not necessarily the safest. The *U.S. Navy Diving Manual Rev. 6* recommends the following guidelines to be used to select the mode of decompression:

- **In-Water Air:** In-water air decompression is most suitable for dives requiring less than 15 minutes total decompression stop time.

- **In-Water Air/O₂:** In-water air/oxygen is strongly recommended when more than 15 minutes total decompression stop time is required in water. It is a good alternative to surface decompression when a chamber is not available, or site conditions such as decontamination after hazmat will compromise the surface interval time. This mode is only an option when the following conditions are met: the system is oxygen clean and oxygen is available and plumbed into the panel.
- **Surface Decompression Using Oxygen:** The preferred method, and safest for the diver is surface decompression using oxygen. This mode reduces the time the diver must remain in the water and allows for visual monitoring of the diver during the decompression phase. Sur D O₂ is also a cleaner, more efficient mode of decompression, physiologically speaking.

All three of the above modes of decompression are included in Table 9-9 Air Decompression Table. The depth is selected in the upper left, and in the column below this are bottom time increments to select a decompression schedule. Moving across the selected decompression schedule, we see there are two breathing gas mixes listed, air and air/O₂. In line (horizontally) with the gas mixes are times. These are the times the diver is required to spend at each decompression stop. By looking straight up above the time, the depth of the in-water stop is indicated. To the far right of Table 9-9 there is a column titled "chamber O₂ periods", which states the number of 30-minute oxygen breathing periods in the chamber, should surface decompression mode be selected. Each mode of decompression has its own procedure.

5.6.2 Procedure for Water Stops (In-Water Air Decompression)
The stop time for the first stop begins when the diver arrives on the stop and ends when the diver leaves. Travel time to subsequent water stops is included in the stop times. All stops are at 10-foot intervals, and the last in-water stop is at 20 fsw. Upon arrival at each stop, the diver should position the pneumo at mid-chest to allow the supervisor to check the stop elevation, whether the diver is in a stage (basket) or on a down-line.

5.6.3 Procedure for Water Stops (In-Water Oxygen Decompression)
If water stops are required deeper than 30 fsw, they are to be performed on air. The first oxygen breathing water stop is at 30 fsw. The time for travel from the 40 fsw air stop (if required) to the 30 fsw stop, including the shift over to oxygen breathing, should not exceed 3 minutes. If no 30 fsw stop is required, the first stop is 20 fsw. Stop time begins when the diver is confirmed on oxygen, once the breathing gas has been changed from air to oxygen, and the diver has ventilated the helmet continuously for 20 seconds. After every 30 minutes of continuous oxygen breathing, an air break of 5 minutes is required but time on air does not count toward the diver's decompression commitment. The only exceptions on the air breaks is when the total decompression time on oxygen is less than 35 minutes or when the final oxygen breathing period is 35 minutes or less. In these two instances, the air break may be skipped. Ascent from the 30 fsw stop to the 20 fsw stop is performed while breathing oxygen. Ascent from the 20 fsw stop to surface is performed while breathing oxygen. If the total time on decompression stops breathing air and oxygen exceeds 90 minutes, surface decompression using oxygen is strongly recommended, due to the possibility of CNS oxygen toxicity.

5.6.4 Proper Ascent Rate
The proper ascent rate when utilizing USN Rev. 6 is 30 fsw per minute (20 seconds per 10 fsw), with variations between 20 and 40 fsw per minute being acceptable. The same rate is used between water stops, and between the last stop and the surface, except in surface decompression.

5.6.5 Correcting Variations in Ascent Rate

The following rules for correcting variations in ascent rate apply to in-water air decompression, in-water O_2 decompression, and also to surface decompression tables from *U.S. Navy Diving Manual Rev. 6*, as found in this training manual.

5.6.5.1 Travel Rate Exceeded

If the ascent rate exceeds 40 fsw per minute, stop the ascent, allow the watches to catch up, and restart the ascent.

5.6.5.2 Early Arrival at the First Decompression Stop

If the first stop is on air, begin the stop time once the required travel time has elapsed.

If the first stop is on oxygen, put the diver on oxygen on arrival at the stop. With the diver confirmed on oxygen, begin the stop time once the required travel time has elapsed.

5.6.5.3 Delays in Arriving at the First Decompression Stop

- **Delays up to one minute:** A delay of up to and including one minute in arriving at the first decompression stop may be ignored.

- **Delays greater than one minute deeper than 50 fsw:** Round up the delay time to the next whole minute and add to the bottom time. Select correct bottom time increment on table. If no change is required, continue with decompression. If a change in the schedule is required and there are stops deeper than the diver's current depth, perform any missed deeper stops at the diver's current depth. Do not send the diver deeper. Once completed, continue decompression from current depth.

- **Delays greater than one minute shallower than 50 fsw:** Round up the delay time to the next whole minute and add it to the first stop time.

5.6.5.4 Delays in Leaving a Stop or Between Stops

- **Delay less than one minute leaving an air stop:** Disregard a delay of less than one minute. Resume the decompression schedule when delay is finished.

- **Delay less than one minute between air stops:** Disregard delays of less than one minute between air stops.

- **Delay greater than one minute leaving air stop or between stops deeper than 50 fsw:** Add the delay to the bottom time and recalculate decompression. If a new schedule is required, enter the new schedule at present stop or subsequent stop if between stops. Ignore missed stops or times deeper than the depth of delay.

- **Delay greater than one minute leaving air stop or between stops shallower than 50 fsw:** Ignore delay. Resume schedule when delay is finished.

- **Delay leaving 30 fsw O_2 stop or between 30 and 20 fsw O_2 stop:** Subtract any delay leaving 30 fsw O_2 stop or travelling between 30 and 20 fsw O_2 stop from the 20 fsw stop time. If delay causes time on O_2 deeper than 20 fsw to exceed 30 min, give diver an air break at 30 min. When problem is resolved, resume O_2 decompression. Time on air is to be considered "dead time."

- **Delay leaving 20 fsw O_2 stop:** Delays in leaving 20 fsw stop may be ignored. If diver's time on O_2 reached 30 min, give an air break and remain on air until problem resolved, then surface on O_2

The following is a sample page from Table 9-9 of the *U.S. Navy Diving Manual Rev. 6*. All of the most important features have been highlighted in color and labeled for easier understanding. The yellow 80 FSW in the upper left corner signifies the dive depth; we call it the 80-foot table. The pink box across the top has the depths (in fsw) for in-water decompression stops. The orange down the left side indicates bottom time of the dive; we call that the schedule, as in 80/60, or the 60-min. schedule on the 80-ft. table. The light blue vertical box just below the pink box indicates the time spent on water stop (in minutes). Farther down the table, the light blue vertical box indicates the ascent time (min:sec) from bottom to the first stop. The pink vertical box indicates the breathing gas used by the diver on water stops. (Note: Oxygen is never used in-water deeper than 30 fsw) The pink horizontal box below that again indicates air stop time. The green horizontal box just below that indicates oxygen stop time. Farther down the table again and toward the right-hand side, the light blue vertical box indicates total ascent time (min:sec – includes stops and travel time). Beside it, the green vertical box indicates oxygen breathing periods in the chamber.

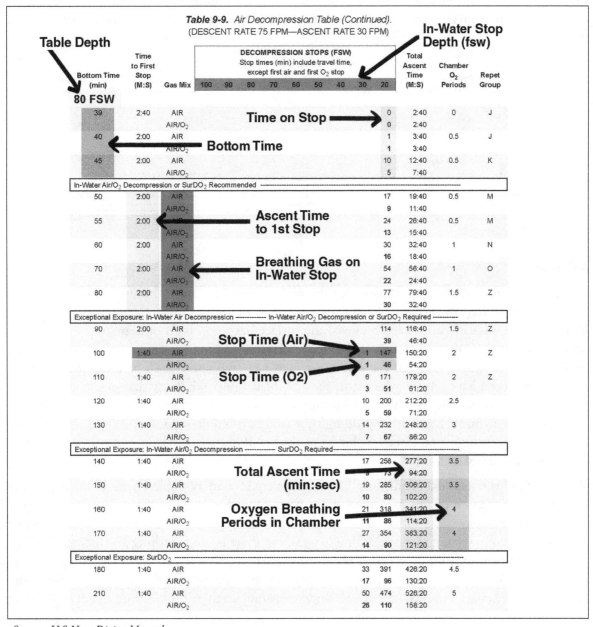

Source: *U.S. Navy Diving Manual*

Knowing that all modes of air decompression are covered by Table 9-9, we will first deal with the two in-water modes before we get into procedures for surface decompression. We saw previously that in-water air decompression is only recommended when the total decompression time is less than 15 minutes. We also saw in-water oxygen is only an option when the diving spread is oxygen compatible (O_2 cleaned) and there is medical oxygen on site and plumbed into the control panel. Therefore, if the conditions for in-water oxygen cannot be met, we have no choice but to use in-water air decompression, and the bottom time should be adjusted accordingly to keep the total decompression time at, or below, 15 minutes. Consider the following example:

Problem:

You are on a salvage project, and your company uses the +5+5 rule and USN Rev. 6. You have to send a diver in to attach air hoses to steel salvage pontoons. The deepest pneumo reading any diver has provided on the job so far is 67 fsw. The only oxygen supply onboard the barge is the chamber supply. Because of the thick oil residue in the water, surface decompression is not an option. What is the maximum bottom time that you can allow your diver? What will the required decompression be?

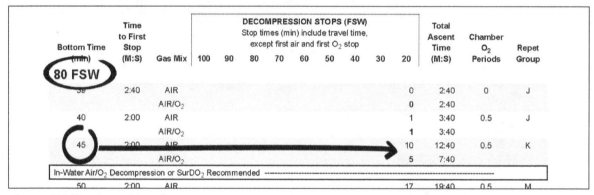

Source: *U.S.Navy Diving Manual*

Solution:

The chamber oxygen must not be used for diving purposes because you must keep the chamber ready in case you have to perform a hyperbaric treatment, so this takes in-water oxygen off the table. You know the thick oil residue has removed the surface decompression option. Your only choices now are in-water air decompression or no-decompression. Assuming your diver gives a pneumo reading of 67 fsw, once you add the correction factor (1 fsw) and the +5 padding the company requires, you then have 73 fsw, which calls for an 80 fsw table. We know that to use in-water air, the decompression should be less than 15 minutes. Therefore, the 45 min. schedule is the one you must use. When you subtract the +5 padding your company requires, you are left with 40 min. The maximum bottom time you can allow for your diver is 40 min. The decompression required will be 10 min. @ 20 fsw on air.

When both of the required conditions (O_2 clean system and an available O_2 supply) for in-water oxygen decompression can be met, then you can use it safely in your diving operation. In-water oxygen decompression, like surface decompression using oxygen, has one great advantage: When the diver is decompressing while breathing oxygen, the diver is not breathing any inert gas (which he/she would be if breathing air). Since the diver is breathing 100% O_2, the gradient from tissue-blood-lungs is increased, therefore the decompression time is cut drastically. The rate of off-gassing, however, is still being controlled (the diver is under pressure), so there is little or no risk of an incident of decompression sickness. Consider this:

Problem:

You have just laid a new 10-inch pipeline, and you need to have your diver take measurements for a spool-piece to be made up, in order to tie in the pipeline to a platform. Your company operates on a +5+5 rule, and you are all set up with several quads of oxygen and O_2 cleaned gear. The diver gives you a bottom pneumo of 123 fsw, and the bottom time is exactly 36 min. Consult the procedures on the previous pages and describe the diver's decompression using in-water oxygen according to Table 9-9, USN Rev. 6.

Bottom Time (min)	Stop (M:S)	Gas Mix	100	90	80	70	60	50	40	30	20	Time (M:S)	O₂ Periods	Repet Group
140 FSW														
10	4:40	AIR									0	4:40	0	E
		AIR/O₂									0	4:40		
15	4:00	AIR									2	6:40	0.5	H
		AIR/O₂									1	5:40		
20	4:00	AIR									7	11:40	0.5	J
		AIR/O₂									4	8:40		
In-Water Air/O₂ Decompression or SurDO₂ Recommended --														
25	4:00	AIR									26	30:40	1	L
		AIR/O₂									14	18:40		
30	4:00	AIR									44	48:40	1	N
		AIR/O₂									23	27:40		
35	3:40	AIR								4	59	67:20	1.5	O
		AIR/O₂								2	30	36:20		
Exceptional Exposure: In-Water Air Decompression ------------- In-Water Air/O₂ Decompression or SurDO₂ Required ----------														
40	3:40	AIR								11	80	95:20	1.5	Z
		AIR/O₂								6	33	48:20		
45	3:20	AIR							3	21	113	141:00	2	Z
		AIR/O₂							3	11	34	57:20		
50	3:20	AIR							7	28	145	184:00	2	Z

Source: *U.S. Navy Diving Manual*

Solution:

The pneumo reading of 123 fsw, with the correction factor, becomes 125 fsw. The company requires a +5 on depth and time, so to select the table we use 130 fsw as his depth of dive, which means that we use the 140 fsw table. The bottom time for this dive is 36 min., and adding the company's +5min, we then have 41 min., which puts us onto the 45 min. schedule. Looking at that schedule, we see the following: ascent to first stop is 3:20 (30 fpm), and there are water stops at 40, 30, and 20 fsw. In our procedures, we learned the deepest oxygen stop used is at 30 fsw. The schedule we selected shows a 40 fsw stop, so the first stop will be done on air. Once the 3 min. air stop has been completed, we bring the diver to his 30 fsw stop, switch to oxygen, and have the diver ventilate the helmet continuously for 20 sec. (see procedure). Once this is done, his time on the 30 fsw stop starts. We see in the schedule that his stop time is 11min. Once the 11 min. has been completed, we start the 20 fsw stop time and bring the diver up to the 20 fsw stop, on oxygen the entire time. According to the schedule, the 20 fsw stop is 34 min., and according to the procedure, after 35min. of continuous oxygen breathing, the diver must have a 5 min. air break. The reason for this is to avoid CNS oxygen toxicity, which could have disastrous consequences if it occurs in the water. The 35 min. figure is the maximum oxygen exposure time without an air break. So after the diver has 20 min. on the 20 fsw stop, we switch him/her to air for 5 min. This air break does not count as oxygen time, so after the air break, we switch him/her back to oxygen, have him/her ventilate the hat, and run another 14 min. on oxygen at 20 fsw. Once this has been completed, we bring the diver to surface, still breathing oxygen. The total ascent time, including travel, stops, air break, and helmet ventilation will be close to 57:20. The total ascent times given on the table are as they would be in a perfect world, which you are not in (you may have noticed) so if the total ascent time is off by a few seconds, you will not face the firing squad. Just follow the procedures and tables as closely as possible, and record the times exactly as they are and not as you think they should be.

The diver in the previous problem had a total ascent time of 57:20 using in-water oxygen. Look now at the schedule for in-water air. That figure is 141:00. The difference in time between the two is less than the bottom time and ascent time on the dive, as shown above, so by using oxygen decompression instead of air for this depth and bottom time, you can manage twice as many dives in the same amount of time.

NOTE:

Once in-water oxygen decompression has been completed, the panel must be switched back to air, the diving helmet and umbilical must be well ventilated prior to the next dive, and this must be recorded in the deck log. Failure to do so may expose the next diver to extremely high ppO$_2$ at depth with serious or fatal consequences.

5.6.6 Exceptional Exposure

If you look at Table 9-9, you will notice horizontal boxes that indicate the recommended cut-offs for in-water air decompression, in-water oxygen decompression, and also the exceptional exposure limits. These limits are not optional; exceeding them increases the risk of decompression sickness to the diver considerably. Two of these are illustrated below:

		AIR/O$_2$		7	67	86:20	
Exceptional Exposure: In-Water Air/O$_2$ Decompression ----------- SurDO$_2$ Required--							
140	1:40	AIR		17	258	277:20	3.5
		AIR/O$_2$		9	73	94:20	
150	1:40	AIR		19	285	306:20	3.5
		AIR/O$_2$	**Exceptional Exposure**	10	80	102:20	
160	1:40	AIR	**Limit**	21	318	341:20	4
		AIR/O$_2$		11	86	114:20	
170	1:40	AIR		27	354	383:20	4
		AIR/O$_2$		14	90	121:20	
Exceptional Exposure: SurDO$_2$ --							
180	1:40	AIR		33	391	426:20	4.5

Source: *U.S. Navy Diving Manual*

Decompression profiles provided beyond the exceptional exposure cut-offs are only to be used in the event of an unforeseen emergency, such as a trapped, injured, or unconscious diver who must be recovered, or the complete failure of the oxygen system requiring in-water air decompression when in-water oxygen was originally planned. These exceptional exposures are never to be used in standard diving operations.

See Apendix V: Procedure for Omitted Decompression for additional information.

5.7 STANDARD PROCEDURE FOR SURFACE DECOMPRESSION

The preferred method of decompression, and the safest for the diver, is surface decompression using oxygen. This mode reduces the time the diver must remain in the water and allows for visual monitoring of the diver during most (or all) of the decompression phase. To calculate the decompression required for any given dive, follow the horizontal row across on the appropriate decompression table/schedule for depth/bottom time. Complete any required in-water decompression stops 40 fsw or deeper. On completion of the 40 fsw water stop, bring the diver to the surface at 40 fsw per minute. If a 40 fsw stop is not required, the diver ascends from bottom to 40f sw at an ascent rate of 30 fsw per minute, and from 40 fsw to the surface at

40 fsw per minute. The allowed 5-minute surface interval starts when the diver leaves the 40 fsw stop or passes 40 fsw on the ascent. The surface interval ends when the diver is at 50 fsw in the chamber, breathing oxygen. Oxygen breathing periods are 30 minutes and half-periods are 15 minutes. The first half period is spent at 50 fsw. If only one half-period is required, the diver is brought from 50 fsw to surface at 30 fsw per minute. If one full period is required, the first half is at 50 fsw and the second half is at 40 fsw. Travel from 50 fsw to 40 fsw is performed on oxygen at a rate of 30 fsw per minute. Travel from 50 to 40 fsw is included in the first oxygen period. Five-minute air breaks are given at the end of each oxygen breathing period. Travel from 40 fsw to surface is at 30 fsw per minute breathing air. If more than four oxygen periods are required, the remaining oxygen periods (beyond period 4) are performed at 30 fsw. Travel from 40 fsw to 30 fsw is performed during the air break and at 30 fsw per minute. Travel from 30 fsw to surface is at 30 fsw per minute breathing air.

5.7.1 Terms and Definitions for Surface Decompression

Term	Definition
Ascent Rate	From bottom to 40 fsw = 30 fpm; from 40 fsw to surface = 40 fpm
Travel Time	Time (min:sec) from leaving bottom to surface or stop; time between stops
Stop Depth (final)	The final in-water stop (air) is at 40 fsw
Surface Interval	Time (min:sec) from 40 fsw (water) to 50 fsw (chamber on O_2), maximum 5 min.
1st Stop (chamber)	First stop is 50 fsw, usually ½ period
2nd Stop (chamber)	Second stop is 40 fsw
3rd Stop (chamber)	Third stop is 30 fsw, only used when total decompression exceeds 4 periods
Oxygen Period	One oxygen period = 30min; one half oxygen period = 15 min.
Air Break	Diver breathes normal air, typical duration 5min.
Safe Way Out	Alternate procedure utilized when diver is unable to equalize in chamber

5.7.2 Surface Interval

As stated above, the surface interval (SI) begins either when the diver leaves the 40 fsw in-water stop or when the diver passes 40 fsw on ascent if no stop is required. It ends when the diver is confirmed to be at 50 fsw in the chamber, breathing oxygen. The maximum allowed surface interval is 5 minutes. If the 5-minute surface interval has been exceeded, proceed as follows:

- **SI greater than 5 min., less than 7 min.:** If the surface exceeds 5 min. but is less than or equal to 7 min., increase O_2 period at 50 fsw to 30 min., ascend to 40 fsw on air break. This penalty is considered normal surface decompression and not an emergency procedure.

- **SI greater than 7 min.:** Take diver to 60 fsw in chamber on O_2. If original schedule called for 2 O_2 periods or less, treat on USN TT5. If original schedule called for 2.5 O_2 periods or more, treat diver on USN TT6.

5.7.3 Procedure for Surface Decompression from 30 fsw and 20 fsw Water Stops

The supervisor has the option to cut short the in-water phase of decompression (air or O_2) and shift to surface decompression using oxygen. This may be desirable in the case of rapidly deteriorating sea-state, if the diver becomes ill, or if other events arise that would impact the diver's in-water decompression. Should the supervisor decide to shift to surface decompression mode, he/she has the option of either prescribing the full number of oxygen breathing periods indicated in the surface decompression schedule or giving the diver credit for time spent decompressing on air or oxygen in-water, thereby reducing the number of oxygen periods.

If surface decompression is elected before the diver has shifted to oxygen, use the full number of oxygen breathing periods shown in the table.

If surface decompression is elected after the diver has shifted to oxygen, compute the number of chamber oxygen periods as follows: multiply remaining time on oxygen at stops by 1.1 and divide the total by 30. Round the result up to the nearest half period. The minimum requirement is ½ oxygen breathing period at 50 fsw.

If surface decompression is elected while the diver is decompressing on air, first convert the remaining air stop time to the equivalent oxygen stop time, then compute the required chamber oxygen periods as detailed below.

To convert stop time on air to equivalent stop time on oxygen, do the following:

- **Diver at 30 fsw:** Divide the 30 fsw air stop time shown in the table by the 30 fsw oxygen time. The result is the *air/oxygen trading ratio.* Divide the remaining air stop time at 30 fsw by the air/oxygen trading ratio. The result is the equivalent remaining oxygen time at 30 fsw. Add the oxygen stop time at 20 fsw shown in the table. Multiply the sum by 1.1 and divide the total by 30. Round up the result to the nearest half-period. The minimum requirement is ½ oxygen period at 50 fsw.

- **Diver at 20 fsw:** Divide the 20 fsw air stop time shown in the table by the 20 fsw oxygen time to achieve the trading ratio. Divide the remaining air stop time at 20 fsw by the air/oxygen trading ratio to establish equivalent remaining oxygen time. Multiply this figure by 1.1 and divide the total by 30. Round up the result to the nearest half period. The minimum requirement is ½ oxygen period at 50 fsw.

5.7.4 Safe Way Out Procedure

If a diver cannot equalize to reach the 50 fsw O_2 stop in the chamber, press diver as deep as he/she can initially equalize. Have the diver begin O_2 breathing at that depth. Continue attempting to press the diver deeper. If the in-water air or air/O_2 schedule for that depth and time called for only a 20 fsw stop, attempt to press to 20 fsw. If the schedule called for a 30 fsw stop, attempt to press to 30 fsw. Double the number of O_2 periods called for in the table and have the diver perform them at the deepest depth the diver can achieve. O_2 time begins when the diver initially starts on O_2. Insert a 15 min. air break every 60 min. Time on air is "dead time" and does not count toward the decompression commitment. Once O_2 time is completed, surface the chamber at 30 fsw per minute. Once on surface, observe the diver closely for signs of DCI. This safe way out procedure is only intended to be used for divers with equalization problems and is not to be used as a substitute for normal surface decompression.

There are requirements that must be met before surface decompression operations can be performed, some of them obvious, some less so. Obviously, a deck decompression chamber must be on site. However, if the project falls under the International Marine Contractors Association (IMCA) Guideline, there must also be a backup deck decompression chamber on site, dedicated for hyperbaric treatments. The reason for this is to avoid becoming "chamber blocked," which means having a diver committed to surface decompression when another diver presents symptoms of pressure related illness. There must be dedicated primary and backup air supplies as well as dedicated primary and backup oxygen supplies to all chambers. More detail on the chambers and their maintenance and operation may be found in Chapter 11: Hyperbaric Chambers. Although you will sometimes see surface decompression operations performed with a down-line, by far the safest way to perform surface decompression (sur-d) dives is with a LARS and stage or wet bell.

As for the diver entering the chamber, there are two schools of thought on this: some choose to have the diver enter chamber with it surfaced and then blowdown, some choose to "transfer under pressure." The reason for using the first option is that if there is a problem with the door seal on the inner lock, you have a second chance with the outer lock seal. However, most times the primary air supply for the chamber is a 5120 LP compressor, and even with a serious leak in a door seal, these units put out enough volume to attain a seal and pressurize the outer lock for a transfer to the inner lock. Once a seal is achieved, most leaks will seal once there is a pressure differential of 10 fsw or so. The proper procedure for transfer under pressure (TUP) is as follows: the inner lock is maintained at the depth of the first stop. The diver is blown down in the outer lock (on BIBS, breathing oxygen), making a "thumbs up" sign in the viewport to indicate there aren't any problems equalizing. As soon as the two locks equalize, the inner lock door will open. The diver enters the inner lock, immediately goes on BIBs, and pushes the inner lock door closed with his/her feet. As soon as this is done, the outer (transfer) lock is surfaced. The faster the outer lock is vented, the better the inner lock will seal in most cases. The chamber operator must watch the gauges carefully, however, as no fluctuation in inner lock depth should occur during the transfer under pressure and the surfacing of the transfer lock. Most operations will require every diver to perform several "dry runs" on the chamber before operating it. A dry run is pressurizing the chamber and going through the entire process with no occupant inside the chamber.

Problem:

You have to send your diver, Myra, down to attach hydraulic lines to a hydraulic actuated valve on a pipeline manifold on the seabed. The company policy requires +5+5 on every dive. Your diver gives a pneumo reading of 124 fsw, and by the time the valve is located, marine growth cleaned off the hydraulic nipples, and hydraulic lines attached, the bottom time is 34:05. You already confirmed the chamber was good-to-go prior to this dive. Describe this diver's decompression.

140 FSW

Bottom Time (min)	Time to First Stop (M:S)	Gas Mix	100	90	80	70	60	50	40	30	20	Total Ascent Time (M:S)	Chamber O$_2$ Periods	Repet Group
10	4:40	AIR									0	4:40	0	E
		AIR/O$_2$									0	4:40		
15	4:00	AIR									2	6:40	0.5	H
		AIR/O$_2$									1	5:40		
20	4:00	AIR									7	11:40	0.5	J
		AIR/O$_2$									4	8:40		
In-Water Air/O$_2$ Decompression or SurDO$_2$ Recommended --														
25	4:00	AIR									26	30:40	1	L
		AIR/O$_2$									14	18:40		
30	4:00	AIR									44	48:40	1	N
		AIR/O$_2$									23	27:40		
35	3:40	AIR								4	59	67:20	1.5	O
		AIR/O$_2$								2	30	36:20		
Exceptional Exposure: In-Water Air Decompression ------------- In-Water Air/O$_2$ Decompression or SurDO$_2$ Required ----------														
40	3:40	AIR								11	80	95:20	1.5	Z
		AIR/O$_2$								6	33	48:20		
45	3:20	AIR							3	21	113	141:00	2	Z
		AIR/O$_2$							3	11	34	57:20		
50	3:20	AIR							7	28	145	184:00	2	Z

Source: *U.S. Navy Diving Manual*

Solution:

Once the pneumo correction factor is added, the depth of dive becomes 126 fsw. You are told to pad this +5, so it then becomes 131 fsw. You select a 140 fsw table. The bottom time of 34:05 is rounded up to 35 min. and with the +5 padding, it becomes 40 min. Therefore, you select the 140/45 schedule. Standard procedure for surface decompression tells us that all in-water stops 40 fsw and deeper are to be completed, and we see that on this schedule, there is a 3 min. stop @ 40 fsw. We are also told the ascent rate is 30 fpm to 40 fsw, and 40 fpm from there to the surface. Knowing both of these facts, you bring your diver, Myra, from bottom at 30 fpm up to the 40 fsw stop. She then spends 3 min. on this water stop. Once her stop is done, you start your surface interval timer and bring her at 40 fpm to the surface. The diver is dressed down as quickly as possible and enters the outer lock. She goes on BIBs and gives the "thumbs up" in the viewport and as soon you hear the surface crew call out "go" (when the door is held shut), you blow her down (taking about 1 minute) to her first chamber stop at 50 fsw. The schedule calls for two O_2 breathing periods, and we know from the sur-d procedure that the first half period is at 50 fsw and the remainder is at 40 fsw. As soon as the diver has completed her first stop (½ period or 15 min.), you bring her (on oxygen) to her second stop at 40 fsw, taking 1min. After 15 min. (including 1min. travel from 50 fsw) at 40 fsw, you then give her a 5 min. air break. On completion of the air break, she goes back on BIBs to do her final 30 min. (one period) at 40 fsw. Once this has been completed, you bring her to surface on air at 30 fpm.

5.7.5 Surfacing the Chamber

It should be noted that on most sur-d operations offshore, after the last stop, the chamber is surfaced on a slow bleed, taking 5 minutes or more to surface, with the diver on oxygen the whole time. While this practice is not according to the procedure in USN Rev. 6, it is totally acceptable. Additional time on oxygen ensures the diver has off-gassed as much as possible, and the slow ascent is much easier on the diver. The air breaks are always inserted to ensure the maximum time on oxygen is 30 min., so when surfacing the diver on a slow bleed, this should be considered. An extra air break may be required.

Problem:

Your diver has completed the dive and is on ascent. Because of the depth, you have selected the 120 fsw sur-d table and due to bottom time, you have selected the 120/50 schedule. The company you are working for requires a 5 min. slow bleed to surface in the chamber. Describe the chamber decompression for this dive.

Bottom Time (min)	Stop to First Stop (M:S)	Gas Mix	100	90	80	70	60	50	40	30	20	Ascent Time (M:S)	Chamber O2 Periods	Repet Group
120 FSW														
	4:00	AIR										4:00	0	F
		AIR/O₂										4:00		
20	3:20	AIR									2	6:00	0.5	H
		AIR/O₂									1	5:00		
25	3:20	AIR									8	12:00	0.5	J
		AIR/O₂									4	8:00		
In-Water Air/O₂ Decompression or SurDO₂ Recommended														
30	3:20	AIR									24	28:00	0.5	L
		AIR/O₂									13	17:00		
35	3:20	AIR									38	42:00	1	N
		AIR/O₂									20	24:00		
40	3:20	AIR									51	55:00	1	O
		AIR/O₂									27	31:00		
45	3:20	AIR									72	76:00	1.5	Z
		AIR/O₂									33	37:00		
Exceptional Exposure: In-Water Air Decompression --- In-Water Air/O₂ Decompression or SurDO₂ Required														
50	3:00	AIR								9	86	98:40	1.5	Z
		AIR/O₂								5	33	46:40		

Solution:

The schedule calls for 1.5 oxygen periods, or 15 min. @ 50 fsw and 30 min. @ 40 fsw. You will run the 50f sw stop and then bring the diver to 40 fsw. Once the diver has spent 5 min. on the 40 fsw stop, you will insert an air break. After the air break, the diver will do 20 min. more on oxygen and then you will give another air break. Then the diver will do the final 5 min. @ 40 fsw on oxygen and then the slow bleed (5 min.) on oxygen to the surface. This timeline ensures the diver's maximum exposure time on oxygen is 20 minutes.

5.8 ASCENT TO ALTITUDE AFTER DIVING

On occasion, the diver may be required to ascend to altitude after a dive or after a hyperbaric treatment for pressure related illness. Examples of this would be: driving through a mountainous region after work, flying home after a trip offshore, or being transported by aircraft for further hyperbaric treatment. In the same way that an existing gas load on the diver must be considered before performing a second dive, it must also be considered before ascent to altitude. Even after decompression, there is always residual nitrogen in the diver's body. This residual nitrogen must be taken into account, or the diver will suffer the consequences. In North America, there are several cases every year of tourists who scuba dive while on vacation, catch "one last dive" before leaving for home, and get bent (sometimes quite seriously) on the flight home. Most diving contractors have a policy for flying after diving but never assume. ***On a recent trip working in West Africa, several of us were booked for a chopper flight one evening, as our offshore hitch was ending. Four of the guys booked for the flight dived earlier in the day. When I asked what altitude the choppers usually use, the answer was "It's only a helicopter, don't worry about it – the other supervisors don't mind." I pushed to find out and was told 1,800–2,000 ft. For years, the other supervisors had been allowing their divers to jump on a chopper after diving, and no one ever asked about the altitude.*** ALWAYS ASK – DON'T ASSUME. Flying by either commercial airliner or helicopter poses a risk to the diver unless residual nitrogen is accounted for.

The following table is from the *Commercial Diver's Handbook* and has been adapted from USN Rev. 6. It may be used to calculate the minimum surface interval (hours:minutes) before ascent to altitude.

(Table 9-6) REQUIRED SURFACE INTERVAL BEFORE ASCENT TO ALTITUDE

Repet Group Designator	Increase in Altitude (feet)									
	1000	2000	3000	4000	5000	6000	7000	8000	9000	10000
A	0:00	0:00	0:00	0:00	0:00	0:00	0:00	0:00	0:00	0:00
B	0:00	0:00	0:00	0:00	0:00	0:00	0:00	0:00	0:00	1:42
C	0:00	0:00	0:00	0:00	0:00	0:00	0:00	0:00	1:48	6:23
D	0:00	0:00	0:00	0:00	0:00	0:00	0:00	1:45	5:24	9:59
E	0:00	0:00	0:00	0:00	0:00	0:00	1:37	4:39	8:18	12:54
F	0:00	0:00	0:00	0:00	0:00	1:32	4:04	7:06	10:45	15:20
G	0:00	0:00	0:00	0:00	1:19	3:38	6:10	9:13	12:52	17:27
H	0:00	0:00	0:00	1:06	3:10	5:29	8:02	11:04	14:43	19:18
I	0:00	0:00	0:56	2:45	4:50	7:09	9:41	12:44	16:22	20:58
J	0:00	0:41	2:25	4:15	6:19	8:39	11:11	14:13	17:52	22:27

Repet Group Designator	Increase in Altitude (feet)									
	1000	2000	3000	4000	5000	6000	7000	8000	9000	10000
K	0:30	2:03	3:47	5:37	7:41	10:00	12:33	15:35	19:14	23:49
L	1:45	3:18	5:02	6:52	8:56	11:15	13:48	16:50	20:29	25:04
M	2:54	4:28	6:12	8:01	10:06	12:25	14:57	18:00	21:38	26:14
N	3:59	5:32	7:16	9:06	11:10	13:29	16:02	19:04	22:43	27:18
O	4:59	6:33	8:17	10:06	12:11	14:30	17:02	20:05	23:43	28:19
Z	5:56	7:29	9:13	11:03	13:07	15:26	17:59	21:01	24:40	29:15

NOTES:

All exceptional exposure dives require a 48-hour surface interval before ascent to altitude.

All treatments for decompression sickness or arterial gas embolism require a 72-hour surface interval before ascent to altitude.

When using this table, use the highest repetitive group factor obtained in the previous 24-hour period.

Cabin pressures in commercial aircraft vary somewhat, but typically are in the 8,000 ft. range.

Surface HeO_2 dives require a 12-hour surface interval for no-decompression; 24 hours if the dive was beyond the no-decompression limit.

Source *The Commercial Diver's Handbook* ©Best Publishing Company

In order to use the table above, you must get the repetitive group letter for the last dive performed. On the left side of the table, find the corresponding letter. Follow the line horizontally to the right until you reach the maximum altitude the diver will reach. The figure in the box is the surface interval (hr:min) required before ascending to that altitude.

Problem:

Joseph, one of your divers, wants to fly home tomorrow because his father was hurt in a car wreck. He did a dive earlier today, and you decompressed him on the 120/25 schedule. He climbed out of the chamber at 1015 hours this morning. Using the table above, when is the earliest he can fly home?

Solution:

Because he was decompressed on the 120/25 schedule, his group letter is J. Looking at the letter J on the table (9-6), we see that in order to travel to 8,000 ft. (standard for commercial airliners), a surface interval of 14:13 is required. Since the diver surfaced at 1015 this morning, he cannot fly until 0028 tomorrow or 28 minutes after midnight.

Problem:

You are diving on a construction job in Washington State near the Canadian border. You want to drive to Calgary, Canada, for a hockey game after work. To drive to Calgary, you have to go through two mountain passes. The highest is Kicking Horse Pass, at 7,600 ft. above sea level. Your dive this morning was on an 80 fsw table, on an 80/80 schedule, and you came out of the chamber at 0830. You really want to get going so you have time to eat before the game – when can you start driving into the mountains?

Bottom Time (min)	Time to First Stop (M:S)	Gas Mix	100	90	80	70	60	50	40	30	20	Total Ascent Time (M:S)	Chamber O₂ Periods	Repet Group
80 FSW														
	2:40	AIR									0	2:40	0	J
		AIR/O₂									0	2:40		
40	2:00	AIR									1	3:40	0.5	J
		AIR/O₂									1	3:40		
45	2:00	AIR									10	12:40	0.5	K
		AIR/O₂									5	7:40		
In-Water Air/O₂ Decompression or SurDO₂ Recommended														
50	2:00	AIR									17	19:40	0.5	M
		AIR/O₂									9	11:40		
55	2:00	AIR									24	26:40	0.5	M
		AIR/O₂									13	15:40		
60	2:00	AIR									30	32:40	1	N
		AIR/O₂									16	18:40		
70	2:00	AIR									54	56:40	1	O
		AIR/O₂									22	24:40		
80	2:00	AIR									77	79:40	1.5	Z
		AIR/O₂									30	32:40		

Source: *U.S. Navy Diving Manual*

Solution:

You dived on an 80/80 schedule, so your group letter after the dive is Z. The highest altitude you will be driving at will be 7,600 feet, which would read as 8,000 feet in Table 9-6. When you follow group letter Z across to 8,000 feet in Table 9-6, you see that the surface interval required is 21:01. So adding 21 hours and 1 minute to your arrive surface time of 0830, you see you can start your ascent to altitude at 0531 the following morning. You are going to want to try to sell your hockey tickets to someone else.

5.9 DIVING AT ALTITUDE

On occasion, the commercial diver will be required to dive at altitude. This could be recovering an aircraft that crashed in a mountain lake or working on a hydro-electric dam in the mountains. Whatever the job entails, one thing holds true for all of them: any dive conducted at altitude requires more decompression than the identical dive performed at sea level. The atmospheric pressure is lower at altitude. Because of this, air decompression tables cannot be used unless they are corrected for the altitude at which they are being used, and depth gauges must be zeroed at the altitude of the dive as well. This includes both the pneumofathometer and chamber gauges. The only alternative to a pneumo is hard measurement – closed depth gauges will not be accurate at altitude. In addition to the corrections to tables and zeroing gauges, the diver must be equilibrated and acclimatized to the altitude as well. When the human body ascends to altitude, it off-gasses nitrogen until it reaches a state of equilibrium with the partial pressure of nitrogen in the atmosphere. This equilibration process takes up to 12 hours. In addition, the body makes adjustments to deal with the lower partial pressure of oxygen. This process is called acclimatization and takes up to 24 hours. Table 9-4 provides sea level equivalent depths in order to correct for various altitudes. The lower portion of the table has depth corrections for various altitudes for decompression stops.

Table 9-4. *Sea Level Equivalent Depth (fsw).*

Actual Depth (fsw)	Altitude (feet)									
	1000	2000	3000	4000	5000	6000	7000	8000	9000	10000
10	10	15	15	15	15	15	15	15	15	15
15	15	20	20	20	20	20	20	25	25	25
20	20	25	25	25	25	25	30	30	30	30
25	25	30	30	30	35	35	35	35	35	40
30	30	35	35	35	40	40	40	45	45	45
35	35	40	40	45	45	45	50	50	50	60
40	40	45	45	50	50	50	55	55	60	60
45	45	50	55	55	55	60	60	70	70	70
50	50	55	60	60	70	70	70	70	70	80
55	55	60	70	70	70	70	80	80	80	80
60	60	70	70	70	80	80	80	90	90	90
65	65	70	80	80	80	90	90	90	100	100
70	70	80	80	90	90	90	100	100	100	110
75	75	90	90	90	100	100	100	110	110	110
80	80	90	90	100	100	100	110	110	120	120
85	85	100	100	100	110	110	120	120	120	130
90	90	100	110	110	110	120	120	130	130	140
95	95	110	110	110	120	120	130	130	140	140
100	100	110	120	120	130	130	130	140	140	150
105	105	120	120	130	130	140	140	150	150	160
110	110	120	130	130	140	140	150	150	160	160
115	115	130	130	140	140	150	150	160	170	170
120	120	130	140	140	150	150	160	170	170	180
125	125	140	140	150	160	160	170	170	180	190
130	130	140	150	160	160	170	170	180	190	190
135	135	150	160	160	170	170	180	190	190	200
140	140	160	160	170	170	180	190	190	200	210
145	145	160	170	170	180	190	190	200	210	
150	160	170	170	180	190	190	200	210		
155	170	170	180	180	190	200	210			
160	170	180	180	190	200	200				
165	180	180	190	200	200					
170	180	190	190	200						
175	190	190	200							
180	190	200	210							
185	200	200								
190	200									
Table Water Stops	Equivalent Stop Depths (fsw)									
10	10	9	9	9	8	8	8	7	7	7
20	19	19	18	17	17	16	15	15	14	14
30	29	28	27	26	25	24	23	22	21	21
40	39	37	36	35	33	32	31	30	29	28
50	48	47	45	43	42	40	39	37	36	34
60	58	56	54	52	50	48	46	45	43	41

Note: ▬▬▬ = Exceptional Exposure Limit

Source: *U.S. Navy Diving Manual*

It is strongly recommended that dives not be performed until at least a 12-hour acclimatization period has passed at altitude, preferably 24 hours. Any time that a dive is performed less than 12 hours after ascent to altitude, it is considered a repetitive dive, with the initial ascent also being considered a dive. To obtain a group letter for the initial ascent to altitude, we use Table 9-5.

Once the repetitive group letter has been established, we use it and the surface interval (begins on arrival at altitude and ends on leaving surface) in Table 9-8 to calculate the residual nitrogen for the dive at altitude.

Table 9-5 Repetitive Groups Associated with Initial Ascent to Altitude

Altitude (feet)	Repetitive Group
1000	A
2000	A
3000	B
4000	C
5000	D
6000	E
7000	F
8000	G
9000	H
10000	I

Source: *U.S.Navy Diving Manual*

Problem:

A diver has been brought from the coast to a dam in the mountains to clean an intake screen. The altitude of the dam is 5,400 feet. His ascent by helicopter started 2 hours before he left surface, and his maximum depth will be 45 fsw. How much residual nitrogen will there be to account for in-bottom time calculations?

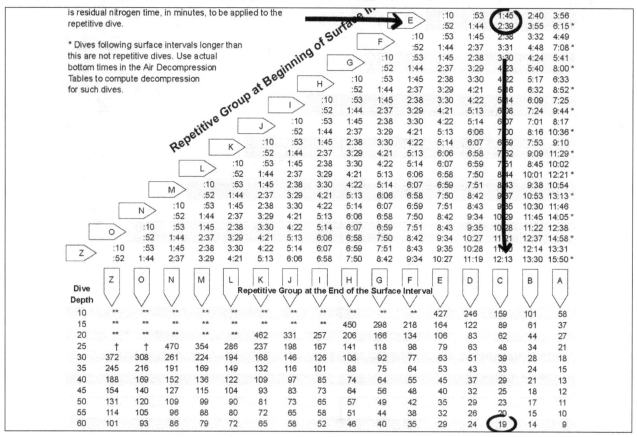

Source: *U.S.Navy Diving Manual*

Solution:

The elevation of the dam is 5,400 feet, so we enter Table 9-5 at 6,000 feet, and see that the diver's group letter is E. Next we correct the depth (45 fsw) in Table 9-4 to 60 fsw. Then we enter Table 9-8 at E, go horizontally to where the 2:00 surface interval lines up, and find that the new group is C. We then follow that column down to 60 fsw and establish the RN for this dive is 19 min.

Problem:

The diver mentioned above takes much longer than expected to clean the intake screen on the dam, and there is only one other diver on hand who must be kept for a standby diver. By the time the diver finishes, he must do in-water decompression, and there is a 30 fsw and a 20 fsw stop. With correction, what depth will the stops actually be?

Solution:

We were told earlier that the altitude of the dam was 5,400 feet above sea level. Table 9-4 is in altitude increments of 1,000 feet, so we calculate for 6,000. On the lower part of Table 9-4, we see that the 30 fsw stop is actually at 24 fsw, and the 20 fsw stop is actually at 16 fsw.

5.10 FINAL NOTES ON AIR DIVING AND DECOMPRESSION

When you, as a diver, are on the job, it will be the responsibility of your supervisor to run your dive. That includes choosing the table and schedule and working out any decompression involved. The smart diver is the one who always checks the math on his/her dive sheet after each dive. As a supervisor since 1981, this author is never offended when a diver asks to check the math on a dive sheet. If your supervisor is offended, you need to ask yourself why, and you need to try to get on another crew. Anyone can make a math mistake, and a wise man appreciates it when someone checks math. If a mistake is caught early on, it can be dealt with much easier, rather than later, after symptoms have presented.

You, as a diver, can do a lot to protect yourself from pressure related illness. One way you can do this is by keeping yourself properly hydrated while on the job. Dehydration is a significant factor in a great many cases of decompression sickness. If you are not properly hydrated, your blood ph will be off; if your blood ph is off, gas transfer in your bloodstream is affected, and you are not going to off-gas as the tables assume that you will. Dehydration may also be caused by alcohol consumption. Most contractors, when performing decompression work on inland or coastal jobs, advise their divers not to drink alcohol in the evenings when they are diving the next day. On offshore projects, this is not an issue, since alcohol is banned offshore.

An issue just as important as hydration when diving is maintaining the proper core temperature. There are a few things you can do to ensure your body is able to properly regulate its core temperature. By eating well-balanced meals and eating regularly, you will keep your body metabolism in the safe zone. A cup of coffee is something many of us feel we cannot do without. But coffee is a diluent, which means it causes blood vessels to expand, therefore allowing the body to cool more quickly. When diving in cold water, have your coffee after your dive and not before. Many prescription medications have an effect on the body's thermoregulation ability, as do some over-the-counter medications. Most cold and flu medications have this problem. When in doubt, find out. If you are using medications, tell your supervisor; if you are noticing symptoms of hypothermia or hyperthermia in water or out, tell your supervisor.

Be aware of any changes in depth. If you are walking on bottom and stumble into a hole, tell your supervisor so he/she can get another pneumo reading. If it feels like you are walking on a slope, tell your supervisor. Typically, the supervisor will take readings every 10 minutes or so, just to be sure. Depending on where you are working, a rising tide may jump you as much as 2 tables deeper during a longer dive.

When you are working mid-water, never drop below your working elevation without permission from your supervisor. If given permission, provide a pneumo reading once you arrive at the deeper elevation. *In late 2003, a young diver was working mid-water on a concrete jacketing job in Newfoundland. Toward the end of his dive, he dropped a socket. He could see it just below him on a crossbeam, so he slipped down and grabbed it, without telling the supervisor. What he did not realize was that by doing that, he jumped from a 40 fsw to a 50 fsw table. The supervisor, not knowing what had happened, ran the young diver close to his no-D limit on the 40 fsw table. As they were cleaning up on the job site (around ½ hour after surfacing) he started to present Type II symptoms. There was no chamber on site, and before they could get him to the nearest chamber, major body organs were shutting down. The young lad was treated several times, and his life was saved. He will never dive again and now requires kidney dialysis. One small mistake had life-changing consequences for him.* Don't be the case study in the next training manual – think before you act, and if you are not sure, ask someone.

Listen to your instructors and old divers; it is better to learn from other's mistakes than your own.

6.0 SURFACE-SUPPLIED DIVING

6.1 MODES OF DIVING

There are three modes of diving today: scuba, surface-supplied, and saturation. Scuba is not considered an acceptable mode of diving in commercial work for two reasons: Scuba equipment provides the diver with a limited amount of breathing gas and is not productive; and scuba does not even come close to meeting what is required by the commercial diving industry regarding safety systems. The only **two modes** accepted by the industry are surface-supplied and saturation diving. The reasons for this are fairly obvious: the nearly unlimited breathing gas supply; the ability to closely monitor the diver through two-way communications and video; and the ability to monitor and control the diver's depth and decompression accurately and safely. This chapter examines surface-supplied diving, the more common of the two. It is known as surface-supplied diving because the breathing gas is supplied to the diver via the umbilical, from the surface.

6.2 OPERATIONAL PLANNING

In order to be successful, a diving operation must meet two criteria: it must be performed safely, and the task must be completed as designed. This does not just happen by chance; the degree of success is directly related to the planning that went into the job. There are several factors that must be considered in order to plan a safe and efficient diving operation, and every conceivable problem must have either a solution or a means of reducing the impact of the problem on the job and crew. A proper job plan includes the following:

1. Risk Analysis
2. Hazard Analysis and Reduction
3. Proper Personnel and Supervision
4. Proper Manning Levels
5. Proper Diving Mode
6. Correct Diving Equipment
7. Correct Tooling
8. Proper Surface Support

The diver may have input into some of the above, including ongoing hazard analysis, the mobilization of the diving equipment, and preparing the tooling. By thinking ahead about the job to be performed and drawing on past experience, the diver can often make suggestions that will be used and greatly appreciated by the supervisor or superintendent.

1. Risk Analysis

Risk Analysis begins when a project is in the planning stages and continues through until project completion. The initial risk assessment plans for everything that can go wrong and how to mitigate (lessen) or eliminate these risks through contingency planning. This process follows three separate tracks: environmental risk, risk of infrastructure damage, and risk of injury or death to job-site personnel or to bystanders. The assessment looks at the underlying causes of the risk: the impact of site conditions such as weather, tides, or current on operations; damage to existing facilities caused by human error or equipment failure; injury or death caused by human error, equipment failure, or site conditions. The risk assessment determines the equipment used on the job: environmental protection gear, diving mode selected, size and type of diving support vessel, and emergency response. Various names are used for these assessments such as risk assessment, risk analysis, high impact risk assessment, etc., but the intent is always the same: **identify and eliminate risk**. These assessments typically do not require any input from the divers.

2. Hazard Analysis and Reduction

Hazard Analysis starts at mobilization and continues throughout the diving project. Called either a job hazard analysis (JHA), or a job safety analysis (JSA), this process identifies any known hazards to the crew, how that hazard can be mitigated, mitigation steps involved, and who is responsible to deal with it. This process utilizes written documents similar to a checklist and involves the participation of every member of the diving crew. The JSA is performed at each new phase of the project or every time a different activity begins. Another part of this process is the daily toolbox safety meeting, which involves input from all members of the diving crew. Sample JSA and toolbox meeting forms may be found in Appendix II: Forms and Checklists Used in Surface-Supplied Diving Operations.

3. Proper Personnel and Supervision

Years ago, diving contractors would pick up hands as they required them and teach them to dive. If the job required underwater welding, they would teach a surface welder to dive. This is no longer considered acceptable practice anywhere in the world. Commercial divers today are required to have formal training, certification proving competence, first aid and CPR training, offshore survival training, and pass a hyperbaric medical exam. The initial hyperbaric medical establishes a base line, so that any changes in the diver's physiology during his/her career can be observed. There is no way to prepare a diving school student for every possible situation encountered while working as a commercial diver. You have heard it said experience is the best teacher; that is the case in this industry. A graduate of a diving school has the knowledge to safely learn on the job. When sufficient practical experience on the job is gained, the graduate goes from being a "green hand" to a diver. In the Gulf of Mexico, the green hands are known as tenders, and elsewhere in the world they are known as "baby divers."

Supervisors also used to be appointed by the employer. These were crane operators, blasters, or pipefitters with absolutely no training or experience in diving. Many accidents over the years were attributed to improperly trained or untrained supervisors. Every country with any type of safety regulation now requires properly trained, qualified supervisors on all diving operations. Supervisor trainees are required to work under a qualified supervisor in order to gain sufficient "panel hours" to become qualified. Although they are still appointed by the employer, they are now required to be divers trained as supervisors.

4. Proper Manning Levels

Each diving operation has its own manpower requirements. The minimum crew required by law for any diving operation depends on where you are. In the United States, the minimum crew size is three, but that is expected to change very soon. The Canadian CSA Standard calls for four men, but in some Canadian provinces a two-man diving crew is legal. In the United Kingdom it is four, but at least one European country accepts two.

To establish what crew size is safe, consider the following: the supervisor should be dedicated (perform no other work); every diver requires a tender; and the primary diver requires a standby diver. A safe diving crew then should have five members. In the *U.S. Navy Diving Manual Rev.6*, you will find the navy's minimum crew size for surface-supplied diving is five. It is strange that the state, provincial, and federal governments in North America and elsewhere would think it would require fewer diving crew members to safely operate on a commercial job than the U.S. Navy requires. In addition to the stated minimum crew, surface-tended tools, such as pneumatic or hydraulic tools, welding or cutting gear, and tethered NDT probes require additional tenders on the jobsite. Various operating conditions also will require different levels of manning. Shallow air, intermediate air, deep air, and surface mixed-gas jobs all require different numbers of people to safely operate, since there are more tasks to perform (chamber operations, for example).

5. Proper Diving Mode

Selecting the proper mode of diving was, at one time, as simple as looking at the depth of water. Depths up to 200 fsw were worked on air, up to 300 fsw were worked mixed gas, and deeper than that was always considered saturation (sat) work. All this has all changed. Now surface air is seldom used deeper than 170 fsw, and mixed gas is not an acceptable mode of diving in most jurisdictions, including the North Sea and Europe. Often now, we see sat diving operations being performed as shallow as 150 fsw. It is not uncommon now to have a surface air diver and a saturation diver working side-by-side on the same job. When selecting the proper mode of diving, we consider the water depth, the bottom time required, and also the equipment and personnel currently available for the work.

6. Correct Diving Equipment

Choosing the correct diving equipment for a project could save someone from being killed or injured, or it could make the difference whether the project is completed on time or not. For a surface-supplied diving operation, the place to start is with the gas supply, deciding between LP or HP supplies. If the operation is taking place in a dusty, smoky, or fume-filled environment, HP gas is the only option. Filtration systems on LP compressors are there to catch what may sneak by; they **are not** designed to remove noticeable contaminants. The duration of the job also plays a part. LP compressors are best for a long-term project, as they save handling gas racks every few days. Included in the gas supply are the bailouts. The bailout needs to have sufficient gas for the working depth. The duration of the bailout at the working depth must be calculated. (The formula for this calculation is found at the end of Chapter 2: Underwater Physics.) Choices must be made concerning the umbilical type and length used. A good rule of thumb for length is this – the umbilical length should be three times the distance from the dive station to the underwater job site. The choice of floating or standard umbilical depends on the site conditions. (See Chapter 4: Diving and Support Equipment.) One must look at the site conditions and measure these against the good and bad points of each type of hose. There are choices to make regarding the helmet to be used. The site conditions will influence the choice of helmet type as well. Most jobs today use either a Superlite 17 or 37 for the primary helmet; many use a band mask for the standby hat, but band masks should never be used without a head protector (shell). The type of diving dress depends on site conditions as well. Temperature is usually the deciding factor as to whether wetsuit, drysuit, or hot-water suits are used. However, for contaminated water, the choice is narrowed to the vulcanized drysuit. These are the only suits that can be adapted for hazmat use.

Diver retrieval (egress) systems are dictated both by site conditions and vessels used. A dive ladder is sufficient if the deck of the support vessel is within six feet of the water, but longer distances will require a man basket, stage, or wet bell, with either a crane or a launch and recovery system (LARS) with A-frame.

Diver in LARS stage
Photo courtesy of Nick Gill

Diver on ladder

Injured diver recovery with winch and harness

The reason for this six-foot rule: A diver falling into the water from a height over six feet has a good chance of being seriously injured. Every crane or LARS used in diving operations must be man riding and inspected, tested, and certified regularly. The recovery of an unconscious or injured diver must be quickly and easily performed with any diver retrieval system used, whether it is the man basket of a LARS or a diver recovery winch and harness used with a ladder.

Whether or not a decompression chamber is used depends both on the depth of the job and if any work is planned outside of the no-decompression limits. The depth at which a decompression chamber is required varies with the jurisdiction, but most regulations state whenever dives are planned that exceed the no- decompression limits, a chamber is required. Regardless of what the regulations state, most reputable diving contractors will have one on site if the depth exceeds 70 fsw.

7. Correct Tooling

The correct tooling for the job sounds like more of an efficiency issue than a safety issue. In the case of hydraulic versus pneumatic tools with the job being in 66 fsw, this would be true. But if the operation involved cutting off a pipeline recently carrying petroleum products, the choice of a guillotine saw instead of cutting gear is most definitely a safety issue. It is important to consider all of the strong points and limitations of tooling, from the standpoint of safety first and then productivity. Diving crew members must be aware of the proper safety and operating procedures for all tools. No tool should be used unless it is working properly and all safety features are fully operational.

8. Proper Surface Support

This author was on a job with a diver on bottom many years ago; the dive spread was on a small steel tugboat in just over 70 feet of water. Halfway through the first dive, without any warning, the tugboat arrived on bottom alongside the diver. Not a good day at work, and it perfectly illustrates the need for proper surface support. Every diving operation requires **suitable and safe** surface support. The definition of suitable and safe is not the same for all operations. On any job where floating surface support is required, the first issue to consider is seaworthiness. Barges or vessels suitable for an inland lake may not be suitable in a harbor; barges or vessels suitable for work in a sheltered harbor may not be suitable for use offshore.

Barges vary in size from small ones used on inshore jobs, to the massive pipe-lay and derrick barges used offshore. Small barges most often use 4-point mooring systems when anchored, while the larger ones mostly use 6- or 8-point mooring systems.

Small barge for harbor diving

Derrick/pipe-lay barge offshore

Barges are towed to their work location and utilize other vessels (tugs) for both moving and anchor handling. The 6- and 8-point barges can often move along at a good clip by simply winching up and slacking off on various anchors. Some specialty barges, like jack-up barges and some pipe-lay barges are occasionally self-propelled; some even are equipped with dynamic positioning systems in order to avoid the need for an anchor array and anchor handling tugs.

Jack-up barge (lift boat)

Diving support vessels range in size from converted fishing vessels used for coastal and harbor work to larger 3- and 4-point anchor moored vessels and dynamically positioned (DP) vessels. Many of the DP vessels utilize a moon pool, which allows for the diving bell or stage to be operated down through the center of the ship, minimizing the impact poor weather has on the diving operations. Regardless of the type of vessel used, it has to be able to remain on station and not "run off" while the diver is in the water. For this reason, anything less than a 3-point mooring is never used on an anchored barge or vessel, and a DP2 is the minimum in dynamically positioned vessels. DP2 indicates the computer and propulsion systems both have dual redundancy built in, and at least two frames of reference (example: beacons and DGPS) are used for positioning.

4-point DSV for air/gas diving

DP2 DSV with moon pool for sat diving

All vessels used on inland and coastal waters must meet Coast Guard standards for seaworthiness and for the machinery and equipment on board. This includes the various safety features. Vessels used offshore must meet both Coast Guard and American Bureau of Shipping (ABS) standards. Periodic surveys (inspections) are performed on vessels in order to renew the Coast Guard and ABS certificates. All diving operations must be performed from vessels or barges that carry an in-date Coast Guard or ABS certificate.

6.3 MARINE TRAFFIC WARNINGS

When engaged in diving operations in navigable waters, all vessels worldwide are required by the "International Collision Regulations" to warn other vessels to stay away when the diving operations are underway. This involves both audio and visual warnings. The audio warnings are "Notice to Shipping" broadcasts, made usually twice daily on VHF and sideband by various national agencies, usually the local Coast Guard, and on-scene VHF radio broadcasts made by the vessels involved. For the visual warnings, the Alpha Flag (letter

A) and day shapes are prominently displayed during daylight hours and "restricted in ability to maneuver" lights are displayed on the main mast at night. Even with the audio and visual warnings, the vessel crew and diving crew should always **remain alert** for vessel traffic.

This author was on a pipe repair project in the Gulf of Mexico a few years ago when a new school graduate noticed a large ship heading toward the diving vessel at a high rate of knots. The vessel ignored repeated calls on the VHF marine radio as well as the rigid "A" flags and day shapes. We physically pulled the diver away from the job (he was not running fast enough) and brought him over until he was at our vessel and safely on the diving ladder. The US Coast Guard investigated the near miss and charges were laid, but if that young diving school graduate had not been on the ball, the ship would have passed over our diver, who was in shallow water and about 100 feet away from our vessel. The incident could have ended badly.

ALPHA FLAG	DAY SHAPES	NIGHT LIGHTS
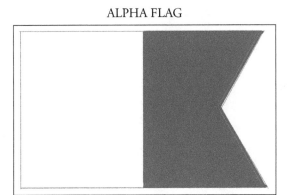		
"Diver working, stay well clear"	"Undersea work ongoing"	"Restricted in ability to maneuver"

Other than sending semaphore messages, the Alpha Flag is only used to warn of diving operations. The black ball/black diamond/black ball day shape is used for any submarine work (diving, trenching, and dredging). The red-white-red lights indicate restricted ability to maneuver and are used for diving operations, dredging, large vessels under tow, and any other circumstance when a vessel cannot give way to an oncoming vessel with the right-of-way.

6.4 PREDIVE PREPARATIONS

The surface-supplied diving equipment (dive spread) will stay set up and ready to go on long-term projects, diving vessels (DSV), and in rapid-response trucks or trailers. On short-term jobs, like a one-day job at a power plant, the equipment will obviously have to be set up (mobilized) and then taken down again (demobilized) after the dives are completed. Diving contractors will usually have load-out lists to ensure needed equipment is taken to the job and it all comes back. For these short-term jobs, there are a few important points the diving crew should remember when mobilizing and de-mobilizing:

- Always use a complete checklist (that includes spares) for both mob and de-mob.

- Test the diving radio batteries and communications before leaving the shop.

- Test cylinder pressures and all fuel and oil levels before leaving the shop.

- Always test the non-return valve on diving helmets prior to putting them online.

- Always cap, bag, or tape up all open fittings and hose ends to keep dirt and debris out.

- PPE (hard hats, gloves, eye protection, safety boots) are required on most job sites.

Once on the job site (or in the case of an ongoing operation or a DSV, as the crew arrives on deck), they perform a JSA, if necessary, and have a toolbox safety meeting. After this safety meeting, a predive system check is performed to ensure all equipment is ready to go before the diving operation begins. If the vessel is dynamically positioned, DP checks are performed by the diving supervisor and the senior DP officer at the same time the diving system checks are performed. These checks are performed before the divers ever dress in. The following are actual predive checklists, as used offshore on a diving support vessel, by one of the major diving contractors.

6.4.1 Predive System Checks
The following items on the spread are to be checked prior to diver dress-in:

- DP checks performed with Vessel Bridge and Dive Control (DP checklist to be used)
- Primary and standby diver LP compressor oil levels in safe range
- All compressor intakes clear of exhaust fumes
- Primary and standby diver backup HP gas banks fully pressurized
- Confirm black box record capability
- Confirm sufficient free space on black box hard drive
- Confirm 2-way communications on both diving helmets
- Chamber air supply topped up
- Chamber backup air supply topped up
- Chamber oxygen supply sufficient and online
- Chamber inner lock at 60 fsw
- Primary and standby diver bailout cylinders topped up full
- Hydraulic supply for LARS 1 and 2 tested
- Backup hydraulic supply for LARS 1 and 2 tested
- LARS 1 and 2 emergency gas cylinders confirmed full
- Diver's hot water unit fueled and ready
- Hydraulic power unit for tools fueled and ready
- Hydraulic tools tested

The above system predive checks are usually performed by the diving crew and supervised by the lead diver while the diving supervisor is busy doing the DP checks and then briefing the diver and the standby diver on the tasks to be performed. Both the diver and standby are included in the briefing, since the standby diver will be the next diver in on the rotation, and it provides continuity on the job when each knows what the other is expected to do. Once the predive system checks and the briefing have been completed, the divers dress in, then the diver predive checks are performed. These checks are performed on the standby diver first, with the primary diver checked just before entering the water.

6.4.2 Standby Diver Predive Checks
- Communications loud and clear in both directions
- Bailout function tested and working properly
- Bailout gas secured (shut off firmly)
- Main gas function tested and working properly
- Diver's suit in good condition; hot water bypass valve working
- Harness on correctly and fastened securely
- Umbilical snap shackle secure and fastened to D ring on harness

- Bailout bottle full (read pressure out loud)
- Diver has a sharp knife and rescue lanyard
- Helmet light working properly
- Helmet camera working properly
- Diver has neck dam on, helmet in lap, and is ready to deploy

The first four items on the standby diver checklist are performed by the standby and the supervisor. The main gas supply is shut off at the panel, and the standby bleeds the pressure off the umbilical by opening the steady flow valve (vent). The diver then turns on the bailout and breathes to function test it. Once it is ensured the helmet will breathe properly on bailout, the bailout is secured, and the supervisor is asked for main gas. The diver tests to make sure the helmet is breathing properly on main gas. The supervisor informs the lead diver via the deck radio that internal checks are complete. The lead diver performs the remaining checks on the list. As each item is checked, it is read over the deck radio, and the supervisor records the entire predive checklist on the black box system.

Standby diver at the ready

6.4.3 Primary Diver Predive Checks

- Communications loud and clear in both directions
- Bailout function tested and working properly
- Bailout gas secured (shut off firmly)
- Main gas function tested and working properly
- Helmet on and secured to the neck dam
- Helmet locking pin (or latch catch) secured
- Helmet light working properly
- Helmet camera working properly
- Diver's suit in good condition; hot water bypass valve working
- Harness on correctly and fastened securely
- Umbilical snap shackle secure and fastened to D ring on harness
- Bailout bottle full (read pressure out loud)
- Diver has a sharp knife and tools required for the job

Performing predive checks on the primary diver

As with the standby diver, the first four items on this checklist involve the diver and the supervisor. Once the supervisor hears "diver has tools required for the job," the crew is instructed to stand the diver up and walk him/her to the LARS. **A fully dressed diver must never walk on deck without assistance.** The correct way to assist the diver is to have one tender carrying a bight of umbilical and another tender with a hand on the diver at all times to prevent the diver from falling on deck.

6.5 DUTIES OF THE DIVING CREW MEMBERS

There is a whole lot more involved in a diving operation than just the diver. If the other crew members do not do their jobs and do them properly, the diver cannot operate safely or efficiently. The following are the basic duties of the crew members on a minimum sized crew.

6.5.1 Diving Supervisor

The person legally responsible for the safety of the crew, the supervisor directs the entire operation, ensuring the work gets done safely and efficiently. Sometimes a timekeeper is used in addition to the supervisor, freeing him/her up from radio-telephone and timekeeping duties. The supervisor (or timekeeper) records the leave surface time, takes regular pneumo readings and records them, records the leave bottom time, and records the total bottom time. Using this information and the tables, the supervisor decides what decompression is required. Typically, one decompression schedule will be preselected for the planned bottom time and another selected if the bottom time varies from the plan. When the job involves surface decompression, the supervisor may elect to operate the chamber or supervise another operator. In the case of treatments for pressure related illness, the supervisor will choose and supervise the treatment.

6.5.2 Primary Diver

Performing the actual work in the water, the diver runs almost all aspects of the job by the supervisor for input. The diver does not leave surface until the supervisor is aware and will not leave bottom until told, except in an emergency. The diver keeps the supervisor informed of everything (underwater conditions and work being performed) which allows the supervisor to control the dive and to monitor job progress.

6.5.3 Tender

The tender dresses the diver before entering the water, helps the diver into the stage or onto the ladder, and constantly holds on to the umbilical while the diver is in the water. During the dive, the tender pays attention, listens for commands from the lead diver or the supervisor, and feels for line-pull signals from the diver (if communications fail). Once the diver returns to surface, the tender dresses the diver down, walks the diver to the chamber (if required), cleans the helmet, and gets prepared for the next diver.

6.5.4 Standby Diver

The standby (for this explanation, a male) is the diver's last hope in times of trouble, so he must always be ready. He should listen to the dive radio or see the helmet video, if possible, because he then stays informed of the conditions at the job site and knows what the diver is doing. In the event deployment is necessary, the standby **always** follows the diver's hose to the diver. Once the standby arrives at the diver, he immediately opens the diver's vent. If there does not appear to be gas entering the hat, the bailout is opened. If neither of these actions provides gas, the pneumo is inserted under the diver's neck dam and the standby asks for air to the pneumo. The standby then attaches the rescue lanyard to the diver's harness, and brings the diver back to the stage or down line. The standby must tell the supervisor exactly what is happening at all times while deployed, and will ensure that the diver reaches the surface safely. The first aid training received is adapted to fit the underwater jobsite, and in the case of an unconscious diver, the standby will ensure a clear airway by keeping the diver's head back. If using a stage, the standby will place the diver in, attach a lanyard and climb aboard with the diver. If using a down line, the standby will accompany the diver to the surface on the down line.

6.5.5 Standby Tender

While the primary diver is in the water, the standby tender is always ready in case he/she has to deploy the standby diver to assist the primary diver in an emergency. If the standby must be deployed, the standby tender's duties mirror the primary tender's duties. On occasion, he/she also assists the primary diver by getting the required tools ready and sending them down to the diver as needed.

6.6 TENDING THE DIVER

The one secret to being a good tender: mentally put yourself in the diving helmet and do everything possible to make the diver's job safer and easier. Before the dress-in, the tender cleans the oral nasal on the helmet, applies a layer of antifog to the inside of the faceplate, and gauges the bailout pressure. Once the tender has dressed the diver and all of the predive checks are complete, the tender assists the diver to the ladder or the LARS stage. Once the diver has a firm grip on the ladder or stage, the tender pays out umbilical until the bight touches the water. This is done in case the diver falls or the stage falls. It will save injury to the diver and keep the tender from being pulled overboard. Once the diver has reached the water, the tender picks the slack hose up and slacks it back out slowly as the diver requires it on his descent. The hose should not be kept tight, but with no more than two feet of slack until the diver reaches bottom.

Once the diver is on bottom, the supervisor will alert the crew. Then the tender will ensure the hose has two-to-three feet of slack, occasionally picking it up gently until the diver can actually be felt. The umbilical is never to be left untended – there must be one pair of hands on it at all times. Only a half-dozen wraps of hose should be left on deck at any time; excess slack hose should be flaked back on the rack. The tender should be alert and ready at all times for line-pull signals, which are used in the event of a loss of communications. There are a lot of line-pull signals posted in various publications to send the diver in different directions, signal lifting operations with cranes, and even for inflating lift bags. If you can name it, there is a line-pull signal for it. But the reality is this: In the event of a loss of communications, diving operations are **terminated immediately**, and we never operate without communications - **ever**. The only line-pull signals you will ever need to know are these:

    1 pull – all stop (if ascending or descending); are you all right (from surface) I am all right (from diver)

    2 pulls – slack the diver (from diver); go down, you have come up too far (if ascending)

    3 pulls – up on slack (from diver); you have gone down too far (if descending); come up, coming up

    4 pulls – leave bottom now (from surface), pull me up (from diver)

Different job conditions require different actions in the event of lost communications. For example, if the diver is welding 20 feet away from the man basket, the diver will have to return to the man basket before it is brought up by the LARS winch. Because all underwater jobs are not the same, every underwater job must have its own printed lost communications protocol, and the entire crew must learn it.

As the diver ascends, the tender follows the diver up with the hose, being careful not to actually pull unless the diver needs to be hauled up. In this case, the tender must depend on the supervisor's directions to speed up or slow down the ascent rate. When the diver has surfaced, the bight of the hose is left in the water (as on entry) until the diver has climbed the ladder or until the LARS stage is on deck, then it is quickly recovered. Once the diver is on deck, he/she is to be walked to the correct area and dressed down quickly, whether the chamber is required or not. If chamber decompression is required, the diver is to be escorted to the outer lock door by the tender. Remember: One set of hands on the diver at all times when the diver is dressed and on deck.

6.7 IN-WATER OPERATIONS

The most important aspect of any diving operation is safety, which is closely linked to control. The control of the diver's descent, bottom time, and ascent are very important because time under pressure determines gas load, and ascent is a part of decompression. Free ascents and descents are usually avoided, except in the case of a dire emergency. A typical diving operation will use a down line, a stage, or a wet bell. Stages and down lines are often used together; the diver may use a stage to enter and exit the water (due to a large air gap) but follow a down line to the job. If the diver rides a stage or wet bell the whole way to the bottom, the stage or wet bell is usually stopped just before it hits slightly above the LARS clump weight.

6.7.1 Using a Down Line for Descent/Ascent

The down line may be fixed to the job or have a heavy weight (clump weight) attached. A ⅝ inch or larger rope is used for a down line. There are two reasons for this: less chance of the down line parting and larger rope is easier for the diver to grip with his/her hands. The proper way to descend and ascend on a down line is to have one half turn on the diver's leg around the line and hands on the line. The line passes inside the diver's thigh and outside the ankle. In this way, the diver's leg acts in the same way as a mountain climber's carabiner when rappelling. The diver does not leave the surface until the supervisor indicates "ready," at which time he announces "leaving surface." This allows the supervisor to start the timer and record clock time. At the end of the dive, the diver leaves bottom only when told to by the supervisor, again informing "leaving bottom," making sure the pneumo is kept at mid-chest level. The supervisor then controls the ascent rate by telling the diver to speed up or slow down the ascent.

6.7.2 Using a Stage or Wet Bell for Descent/Ascent

The diver keeps a firm grip on the handholds inside the stage or wet bell, avoiding letting the hands get near the outside where they could get crushed as the stage travels. Once the helmet is in the water, the diver informs the supervisor he/she is leaving surface. When riding a stage, the diver should be constantly on the lookout for obstructions that the stage may catch on. The diver's umbilical is either fed through the top of the stage or through the back (the side toward the vessel) instead of straight down from the surface, and the diver exits through the front (side away from the vessel). Tending the hose through the stage allows the diver to easily find the stage again after the diver has left to perform work. The diver typically asks to have the stage stopped before it touches down on the clump weight (which itself is usually about four feet off bottom). This keeps the winch wires from going slack, keeps the stage up out of the way of the work, and keeps the umbilical from fouling by keeping it off bottom. When the diver leaves bottom in the stage, he/she informs the supervisor and keeps the pneumo at mid-chest. The supervisor instructs the LARS operator to speed up or slow down the winch as required, to keep the proper ascent rate for the diver.

6.7.3 Establishing Depth of Dive

Whether the diver is in a stage or on a down line, the first thing when reaching bottom is to provide the supervisor with a good clean pneumo reading. To do this, the end of the pneumo hose is held down to the bottom, if possible, or at least down to ankle level. There are a few areas (Cook Inlet, Alaska and Bay of Fundy, Canada) that have extreme tidal ranges, with the difference between high and low tide approaching or exceeding 30 feet. When diving operations are performed in these areas, pneumo readings must be taken at least every 15 minutes. This is because the rising tide can cause a diver to jump several tables over the course of one dive. In areas with less tidal range, the supervisor may only take a pneumo reading every half hour. The diver must inform the supervisor every time he/she changes elevation. A fall into a six-foot-deep hole can jump a table and drastically change the dive profile. If the supervisor is not aware, this is not noted on the pneumo readings, the proper table will not be selected, and the decompression will not be sufficient for the gas load carried. To put it simply, you'll likely get bent if you say nothing.

6.7.4 Using the Diving Helmet

The two most popular helmets used in the diving industry today are the Kirby Morgan Superlite 17 and the Kirby Morgan 37, also of the Superlite line. The 17 has been produced since the mid-1970s but remains in high demand today. The illustrations below show some of the important features of both the 17 and the 37.

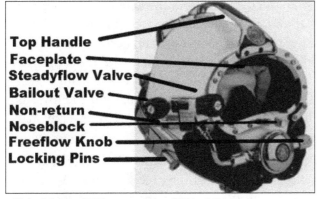

Top Handle
Faceplate
Steadyflow Valve
Bailout Valve
Non-return
Noseblock
Freeflow Knob
Locking Pins

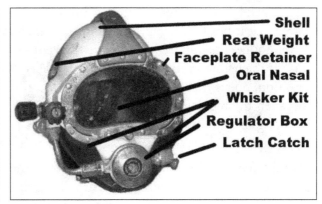

Shell
Rear Weight
Faceplate Retainer
Oral Nasal
Whisker Kit
Regulator Box
Latch Catch

Kirby Morgan 37 Photo courtesy of Kirby Morgan   Superlite 17

Prior to dressing in, the diver should know what neck dam is worn. They come in S, M, L and XL, and one size does not fit all. The neck dam should be snug, but not tight, or it will restrict blood flow in the carotid artery and jugular vein. When dressing in, the diver first dons the suit, zips it up, and dons the neck dam. The crew usually sits the diver down, assists the diver to don harness, weight belt, and bailout (or all-in-one if using the integrated recovery vest). The crew takes the helmet by the top handle and sets it on the diver's head. This is the point where many divers screw up; the diver should take a moment or two to move his/her head around inside the helmet to get it seated comfortably. Holding the helmet with one hand, he/she should put the other hand up in and make sure the oral nasal pouch is seated properly and not folded over on the edge. A folded oral nasal will allow the diver to inhale carbon dioxide from inside the helmet shell and will guarantee a severe headache later in the dive. Once the diver is sure the oral nasal is fitting properly, the chin strap is tightened. Then the crew will mate the helmet to the neck dam, close it, and set the latch catch (on the SL17) or the locking pins (on the SL37). Once in the helmet, the diver will ask the supervisor to secure the main gas. When the supervisor confirms this, the diver opens the vent (steady-flow valve) to purge the air from the hose and hat. Then the diver turns the bailout valve on, breathes with the bailout, and tells the dive supervisor the bailout is tested and functioning. As soon as the supervisor acknowledges this, the diver secures (turns off) the bailout and asks for main gas. The supervisor turns the main gas back on, and the diver then function tests the helmet on main gas. Now the diver is ready for the external predive checks.

Diving helmets are not "smart hats"; they require the diver to operate them. As the diver descends, the free-flow adjustment knob must be periodically adjusted (sometimes called dial-a-breath) to allow for the change in ambient pressure. The knob is turned out until the regulator starts to free flow, then back in just until it stops. This process should then be repeated in reverse on ascent. Failure to adjust the free-flow will cause the diver to have increased "work of breathing." This will cause several problems: premature fatigue, carbon dioxide build-up, increased susceptibility to nitrogen narcosis, and improper inert gas exchange. The diver should form the habit early on of free-flow adjustment.

Also on descent, the diver may have to use the nose block device (sometimes called the plunger). The V- shaped neoprene covered metal device is designed to block the nostrils and allow easier equalization. This author could never use the nose block (nose broken too many times) and wiggled his jaw or swallowed in order to get his ears to equalize. If the plunger does not reach your nostrils so you can use it, do not step in front of a bus. There are other ways to equalize. If you do use the plunger, make sure to pull it back out once you have equalized. It has an effect on your speech and pronunciation, and your supervisor has enough problems already without you adding to them.

On deeper descents, the diver will ventilate the hat using the steady-flow valve (sometimes called the vent), just before reaching bottom. This removes all accumulated CO_2 from the helmet, and gives the diver a clear head (remember, CO_2 buildup increases the susceptibility and impact of narcosis). If the diver notices the initial effects of narcosis, venting the hat will often help keep from becoming "gooned up." If the helmet starts to fill with water (called flooding), the diver positions the head in the upright position, opens the vent, and the water is forced out of the main exhaust (in front of the helmet shell between the regulator box and the neck dam). Slight flooding is normal, particularly if the diver is working in a heads-down position, and it does not mean that life, as you know it, is over. If the hat starts to flood, don't panic, get upright, and open the vent.

Another use for the steady-flow valve is when the diver performs strenuous work. Opening the valve for a few seconds provides significant relief, helps to check shallow breathing (gets rid of CO_2 in the lungs this time), and avoids fatigue. One more use of the vent valve is defogging the faceplate. Most times a defogging agent (often non-ionic dish detergent) is used on the faceplate, but it eventually wears off. The air from the vent valve will clean the steam off the faceplate temporarily. The vent is also used periodically during decompression stops, to ensure there is no CO_2 buildup, and it is used to flush the helmet and hose on all breathing gas changes.

The bailout valve is only used during the predive checks and when there is a loss of breathing gas. The bailout is **NEVER** activated unless the supervisor has been made aware. Once the bailout has been activated, the diver must proceed to the down line or stage immediately in order to leave bottom. The steady-flow valve should not be used when the diver is on bailout unless the helmet is flooding severely and breathing is affected, as the bailout volume is limited. Remember these two things: You **never** activate the bailout without telling the supervisor, and you **never** work when on bailout.

6.7.5 Using the Down Line for Working Underwater

The first diver in on any given job usually establishes a down line close to the job before anything else. There is a good reason for this: The down line is not only the diver's "road to work," but it is also the "supply route." Messenger lines are used to lower tools and materials, and they follow the down line directly to the diver. A traveling shackle is used to keep the tool at the down line. This saves having the diver search for the tool; it will be sliding down the down line to the diver. On projects more than a dozen feet long, a second down line is often installed at the opposite end. The surface crew tends messenger lines and tool lines away from where the down line is secured on deck. A messenger line tended beside a down line may get tangled. Ideally, there should be a "spread" of about half of the water depth between the lines to keep the proper angle. Occasionally, items may be sent "express." This means the item is attached to the down line and dropped overboard without a messenger line attached. If sending an item express, you must make sure the supervisor keeps the diver away from the down line until the item has reached bottom. A diver was killed offshore in Saudi Arabia in 2007 when a 50-ton shackle sent "express" hit him in the back of the head. The diver was wearing a band mask with no shell when this happened.

The diver's umbilical is also tended from a spot well away from the down line and messengers, to avoid entanglement.

6.8 SURFACE-SUPPLIED OPERATIONS FROM SMALL CRAFT

Surface-supplied diving operations are performed from small boats on many inland jobs, and it occasionally happens offshore, as well. For a few years, scuba was used offshore, when divers had to work away from the diving support vessel. After many deaths, the regulatory agencies finally put it together: Scuba is not safe to use when working. The idea of using a small diving crew, with a portable surface- supplied diving spread was approved as a "replacement" for using scuba. These portable spreads on small boats are now known as scuba replacement packages (SRP). Most of the time, SRP work is performed using rigid hull inflatable boats (RIB), but small, heavy-duty fiberglass or aluminum boats are used as well. Whatever type of boat used, it must be large enough to carry the SRP pack and diving crew and be seaworthy with all of this weight onboard. The SRP pack is a steel frame with lifting eyes that holds 4 HP cylinders (main and standby gas for both the diver and standby). Usually, there are horns on the steel frame to flake the two umbilicals onto and a shelf to hold a portable dive control panel. The ladder is a small aluminum or steel ladder that attaches to the boat and extends 3 rungs below surface. If the SRP pack moves in a small boat due to sea conditions, it will likely sink the boat. These boats must always have cleats or pad eyes for securely fastening both the SRP pack and the dive ladder.

SRP boat on pipe-lay barge, Saudi Arabia 2007

SRP crew offshore, West Africa 2014

IMCA has a few guidelines for SRP operations, and these are followed closely offshore. These guidelines detail the minimum safety equipment carried onboard (flares, portable radios, medical kit, portable oxygen kit); the maximum distance from the mother ship (within line of sight); the maximum water depth (100 fsw) for SRP diving; and the hours of operation (never after dark). One item IMCA does not address in relation to SRP work is live boating. Live boating should not be considered unless the following conditions are met: less than 60 fsw, floating umbilical, propeller guard on the vessel that will not allow the umbilical to enter, and the operator must have an unobstructed view of the diver's umbilical at all times.

6.9 JOB-RELATED PAPERWORK

Diving operations have no shortage of job-related paperwork. The diving supervisor is required to keep a deck log to record everything that happens on the job and the exact time it happens. This deck log is required on most operations (all IMCA jobs), and it is in the crew's best interest. Since it is a written, chronological record, it is considered a legal document and can prove things were done when they should have been done, which proves the crew and supervisor did their jobs properly. In addition to the JSA and toolbox meeting form, the supervisor also keeps a written record of each dive on a dive sheet (sometimes called a dive chart).

The dive sheet includes the following: diver's name, location, date, leave surface time, pneumo readings, maximum depth, leave bottom time, total bottom time, table/schedule used, and decompression details. The dive sheets used for single or repetitive dives are usually different than those used for surface decompression dives. There are sample dive sheets found in Appendix II: Forms and Checklists Used in Surface-Supplied Diving Operations. If an accident occurs, there are, of course, forms to be filled in. Hyperbaric treatments require a treatment sheet (specialized dive sheet) to be completed. The diving supervisor's personal logbook has to be filled in daily. All of the paperwork, however, is not the supervisor's responsibility. Each diver has a logbook to record the details of every dive and every hyperbaric treatment. This logbook is also a legal document, and each page requires the signature of the supervisor (or other diving company representative), and each page must be stamped with the diving contractor's legal stamp. Make sure you, as a diver, have your logbook filled out and signed daily. In the past five years, this author has seen at least six divers removed from projects for not having up-to-date logbooks. Company reps, safety men, and Coast Guard inspectors will ask to see logbooks, usually with no advance warning. In addition to a logbook, the diver is required to carry a copy of a current hyperbaric medical examination and a diving certificate copy to every job. Most divers carry all of this in a sealed, waterproof container in their sea bag.

6.10 BREATHING GAS REQUIREMENTS

6.10.1 Gas Purity

All breathing gases used in diving operations must meet preset purity standards. These standards are set by different regulatory agencies in different countries, but all are essentially the same (See Components of Dry Atmospheric Air Table in Chapter 2: Underwater Physics). Most safety regulations require 3rd party purity testing every six months. This is done by obtaining a sample cylinder and sending it to a laboratory for analysis. Most contractors keep a Dräger pump and tubes for random onsite testing as well. Dräger gas sampling tubes are available for measuring everything from contaminants such as hydrogen sulfide, oil mist, and carbon monoxide, to the actual breathing gas components, such as oxygen, nitrogen or helium. This system is simple to operate. The pump is hand operated, with a stroke counter built in. The tubes are made of glass and come in plastic boxes, marked as to what the tubes sample. On the box label there are instructions on how many strokes are required on the pump for the gas or contaminant you are testing for. The two ends are snapped off the glass tube, the tube is inserted into the pump, and the pump is operated. Then the results are read on the side of the glass tube. The whole process often takes less than 2 minutes per sample, depending on the test being performed.

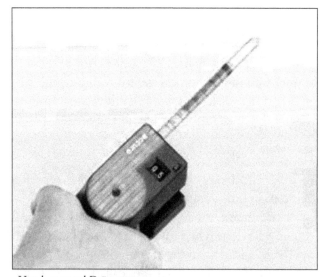

Hand-operated Dräger pump

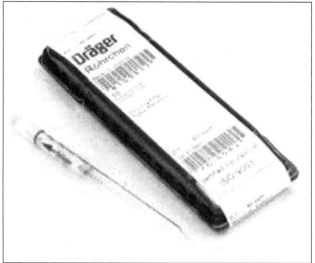

Dräger gas sampling tubes

6.10.2 Supply Volume

Diving helmets require an adequate supply volume of breathing gas in order to operate correctly and enable the diver to breathe easily with minimal carbon dioxide buildup. Adequate volume is also needed in order to allow ventilating, which, as we saw when reading about helmets, must be done periodically. The formula for calculating gas volume requirements when using an LP compressor is:

$$SCFM = ATA \times ACFM \times N$$

Where:
SCFM = standard cubic feet per minute
ATA = atmospheres absolute
ACFM = actual cubic feet per minute
N = number of divers

The formula for calculating gas volume requirements using an HP quad is: $SCF = ATA \times ACFM \times N \times T$

Where:
SCF = standard cubic feet
ATA = atmospheres absolute
ACFM = actual cubic feet per minute
N = number of divers
T = time (in minutes)

The following gas consumption rates are used with the formulas above: Free-flow helmet – 4.5 ACFM; Demand helmet – 1.4 ACFM; BIBS mask – 0.3A CFM.

Problem:

Using the formulas above, calculate the LP compressor volume required to operate 2 Kirby Morgan 37s in 60 fsw in demand mode, with minimal ventilating.

Solution:

The correct formula is $SCFM = ATA \times ACFM \times N$. The depth is 60 fsw, or 2.81 ATA, the helmets require 1.4 ACFM, the number of divers is 2, so SCFM = 2.81 × 1.4 × 2, or SCFM = 7.868.

Problem:

Using the formulas above, calculate the amount of oxygen required to keep a diver on BIBs at 50 fsw in the chamber for 15 minutes, and 40 fsw for 30 minutes.

Solution:

The correct formula is $SCF = ATA \times ACFM \times N \times T$, and because there are two depths and times, we will have to run the formula twice, and add the results. First, we will calculate the requirement for the time at 50 fsw. The depth (50 fsw) is 2.52 ATA, the BIBS uses 0.3 ACFM, the number of divers is 1, and the time in minutes is 15, so:SCF = 2.52 × 0.3 × 1 × 15, or SCF = 11.34.

Next we calculate for the oxygen required at 40 fsw. The depth is 2.21 ATA, the BIBS uses 0.3 ACFM, the number of divers is 1, and the time in minutes is 30, so SCF = 2.21 × 0.3 × 1 × 30, or SCF = 19.89.

The figure 11.34 SCF at 50 fsw is added to 19.89 SCF at 40 fsw and we determine that 31.23 SCF of medical oxygen will be required to keep the diver on BIBS for the times and depths specified.

6.10.3 Delivery Pressure

The demand regulator on the Kirby Morgan 37 and the Superlite 17 has a minimum pressure requirement in order to operate properly and keep the work of breathing to a minimum. The table below has the depths (fsw) and minimum over bottom pressures required.

To determine the actual delivery pressure, we add the over bottom pressure from the table to the bottom pressure at the diver's working depth. We use this formula: bottom pressure = Depth (fsw) × .445 to determine bottom pressure in psig.

Depth in Feet Sea Water	Over Bottom Pressure
0 – 60	90 psig
61 – 100	115 psig
101 – 132	135 psig
133 – 165	165 psig
166 – 220	225 psig

Problem:

Your crew will be working in 140 fsw for the next two weeks with a 17B. The portable panel you have will give you a maximum delivery pressure of 175 psig. Is this sufficient delivery pressure for the depth?

Solution:

First, we establish the ambient pressure at depth. Bottom pressure = 140 × .445, or 62.3 psig. Then we add that to the over bottom pressure of 165 (from table above) and we get a result of 227.3 psig required. The answer to the question above is no, the delivery pressure of the portable panel is not sufficient.

6.11 DIVER AND DIVE SITE EMERGENCIES

Detailed planning and safe practice will usually avoid emergencies on the job site, but occasionally there is an unplanned, unforeseen event that will put the diver (and sometimes the surface crew) at risk. Well-planned diving operations have contingency plans in place to deal with any emergencies that could possibly occur; we will examine the most common of these, how to deal with them, and how best to prevent them.

6.11.1 Fire in Dive Control

The thought of fire being a threat to a diver may seem strange, but fire on the vessel or fire in Dive Control is a serious threat to the diver, since the breathing gas supply, decompression, and surface support are put in danger. Coast Guard and ABS regulations require fire-fighting equipment on all working vessels, but the dive control area or van must have dedicated fire extinguishers. In addition to the fire extinguishers, a breathing air (BA) set must be supplied for the supervisor, to allow the supervisor to continue to run the dive with smoke or fumes in Dive Control. Usually, the BA set is an Aga mask with a supply hose tapped into the backup supply. To avoid fire in Dive Control, good housekeeping is very important: keep scrap paper, rags, garbage, etc. out of the dive control area. Kerosene, propane or other flame heaters must not be used in a dive control van. Electrical problems must be dealt with immediately. Oil, fuel and other flammable products must not be allowed in Dive Control. Smoking should not be allowed in Dive Control.

DSV fire, Bombay High Field. Divers were in saturation but all survived.

6.11.2 Fouled Umbilical / Fouled Diver

The diver's umbilical, though it is his/her lifeline, may cause problems when it becomes fouled in down lines, messenger lines, dive ladders, subsea structures, or bottom debris. Although not immediately life threatening, a fouled umbilical is serious, since the diver may not be able to ascend until it is clear. Fouled umbilicals usually (but not always) can be cleared without deploying the standby diver. The diver should remain calm, try to determine what the umbilical is fouled on, and attempt to clear it, provided the supervisor agrees. The diver should not use a knife around the umbilical, particularly if visibility is limited. If the both the diver and the standby are unable to free the umbilical, the last resort will be an in-water change-out of umbilicals. The best way to avoid a fouled umbilical is through proper umbilical management; this involves both the diver and the surface crew. Other ways to avoid this are to keep lines in the water on the job site to a minimum and use a floating umbilical when there is debris on the seabed.

Occasionally the diver and not the umbilical will become fouled, most often in excess ropes and lines left trailing from the underwater job site. Another common cause of diver fouling is discarded fishing net. Most often the fouling occurs when lines or net become caught on the helmet valves, the diver's harness, or the bailout cylinder. Often the diver cannot be freed without using a knife. In cases like this, the standby diver must be deployed. The diver must never try to cut nets or lines behind him/her, beside or behind the helmet or out of the diver's range of vision. To avoid diver fouling, remove unused lines and abandoned fishing nets from the underwater job site before proceeding with the work.

6.11.3 Loss of Breathing Gas

With the redundant backup systems on today's surface-supplied diving spread, a loss of breathing gas is not as likely to happen and not as serious as it was in the past. It still is, however, a serious incident to be dealt with properly. If there is a loss of the main gas supply, the diver is immediately switched to the backup supply at the panel, and the cause of the interruption is identified. If the main supply cannot be restored immediately, the dive is aborted. The diver does not ever work while breathing from the backup supply. Occasionally, the problem is between the panel and the diver. In this case, the diver goes on bailout, immediately informs the supervisor, and makes his/her way back to the stage or down line. Usually it will not be a kinked hose, as modern diving hose is "non-kink" hose, unable to be completely flattened. Any time the diver has to engage the bailout, the dive is terminated. To prevent a loss of breathing gas, deck whips and umbilicals should be regularly inspected, panel gauges must be in good working order, gas system valves must be fully opened or fully closed, and gas bank pressures must be closely monitored.

6.11.4 Loss of Communications

Although it does not happen as often as it did years ago, occasionally a loss of communications will occur while the diver is in the water. If this occurs, the diver is instructed by line-pull signals to quickly return to the stage or down line. If there is no response to line-pull signals, the standby diver must be immediately deployed. As with the breathing gas, if communications can be restored immediately, the dive may continue, otherwise, it must be aborted. To prevent communications loss, regularly inspect the radio-telephone power supply, the communications wire on the umbilical, the connectors on the helmet, and the communications components or modules in the helmet.

6.11.5 Blowup (uncontrolled ascent)

Blowup is a term used for the uncontrolled ascent of a diver, and it is a situation that can, depending on the circumstances, have very serious consequences for the diver. Blowup may be caused by several factors including: overinflated or stuck inflator on drysuit; dropped weights; umbilical swept away by current; large sea creatures becoming entangled in the umbilical; and umbilical fouled in an unsecured lift bag or crane wire. If a blowup happens, there are two things the diver should do, or attempt to do: tilt head back to maintain an open airway while exhaling hard and spread the arms and legs to increase drag. How the blowup is dealt with depends on the circumstances as outlined below:

- Shallow Water No-Decompression: Recover diver quickly, remove helmet, and observe for signs of AGE.
- Deep Water No-Decompression: If diver shows no adverse symptoms, return diver to 20 fsw and decompress for the normal ascent time for the depth of dive according to *U.S. Navy Manual Rev. 6*.
- Beyond No-Decompression Limits with No In-Water Stops 40 fsw or Deeper: If no symptoms, place diver in chamber, press to 50 fsw, and decompress according to *U.S. Navy Manual Rev. 6* as a surface decompression dive.
- Beyond No-Decompression Limits with In-Water Stops 40 fsw or Deeper: If no symptoms, place diver in chamber, press to 60 fsw, and begin a USN Treatment Table 6.
- Diver Presents Any Symptoms of AGE: Press to depth of significant relief; starting at 60 fsw (observing for 5 minutes) and pressing deeper by 10 fsw increments until depth of relief, entering USN Treatment Table 6A at the depth of relief. (See Chapter 10: Hyperbaric Emergencies.)

The following measures will help prevent blowup: never use quick release weights; never overinflate dry-suit to lift heavy objects; when using drysuit, wear ankle weights; when using lift bags, always use hold backs and inverter lines; when working in areas where whales, large manta rays, and other sea life are common, use a stage or wet-bell system; and practice proper umbilical management.

6.11.6 Trapped Diver

Fortunately, a trapped diver is not a common occurrence in underwater operations. A trapped diver is a serious incident for three reasons: we are limited in the help we can get to the diver; despite having primary and backup gas supplies, there is still a limit to how long they will last; and the longer the diver is trapped, the more the decompression commitment increases. Divers may become trapped in different ways: under a heavy object that has been lowered or shifted; buried in an excavation by sand or silt; or by the suction of differential pressure. In the case of a heavy object, the best method of rescue (if possible), is to lift the object enough with a crane or lift bags to free the diver. Extracting the diver via excavation around the diver is the only other way but care must be taken not to further de-stabilize the object. Burial in sand or silt is a more common occurrence, often (but not always) happening in an improper underwater excavation. Rescue in this case will require an airlift or a jet pump. An airlift moves the material farther away and quicker, so it is the better method. The most common way divers become trapped is suction due to differential pressure. To rescue a diver trapped by suction, the suction must be eliminated, significantly reduced, or diffused. This may require closing a valve, filling a de-watered space, or opening alternative holes to allow suction to bypass the diver. Whatever method is used, the standby diver must be careful – the suction that has one diver trapped can (and often does) trap the second diver.

To prevent diver entrapment with heavy objects, the following precautions should be taken:

- Keep the diver well clear of heavy lifts until they are on or very close to bottom. Ensure the lifts are firmly on bottom and sitting level before disconnecting the crane. Keep umbilical clear of lifts with proper umbilical management.
- Never attempt to excavate with airlift or jet pump underneath or adjacent to any heavy object, unless it is a secure, immoveable structure such as a jacket, dock, or seawall.

To prevent diver entrapment by burial, the following precautions should be taken:

- Always use the 3 to 1 rule: The top of any excavation must always be 3 times wider than the depth of the excavation. This keeps the sides sloped at a stable angle.
- Never excavate deeper than 3 feet unless using a "trench box." A trench box is a reinforced steel box lowered into the excavation as the digging progresses.
- When excavating or "jetting in" subsea pipelines or cables, always keep a recue airlift ready in case of trapped diver.

To prevent diver entrapment by differential pressure, use the following precautions:

- Perform lockout/tagout procedure on all pumps and manual suction devices before any diving operations commence.
- For differential pressure areas such as dams, tanks, and locks, keep the diver away from danger zones, such as the bottom of power plant gates, drain pipe intakes, etc. If they must approach the danger zones, use a "diffuser cage" or other device to protect the diver from entrapment.
- Never lower empty pipelines, flex hoses, or tanks underwater. Always prefill such devices, or remove all blind flanges to allow complete flooding as they are lowered subsea.

6.11.7 Pressure-Related Illness

Due to the nature of underwater operations, pressure-related illness (decompression sickness or arterial gas embolism) is always a possibility. Many mistakenly believe working within the no-decompression limits will guarantee there will not be an incident. Many also believe that pain only (Type I decompression sickness) is not serious and does not require treatment. Every case of decompression sickness is serious, and like AGE, must be treated, and even dives within the no-decompression limits can have incidents. The key to successful treatment of any pressure-related illness is to recognize symptoms quickly, perform treatment in a timely manner, and perform the treatment properly. Every diver must be familiar with the signs and symptoms of both arterial gas embolism and decompression sickness. (See Chapter 3: Underwater Physiology.) The four ways to avoid these illnesses are to always use a pneumofathometer, ensure the pneumofathometer is properly calibrated, follow the instructions for usage with the decompression tables, and always pad the tables being used.

6.12 TIPS FROM AN OLD DIVER FOR WORKING IN-WATER

Bottom time is like youth – once it is gone, you cannot get it back. The diver must make every second count while in the water. The best way is to discuss a plan with the supervisor without being stuck to the plan. Plan ahead but also think on your feet, changing the plan (and letting topside know) as conditions change. There are a few simple tips to help you out:

- Don't use decongestants if you are having trouble equalizing. The old navy divers always snuffed a handful of clean saltwater up the nostrils. It feels exactly like you have been hit in the face with a garden rake, but it really works to help you equalize.
- Remember to use the free-flow adjustment knob and the steady-flow valve on your hat. Any increase in the work of breathing has a direct and definite influence on the amount of time you will require to complete a given task, as will excessive carbon dioxide buildup.
- Try to orient yourself on the underwater job site. Be aware of where the barge or vessel is in relation to you (behind you, in front, to either side), and it will help in various tasks, such as lowering materials. Try to always know where your down line is, to avoid searching for it.

- If you want to be an efficient diver, learn to think ahead and ask instead of waiting for tools. Better to have a tool ready and not need it than to burn precious bottom time blowing bubbles waiting.

- Grow a "third hand." Keep 1 ½ fathoms of ⅜" rope coiled, taped, and tied on your harness or your belt. With the proper knot, this can hold or secure almost anything while you work on it. Just remember to retrieve your third hand every time you use it.

- Take the time and make sure the tools you will need are ready before you dress in. Sharpen knives and chisels, make sure you have the proper size wrenches, etc.

- In the military you are taught to completely disassemble and reassemble your weapon with your eyes shut. The tools you use underwater are your weapons. Get to know your tools, exactly how they operate, how to repair them, and how to use them most effectively.

- When you finish with a tool underwater, don't just drop it on bottom. Put it back on the messenger line, in the tool basket, or store it in a safe place (and tell topside where it is). Don't be "that person" who always loses the tools. No one wants "that person" on their crew, ever.

- Remember you have a topside crew and use them to help you work. If you have to move a 100 lb. valve a distance of 10 feet, 3 people on the surface can lift it while you guide it into place with a lot less effort and a lot faster than you can do it yourself.

- Let your supervisor know what is going on down there and what you are planning to do. The supervisor can't give you ideas or help if he/she doesn't know what is happening.

- Listen to and watch the older hands on the job and find out how they do things. Sometimes new ideas will work; sometimes not. If you plan on doing something different, make sure you ask permission before doing it. Then if it causes a problem, you are off the hook.

7.0 MIXED-GAS DIVING

In the field of commercial diving, any breathing medium supplied to the diver other than atmospheric air is considered to be a mixed gas. Mixed gas is used for the diver's breathing gas when the use of air is either impossible due to the properties of the component gases in air or less productive due to the decompression required when using air. There are two mixed gases accepted for use in commercial diving: N_2O_2 (nitrox) and HeO_2 (heliox). In many jurisdictions today, heliox is only allowed when used in saturation diving.

7.1 N_2O_2 (Nitrox)

In recent years, a mode of diving called nitrox (represented as N_2O_2) has been seeing more usage on commercial diving job sites. Nitrox is typically used in the intermediate air range to increase no-decompression bottom times. Although it is sometimes called oxygen-enriched air, this is a misnomer. Nitrox is a mixed gas, since it is not atmospheric air, and the breathing medium must be mixed prior to its use. Varying mixes are used, from 75/25 to 60/40, and as a treatment gas in chambers 50/50. Nitrox is becoming more widely used in commercial diving, as both contractors and clients become more comfortable with its use. Nitrox is most useful and advantageous in the range between 40 and 80 fsw. See table below:

No-Decompression Limits at Various Depths Using Various Breathing Gasses

Breathing Gas Used	30fsw	40fsw	50fsw	60fsw	70fsw	80fsw	90fsw	100fsw	110fsw
Air	371	163	92	60	48	39	30	25	20
68/32	595	371	163	92	60	48	39	30	25
60/40	unlimited	595	371	163	92	74	XXXX	XXXX	XXXX

In depths of less than 40 fsw, the no-D limits times are so long, there is little advantage in using nitrox instead of air. But at 40 fsw and 50 fsw, the advantages are huge – the no-D time is almost quadrupled if the diver is breathing a 40% mixture. There is still a noticeable advantage up to 80 fsw. Beyond 80 fsw, the advantages of a 32% mixture are very limited, and a 40% mixture cannot be used deeper than 80 fsw.

7.1.1 Nitrox Theory

The oxygen in any given breathing mixture does not factor into decompression; it is the partial pressure of the inert gas that determines decompression based on bottom time at a given depth. The theory behind nitrox is this: by decreasing the percentage of nitrogen in the diver's breathing gas, the no-decompression bottom time is maximized and the decompression required after dives is reduced. This may be accomplished either by removing the nitrogen from or adding oxygen to breathing quality air, thereby reducing the partial pressure of the inert gas, nitrogen. The advantages and disadvantages are as follows:

Advantages of Nitrox
- Extended bottom times without decompression
- Reduced decompression required for longer dives
- Reduced residual nitrogen after dives
- Reduced risk of decompression sickness

Disadvantages of Nitrox
- Increased risk of CNS oxygen toxicity
- Special equipment required for mixing
- Special cleaning required for all equipment used, including diving gear (see Section 7.4)
- Repeated long exposures can result in pulmonary oxygen toxicity
- More expensive than air diving
- Maximum depth of 110 fsw

7.2 OXYGEN TOXICITY

Oxygen toxicity is a factor to be considered when using nitrox or any mixed gas. As a general rule, CNS oxygen toxicity is a threat to the diver any time the partial pressure of oxygen (ppO_2) approaches or exceeds 1.6 ATA, but it can be an issue even with lower partial pressures and longer exposures. Breathing atmospheric air, the diver can exceed 200 fsw (actually, 218 fsw) before this becomes an issue. By comparison, when breathing a 60/40 blend, the ppO_2 hits 1.6 ATA at 99 fsw, and when breathing a 68/32 blend, the 1.6 ATA threshold is reached at 132 fsw. To reduce the risk, most commercial operations do not exceed 1.4 ATA on the in-water working portions of the diving operation. The included EAD table has a 1.4 ATA cut-off built in. Pulmonary oxygen toxicity, although seldom resulting in death, damages the lungs, leading to a marked decrease in pulmonary function. Repetitive long duration dives would be required to cause pulmonary oxygen toxicity with the ppO_2 above 1.0 ATA. The effects of pulmonary toxicity are cumulative. In addition, some in the diving medical community now believe repeated long exposures to high partial pressures of oxygen may lead to disbaric osteonecrosis (bone necrosis), which for years was assumed to be the result of exposure to high partial pressures of inert gas, nitrogen in particular. Long duration dives and multiple repetitive dives with high ppO_2 should be avoided in any case.

WARNING: Do not exceed the deepest recommended depth for each nitrox mix. Doing so puts the diver at risk for CNS oxygen toxicity occuring at depth, with a high probability of fatal results. Always check the precentages before using the mixture. Always use a calibrated, panel-mounted oxygen analyzer when using mixed gas. Always have the same mixture in the bailout that is running through the panel.

7.3 CALCULATING DECOMPRESSION FOR NITROX DIVES

To calculate the required decompression for a nitrox mixture, we find the depth on atmospheric air that has the same partial pressure of nitrogen (equivalent air depth), and follow the air diving table for that depth, whether it is a standard air or surface decompression table. For example; using a 68/32 mix on a dive to 63 fsw, the ppN_2 is 2.0 ATA, and using atmospheric air, the ppN_2 at 50 fsw is 2.0 ATA, so the equivalent air depth (EAD) for a dive to 63 fsw on 32% is 50 fsw. The formula for calculating EAD is as follows:

$$EAD = \frac{(1 - O_2\%) (D + 33)}{0.79} - 33$$

Where:

EAD = Equivalent Air Depth
$O_2\%$ = the oxygen percentage of the gas blend expressed as a decimal
D = the depth (in fsw) of the diver breathing the gas blend

Problem:

You are planning a dive to 55 fsw to clean marine growth and inspect anodes on a jacket leg. You have two full quads of 60/40 N_2O_2 available to use for the dive. How long can you run each diver no-D?

Solution:

Using the formula above as follows: $EAD = \frac{(1 - 0.4) (55 + 33)}{0.79} - 33$

$EAD = \frac{0.6 \times 88}{0.79} - 33$ EAD = 33.84. The Equivalent Air Depth of this dive is 34 fsw.

Using Table 9-7, we can see that the no-D limit for 35 fsw is 232 minutes, so that is the maximum bottom time without decompression you can give each diver in this case. Remember, this will also be padded.

30	371	17	27	38	50
35	232	14	23	32	42
40	163	12	20	27	36

Source: *U.S.Navy Diving Manual*

EQUIVALENT AIR DEPTH TABLE

Depth (fsw)	Oxygen Percentage in Breathing Media								
	32	34	36	38	40	42	44	46	48
20	13	12	10	9	8	6	5	4	2
22	15	13	12	11	9	8	6	5	4
24	17	15	14	12	11	9	8	6	5
26	18	17	15	14	12	11	9	8	6
28	20	18	17	15	14	12	11	9	8
30	22	20	18	17	15	14	12	11	9
32	23	22	20	18	17	15	14	12	10
34	25	23	22	20	18	17	15	13	12
36	27	25	23	22	20	18	16	15	13
38	29	27	25	23	21	20	18	16	14
40	30	28	27	25	23	21	19	17	16
42	32	30	28	26	24	23	21	19	17
44	34	32	30	28	26	24	22	20	18
46	35	33	31	29	27	25	23	21	19
48	37	35	33	31	29	27	25	23	21
50	39	37	35	33	30	28	26	24	22
52	41	38	36	34	32	30	28	26	23
54	42	40	38	36	33	31	29	27	25
56	44	42	40	37	35	33	31	28	26
58	46	43	41	39	37	34	32	30	27
60	47	45	43	40	38	36	33	31	29
62	49	47	44	42	40	37	35	32	30
64	51	48	46	44	41	39	36	34	
66	53	50	48	45	43	40	38	35	
68	54	52	49	47	44	42	39		
70	56	53	51	48	46	43	40		
72	58	55	53	50	47	45			
74	60	57	54	51	49	46			
76	61	58	56	53	50	48			
78	63	60	57	54	52				
80	65	62	59	56	53				
82	66	63	61	58	55				
84	68	65	62	59					
86	70	67	64	61					
88	72	68	65	62					
90	73	70	67						
92	75	72	69						
94	77	74	70						
96	78	75							
98	80	77							
100	82	79							
102	84	80							
104	85								
106	87								
108	89								
110	91								
112									

Source: *The Commercial Diver's Handbook* © Best Publishing Company

The table on the previous page allows for quick determination of the EAD without having to perform the calculations. The depth of the proposed dive is read on the far left column (blue), and the row is followed across horizontally to line up with the oxygen percentage in the nitrox mix (read across the top in green), and the resulting number is the EAD. For example: A proposed dive will be to 66 fsw, using a 60/40 mix. The EAD for this dive will be 43 fsw, so decompression follows the USN 50 fsw Air Decompression Table.

A real concern in nitrox diving is the partial pressure of oxygen at depth. Because of the elevated oxygen percentages, the partial pressures are very high, particularly at the deeper depths for each mixture. The universally accepted cutoff for partial pressure of oxygen is 1.4 ATA. This is reflected on the EAD table: The lower right corner is in red, with no equivalent air depths given. When using nitrox, it is necessary to have an in-line oxygen analyzer on the panel and to be alert for signs of CNS oxygen toxicity when diving at the higher partial pressures.

7.4 USING NITROX SAFELY

Nitrox gas must be handled differently than air. In the United States, any gas with an oxygen percentage lower than 40 may be handled as if it was air. However, in most countries, any gas mixture with oxygen content higher than 25% is considered pure oxygen. IMCA, in its guidance notes also uses 25% as the cutoff point, and most diving operations offshore follow IMCA. Pressurized oxygen requires special safety measures. The two mixtures most commonly used in commercial diving work are 60/40 (0 – 80 fsw) and 68/32 (80 – 110 fsw). Both of these mixes are obviously above 25%, so both require the same treatment and safety measures as 100% oxygen.

All equipment used in nitrox diving operations must be oxygen cleaned. This includes cylinders, deck whips, panels, regulators, umbilicals, bailouts, and helmets. Failure to follow oxygen cleaning and safety guidelines may result in explosion and fire causing injury or death.

Due, in part, to the explosion and fire hazard, and in part to the oxygen toxicity hazard, diving with nitrox also requires special procedures and some special equipment. These are as follows:

- A calibrated oxygen analyzer is used on the diver's breathing mixture at all times.
- Two independent supplies of nitrox must be available to each working diver.
- All storage cylinders and bailouts must be analyzed prior to diving operations.
- The diver's bailout must contain the same nitrox blend used for the dive.
- All storage and bailout cylinders must be labeled (mixture and cutoff depth).
- All gas supply whips and panel plumbing must be oxygen cleaned.
- The diver's umbilical and helmet must be oxygen cleaned.
- The diver's bailout regulator must be oxygen cleaned.

There are two reasons an oxygen analyzer is used on the panel when using nitrox: If the oxygen level drops too low, the EAD used will not be accurate; and if it climbs too high, there is a risk of toxicity. The analyzers must also be calibrated regularly to ensure they are reading correctly. This is done by running calibration gas through the units and adjusting the readout, usually zero, twenty, and forty gases. Accuracy in oxygen analyzers is required to be less than 0.5%. The acceptable range for oxygen percentage is ±2% when using nitrox in a diving operation. Any time the percentage varies outside of this range, another EAD must be used. To avoid encountering this problem with a diver in the water, the gas is always analyzed before it is put online to the panel.

When performing diving operations with nitrox, the diver must always have the exact same mix in the bailout that is running through the panel. Since it is common to have both air and nitrox operations on the same vessel, nitrox bailouts must be clearly marked as indicated below, with a tag on the cylinder valve showing the percentage of the blend in the cylinder.

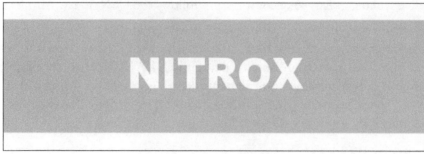

Marking found on nitrox bailout cylinder

Panel-mounted and portable oxygen analyzers

7.5 MIXING NITROX

The oxygen percentage in pre-packaged nitrox gas often varies widely from what it claims to be. Also, the mixing of N_2O_2 on site can be significantly cheaper than buying pre-packaged gas. There are a few methods of mixing nitrox: oil-less HP compressor with an oxygen injection system; oil-less HP compressor with a molecular sieve; LP compressor with a nitrox membrane; and HP mixing using breathable compressed air and medical oxygen. HP mixing, also known as partial-pressure mixing, tends to be used most often offshore and will be reviewed here. Oxygen must be handled with care during mixing, and only O_2 cleaned equipment can be used. When mixing gas in a cylinder (or even in a sat bell or sat chamber for oxygen makeup), often one gas will drop and the other rise, not mixing initially but gradually mixing over time. This condition is known as **stratification** or layering. To avoid stratification in a sat system, saturation divers sometimes wave towels to help mix the gas and newer systems have circulation fans. The larger the area over which the two gases are exposed to one another, the better they will mix. Cylinders or quads used for mixing are laid down horizontally, which gives a greater area of exposure for the two gases to mix. Blending takes time, so the nitrox is not used for at least 24 hours after mixing, and the oxygen percentage is tested before and during use with an oxygen analyzer. Mixing gas involves working with high pressure gases but it also involves working with 100% oxygen under high pressure. Because of this, there are safety precautions to be followed **every time**. These safety precautions are as follows:

- Never pump or attempt to compress oxygen other than with an industry-approved gas transfer pump, certified for oxygen service.

- Ensure all hoses and fittings used are oxygen cleaned.

- Ensure all hoses used are approved for oxygen transfer (Synflex or equivalent).

- Ensure that the cylinders or quads used to mix and store the mixture are oxygen clean.

- Always cascade the oxygen first, metering flow with the valve on the oxygen cylinder.

- When opening valves, stand to one side, look away, and open slowly.

- Wear all personal protective equipment when gas mixing.

- Test the breathing air source regularly with Dräger tubes for oil mist (maximum 0.1 mg/m^3)

When starting to mix the gas, cascade the oxygen first. It is recommended there be at least 100 psi of N_2O_2 or breathing air in the mixing quad before adding the oxygen. This helps to reduce the risk of adiabatic compression temperature increase, which can have disastrous consequences. Control the flow of oxygen with a metering valve or the king valve on the oxygen quad and not the king valve on the mixing quad. Once the correct amount of oxygen has been cascaded, close the oxygen valve first, then the valve on the mixing quad. Add breathing air as required to bring the mixing quad up to final pressure. Keep the mix cylinders lying horizontal to avoid stratification, and do not use the mix for at least 24 hours. Once the mixing operation is complete, ensure that the nitrox cylinders are clearly marked for content, showing the percentage of nitrogen and oxygen (example: N_2O_2 68/32) and the date and time it was blended. Variations of ±2% in oxygen content are typically accepted.

After allowing the mix to settle for 24 hours, test oxygen percentage with a calibrated oxygen analyzer. Never use a batch of mixed gas unless it has had a full 24 hours to settle. Always use an oxygen analyzer on the panel while running surface-supplied nitrox. Regularly test the air supply for mixing to ensure the oil mist stays below the 0.1 mg/m^3 level.

7.6 USING NITROX AS A DECOMPRESSION GAS

Sometimes when performing dives deeper in the air range using in-water decompression, nitrox is used as a breathing gas for decompression stops. This is only done, of course, when nitrox is online to the panel, and the diving system has been oxygen cleaned. The lower partial pressure of nitrogen in the gas allows the diver to off-gas more thoroughly, making a bend far less likely. When using nitrox as a breathing gas for decompression, no change is made to the schedule – decompression is performed exactly as it would be if the diver were breathing air. Usually, 60/40 is used, but if only 68/32 is available, it still provides a huge advantage over air. This practice almost guarantees an incident-free decompression.

7.7 USING NITROX AS A TREATMENT GAS

Occasionally, a Type II bend or arterial gas embolism case will be encountered when the symptoms seem to really hang on. Relief will occur, then as the treatment progresses, a recurrence of symptoms happens. In cases like these, nitrox is used instead of air on the deeper end of Treatment Table 6A. Since the use of 100% oxygen is not possible deeper than 60 fsw on treatments, nitrox provides a gas with a lower partial pressure of nitrogen, thereby allowing more thorough off-gassing, and allowing the removal of the more stubborn inert gas bubbles. Typically, 32% nitrox is used at 100 fsw and shallower, while 40% is used at 80 fsw and shallower. There are also times when a patient will not be able to stand 100% oxygen without oxygen toxicity symptoms but will tolerate 50% oxygen. In these cases, 50/50 will often be used on an air treatment table with favorable results.

7.8 HELIUM-OXYGEN GAS (HeO₂ Heliox)

The other mixed gas commonly used in commercial diving is heliox. Dan Wilson built the first commercial mixed-gas diving helmet in 1962, and Bob Kirby followed with his version in 1963. This was the same time period when the first working dives performed by civilians with heliox were being done in oil fields of the Santa Barbara Channel and the Gulf of Mexico. Heliox has been in the commercial diving toolbox ever since. In the early days, any work shallower than 200 fsw was done on air; mixed gas was used between 200 and 400 fsw and often even deeper. Although helium was an expensive gas, it was the only practical way for a diver to perform work in the deeper depths. These days, in order to cut back on the cost of the helium, reclaim technology is being used. In the reclaim process, the exhaled gas is returned to the surface where the carbon dioxide is removed, the helium is recompressed, and fresh oxygen is added. With the advances made over the years, reclaim technology today reuses over 80% of the original helium.

7.8.1 Heliox Theory

Inert gas is necessary in the diver's breathing mix in order to carry the oxygen necessary to maintain life. Oxygen becomes toxic as the partial pressures increase, so the deeper a diver descends, the more inert gas is required in the breathing mixture to lower the partial pressure of oxygen. The inert gas in atmospheric air, nitrogen, unfortunately has narcotic properties that increase as the partial pressure increases at depth. Many divers cannot dive deeper than 170 fsw due to nitrogen narcosis, and very few can manage to keep their head on straight beyond 220 fsw. But by using helium-oxygen mixtures, anyone can dive deep without suffering from narcosis. Helium, when used as the inert gas carrier in a breathing mixture, does not appear to have any of the narcotic properties of nitrogen at any depth.

Advantages of Using Heliox
- No narcotic effects as encountered when breathing air
- Better productivity due to lack of narcotic effect
- Safer for the diver due to lack of narcotic effect

Disadvantages of Using Heliox
- Possibility of HPNS on descent
- Diver has serious speech distortion
- Diver has rapid loss of body heat
- Helium is very expensive

7.9 USING HELIOX AS A BREATHING GAS

When divers first began using heliox on dives, one problem became apparent immediately. Divers talked like Donald Duck. Helium is much less dense than air, and the human vocal chords were designed for use in air. Eventually, the manufacturers of radio-telephones came up with the "helium unscrambler" which allows the supervisor to adjust the tone of the diver's voice to be better understood.

The second problem encountered was much more serious: divers got cold very fast when breathing heliox. There are two reasons for this: the increased thermal conductivity of helium (see Chapter 2: Underwater Physics) and the reduced density, which allowed divers to exhale the gas much quicker, expelling more of their body heat. The U.S. Navy experimented with electrically heated underwear, similar to those used by fighter and bomber pilots at high altitude. Although it helped, it was obvious a better alternative was necessary—a hot water suit. The first commercial saturation project (Smith Mountain Dam, 1965) was also the first time that hot-water suits were used. These suits were a huge improvement, keeping the divers warm enough to work comfortably while breathing heliox, but the diver's wrists and ankles were burned by the hot water.

Not until 1971, when Dick Long of DUI patented his hot water suit was the problem truly solved. The hot water suit is now used on virtually every working heliox dive (and many air dives as well), and with the hot water hose alongside the gas hose in the umbilical bundle, the gas is warmed slightly on its way to the diver.

The third problem was not noticed until dives were attempted beyond 450 fsw in the mid-1960s. Many divers would suffer from tremors, muscle twitching, dizziness, and nausea. It was given the name helium tremors, since it was thought to be a result of breathing helium. With testing, it was proven the condition was the result of too rapid compression, not breathing helium. Now known as high pressure nervous syndrome (HPNS), it is avoided by using slower descent rates and stopping the descent occasionally once the 400 fsw level has been reached.

The accepted partial pressure of oxygen for in-water work in the industry today is reckoned at 1.4 ATA to avoid CNS O_2 toxicity. This means different mixes are used for different depths of dive. On any given job you may see 50/50, 84/16, 90/10 HeO_2, or any number of other blends, plus air and oxygen. Usually, a surface gas job will use one HeO_2 blend for bottom mix and a different one for mid-water. Although some contractors will have the diver leave surface on air and perform a gas switch at about the 100 fsw range, it is best practice to leave surface breathing HeO_2 (84/16 or higher O_2). This avoids the condition known as isobaric DCS, which can occur after switching from air to HeO_2. Provided the O_2 level is high enough, HeO_2 from the surface is the way to go. The descent rate is kept at 60 fpm or slower, and the ppO_2 is kept below 1.4 by gas changes. A gas change is performed at the panel, and the diver ventilates the hat for 20 seconds after the proper oxygen percentage is read on the O_2 analyzer on the panel. When changing gas to air on ascent, the diver ventilates until a voice change is heard. The diver's ascent procedure will depend on the decompression tables being used.

The U.S. Navy mixed-gas tables in Revision 6 call for the diver to breathe bottom mix throughout the entire dive, unless the O_2 percentage is below 16. In this case, the diver leaves surface on air, and switches to bottom mix at 20 fsw. Following the dive, the diver leaves bottom on bottom mix, proceeds to 90 fsw and switches to 50/50 HeO_2. All required stops are performed on 50/50 until 30 fsw is reached. Then, the diver is switched to 100% O_2 for any remaining stops to the surface. Air breaks are inserted after every 30 minutes of oxygen breathing. When using surface decompression, the final water stop is 40 fsw.

The Canadian Navy tables (most commonly used outside the United States) call for the diver to breathe the same mix (84/16) throughout the entire dive and to remain on HeO_2 only until the first decompression stop, where the diver switches to air. All decompression is performed on air until the diver reaches 30 fsw, where he/she is switched to 100% O_2. Air breaks are inserted after every 30 minutes of oxygen breathing. When surface decompression is to be used, the final water stop is at 30 fsw.

There are several other heliox tables in use; the table depends on the contractor's preference. Surface-supplied heliox diving is no longer used in many areas; the clients and regulatory agencies now insist on saturation diving for any work beyond 170 fsw. The areas where it is still used regularly now are in the United States, Canada, and some areas in Southeast Asia. Although IMCA does approve heliox diving, it restricts the depth to 250 fsw, and restricts the bottom time to 30 minutes.

7.10 SAFETY NOTES ON HELIOX

Heliox dives should never be performed using only a down line. The use of an enclosed stage or wet bell complete with onboard emergency gas supply is **STRONGLY RECOMMENDED**. Onboard emergency gas supply should include (clearly marked) HeO_2, air, and O_2 for decompression. Helium-oxygen dives must never be performed without a chamber on site. Always ensure that in addition to decompression tables, abort and emergency decompression tables are on site prior to commencing operations.

8.0 SATURATION DIVING

Although this chapter examines saturation diving, it is only a very brief overview. Saturation diving is beyond the scope of this text, and additional training will be involved should the reader wish to engage in this particular mode of diving. If you wish to train as a saturation diver, it is recommended that you spend no less than five years working offshore as an air diver prior to saturation diving training.

8.1 WHY SATURATION IS USED

In the surface-supplied diving mode, all dives must have the decompression commitment dealt with immediately; every dive that requires decompression must have the decompression done at the end of the dive. For dives at the deeper end of the air range and surface mixed-gas dives, the decompression phase of the dive is far longer in time than the actual time spent working. You will recall from Chapter 3: Underwater Physiology that a diver under pressure takes on inert gas up to the point of total saturation. From that point of saturation on, there is no longer any uptake of inert gas, provided there is no depth increase once saturated. Once the diver has reached the point of total saturation (approximately 24 hours), it doesn't matter whether he/she stays saturated for 2 or 22 days. The same amount of decompression to remove the inert gas is needed. Because of this, it makes good sense from an economic and productivity standpoint to pressurize a crew of divers to a given depth and keep them saturated as long as possible to maximize on bottom time and also minimize the decompression commitment. The surface diver can stay underwater an hour, and decompress for three, while a saturation diver at the same depth can work every day for several days and only decompress once when finished. The IMCA guideline has stipulated 28 days seal to seal, which has become the industry standard. A 656 fsw (200 meter) dive for 28 days requires 8 days, 9 hours, and 20 minutes decompression. Therefore, divers can work for 19 ½ days, then decompress for the required time, to reach surface within the allowable 28 days.

Obviously, it is not practical to keep divers in the water while they are in saturation. The diving crew is kept in a series of interconnected deck chambers, known as a saturation system or a sat spread. The crew eats, sleeps, showers, uses the toilet, and relaxes in the sat system chambers. When it is time for the divers to go to work, they transfer through a lock to a closed bell and are lowered to the subsea job site, staying pressurized the entire time.

Testing a new bell

Sat diver on clump weight
Photo courtesy of Oceaneering International

8.2 HOW SATURATION IS PERFORMED

One chamber in the sat system is usually used for blowdown and decompression. When divers are going in for a sat, they take their kit bag (toiletries, books, i-Pad) and climb into the chamber. The initial blowdown is on 20/80 heliox mix to about 30 fsw, then the rest of the pressurization is on the heliox bottom mix. The blowdown continues until the divers reach a predetermined depth, known as the storage depth. Then the new divers enter the system. If it is a long-term job, there will be three or four divers waiting to climb into the travel chamber to start decompressing. The entire saturation system is maintained at the storage depth at all times. The storage depth is within 15 to 20 feet of the depth the divers will be working, and the divers are allowed short upward and downward excursions from this storage depth in order to perform their work. Each team of 2 or 3 men (depending on the system) has a shift (usually 8 hours) when they are required to dive. When their shift starts, they will climb through a short trunking into the bell. Then the sat supervisor and one of the divers will perform bell checks. These are the predive checks on the bell when every valve and gauge is checked. Once the bell checks are complete, the second (or third, if a 3-man bell) diver closes and dogs the chamber door while climbing through the trunking, then closes the bell hatch. The pressure on the trunking is bled off to surface pressure. Once the trunking has been bled off, the bell mating clamp is released, and the bell is picked up by the LARS and lowered into the moon pool (or over the side, depending on the vessel). The LARS system is similar to those on the surface diving systems. There are separate winches for the clump weight and bell, and a large roller for the bell umbilical. Once the bell reaches the water depth equivalent to the storage depth, the hatch is opened and the first diver dresses and does predive checks. In a 2-man bell run, each diver will spend around 3½ hours in the water. Diver 1 will leave the bell while his/her partner (the bellman) tends the hose and keeps an eye on delivery gas pressure from the surface. The bellman will also adjust and monitor the reclaim pressure as the diver's gas is "reclaimed" and sent back to the surface for CO_2 scrubbing, O_2 injection, and subsequent reuse. Helium is a very expensive gas, and the dive companies always try to get the best reclaim percentage. This cuts down on cost as well as the amount of heliox that must be stored on board. In a 3-man team, 2 divers dive concurrently, while the bellman only leaves the bell in the case of extreme emergency. The divers take turns acting as the bellman, so every third bell run a team does, the diver is bellman and never leaves the bell in the 8-hour bell run. Three-man teams have the advantage of 2 divers working in the water together for upwards of 6 hours at a time. When the shift is completed, they close the hatch and the LARS lifts the bell. Once on the surface, the bell is clamped back onto the trunking, and the trunking is pressurized. This allows the divers to open the hatch, climb through the trunking, and into the chamber. At each shift change, this process is repeated.

8.3 THE SATURATION DIVING SYSTEM

The typical saturation system consists of 3 or more main chambers, bolted together or connected by trunking, a bell complete with LARS, and a hyperbaric rescue craft (HRC) with a dedicated LARS. The HRC is required because the crew in saturation must have a way to escape under pressure if the vessel is in peril. Older HRCs were often set up to "float off," but now they usually either have a LARS or other launch mechanism to ensure

that the HRC will get clear of the vessel in the event of an emergency. Often, there is a long section of pressurized pipe known as an "escape trunking" for the crew to scramble through in order to board the HRC. A very few years ago, sat systems did not have any provisions for the rescue of the divers under pressure. Even today, there are non-IMCA systems without rescue capability. The *Koosha I* sank in the Persian Gulf in October 2011 with the loss of the entire saturation crew as well as the life support supervisor who had tried (unsuccessfully) to save them by pressurizing the system over bottom pressure.

Hyperbaric rescue craft undergoing IMCA D024 test

12-man saturation system being mobilized on barge

Chambers below deck on a DSV

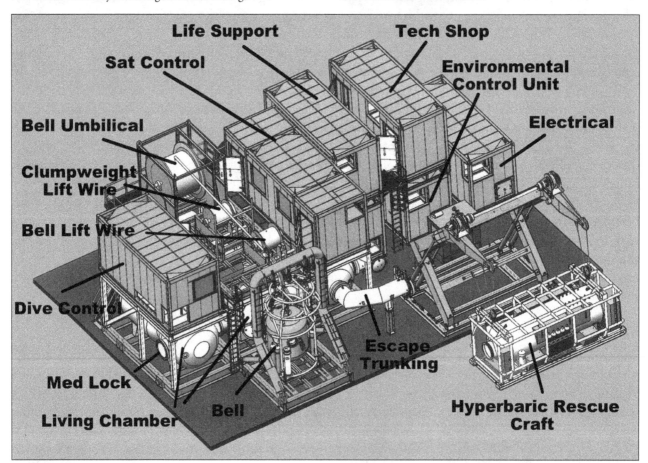

3-D view of deck-mounted sat system

Usually the chambers and LARS are mounted on the lower level of a two-level I-beam skid secured to the deck of the vessel, with the various sea containers and winches mounted on the upper level. In the 3D drawing above, the various components are labeled. Dive control is where the sat supervisor runs the actual working dives, and sat control is where the life support supervisor and crew manage the day-to-day conditions in the various chambers of the saturation system. There are other containers (vans) for the system technician's supplies (electrical and mechanical), for technician workshops, for environmental control (both heating and cooling), for life support (managing all of the system's breathing gas), and for housing electrical systems, compressors, reclaim pumps, etc. In the same way all offshore surface diving systems are maintained and inspected to IMCA D023, saturation systems are likewise maintained and inspected to their own standard, known as IMCA D024.

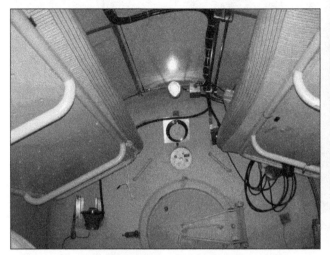

Interior of living chamber with bunks folded up
Photo courtesy of Greg Ingalls.

Gas storage tubes (Kelly Tubes) below deck
Photo courtesy of Greg Ingalls

The medical locks on the sat chambers are much larger than those on an air chamber and are used to transfer everything from hot meals and laundry to medical supplies, if required. The bell umbilical consists of many gas and fluid hoses, along with electrical and digital cables, all bundled into one tether with a woven coating (usually kevlar) to protect it from abrasion. The bell umbilical carries gas to the bell, gas to the helmets, gas from the bell, gas from the helmets, hot water to the bell and the divers, electricity to the bell and the helmets, digital video signal from the bell and helmets up to dive control, communications to and from the bell and the helmets, and bell and diver pneumo hoses. Each of these lines typically has a spare also contained within the umbilical bundle. The typical bell umbilical is over 5 inches in diameter.

Top mount saturation bell, top view

All bells are used in conjunction with a clump weight. The clump weight serves a few different purposes: it dampens any pendulum action of the bell, it keeps the bell aligned below the LARS in current, it keeps the bell from rotating as it is lowered and raised, and some clump weights have a standoff that keeps the bell up enough to allow the diver to more easily exit and enter the bell. The clump weight is also used as a secondary recovery device. If there is a main winch failure or severed main wire and umbilical, the clump weight can be used to recover the bell to the A-frame on the Bell LARS. Older systems were designed so the clump weight could recover the bell to the surface only where an air diver would be deployed to connect the crane or other lifting device to the bell. Then the bell could be recovered safely to the deck in the case of a severed wire emergency. Some LARS also have cursors or bell catchers to help maintain the alignment of the bell when moving through the moon pool or the air-water interface and help to align it on the capture flange for clamping onto the system.

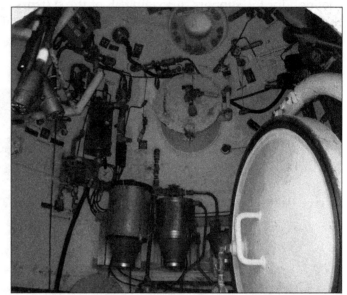

Bell interior with dive gear removed

8.4 PERSONNEL INVOLVED

The smallest saturation crew used in the past was 7, as indicated in IMCA DO22. It was the bare minimum: a supervisor, two bell divers, a surface standby and tender, and an LSS and LST. This was very rarely seen and would be utilized only for a small short-term job. The smallest saturation crew commonly seen today is 14, but most saturation crews are considerably larger than that. Every sat job now has a superintendent, four sat supervisors (6 hrs on the panel each), a life support supervisor, 2 life support technicians, 2 assistant life support techs, 2 mechanical techs, 1 electrical tech, at least 4 divers not in saturation who tend the tools for the sat divers and perform surface diving if required, and, depending on the system, either 6 or 9 divers in the system (3 – 2-man teams or 3 – 3-man teams to provide 24-hour coverage) to perform the actual diving.

The saturation superintendent is in charge of the entire operation: ensuring the safety and competence of the surface and diving crews, ensuring project productivity, and representing the diving contractor to the client. The superintendent typically lays out how a given project is to happen, and passes that information on to his sat supervisors, who ensure things happen that way.

The sat supervisor (bell dive supervisor) runs the actual dives. He/she ensures the bell and LARS are properly maintained by the techs, performs bell checks before launching, supervises the deployment and recovery of the bell, supervises all of the required predive checks on the divers, ensures the divers have sufficient gas delivery pressure, ensures the gas reclaim system is operating properly, and supervises all of the work performed during a bell deployment (bell run). The supervisor monitors the gas delivery pressure, hot water temperature, and hot water flow rate throughout the entire dive until the bell is locked back on to the system. Although the dive superintendent is in overall charge and makes the

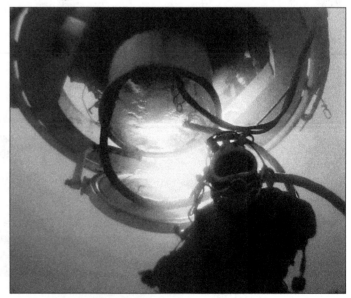

Sat diver leaving the bell
Photo courtesy of Nick Gill

call to launch the hyperbaric lifeboat in the case of an emergency, the sat supervisor that has "signed on" in the logbook as running the dive is the one legally responsible for the safety of the divers.

The life support supervisor (LSS) is responsible for pressurizing and decompressing the divers, monitoring the gas mixtures, maintaining the storage depth in the system, keeping the system's internal temperature in the proper range, and monitoring gas supplies. Once the bell locks off, the LSS has little to do with the divers. The mission of the LSS is to keep the divers alive and comfortable while in the chambers. Once the bell locks off, the sat supervisor may call upon the LSS to "change quads" that supply the diver or to change the Sodasorb in the reclaim system. Sodasorb eventually becomes saturated with CO_2 and will absorb no more CO_2. The LSS may either do this or delegate the task to the LST or ALST.

The life support technicians adjust the gas mixtures in the system (including adding oxygen as required and scrubbing carbon dioxide) as directed by the LSS. They maintain the system temperature and depth as directed by the LSS, flush the hyperbaric toilets as directed by the divers and remove the sewage, obtain meals as requested by the divers and send them in through the med lock, and look after laundry for the divers. They are helped in their duties by assistant life support technicians.

The system technician (mechanical) maintains the pressure vessels (chambers, bell, HRC), the plumbing and valves on the systems, the LARS hydraulics, and basically repairs and maintains anything mechanical on the system according to the planned maintenance system. One of the mechanical techs is certified to service the diving helmets and reclaim systems as well. The system technician (electrical) maintains all electrical and electronic systems on the sat spread, from the deck lights to the diver's helmet camera and communications.

8.5 WORKING AS AN AIR DIVER WITH A SATURATION CREW

With the trend today to work saturation in depths as shallow as 80 fsw, it is common for air divers to be kept on sat vessels as sat support crew. The air divers may be required to perform the following tasks:

- Position or recover tripod beacons for the vessel's DP system on the seafloor
- Assist with surface tending tasks (bell mating clamps, tending tool messengers, or burning gear)
- Sat system maintenance (cleaning bell, clump weight, LARS)
- Tool maintenance (cleaning and servicing hydraulic tools, burning gear, etc.)
- Work alongside and assist the saturation divers on project tasks
- Vessel-related tasks (sea-chest cleaning, etc.)
- Assist in clearing fouled gear the saturation diver cannot get to (i.e. burning gear fouled in down line near surface)

Should the air diver work as a support diver on a saturation vessel, there are a few very important points to remember:

- When asked to perform any function on the sat system (operating LARS, closing or releasing bell mating clamp), make sure you know exactly how to perform the task. If you are at all unsure, ask someone for help. If there is a way to practice first, do so.
- Never enter a surfaced bell or chamber on a sat system unless you know the oxygen level inside is safe above 16% prior to entering. A bell working at a depth of only 200 fsw surfaced for maintenance may only have an oxygen level of 7% inside. While this would be fine for a diver at 200 fsw, it will be lethal to a diver climbing in on the surface. Bells and chambers must always be flushed with air until it is suitable for entry. Test oxygen levels with a portable O_2 monitor.
- Pay attention to what is happening around you on deck, and stay alert.

9.0 EMERGENCY MEDICAL CARE (FIRST AID)

First aid is classically defined as the immediate, temporary assistance provided to a victim of injury or illness before the services of emergency medical personnel or a physician can be obtained. The purpose of first aid is to prevent further injury or worsening of the victim's condition. When an accident occurs, the proper response can mean the difference between life and death, temporary or permanent disability, and short- or long-term hospitalization. In the diving environment, due to time delays inherent in the distances from medical treatment and medical facilities, the classic definition of first aid is frequently obscured by circumstances. It is for this reason everyone involved in diving operations should have more than just an understanding of the basics of first aid. All divers should complete a comprehensive first aid and cardiopulmonary resuscitation course as offered by St John Ambulance, the National Safety Council First Aid Institute, or the American or Canadian Red Cross. More appropriately, at least one diver per crew/shift should be trained and certified as a diver medical technician; two per shift if the DMTs are performing dives.

9.1 EMERGENCY MEDICAL RESPONSE PLAN

Every diving operation requires an emergency medical response plan (EMRP). Offshore, copies of this plan are kept on the bridge of the vessel, the diving superintendent's office, and in dive control. On smaller jobs (inland and coastal), it will be kept with the diving manual. It is a printed document with an accompanying laminated flowchart, which has the following information: on-site location of medical equipment and supplies; names of designated on-board medical response personnel for each shift; names and contact information for on-call hyperbaric physician; contact information for patient transport, such as med-evac vessels or aircraft; contact details for on-call medical facility or hospital; and for smaller projects, the location of the nearest chamber. A sample EMRP is found at the end of this chapter.

9.2 MEDICAL EQUIPMENT

Most diving operations worldwide are performed according to the IMCA International Code of Practice for Offshore Diving, most often referred to as the IMCA Guideline. IMCA has a diving medical advisory committee (DMAC), which consists of hyperbaric physicians from around the world. DMAC advises the diving contractors on diver's health issues, diver's medical fitness, treatment techniques and emergency medical equipment (DMAC-diving.org). The medical kits used offshore are the DMAC trauma kit and the DMAC chamber internal medical kits The contents list for the DMAC medical kits (DMAC 15) is updated often. The current list is Revision 4 and is found in Chapter 10: Hyperbaric Emergencies.

9.3 BASIC PRINCIPLES OF EMERGENCY MEDICAL CARE

The first step in administering first aid is to evaluate the victim's condition quickly and accurately and to elect an appropriate course of action. This evaluation must be done systematically, quickly, and comprehensively. In caring for the victim of a medical or trauma emergency, there are several steps involved in immediate assessment and intervention. Too often these have been viewed as separate components. In reality, assessment and care constitute a continuum.

9.3.1 Accident Scene Safety
The first concern of any rescue operation is scene safety. When rescuers jump head first into a situation without any concern for their own safety, they often become another victim, drawing more resources and thereby fail to contribute at all to the rescue. The scene may never be completely safe, but steps can be taken to mitigate the risk. On diving operations, rescuers need to pay attention to threats to themselves first: the sea state and current, hazardous marine life, unsecured deck gear or loads, mechanical or electrical hazards, or areas with poor air quality. Once reasonably assured of rescuer and victim safety, a quick examination of the victim begins to identify problems that present an immediate threat to life. These include problems associated with ABC (airway, breathing, and circulation).

9.3.2 Primary Assessment

Once immediate threats to safety have been addressed, the victim can be tended. First, establish responsiveness. If the victim is responsive, even minimally, they obviously have a pulse and are breathing. If no response, do a quick scan of the victim to determine if he/she is breathing. At this point, there obviously exists an emergent condition and help should be summoned. Depending on the location, this could be calling 911, the Coast Guard, or radio back to the ship. Designate someone to do this task, and check for a pulse. This may require rapid removal/cutting of the exposure suit, even if it is an expensive drysuit. If there is no pulse, the treatment is simple – chest compressions. Meanwhile, another rescuer should be getting the AED and preparing the oxygen kit to assist ventilations.

9.3.3 Secondary Assessment

Once immediate threats to a victim's life have been corrected or eliminated, a more comprehensive examination is carried out. In a trauma victim, this is a thorough head-to-toe evaluation of all body parts and systems. In a medical emergency, the secondary survey may be more focused on those body parts and systems that have the greatest likelihood of being involved based on the victim's chief complaint. It is possible during the secondary survey, the rescuer may identify problems that, if left unchecked, might develop into life-threatening circumstances. During this phase of the care continuum, additional treatment and stabilization may be provided beyond that initiated during the initial assessment. Never should an assessment delay transport by the EMS to an appropriate medical facility. Although generally not viewed as a part of out-of-hospital emergency medical care, it is possible that even though the rescuer is not a medical professional, he/she may be called upon to deliver definitive care in the diving setting.

9.3.4 Infection Control

It is important to eliminate direct contact with the casualty's blood or other bodily fluids, mucous membranes, wounds, or burns. The tools that rescuers should employ to protect themselves include the following:

- Good quality, disposable latex, nitrile, or vinyl gloves. Fit is not as critical as protection. If gloves are too small, there is the risk of having the gloves tear when being applied or during use, an event to be avoided at all costs.

- A pocket mask with a one-way valve (and an oxygen adapter) should it be necessary to provide artificial ventilation to the victim using the mouth and lungs as the means for restoring or supplementing the victim's breathing. The pocket mask is the minimum required – a bag valve mask is a better choice.

- Eye protection in the form of eyeglasses that are wide enough to prevent fluids from becoming splashed in the eyes. More appropriately, medical kits used in the diving environment should contain inexpensive goggles designed for emergency medical care.

- A disposable, medical face mask will prevent the inhalation of infectious organisms in airborne droplets. Though in the marine setting the rescuer is unlikely to encounter such situations, there are certain infections for which a face mask may also be appropriately put on the victim as well as the rescuer—meningitis and tuberculosis, for example.

Each of these items is relatively inexpensive and should be a part of a personal kit or the medical kit carried on board every boat.

9.4 THE PRIMARY SURVEY – A DETAILED LOOK

If the body loses its ability to take in oxygen and release carbon dioxide through the respiratory system or can no longer move life-sustaining oxygen through the circulatory system, then tissues and organs and, eventually, the person will die. Likewise, if there is no detectable circulation, the patient may die. The main purpose of the primary assessment is the establishment and/or maintenance of an adequate airway, to ensure the victim is breathing, and adequate circulation is present. These are the first steps to take in BLS (basic life support), also known to many as cardiopulmonary resuscitation (CPR). In 2010, the AHA (American Heart Association) changed the ABC's to "CAB" (compressions, airway, breathing) based on clinical and evidence-based research. The first step is to determine whether the victim has only fainted. Assuming there are no signs/symptoms of injury to suggest spinal trauma, roll the victim into a face-up position on a firm surface like the deck of a boat or the firm sand on a beach. Gently shake the victim and shout, "Are you OK?" Should trauma be a possibility, spinal stabilization must be considered. In such cases, do not shake the victim but tap on the victim's shoulder firmly and shout. If the victim has only fainted, he/she will usually regain consciousness immediately or soon after lying down. If the victim does not respond or regain consciousness, ask bystanders to notify whatever emergency medical services are available. If the victim regains consciousness and is breathing adequately, then continue to the initial assessment, again provided no life-threatening bleeding is present. The rescuer should perform a scan of the victim looking for breathing and other signs of life. Rescuers trained in BLS for the HCP (health care provider) are trained to check for a pulse at this point. If not trained in this procedure, proceed directly to compressions if no signs of life are present. The action, once known as "look-listen-feel," has been removed from the BLS algorithm. By performing CAB, the first step has been taken in the performance of BLS. CAB is broken down into the following steps:

- **Compressions**: As soon as it has been determined the patient is unresponsive and not breathing, chest compressions must be administered. Without spontaneous heartbeat, the oxygen being supplied through the lungs cannot reach the body's tissues and organs. According to 2010 AHA guidelines, begin with 30 chest compressions, followed with 2 breaths. Chest compressions should be started immediately if there is no breathing or if there is only agonal breathing, which are slow, gasping-type breaths. If trained, such as in BLS for the HCP, a pulse may be checked. However, if there is any question that a pulse may be absent, or if one is not sure they feel a pulse, chest compressions should be started immediately. Chest compressions should be done at a rate of at least 100 per minute and at least 2 in. in depth.

- **Airway**: To open the victim's airway, use the head-tilt, chin-lift method, which puts a hand (the one closest to the victim's head) on the victim's forehead, while two or three fingers of the other hand are placed under the bony portion of the victim's jaw. By lifting with the fingers under the jaw and at the same time, pressing gently on the victim's forehead, the head is tilted back into a hyper-extended position. This lifts the tongue and keeps it from blocking the airway of the victim. Sometimes, opening the airway is enough to start the victim breathing spontaneously.

Ensure the victim is conscious enough to maintain his/her airway or manually open the airway to make certain it is maintained. If it is suspected there might be injury to the victim's cervical spine, a special method for opening the airway should be employed as follows:

If it is suspected the victim may have sustained a spinal injury, then the technique used for opening the airway is called the "jaw thrust maneuver." Take both thumbs, and place them pointing downward on the large bones under the victim's eyes – the cheek bones. With the thumbs in this position, the rescuer should be able to get his/her fingers behind the victim's jaw at the point where the bend in the lower jaw, or mandible, can be felt. With the thumbs and fingers in this position, and using the opposing forces of the thumb against the fingers, the rescuer will be able to move the jaw forward. This will lift the tongue off the back of the throat and establish an open airway. All of this must be done without any manipulation of the spine, which must be maintained in a neutral position.

- **Breathing**: Once an adequate airway has been established, then breathing must be evaluated and either restored or aided. If the victim is not breathing, initiate ventilations according to the agency you were trained by, which in most cases is 1 breath every 3-5 seconds if giving rescue breaths only, or 2 breaths per 30 chest compressions if performing CPR. Use an oxygen-powered positive pressure valve or a bag-valve mask connected to an oxygen source. If neither of these are available, perform mouth-to-mask ventilations. Ideally, all victims should receive supplemental oxygen as part of breathing restoration, but this is particularly true when dealing with a diving emergency.

After each ventilation, allow the victim to passively exhale. To ventilate the patient, use a pocket mask, tru-fit mask, or other oral-nasal type mask. To seal the mask on the victim's face, make the OK sign to demonstrate the preferred hand position for the hand grasping the mask device. The thumb and index finger circle the port through which the rescuer ventilates the victim while the remaining fingers are used to assist in maintaining the seal of the mask over the victim's face.

The circular device appearing above the thumb and index finger is the one-way valve incorporated in the mask, which prevents the victim's exhaled air or other expired or regurgitated matter from entering the caregiver's mouth or airway. Use of these one-way valves is consistent with the concept of self-protection when providing care to a victim. The oral-nasal mask is placed over the victim's mouth and nose, with the opening of the breathing tube directly over the victim's mouth. The fingers of the right hand are used to lift the jaw, while the left hand is on the forehead. Even with the pocket mask device, the head-tilt, chin-lift technique must be utilized to maintain an open airway. With the left and right hands in proper position, the caregiver ventilates the victim for 1½ to 2 seconds per ventilation and allows the victim to exhale passively between breaths. Using peripheral vision, the caregiver can also monitor chest rise with each ventilation to be certain the breaths are properly entering the victim's lungs. If chest rise is not observed during efforts to ventilate, the head-tilt, chin-lift maneuver should be repeated, since the airway may be blocked by the victim's tongue or other anatomic structures. If such repositioning does not result in successful ventilation of the victim, then there may be an airway obstruction that cannot be corrected by repositioning. In these cases, the foreign body airway obstruction technique learned in formal CPR training should be employed.

Next, it is vital to determine if there is life-threatening bleeding; if such bleeding is found, it must be stopped. Once a conscious victim can speak clearly, seems to be properly oriented to the surroundings, and there is no obvious life-threatening bleeding, the primary assessment has been completed.

9.4.1 Emergency Airway Management and Artificial Ventilation

It is desirable to have the victim's airway maintenance supplemented by using an oropharyngeal airway if, as a part of the life support provided, artificial ventilations are required. Ventilations may be provided using mouth-to-mask ventilation, or more preferably, ventilation utilizing a manually-triggered, oxygen-powered positive pressure/demand valve or a bag-valve mask connected to an oxygen source. If the victim is breathing, then a decision must be made whether the breathing is adequate or if some supplemental ventilation is required. Most victims of serious illness or injury will be breathing relatively rapidly. In some cases, this is a positive finding, but if the victim is breathing too rapidly, there may not be enough air moving in and out of the lungs with each breath. In such cases, the breathing must be managed. Using a watch, count the number of breaths the victim takes during 15 seconds. Multiply that by four to determine the number of times the victim is breathing each minute. If the victim is breathing at a rate of less than ten breaths per minute and is symptomatic, supplementing respirations may be required.

9.4.2 Adult One-Rescuer CPR

Artificial ventilation is done by mouth-to-mouth resuscitation or utilizing a supplemental device as described above, while artificial circulation is done by external cardiac massage. Together, they are called CPR. Though the material presented here is thorough, every diver should complete a CPR course from a recognized training agency. Some of those include the American National Red Cross, American Heart Association, and National Safety Council First Aid Institute.

CPR's goal is to supply the victim's body with oxygen and rid the body of excess carbon dioxide. The purpose of CPR may also include the establishment and maintenance of the victim's circulation until more advanced life support can be initiated or until normal breathing and heartbeat are restored. Once begun, CPR is continued until relieved by emergency medical services personnel or until the rescuer is unable to continue.

For the sake of simplicity, this discussion deals exclusively with one rescuer CPR. In the event CPR is required for an extended period of time, other divers can continue one rescuer CPR should the rescuer become overly fatigued. If trained in HCP BLS, check the victim's pulse. Otherwise assess respirations as previously described and begin chest compressions as instructed by your BLS course. Do this by sliding two fingertips gently into the groove-like indentation between the trachea (windpipe) and the large muscle (sternocleidomastoid) running down the side of the victim's neck. If the heart is beating adequately, a pulse may be felt in a major artery found in this anatomic landmark – the carotid artery. Take 5 to 10 seconds to detect the victim's pulse before going any further. The 5-to-10-second delay serves two purposes. First, it may take a few seconds to discern a weak pulse. Second, if the victim's heart is beating slowly but still beating spontaneously, it may take that long to feel more than one pulse beat. This would be true in cases of severe hypothermia and certain depressant drug overdose. If there is a pulse, then the victim's heart is still beating, and chest compressions are not needed.

However, if the victim is still not breathing, then give the victim rescue breaths at a rate of 1 breath every 5 seconds (8-10 breaths per minute). Check the pulse every few minutes to be certain the victim's heart is still beating. It is generally believed that, in an adult, the presence of a pulse in the carotid artery is consistent with a blood pressure adequate to keep the brain sufficiently perfused. If a pulse is present, the victim has blood pressure sufficient to sustain life. If no pulse is felt, then the victim's heart is not beating, or it is not beating adequately. Another possibility is the victim's heart is not beating in an organized fashion and may require defibrillation. Initiate chest compressions along with ventilations. Expose the victim's chest, if it is not already bared. Place the heel of the other hand, which is closest to the victim's head, on the lower half of the sternum, with the other hand placed on top of the first. It helps to interlock your fingers to avoid putting pressure on the ribs. Compress the sternum at a rate of at least 100 compressions per minute. Each compression should be at least 2 in. in depth. After compressing the victim's chest for 30 strokes, ventilate the victim 2 more times and then continue alternating 30 chest compressions with 2 ventilations. After 5 cycles of compressions and ventilations, recheck the pulse. If the pulse has returned, stop chest compressions but continue artificial ventilations as needed. If there has been no return of pulse, then the victim should be ventilated and chest compressions and artificial ventilation should continue in the same 30:2 configuration. CPR is continued in this manner until the victim begins to breathe spontaneously or if the rescuer is too weak to continue, is relieved by someone else who knows how to do cardiopulmonary resuscitation, or the victim is placed in the care of emergency medical services personnel.

9.4.3 Early Defibrillation

CPR by itself may not be adequate to save lives in cardiac arrest. The 1992 National Conference on Cardiopulmonary Resuscitation (CPR) and Emergency Cardiac Care (ECC) concluded more widespread use of early defibrillation intervention was needed. While basic CPR prolongs the life of the victim for a few minutes, most victims of sudden cardiac arrest will not ultimately survive unless there is further intervention. An automated external defibrillator (AED) should be kept on site at all commercial diving operations. Sudden death secondary to cardiac disease is a leading cause of death in the United States. If all the links in what is called the "chain of survival" are intact, it is estimated about 49% of all victims of sudden cardiac death might survive to discharge. The critical links in the chain of survival include:

- Early recognition of the problem and mobilization of the EMS response
- Early CPR intervention
- Early defibrillation
- Early advanced cardiac life support

According to the AHA guidelines, a diver trained in CPR can be instrumental in performing the key functions in the first three links in the chain, i.e. call for help, CAB, and defibrillation. Certain heart rhythm abnormalities respond favorably to the delivery of a direct current shock through the heart muscle. One of these rhythms is called ventricular fibrillation. The heart quivers without any blood being pumped. The AHA guidelines state, "the majority (80–90%) of adults with sudden, non-traumatic, cardiac arrest are found to be in ventricular fibrillation when the initial electrocardiogram is obtained." Most survivors of ventricular fibrillation receive early defibrillation. Survival dramatically falls if the first defibrillation effort is not delivered within 8-10 minutes of the initial arrest. The emphasis on early defibrillation is so great, the implication of the 2010 report is optimally, automated external defibrillators should be available to deal with sudden cardiac death.

The AED is a medical device that not only analyzes a victim's cardiac rhythm but also guides the rescuer through the steps to deliver the potentially lifesaving shock. Automated external defibrillators sold today are described as semiautomatic in their method of operation. The semiautomatic defibrillator analyzes the cardiac rhythm and determines if a shock is warranted. The shock cannot be delivered without some physical action by the rescuer. The material below shows the steps in the utilization of this device. (Note: As with most material in this section, the brief presentation does not constitute training but provides material to supplement appropriate training by the agencies previously cited.)

Automated defibrillators not only analyze cardiac rhythms but also provide voice prompts to the caregiver. For example, some of the "spoken" computer-generated commands heard from the automated defibrillator's speaker include: "stand clear," "analyzing," "charging," "press to shock," "check pulse," "start CPR," "stop CPR," "check victim," etc.

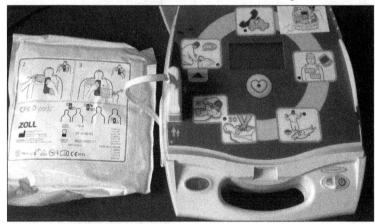

AED unit, with a sealed package of single use pads
Photo courtesy of John McElligott

The victim is checked for responsiveness, breathing, and pulse. In the non-breathing and pulseless victim, ensure someone has activated the EMS system. At the same time, have someone bring the automatic defibrillator to the victim and place it beside the victim. If there is more than a momentary delay until the automated defibrillator is deployed, perform basic CPR and, if possible, the victim's breathing should be supported with supplemental oxygen.

The automated defibrillator, due to its sophisticated computer technology, is not the sort of device a diver will purchase. However, on projects that fall under the IMCA guidelines, AED units, as well as trauma kits, are a requirement on all dive support and offshore construction vessels. A list of contents for these DMAC trauma kits may be found in Chapter 10: Hyperbaric Emergencies.

9.4.4 Stopping Life-Threatening Bleeding

Once the presence of a pulse and the patient airway and breathing have been verified, the last phase of the primary assessment/intervention is control of any visible, life-threatening, or severe bleeding. It is unusual that any external bleeding will require care beyond direct pressure to the site of the bleeding and, if the injury is to an extremity, lifting it above the level of the heart. It is important, particularly when bleeding is present, to be cognizant of the infection risks and take the steps necessary for protection. Remove the disposable gloves from their packaging and put gloves on before proceeding.

Provided there is time, a sterile dressing should be removed from its packaging in a manner to maintain sterility. The sterile dressing should be firmly held against the wound with a gloved hand, and, if the wound is in an extremity, the extremity should be lifted above the level of the victim's heart. The force of gravity working against the movement of blood will, in a small part, contribute to the slowing of the rate of bleeding. If direct pressure with the dressing substantially slows but does not entirely stop the bleeding, do not remove the dressing. Instead, apply another dressing on top of the blood-soaked dressing and continue this process until the soaking of the dressings subsides or until it is determined more aggressive methods must be employed to stop the bleeding.

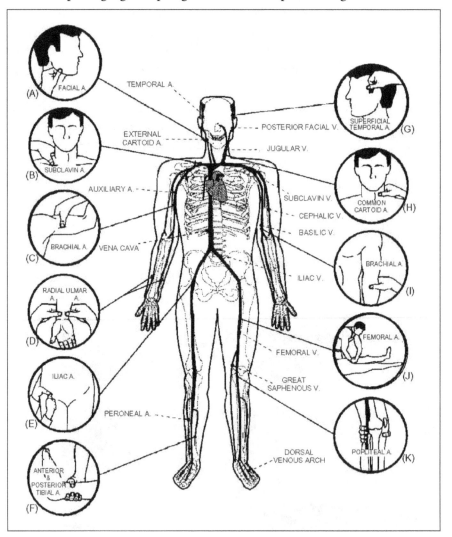

Pressure Points
Source: *U.S. Navy Diving Manual*

If direct pressure and elevation do not significantly reduce the rate of the flow of blood, then it may be necessary to use alternative means to stop the bleeding. If the uncontrolled bleeding is in the upper arm, pressure should be applied to the brachial artery, found on the inside of the upper arm. Apply pressure where there is a pulse. This will compress the artery against the bone of the upper arm. The pressure point to use for bleeding in the leg is the femoral artery. Feel along the crease in the groin on the inside of the upper leg to find a pulse. Use the heel of one hand to compress the artery against the bone.

A tourniquet is the absolute last resort in an effort to control bleeding from an extremity. The "litmus test" to determine if the use of the tourniquet is needed is when the risk of the loss of a portion of the limb is an acceptable tradeoff for the stopping of the bleeding. A 3- to 4-inch band of cloth makes a good tourniquet, usually a triangular bandage folded into a cravat. The cravat should be placed between the victim's heart and the wound, about one inch above the wound. The cravat is wrapped around the extremity and an overhand knot is tied in the cravat to hold it in place. A stout stick is needed, or on a boat, a wrench is usually available, at least 6 in. in length. Place it over the overhand knot and tie it in place with a square knot. Twist the stick in circles until the bleeding stops. Once the bleeding has stopped, take another cravat and use it to tie the stick in place. Remember, the tourniquet is a last-ditch effort to stop bleeding that cannot be stopped by direct pressure, elevation, or the use of pressure points. There are also several commercially manufactured tourniquets on the market. Be certain the direct pressure and elevation method or pressure on an arterial pressure point have been given adequate time before making the decision to apply a tourniquet.

If the tourniquet is used as other than a short-term, stop-gap measure, take a marking device and write the initials "TQ" on the victim's forehead as well as the time the tourniquet was applied. Finally, in preparing the victim for transport, never allow the tourniquet to be covered since it may be missed or accidentally dislodged. Keeping the tourniquet in sight will make all those involved in the care or handling of the victim aware of the tourniquet's presence.

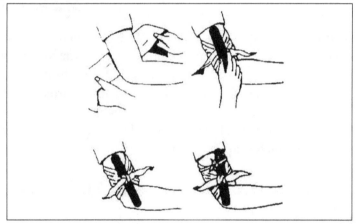

Applying a tourniquet
Source: *U.S. Navy Diving Manual*

9.4.5 Managing the Victim with Suspected Spinal Injury

Always consider the possibility that in-water trauma may have caused injury to the victim's spinal cord. Some mechanisms of possible spinal injury include the victim's head hitting the bottom of a boat, victim struck by a crane load, boat, or watercraft, or victim thrown around uncontrollably in the surf. These examples presume a spinal cord injury has taken place, and inappropriate management of the victim may lead to further and permanently disabling injury.

The section of the spinal cord most frequently injured in such accidents is the cervical spine, the section of the spinal column in the neck. The most critical aspect of managing such victims is maintaining the cervical spine in a neutral inline position. A rescuer should try to keep the victim's neck in a position that approximates the normal position the neck is in when the victim is standing upright with the head looking straight forward.

When moving a victim in the water, manual support to keep the head in that position is supplemented by the buoyant effect of the water. The water can provide some of the splinting effect necessary. In the water, cradle the victim's head between your forearms while stabilizing the head relative to the spine by placing your hands on the victim's torso. It is impossible to stabilize the cervical spine by holding only the head while floating in the water. It is important that the rescuer get assistance in managing such a victim immediately, since maintaining a victim in this position, while keeping the body aligned, is difficult to do alone. In wading water, the victim needs to be towed with one arm being utilized to stabilize the spine, while the other hand is used to maintain the head in a neutral position. Again, assistance of other trained individuals or bystanders should be enlisted as soon as possible. If the victim is otherwise stable, the victim should be maintained in the water until additional assistance arrives with appropriate equipment for removing the victim from the water and replacing the manual stabilization technique being employed.

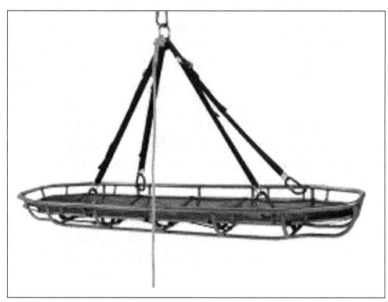

Aluminum Stokes litter c/w lift harness
Photo courtesy of CMC Rescue

Removing a victim from the water can be a difficult process, particularly if the victim needs to be lifted over a gunwale or transom. After getting the maximum amount of help, stabilize the victim onto a backboard or basket litter (Stokes litter). A door from one of the boat's hatches might be removed from its hinges and used for this purpose if no Stokes litter is available. While still in the water, use the slings on the Stokes litter (or appropriate lifting device) and lift the victim from the water with the recovery winch or other davit. The best method is to firmly tie the Stokes litter down in the LARS basket at water level, and winch it up onboard.

9.5 THE SECONDARY SURVEY - A COMPLETE VICTIM ASSESSMENT

9.5.1 The Head-To-Toe Examination

The secondary survey is initiated after completing primary victim care, having identified and managed those problems which might be life threatening. The secondary survey by first responders in the field should never delay formal EMS transport to an emergency department. If EMS personnel have not arrived and time permits, the secondary survey should proceed.

A rescuer reevaluates the victim to be certain no potentially life-threatening problems were missed during primary victim care. Problems not life threatening should be identified and managed, and then noted at the conclusion of the secondary survey. During this integrated process, the victim is interviewed to learn any significant facts regarding the victim's medical history and what caused the problem.

For a victim suffering an illness, the secondary survey may take on a different pattern than for the victim suffering from injury (trauma). The trauma victim requires a complete head-to-toe check, while in illness emergency surveys, a rescuer will generally focus on those parts of the body the victim is complaining about. This discussion will explain the secondary survey as it relates to a trauma victim. If you want to use these techniques on an illness victim, use any applicable procedures that would apply to the part of the body about which the victim is complaining. In both injury and illness.

The eyes and hands are the tools every rescuer will need to conduct a secondary survey. Visualization and recognition of abnormalities, as well as touching the victim, are the primary methods used by every caregiver, including physicians. Remove all unnecessary body covering so the victim's body surfaces can be seen and touched. In all cases, this is done with discretion and concern for the victim's emotional and physical welfare. If it is necessary to remove a woman's clothing, for example, be careful to cover her breasts with a sheet or towel in the interest of modesty. The same sensitivity applies when the genital area of either sex is exposed. If a wetsuit must be removed, start by cutting at the neck of the suit down the sleeve. Removal of coverings to expose the victim begins at the upper body since there is greater risk to the victim from injuries to the neck, chest, and abdomen than from injuries to the lower extremities. As much as possible, cut apparel at or near the seams so that the wetsuit or garment may possibly be repaired later. However, never jeopardize the victim for the sake of a garment. As garments are removed, constantly scan the victim's exposed body for signs of injury. Rather than exposing a little of the victim and assessing, it will keep the process more organized and more thorough to expose the victim all at once. Then return to the victim's head to begin the thorough head-to-toe evaluation.

Using proper personal protective equipment, begin the secondary assessment of the victim by gently palpating (feeling) the victim's scalp and noting any deformities or places where fluid that may be blood is present. External bleeding hidden by the hair will be evident from the appearance of blood on the gloved fingers. Note any reaction the victim may have to being touched that appears to indicate feeling pain. Examine the ears for any bleeding or discharge.

Next, slide both hands to the back of the victim's neck to feel for any noticeable deformities and any indication that pain is present. If it appears an injury mechanism may have caused injury to the spine, or if neck pain response is elicited, stabilize the neck. Enlist the assistance of another caregiver or a bystander to hold the victim's head in a neutral position. Additionally, if the victim is conscious and oriented, caution the victim of the importance that no head movement take place since it might lead to further injury.

Using your hand, cover one of the victim's eyes. While doing so, watch the pupil (black, central portion of the eye) to observe if it dilated (got larger) while it was shaded. If it did not, it may indicate some serious problems either to the eye itself or the brain. When the hand shading the eye is removed, the pupil should constrict (get smaller). This procedure should be repeated with the other eye. Again, failure of the pupil to react in this fashion is a sign of possible abnormality and should be noted.

Move the fingers down to the prominent bones under the eyes and press gently. Feel for deformity and watch the victim for a response to pain when these bones are pressed. While doing this segment of the assessment, also examine the nostrils for the discharge of blood-like fluid. Do one side of the victim's face and then the other, so as to specifically identify an area where an injury has occurred.

The victim's mouth should be opened either voluntarily or by the rescuer. Note any pain when the victim's mouth is opened and examine the inside of mouth for any debris, broken teeth, blood clots, etc. If any loose or foreign matter is noticed, carefully remove it with your fingers. Be careful not to push such material deeper into the victim's airway, and do not reach too far back into the victim's throat to remove the object or vomiting may be stimulated.

Examine the front portion of the neck visually for open wounds or signs of injury, such as abrasions or discoloration. The entire neck should be gently palpated with the finger tips, particularly in diving accidents. If little blister-pack-like bubbles are felt under the skin or noises that sound like Rice Krispies® are heard when pressing on the tissues, it probably indicates the presence of subcutaneous emphysema, the presence of free air bubbles under the skin. This is usually found in severe lung injuries where air has escaped from the lungs and chest cavity and migrated under the skin to the neck region.

A visual scan of the skin over the collarbone (clavicle) is performed to identify injuries or discoloration, usually bruising, consistent with injury. Use fingers to press gently along the length of each collarbone, the most commonly fractured bone in the body. By checking these bones and others separately rather than using both hands and doing them simultaneously, the rescuer only has to elicit a painful response from the victim once, since it is evident when palpating a victim unilaterally which side the injury is on. If both bones are palpated at the same time and the victim is not completely lucid, a painful response may be difficult to isolate relative to location without repeating the stimulation that caused pain.

Re-examine the chest. Remember it was visually scanned at the time the garments were removed. If any open wounds are noted that look like they are through the chest wall or are bubbling, have someone place a gloved hand over the wound to prevent further passage of air in and out. Later, after the examination is complete, the bystander's hand can be replaced with some form of dressing which will prevent air from entering the chest. The Asherman Chest Seal®, developed by a U.S. Navy SEAL, is a device specifically designed for rapid treatment of such chest injuries.

Use one hand to stabilize the chest on the side opposite the section of the chest that will be palpated. Use fingers to feel for each rib to be palpated. In finding a rib, pressure should be applied and the rib evaluated for stability. Does it feel loose or are there pieces of a broken rib rubbing against neighboring, damaged bone? This process is repeated for every rib that can be felt, and then is done in exactly the same fashion on the other side. In addition to feeling for lack of stability, watch for a painful response from the victim.

Imagine there are two lines drawn on the front of the victim's body. One of these lines goes from the chin down the middle of the body through the belly button. These two imaginary lines subdivide the victim's abdomen into four quadrants. First visually scan the abdomen for signs of injury, and then palpate each of these four quadrants separately, noting if it is hard, is stiffened by the victim when pressed upon, or causes a painful response from the victim when pressed on. A rigid abdomen is typically a sign of internal bleeding and represents a serious medical emergency. Each quadrant of the abdomen is palpated separately. Mentally note the findings. Other than managing any open wounds found on the abdomen, the rescuer's only role in this phase of the assessment is to identify anything abnormal.

When reporting the findings to emergency medical services personnel, describe in which of the four areas of the abdomen the findings were present. Going back to the imaginary lines from above, the abdomen is described as the right upper quadrant (RUQ), left upper quadrant (LUQ), right lower quadrant (RLQ), and left lower quadrant (LLQ). Left and right in this regard, as in all other descriptions relative to left and right on a victim, refer to the victim's right and left. The major organs of the RUQ are the liver and the gall bladder. The LUQ contains the stomach and the spleen. The appendix is found in the RLQ. Small and large intestine can be found in both of the lower quadrants, with the major structure in the LLQ being the terminal segments of the large intestine. The urinary bladder is located in the middle of the bottom of the abdomen as is a woman's uterus. The female reproductive organs and ovaries are found in both the RLQ and the LLQ.

Now place both palms on the "wings" of the pelvis (anatomically described as the superior iliac crests). With hands in this position, push them toward each other and "squeeze" the pelvis toward the middle of the victim's body, noting any feeling of instability or any painful response.

If the above evaluation did not elicit any response from the victim, shift position slightly so that your body is over the victim's pelvis and shift hand position slightly. With the hands in this position, push on both sides of the pelvis simultaneously. Again, try to note any instability of the pelvis and any painful response on the part of the victim.

Visually examine each leg, looking for any obvious deformity of the legs and joints, unevenness in size (indicating swelling), open wounds, abrasions, or bruising. With both hands, palpate the entire length of each leg separately. This palpation should be fairly deep since the objective is to feel for the bones underneath. One must at least press deeply enough to stimulate a painful response to pressure from the victim if injury is present.

Having completed the visual and manual evaluation of each leg, use one hand to stabilize the bottom of the legend if the victim is conscious, ask the victim to wiggle his/her toes on the leg being held. Then stroke the foot with fingertips and ask the victim if the touch was felt. This procedure is then repeated on the opposite leg. This method is used to determine if the nerves to the leg are functioning properly from a sensory standpoint and whether or not the victim is capable of voluntarily moving the lower extremities, also a nerve-involved assessment step.

Now evaluate the victim's arms. As with all other parts of the body, the first step is to visually scan the arms for obvious deformities or injuries. Next, in a fashion similar to the procedure used with the legs, the bones of the arms are palpated, checking one arm at a time.

Finally, the arm is stabilized with one hand similar to the leg procedure. Ask the victim to wiggle his/her fingers first, then stroke the hand with your fingers and ask the victim if the touch can be felt. This procedure is performed on both arms. Similar to the steps used for the legs, this procedure determines if the nerve pathways to and from the arms are intact. When reaching the victim's wrist, feel for the presence of a radial pulse. This pulse is found on the underside of the arm at the same side of the wrist where the thumb is on the hand. If a pulse is present, it is a good sign the victim's blood pressure is not dangerously low. If a watch is available, count the pulse beats in 15 seconds. Taking that number and multiplying by four will yield the victim's heart rate for one minute. Alternatively, count the pulses for 30 seconds and double the result. If there are no injuries to the lower extremities and no head injury, it may be appropriate to elevate the lower extremities. This allows gravity to assist with the shifting of some of the victim's blood from the legs to the body core. If the victim complains of increased discomfort in the head or the victim finds it more difficult to breathe with the legs in this position, then the victim should be maintained in a flat position.

If no pulse is felt at the wrist on either arm, the victim may be in shock. If so, oxygen needs to be administered as soon as possible, as well as measures taken to conserve the victim's body heat. The technical definition of shock is inadequate tissue perfusion. The circulatory system is incapable of delivering adequate oxygen and nutrients to the tissues, most significantly the vital organs. At the same time, potentially toxic byproducts of the body's metabolism are no longer being removed adequately. The grave results of this process, without appropriate recognition and intervention, may be death to tissues, organs, or in the most extreme cases, the victim. The simplest means of identifying impending or present shock is observable in the physical appearance of the victim along with an increased heart rate. A drop in blood pressure is also a significant sign of shock but may only occur later.

The body's natural defenses against shock will cause the victim to appear pale and the skin will feel cool to the touch. The victim's skin surface will usually be moist (often described as clammy). This victim needs immediate, aggressive care which, for the most part, is beyond the scope of the basic caregiver. The principal steps to take when shock is suspected include the following:

- Keep the victim lying down.
- Prevent the loss of body heat, and make sure the victim is dry to limit evaporative heat loss.
- Administer oxygen to the victim as soon as these signs of shock are recognized.

The pulse should be felt at the neck and the heart rate determined by counting those pulses for 15 or 30 seconds and multiplying as described above.

Now, observe the rise and fall of the victim's chest and count the number of respirations in 15 seconds, multiplying in the same way as with the pulse. The victim's breathing rate may be assessed.

The last step in the secondary assessment or survey is to record the findings. On a smaller vessel or open boat, a dive slate is the best device to record information. The slate is waterproof, so the notes will not disintegrate if they get wet and the ink will not smear. On a larger vessel or an inland project, pen and paper will do fine.

All information is recorded: the presence or absence of motor control, feeling in the four limbs, the presence or absence of a radial pulse, heart rate, and breathing rate. Also record observations relative to "what happened" to cause the victim's condition. If decompression sickness is suspected, a complete neurological assessment should be performed by a diver medic if the victim is in stable condition.

9.5.2 Taking the Necessary History

Aside from the immediate medical or injury problems (medically referred to as acute conditions), it is also important for all medical caregivers to know something about the victim's medical history that might have some relevance to the current problem. If, during the secondary survey, problems have been identified that require treatment quickly, then the performing of the medical history interview can be delayed until those conditions are cared for. Some examples of problems that might need immediate attention are listed below.

- The victim's airway or breathing is deteriorating.
- The victim's overall condition is failing, consistent with shock.
- Wounds need to have bleeding stopped and dressings applied.
- Injuries to the bones or joints need to be splinted.
- Diving illnesses need the immediate administration of oxygen.
- Marine life injuries need immediate treatment in order to relieve significant victim discomfort.

Failing any of the problems listed above, the victim history taking interview should follow immediately after recording the findings from the primary and secondary assessments.

First, explain to the victim the importance of obtaining the medical history. Both EMTs and DMTs use a mnemonic to easily learn the necessary components of the complete medical history. The mnemonic is SAMPLE, and each letter represents a vital component of the victim's medical history.

S - Signs and symptoms (signs are visible to the medic; symptoms are what the victim tells the medic)

A - Allergies

M - Medications.

P - Past illnesses or injuries; past medical history

L - Last meal or last oral intake

E - Events leading up to the injury or illness

As part of the medical history interview, the victim should describe his/her symptoms. Is pain present? If so, what does it feel like? Does anything make the pain worse or better? How long has the pain been present and has its intensity changed during that period? Does the pain remain in one place or does it seem to radiate or travel to other parts of the body? Have the patient rate the pain on a scale of 0 to 10, with 10 being the worst pain possible.

All information learned during this part of the interview should be recorded and related to medical care personnel, who assume responsibility for the victim. Signs and symptoms include the patient's chief complaint, location and severity of pain, and allergies. Allergies are important as some acute allergic reactions, called anaphylactic responses, may trigger breathing difficulties and may also lead to the victim slipping into a severe shock state. Sometimes, people have such reactions from the consumption of certain seafood. At other times, stinging insects may precipitate allergic reactions in people. In the marine setting, though quite rare, true anaphylactic reactions have been observed after a victim has sustained a marine life sting. If the victim does have an allergic history from bites and stings or past allergic reactions to certain foods, it is important to monitor the victim closely. Be on the alert for breathing difficulties or severe deterioration of the victim, since this may be the early signs of a major crisis.

A rescuer is not expected to know what certain medications do, but a rescuer should know why a victim is taking certain medications. If a victim is taking "water" or "pressure" pills, there may be a history of heart or high blood pressure problems, which may have caused the present emergency. If the victim takes "sugar" pills or medication for "sugar," suspect diabetes. Low blood sugar (hypoglycemia) may be a cause of instability in both diabetics and non-diabetics alike. People with seizure disorders should not be cleared for diving. Persons with epilepsy may take medications such as Dilantin®, Tegretol®, or phenobarbital. Divers who have trouble clearing their ears while diving sometimes use decongestants. These medications have a finite effect which may wear off while diving. This can carry a "rebound effect," which may contribute to a diving related injury.

In the diving and marine environment, the illnesses that may lead to serious problems include heart disease, respiratory diseases (such as asthma), high blood pressure (hypertension), diabetes, and seizure disorders.

What a victim has ingested orally may be a cause of a victim's difficulty. Determine whether the victim has eaten within a reasonable period of time prior to the illness or injury. In the marine setting, ingestion of certain marine life can lead to various illnesses. Dehydration has been implicated as a contributing factor to diving injuries. Question a diving injury victim relative to adequate non-alcoholic fluid intake during the prior 24 hours. Alcohol or other drugs of abuse may be contributors to a victim's injuries. Query the victim relative to the use of alcohol or drugs during the period of time coincident with the injury or illness.

Perhaps the most significant part of the medical history interview involves events leading up to the injury or illness. This is the "what happened" part of the interview. In diving accidents, it is important to learn the dive profile, not that it influences treatment, but to avoid a repeat of the problem. The diving equipment the victim was using should be kept together in one place, just in case investigators require it for inspection.

In the case of non-diving related trauma, it is significant to ask the victim if everything was normal before the injury. Was the injury an accident or was there some medical problem that precipitated the victim's injury. It may be useful to learn what caused the accident resulting in the trauma in order to prevent future similar accidents. As far as possible, record in the victim's own words what took place before an accident. What activity was the victim involved in? Was the victim at rest or performing a specific strenuous activity? What had the victim been doing in the hours immediately preceding the onset of illness? Did the victim notice any unusual feelings during those hours that were not normal but did not seem too severe?

9.6 ELECTROCUTION

Electrocution may result from the careless handling, poor design, or poor maintenance of power equipment such as welding and cutting equipment or electric underwater lights. All electrical equipment used underwater should be well insulated. In addition, divers should be properly insulated from any possible source of electrical current.

Another source of electrocution and electrical burns is lightning. Prevention of electrocution from lightning is a matter of divers not permitting themselves to remain out in the open, particularly on a small open boat, when there is obviously the threat of lightning from thunderstorms. The IMCA Guideline recommends ceasing diving operations at the first sign of an electrical storm. When seeking shelter from storms, it is important to avoid places and structures where one might reasonably expect lightning to strike (i.e. under trees or in structures that stand alone in an open area).

When leaving the water to board a vessel, divers should not carry an energized electric tool, surface powered light, or welding lead. Victims often are not able to separate themselves from the source of the shock. Before intervening, the rescuer must be certain he/she will not be exposed to an electrocution hazard. When attempting to separate the electrocution victim from the source of the electricity, make certain that a non-conducting material is used to facilitate the separation. Non-metallic poles, long pieces of dry lumber (like a wooden oar) are objects that might be found in the diving environment suitable for separating the victim from an electrical source. If an electrical extension cord is involved, it might be most effective to find the plug and disconnect the cord. The victim of electrocution may have the following signs and symptoms:

- Unconsciousness
- Seizures
- Cardiopulmonary arrest
- Burns (Electrical burns rarely appear as severe as the actual tissue damage that has occurred.)

The victim, if unresponsive after being separated from the electrical source, must have a primary assessment performed and may require CPR. Since many electrocutions place the victim into ventricular fibrillation, rapid deployment of the AED is a prudent action. Even when an electrocution victim seems normal after the event, evaluation at a medical care institution is required. Potentially lethal side effects of electrical injury include heart dysrhythmia, kidney abnormalities and failure, and methemoglobinemia, a severe and life-threatening condition precipitated by the unseen breakdown of tissues following serious injury.

9.7 WOUNDS

Open wounds, most often lacerations, are frequently encountered in the marine environment. The primary concern is to stop the bleeding and prevent any further contamination of the wound. Since blood will undoubtedly be present, caregivers must don disposable gloves for protection. Dressing packages should be opened to minimize contamination of the dressing. The dressing is placed over the victim's wound and pressure is applied until all bleeding has stopped. Bleeding extremities are also elevated while direct pressure is applied. Both pressure and gravity are used to slow bleeding. If the bleeding continues and soaks through the first dressing applied, apply an additional dressing on top of the first. This process of adding dressings continues until the bleeding stops with blood-soaked dressings remaining in place.

With the bleeding stopped, apply a self-conforming bandage to hold the dressing in place. The first step in this process is to utilize some technique to keep the bandage from "spinning" around the victim's wound as it is applied. By wrapping one corner of the end of the bandage and "locking" it under the first wrap of the bandage, the conforming bandage can be stabilized on any body part. Most bandaging techniques employ the open spiral/closed spiral technique. The open spiral is wrapping the bandage so the dressing is held in place but is not overlapped sequentially. That will be executed during the closed spiral phase. When holding a roll of conforming bandage, it is held in such a way that the additional material is released from "under" the bandage roll rather than from the "top." This method makes it easier to maintain appropriate tension on the bandage as well as make it less likely for the bandage will "get away."

After securing the dressing in place with the open spiral, wrap the bandage in the opposite direction utilizing the closed spiral technique. In this wrapping of the bandage, each wrap overlaps the previous wrap so that the dressing is completely covered by the bandage. When applying a bandage to a victim, several options are available at the end of the procedure to secure the bandage in place. One approach is to tape the bandage in place. The bandage may also be split along its length with an overhand knot tied in the resulting "tails." These tail pieces will be used to tie the bandage in place by encircling the extremity and tying a square knot. Another common technique which helps create a pressure dressing is to create a loop in the bandaging material at the end of the bandaging process. The bandage is then taken back in the opposite direction until it can be passed through the loop. Secure the dressing using an overhand knot tied in the bandage. Be certain the knot is not made so tight that the circulation is impaired. A finger should fit under the tied part of the bandage without too much effort.

After the bandage is tied, trim excess bandaging material from the ends so these pieces will not become entangled in anything and compromise the management of the victim. With the dressing tied in place by the bandaging method chosen, periodically touch the victim's hand or foot, depending upon the extremity bandaged, to make sure it remains as warm as the opposite extremity. Monitor the skin color as well. If there is any abnormality, there is a possibility the bandage has impaired the victim's circulation or swelling has caused such impairment. The bandage should be untied and retied more loosely.

When treating smaller wounds and unable to get the victim to medical assistance immediately, the small wounds may be washed with soap and water and then dressed in the same manner as above. The only difference is there will not be any substantial bleeding that needs to be stopped.

9.8 BURNS

When one is exposed to boats, there are many sources of heat that may cause burns. Manifolds, stuffing boxes, generators, compressors, and gas or alcohol stoves are just a few of the heat sources to cause such burns. Burns can be particularly insidious injuries leading to infection, severe scarring, and partial disability of the burned area.

There are three generally accepted classifications of burns with which you should have some familiarity:

- **Superficial or First Degree:** A burn only involving the epidermis. Often referred to as superficial burns, they redden the skin but initially cause no other damage. Treat such burns by immersing the affected body part in cool water to stop the burn. The objective is to reduce the temperature of the affected tissues to limit the damage and reduce the victim's discomfort. If on board a boat and looking for some immediate relief for minor burns, Burn Gel® or other similar products can be used. This is a gel material to spread on minor burns, but most significantly, it contains 2% lidocaine HCl, a topical anesthetic.

- **Partial Thickness or Second Degree**: A burn involving the epidermis and the dermis but not penetrating the dermis. Sometimes called partial-thickness burns, they are more severe than first-degree burns as there is more extensive tissue damage. Blistering is a strong indication of a second-degree burn. For small burns of this classification, the same type of treatment as for first-degree burns may be initially utilized. This should be followed with the application of sterile dressings or specialized burn dressings, discussed below. Though blisters may not be attractive, care should be taken to keep the blisters intact since they are a natural "bandage" covering injured tissue below and protecting from infection.

- **Full Thickness or Third Degree**: A full thickness burn with all layers of the skin receiving damage. While they are sometimes confused with second-degree burns, a strong indicator are dry, white, and even charred black areas. The patient may complain of severe pain or no pain at all, which indicates severe nerve damage (although there will usually be pain around the periphery of the third-degree burn). Third-degree burns may involve permanent nerve damage, respiratory arrest, and other major complications. Victims should be transported immediately to a medical facility.

There has been a tendency among first aid providers over the years to want to put something on burns. A very simple rule is: Don't. Most topical substances commonly used do nothing to enhance healing, and most are suspended in material which has limited bacteriostatic strength but can act as a "glue" for particulate matter. Since all serious burns should be assessed medically, these substances will have to be removed by medical personnel so that the burn may be appropriately evaluated and treated.

All but the most minor superficial burns should be evaluated at a hospital emergency department. In addition, there are several types of burn situations that need to be treated in hospitals designated as burn centers. Local emergency medical services personnel should be aware which facilities are designated burn centers. If there is any doubt, the victim should be transported to the nearest trauma center. Those burn injuries which require such special attention include the following:

- Partial-thickness burns covering more than 15% of body surface area
- Full-thickness burns covering more than 5% of body surface area
- Any significant burns involving the hands, face, feet, or genital area
- Any high voltage electrical burns
- Any inhalation or airway burns
- Any chemical burns from chemicals that may continue to destroy tissues
- Any burns which occurred with associated significant other injuries

The simplest to determine percentage of surface-area burns is a method of estimation based on the surface area of the victim's palm. Each "palm" is equal to 1% of the victim's body surface. Visually estimate the surface area of the victim's palm and then make an estimate as to how many of those palm surface areas would cover the burned area. So, if the estimate is 10 of the victim's palms might cover the burned area, that would equal a 10% burn. Another common method is the rule of nines. For this method, each full arm is 9%, the front of each leg is 9%, and the back of each leg is 9%. The upper front torso is 9% as well as the lower front torso (abdominal area), with the corresponding back area each being another 9%. The head is the final 9% bringing the total of these 11 areas to 99%. The pubic area is the final 1%.

9.9 FRACTURES AND SPRAINS

"Slip and fall" injuries are a problem, particularly with wet boat decks. Detailed diagnosis of bone and joint injuries are left to trained medical personnel. A rescuer must recognize there is an injury that may involve the bones and joints. If a victim has suffered a falling or twisting injury and complains of severe pain in a bone or joint, the initial presumption should be an injury. Swelling and discoloration may confirm such injuries. Injuries like this need to be evaluated by a medical professional, preferably in a hospital emergency room. Even if there is no fracture present, there may be significant injury to the tissues surrounding a joint, and the injury needs to be managed as a fracture.

Principles of bone and joint injury management are universal. The primary objective is to immobilize the bones and joints immediately above and immediately below the site of the injury. The ankle is a commonly injured joint in the marine environment, and management can take advantage of some available materials. For an injured ankle, one may use a wetsuit, blanket, or two large towels for splinting. The folded wetsuit (or alternate materials mentioned) is pulled up the victim's leg to be certain the area covered is adequate to immobilize the ankle. The cravat (triangular bandage) is first brought under the victim's foot that has been wrapped in the folded wetsuit. In larger victims, two cravats may have to be tied together to have sufficient length for application of the bandage. Take the long ends and cross them behind the victim's leg, then bring the ends around and across the top of the victim's foot. The "tails" are now slipped through the material originally taken behind the victim's leg. With the long ends pulled through the "stirrups" formed by the material, and with steady upward pressure, the ankle and foot are secured with the cravat and wetsuit material. The ends of the cravats are tied off on top of the victim's foot. Though not as rigid as a cast, this method immobilizes an injured ankle adequately and will enable the victim to be moved with limited additional risk of further injury.

The forearm bones are commonly fractured either by falls or having heavy objects falling upon them. Managing such an injury ideally requires the assistance of a bystander or another caregiver during the initial stages so that any additional movement of the injured extremity is minimized. The victim's upper arm, elbow, wrist, and hand are stabilized manually first. Due to the interconnections between the hand and the arm, it is important to be certain the hand is immobilized in the position of function. This will prevent unnecessary pain and further injury to the victim. One of the simplest methods of doing this is by placing a roll of self-conforming bandage gently into the victim's grip while the support of the arm is manually maintained.

Another caregiver or bystander can manage the manual support of the injured extremity while the rescuer shapes a SAM® splint to the victim's arm. The SAM® splint was developed by orthopedic surgeon Sam Scheinberg and is an ideal device for the marine environment. It is impervious to the environment, light in weight, and when rolled up, takes up little space. This splint can also be reused and is suitable for bone and joint injuries of the arm as well as wrist, shoulder, and, when two splints are used together, can be used to splint the leg or ankle. The splint is secured in place using a self-conforming bandage in the same manner as discussed in wound management.

For upper extremity injuries, the splint is only the first part of care and the arm should be further supported and immobilized using a sling and swathe. To prepare a sling for the victim, tie an overhand knot in the point of the triangular bandage that will be used as the splint. If a triangular bandage is laid out flat, two "long arms" and one "short arm" will be noticed. The knot should be tied at the very end of the short arm. The knot will help to form the "cup" at the victim's elbow when the sling is applied.

When applying the sling to the victim, take the portion of the triangular bandage closest to the victim's body and pass it around the side of the neck on the same side as the injury. The other end of the triangular bandage, the portion which is on the outside of the victim's arm, is passed over the shoulder opposite the victim's injured arm. The sling is tied behind the victim's neck with a square knot, but the knot should rest to the side of the neck in the interest of the victim's comfort. As a final safeguard, take another triangular bandage and bring it over the outside of the upper arm and tie it off under the victim's opposite arm. This is described as the swathe and yields a full immobilization of the injured arm. With slight modifications, this same sling and swathe technique is useful for the management of upper arm, shoulder, and collar bone injuries.

9.10 POSSIBLE MEDICAL PROBLEMS

Though most people encountered on a diving operation are generally healthy, it is possible that on board a boat, divers may be exposed to certain medical emergencies. None of these will be discussed in great detail, but some thoughts are offered relative to the initial management of several illnesses.

9.10.1 Respiratory Emergencies

Respiratory problems involve victims breathing too fast, those breathing too slowly, or those whose breathing is impaired due to some internal obstruction.

9.10.1.1 Hyperventilation

Breathing too fast (tachypnea) may be a natural response to injuries or to blood loss and need not be treated. Instead, deal with the underlying problems in a manner previously discussed. Tachypnea may also be a result of diabetes or other metabolic emergencies and needs the attention of medical professionals, as it may be a sign of a serious medical condition.

However, the hyperventilation syndrome can be a problem. By definition, hyperventilation means increased ventilation, which depletes blood CO_2 below 35 to 38 mm Hg. This may lead to an imbalance of respiratory gases in the body that need to maintain a relatively delicate balance. It is usually precipitated from some emotional response, but once started, appears to be self-sustaining and beyond the voluntary control of the victim.

The victim will usually breathe from 35 to 50 times per minute and may complain of numbness and tingling around the mouth and nose. The victim is anxious and appears to be suffering from air hunger and may also exhibit cramping of the hands and forearms. Management of this type of hyperventilation is directed at getting the victim's respiratory gases back into balance and requires two immediate actions.

1. Continue to reassure the victim everything is OK, and he/she needs to concentrate on trying to slow the breathing down.

2. Using either a paper bag or an oxygen mask not connected to any oxygen, have the victim rebreathe his/her own exhaled air. This will increase the level of carbon dioxide in the blood, the gas that has been depleted via hyperventilation, and bring the respiratory rate back under control.

If the victim's breathing does not quickly come under control, the victim needs to be treated by more advanced emergency medical personnel.

9.10.1.2 Inadequate Breathing (Hypoventilation)

This type of problem can be the result of a disease process, extreme weakness, or some injuries that cause the victim to limit chest wall movement. An inadequate volume of gas is being exchanged each minute, with too little oxygen being taken into the system and too little carbon dioxide being exhaled. The rescuer may observe a very slow breathing rate of less than 10 breaths per minute. Shallow breathing or cyanosis (a bluish color change seen in the nail beds and around the lips) may be present. Any of these findings should be treated by administering oxygen and providing ventilatory support to the victim.

9.10.1.3 Obstructive Problems

Diseases such as chronic bronchitis, emphysema, and asthma result in some degree of blockage or impairment of normal gas exchange. If a victim has one of these diseases and is in respiratory difficulty and in obvious distress, oxygen should be administered and supplementary ventilation considered. Such victims are almost always more comfortable if maintained in a sitting position. These are emergencies that need to be transferred immediately to the emergency medical services system for care.

9.10.2 Cardiovascular Emergencies

One of the leading causes of unnecessary deaths from heart disease occurs because of delay in reaching appropriate care. Do not contribute to the problem. Certain chronic cardiac problems, the most common being chronic or congestive heart failure, will usually involve a victim in respiratory distress. Other heart conditions usually present with a victim having any one of the following signs and symptoms:

- Chest pain (this pain will usually be described by the victim as crushing or squeezing and will not be relieved by any change of position or with breathing)
- Respiratory distress
- Nausea or vomiting
- Unusual fatigue
- Skin color and quality that may be shock-like as previously described or cyanotic

Angina is a condition where a victim usually has the chest pain precipitated by either physical or emotional stress. The pain of angina is brought on by inadequate blood flow to the heart muscle and might be compared to a cramp of the heart muscle. However, it is often difficult to distinguish the pain of angina from a more serious cardiac problem. The rescuer should take several steps if it appears angina is the victim's problem.

1. Calm and reassure the victim and keep the victim in a position where they are most comfortable, often a sitting position.

2. Administer oxygen to the victim.

3. If the victim has medication for angina, assist the victim in taking the medication. If the medication is nitroglycerin in tablet form, wear disposable gloves when handling the medication, since it can be absorbed through the skin and give the caregiver a severe headache.

4. Give an adult aspirin to the patient if not allergic.

Very often, the symptoms of the angina will quickly disappear when the victim has been calmed, oxygen has been administered, and the victim's own medication has been taken. If the victim's pain and discomfort does not quickly subside, it must be presumed angina is not the problem. The victim may be having an acute myocardial infarction (heart attack) and may be in imminent threat of death. Treatment for the heart attack victim is the same as for angina victim at the basic level, except the victim must be cautioned not to assist in any movement in any way and allow you to move him/her at all times. If the victim is in a tight-fitting wetsuit or similar garment, these restricting garments must be loosened in order to allow the victim to breathe with as little effort as possible. The AED should be accessible in the event the victim becomes unresponsive.

9.10.3 Stroke (Cerebro-Vascular Accident)

Strokes are usually precipitated by either a blockage of a blood vessel leading to the brain or a rupture of a vessel in the brain. Most often, victims of these problems have a history of high blood pressure. On occasion, a stroke may occur, as in the case of heart attacks, without any prior medical history or warning. A victim suffering from a stroke will exhibit one or more of the following signs and symptoms:

- Headache (sometimes described as the worst headache the victim has ever had)

- Visual disturbances (the victim will tell caregiver vision is distorted or there is blindness in or both eyes
- Abnormalities of speech
- Inability to move one side of the body or weakness or loss of feeling to one side of the body
- Memory loss or disorientation
- Seizures
- Loss of consciousness

With recognition of any of these signs or symptoms, activate emergency medical service resources. The following immediate care must be given to the victim:

- The victim's breathing status needs to be monitored since stroke victims sometimes have difficulty protecting their own airway. If any difficulty is noticed, position the victim in a way breathing is unobstructed.
- Keep the victim calm and reassured. If the victim is still responsive, place him/her in a comfortable position, preferably the recovery position, and pay constant attention to the airway.
- Administer oxygen.
- Make sure the victim's body temperature is maintained and no additional body heat will be lost.
- If the victim is unresponsive, place the victim on his/her side so any saliva or vomit will drain out of the mouth rather than being inhaled.

This care and vigilant monitoring should continue until the victim is transferred to emergency medical services personnel.

9.10.4 Convulsions (Seizure)

Seizures are a short circuit in the victim's brain, which may result in involuntary action of an isolated segment of the victim's body. Generalized motor seizures or convulsions are a major medical emergency and require intervention beyond the basic level. Contact local emergency medical services personnel. With a seizing victim, certain essential care must be performed while awaiting the arrival of emergency care personnel.

- Do not try to restrain the victim in any way.
- Move any objects away from the victim that might cause injury.
- Ensure the victim's airway is maintained. This is particularly important after the active seizing stops. Most seizures are followed by a period of unconsciousness, when the airway may become impaired. Position the victim in the same way as an unconscious stroke victim.
- After the active seizure, do not try to arouse the victim if sleeping. This is a natural aftermath to a major seizure.

Take notes relative to the progression of the seizure (what part of the body it started in) and the duration of the active seizing. This information, along with any other known medical history, should be given to emergency medical services personnel upon their arrival.

9.10.5 Diabetic Emergencies

The disease processes involved with diabetes are extremely complex, with one of the principal problems being microangiopathy (a disease caused by blood vessels being small). This, as well as some of the other manifestations of diabetes, is the reason diabetic persons cannot be cleared medically for diving. However, other personnel on the job site or offshore may indeed be diabetic, and for this reason, diabetic emergencies are covered herein.

This disease tends to be complicated in the way it manifests itself, but the problems typically encountered will have to do with insulin, glucose, or both. Insulin is a chemical produced by the body that enables the body to utilize glucose, a sugar that serves as the body's primary energy source. If an individual does not have enough insulin, the glucose present cannot be utilized. At the other extreme, if the individual has enough insulin but no glucose, other problems will arise. The two significant diabetes-related emergencies the rescuer may encounter are hypoglycemia (low blood sugar) and diabetic ketoacidosis, at one time called diabetic coma.

Hypoglycemia usually develops rapidly due to a quick drop in the blood sugar level (glucose). It may be precipitated by strenuous activity beyond the diabetic victim's normal activity level. The blood's sugar level drops and the body, particularly the brain, is precipitately deprived of the primary source of energy. Notice the following signs and symptoms:

- Mental status altered, with confusion, bizarre behavior, combativeness, and irritability
- Cold, clammy skin similar to shock
- Weakness and uncoordinated, if still responsive
- Rapid pulse but may be bounding since there has been no loss of blood
- Seizures

If the victim is still conscious enough to protect his/her airway, administer sugar to the victim. Simple sources include non-diet soft drinks, sugar and water syrup, and fruit juices. Other sources made particularly for emergency care include thick sugar gels contained in tubes and can be expelled under the victim's tongue. This allows the glucose to be quickly absorbed by the numerous blood vessels under the tongue. Monitor the victim's airway, and protect the victim from injury during seizure. The victim will quickly respond to this type of care, but any delay in response to oral sugar administration requires immediate notification of emergency medical services for assistance.

Diabetic ketoacidosis is a far more serious diabetic emergency, since a simple dose of glucose will not provide any "quick fix" for the victim. Instead, the victim needs immediate, sophisticated medical intervention only available at a hospital. Expediency in getting the emergency medical services mobilized is critical for the victim's well-being and needs to take the highest priority. The victim of diabetic ketoacidosis usually has the following signs and symptoms:

- Confusion and headache
- Thirsty but produces excess amounts of urine
- Dehydration with warm, dry skin
- Deep, sighing breathing with a fruity breath odor
- General feeling of "unwellness" for a prior period of days

Keep the victim comfortable until emergency medical services personnel can take over care. The victim's airway must be monitored, since a comatose victim may be unable to maintain a clear airway. Oxygen administration is desirable, and, if the victim is conscious and able to protect the airway, small quantities of water (no more than 8 oz. (~250 ml.) every 15–30 minutes) may be helpful to relieve some of the dehydration. If in doubt whether the victim is suffering from diabetic ketoacidosis or is hypoglycemic, oral administration of sugar as in hypoglycemia will do little harm to the victim and if the victim is hypoglycemic, the oral sugar administration may assist the victim.

9.11 HEAT ILLNESSES

The two serious heat emergencies in diving are heat exhaustion and heat stroke. Prevention is one area every diver can play a part. When individuals work in a heated environment (i.e. below decks on a boat), be certain everyone takes frequent breaks to cool themselves and make sure adequate fluid consumption is continuing throughout the work day. Despite the availability of numerous commercially available beverages, water remains the best fluid for hydration. In the diving environment, on particularly warm days, do not let divers spend too much time in wet- or drysuits while not in the water. These garments retain body heat, and divers can sustain a significant rise in body temperature.

9.11.1 Heat Exhaustion

Heat exhaustion is caused by excessive fluid loss from the body, as well as loss of sodium, most often due to profuse sweating. This problem can be made worse by vomiting, diarrhea, and heavy alcohol consumption. The victim of heat exhaustion may have the following signs and symptoms:

- Rapid pulse
- Dizziness, anxiety, irritability, headache, and vision problems
- Normal to slightly elevated body temperature
- Cold, clammy skin with pallor similar to shock
- Mild cramps, nausea, and sometimes vomiting.

Keep the victim calm and remove unnecessary clothing. The purpose is to lower the victim's body temperature. If the victim is conscious and capable of protecting his own airway, it is advisable to give the victim a solution consisting of 1 tsp. (~5 ml.) of salt dissolved in 8 oz. (~250 ml.) of water. Have the victim drink this slowly over a period of 15 minutes to avoid precipitating vomiting. As it may be difficult to determine if the victim is suffering from heat exhaustion or heat stroke, discussed below, it is important to remove the victim from the source of excessive heat, as well as to remove any body covering that may be causing additional internal heat build-up. If in doubt relative to the heat related problem from which the victim is suffering, treat for heat stroke.

9.11.2 Heat Stroke

A life-threatening emergency, heat stroke causes the victim's core temperature to rise to a potentially deadly level and the body's natural "thermostat" to fail. The signs and symptoms of heat stroke may be similar to heat exhaustion, or the victim may present the following classic heat stroke signs and symptoms:

- Rapid pulse and respiration
- Hot, dry, reddish skin (This may not be evident in victims who are in excellent physical condition.)
- Headache, weakness, dizziness
- Anxiety and fatigue
- Sweating has ceased

The key difference between heat exhaustion and heat stroke is a change in mental status. Treatment of the victim of heat stroke requires immediate, aggressive intervention in order to save the victim's life. The rescuer, ideally, should have someone else immediately initiate the mobilization of emergency medical services while turning full attention to the victim. Top priority is to lower the body core temperature. The following actions should take place:

- Remove all of the victim's clothing and cover the victim with a cool, water-soaked sheet.
- Place the victim in an air-conditioned area, if available.
- Administer oxygen while maintaining the victim's airway.

- Place chemical cold packs or bags of ice under the victim's arm pits, at the groin, around the head and neck, and anywhere else the source of cold can be placed near a major supply of moving blood.
- Be prepared to manage the victim in the event convulsing begins.

The need for rapid cooling of these victims cannot be overemphasized. Without rapid cooling, the victim of heat stroke will either die or, if they survive, suffer permanent, debilitating brain injury.

9.12 HYPOTHERMIA

Water possesses the physical property of drawing heat from the human body faster than air. Body heat is lost 25 times faster in water than in air of the same temperature. There is a risk of significant body heat loss even in temperate exposures. As an example, though 70°F (21 C) water is not viewed as frigid, an individual tossed into such water for a period of 4 hours has experienced an environmental exposure equivalent to standing naked in 70°F (21 C) air for 100 hours. On a diving project, a rescuer may care for individuals who have been subject to significant exposures to cold.

Hypothermia is a drop in the body's core temperature to less than 95°F (35 C). (For reference, normal body temperature is 98.6°F (37 C).) Any time a victim has been subject to immersion in water, the victim should be cared for as though hypothermia is present. Hypothermia is classified as mild, moderate, or severe based upon core temperature. Some of the signs and symptoms of the varying classes of hypothermia include the following:

- **Mild Hypothermia**: shivering, slurred speech, apathetic, motor difficulties (wobbling gait, awkward manual control), memory loss (amnesia)
- **Moderate Hypothermia**: shivering ceases, state of stupor, slow heart beat and respirations, pupils may be dilated.
- **Severe Hypothermia**: At this point, the core temperature is down to nearly 80°F (27 C). The victim has lost voluntary movement capabilities and most reflexes are gone. Respiratory difficulties may become more severe due to accumulation of fluid in the lungs brought on by the hypothermia. These victims are also at great risk for cardiac arrest.

9.12.1 Hypothermia Management

First, prevent any further heat loss to the victim. Most hypothermia victims encountered in diving will have suffered extended immersions. The victim's clothing must be removed and the victim must be dried. Be careful to handle these victims gently, since rough handling may bring on cardiac arrest or cause irreversible organ damage in severely hypothermic victims. Additional required care includes the following:

- Maintain the victim's airway, and, if trauma is suspected, provide immobilization of the cervical spine while maintaining the airway.
- If necessary, all normal basic life support procedures must be carried out, including CPR. The basic tenet in caring for dead hypothermic victims is the "victim is not dead until they are warm and dead." This means the rescuer and emergency medical services personnel must continue resuscitative efforts until the victim has been transferred to a hospital.
- If there will be any significant delay in getting the victim to advanced care, the victim should be wrapped in blankets and re-warmed. However, if the transfer to EMS personnel will be quickly accomplished, then the aggressive re-warming should be delayed until re-warmed from the inside out using sophisticated medical interventions. (Re-warming a hypothermia victim

from the outside in presents a risk of a problem called "after drop" where colder blood from the body's surface and extremities moves into the body's core and may actually drop the body core temperature further.)

- The victim can be re-warmed by wrapping the naked victim in a blanket with a naked companion. The non-hypothermic person's body heat will help re-warm the victim.

- If the victim does not have an impaired gag reflex, they can then be given warmed fluids by mouth. Warm juices, water, and thin soups are appropriate. Any fluids containing caffeine (coffee, tea, hot chocolate) and any beverages containing alcohol should not be given to the victim.

- If basic life support is required, oxygen should be preheated, since it will tend to reduce the victim's core temperature further. We preheat oxygen by putting several coils of the oxygen hose in a pail of hot water. This ensures the oxygen gas is prewarmed before it arrives at the mask.

The victims must be handled gently, rewarmed, and transferred to a hospital as soon as possible.

9.13 SEASICKNESS (MOTION SICKNESS)

Diving should not be attempted when a diver is seasick, as vomiting while submerged can cause respiratory obstruction and death. Occasionally, a diver will become seasick on an in-water decompression stop or when working in shallow water close to the splash zone. The victim of motion sickness may have the following signs and symptoms:

- Nausea

- Dizziness

- Feelings of withdrawal and fatigue

- Pallor or a sickly complexion

- Slurred speech

- Vomiting

There is no effective treatment for seasickness except to return the victim to a stable platform, preferably shore. Some people are more susceptible than others, but repeated exposures tend to decrease sensitivity. The susceptible person should eat lightly just before exposure and avoid diving with an alcohol-related hangover. Seasick individuals should be isolated to avoid affecting others on board adversely. Drug therapy is of questionable value and must be used with caution because most motion sickness preparations contain antihistamines that make the diver drowsy and could affect a diver's judgment. The use of scopolamine via a skin patch has been shown to be useful in preventing seasickness, but this drug has been known to cause psychotic behavior in sensitive persons. Those choosing to use the scopolamine patch are cautioned not to touch their eyes after touching the patch as this will cause dilation of the pupil. Drugs should be used only under the direction of a physician who understands diving, and then only after a test dose on non-diving days has been shown not to affect the individual adversely. One side effect of seasickness is dehydration. Divers should be aware of the role dehydration plays in decompression sickness and rehydrate accordingly before diving to prevent unnecessary risk.

Sample Emergency Medical Response Plan

MEDICAL EMERGENCY RESPONSE PLAN	
ONBOARD AND SHORE-BASED EMERGENCY INFORMATION AND CONTACTS	
VESSEL: DP Barge Saint Patrick	**LOCATION**: Exxon/Mobil Field, Gulf of Guinea, Nigeria
ON-CALL HOSPITAL: Victoria General, Lagos **PHONE**: +234 XXX - XXXX	**ON-CALL PHYSICIAN**: Adesola Odesippe, MD **PHONE**: +234 XXX-XXXX
BRORON CONTACT: Aiden O'Connor, HSE **PHONE**: +234 XXX - XXXX	**EXXON/MOBIL CONTACT**: Shift Supervisor **PHONE**: +234 XXX - XXXX
First Aid Kit Locations: Bridge, Barge Clinic, Diving Department Office, Dive Control	**DMAC Kit Locations**: Diving Department Office, Chamber Van
Stokes Litter Locations: Barge Clinic, Diving Department Office, Chamber Van	**Satellite Phone Locations**: Dive Control Van, Vessel Bridge
Designated First Aiders: Barge Medic, Day Shift DMT, Night Shift DMT, Rigging Foreman	**Designated Diver Medics**: Diving Day Shift – two, Diving Night Shift – two
MEDICAL EVACUATION: Bristow Helicopters **PHONE**: +234 XXX - XXXX	**SPECIAL NOTE**: DCS and AGE incidents require immediate notification of diving superintendent, regardless of the time (Phone 105). Superintendent will notify all other parties.
ALTERNATE EVACUATION: Bourbon Ships **PHONE**: +234 XXX - XXXX (VHF channel 06)	
SERIOUS INCIDENT RESPONSE PROCEDURE	

PRESSURE RELATED ILLNESS:	TRAUMA INCIDENT:
1. Notify on-shift DMTs and superintendent.	1. Notify barge medic and/or on-shift DMT.
2. Press casualty to 60 fsw on O_2.	2. Locate nearest first aid kit and stabilize casualty.
3. Start TT5, TT6 or TT6A (as per USN Flowchart).	3. Transport casualty to Barge Clinic.
4. Perform rapid neurological examination.	4. Notify contractor office and Exxon Mobil.
5. Notify on-call hyperbaric physician.	5. If hospitalization required, notify on-call hospital and medical evacuation chopper or vessel.
6. Notify contractor office and Exxon/Mobil.	6. Log all incident details and treatment details.
7. Log events on treatment record and deck log.	7. Diving crew will keep incident details quiet until such time as the company releases a statement.
8. All diving operations cease during treatments.	
9. Diving crew will keep incident details quiet until such time as the company releases a statement.	

10.0 HYPERBARIC EMERGENCIES

Since the majority of diving projects occur in remote locations and hyperbaric treatment facilities are not found in most hospitals, divers have traditionally treated their own as far as pressure-related illness and injury is concerned. This has been true especially with those incidents requiring hyperbaric treatment. In the past, every diver on the crew was expected to know the basics of diving medicine, and usually every crew had one person who really knew "his stuff," keeping up on all of the latest treatments, medical procedures, and medical equipment. Twenty years ago, it was not an easy task to find a hyperbaric physician (even in larger population centers) and the training for and designation of diving medical technician did not yet exist.

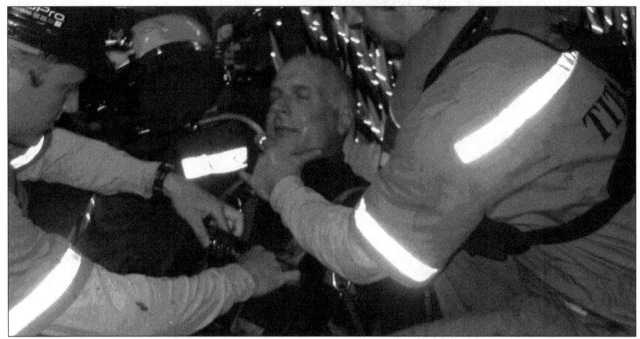

Two DMTs dressing down a stricken diver to prepare for hyperbaric treatment

The diving crew of today has more hyperbaric physicians available, better communications with the hyperbaric physicians ashore, and the diving medical technician is the one who typically administers on-site care. We have more modern medical equipment, better chambers, more up-to-date treatment protocols, but even with all of this – the prevention, diagnosis, and on-site treatment of diving-related injury and illness still involves the diving crew. How we perform these duties at the dive site will determine whether the stricken diver will be able to work in the water again, and in some cases, whether the diver will live or die.

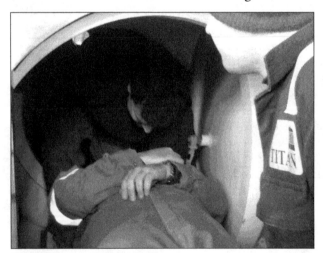

Patient being loaded in a chamber

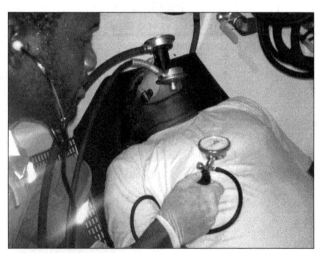

Taking a blood pressure reading
Photo courtesy of John McElligott

10.1 TREATMENT WITH HYPERBARIC OXYGEN

Hyperbaric oxygen is regularly used to treat pressure-related illness such as Type I and II decompression sickness (DCS) and arterial gas embolism (AGE). It is also used therapeutically for many non-diving conditions as indicated in the following table:

Table 20-3. *Guidelines for Conducting Hyperbaric Oxygen Therapy.*

Indication	Treatment Table	Minimum # Treatments	Maximum # Treatments
Carbon Monoxide Poisoning and Smoke Inhalation	Treatment Table 5 or Table 6 as recommended by the DMO	1	5
Gas Gangrene (Clostridial Myonecrosis)	Treatment Table 5 TID × 1 day then BID × 4-5 days	5	10
Crush Injury, Compartment Syndrome, and other Acute Traumatic Ischemia	Treatment Table 9 TID × 2 days BID × 2 days QD × 2 days	3	12
Enhancements of Healing in Selected Wounds	Treatment Table 9 QD or BID	10	60
Necrotizing Soft-Tissue Infections (subcutaneous tissue, muscle, fascia)	Treatment Table 9 BID initially, then QD	5	30
Osteomyelitis (refractory)	Treatment Table 9 QD	20	60
Radiation Tissue Damage (osteoradinecrosis)	Treatment Table 9 QD	20	60
Skin Grafts and Flaps (compromised)	Treatment Table 9 BID initially, then QD	6	40
Thermal Burns	Treatment Table 9 TID × 1 day, then BID	5	45

QD = 1 time in 24 hours   BID = 2 times in 24 hours   TID = 3 times in 24 hours
For further information, see Hyperbaric Oxygen Therapy: A Committee Report, 2003 Revision.

Source: *U.S. Navy Diving Manual*

The above table has been included for information only, and the treatments listed (with the possible exception of the treatment for carbon monoxide poisoning) will be performed onshore and not on the offshore dive site. The primary focus of this chapter will be on the treatment of pressure related diving disorders, as performed offshore on diving operations.

10.2 DIAGNOSIS OF DECOMPRESSION SICKNESS OR ARTERIAL GAS EMBOLISM

In order for a diagnosis of DCS or AGE to be made, the casualty must have been either breathing gas under pressure or exposed to high altitude. Even though some diving safety regulations require that divers carry a copy of their dive record (dive sheet) after decompression dives, the depth and duration of a dive are **not in any way** relevant to treatment. Hyperbaric treatment is **always** based on symptoms presented. A diagnosis of DCS does not require the diver to have exceeded the no-decompression limits or to have improperly followed decompression tables; DCS can and has occurred in divers who were well within the no-decompression limits and followed decompression tables exactly as they were designed. Proper and timely diagnosis and treatment of AGE and DCS is critical to maintain life and to minimize physiological damage and long-term (residual) effects. The signs and symptoms listed below are those used in diagnosis. Every working diver must know these.

10.2.1 Signs and Symptoms of Arterial Gas Embolism
- Chest pain, severe headache, cough, shortness of breath
- Bloody sputum, bloody froth around nose and /or mouth
- Impaired or distorted vision, blindness (partial or complete)
- Numbness, tingling, weakness or paralysis, dizziness, confusion
- Sudden unconsciousness (usually immediately upon surfacing)
- Respiratory arrest, death

10.2.2 Signs and Symptoms of Type I Decompression Sickness
- Joint or muscle pain – a dull ache that does not move and is present at rest
- Lymph nodes – swelling and pain in the lymph nodes and surrounding tissue
- Skin symptoms – welts (resembling purple hives), itching with a mild reddish rash

10.2.3 Signs and Symptoms of Type II Decompression Sickness
- Skin symptoms – marbling or mottling (starts as itching, redness, then becomes bluish rash)
- Unusual extreme fatigue, numbness, tingling, muscle weakness, paralysis
- Vertigo, dizziness, hearing loss, ringing in the ears, vision problems, blindness
- Disrupted motor performance, lack of coordination, disrupted mental status
- Difficulty walking, balance problems, difficulty in urination
- Cardio-respiratory symptoms (chokes) – chest pain, cough, rapid shallow breaths

Many of the symptoms of AGE and Type II DCS are very similar. Both conditions call for the same initial treatment protocol (initial press to 60 fsw on oxygen and a neurological exam), so differentiating between them, at least initially, is not critical. There is, however, a good rule of thumb to use: Incidents with neurological involvement presenting less than 5 minutes after surfacing are usually considered to be AGE; incidents with neurological involvement presenting more than 5 minutes after surfacing are usually considered to be Type II DCS. Symptoms of AGE occur just as the diver is arriving at surface or immediately after surfacing, and they are almost always very sudden and very dramatic. With Type II DCS, symptoms present a little later on, and in most cases, the victim will notice difficulty in urination, regardless what other signs and symptoms are presented.

Portable oxygen administration kit
Photo courtesy of John McElligott

The following are important points to remember with pressure-related illness:

- Always treat based on signs and symptoms
- Always treat in a timely manner – initiate treatment as soon as possible
- Always follow the flowcharts and treatment tables as they are presented
- Never deviate from the treatment tables
- Never attempt to run a treatment from memory – read the tables every time

10.3 TREATMENT OF DECOMPRESSION SICKNESS OR ARTERIAL GAS EMBOLISM

There is only one way to treat DCS or AGE – recompression in a hyperbaric chamber. To perform treatments, we use the flow charts and treatment tables as found in the *U.S. Navy Diving Manual*, according to the rules in the following table:

Table 20-1. Rules for Recompression Treatment.

ALWAYS:

1. Follow the treatment tables accurately, unless modified by a Diving Medical Officer with concurrence of the Commanding Officer.
2. Have a qualified tender in chamber at all times during treatment.
3. Maintain the normal descent and ascent rates as much as possible.
4. Examine the patient thoroughly at depth of relief or treatment depth.
5. Treat an unconscious patient for arterial gas embolism or serious decompression sickness unless the possibility of such a condition can be ruled out without question.
6. Use air treatment tables only if oxygen is unavailable.
7. Be alert for warning signs of oxygen toxicity if oxygen is used.
8. In the event of an oxygen convulsion, remove the oxygen mask and keep the patient from self-harm. Do not force the mouth open during a convulsion.
9. Maintain oxygen usage within the time and depth limitations prescribed by the treatment table.
10. Check the patient's condition and vital signs periodically. Check frequently if the patient's condition is changing rapidly or the vital signs are unstable.
11. Observe patient after treatment for recurrence of symptoms. Observe 2 hours for pain-only symptoms, 6 hours for serious symptoms. Do not release patient without consulting a DMO.
12. Maintain accurate timekeeping and recording.
13. Maintain a well-stocked Primary and Secondary Emergency Kit.

NEVER:

1. Permit any shortening or other alteration of the tables, except under the direction of a Diving Medical Officer.
2. Wait for a bag resuscitator. Use mouth-to-mouth resuscitation with a barrier device immediately if breathing ceases.
3. Interrupt chest compressions for longer than 10 seconds.
4. Permit the use of 100 percent oxygen below 60 feet in cases of DCS or AGE.
5. Fail to treat doubtful cases.
6. Allow personnel in the chamber to assume a cramped position that might interfere with complete blood circulation.

Source: *U.S. Navy Diving Manual*

10.3.1 How Hyperbaric Treatment Works

If bubbles of inert gas occur in the bloodstream (AGE) or in body tissue (DCS), a diver is recompressed in the chamber. The bubbles of inert gas are compressed back down and return to solution within the tissues and blood. Through the "treatment," the inert gas is allowed to come out of solution slowly (without bubbling) and to be exhaled by the diver. By using different "treatment gases" as the diver's breathing media, the inert gas partial pressure is kept very low in the respiratory and arterial side of the circulatory systems, while the pressure on the diver's body is kept high enough to keep the gas in tissues and blood from bubbling as off-gassing occurs. This is same technique used in surface decompression using oxygen. Different treatment gases may be used: medical oxygen, oxygen enriched air (nitrox), and various helium/oxygen mixes. Medical oxygen is the most common treatment gas used. It is important to use the exact treatment gas prescribed for the treatment table used and follow the tables to the letter.

10.3.2 Life Support Considerations During Treatments

The shorter treatment tables (Treatment Tables 5, 6, 6A, 9, and Air Treatment Tables 1A and 2A) are short enough in duration that they will only involve one crew and should not be too hard on the gas supplies and equipment. The longer treatment tables (Treatment Tables 3, 4, 7 and 8) will require additional crew and will be very hard on the gas supplies, consumables, and equipment. The good news is that the longer tables are seldom, if ever, used. Due to the duration (considerably longer than surface decompression) of the treatment tables and the fact that they are an emergency medical treatment, issues such as manning, patient monitoring, and chamber environmental control come to the forefront.

10.3.2.1 Minimum Manning Requirements for Treatments

The following are the minimum crew that will be required on site to perform a treatment:

- **Supervisor**: Selection and supervision of the hyperbaric treatment, chamber operations, and timekeeping for the occupants
- **Outside Tender**: Monitor gas supplies, assist occupants with entry and exit from chamber
- **DMT**: Perform emergency medical procedures as required on the casualty, liaision with the on-call hyperbaric physician regarding the treatment
- **Inside Tender** (optional): Monitor the casualty, as required, eliminating the need to keep the DMT inside the chamber throughout the entire treatment

Although the minimum crew specified above will suffice in most cases, it is better to have a second outside tender to operate the chamber, freeing up the supervisor. Additional inside tenders will be required in incidents where CPR or assisted breathing is necessary. Also, additional inside tenders are required for longer treatments. The long tables will require at least one crew change, possibly more, depending on the point in the original shift that the treatment was initiated.

10.3.2.2 Temperature Control

The internal chamber temperature becomes more important on the treatment tables, as the diver/patient is in the chamber environment for a longer period of time, and the diver/patient is undergoing an emergency medical procedure that is temperature sensitive. Although the table below shows maximum tolerance times for various temperatures up to 104° F, it is **strongly recommended** that the internal temperature of the chamber be kept below 85°F for all applications, whether regular surface decompression or performing a treatment. When treating for arterial gas embolism and neurological symptoms in decompression sickness, the patient's core temperature must be kept as close as possible to the normal range. This becomes more difficult when the chamber is too warm. In addition, temperature significantly affects the patient's ability to tolerate hyperbaric oxygen. The best way to maintain optimum internal temperature is to have the chamber inside a climate-controlled compartment or sea container. Other methods of dropping internal temperature include heater/chiller, venting the chamber, shading the chamber, and placing water-soaked blankets or burlap on the top of the chamber.

Table 20-4. *Maximum Permissible Recompression Chamber Exposure Times at Various Temperatures.*

Internal Temperature	Maximum Tolerance Time	Permissible Treatment Tables
Over 104°F (40°C)	Intolerable	No treatments
95–104°F (34.4–40°C)	2 hours	Table 5, 9
85–94°F (29–34.4°C)	6 hours	Tables 5, 6, 6A, 1A, 9
Under 85°F (29°C)	Unlimited	All treatments

NOTE:
Internal chamber temperature can be kept considerably below ambient by venting or by using an installed chiller unit. Internal chamber temperature can be measured using electronic, bimetallic, alcohol, or liquid crystal thermometers. Never use a mercury thermometer in or around hyperbaric chambers. Since chamber ventilation will produce temperature swings during ventilation, the above limits should be used as averages when controlling temperature by ventilation. Always shade chamber from direct sunlight.

Source: *U.S. Navy Diving Manual*

Of equal importance is the minimum internal temperature, which becomes an issue in colder climates as found in the non-tropical regions. Although chamber blankets are normally provided, the internal temperature should never be allowed to drop below 70° F. Lower temperatures for extended periods will affect the metabolism of the occupant, and gas elimination will not occur at the proper rate, either in normal surface decompression or in hyperbaric treatment.

10.3.2.3 Oxygen Levels in the Chamber

Since most chambers today are equipped with an oxygen monitor, it is relatively easy to maintain the proper oxygen level in the chamber environment during treatments. As always, the level must not be allowed to climb too high, thereby presenting a risk of fire. But with inside tenders breathing air, it must not be allowed to drop too low. Oxygen levels should be maintained in the 20-22% range, never being permitted to drop below 19%, nor climb above 25%. Venting the chamber (while maintaining depth) will help in both cases. It is imperative the chamber depth not fluctuate while venting.

10.3.2.4 Carbon Dioxide Levels in the Chamber

Carbon dioxide must be maintained below 1.5% in the chamber environment. This is best accomplished when the chamber has a CO_2 monitor. Most CO_2 monitors are installed on the surface side of the exhaust line, so the maximum CO_2 reading should be 0.78% when the chamber is at 30 fsw, 0.53% when at 60 fsw, and 0.25% when at 165 fsw to maintain 1.5% at pressure. CO_2 monitors that take their reading internally need not be corrected. Although many newer chambers have CO_2 scrubbers, when there is work being performed by more than one person, (CPR) ventilation will also be required to maintain the CO_2 level. If the chamber has neither a CO_2 monitor nor a scrubber, the standard rates of ventilation will apply: 3 scfm per occupant at rest, 6 scfm per occupant at work (CPR). The formula to calculate ventilation rates is:

$$R = \frac{V \times 18}{T \times \frac{(P + 33)}{33}}$$

Where: R = ventilation rate in acfm
V = chamber volume in cubic feet
T = time (in seconds) to change chamber depth by 10 fsw
P = chamber gauge pressure in fsw

When in doubt, ventilate 1 out of every 5 minutes with occupants resting and 2 out of every 5 minutes with occupants performing strenuous work.

Remember: Scrubbers do not necessarily eliminate the need for ventilation. With multiple occupants, particularly if they are working strenuously, ventilation will be required even with a scrubber. Scrubber absorbent should be changed prior to the level of carbon dioxide in the chamber reaching 1.5%.

10.3.2.5 Patient Hydration

Successful treatment of DCS depends upon adequate hydration of the patient. Thirst is an unreliable indicator of necessary water intake, particularly if the chamber occupants are sweating heavily. At temperatures above 85°F, patients and tenders should drink at least one liter of water per hour; below 85°F they should drink one half liter of water per hour. Only fully conscious patients may be given fluids by mouth. Water, fruit or vegetable juice, and non-carbonated sports drinks such as Gatorade may be given by mouth. Semi-conscious and unconscious patients should be started on intravenous immediately, using normal saline at a rate of 75 – 100 cc/hr until specific IV instructions can be issued by a hyperbaric physician. Do not use glucose or dextrose solutions if brain or spinal cord involvement is suspected. Patients presenting Type II or AGE symptoms should be considered for IV hydration, even if conscious. The patient's ability to void the bladder should be assessed as soon as possible. If the patient cannot empty a full bladder, a urinary catheter must be inserted as soon as possible by a DMT experienced in invasive procedures. Urine output at or above 0.5cc/kg/hr is a reliable indication of adequate hydration, however clear colorless urine in both the patient and the tender is the best indicator.

10.3.2.6 Breathing Gas

Any time the chamber is pressed deeper than 45 fsw, at least one occupant (inside tender) will be breathing air. At depths of less than 45 fsw, the inside tender may breathe oxygen but should not strap on the BIBS mask. The treatment tables that follow have instructions for tender oxygen breathing. High oxygen treatment gasses are now being utilized deeper than 60 fsw, since a high partial pressure of oxygen offers a significant therapeutic advantage over air. The target zone is typically a partial pressure of 1.5 to 3.0 ATA of oxygen at treatment depth. This is achieved using either N_2O_2 or HeO_2 at depths up to 165 fsw and at depths beyond 165 fsw with HeO_2 only.

Depth (fsw)	Breathing Gas	O_2 Percentage	ppO_2
0 – 60	Oxygen	100%	1.00 – 2.82
61–165	N_2O_2 or HeO_2	50%	1.42 – 3.00
166 – 225	Helium/Oxygen Mix	36%	2.17 – 2.81

Decompression sickness following helium dives may be treated with either N_2O_2 or HeO_2. For treatment requiring depths beyond 165 fsw (which is extremely rare), HeO_2 is strongly recommended to avoid nitrogen narcosis. For treatment of decompression sickness following air or N_2O_2 dives, helium should be avoided as the breathing medium, as studies have indicated that in these cases, helium may do more harm than good.

In cases where the patient cannot tolerate 100% oxygen at 60 fsw or shallower (CNS toxicity), high oxygen treatment gasses are often a good alternative, since they keep the ppO_2 significantly higher than air.

10.4 OXYGEN PROBLEMS OCCURING DURING TREATMENT

Oxygen is the therapeutic gas for many of the treatment tables, and a failure of the oxygen system requires the proper action. Likewise, CNS oxygen toxicity may develop on any oxygen treatment table and pulmonary oxygen toxicity may develop on Tables 4, 7, 8 or on a Table 6 if repeat treatments are required.

10.4.1 CNS Toxicity

On oxygen treatment tables, the chamber operator and the inside tender or DMT must be continually watching for initial signs and symptoms of CNS oxygen toxicity. The acronym CON-VENTID will help to remember the signs and symptoms: convulsions, vision, ears, nausea, twitching/tingling, irritability and dizziness. At the first sign of CNS toxicity, the BIBS mask must be removed. Unfortunately, convulsions do occur sometimes with no other warning signs. CNS toxicity is unlikely to occur in a resting individual at 50 fsw and shallower and highly unlikely to occur at 30 fsw and shallower, even when active. Patients with arterial gas embolism or severe Type II decompression sickness may be more susceptible to CNS oxygen toxicity. Also, seizures occurring as a result of these conditions may be hard to distinguish from convulsions due to CNS oxygen toxicity.

10.4.1.1 Procedures for CNS Oxygen Toxicity During Treatment

At the first sign of oxygen toxicity, the patient must be removed from oxygen and allowed to breathe chamber air. Fifteen minutes after the last symptom has subsided, resume oxygen breathing. For Tables 5, 6 and 6A, resume oxygen breathing at the point of interruption. For Tables 4, 7 and 8, no lengthening of the table is required due to the interruption. If oxygen toxicity symptoms develop again, or if the first symptom is a convulsion, take the actions detailed below:

When using Treatment Table 5, 6 or 6A:
- Remove the BIBS mask from the patient.
- Wait for all symptoms to completely subside, and then ascend 10 fsw at a rate of 1 fsw/min. For convulsions, travel after the patient is fully relaxed and breathing normally.
- Resume oxygen breathing at the shallower depth at the point of interruption.
- If another toxicity symptom occurs after ascending 10 fsw, consult the on-call hyperbaric physician about modifications to the treatment.

When using Treatment Table 4, 7 or 8:
- Remove the BIBS mask from the patient.
- Consult the on-call hyperbaric physician before resuming oxygen breathing. No lengthening of the tables will be required to compensate for the interruption.

10.4.2 Pulmonary Oxygen Toxicity

When using Treatment Tables 5, 6 or 6A pulmonary oxygen toxicity is highly unlikely. When using Treatment Table 4, 7 or 8, or with repeated uses of TT5, 6 or 6A (particularly with extensions), the long periods of oxygen breathing may result in pulmonary toxicity. Patients will present end-inspiratory discomfort, which may progress to substernal burning and severe pain on inspiration. If a patient shows a good response to treatment but complains of substernal burning, discontinue oxygen and consult with the hyperbaric physician. If, however, neurological deficit remains and improvement is noted (or if condition deteriorates when oxygen is stopped), oxygen should be continued as long as is considered beneficial or until pain limits inspiration. If oxygen breathing must be continued beyond the onset of substernal burning, or if the 2-hour air breaks found in TT4, 7 or 8 cannot be used due to deterioration in patient condition on the discontinuance of oxygen, the O_2 breathing periods should be changed to 20 minutes on O_2 followed by a 10-minute air break. Alternatively, a treatment gas with a lower percentage of oxygen may be used. The course of action will be decided by the on-call hyperbaric physician.

10.4.3 Loss of Oxygen During Treatment

The loss of oxygen to the BIBS during a treatment should be handled as indicated below:

If oxygen supply can be restored within 15 minutes:

- Maintain depth until oxygen is restored.
- Once oxygen is restored, resume treatment at the point of interruption.

If oxygen supply can be restored after 15 minutes but before 2 hours (table selected TT5, 6 or 6A):

- Maintain depth until oxygen is restored
- Once oxygen is restored, complete treatment with maximum number of O_2 extensions

If oxygen supply can be restored after 15 minutes but before 2 hours (table selected TT4, 7 or 8):

- Continue decompression as with oxygen, changing back to oxygen when it is restored
- If the patient has worsening symptoms without oxygen, the decompression must be stopped. Once oxygen is restored, continue treatment from point where it was stopped.

If oxygen supply cannot be restored within 2 hours, switch to the comparable air treatment table at the current depth if at 60 fsw or shallower. Ascent rate must not exceed 1 fsw per minute between stops. If it becomes apparent symptoms are worsening and a depth deeper than 60 fsw is needed, use TT4.

10.5 POST-TREATMENT CONSIDERATIONS

Inside tenders on Treatment Table 5, 6, 6A, 1A, 2A, or 3 will require a minimum 18-hoursurface interval prior to performing no-decompression dives and a minimum 24-hour surface interval prior to decompression dives. Inside tenders on Treatment Table 4, 7 and 8 will require a minimum 48-hour surface interval prior to performing any dive.

Inside tenders should remain near the chamber for 1 hour after a treatment. If they were inside tender on a TT4, 7 or 8, they should remain within 1-hour travel of the chamber for 24 hours.

INSIDE TENDER OXYGEN BREATHING REQUIREMENTS

Treatment Table Utilized	O$_2$ Time (min)
TT 5 with or without extension @ 30 fsw	:00
TT6 with up to one extension @ either 60 fsw or 30 fsw	:30
TT6 with more than one extension	:60
TT6A with up to one extension @ either 60 fsw or 30 fsw	:60
TT6A with more than one extension	:90

Note 1: Tender O$_2$ breathing times are at 30 fsw, and tenders breathe O$_2$ on ascent from 30 fsw to the surface
 Note 2: If tender has had hyperbaric exposure within the previous 18 hours, use the following guidance:
     For TT5, add an additional 20-min. O$_2$ period to the times in the table.
     For TT6 or TT6A add an additional 60-min. O$_2$ period to the times in the table.	

Source: *U.S. Navy Diving Manual*

10.5.1 Observation Period

Patients treated on a Treatment Table 5 that have had complete relief must remain near the chamber for 2 hours. Patients treated for Type II symptoms or patients treated on a Treatment Table 6 for Type I symptoms that have had complete relief must remain near the chamber for 6 hours. Any patient treated on a TT6, 6A, 4, 7, 8 or 9 is likely to require at least some hospitalization. The hyperbaric physician will determine whether hospitalization is required, and the length of observation time. Regardless, all patients undergoing treatment should remain within 1-hour travel time from the chamber for 24 hours and be accompanied for that period by a person able to recognize the recurrence of symptoms.

10.5.2 Flying After Treatment

Patients presenting any residual symptoms must not fly without first consulting a hyperbaric physician. Patients experiencing complete relief after treatment for AGE or DS must not fly for a minimum 72 hours after treatment.

Inside tenders on Treatment Table 5, 6, 6A, 1A, 2A or 3 must not fly for at least 24 hours. Inside tenders on Treatment Table 4, 7 or 8 must not fly for at least 72 hours.

10.5.3 Air Evacuation

Occasionally patients will require air evacuation to a shore-based medical or treatment facility immediately upon the completion of treatment. They will not meet the surface interval requirements mentioned above. These evacuations are only done on the advice of the on-call hyperbaric physician. Aircraft with a cabin pressurized to 1 ATA should be used if possible, or if an unpressurized cabin, the aircraft must stay below 1,000 feet above sea level. The patient should be maintained on 100% oxygen during transit. If available, load the patient into a hyperbaric stretcher for the evacuation and maintain the pressure at 1 ata.

10.5.4 Residual Symptoms

After treatment, if a complete medical evaluation indicates Type II symptoms remain, additional treatments will most likely be prescribed by the hyperbaric physician. These will be better performed at a shore-based facility, since most offshore sites do not have the capacity to maintain daily treatments along with the day-to-day operations of the diving crew. Sometimes the physician will allow the patient to return home if there is a treatment facility nearby. If the patient is ambulatory and is traveling home or to a treatment facility, someone must escort the patient who has a basic knowledge of diving medicine and be familiar with the patient's case.

10.5.5 Returning to Diving after Treatment

Divers presenting Type I symptoms and meeting all the criteria to allow them to be treated on a Treatment Table 5 who have had complete relief may return to diving 48 hours after completion of treatment, providing there was no doubt about the presence or absence of Type II symptoms. If there was some doubt about Type II symptoms, the diver will be required to consult with the hyperbaric physician before resumption of diving.

Divers presenting Type I symptoms but requiring treatment on Treatment Table 6 who have had complete relief of all symptoms may return to diving after 7 days.

Divers presenting symptoms and diagnosed with Type II decompression sickness or arterial gas embolism may be cleared to dive 30 days after treatment by the hyperbaric physician provided no evidence exists of neurological deficit.

10.6 NON-STANDARD TREATMENTS

All treatment recommendations presented here are as found in the *U.S. Navy Diving Manual Rev. 6* and should be followed as closely as possible unless it becomes evident they are not working. Only a hyperbaric physician may recommend changes to the treatment protocols, and any changes should then be approved by the corporate diving manager. These treatment tables are considered the minimum required and should in no case be shortened, except when either the patient is declared dead or the vessel on which the chamber is located is afire or in imminent danger of sinking. In these cases, the abort procedures should be followed.

10.7 TREATMENT ABORT PROCEDURES

All treatments must be followed through to the end unless the patient is declared dead or a condition arises that puts the chamber occupants and operators in mortal danger. Abort procedures are explained below.

10.7.1 Abort Due to Death During Treatment

If it appears a diver undergoing treatment has died, the decision to abort must be made by the on-call hyperbaric physician. Once the decision to abort has been made, there are different options available for decompressing the inside tender(s), depending on the depth and the profile of the treatment table.

- If death occurs following initial recompression to 60, 165, or 225 on Treatment Tables 6, 6A, 4 or 8, decompress on the air/oxygen schedule in the air decompression table having the next deeper depth and next longer time than those achieved in the treatment. Even if N_2O_2 or HeO_2 were the breathing medium, the air/oxygen schedule still may be used.
- If death occurs after leaving initial treatment depth on a TT6 or 6A, decompress at 30 fsw/min to 30 fsw, then begin oxygen breathing at 30 fsw for the time indicated in the table below. Once oxygen breathing at 30 fsw is completed, ascend to surface breathing oxygen at a rate of 1 fsw/min.
- If death occurs after leaving the initial treatment depth on TT4 or 8 or after beginning treatment on TT7 at 60 fsw, decompress by continuing the table as written. Alternatively, follow the table as written to 60 fsw. At 60 fsw, have tender breathe oxygen for three 30-minute periods, separated by 5-minute air breaks. Ascend at 30 fpm to 50 fsw. Perform two 30-minute O_2 periods separated by a 5-min. air break. Ascend at 30 fpm to 40 fsw. Perform a 60-min. O_2 period with a 15-min. air break at the end. Ascend at 30 fpm to 30 fsw. Perform a 60-min. O_2 period followed by a 15-min. air break. Ascend at 30 fpm to 20 fsw. Perform two 60-min. O_2 periods, separated by a 15-min. air break. After the final O_2 period at 20 fsw, ascend to surface at 30 fpm. Observe for signs of DCS.

10.7.2 Abort Due to Impending Disaster

If an impending disaster (vessel in danger of sinking, catastrophic mechanical failure, fire on board) forces the treatment to be aborted, the previous abort procedure (10.7.1) may be used for all occupants. If there is insufficient time available, the following actions may be followed:

1. If deeper than 60 feet when deciding to abort, start travel immediately to 60 feet.

2. Once at 60 feet, put all chamber occupants on oxygen. Select the air/oxygen schedule in the air decompression table that corresponds to the deepest depth and total time attained in treatment.

3. If at 60 feet when deciding to abort, put all chamber occupants on O_2 for a period of time equal to all decompression stops 60 feet and deeper according to the air/oxygen schedule, then continue decompression according to the air/oxygen schedule. Complete as much of the oxygen breathing as possible.

4. When no more time is available, surface the chamber (without exceeding 10 fpm if possible) and try to keep all occupants on oxygen during evacuation.

5. Evacuate all chamber occupants to the nearest hyperbaric facility and treat according to the flowchart Treatment for Arterial Gas Embolism or Serious Decompression Sickness. If no symptoms presented between abort and arrival at the facility, follow TT6.

10.8 DMAC MEDICAL KITS

As mentioned in Chapter 9: Emergency Medical Care, offshore commercial diving operations are required by IMCA to have DMAC medical kits, the large primary medical kit (trauma kit) outside the chamber, and the chamber internal kit inside. These kits are based on, and very similar to those found in the *U.S. Navy Diving Manual*. It is the responsibility of the diving medical technicians to maintain these kits, regularly inventory the contents, and ensure that replacement supplies are ordered as supplies are depleted. The contents list for both the DMAC Primary Medical Kit and the DMAC Chamber Internal Medical Kit, as well as the list of required drugs may be found at the end of this chapter.

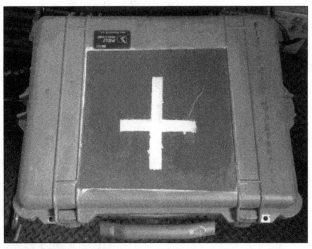

DMAC 15 trauma kit
Photo courtesy of John McElligott

10.9 NEUROLOGICAL EXAMINATION AND EXTREMITY STRENGTH TESTING

The Neurological Exam and Extremity Strength Test is the primary method we use to determine whether neurological deficit exists in a diver stricken with DCS or AGE. There are various neurological examinations out there to choose from, but the neuro exam should assess the following areas: 1) mental status 2) cranial nerves 3) motor function 4) sensory function, and 5) balance and coordination. Nearly 60% of cases of decompression sickness are considered Type I with no neurological involvement, but we must have a method to definitively state there is no neuro involvement. We also need to identify and locate any deficit found in Type II cases, and to establish a base line to determine if treatment is effective and to what degree it is effective. A deficit is more likely to be noticed in the extremity strength test than the neurological exam. Evidence of deficit in either exam requires e stricken diver be treated for Type II DCS or AGE.

There has been a debate ongoing for years as to the need for patient history (including the dive profile) for hyperbaric treatment of pressure-related illness. Treatment for pressure-related illness is symptom based, but there are cases where the history can help to explain the patient's response to a given treatment protocol or even explain residual symptoms. Most hyperbaric physicians will want to see the patient's history, so even if you are inclined to disagree – record it.

Treatment is not delayed for a neurological exam, but the initial assessment can take place while the crew is mustering and readying the chamber and medical equipment. The initial assessment will often indicate the nature of the problem (whether Type I or Type II DCS). In the case of AGE, there is usually no question, and no time for an initial assessment. For the initial assessment, the stricken diver is questioned about his symptoms. The DMT or diving crew member assessing the diver should watch closely (while the diver is questioned and walks to the chamber) for the following:

- Is the diver having difficulty understanding questions, concentrating or remembering?
- Does the diver appear to be unusually irritable or moody?
- Are the diver's pupils equally sized, and do they track smoothly?
- Is the diver having difficulty with speech or enunciating words?
- Is there evidence of hearing difficulty or vision problems? (look for a squint)
- Is the diver experiencing balance problems? (unsteady on feet, stumbling gait)

The above observations are an excellent initial check for neurological problems. They will give a good indication of mental status, balance/coordination, motor coordination, and sensory ability. The only information not gained here is the reflexes. Make careful note of any and all deficiencies.

If the only symptom presenting is pain, have the patient answer the following:

1. Describe the pain (sharp, dull, throbbing)
2. In what area of the body is the pain?
3. Is the pain localized or hard to pinpoint?
4. Is the pain fixed or radiating?
5. When was the pain first noticed? (prior to, during, or after the dive)

If symptoms other than localized pain are presenting, have the patient answer the following:

1. Describe the symptoms (dizziness, vertigo, radiating pain, abnormal sensation, nausea, etc)
2. Does the diver feel unusually fatigued for the amount of effort expended on the dive?
3. How long after the dive were the symptoms first noticed?

   If the symptom was first noticed during the dive, determine if it was during descent, on bottom, during the ascent, or on decompression stops. Are the symptoms remaining the same or worsening with passing time? Are any additional symptoms developing? Has the diver ever experienced similar symptoms? Does the diver have any underlying medical conditions that might explain the symptoms? Has the diver ever suffered from decompression sickness or arterial gas embolism in the past?

If any symptoms other than localized pain presented, or if the initial assessment indicated any deficit, the remainder of the neuro exam and extremity strength test should be performed once the diver has been recompressed to 60 fsw. Details of the dive (depth, bottom time, profile) may be recorded after blow down. The following forms may be used to record the results of the neurological exam and extremity strength test.

10.9.1 Neurological Examination Checklist (Page 1)

NEUROLOGICAL EXAMINATION CHECKLIST

(Sheet 1 of 2)

(See text of Appendix 5A for examination procedures and definitions of terms.)

Patient's Name: _____Date/Time: _____

Describe pain/numbness: _____

_____

HISTORY

Type of dive last performed: _____ Depth: _____ How long: _____

Number of dives in last 24 hours: _____

Was symptom noticed before, during or after the dive? _____

If during, was it while descending, on the bottom or ascending? _____

Has symptom increased or decreased since it was first noticed? _____

Have any other symptoms occurred since the first one was noticed? _____

Describe: _____

Has patient ever had a similar symptom before? _____When: _____

_____

MENTAL STATUS/STATE OF CONSCIOUSNESS

_____

_____

COORDINATION		STRENGTH (Grade 0 to 5)		
	Walk: _____	**UPPER BODY**		
	Heel-to Toe: _____	Deltoids	L ____	R ____
	Romberg: _____	Latissimus	L ____	R ____
	Finger-to-Nose: _____	Biceps	L ____	R ____
	Heel Shin Slide: _____	Triceps	L ____	R ____
	Rapid Movement: _____	Forearms	L ____	R ____
		Hands	L ____	R ____
CRANIAL NERVES		**LOWER BODY**		
	Sense of Smell (I): _____	**Hips**		
	Vision/Visual Fld (II): _____	Flexion	L ____	R ____
Eye Movements, Pupils (III, IV, VI): _____		Extension	L ____	R ____
	Facial Sensation, Chewing (V): _____	Abduction	L ____	R ____
	Facial Expression Muscles (VII): _____	Adduction	L ____	R ____
	Hearing (VIII): _____	**Knees**		
Upper Mouth, Throat Sensation (IX): _____		Flexion	L ____	R ____
	Gag & Voice (X): _____	Extension	L ____	R ____
	Shoulder Shrug (XI): _____			
	Tongue (XII): _____			

Figure 5A-1a. Neurological Examination Checklist (sheet 1 of 2).

Source: *U.S. Navy Diving Manual*

10.9.2 Neurological Examination Checklist (Page 2)

NEUROLOGICAL EXAMINATION CHECKLIST
(Sheet 2 of 2)

REFLEXES
(Grade: Normal, Hypoactive, Hyperactive, Absent

Biceps	L ____	R ____	**Ankles**			
Triceps	L ____	R ____	Dorsiflexion	L ____	R ____
Knees	L ____	R ____	Plantarflexion	L ____	R ____
Ankles	L ____	R ____	**Toes**	L ____	R ____

Sensory Examination for Skin Sensation
(Use diagram to record location of sensory abnormalities – numbness, tingling, etc.)

LOCATION

Indicate results
as follows:

|||| Painful
Area

＝ Decreased
＝ Sensation

COMMENTS

_____
_____
_____
_____
_____
_____
_____
_____

Examination Performed by: _____

Figure 5A-1b. Neurological Examination Checklist (sheet 2 of 2).

Source: *U.S. Navy Diving Manual*

10.9.3 Extremity Strength Test Procedure

Table 5A-1. *Extremity Strength Tests.*

Test	Procedure
Deltoid Muscles	The patient raises his arm to the side at the shoulder joint. The examiner places a hand on the patient's wrist and exerts a downward force that the patient resists.
Latissimus Group	The patient raises his arm to the side. The examiner places a hand on the underside of the patient's wrist and resists the patient's attempt to lower his arm.
Biceps	The patient bends his arm at the elbow, toward his chest. The examiner then grasps the patient's wrist and exerts a force to straighten the patient's arm.
Triceps	The patient bends his arm at the elbow, toward his chest. The examiner then places his hand on the patient's forearm and the patient tries to straighten his arm.
Forearm Muscles	The patient makes a fist. The examiner grips the patient's fist and resists while the patient tries to bend his wrist upward and downward.
Hand Muscles	• The patient strongly grips the examiner's extended fingers. • The patient extends his hand with the fingers widespread. The examiner grips two of the extended fingers with two of his own fingers and tries to squeeze the patient's two fingers together, noting the patient's strength of resistance.
Lower Extremity Strength	• The patient walks on his heels for a short distance. The patient then turns around and walks back on his toes. • The patient walks while squatting (duck walk). These tests adequately assesses lower extremity strength as well as balance and coordination. If a more detailed examination of lower extremity strength is desired, testing should be accomplished at each joint as in the upper arm.

In the following tests, the patient sits on a solid surface such as a desk, with feet off the floor.

Test	Procedure
Hip Flexion	The examiner places his hand on the patient's thigh to resist as the patient tries to raise his thigh.
Hip Extension	The examiner places his hand on the underside of the patient's thigh to resist as the patient tries to lower his thigh.
Hip Abduction	The patients sits as above, with knees together. The examiner places a hand on the outside of each of the patient's knees to provide resistance. The patient tries to open his knees.
Hip Adduction	The patient sits as above, with knees apart. The examiner places a hand on the inside of each of the patient's knees to provide resistance. The patient tries to bring his knees together.
Knee Extension	The examiner places a hand on the patient's shin to resist as the patient tries to straighten his leg.
Knee Flexion	The examiner places a hand on the back of the patient's lower leg to resist as the patient tries to pull his lower leg to the rear by flexing his knee.
Ankle Dorsiflexion (ability to flex the foot toward the rear)	The examiner places a hand on top of the patient's foot to resist as the patient tries to raise his foot by flexing it at the ankle.
Ankle Plantarflexion (ability to flex the foot downward)	The examiner places a hand on the bottom of the patient's foot to resist as the patient tries to lower his foot by flexing it at the ankle.
Toes	• The patient stands on tiptoes for 15 seconds • The patient flexes his toes with resistance provided by the examiner.

Source: *U.S. Navy Diving Manual*

10.9.4 Form for Extremity Strength Test

Test Performed	Left Side		Right Side	
	Normal	Abnormal	Normal	Abnormal
Deltoid Muscles				
Latissimus Group				
Biceps				
Triceps				
Forearm Muscles				
Hand Muscles				
Lower Extremity Strength				
Hip Flexion Upward				
Hip Flexion Downward				
Hip Abduction				
Hip Adduction				
Knee Extension				
Knee Flexion				
Ankle Dorsiflexion (flex foot toward rear)				
Ankle Plantarflexion (flex foot downward)				
Toes				
Additional comments:				
Patient Name:				
Examination performed by: Date:				

EXTREMITY STRENGTH TEST RESULTS

If time permits, extremity strength tests are best performed on deck due to limited space in most offshore chambers. However, if the chamber and all personnel are ready and it is apparent that Type II symptoms are presenting, it is not advisable to delay recompression to perform the extremity strength test. Most components of the test can be performed in the chamber.

10.9.5 Deep Tendon Reflex Test

Table 5A-2. Reflexes.

Test	Procedure
Biceps	The examiner holds the patient's elbow with the patient's hand resting on the examiner's forearm. The patient's elbow should be slightly bent and his arm relaxed. The examiner places his thumb on the patient's biceps tendon, located in the bend of the patient's elbow. The examiner taps his thumb with the percussion hammer, feeling for the patient's muscle to contract.
Triceps	The examiner supports the patient's arm at the biceps. The patient's arm hangs with the elbow bent. The examiner taps the back of the patient's arm just above the elbow with the percussion hammer, feeling for the muscle to contract.
Knee	The patient sits on a table or bench with his feet off the deck. The examiner taps the patient's knee just below the kneecap, on the tendon. The examiner looks for the contraction of the quadriceps (thigh muscle) and movement of the lower leg.
Ankle	The patient sits as above. The examiner places slight pressure on the patient's toes to stretch the Achilles' tendon, feeling for the toes to contract as the Achilles' tendon shortens (contracts).

Source: *U.S. Navy Diving Manual*

10.9.6 Dermatomal Areas Correlated to Spinal Cord Segment (Posterior)

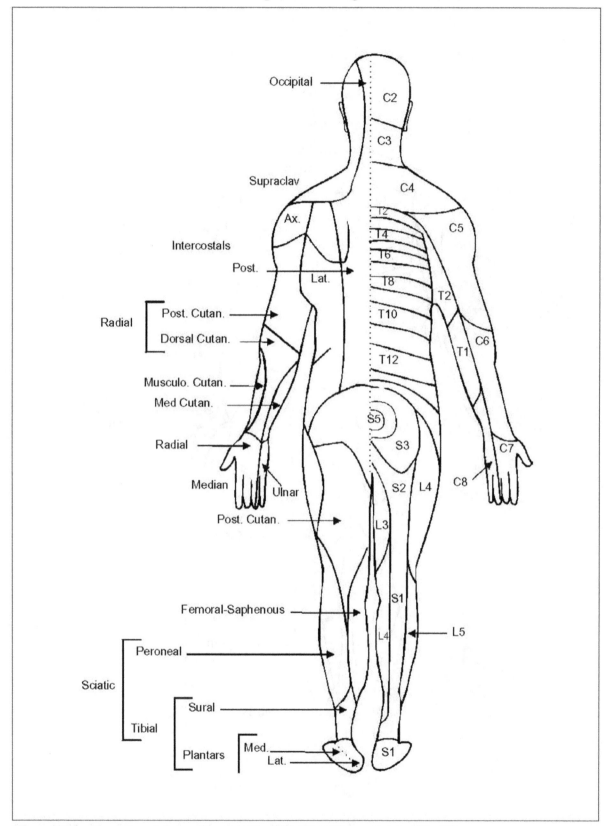

Figure 5A-2a. Dermatomal Areas Correlated to Spinal Cord Segment (sheet 1 of 2).

Source: *U.S. Navy Diving Manual*

10.9.7 Dermatomal Areas Correlated to Spinal Cord Segment (Anterior)

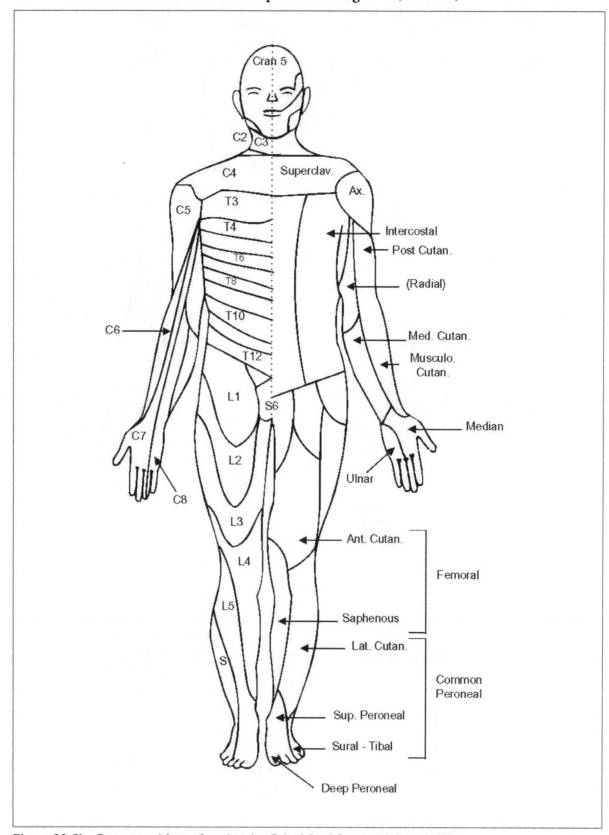

Figure 5A-2b. Dermatomal Areas Correlated to Spinal Cord Segment (sheet 2 of 2).

Source: *U.S. Navy Diving Manual*

10.9.8 Rapid Neuro Exam (4 Minute Neuro)

The following is the Rapid Neuro Exam developed by the Canadian Navy. This thorough exam is approved and recommended by the Undersea & Hyperbaric Medical Society and can be performed on deck while the chamber is being made ready. Although it can be performed in only four minutes, all of the major indicators of neurological involvement are covered in this single examination.

4-Minute Neuro

Patient's Name: _____ Place: _____ Date: _____ Time: _____

HEAD AND NECK	Normal	Abnormal
Orientation *(time, person, place)*	_____	_____
Visual Acuity *(count fingers; ask about double vision)*	_____	_____
Visual Fields *(bring fingers from behind patient's head)*	_____	_____
Pupils equal and reactive to light	_____	_____
Eye movement *("H" pattern; nystagmus)*	_____	_____
Clench teeth *(check jaw muscles)*	_____	_____
Furrow brow	_____	_____
Shut eyes tight *(check muscles above and below eyes)*	_____	_____
Check hearing/noises	_____	_____
Smile or grimace	_____	_____
Swallow	_____	_____
Protrude tongue *(check for deviation to one side)*	_____	_____
Shrug shoulders *(apply force both shoulders; check resistance)*	_____	_____

SENSATION

	Normal	Abnormal
Ask if any unusual sensation	_____	_____

Sensation (draw fingernails [along] both hands simultaneously, inside and out along length & across opposing sides. Do both feel the same?)

Check sensation of:		Normal	Abnormal
	cheeks	_____	_____
	forehead	_____	_____
	lower jaw	_____	_____
	arms	_____	_____
	trunk	_____	_____
	back	_____	_____
	legs	_____	_____
Sensation same on both sides		_____	_____

MOTOR FUNCTION

		Normal	Abnormal
Finger squeezes bilaterally		_____	_____
Thumbs up & down, resist pushing arms together and apart		_____	_____
Flexion and extension	hip	_____	_____
	knee	_____	_____
	ankle	_____	_____
Plantar Reflex (Babinski) *(toes down = normal)*		_____	_____

RAPID NEUROLOGICAL EXAMINATION COMMENTS

Source: *Royal Canadian Navy*

10.10 FLOWCHARTS AND TREATMENT TABLES (*U.S. NAVY DIVING MANUAL*)

10.10.1 Flowchart for AGE or Type II

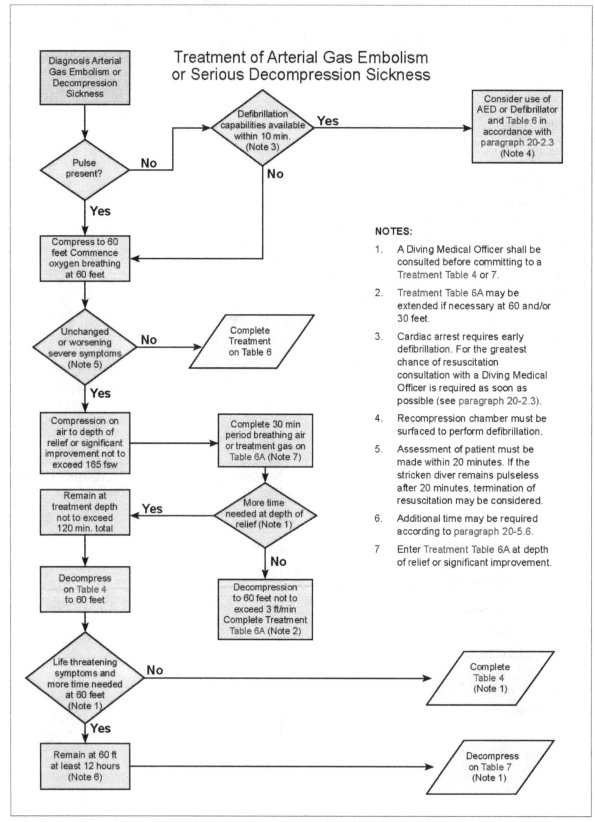

Figure 20-1. Treatment of Arterial Gas Embolism or Serious Decompression Sickness.

10.10.2 Flowchart for Type I

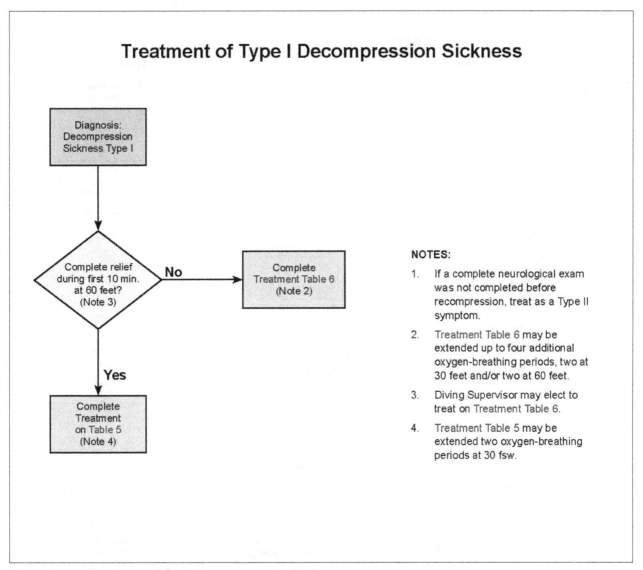

Figure 20-2. Treatment of Type I Decompression Sickness.

10.10.3 Flowchart for Symptom Recurrence

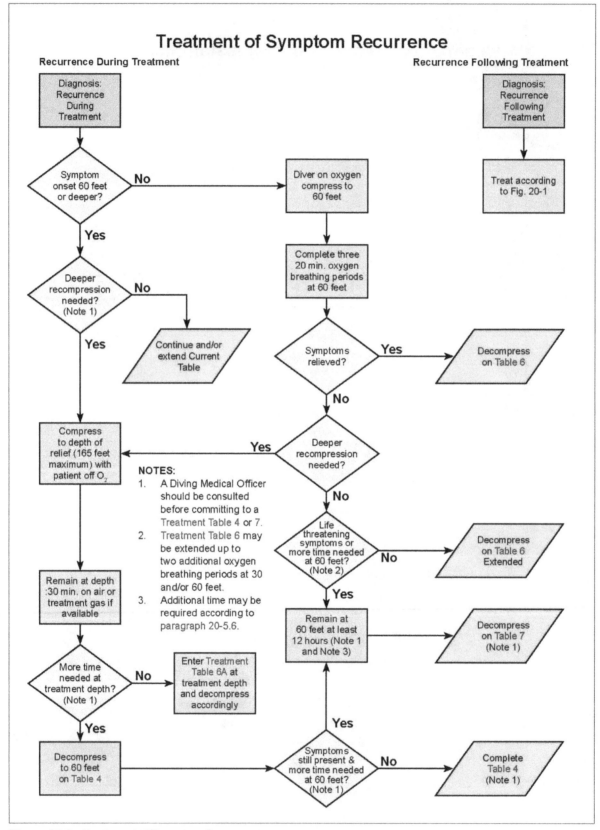

Figure 20-3. Treatment of Symptom Recurrence.

10.10.4 Treatment Table 5

Treatment Table 5

1. Descent rate - 20 ft/min.

2. Ascent rate - Not to exceed 1 ft/min. Do not compensate for slower ascent rates. Compensate for faster rates by halting the ascent.

3. Time on oxygen begins on arrival at 60 feet.

4. If oxygen breathing must be interrupted because of CNS Oxygen Toxicity, allow 15 minutes after the reaction has entirely subsided and resume schedule at point of interruption (see paragraph 20-7.11.1.1)

5. Treatment Table may be extended two oxygen-breathing periods at the 30-foot stop. No air break required between oxygen-breathing periods or prior to ascent.

6. Tender breathes 100 percent O_2 during ascent from the 30-foot stop to the surface. If the tender had a previous hyperbaric exposure in the previous 18 hours, an additional 20 minutes of oxygen breathing is required prior to ascent.

Treatment Table 5 Depth/Time Profile

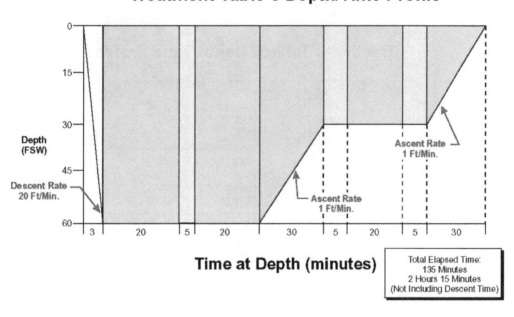

Figure 20-4. Treatment Table 5.

10.10.5 Treatment Table 6

Treatment Table 6

1. Descent rate - 20 ft/min.

2. Ascent rate - Not to exceed 1 ft/min. Do not compensate for slower ascent rates. Compensate for faster rates by halting the ascent.

3. Time on oxygen begins on arrival at 60 feet.

4. If oxygen breathing must be interrupted because of CNS Oxygen Toxicity, allow 15 minutes after the reaction has entirely subsided and resume schedule at point of interruption (see paragraph 20-7.11.1.1).

5. Table 6 can be lengthened up to 2 additional 25-minute periods at 60 feet (20 minutes on oxygen and 5 minutes on air), or up to 2 additional 75-minute periods at 30 feet (15 minutes on air and 60 minutes on oxygen), or both.

6. Tender breathes 100 percent O_2 during the last 30 min. at 30 fsw and during ascent to the surface for an unmodified table or where there has been only a single extension at 30 or 60 feet. If there has been more than one extension, the O_2 breathing at 30 feet is increased to 60 minutes. If the tender had a hyperbaric exposure within the past 18 hours an additional 60-minute O_2 period is taken at 30 feet.

Treatment Table 6 Depth/Time Profile

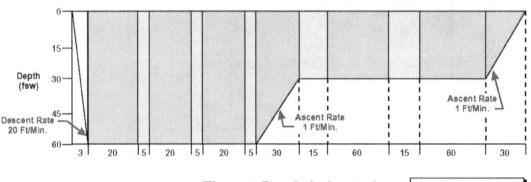

Figure 20-5. Treatment Table 6.

10.10.6 Treatment Table 6A

Treatment Table 6A

1. Descent rate - 20 ft/min.

2. Ascent rate - 165 fsw to 60 fsw not to exceed 3 ft/min, 60 fsw and shallower, not to exceed 1 ft/min. Do not compensate for slower ascent rates. Compensate for faster rates by halting the ascent.

3. Time at treatment depth does not include compression time.

4. Table begins with initial compression to depth of 60 fsw. If initial treatment was at 60 feet, up to 20 minutes may be spent at 60 feet before compression to 165 fsw. Contact a Diving Medical Officer.

5. If a chamber is equipped with a high-O_2 treatment gas, it may be administered at 165 fsw and shallower, not to exceed 3.0 ata O_2 in accordance with paragraph 20-7.10. Treatment gas is administered for 25 minutes interrupted by 5 minutes of air. Treatment gas is breathed during ascent from the treatment depth to 60 fsw.

6. Deeper than 60 feet, if treatment gas must be interrupted because of CNS oxygen toxicity, allow 15 minutes after the reaction has entirely subsided before resuming treatment gas. The time off treatment gas is counted as part of the time at treatment depth. If at 60 feet or shallower and oxygen breathing must be interrupted because of CNS oxygen toxicity, allow 15 minutes after the reaction has entirely subsided and resume schedule at point of interruption (see paragraph 20-7.11.1.1).

7. Table 6A can be lengthened up to 2 additional 25-minute periods at 60 feet (20 minutes on oxygen and 5 minutes on air), or up to 2 additional 75-minute periods at 30 feet (60 minutes on oxygen and 15 minutes on air), or both.

8. Tender breathes 100 percent O_2 during the last 60 minutes at 30 fsw and during ascent to the surface for an unmodified table or where there has been only a single extension at 30 or 60 fsw. If there has been more than one extension, the O_2 breathing at 30 fsw is increased to 90 minutes. If the tender had a hyperbaric exposure within the past 18 hours, an additional 60 minute O_2 breathing period is taken at 30 fsw.

9. If significant improvement is not obtained within 30 minutes at 165 feet, consult with a Diving Medical Officer before switching to Treatment Table 4.

Treatment Table 6A Depth/Time Profile

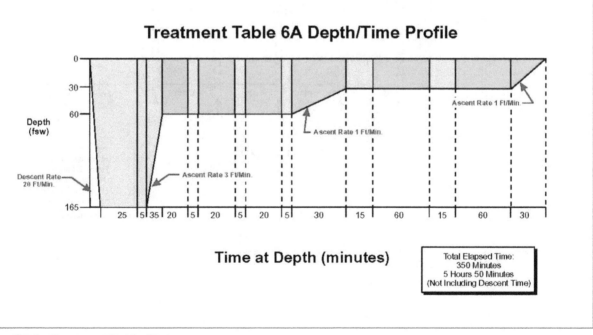

Time at Depth (minutes)

Total Elapsed Time:
350 Minutes
5 Hours 50 Minutes
(Not Including Descent Time)

Figure 20-6. Treatment Table 6A.

10.10.7 Treatment Table 4

Treatment Table 4

1. Descent rate - 20 ft/min.

2. Ascent rate - 1 ft/min.

3. Time at 165 feet includes compression.

4. If only air is available, decompress on air. If oxygen is available, patient begins oxygen breathing upon arrival at 60 feet with appropriate air breaks. Both tender and patient breathe oxygen beginning 2 hours before leaving 30 feet. (see paragraph 20-5.5).

5. Ensure life-support considerations can be met before committing to a Table 4. (see paragraph 20-7.5) Internal chamber temperature should be below 85° F.

6. If oxygen breathing is interrupted, no compensatory lengthening of the table is required.

7. If switching from Treatment Table 6A or 3 at 165 feet, stay a maximum of 2 hours at 165 feet before decompressing.

8. If the chamber is equipped with a high-O_2 treatment gas, it may be administered at 165 fsw, not to exceed 3.0 ata O_2. Treatment gas is administered for 25 minutes interrupted by 5 minutes of air.

Treatment Table 4 Depth/Time Profile

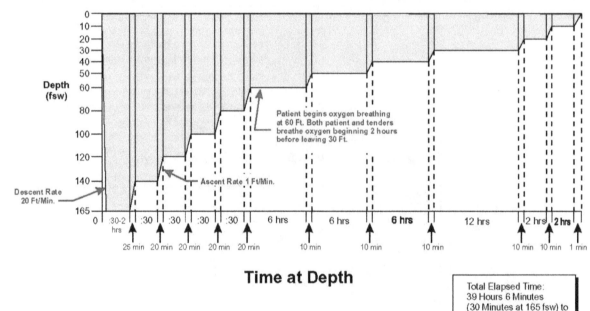

Depth (fsw)

Descent Rate 20 Ft/Min.

Ascent Rate 1 Ft/Min.

Patient begins oxygen breathing at 60 Ft. Both patient and tenders breathe oxygen beginning 2 hours before leaving 30 Ft.

Time at Depth

Total Elapsed Time:
39 Hours 6 Minutes
(30 Minutes at 165 fsw) to
40 Hours 36 Minutes
(2 Hours at 165 fsw)

Figure 20-7. Treatment Table 4.

10.10.8 Treatment Table 7

Treatment Table 7

1. Table begins upon arrival at 60 feet. Arrival at 60 feet is accomplished by initial treatment on Table 6, 6A or 4. If initial treatment has progressed to a depth shallower than 60 feet, compress to 60 feet at 20 ft/min to begin Table 7.

2. Maximum duration at 60 feet is unlimited. Remain at 60 feet a minimum of 12 hours unless overriding circumstances dictate earlier decompression.

3. Patient begins oxygen breathing periods at 60 feet. Tender need breathe only chamber atmosphere throughout. If oxygen breathing is interrupted, no lengthening of the table is required.

4. Minimum chamber O_2 concentration is 19 percent. Maximum CO_2 concentration is 1.5 percent SEV (11.4 mmHg). Maximum chamber internal temperature is 85°F (paragraph 20-7.5).

5. Decompression starts with a 2-foot upward excursion from 60 to 58 feet. Decompress with stops every 2 feet for times shown in profile below. Ascent time between stops is approximately 30 seconds. Stop time begins with ascent from deeper to next shallower step. Stop at 4 feet for 4 hours and then ascend to the surface at 1 ft/min.

6. Ensure chamber life-support requirements can be met before committing to a Treatment Table 7.

7. A Diving Medical Officer should be consulted before committing to this treatment table.

Treatment Table 7 Depth/Time Profile

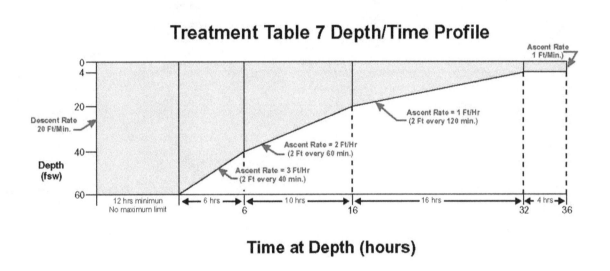

Figure 20-8. Treatment Table 7.

10.10.9 Treatment Table 8

Treatment Table 8

1. Enter the table at the depth which is exactly equal to or next greater than the deepest depth attained in the recompression. The descent rate is as fast as tolerable.

2. The maximum time that can be spent at the deepest depth is shown in the second column. The maximum time for 225 fsw is 30 minutes; for 165 fsw, 3 hours. For an asymptomatic diver, the maximum time at depth is 30 minutes for depths exceeding 165 fsw and 2 hours for depths equal to or shallower than 165 fsw.

3. Decompression is begun with a 2-fsw reduction in pressure if the depth is an even number. Decompression is begun with a 3-fsw reduction in pressure if the depth is an odd number. Subsequent stops are carried out every 2 fsw. Stop times are given in column three. The stop time begins when leaving the previous depth. Ascend to the next stop in approximately 30 seconds.

4. Stop times apply to all stops within the band up to the next quoted depth. For example, for ascent from 165 fsw, stops for 12 minutes are made at 162 fsw and at every two-foot interval to 140 fsw. At 140 fsw, the stop time becomes 15 minutes. When traveling from 225 fsw, the 166-foot stop is 5 minutes; the 164-foot stop is 12 minutes. Once begun, decompression is continuous. For example, when decompressing from 225 feet, ascent is not halted at 165 fsw for 3 hours. However, ascent may be halted at 60 fsw and shallower for any desired period of time.

5. While deeper than 165 fsw, a helium-oxygen mixture with 16-36 percent oxygen may be breathed by mask to reduce narcosis. A 64/36 helium-oxygen mixture is the preferred treatment gas. At 165 fsw and shallower, a HeO_2 or N_2O_2 mix with a ppO_2 not to exceed 3.0 ata may be given to the diver as a treatment gas. At 60 fsw and shallower, pure oxygen may be given to the divers as a treatment gas. For all treatment gases (HeO_2, N_2O and O_2), a schedule of 25 minutes on gas and 5 minute on chamber air should be followed for a total of four cycles. Additional oxygen may be given at 60 fsw after a 2-hour interval of chamber air. See Treatment Table 7 for guidance. If high O_2 breathing is interrupted, no lengthening of the table is required.

6. To avoid loss of the chamber seal, ascent may be halte at 4 fsw and the total remaining stop time of 240 minute taken at this depth. Ascend directly to the surface upon completion of the required time.

7. Total ascent time from 225 fsw is 56 hours, 29 minutes. For a 165-fsw recompression, total ascent time is 53 hours, 52 minutes, and for a 60-fsw recompression, 36 hours, 0 minutes.

Depth (fsw)	Max Time at Initial Treatment Depth (hours)	2-fsw Stop Times (minutes)
225	0.5	5
165	3	12
140	5	15
120	8	20
100	11	25
80	15	30
60	Unlimited	40
40	Unlimited	60
20	Unlimited	120

Figure 20-9. Treatment Table 8.

10.10.10 Treatment Table 9

Treatment Table 9

1. Descent rate - 20 ft/min.

2. Ascent rate - 20 ft/min. Rate may be slowed to 1 ft/min depending upon the patient's medical condition.

3. Time at 45 feet begins on arrival at 45 feet.

4. If oxygen breathing must be interrupted because of CNS Oxygen Toxicity, oxygen breathing may be restarted 15 minutes after all symptoms have subsided. Resume schedule at point of interruption (see paragraph 20-7.11.1.1).

5. Tender breathes 100 percent O_2 during last 15 minute at 45 feet and during ascent to the surface regardless of ascent rate used.

6. Patient may breathe air or oxygen during ascent.

7. If patient cannot tolerate oxygen at 45 feet, this table can be modified to allow a treatment depth of 30 feet. The oxygen breathing time can be extended to a maximum of 3 to 4 hours.

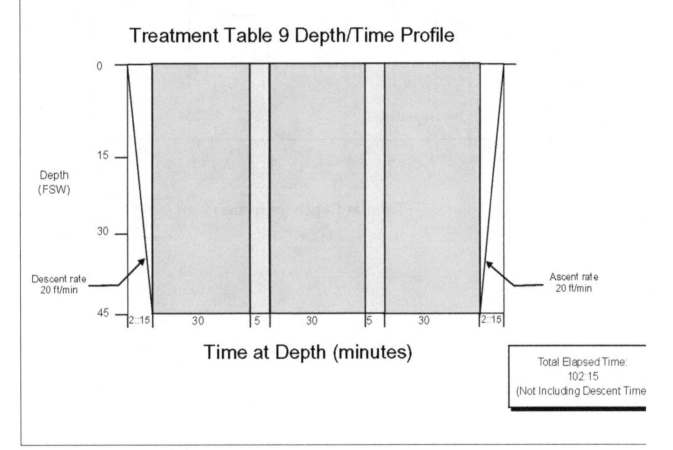

Figure 20-10. Treatment Table 9.

10.10.11 Treatment Table 1A

Air Treatment Table 1A

1. Descent rate - 20 ft/min.

2. Ascent rate - 1 ft/min.

3. Time at 100 feet includes time from the surface.

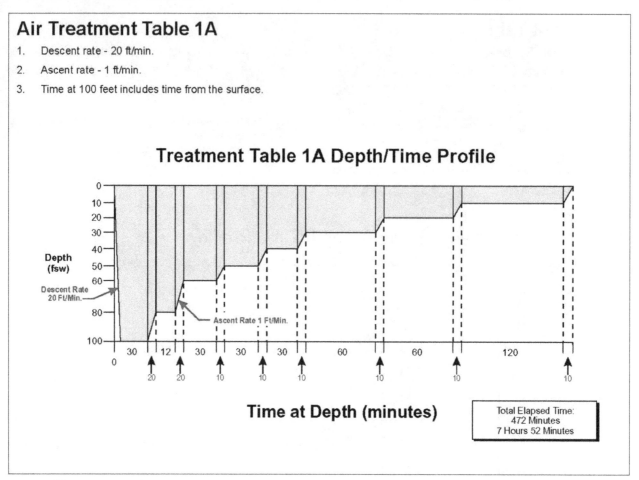

Figure 20-11. Air Treatment Table 1A.

10.10.12 Treatment Table 2A

Air Treatment Table 2A

1. Descent rate - 20 ft/min.
2. Ascent rate - 1 ft/min.
3. Time at 165 feet includes time from the surface.

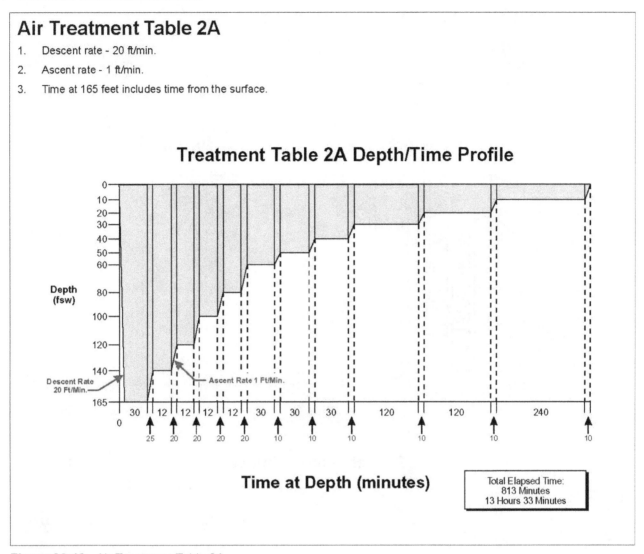

Figure 20-12. Air Treatment Table 2A.

10.10.13 Treatment Table 3

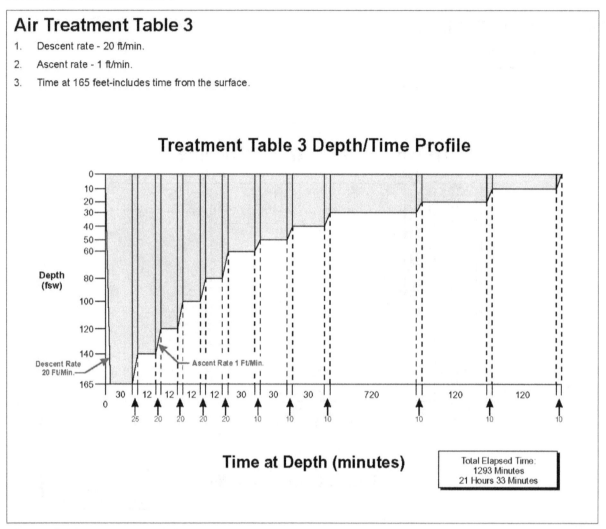

Air Treatment Table 3

1. Descent rate - 20 ft/min.

2. Ascent rate - 1 ft/min.

3. Time at 165 feet-includes time from the surface.

Figure 20-13. Air Treatment Table 3.

10.11 PRACTICE EXERCISES

The following exercises are presented to familiarize the reader with the usage of the flowcharts and treatment tables as found in the *U.S. Navy Diving Manual Revision 6*.

Problem:

A male diver has reported serious, non-radiating pain in his right elbow. He dove earlier today. H is depth of dive was 64 fsw, his bottom time was 53 min., and since your company goes by the +5+5 rule, he was on an 80 fsw table on the 80/60 schedule. He spent 30 minutes breathing air on a 20 fsw water stop and came to surface 35 minutes ago. How would you diagnose his condition, and how would you treat it?

Solution:

Although you will make note of the depth, duration, and decompression of the dive, it will have no bearing on the diagnosis or treatment. The diver is reporting pain only, so we suspect Type I DCS. The chamber is going to be 5 minutes until it is ready, so we first perform a Rapid Neuro Exam to eliminate the possibility of Type II DCS. As soon as the chamber is ready, we blow him down to 60 fsw, and look at the flowchart.

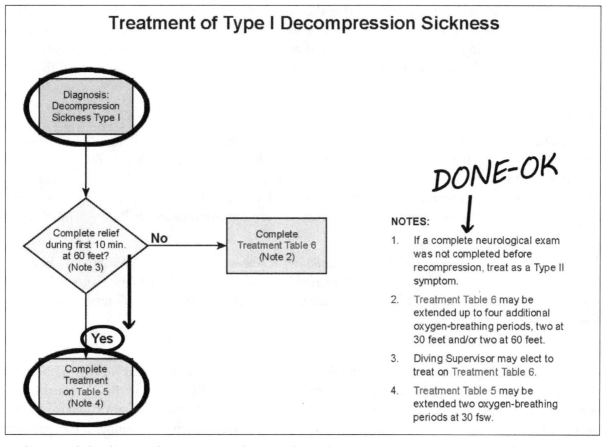

We diagnosed the diver with Type I DCS because his only symptom was pain. Waiting for the chamber to be made ready, we performed a Rapid Neuro and found no deficit. After just 5 minutes breathing oxygen at 60 fsw, the diver reported complete relief, so we proceed with Treatment Table 5 (TT5). When using the treatment tables, green represents time breathing oxygen and blue represents time breathing air.

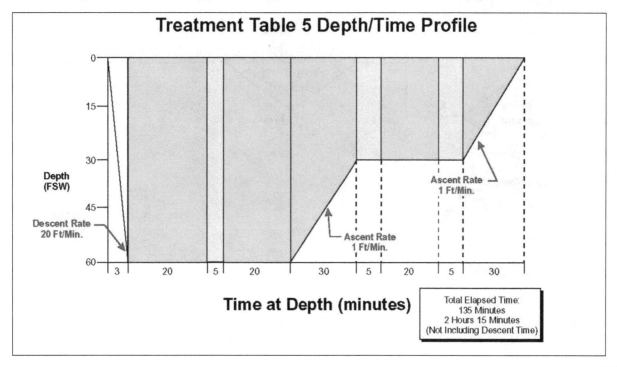

Looking at the previous table, we can see that the diver has two 20-min. oxygen breathing periods at 60 fsw, separated by a 5-minute air break. Then he takes 30 minutes to travel from 60 fsw to 30 fsw (1 fsw/min) also breathing oxygen. Once at 30 fsw, there is a 5-min. air break and then a 20-min. oxygen breathing period. This is again followed by a 5-min. air break and then the 30-min. travel to surface starts, again at 1 fsw/min.

NOTE:

As mentioned in Chapter 3: Underwater Physiology, there are two schools of thought on treating DCS: the first using TT5 for Type I cases and TT6 for Type II; the second using TT6 for all. The first method is illustrated in the example above but the second method is completely acceptable as it provides a safer alternative. Many diving contractors now insist on using TT6, regardless of symptoms, and only use TT5 for asymptomatic omitted decompression or for surface decompression delays shallower than 40 fsw.

Problem:

A female diver has just arrived on surface and cannot walk. She was fine while in the water, but she cannot seem to keep her balance and had to be half-carried from the stage. While the tenders are dressing her down, you notice that one pupil is twice the size of the other. The chamber is all ready. How do you diagnose and treat this diver?

Solution:

It is obvious the diver has neurological involvement: balance and/or weakness preventing her from walking unaided and unequal sized pupils. Since it occurred immediately upon arriving at surface, this points strongly toward AGE rather than Type II DCS. In this case, the diver is immediately placed in the chamber, along with a DMT. The Rapid Neuro can be performed in the chamber under pressure.

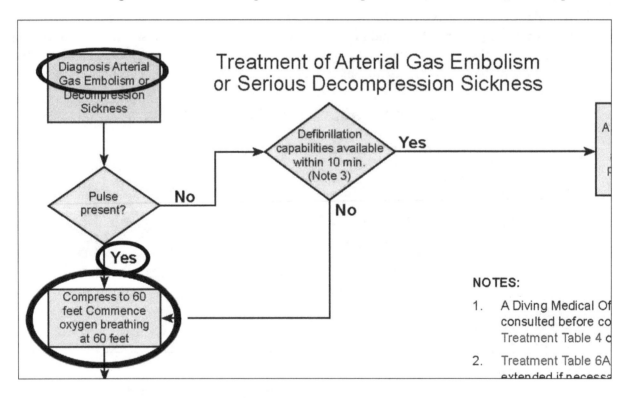

We can see by the flowchart above that for either AGE or Type II DCS, provided the diver has a pulse (which she does), we immediately blow her down to 60 fsw and get her on BIBS and breathing oxygen.

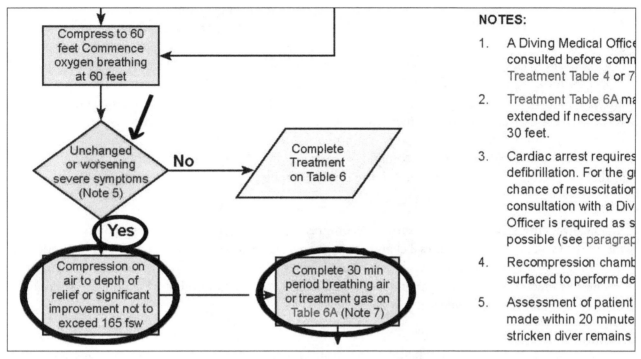

NOTES:

1. A Diving Medical Office consulted before comm Treatment Table 4 or 7

2. Treatment Table 6A ma extended if necessary 30 feet.

3. Cardiac arrest requires defibrillation. For the g chance of resuscitation consultation with a Div Officer is required as s possible (see paragrap

4. Recompression chamb surfaced to perform de

5. Assessment of patient made within 20 minute stricken diver remains

We kept our diver at 60 fsw for 15 minutes, and she did not get relief. The Rapid Neuro exam was showing deficit in a few areas, which has confirmed our initial diagnosis. We take the diver down to 70 fsw and wait for 15 minutes. She seems to feel better generally, but she still has impaired strength in her limbs, and her pupils are still unequal. We then press the chamber to 80 fsw and almost immediately the diver says she feels almost normal. We then perform another extremity strength test, which indicates both sides equal and normal strength for arms and legs. The pupils are almost equal in size and appear to be getting closer by the minute. This establishes 80 fsw as the "depth of relief." According to the flowchart above, we then enter TT6A at the 80 fsw point. The chamber that we have onboard is not plumbed for any other treatment gases; it has oxygen only, so we start our diver off breathing chamber air. Because of this, we are going to need to do two things: 1) closely monitor both the CO_2 and oxygen levels; and 2) regularly ventilate the chamber to keep both levels within the proper range. According to the flowchart, we are to give the diver 30 minutes breathing air at the initial depth (depth of relief or 80 fsw). From this point on, we follow Treatment Table 6A, exactly as it is written.

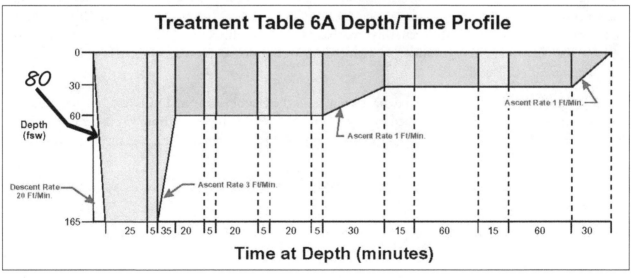

According to the treatment table on the previous page, once the diver has completed her 30 minutes at 80 fsw, she then has to travel to 60 fsw, with a travel rate of 3 ft./min. Once at 60 fsw, the diver immediately goes on BIBS, and she begins the first of 3 oxygen breathing periods, each 20 min. in duration, separated by 5-min. air breaks. The DMT observes the diver throughout the entire treatment and performs exams during air breaks. At the end of the third air break, the diver travels to 30 fsw at a rate of 1 ft/min. Upon arrival at 30 fsw, the diver has a 15-min. air break, followed by a 60-min. oxygen breathing period. There is one more 15-min.air break, and then both the diver and the DMT go on BIBS. There is one final 60-min.oxygen breathing period at 30 fsw, and then both stay on oxygen while traveling to surface at a travel rate of 1 ft./min. The above scenario is assuming there have been no recurrences of symptoms as the diver ascends toward the surface on the treatment table.

Problem:

A male diver enters the chamber for surface decompression using oxygen. He was on an 80 fsw table, on the 80/100 schedule, so he requires 2 chamber oxygen periods. At 14:35 on BIBS at 50 fsw, he suddenly pulls off the BIBS mask and vomits all over himself. He is having great difficulty hearing when you try to talk to him, and he is getting angry because he thinks you are mumbling when you are speaking. How would you diagnose and treat this diver?

Solution:

When using the U.N Revision 6 Tables, occasionally a diver will suffer CNS Oxygen Toxicity on the 50 fsw stop and it will usually occur late in the stop. The Acronym CON-VENTID is used to identify the signs and symptoms of CNS O_2 Toxicity. The first sign is increasing tunnel vision, but it is often unreported. This is followed by ringing in the ears, with an increasing difficulty in hearing. Next, one of two things will happen – the diver will begin to convulse in a violent manner, or he will vomit (often projectile vomiting). Irritability and dizziness are noticed usually once the convulsions or vomiting have subsided. The tingling sensation in the skin is often felt when no other symptoms present: some divers feel a tingling around their lips almost every time they are in the chamber and on BIBS, breathing oxygen but it progresses no further.

The diver in this case is obviously suffering from CNS Oxygen Toxicity. The first course of action is to get him off BIBS, which he has done in order to vomit. We then keep him breathing chamber air (watching the oxygen and CO_2 levels) until he has no more symptoms. From that point, we keep him on chamber air for a further 15 minutes. We then have him go back on BIBS, breathing oxygen. 30 seconds after he is back on oxygen, we travel the chamber to 40 fsw and complete his decompression as scheduled. It is extremely rare for an incident of CNS Oxygen Toxicity to occur at 40 fsw, but it occasionally does happen. In the event this diver has a recurrence, his decompression must be completed on air. The *U.S. Navy Diving Manual* has a procedure to complete oxygen decompression on air, found in Chapter 9 (9-12.8 and 9-12.9).

The situation above illustrates the need to have a tender in the chamber on Sur-D-O_2 (as U.S. Navy does) or at the very least, have the BIBS plumbed in such a way as to be able to switch from O_2 to air from outside the chamber rapidly. CNS O_2 Toxicity does not happen often, but when it does, it is always serious.

10.12 DMAC 15 PRIMARY MEDICAL KIT CONTENTS

10.12.1 Diagnostic Equipment

- 1 penlight
- 1 electronic thermometer
- 1 stethoscope
- 1 aneroid sphygmomanometer
- 1 reflex hammer
- 1 tape measure
- 2 tuning forks (128 and 256 Hz)

- pins for testing sensation (neurotips)
- blood sugar test strips
- urine test strips
- tongue depressors
- 1 auroscope (c/w spare bulb, batteries, and disposable ear pieces)

10.12.2 Thoracocenticis

- 2 intercostal drain and drainage kits – preferably those without sharp metal "trocar" inducers (portex flexible introducer type)
- 4 large bore intravenous canulae (approx. 14 g)
- 2 Heimlich valves

10.12.3 Urinary Catheterization

- 2 urinary catheters, size 16 and 18 (Foley type)
- 2 urine collection bags

- 2 catheter spigots (optional)
- 2 × 20 ml. sterile water
- 2 urethral anesthetic gel

10.12.4 Dressings

- 10 packets gauze squares 2 × 2 in.
- 5 packets cotton balls
- 4 triangular bandages
- 4 trauma care bandages
- 12 safety pins
- 2 adhesive bandages 3 in. × 10 ft.
- 2 adhesive bandages 1 in. × 10 ft.
- 2 crepe bandages 6 in,

- 2 crepe bandages 3 in.
- 2 large dressings
- 2 medium dressings
- 40 adhesive plasters
- 2 dressing bowls
- 4 eye pads
- 1 eye wash kit

10.12.5 Sterile Supplies – General

- 4 universal containers
- 2 drapes
- 10 alcohol swabs or sachets of skin disinfectant (Cetrimide solution)
- 5 boxes of surgical gloves (selection of sizes, preferably non-latex)
- 6 sutures non-resorbable (nylon) size 2/0 and 3/0, preferably with cutting needles attached
- 2 resorbable sutures, size 2/0 and 3/0 preferable with needles attached
- 5 × 20 ml syringes
- 5 × 10 ml syringes
- 5 × 2 ml syringes
- 10 × 18 g needles
- 10 × 21 g needles

10.12.6 Sterile Instruments
- 2 × 5 in. forceps (Spencer Wells)
- 1 mosquito forceps
- 1 dressing forceps
- 2 fisposable scalpels
- 1 forceps – fine toothed
- 1 dressing scissors
- 1 scissors – fine pointed
- 1 stainless steel ring cutter (for removal of rings and other piercings) – not required to be sterile

10.12.7 Intravenous Access
- 3 giving sets
- 4 IV cannulae 16 g
- 4 IV cannulae 18 g
- 4 butterfly infusion sets 19 g (optional)
- 2 magnetic hooks
- 1 intraosseous infusion (IO) system. It is recommended that spring-loaded placement systems are used. DMTs must be trained and up-to-date in the system used by the diving company. Battery-operated placement systems are not advised for use in hyperbaric chamber environments.

10.12.8 Resuscitation
- resuscitator to include reservoir and connection for BIBS gas (e.g. Laerdal type)*
- 3 resuscitation masks with silicone face seals (various sizes)
- 1 pocket resuscitator with one-way valve (e.g. Laerdal pocket mask with silicone face seal and non-return valve) or face shield for mouth-to-mouth ventilation
- 4 supraglottic airways sized for adult males (e.g. IGel size 3, 4 and 5 or Combitube) with catheter mounts and filters. (If female divers are onboard, ensure correctly sized airways are available.)
- endotracheal (ET) tubes (optional) sizes 7, 8 and 9 with catheter mounts and filters**
- laryngoscope (optional) with batteries and spare bulbs. The use of laryngoscope with fiber-optic disposable blades is encouraged, required if ET tubes are stored.
- 2 oropharyngeal airways, sizes 3 and 4 (e.g. Guedel type)
- 1 foot-operated suction device
- 1 tourniquet to aid with venous access
- 2 endotracheal suction catheters
- 2 wide bore suckers
- 1 automated external defibrillator

* Resuscitators may require modification to gas inlet to ensure adequate filling at treatment pressure

** Endotracheal tubes for use by physician only

10.13 DRUGS REQUIRED

Anatomical Therapeutic Chemical (ATC) codes are provided in brackets for guidance.

10.13.1 Anesthesia

Lidocaine injection without adrenalin (N01B B02)

Suggested: Lidocaine 10 mg/ml or 20 mg/ml ampoules 5 × 10 ml

Indication: Lidocaine is a useful anesthetic in concentrations up to 20%

10.13.2 Analgesia

Soluble aspirin tablets (N02B A01)

Suggested: Soluble aspirin 20 × 300 mg or 20 × 500 mg tablets

Indication: Mild to moderate pain, pyrexia (fever), chest pain of suspected cardiac origin

1 to 2 tablets every 4 to 6 hours

Paracetamol tablets (N02B E01)

Suggested: Paracetamol 25 × 500 mg tablets

Indication: Mild to moderate pain, pyrexia

1 to 2 tablets every 4 to 6 hours to a maximum of 8 tablets in 24 hours

Codeine or dihydrocodeine tablets (N02A A08 or R05D A04)

Suggested: Codeine or dihydrocodeine tablets 20 × 25-30 mg tablets

Indication: Moderate to severe pain

1 × 25 or 30 mg tablet every 4 to 6 hours as necessary

Morphine injection (N02A A01)

Suggested: Morphine 5 × 10 mg ampoules

Indication: Severe and acute pain

Patients must be closely monitored for pain relief and side effects, particularly respiratory depression

Naloxone injection (V03A B15)

Suggested: Naloxone 0.4 mg/ml ampoules – 2 × 1 ml

Indication: Opioid (morphine) overdose, respiratory depression due to the administration of morphine. Respiratory depression is a major concern with opioids and may be treated by artificial ventilation or be reversed by naloxone. Naloxone will immediately reverse respiratory depression, but the dose may have to be repeated due to the short duration of action of naloxone. However, naloxone will also antagonize the analgesic effect.

The following drug is useful and acceptable as analgesia for moderate to severe pain in cases where it is impossible to stock morphine:

Tramadol injection (N02A X02)

Suggested: Tramadol, 5 × 100 mg ampoules

Indication: Moderate to severe pain

10.13.3 Resuscitation Drugs (refer to the appropriate resuscitation guidelines)

Adrenaline/Epinephrine injection (C01C A24)

Suggested: Adrenaline, 10 × 10 ml ampoules 100 µg/ml ampoules (1 in 10,000)

Indication: Emergency treatment for cardiopulmonary resuscitation

Important: Intravenous route or intraosseous route used in resuscitation during CPR only

Amiodarone injection (C01B D01)

Suggested: Amiodarone 6 × 150 mg ampoules

Indication: Amiodarone is used for the treatment of arrhythmias, particularly during CPR, and particularly when other drugs are ineffective or contraindicated.

In some countries, Amiodarone is sold as a powder. If this is the case, ensure that the proper amount of solute is included.

Important: Intravenous route or IO route to be used in resuscitation during CPR only

Furosemide injection (C03C A01)

Suggested: Furosemide 5 × 40 mg ampoules

Indication: Oedema, pulmonary oedema, resistant hypertension

10.13.4 Nausea and Vomiting

Fentiazin or prochlorperazine injection (preferred) or oral (optional) (N05A B)

Suggested: Prochlorperazine 5 × 25 mg ampoules or Prochlorperazine 20 × 5 mg tablets

Indication: Severe nausea, vomiting, vertigo, labyrinthine disorders (not for use in motion sickness)

Where available, Prochlorperazine in 3 mg buccal tablets (dissolves sublingually) is a good choice as opposed to standard tablets as there is no need to swallow a tablet; 10 × 3 mg

Hyoscine hydrobromide (Scopolamine) tablets / dermal patches (A04A D01)

Suggested: Hyoscine 40 × 300 µg tablets (e.g. Kwells)

Indication: Short-acting drug for sea sickness or hyperbaric evacuation (chewable tablets)

Suggested: Scopolamine 20 × dermal patches (e.g. Scopolamine plasters)

Indication: Long acting slow release drug for sea sickness or hyperbaric evacuation. One patch behind ear

10.13.5 Allergic Reactions

Antihistamine for injection (R06A B)

Suggested: Chlorpheniramine 2 × 10 mg ampoules or dekschlorpheniramine 2 × 5 mg ampoules

Indication: Symptomatic relief of allergy, urticaria, emergency treatment of anaphylactic reaction

Oral antihistamine (R06A E)

Suggested: Cetirizine 20 × 10 mg tablets

Indication: Symptomatic relief of allergies – non-sedating. Other non-sedating oral antihistamines may be substituted as required.

Corticosteroid for injection (H02A B)

Suggested: Hydrocortisone 5 × 100 mg ampoules

Indication: Hypersensitivity reaction (anaphylaxis, angiodema, asthma)

Adrenaline / epinephrine auto-injector (C01C A24)

Suggested: Epinephrine auto-injector (EpiPen auto-injector) 0.3 mg of 1 in 1000 (1 mg/ml) adrenaline (giving 3 mcg) 2 ml auto-injector

Indication: Emergency treatment of acute anaphylaxis

10.13.6 Drugs Various

Atropine injection (A03B A01)

Suggested: Atropine 4 × 1ml ampoules (600 μg/ml)

Although atropine is no longer recommended in the treatment of asystole or pulseless electrical in the European resuscitation guidelines, it may be useful in the treatment of bradycardia

Glucose injection (B05B A03)

Suggested: Glucose 2 × 500 mg/ml 50 ml

Indication: Hypoglycemia

Glyceryl trinitrate sublingual tablets (C01D A02)

Suggested: Glyceryl trinitrate sublingual tablets × 10 tablets

Indication: Cardiac chest pain

Intravenous fluids (B05B B01)

Suggested: Crystalloid infusion – 6 liters

Sodium chloride infusion 0.9% and/or Hartman's or Ringer's lactate

Diving company doctor to advise on exact make-up

Anti-psychotic drug for injection (N05A A)

Suggested: Chlorpromazine 2 × 50 mg ampoules, or Levomepromazine 2 × 25 mg ampoules

Indication: For relief of acute symptoms of schizophrenia and other psychoses or mania, short-term adjunctive management of severe anxiety, psychomotor agitation, excitement, violent or dangerously impulsive behavior

Anxiolytics for injection (N05B A)

Suggested: Diazepam 5 × 10 mg ampoules

Indication: Short-term use for anxiety or insomnia, status epilepticus and for muscle relaxant effect

Anxiolytics for oral use (N05B A)

Suggested: Diazepam 10 × 5 mg tablets

Indication: Short-term use in anxiety or insomnia, status epilepticus

Anxiolytics for rectal use (N05B A)

Suggested: Diazepam 10 × 5 mg suppositories

Indication: Short-term use in status epilepticus

COMMERCIAL DIVER TRAINING MANUAL

10.13.7 Treatment of Burns

Sulfonamides for topical (skin) use (D06B A01)

Suggested: Silver sulphadiazine cream, 1 tube of 1%

Indication: For example prophylaxis and treatment of infection in burn wounds, as an adjunct to short-term treatment of extensive abrasions, for conservative management of finger-tip injuries

10.13.8 Antibiotics

Broad spectrum antibiotics for oral use (J01C A, J01C F, or J01C R02)

Suggested: Co-amoxiclav 21 × 625 mg tablets (3 times per day for 7 days) or dicloxacilline 30 × 500 mg

Indication: Broad-spectrum antibiotic

If this drug is not available, company doctor may recommend a similar penicillinase resistant antibiotic

Macrolide antibiotic for oral use (J01F A)

Suggested: Clarithromycin 14 × 250 mg tablets (twice daily for 7 days) or erythromycin 30 × 250 mg tablets (2 tabs twice daily for 7 days)

Indication: Susceptible infections in patients with penicillin hypersensitivity

Antibiotic and corticosteroid ear drops (S03C A)

Suggested: Sofradex (framycetin sulphate/dexamethasone/gramicidin) ear drops or hydrocortisone / polymyxine B ear drops one bottle (2 – 3 drops 3 – 4 times per day)

Sofradex drops may also be used for eye infections

Antifungal drug

Suggested: Clotrimazole cream

Indication: For fungal skin infections

10.14 DMAC 15 CHAMBER INTERNAL MEDICAL KIT CONTENTS

- 1 arterial tourniquet (e.g. CAT tourniquet)
- 3 polyethylene bags – used to cover burns or a waste bags
- 1 resuscitation mask (with silicone seal and non-return valve) for mouth-to-mouth
- 2 oropharyngeal air way (size 3 and 4)
- 1 tuff cut scissors
- 1 medium dressing
- 1 large dressing
- 2 triangular bandages

- 1 roll of 1in adhesive tape
- 2 crepe bandages – 3 in.
- 1 hand-powered suction pump
- 1 watertight bag
- 1 suction catheters, sizes 12 and 14
- 1 adult adjustable cervical spine collar
- 2 pairs non-sterilized gloves, sized for DMTs, non-latex if possible
- 2 space blankets

The above equipment is to be stored in a water tight, vented container or bag either inside the deck decompression chamber or very close by in order to be taken in by diver medical technicians as required.

11.0 HYPERBARIC CHAMBERS

The hyperbaric chamber is a unique piece of equipment in that it allows the user to duplicate the effects of being underwater on the human body, but in a dry, controlled environment. The chamber has three primary functions in our industry: surface decompression, saturation, and the recompression treatment of pressure-related illness or injury. In the health-care field, hyperbaric chambers are used to treat a variety of conditions with hyperbaric oxygen therapy (HBOT), including muscular sclerosis, osteo-arthritis, gangrene, burn and crush injuries, carbon monoxide poisoning, and necrotizing fasciitis (flesh-eating disease).

11.1 TYPES OF HYPERBARIC CHAMBER

All chambers are classified as Class A, B, or C. Class A are multiplace, with an inner lock and an outer or transfer lock, Class B are monoplace with a single lock, and Class C are test chambers, used for testing equipment or research involving animals. The chamber size is based on the internal diameter. Those used in air and mixed-gas diving are always Class A and 54 or 60 inch units; older chambers may be 42 or 48 inch units. Deck chambers used in diving are skid mounted and average about 13 feet long. Chambers used in saturation are much larger, built to accommodate a 6-, 8-, or 12-man diving crew for weeks at a time. Chambers used in the health-care industry are often up to 8 feet in diameter to allow users to enter by walking, as opposed to climbing through a manway. This chapter will deal primarily with the deck decompression chambers used in air and mixed-gas diving operations.

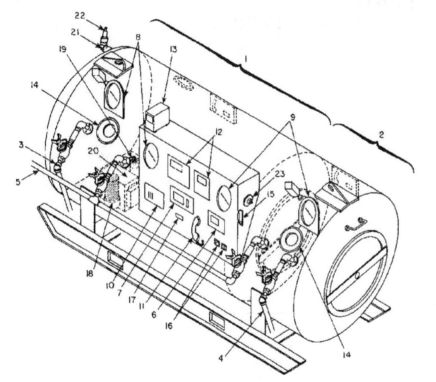

1. Inner Lock
2. Outer Lock
3. Gas Supply – Inner Lock
4. Gas Supply – Outer Lock
5. Gas Exhaust
6. O_2 Analyzer
7. CO_2 Analyzer
8. Inner-Lock Depth Gauges (2)
9. Outer-Lock Depth Gauges (2)
10. Communications Panel
11. Sound-Powered Phone
12. Pipe Light Control Panel
13. Ground Fault Interrupter
14. View Ports (5)
15. Flowmeter
16. Stopwatch/Timer
17. Telethermometer
18. CO_2 Scrubber
19. Fire Extinguisher
20. Chiller/Conditioner Unit
21. Gag Valve
22. Relief Valve – 110 psig
23. BIBS Overboard Dump Regulator – Outer Lock

Features of a Navy Double Lock Deck Decompression Chamber (DDC)
Source: *U.S. Navy Diving Manual*

11.2 CONSTRUCTION OF HYPERBARIC CHAMBERS

Chambers are pressure vessels, and they must be constructed and inspected to very stringent standards. The standard for chamber construction in the United States is the Boiler and Pressure Vessel Code, provided by the American Society of Mechanical Engineers (ASME) and in Canada, the Canadian Standard CSA B-51 is nearly identical. In Europe, chambers are usually certified by Lloyd's Register of Shipping. ASME requires a U stamp on new builds, and an R stamp on refits; in Canada, chambers are required to have a Canadian Registration Number (CRN) from the chief boiler inspector; and in Europe, chambers will have an LR stamp. In most countries, hyperbaric chambers have the designation "pressure vessel for human occupancy" (PVHO). Every PVHO must have a specification plate; if it does not, it cannot be inspected, and therefore, cannot be legally used. These plates may be found in one of the following locations: on the bulkhead above the interior or the exterior manway or on the hull beside the control panel. The specification plate will have the following information printed on it with stamped or raised letters: manufacturer's name, date of manufacture, serial number, certification number, design pressure, hydrostatic test pressure, maximum operating temperature, internal diameter, shell thickness, bulkhead thickness, and the original inspector's U stamp. Chambers are usually built with 44W (300W) hot rolled steel. Every weld on the pressure hull is magnetic-particle tested and X-rayed during the initial inspection which is performed when the chamber is first certified. This initial inspection is when the chamber gets her specification plate and that plate is required to stay with the chamber for its entire working life. Any modification of a pressure vessel by welding, cutting, or drilling makes the inspection null and void. Modifications must be approved first by the boiler inspector, and then a new inspection will be performed after the modification or refit, and the vessel will be re-stamped with an R stamp.

ASME U stamp   Lloyd's Register stamp   ASME R stamp

Along with a specification plate, there must be certification paperwork for the chamber. This paperwork usually stays in the office of the owner. **Do not operate a chamber that does not have a specification plate or has not been maintained in good operating condition.** Every jurisdiction in the world requires a specification plate and supporting paperwork for all chambers used in commercial diving operations.

Specification plate on chamber in the United States
Photo courtesy of Divers Supply Inc.

Specification plate on a chamber in Congo

Chamber viewports may be constructed of tempered glass or acrylic. Because they are a part of the pressure hull of a PVHO, they must have a pedigree. This is paperwork that details all of the steps in the manufacturing process and the tests performed on them. The viewport pedigree paperwork will be found in the chamber certification pack, with the chamber builder's paperwork. When chambers are stored and not in use, all of the viewports should be covered with deadlights to protect them. **Do not operate a chamber with viewports that are cracked or have obvious damage.**

There are two types of door seals used on hyperbaric chambers: flat gasket and O ring. The O ring type of seal performs much better than the flat gasket. The door seals are critical to building and maintaining pressure and must be maintained in good condition.

Plumbing, fittings, and valves on hyperbaric chambers must be brass, stainless steel, or tungum, and never black iron. Threaded fittings are taped with 02 safe Teflon tape. Although the U.S. Navy has color codes for chamber plumbing, these codes are not used in commercial work. Instead, all lines are clearly marked to indicate what they carry, and all valves are clearly marked to indicate what their function is. All of the valves on PVHOs are ¼ turn ball valves, with the exception of the valves on the chamber gauges and the valves on the oxygen supply. These are needle valves.

The pneumofathometer gauges used on hyperbaric chambers must have a valve and a quick-disconnect fitting between the gauge and the through hull penetrator. This allows the rapid replacement of a malfunctioning gauge. The gauges must be accurate to 0.25% over the range of the gauge, which in the case of chamber gauges, is usually 0 – 250 fsw. These gauges are required to be calibrated on a regular basis by a third party organization; most jurisdictions require a twice-annual calibration. Between calibrations, the gauges should be tested by comparison between the two locks. Good quality gauges have a zero set adjustment screw. This should be adjusted when ever the zero is off.

11.2.1 Required Features

There are some features that are required on every deck decompression chamber (DDC) used in diving operations. These features are as follows:

- Twin locks – monoplace chambers are no longer legal for use in diving
- Accessible manways – large enough to move an unconscious patient easily
- Minimum of three viewports – one in outer lock, two in inner lock
- Through hull penetrators – minimum of nine required per lock
- Pressure relief valves – one per lock, complete with gag valves
- Fire-fighting capability – hyperbaric extinguisher (pail of water in some jurisdictions)
- Main air supply – with the ability to pressurize to 6 ATA, ventilate and maintain for one hour
- Backup air supply – with the exact same ability as the main air supply
- Calibrated pneumofathometer gauges – one required per lock
- Medical oxygen supply – sufficient quantity for decompression and treatment
- BIBS – built in breathing system complete with overboard dump capability
- Primary communications system – wired intercom or sound-powered phone
- Secondary communications system – sound-powered phone or signal hammer
- Lighting system – internal or external

11.2.2 Optional Features

There are optional features on a deck decompression chamber.

- Caisson gauges – for interior depth monitoring
- Panel cover – to protect the chamber controls
- Deck plates – to keep the occupants off of the shell
- Mattresses and bedding – fireproof
- Medical lock – usually 18 inch
- CO_2 scrubber
- Oxygen analyzer
- Heater/chiller system – good for outside chambers
- Dual controls – interior and exterior (exterior override)
- Hull insulation
- Bunks and benches
- Sprinkler system

11.3 CHAMBER GAS SUPPLY

The chambers used in surface diving (air and gas) use breathing quality air as the internal environment, and specialized gases such as oxygen are delivered through a BIBS. Chambers require a main air supply, which is often LP air, supplied by a 5120 compressor. Also required is a backup supply, which may be either LP or HP. If the chamber is being used for surface decompression, the main supply must be sufficient to pressurize the chamber as required for the normal decompression and also to pressurize for a Treatment Table 6A, including ventilation. The backup supply must be able to pressurize the chamber for a TT6A also. The air quality is required to be breathable compressed air. If HP air is used for the main supply, a 16-cylinder quad is used, refilling by HP compressor as it is depleted.

11.4 MAINTAINING THE CHAMBER ENVIRONMENT

The chamber environment must be maintained (gas partial pressures and temperature). The gas partial pressures are important to maintain life, ensure proper rates of off-gassing, and prevent fire. The internal temperature is important for off-gassing. The internal temperature must be maintained between 70° and 85°F, and this is best achieved by having the chamber in a climate-controlled van. If that is not an option, heater-chiller units are available for chambers. The two gas partial pressures that are closely watched are oxygen and carbon dioxide. Oxygen must be kept in the 20 to 23.5% range at all times. When allowed to drop lower, it is insufficient for breathing; when allowed to climb higher, there is a risk of fire.

High carbon dioxide levels are caused by chamber occupants breathing the air in the chamber environment and exhaling into that environment. High oxygen levels are caused by one of two things: a leak in the BIBS or an improperly fitting BIBS mask. The leaks are caught in regular chamber maintenance; improper fit on the BIBS mask is corrected by the occupant or the DMT. Most modern chambers monitor oxygen

Oxygen analyzer

levels with an oxygen analyzer, which has a readout showing the percentage in the chamber atmosphere (taken at the exhaust). Carbon dioxide monitors are less common, but many chambers are equipped with scrubbers. These are a fan that circulates the chamber air through a cylinder where it passes through soda-lime, removing the carbon dioxide. These scrubbers use the exact same technology used in submarines, spacecraft, and atmospheric diving systems. A scrubber will handle the CO_2 generated during surface decompression or a treatment unless there is a lot of physical activity in the chamber, as there would be if CPR was being performed. Both oxygen and carbon dioxide percentages that are too high are dealt with in the exact same way: ventilating the chamber. Ventilation is usually performed one out of every five minutes when a

Carbon dioxide scrubber

chamber does not have a scrubber and the occupants are breathing air from the chamber environment. The recommended rate for ventilation is 2 acfm per occupant at rest, and at least 4 acfm for each occupant engaged in strenuous activity (performing CPR).

Chamber ventilation must always be performed without causing any fluctuation in depth. If the chamber gauge needle moves during ventilation, it is not being done properly. To avoid depth fluctuations, open the inlet valve, followed closely by the exhaust valve. The operator should not touch the inlet valve again until venting is completed. The rate of ventilation is controlled by adjusting the position of the exhaust valve only, and the only way you will get good at ventilating is through practice.

11.5 BUILT-IN BREATHING SYSTEMS (BIBS)

The BIBS consists of a breathing gas supply (separate from the chamber gas supply) regulated down below 125 psi, an oral-nasal demand mask, and an exhaust system. There are a few manufacturers of BIBS masks, but the most common is produced by Scott Aviation, the Pressure-Vac II.

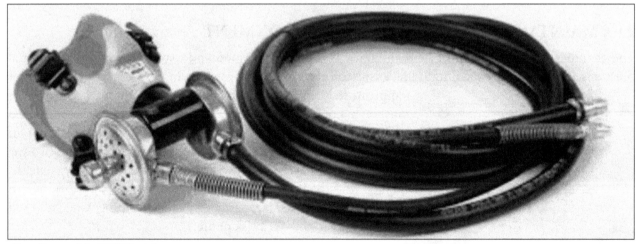

Scott Pressure-Vac II BIBS mask

The Scott mask has a free-flow adjustment on the right-hand side, which is the inlet side of the mask. The left-hand, or exhaust side has a slightly larger bore hose, to reduce exhaust drag. There is a head harness on the Scott mask, only to be used if the mask can be immediately switched from oxygen to air. To be properly outfitted, the BIBS should be arranged to deliver at least medical oxygen and breathing air, with the option of other treatment gases (HeO$_2$ and N$_2$O$_2$). The BIBS must also have an overboard dump, which means the exhaled breathing gas goes outside the chamber environment, thereby keeping the oxygen levels lower and reducing the risk of fire. The delivery pressure to the Scott BIBS mask must be maintained between 110 and 125 psi. If it exceeds 125 psi, damage to the masks will result. If BIBS are to be used deeper than 60 fsw, a back-pressure regulator must be installed on the exhaust system.

11.6 CHAMBER OPERATIONS

Chamber operators use a checklist to ensure everything is ready to go on the chamber. Each operator should run through his/her own checklist if more than one operator is utilized during a shift. If an operator hasn't run chamber in a while, he/she should perform a dry run of the chamber. A dry run involves pressurizing the empty chamber, checking the operation of all of the systems, and familiarization with the vessel's controls. Once a dry run has been performed, the operator and the chamber are ready to go. The following is a sample chamber predive checklist.

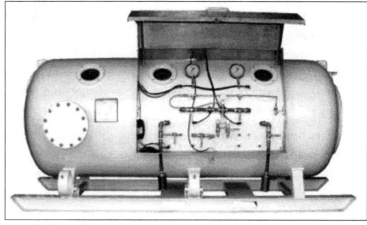

Standard 54-inch deck decompression chamber
Photo courtesy of Divers Supply Inc.

- Chamber clean and free of odors
- Chamber doors and door seals undamaged and working properly
- Pneumo gauges comparison checked and working properly
- Chamber free of unnecessary equipment
- Primary air supply (check fuel and oil, check filters)
- Supply and inlet valves all closed
- Exhaust valves closed
- Chamber drain valves closed on both locks
- Standby air supply (bank pressures, regulator delivery pressure setting)
- Standby supply valve closed
- Medical oxygen supply (full cylinders online, regulator preset for BIBS)
- Oxygen supply valve closed

- BIBS masks clean and tested
- Overboard dump tested
- Primary and standby communications tested
- Lighting system tested
- Firefighting supplies in chamber
- Mattress and blankets in chamber
- Waste bucket in chamber
- Inside medical kit in chamber
- Primary medical kit outside chamber
- Watch and two stopwatches
- Decompression tables
- U.S. Navy flowcharts and treatment tables
- Treatment sheets
- Clipboard and pen
- Emergency procedures manual

The pressurization (known as the blowdown) of the chamber is critical in surface decompression, and in treatments. While it is important to get the occupant to the required depth as quickly as possible, it is also important not to hurt the occupant while achieving this goal. To avoid this, the occupant always holds his/her hand in the viewport during blowdown, with a "thumbs up" to indicate there are no problems equalizing. There are different methods used for blowdown. The most common method is the "transfer under pressure." To perform this blowdown, you store the inner lock deeper than the first stop, have the occupant enter the transfer lock, bleed air from the inner to the outer lock until both locks are equalized, and have the occupant to transfer under pressure to the inner lock. Once in the inner lock, the occupant pushes the door shut with his/her feet, and the operator quickly returns the transfer lock to surface pressure, so it can be used to get a tender inside in an emergency. On chambers where the cross-over valves are too slow, the inner lock is stored at the depth of the first stop. The occupant enters the transfer lock and it is blown down to the stop depth using the air inlet valve instead of bleeding it from one lock to the other.

Control panel on deck chamber

The other method of blowdown is to have the occupant enter the inner lock, have a tender hold the inner door shut, and pressurize only the inner lock to the stop depth. There are many diving supervisors who will only use this method. There are a couple of reasons for this. If there is a failure of the door seal on the inner door, you have a "second chance" with the outer door seal, whereas when using the transfer under pressure method, you have only one door seal to count on, unless you bleed the entire chamber down. The other reason that some supervisors prefer this method is many older chambers only have BIBS in the inner lock, and they want the occupant on O_2 while being blown down.

Regardless of the blowdown method used, the operator must ensure the occupant is able to equalize on descent. The *U.S. Navy Diving Manual* has made provision for an occupant unable to equalize. It is known as the "Safe Way Out" procedure and is detailed in Chapter 5: Air Diving and Decompression.

Once the chamber is blown down, the operator must regularly look in on the occupant. The operator should be watching first for signs of oxygen toxicity. To do this, the operator will look over the occupant's entire body, from feet to head, watching for tremors or jerky movements (convulsions). The operator will make eye contact with the occupant, looking for squinting (a sign of vision problems), and also around the edges of the BIBS mask for twitching facial muscles. Chamber operators must know the signs and symptoms of CNS Oxygen Toxicity (CON-VENTID). The operator must ensure the occupant does not sit or lie in such a way as to restrict blood flow; this may cause a bend. Crossed or bent legs or arms must be avoided.

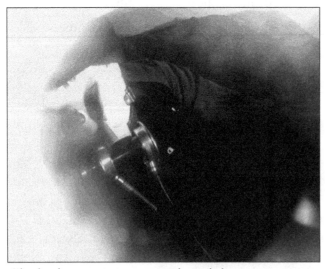

The chamber operator must constantly watch the occupant

The internal temperature of the chamber must be maintained at a comfortable level. If it is very hot and the chamber is not equipped with a chiller, burlap or blankets laid over the chamber, soaked down with water will effectively cool it. Tarps to keep the sun off the chamber help as well. To keep the chamber warm in cold weather, internal heaters are available, but a temporary heated enclosure will work fine. The best answer is a climate-controlled container in both cases, but they are not always available. Remember – body temperature has a direct effect on metabolic rates and changes in the metabolic rates change the rate the body off-gases. Keep your chamber occupant comfortable.

The operator must also ensure there is adequate ventilation to keep the oxygen level in the safe zone (above 20% and below 23.5%). When the chamber is equipped with an oxygen analyzer, the operator ventilates the chamber when the oxygen level indicates it is time to do so. Otherwise, use the 1 in 5 rule: Ventilate the chamber 1 minute of every 5.

The chamber operator is also required to keep time for chamber stops at various depths, travel time, time on oxygen, and air break times. All of these times must be recorded on the dive sheet for surface decompression or the treatment sheet when performing hyperbaric treatments. Time on oxygen and air break time are straightforward, but travel times can be difficult to adhere to. If the travel between stops or from the last stop to the surface is lagging, do not try to "catch up" by increasing the travel rate at the end of the travel period. Adjust the times on the sheet accordingly. Travel periods, or slides, as they are sometimes called, are usually performed with the occupant breathing oxygen (depending on the table), and an extra minute or two breathing oxygen will not hurt the occupant. Exceeding the travel rate, however, can certainly hurt the occupant. Stay as close as possible to the table.

During surface decompression diving operations, the chamber operator must stay in contact with the diving supervisor to let the supervisor know exactly when the chamber will be free for another occupant. This will avoid having a diver ready to enter the chamber before the chamber is surfaced and empty, a condition known as being "chamber blocked." There is usually a second chamber on hand, but avoid the nasty surprises.

The two most common causes of incidents requiring hyperbaric treatment are equipment failure and math or calculation mistakes. Math and calculation mistakes can usually be traced back to inattention or distraction of either the supervisor or the chamber operator. Pay attention, do not allow yourself to be distracted, and double check your math and the supervisor's math.

The chamber operator must pay attention

11.7 CHAMBER FIRES

As you learned in your physics, as air pressure is increased, the partial pressure of the gases in the air increases. Because air contains approximately 21% oxygen, the threat of fire in the chamber environment is increased somewhat. Prior to development of surface decompression using oxygen (sur-d-O_2) procedures, surface decompression was accomplished with air. It was not uncommon to see a "butt can" inside the chamber for discarded cigarette butts. Everyone smoked in the chambers, and it was accepted. The development of the sur-d-O_2 procedures changed all of that. Not only was there the high partial pressure of oxygen in the chamber air, but now the occupants were breathing 100% medical grade oxygen. In the early years of sur-d-O_2, there were a lot of chamber fires. The first BIBS masks were single hose and exhausted the exhaled breath into the chamber environment, creating very high oxygen levels. In a chamber fire, not only does the occupant have nowhere to run to escape, but fire produces poisonous gases, and a fire in a chamber environment burns until it uses all available oxygen and extinguishes itself. There are no happy endings in a chamber fire. With the invention of the overboard dump system, and increased training for chamber operators, there has been a marked reduction in chamber fires to the point that they are, thankfully, a very rare thing today.

11.7.1 Fire Prevention

You may have heard it said "an ounce of prevention is worth a pound of cure"; that was never truer than when dealing with chamber fires. The three steps in chamber fire prevention are:

1. Control what enters the chamber

2. Control the oxygen level

3. Routine chamber maintenance

1. The interior of the chamber is considered a foreign material exclusion (FME) zone. In other words, only those materials and products approved for use in a hyperbaric environment may enter beyond the transfer lock manway. FME can be a matter of life and death. For example, a butane cigarette lighter accidently dropped from a shirt pocket in the chamber will mean certain death for chamber occupants (and probably the operator) if it is not removed prior to pressurization. All personnel entering the chamber (even for maintenance and cleaning) must remove footwear, empty pockets, and remove any dirty clothing or coveralls. All mattresses, blankets, pillows, etc. must be chamber safe. Clothing worn by occupants must be chamber safe (100% cotton or Durrett material). Petroleum and petroleum products must **never** be allowed to enter the chamber. If a diver is covered in oil and requires decompression, the diver must be scrubbed completely clean prior to entering the chamber, even if it means treating for omitted decompression. Divers, tenders, and any other personnel entering beyond the outer door must remove footwear. Foreign material tracked into the chamber can be a fire hazard.

2. To control the oxygen levels in the chamber environment, the operator must ventilate by using the air inlet and exhaust valves. Even with a BIBS system with overboard dump, the oxygen level can rise simply by having a poor seal between the occupant's face and the BIBS mask. The oxygen level must be kept below 23.5%. Watch the oxygen analyzer or vent for 1 out of every 5 minutes.

3. Routine maintenance (cleaning) plays a big part in chamber fire prevention. Washing the chamber down is the best way to control the accumulation of dust and dirt, which often has flammable material in it.

11.8 CHAMBER MAINTENANCE

The hyperbaric chamber, even though it is used every day on the job, is considered a piece of emergency equipment. It must be kept ready to go at all times. Do not allow the crew to use the chamber as a storage locker for clothing, tools, or diving gear. When the chamber is not being used, keep the doors dogged – it will keep foreign material out, and it will keep the doors from banging around if the weather gets rough.

Check the door seals at least every day. Lubricate the seals often. Use only a food grade non-flammable O-ring lube, such as Dow Corning 111. Do not allow an excessive build up of lubricant. Any excess lubricant should be wiped off.

Wash the chamber often; you are helping to prevent fire and stopping bacteria growth. Use potable water and TSP (trisodium phosphate) to wash it down. If TSP is not available, use non-ionized dish soap and water. Scrub all surfaces in the chamber (except the viewports) with the drains open. Soak up any water that does not drain. Don't leave standing water. Don't use corrosive cleaners in the chamber.

When cleaning the chamber viewports, never use strong detergents or powdered cleansers. Use only clear, potable water to clean the viewports.

An important part of chamber maintenance is painting. Chamber interiors were in the past painted with non-flammable and non-toxic epoxy paints. Now, however, the paint used for interiors is a good quality exterior latex (water-based) paint. It is important to keep paint buildup to a minimum. For this reason, when repainting a chamber interior, all old paint is removed by sanding to the bare steel. Viewports are removed first, as are the door seals and deck plates. All interior plumbing is then covered with masking tape. A primer is then applied, and then no more than two thin coats of the finish paint. The paint must be allowed to fully dry before replacing the door seals and viewports.

Any time the viewports and door seals have been removed or altered, a leak test must be performed. When replacing the viewports, the retainer plates should only be tightened down enough to put a slight compression on the viewport gasket. The retainer plate bolts should be tightened down evenly. When replacing door seals, get the measurement for the new one from the old one and not from the door seal groove. Door seals are larger than the seal grove and must be worked into place.

Exterior painting is also important on chambers. Any exterior metal paint may be used, but usually an epoxy is chosen, due to durability. Viewports must be removed to paint the exterior as well because paint on an acrylic viewport will destroy it. Exterior plumbing is masked or removed, and the old paint is sanded down. Chipping hammers, needle guns and grinders must never be used on a chamber. Sanding and scraping are the only acceptable ways to remove the old paint. As with the interior, when painting the exterior, the paint must be completely dry before replacing the viewports.

Mattress covers and blankets should be removed daily and dried. Damp or wet bedding will mildew, and bacteria flourish in a damp environment. When storing a chamber unused, remove the BIBS masks, bedding, and mattresses. Cover viewports for storage.

When transporting a chamber, remove any loose items inside, such as fire extinguishers. Remove BIBS masks and hoses. Close and firmly dog all doors, including medical lock. Remove chamber gauges. Close all valves, and tape up open fittings. Cover viewports with deadlight covers. Only lift with rated slings, using the chamber's lifting eyes.

11.9 OXYGEN SAFETY

Oxygen, when combined with many other substances under pressure, will promote rapid burning and/ or cause an explosion. Many people are aware of this when it comes to petroleum or other hydrocarbon products. But common dust in an oxygen valve or hose will burn or explode. Using the wrong type of hose to transport oxygen will also cause an explosion. Common sense is not enough when it comes to the safe use of oxygen. What you don't know, can hurt you. Follow these simple rules:

- Crack it first. Always "crack" the valve on oxygen cylinders before installing regulators or manifolds. This will help blow any foreign material out of the valve.

- Open oxygen valves slowly. Low-pressure oxygen valves are rising stem or "needle" valves. The ¼-turn ball valves used for air must not be used for oxygen.

- Never use oil or grease on any high pressure gas lines, fittings, valves, or gauges.

- Oxygen equipment that requires lubrication must be lubricated with an oxygen compatible lubricant, such as Krytox, Christolube, or Dow Corning 111.

- When working on oxygen systems, clean all wrenches and tools off before you proceed with the work. Make sure oil and grease are cleaned off the tools.

- Keep oxygen hoses to a minimum. Use pipe whenever possible.

- Oxygen system piping should not be made of stainless steel. It should be brass, copper, or tungum.

- Never use oxygen regulators or hoses to transport any gas other than oxygen.

- Only use certified "O$_2$ safe" hose to transport oxygen (Synflex or equivalent, **never** rubber).

- When using O-rings or pressure seals in oxygen service, they must be constructed of an oxygen compatible material such as Viton.

- If oxygen equipment has been contaminated by hydrocarbons, do not use it until it has been properly O_2 cleaned and inspected.

- Use the "bag and tag" system. Once oxygen equipment has been inspected and found O_2 clean, keep it sealed in an airtight bag until use. All oxygen equipment should be stored in sealed bags.

Any components used in oxygen storage and delivery (from the cylinder to the mask) are always to be kept O_2 clean. There are various products on the market for oxygen cleaning marketed under different names (BIOX, Simple Green, Blue Gold). To establish the best product to use, talk to your local industrial gas supplier. They do more oxygen cleaning than you will ever have to do. Before using these cleaners, check out the WHMIS information and find what safety precautions you must take, if any, when using them. To inspect the oxygen equipment to ensure it is O_2 clean, use ultraviolet (black) light. Any problem areas will show up easily under the light.

11.10 CHAMBER SAFETY GUIDELINES

The hyperbaric chamber, being a pressure vessel and having an oxygen supply, has the potential to be a dangerous piece of equipment. That potential can be mitigated by cleanliness, proper maintenance, and careful operation. The following safety guidelines will help in this respect:

- Never allow petroleum or any petroleum products to enter the chamber.

- Do not allow any flammable substances to enter the chamber.

- Do not use oil on oxygen or air fittings, valves, regulators, or gauges.

- Never permit the chamber to be used for gear storage or as a bunkhouse.

- Do not allow footwear to be worn inside the chamber.

- Do not permit diving suits of any kind to be worn in the chamber.

- Have all personnel in street clothes empty pockets before entering the entrance lock of the chamber.

- Do not allow cell phones or other electronics to enter the chamber.

- Check door seals and door dogs on a regular basis (daily).

- Do not allow doors to remain dogged after blowdown.

- Do not allow medical oxygen supply for BIBS system to run below 100 psig or above 125 psig.

- Perform a checklist at the start of every shift as a chamber operator.

- When operating chamber, do not allow yourself to be distracted.

- Look in on the chamber occupant often, watching for any adverse symptoms.

- Do not perform repairs or modifications to the chamber unless you are qualified and authorized to do so.

- Practice good chamber maintenance, particularly regular and thorough wash downs.

11.11 DECK DECOMPRESSION CHAMBER TESTING

Every chamber must undergo commissioning prior to use with human occupants, whether it is a DDC or a medical hyperbaric chamber. This commissioning involves a detailed inspection and function testing of all of the major components and safety systems of the chamber, a thorough cleaning of the chamber, and depending on the circumstances, a pressure/leak test may be required. The pressure/leak test is based on the U.S. Navy's own test and is required under the following conditions:

- Every two years, regardless of number of times used
- Every time the chamber is moved to a different location
- Every time changes have been made (e.g. replacement of plumbing)
- Every time viewports have been removed and replaced

The commissioning inspection, function testing, and cleaning takes place in the following instances:

- Upon delivery of a new-build or rental chamber
- Upon removal from storage or lay up
- Upon transfer to a different vessel

Commissioning of a chamber is similar to, but performed separately from, the DDC inspection and function testing required by the IMCA D023 Air Diving System Audit. The paperwork for the commissioning and pressure/leak test may be found on the following pages.

HYPERBARIC CHAMBER PRESSURE/LEAK TEST

Location:	Date:
Chamber S/N:	Tested by:

STEP	REQUIRED OPERATION
1	Open the inner med-lock door, close the inner chamber door, and pressurize the inner lock to 100 fsw. Snoop all penetrators, welds, viewports, door seals, valves, fittings, and pipe-joints.
2	Mark all leaks, depressurize chamber, and adjust, repair, or replace chamber components as necessary to eliminate leaks.
3	Repeat steps 1 and 2 as required until all leaks are eliminated.
4	Pressurize the inner lock to 225 fsw and hold, adding air as required, for 5 minutes. Disregard small leaks at this pressure.
5	Depressurize the chamber to 165 fsw. Hold for 1 hour. Do not add air. If pressure drops below 145 fsw in 1 hour, locate and mark leaks. Depressurize the chamber and repair according to step 2. Repeat procedure until pressure holds above 145 fsw in 1 hour.
6	Repeat steps 1 through 5 with inner lock door open. Leak test only the outer lock of the chamber.

Start time IL:	End time IL:
Max depth fsw:	Status (satisfactory/not)
Start time OL:	End time OL:
Max depth fsw:	Status (satisfactory/not)

Comments:

Signature _____

Dated _____

INITIAL COMMISSIONING SIGN-OFF FOR PVHO

Description of Pressure Vessel:

Mfg:	Serial No:
PVHO No:	CRN No:
Mfg Date:	Design WP:
Max WP:	Commission Date:

Test Details (indicate with X)

Cleaning of Vessel		Oxygen/CO$_2$ Analyzer Function	
Flush of Plumbing		Gauge Comparison to Master	
Pressure/Leak Test		Communications Function Test	
BIBS Function Test		Sound Powered Phones Function Test	
Valve Function Test		Interior Lighting Function Test	

Close Visual Inspection Details

Specification Plate		Pipework and Plumbing	
Certification Package		Valve Placement	
Viewports		Whips and Feed Lines	
Manway O-ring seals		Overpressure Relief Valves	
Medical Lock O-ring seals		Fire-Fighting Appliances	
Thru-Hull Penetrators		Mattresses and Blankets	

Comments:

Vessel Inspected and Tested to (Standard or Regulation) _____

Testing and inspection performed under the direction of _____
                                                              Printed Name

Signature _____   Date _____

12.0 MARINE CONSTRUCTION

Humans have been engaged in construction in marine environments for as long as they have been sailing the seas. Marine construction projects have evolved from simple piers and docks to today's large, high-technology oil drilling platforms. All of these facilities employ commercial divers, at least occasionally, for construction, maintenance, and repair. Therefore, the commercial diver needs to be familiar with the tools, techniques, and materials of marine construction. Construction work that may employ divers includes dredging, cribwork, and concrete and steel construction. Also, divers are often used in pre- and post-construction survey work. This section covers the basic skills the construction diver needs to have to perform this work safely and effectively.

12.1 DREDGING

Dredging is the process of removing material from underwater, whether for maintaining harbor and channel depth or for installing a new marine structure or bridge pier. The material removed by the dredge is known as dredge spoils. The dredging of large areas is always performed by some type of mechanical dredge and smaller areas, such as cofferdams, are often done manually. It is the first operation on any construction job.

Divers are not used in the day-to-day operations of the mechanical dredges but are quite often called on for maintenance and repair of the vessels used in the operation. If the dredging is being performed to allow construction, usually divers will perform a pre- and post-dredge survey.

12.1.1 Mechanical Dredging

There are five types of mechanical dredge: conveyor, clamshell, suction, sand pump, and backhoe. All five of these types of dredge have the same problem: They must stay on location while dredging but be able to move quickly as the work progresses. The system dredges most often use is "spudding in." Steel beam or pipe "spuds" are lowered to the seabed through "spud pockets" in the sides of the barge. The weight of the spuds holds them on bottom, and they hold the dredge barge in place. Dredge spoils are either deposited on shore by means of a pipeline or into a dump scow, which, once it has been filled, takes the spoils to a pre-selected dumping area. Dump scows may be either self-propelled vessels or towed by a dedicated tugboat.

Conveyor Dredges

Conveyor dredges, also called bucket-ladder dredges, have, as the names suggest, a conveyor with steel buckets attached. One end of the conveyor is lowered to the bottom, while the other end extends over the dump scow. As the conveyor operates, full buckets are continually dumping into the scow as the empty ones at the lower end are filled. Conveyor dredges are always barge or ship based.

Clamshell Dredges

Clamshell dredges are the most common unit seen in marine construction. Basically, a clamshell dredge is a conventional crane with a clam bucket. They are used both on barges and on land and work well in any depth, with any type of overburden (the overlying material to be removed). In marine-based clamming, self-dumping barges, called dump scows, are used to transport spoils. In land-based clamming, usually dump trucks haul the spoils away.

Suction Dredges

Suction dredges have a huge pump with a large suction pipe lowered to the bottom. Discharge is either loaded into dump scows or run ashore through floating pipeline. These units often have a cutter head, for hard bottom, attached to the dredge intake. Usually, they are barge or ship mounted. Suction dredges are routinely used in the state of Florida for beach restoration. As the unit dredges the navigation channels, the sand is piped ashore to rebuild the beaches that have suffered from ocean erosion.

Sand Pump Dredges

Sand pump dredges, like suction dredges, have a large pipe lowered to the bottom. The main difference is that sand pump dredges have a submergible pump mounted on the lower end of the pipe. These pumps occasionally have cutters attached. These units are mounted on a ship or barge and are only used for sand or light silt bottoms.

Backhoe Dredges

Backhoe dredges are used primarily for shallower dredging projects. Often, a hydraulic excavator is mounted on a barge, but there are also units especially made for this purpose. Long-reach backhoes are often used for land-based shallow dredging. Backhoe dredges are useful on projects involving cable and pipeline shore landings.

12.1.2 Manual Dredging

Manual dredging with a diver is usually done only when a mechanical dredge will not do the job or will damage existing infrastructure. For example, manual dredging is required near submarine cables or pipelines, inside cofferdams, or inside intake structures or pipelines.

The Airlift

The most commonly used method of manual dredging is the airlift, a suction device utilizing a length of pipe modified to allow the injection of air about 12 inches above the bottom end. The air, being lighter than water, rises rapidly up the pipe and creates a Venturi effect at the bottom end. When the airlift is running, anything near the bottom end is sucked up the pipe. These are efficient tools that work well in silt, sand, and gravel. Airlifts may be built in any size, but anything over 14 inches in diameter is difficult for a diver to handle. These units should always have a grate on the intake, constructed in such a way that, should a diver be sucked against it, water will bypass the diver. This will prevent serious injury to the diver, but the diver will be stuck there until the air is shut off. Therefore, a ¼-turn ball valve should always be mounted on the air supply at the diver's end, with another at the dive station.

Suction Pumps

Suction pumps are occasionally used for manual dredging. Suction pumps may consist of a large bore centrifugal pump with a flexible intake hose or a submergible hydraulic pump, with a short flexible hose on the intake, and a long hose on the discharge. Suction pumps are most effective in silt and very fine sand but are used routinely in diamond mining to move gravel. The drawback to these units is they cannot be controlled from the diver's end. South African diamond divers do use a flow diversion device that protects the diver to a limited degree. Pumps are less violent than airlifts, but less effective in some applications.

Water and Air Jetting

Probably the least effective method of dredging is jetting. Water jets are typically a large diameter (6 inches or more) high volume pump that is reduced to 2.5 or 3 inches at the discharge. The jet hose is high pressure hose, and at the business end, the jet nozzles reduce the size down to 1 inch. The nozzles are balanced, having opposing streams through a T-shaped head that makes it easier for the diver to control. These units can generate pressures in excess of 300 psi and must be used with caution. The most common use of water jets is in pipeline construction and repair. Jets push material, as opposed to removing it, to another location and for that reason are less effective. Air jets are similar in operation to water jets but feed LP air from a compressor to an "air lance," which is a piece of pipe attached to the end of the air hose. The most common use for air jets is in salvage work, where they are used to feed lifting slings under an object resting on the seafloor.

Hand Dredging

Occasionally, dredging must be performed in areas where even pumps and airlifts cannot be used, such as up inside an intake pipe. In these cases, the standard way of removing spoils is on a cart or sled, which is winched out of the pipe after it is full. A snatch-block is rigged inside the pipe so the sled can be hauled in both directions by the winch. The diver utilizes a shovel to fill the cart or sled with spoils; then the spoils are hauled away.

12.2 Pile Driving

Pilings are used in marine work to support structures such as piers and bridges in the construction of cofferdams and as forms for concrete work. Most pile driving jobs are done by dock builders and pile drivers, who often use divers in their work. As with any part of a man-made structure exposed to a marine environment, piles will, with time, require repair or replacement. Usually, this will involve a diving contractor. There are also some preventive measures that may be taken to extend the service life of piling. Additionally, false work, by design, must be removed. Often this work requires divers.

12.2.1 Types and Uses of Piling

There are four materials commonly used for piling: timber, steel, precast concrete, and recycled plastic.

Timber Piles

For centuries, timber piles have been used in the construction of marine structures. Timber piles may be either hard- or softwood and are often pressure treated with a wood preservative. When used as load-bearing members, timber piles are often driven with a steel "shoe" to allow driving to refusal. Timber piles are often used to support temporary decks to allow for construction using other materials. These temporary decks and piles are known as false work. Often, timber is the material of choice for fender piles, which are piles that are used as "bumpers" between piers and vessels, as well as other applications.

Steel Piles

The most common material used in piling today is steel. Steel may be seen in H piles, pipe piles, or in sheet piles. The details of each type of pile are found below:

Steel sheet piles   Steel H pile   Steel pipe piles

Steel H Piles

Depending on the design loads, steel H piles vary in size from 8 to 48 inches. Web and flange thickness varies as well. H piles are used for bearing piles, fender piles, and also as false work. They sometimes have a protective coating applied before driving.

Steel Pipe Piles

Steel pipe piles vary in size from 12 to 60 inches. They have different wall thicknesses and may or may not be coated. Pipe piles are used for bearing piles and occasionally for false work.

Steel Sheet Piles

Steel sheet pile is available in different configurations and thicknesses. The most common is the AZ configuration, which looks almost like the letter W. Sheet pile is used for backfill retention, wave breaks, flow diversion, and also to form cofferdams. Sheet pile sections have locks on both edges, so several sheets may interlock to form a solid steel wall. When it is used in a permanent installation, sheet pile is usually coated prior to driving.

Precast Concrete Piles

Precast concrete piles are available in square, octagon, and round configurations. They are often cast with a hollow core to minimize weight in handling. Size usually ranges from 12-inch square to 24-inch round, depending on design loads. These piles are usually used as bearing piles.

Concrete pile dock

Recycled Plastic

Plastic piles are used only as fender piles and are available in various sizes. They are proving to be an efficient and economical alternative to timber or steel.

12.2.2 Methods of Pile Driving

Pilings are driven into the bottom with a pile driver, using one of five methods: drop hammer, diesel hammer, air hammer, vibratory hammer, and rock socketing. Piling are often driven to refusal: This is the point at which the piling basically bounces when hit. It cannot be driven any farther.

Drop Hammer

The oldest method of driving pile is the drop hammer; it is often still the method of choice. A drop hammer is a very heavy weight (called a pig) winched up a track or cage (called the leads) and then let free fall down to hit the pile with enough force to drive it into the ground or the seafloor. Drop hammers, depending on the length of the leads and the weight of the pig, often hit the pile with sufficient force to damage (broom up) the top of the pile. For this reason, a steel driving cap is often placed on the piles before driving begins. The winch used must have free-fall capability, so conventional cranes are usually the only type used with a drop hammer.

Drop hammer

Diesel Hammer

The diesel hammer is a heavy, cast steel piston and cylinder. The cylinder has inlet valves for both diesel fuel and air and an exhaust port at the maximum stroke of the piston. The cylinder sets on top of the pile; a crane lifts the piston and drops it. When the piston falls, it compresses the air/diesel mixture, causing it to explode. This explosion drives the piston back up to keep the diesel hammer running. To stop the diesel hammer, a decompression valve is mounted on the cylinder, which is operated by the rigger.

Air Hammer

Like diesel hammers, air hammers have a piston and a cylinder. Air hammers, however, use compressed air instead of internal combustion to operate. Although these are efficient hammers, they require a large compressor to operate.

Vibratory Hammers

Vibratory hammers use rapid vibration instead of blunt force to drive the pile. These hammers are powered by air or hydraulics and may be used for both driving and extracting piles. Vibratory hammers are used to drive sheet pile; they are also used underwater when installing mooring system piles for single-buoy moorings, floating production storage, and offloading vessels.

Rock Socketing

Used only with steel pipe piles, this method is used when there is a rock bottom. The pile is first driven to rock, then a drill is fed down the center of the pile. Next, a socket is drilled into the rock, and concrete is pumped into the socket and the pile in a monolithic pour. Often there are dowels inserted very deep below the socket to provide additional shear strength. This system is used when installing jacket platforms.

Air hammer

12.3 PILING REPAIRS

Divers are often involved in the maintenance and repair of pile-work structures. The tools, techniques, and materials required for the job are determined by the type of structure and the type of repair needed.

12.3.1 Concrete Jacket Repairs

The most effective and structurally sound method of pile repair is the concrete jacket, which is a reinforced concrete encasement over part or all of a piling. Jackets may be used on wood, steel, or concrete piling. There are many different materials used in constructing forms for concrete jackets, but they are referred to as bag forms and rigid forms.

Bag Forms

Bag forms are typically used for shorter jackets and are constructed of nylon, polyester, or a similar fabric, with a rugged zipper up one side. They usually have welded wire mesh inside against the pile for reinforcing. They are filled from the top, using a pump. The fabric is designed to bleed any entrapped water, while at the same time retaining the concrete or grout.

Rigid Forms

Rigid forms (used for any length of repair) are constructed of fiberglass, steel, or aluminum. Rigid jacket forms are cylindrical in shape, with two halves bolted together on a bottom plate. Rigid forms may be used with wire mesh, rebar, or steel fiber as the reinforcing. Rigid forms may be filled from the top, but the best results are achieved when they are bottom pumped. In most instances, rigid forms are removed and reused. A big advantage of the rigid forms is that form vibrators can be attached to them to aid in consolidation of the pour.

12.3.2 Repairs Without Concrete

Occasionally, steel pilings are repaired without concrete. For example, steel H piles often are repaired by positioning gusset plates over severely corroded areas and welding to solid steel both above and below the corrosion. Usually, gusset plates are constructed as channels that fit against each side of the web. Occasionally, rectangular plates are welded to the flanges. Steel pipe piles often are repaired by installing rolled plate patches over corroded areas. Sometimes corrosion is so extensive that steel jackets are installed to cover the entire circumference of the pile, reaching well above and below the corroded area.

12.3.3 Preventive Measures

Measures to prevent damage to marine structures are often carried out by divers. These measures usually take the form of pile-wrap or cathodic protection.

Pile Wrap

The most common preventive measure taken with piling is pile wrap. Several manufacturers have products available, but all are similar. Pile wraps always have an inner layer that helps keep electrolysis from occurring (steel) or worms from eating wood and an outer protective layer (usually a vinyl). Concrete piles may be protected from freeze-thaw by insulating pile wrap using a material such as Styrofoam, with a protective vinyl coating.

Insulating pile wrap on concrete piling

Cathodic Protection

Another common preventive measure for steel is cathodic protection. Cathodic protection may be in the form of sacrificial anodes or an impressed current system. Sacrificial anodes (aluminum or zinc) are bolted to brackets welded to the piles. These anodes have a limited lifespan and must be replaced periodically. In recent years, a common practice has been to place the sacrificial anodes on a "sled," with the sleds attached to the piles with heavy, coated wire. Brackets are welded to the piles for these wires to attach to. Cathodic protection of steel structures is covered more fully in Chapter 16: Non-Destructive Testing.

Diver welding anode on pipe pile

12.3.4 Removal of False-Work Piling

False work are piling driven to hold a temporary deck, used for construction. False work is used during the construction of bridges and docks to allow cranes to set up and drive the permanent bearing piles. Since the invention of the pile extractors, there has been less initial work for divers in the removal of false work. Quite often, however, for one reason or another, extractors fail to do the job. Divers are then used to cut steel H piles, pipe piles, sheet piles, or timber piles. If the false work is in a navigable waterway, excavation may be required before cutting in order to get the cut off elevation deep enough.

12.3.5 Bridge Pier Cofferdams

Modern bridge construction typically uses concrete piers, poured in a sheet pile cofferdam. These cofferdams often have a large number of steel H piles, driven on a batter, as bearing piles. These steel H piles are cut to a specific elevation by divers. After the pier base and pier are poured, the sheet piles are extracted. Frequently, it is difficult to extract them because a bond forms between the concrete and the sheet pile itself. In these cases, divers are required to cut the sheet pile off flush with the top of the pier base.

12.4 CRIBWORK

Cribwork has been used in marine construction for hundreds of years. Prior to the invention of rock socketing, it was the only method of construction upon bedrock. Though more expensive than pile work, cribwork is still used when backfill is required to reclaim land on the inshore side of a marine structure.

Timber and concrete are the two most common materials used to construct cribwork.

12.4.1 Timber Cribwork

Originally, the only material used in the construction of cribwork was wood, but timber is seen less often today than concrete. The original timber cribs were built with round logs and filled with beach stone. Timber cribs today are built with square sawn timber, usually pressure treated with preservative. They are fastened with galvanized steel hardware and filled with large quarry stone. The crib is built to the stage where it will set on bottom, yet extend above the water's surface. Then the crib is floated into its final position and loaded with ballast stone to sink it. The crib is then completed, with ballast stone added as the construction progresses.

In the past, when the timber crib was completely filled with ballast, a timber deck was installed and fittings such as bollards (for ship's lines) were installed. Today, however, the deck is cast-in-place concrete, with the deck fittings set into the pour.

Timber cribs may be built to fit the bottom profile (with bedrock) but usually they are placed on a rock mattress. Bedrock is blasted and removed and a mattress of crushed stone is placed and leveled. When overburden exists, the first few feet are usually dredged and a mattress placed. Rock mattress material is two-inch clear stone.

12.4.2 Concrete Cribs

Concrete cribs, also called caissons, are huge, reinforced concrete boxes floated into place, sunk, and then filled with ballast stone. When they are constructed, valves are installed in the floor to allow flooding, and interior walls are poured for lateral strength. When the size permits, concrete cribs are often constructed in a dry dock. Otherwise, cofferdams, tilting platforms, or sinking barges are used to facilitate building and launching.

Concrete cribs are used for wharf and dock structures, bridge piers, and, recently, they have been used for offshore oil production platforms. When concrete cribs are used for offshore oil platforms, they are not classified as cribs but as "gravity base structures."

Concrete cribs, like timber, are usually placed on a rock mattress. When multiple cribs are used to create a wharf structure, the ends of the cribs have a slot cast in the end walls, which is used to hold a precast concrete "key." The key is placed in the gap, or "keyway," between the ends of the cribs. Its purpose is to retain the stone and gravel backfill that is placed behind the cribs. After the cribs are placed and completely filled with ballast, they usually have a concrete deck poured in place. Fittings such as bollards, bull rails, and curbs are incorporated into the deck.

Recently, a new type of concrete cribwork construction has been introduced; it is known as "reinforced earth" construction. In reinforced earth, a rock mattress is placed and leveled. Formwork is put in place, and a wide concrete footing is poured, with steel reinforcing and anchor bolts at precise spacing. Steel I beams are installed vertically on the anchor bolts. Precast concrete panels are then placed between and fitted into the web of these I beams. Galvanized steel tie-backs run from one side of the structure to the other, providing lateral strength. The entire structure is then filled with common backfill, which is compacted. A deck is installed, either with cast-in-place concrete or precast panels.

12.4.3 Diving Work on Cribs

On timber cribwork, there is usually little or no diving work during the initial construction, but rock mattresses are prone to scour because of current, storms, or propeller wash. Regardless of the cause, scour undermines cribs and will cause them to settle; this places unplanned-for stresses on the structure. Divers are used to repair scour areas on rock mattresses under timber cribs, throughout the lifespan of the crib.

Divers are often used on concrete cribs to control the flood valves during placement; additionally, the keyway measurements are taken using a diver. Keyway repairs are usually performed by inserting dowels into the cribs, installing a rebar mat, installing formwork flush with the outer face of the crib, and pumping the formwork full of concrete. This keyway work is all performed by divers.

Reinforced earth requires divers to place the formwork for the footing; this is not a small task. The footing must be precise so that the panels will line up. Divers are required to perform the footing pour, consolidate the concrete, and screed it (level it off). Stripping formwork is all done underwater, and placement of the I-beams and the lower precast concrete panels also require divers.

As with timber cribs, the rock mattress under a concrete crib is prone to scour, which, in turn, undermines the crib. Over time, concrete cribs usually settle, even when they have not been undermined. This will cause the keys to shift in the keyways, allowing backfill to escape. Rock mattress scours are most often repaired with concrete. This concrete may be pumped into rigid formwork or fabric "bag" forms.

12.5 CONCRETE CONSTRUCTION

Underwater concrete is often used in both new construction and in the repair of existing marine infrastructure. Regardless of the application, great care must be taken in all aspects of the work to ensure the pour is successful and the quality of the concrete remains high.

Concrete sets as a result of chemical reaction, not drying out, so concrete hardens nearly as quickly underwater as on dry land. Therefore, underwater concrete placement, when performed properly, will produce a finished product no different than if it were poured on the surface. In many respects, the rules and recommendations for underwater concrete are the same as those for conventional concrete on land. Properly mixed concrete is a stable material with a density more than twice that of water. Once it is in position, it will remain unaffected by the water in which it is immersed unless it is subjected to agitation or other movement while it is setting.

Typically, the mix designs used for pours underwater are 20 to 30% richer in cement to offset any possible washout. Admixtures are also used to prevent washout. The main way washout is prevented, however, is through the method of placement.

12.5.1 Concrete Formwork

When concrete is placed, it requires formwork to hold it in the required shape until it has cured. The formwork must be strong enough to withstand not only the weight (outward force) of the wet concrete but also the increased pressure caused by consolidation, and in some cases, the pump pressure.

Formwork Composition

Formwork may be constructed of wood, steel, fiberglass, aluminum, fabric, or plastic, depending on the application. The most common material used, however, is steel. Concrete formwork must be designed by a professional engineer, or the design should be approved by an engineer to avoid structural failure. Concrete is permanent and is difficult to remove if a form fails.

Any formwork used underwater needs to be tight-fitting, with cracks and gaps kept to a minimum to prevent washout. Any cracks in the formwork should be sealed prior to concrete placement. All tie rods, anchor bolts, and formwork bolts must be checked for tightness. Double nuts on all bolts is a good practice.

Usually, formwork will be removed after curing. To allow easy removal, a bond breaker or form release is used. When a form release is used, it must be compatible with all admixtures and components of the concrete. As well, the form release must not be water soluble.

12.5.2 Concrete Materials
Conventional concrete consists of a cement, usually Portland cement, fine aggregates such as sand, coarse aggregates (usually crushed stone), and water. Admixtures include air entraining, anti-washout, super-plasticizer, and retarder.

Concrete Ingredients
For underwater work, the minimum size of coarse aggregate should be over 20 mm (¾ inch); that is, not more than 10% passing a 20 mm (¾ inch) test sieve. The maximum size stone is governed only by the circumstances of the pour. The exception to this is when the concrete is being placed by pump. Within the past few years, engineers have found that manufactured stone is a superior aggregate to natural stone. The angular surfaces found on manufactured (crushed) stone gives the concrete a higher compressive strength than the round surfaces of natural stone. The aggregate should be clean and free from dust when it is placed because it will not be subjected to any mixing action that might otherwise remove traces of dirt.

Any clean sand suitable for normal concrete may be used. The grading of the sand is important and will depend on the particle shape of both the coarse and fine aggregates. Field tests should normally be carried out to ensure grouting operations will run efficiently with the selected sand.

Normal Portland cement is the most commonly used cement for underwater concrete. Any special requirements are addressed with admixtures (e.g. air entraining to address freeze/thaw). Regardless what type of cement is used for the paste of the concrete and regardless what admixtures are chosen for the mix, the cement quantity should be well above 600 pounds per cubic yard. Blast furnace slag or pozzolanic cements may also be used underwater. The decision to use sulphate-resisting or other special cements should be based on the same criteria that would apply to any concrete in the same environment.

Admixtures, such as fly ash, set accelerators or retarders, water reducing admixtures, air entraining admixtures, expanding agents, and others may be advantageous in some instances as determined by the nature of the work. Air entraining creates micro-bubbles of air in the cured concrete that give improved freeze-thaw qualities. Anti-washout, as the name implies, prevents washout of the cement prior to curing. Super-plasticizer causes the mixture to be more fluid during placement while not adding more water to the mix. Retarders allow a slower initial cure of the concrete, allowing more time to work prior to setting. Care must be taken, however, when using admixtures, as not all admixtures are compatible. In addition, often super-plasticizer and retarder cause a "flash set" or a rapid initial cure at the end of the workability period.

12.5.3 Concrete Reinforcement
Concrete reinforcement serves two purposes. It adds tensile and shear strength, and it absorbs some of the thermal expansion and contraction of the concrete.

Within the obvious limitations imposed by working underwater, placing reinforcement is possible. But placing the concrete is not as certain a process underwater as in the dry, so the results obtained may often be suspect. If it is necessary to use reinforcement, simple details must be observed. Congested reinforcement must be avoided because even nominal amounts of steel may impede the concrete flow, causing voids with consequent deficiencies in bond strength. Where possible, the reinforcement should be assembled in the dry and lowered into position as a cage. In some cases the reinforcement may be fixed to the formwork before it is lowered into position. Reinforcing is provided by one of the following: deformed reinforcing bars (rebar), wire mesh, or fibers.

Rebar

Rebar is most often steel, but fiberglass is becoming more common. Rebar comes in various diameters and lengths and is often epoxy coated to prevent corrosion. It is placed at specified spacing with intersecting lengths tied with wire or welded. Bends in rebar are usually made in a shop; field bending of rebar is not a good practice.

Wire Mesh

Welded wire mesh is available in plain steel or galvanized steel. Overlapping sheets of wire mesh are tied together with wire or galvanized wire when using galvanized mesh.

Fiber

Fiber, used primarily in repair work, may be steel or fiberglass. The fibers are placed into the concrete mix in measured quantities prior to pouring (usually on site).

12.5.4 Concrete Placement and Consolidation

When a mass of fresh concrete moves through the water, or when water flows over the surface of fresh concrete, the cementatious material is separated from the aggregates when the mix comes into direct contact with the water in a process know as segregation. Thus the aim, when placing concrete underwater, is to keep as much of the concrete as possible out of direct contact with the water and to avoid any rapid movement or agitation of the exposed surfaces. While the traditional methods of placing concrete underwater are by tremie, by skip, or a similar device, pumping has become the most common method and pumping achieves the most favorable results as the possibility of segregation is drastically reduced.

The Tremie

The tremie is a steel, plastic, or rubber tube, suspended vertically in the water, with a hopper fixed to the upper end to receive the fresh concrete. The tube or pipe must be watertight, and joints, where necessary, should have watertight meeting faces. It should be smooth-bored and have adequate cross-section for the size of aggregate to be used. A diameter of 150 mm (6 in.) is commonly regarded as the minimum for 20 mm (¾ in.) aggregates and 200 mm (8 in.) as the lower limit for 40 mm (1½ in.) aggregates.

The hopper acts as a reservoir to convert an intermittent supply of concrete into a steady flow down the pipe. It should be a size that it will enable the level of concrete to be maintained generally within its depth. The assembled pipe and hopper must be provided with a means of rapid raising and lowering when charged with wet cement. Simple blocks and tackle, unless power assisted, are generally inadequate for this purpose. Powered systems, such as cranes, are preferable.

The tremie is erected vertically over the area to be concreted with the lower end of the pipe resting on the bottom. Various methods

Concrete hopper and tremie pipe

can be used for sealing the bottom of the pipe to keep out water and to enable the pipe to be filled while dry. It is difficult to provide a means of opening the bottom that is reliable and, at the same time, does not obstruct the flow of concrete or the removal of the pipe after use. Furthermore, the flotation of an empty pipe can be a nuisance when the assembly is being placed in position. For these reasons, it is now common practice to place a traveling plug in the top of the pipe as a barrier between the concrete and the water. The water in the pipe is then displaced as the weight of the concrete forces the plug to the bottom. Cement bags or sacks, folded into shape, are most commonly used for the traveling plug, but in recent years, foam plastic plugs and inflated balls have also been used. Purpose-built buoyant plugs are expected to extricate themselves from the concrete and rise to the surface; otherwise, plugs are generally not recovered. If they are buried in the depths of the concrete, their effect is insignificant. More damage may be caused by attempting to remove plugs than by allowing them to remain in place.

After the pipe has been filled with concrete, it is raised a few inches off the bottom. The concrete begins to flow, quickly burying the end of the pipe. Thereafter, the flow of concrete should continue to feed the interior of the heap of placed concrete.

The Skip

The skip is a hopper-like container for placing concrete. The skip should be of the bottom-opening type with double doors that can be operated automatically or manually. It should be straight-sided, perfectly smooth, and vertical inside with no taper at the bottom. Skirts are sometimes fitted at the bottom. These may provide an advantage in some circumstances by confining the concrete while it is being deposited.

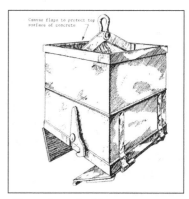

Skips must be completely filled before the top covers are placed. They must be lowered slowly, particularly when entering the water, to avoid disturbance of the concrete under the top cover, and again when nearing the bottom to avoid excessive disturbance of the previously placed concrete.

Illustration of a skip

After it settles on the bottom, the skip must be lifted gently and slowly so that the released concrete causes no turbulence in the water around it. The aim is to deposit fresh concrete from the skip into the body of previously placed concrete and to displace the existing sloping surface of the mass forward in the formwork. Except for pours in confined spaces, it is desirable to have a diver to control the placing of the skips, even when the release mechanism is automatic.

The intermittent nature of skipwork and the way in which the pour is built up from a number of individual discharges subjects a greater proportion of the concrete to the risk of local washing out. Furthermore, the chance of trapping silt or slurry is more likely than would be the case in properly executed tremie work. Skips are more practicable for thin pours and for work requiring a screeded (smoothed off) finish.

Pumping

Recent improvements in the design of concrete pumps have made it possible to consider them for the direct placing of concrete underwater. These pumps range from 2-inch grout pumps to 8-inch tandem concrete pumps capable of handling concrete with 2-inch aggregate. Many of these larger units are capable of pumping ready-mix concrete as fast as it can

Installing concrete pump lines

be delivered and pushing it up through vertical pipeline to heights in excess of 500 feet. Although concrete pumping flex hose is available, concrete should be pumped through steel pumping lines, using long-radius elbows for corners. Flex hose may be required to make up the final transition to the form: if so, keep the length as short as possible.

Loading the concrete pump

Tremie Pumping of Concrete

Pumping the concrete under pressure directly into the mass cuts out the necessity for frequent lifting of the pipe and ensures the desirable constant flow of concrete into the mass. Before pumping commences, the pipe should be adjusted to give a few inches clearance above the formation and a suitable plug inserted in the pipeline adjacent to the pump. Often, a child's neoprene sponge ball (nerf ball) is soaked in form release and used for this purpose.

Concrete pouring should proceed at a fast rate, especially during the initial stages when the bottom of the pipe is being buried. It is desirable to pump for as long as possible, lifting the pipe only when necessary. Caution must be exercised, as excessive lengths of buried pipe in the mass, coupled with a slow rate of pour, can result in new concrete being pushed up underneath concrete that has already begun to set up.

The more workable concretes suitable for pumping can be used for pumping directly into the mass, or for tremie work, but the converse is not necessarily true. The concrete will need a slump in the region of 125 mm (5 in.), but the slump test, while a good test for workability, does not say anything about the other desirable qualities required. Good flowability and cohesion without stickiness are also necessary. These qualities are common requirements for both tremie and pump concretes. Virtually all concrete mix designs require superplasticizer to be pumpable.

Bottom Pumping of Concrete

Now often considered the best method of underwater concrete placement, bottom pumping has the advantage of delivering the concrete continuously into the bottom of the formwork, forcing the water out through the open top of the form. The major advantages of bottom pumping are that the possibility of segregation of aggregates and voids in the concrete mass are greatly reduced. The disadvantages are that high pump pressures are involved, rebar (when used) tries to float up with the concrete, and pumping line connections are difficult to achieve in strong current and reduced visibility.

Formwork used for bottom pumping must be strong due to the high pump pressures. The pumping line attaches to a nipple which is incorporated into the bottom or the bottom of one side of the formwork. To allow the disconnection of the pumping line, a guillotine valve is placed on the nipple. Often, pneumatic form vibrators are bolted to brackets on the sides of the form. When form vibrators are to be used, it is imperative all form bolts be locked tight.

Bottom pumping rigid form   Concrete jacket with form removed

12.5.5 Diving Work on Underwater Concrete Jobs

Underwater concrete job opportunities for divers include finish work such as screeding, site preparation between lifts, and removal of defective concrete (make good). Also, divers are required on pumping operations to connect and disconnect pumping lines, install and remove form vibrators, and install and remove the concrete formwork.

Screeding

Screeding is the process of finishing off the top of the pour to a smooth finish. Besides removing any excess concrete, the screeding process causes a layer of cement to float to the top. This effect covers any aggregate near the surface, which helps to seal the concrete. Screeding is performed by two divers vibrating a flat board across the top of the pour in a see-saw motion.

When screeding concrete underwater, it is essential to have an adequate load of concrete ahead of the screed so that no slacks or hollows can form. It is difficult or impossible to place extra concrete to fill these in. Screeding widths of up to 6 m (20 ft.) are possible in good conditions with experienced divers, but a lesser width is preferable. The screed, which must be heavy, is managed with only two divers because they must operate clear of the concrete. The screed is usually worked off the top of the forms, which should be designed with this in mind.

Skip-placed concrete is generally more suitable for screeding work because the right amount can be delivered to the divers where they require it. A level surface must be created in a single pass. It is possible for divers to achieve accurate finishes, but whenever possible, tolerances should be generous compared to those for a similar class of work in the dry.

Preparation between Lifts

Laitance is an accumulation of fine particles that forms on the top surface of the concrete no matter how carefully the concrete is poured. As soon as the concrete has hardened sufficiently, the laitance should be removed by means of water jet, water-blast, shovel, broom, air lift, etc., until a clean and hard surface is reached. Horizontal construction joints should be avoided wherever possible, but where the volume of concrete makes them necessary, the greatest care must be taken to clear laitance.

Making Good

Satisfactory repair of underwater concrete is virtually impossible. Where concrete is defective, it may be necessary to cut out a relatively large section to ensure that it can be replaced properly. Alternatively, in certain circumstances it may be possible to extend the work to achieve the equivalent result. Pneumatic or hydraulic tools are necessary for the removal of hardened concrete.

Installing and Removing Formwork

Concrete formwork used underwater is usually constructed of steel and designed to be bolted together. All joints in the formwork must be made tight, in order to avoid washout. All sections of formwork must be coated with a non-water soluble form release agent prior to placement underwater. Coating the formwork bolts as well helps to clean them in order to strip the formwork after the pour. When removing formwork, care must be taken not to mark the fresh concrete with pry bars and tools. Where possible, wood wedges should be used to pop the formwork off.

Connecting and Disconnecting Pumping Lines

For underwater concreting, any time the steel pumping line can be run right to the form, that is best practice, but often flex hose must be used. When using flex hose, the best alignment is one with gradual and smooth curves. Sharp curves will restrict concrete flow and cause the pump to plug. Wherever possible, the hose should be supported with rope or chain, being careful not to cause a kink in the line. After the pour, ensure that the inlet valve on the form has been closed and the pump has been reverse stroked to take pressure off the pumping line before you disconnect. Any spilled concrete should be washed out with a high volume of water (fire hose will do).

Installing Form Vibrators

All form vibrators should be tested ahead of time to ensure they work. Vibrators should be installed just before the pour starts. Make sure all vibrator bolts are tightened securely. Tie the air hose off in such a way as to ensure that it will not kink and restrict the air to the vibrators.

12.6 STEEL CONSTRUCTION

Steel is used extensively in the construction and repair of many different marine structures and, of course, in ships. Steel may be mechanically fastened (bolts, studs, etc.), or fusion fastened (welding).

12.6.1 Mechanical Fastening

Mechanical fastening of steel is the alternative used when fusion fastening is not possible or desirable. Because some engineers are not well informed and are convinced quality welds are not possible underwater, they specify mechanical fastening.

Bolting

Bolting is the most common method of mechanical fastening. Often, members are predrilled to avoid drilling underwater. When members are not predrilled, there are several methods to make bolt holes, including hydraulic punch, burning and reaming, and drilling. The fastest of these methods is the hydraulic punch, but these units are heavy and best used with a crane. Burning and reaming is somewhat slower because it involves two operations. The bolt holes must be perfectly round in structural applications, and burning alone leaves an irregular opening. Drilling, depending on the drill used, is very effective. The best drill is a "slugger," a core drill that takes a slug from the steel. On structural steel, there are torque specifications that indicate the amount of torque to be applied to the bolts. Impact wrenches must always be tested to ensure the bolts are being properly torqued. Many of the bolts used today on structural steel are designed to stretch, eliminating the need for lock washers.

Studs

Studs are also used to fasten steel, although usually only on temporary repairs. Studs are a pin driven through or into the steel. These studs may directly fasten two pieces of material, or they may be threaded to bolt additional material. Studs are installed using an explosive charge, similar to those in small arms ammunition. Most stud guns require contact with a hard surface in order to be fired. Extreme care must be taken when working with a stud gun.

12.6.2 Welding and Burning

Underwater welding uses the same basic skills as does surface welding, and most of the same principles apply. On the surface, metals are fused by brazing, arc welding (stick and wire), friction welding, or cad welding. Underwater, brazing and cad welding are not possible, but arc welding and friction welding are routinely performed.

Navy diver welding
Photo courtesy of U.S. Navy

When welding underwater, as on the surface, a steady hand produces the best work. Whenever possible, a staging should be used. The diver needs to take the time to get in a comfortable position and make sure the diving equipment is adjusted properly and working well before starting to weld.

12.6.2.1 Wet Welding

Like surface welding, wet welding is only as good as the surface preparation. All surfaces to be welded must have coatings and marine growth removed, be ground smooth, and be wire brushed prior to welding. Where each new rod starts, slag must be completely chipped and brushed from the previous bead to ensure there are no trapped impurities. The same is true for multiple passes; the slag must be removed, and rough beads must be ground smooth. Rods should be kept dry as long as possible. Unless a dry quiver is used, the diver should carry as few rods at a time as possible.

Wet welding is always performed with direct current and straight polarity, meaning the electrode is negative. The acronym always used is DCEN (direct current, electrode negative). To test for polarity, the diver should place the ground clamp and the stinger in a pail of water roughly four inches apart. With the knife switch hot, small bubbles will form on the rod if the polarity is correct. If they form on the ground, the polarity is wrong. There are a few points to remember to help you weld underwater:

- Watch the puddle. If the puddle is not visible, stop welding and get into a better position. Anything above a number nine lens is too dark for wet welding.
- The diver should actually feel the penetration of the rod into both metal surfaces through the rod to make sure of the proper penetration. The nicest looking bead in the world is useless without good penetration.
- The amperage settings in the rod manufacturer's literature are only guidelines. Colder water requires more amperage to achieve the same results. Long lengths of cable also require more amperage to compensate for line loss.
- Always maintain the gear. Fine sand paper and emery cloth are used to clean all metal parts on the cutting and welding gear. Corroded parts mean poor electrical contact. Poor contact compromises both the quality of the work and the safety of the diver. Keep the gear clean.

12.6.2.2 Underwater Cutting (Burning)

Underwater cutting is performed in much the same way as oxy-acetylene cutting on surface. The material to be cut is first heated to the point of melting, and then it is blown through. The big difference is this: With the temperature achieved by oxy-arc gear ($\pm$10,000° F), it all happens so quickly that you don't realize it. The same acronym is used in underwater cutting to ensure proper polarity: DCEN. Divers who do a lot of cutting push the rod when cutting, instead of dragging the rod. Here are a few tips for underwater cutting:

- Always make sure you have a good ground. Most problems cutting involve a poor ground.
- Always make sure the cutting gear is cleaned up. Polish the brass parts inside the torch head with fine sand paper. Corrosion is your worst enemy in underwater welding and cutting.
- Adjust the oxygen delivery when preparing to burn so that there is at least a three-inch-straight stream at the tip of the rod at the depth where the cutting will be done. Always test delivery pressure at depth.
- Only use the minimum amperage required to light the rod. If you are using Broco rods, that should be around 130 amps.
- Make the knife switch hot only when you are ready, and only keep it hot long enough to light the rod.

- Cold cutting is just as efficient and easier on the gear. As soon as the rod lights, make the gear cold. Do not burn rods less than two inches from the torch.

- The thinner the metal to be cut, the closer the rod should be to parallel to the metal. Thicker metal cuts should be with the rod almost perpendicular to the metal.

- For precision cutting, or in zero visibility, if possible, use a template to guide cutting. Wood or non-ferrous material makes the best template.

- Heavy scale (rust) on steel will not cut, it will melt. When cutting steel with heavy scale, take a few minutes and knock the scale off with a short-handled sledge hammer. Then cut it and look like a pro. It may seem a waste of time, but knocking the scale off will save a lot of time.

12.6.3 Safety Tips for Wet Welding and Cutting

- Make sure that you have a dry hat. A helmet that floods while welding will cause any metallic fillings in the teeth to disappear due to electrolysis and may cause a reverse squeeze that can rupture a tooth.

- Use the DCEN formula for welding and burning. Always check for proper polarity before entering the water or before the gear is sent down.

- When welding and burning, use anodes on the helmet. One is required for the faceplate retainer and one for the side block assembly. Electrolysis destroys life-support gear.

- Never "hot rod." Always make the gear cold before changing cutting or welding rods.

- Never cut or weld underwater without a knife switch installed in line.

- Never have the cutting or welding gear hot, unless the diver is actually cutting or welding. The electric current in welding and cutting causes the hydrogen in water molecules to become disassociated from the oxygen. This hydrogen, when combined again with oxygen, is very explosive and poses a very real threat to the diver. In addition, exothermic cutting rods often produce temperatures of 10,000°F or more at the tip. This heat also causes disassociation, becoming a further source of hydrogen gas.

- Never cut into enclosed structures (tanks, pipes, compartments) unless they have been vented properly. Hydrogen and oxygen produced by the cutting process must be vented and purged out of structures prior to cutting. These gases, if ignited, will explode. Overhanging structures also pose a threat of accumulation. Every year, several divers die due to explosions while cutting. Bear in mind: One cubic foot of hydrogen gas contains the same explosive power as one stick of conventional dynamite. **Do not become a statistic – vent before you cut.**

- When burning, always purge the rod with oxygen prior to striking the arc. Failure to do this may cause an explosion of accumulated hydrogen in the rod.

- Never use a "water ground" or a "floating ground." In some locations, particularly in the offshore, it has become common practice to hang the ground clamp over the side and boost the amperage, thereby saving on having a ground cable running to the job. **Common practice isn't always safe practice.** Always attach the ground firmly to the metal that you are working on. Boosting amperage and using a "water ground" is unsafe and will cause rapid metal loss on cutting gear, welding gear, and life-support gear. Also this makes it impossible for the diver to keep himself from coming between the ground and the work. <u>**Never get between the ground and the work.**</u>

12.7 CONSTRUCTION TOOLS USED UNDERWATER

12.7.1 Hand Tools

The underwater construction project uses most of the same tools the surface project does, with the exception, of course, of electric tools. Hand tools are the same, with some modification. Every tool used underwater should have a short rope lanyard attached. This is used to raise and lower the tool and aids the diver in finding a lost tool, particularly on a silt bottom. Any moving parts on hand tools (jaws on wrenches, tighteners on hacksaws) must be thoroughly lubricated after the tool returns to surface or the moving parts will become fixed in place. Ratchet wrenches must be thoroughly cleaned and lubed as well. Storing these types of tools in light oil such as diesel fuel or vegetable oil works well. Tools such as hammers and crowbars require little or no maintenance. Tool lines or messenger lines are always used to lower tools. Often an open topped canvas tool bag (feed bag) is used to lower tools. Knives, drill bits, and chisels must be sharpened at the end of each dive, if used.

12.7.2 Power Driven Tools

Since electric tools cannot be used underwater, air-powered (pneumatic), and oil-powered (hydraulic) tools are used instead. For the most part, any tool available in electric is available also in pneumatic or hydraulic power. Hydraulic tools are more powerful than air but require heavier hose and are harder for diver and surface crew to handle. For that reason, pneumatic tools are used whenever possible. Pneumatic tools will work well in depths less than 60 feet. Hydraulic tools have no depth limitations: they have been used on ROVs in depths of over 3,000 feet. Any power tool used should have a "dead man" style trigger. This means that in the event the diver loses his grip, the tool will automatically de-energize. All pneumatic tools should be charged before being lowered overboard – this keeps water from being introduced into the system. After use, pneumatic tools must be disconnected, filled with light oil, and flushed with air (best done in an empty barrel). This flushing must be done twice. This ensures all water is purged from the tool and that moving parts are lubricated. Hydraulic tools do not require flushing, but trigger assemblies, and external moving parts must be well cleaned with light oil.

Filling oiler on pneumatic drill

Diver with hydraulic impact gun

12.8 CONSTRUCTION SAFETY TIPS

Before starting any job, all crew members and the supervisor should discuss the project in detail, addressing any safety concerns, and perform a job hazard analysis. If the job to be performed cannot be done safely, the job should not be attempted. Employees have the right to refuse work that is unsafe. The following safety tips must be followed by diving crews working on marine construction projects:

- Do not report for work under the influence of drugs or alcohol. Anyone under the influence should be reported to the supervisor. One crew member under the influence can put the entire crew at risk.

- Pay attention to the job and the work going on around the job. Totally unrelated operations on the job site may put the diver or the support crew at risk.

- Make certain to know where the nearest first-aid kit, fire extinguisher, and telephone are located.

- Keep first aid, Workplace Hazardous Materials Information System (WHMIS), and safety training up to date. It could save a life.

- Make sure you understand exactly what your job entails and what is required of you.

- Pay attention to barrier tapes. Use caution crossing yellow barrier tapes. Never cross a red barrier tape.

- Never pass under a suspended load and never swing a load over other workers. Bystanders must be kept away when lifting loads.

- When a backup alarm sounds close by, stop and look for the source.

- Wear ear protection when working in a loud environment. Hearing loss is usually gradual and becomes permanent. When walking in or crossing roads or high traffic areas, always remove ear protection.

- Find out where and when radiography is being used on the jobsite. Stay clear of radiography work.

- Always wear a safety helmet when working in designated areas or when overhead work is being performed.

- Wear safety glasses or goggles in designated areas or when in the vicinity of workers using any tools.

- Never operate tools without safety glasses.

- Always wear the appropriate PPE for the job you are doing.

- Always wear the proper safety footwear.

- When working on or near the water, always wear a life jacket or personal flotation device. Both pieces of a two-piece PFD should always be worn, never just the pants.

- Always wear or carry a sharp knife, in or out of the water. Take care of it and sharpen it regularly.

13.0 OFFSHORE OIL WORK

It would be hard to overstate the importance of petroleum and petroleum products to the world economy today. Despite much talk of "alternative energy sources" and lobby groups pushing their own agendas, nothing has been found that will take the place of hydrocarbon fuels and lubricants. With the rapid industrialization of the third-world countries, demand has grown exponentially. At the same time, the new deposits found are in more remote and difficult-to-access locations, including offshore.

Technology and expertise in the oil industry have grown at a remarkable rate in recent decades and have allowed expansion into areas previously inaccessible. Oil drilling and recovery is taking place offshore in the Gulf of Mexico, the Arctic, the North Atlantic, Gulf of Alaska, the Pacific Coast of North and South America, the Mediterranean, the Caspian Sea, the Black Sea, the Persian Gulf, the Indian Ocean, the South China Sea, Russia (Siberia and Sakhalin Island), and West Africa.

Once geophysical studies have determined an area is a likely candidate for oil or gas deposits, exploratory drilling takes place. This is the only method of determining the feasibility and potential of a field. The depth and conditions of the water determine what type of vessel will be used for this operation. Test wells determine the extent, reserves, flow rates, and the feasibility of the reservoir. Once this information has been obtained and a decision has been made to utilize the reservoir, construction and installation of a production system begins. These normally take the form of concrete gravity or steel pile structures. In locations with deeper water, guyed tower, tension leg, and remotely operated seabed designs are used. After production begins, the product is transported to shore by means of vessels or pipelines.

As the oil industry continues to expand and diversify, the oil-field diver will continue to be in demand. In fact, the demand for professional, skilled divers in the offshore oil industry increases each year. However, the diver will have to be a technician with the necessary training, expertise, and skills in order to keep pace with the industry. As a member of an offshore drilling or production crew, the oil-field diver needs to have fundamental skills in a variety of related trades: welding, burning, explosives, mechanics, and rigging.

Commercial divers work in all phases of oil-field drilling and extraction: exploration, construction, pipeline laying, production, oil-field maintenance, and decommissioning. The phase of oil-field work that employs the most divers today, however, is oil-field maintenance, now known as IRM work (inspection, repair and maintenance). These divers maintain the entire field infrastructure from the well head to the beach.

13.1 OIL EXPLORATION (DRILLING)

Commercial offshore oil-field drilling is conducted throughout the oceans of the world and other bodies of water. Offshore operations begin by searching for oil with seismic test equipment. The seismic vessel tows a test unit or sends a test unit to the seafloor. This test unit sends a shock wave into the sea bottom. The shock wave works in the same way a sonar does in water. It bounces back to the ship and indicates the properties of the rock below the seafloor. The seismic testing indicates any reservoirs of oil within the rock, and by following preselected grids, the seismic crews are able to estimate the size of the deposits. In the past, seismic testing was done with explosives; these days, it is usually done with high pressure air. Once seismic tests have identified potential deposits, specially equipped exploratory drill ships are brought in, marine versions of their land-based counterparts. The primary differences are the distances between the drill floor and solid ground and the behavior of the water in between.

Offshore oil drilling operations may be supported on bottom-supported rigs or on floating rigs or ships that are not bottom supported during the drilling operations. Offshore oil drilling has been going on for nearly 100 years, and there are still new wells being drilled. Drilling for oil has provided a considerable amount of work for divers over the years and will continue to do so for the foreseeable future.

13.1.1 Bottom Supported Rigs

Jack-up Drill Rigs

A jack-up is a bottom-supported barge with three or more vertically adjustable legs (spuds) that provide a stable platform at a height of 30 feet or more above the surface of the water. Jack-ups can operate in water only as deep as their legs allow; maximum practical depth for drilling is about 150 feet. The barge is towed or self-propelled from site to site with its legs jacked up. As this is a rather unstable configuration, the jack-up requires relatively calm weather conditions for transportation. At the drill site, the legs are lowered to the seabed. The barge is then jacked up on its legs until it is clear of the water. After the drilling operation has been completed, the barge legs are jacked up and it proceeds to the next site.

Jack-up rig

Jack-up Rig Diving Work

Before a jack-up reaches its drilling location, survey normally positions buoys to mark off the center and leg positions. Then survey boats tow side-scan sonar units in a grid pattern to ensure there is no debris on the seabed. If debris is detected by the sonar units, divers locate the debris and remove it.

Divers may be required to measure the depth of penetration of the mud mats (spud cans) using an air probe. In areas of strong currents, divers will have to check for scouring around the mats and, if necessary, fill the scour area with sandbags and build a protective wall around the base of the mat and leg area. Because of the shallow depths involved with jack-up rigs, usually only air diving is necessary.

Jack-up rig Magellan drilling a new well offshore West Africa (2014)

13.1.2 Floating Rigs

Semisubmersible Drill Rigs

A semisubmersible is a unit consisting of a working deck similar to a jack-up rig attached to a floating framework of vertical columns and horizontal pontoon tubes. It is stabilized by the ballasting

Semisubmersibles Thunderhorse and Balder in the U.S. Gulf of Mexico

of pontoons and columns to a predetermined depth. This rig can drill in water depths of 3,000 feet. Generally, the platform is lowered to maximum depth to give greater stability. Many semisubmersibles are capable of operating year-round in varying sea conditions, and though some older semisubs use anchors, many now are fitted (or retrofitted) with DP thrusters to move as well as to hold station at the drilling location.

Semisubmersible Diving Work

When in shallow water with a mud bottom, the semisubmersible may rest on the bottom. Divers may be required to check the pontoons to make sure no penetration occurred when the pontoons sank. In this case, divers will be required to fill scours or to build protective walls with sandbags around the pontoons. Divers may also be utilized to inspect thrusters, pontoons, and sea chests on the structures, assist with rigging of anchor pendent wires, and assist with the recovery of any lost or damaged equipment. Diving operations from a semisubmersible platform can include air, mixed gas, bell bounce, or saturation diving. Deep water work (in excess of 1,000 fsw) is performed by large work class ROVs.

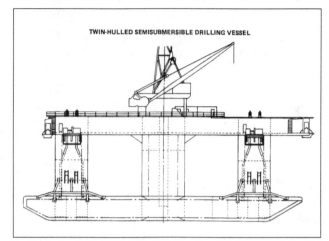

Twin-hulled semisubmersible drilling vessel

NOTE: Because of the usually inconvenient location of deck decompression chambers on semisubmersible rigs (often as many as two decks above the diving station), dives should be kept as short as possible and never go into the exceptional exposure schedules. It may not be possible to maintain the five minutes recommended surface interval time when performing surface decompression due to distances between the diver dress-down area and the chamber.

Drill Ships

Drill ships or drill barges are usually a self-propelled, conventional, or catamaran-hulled vessel with a derrick and drilling equipment. They may be either conventional vessels converted for drilling or may be custom-built. Most have a derrick constructed over a moon pool through which the drill string is run.

Drill ships can drill in depths of over 5,000 feet. They typically use dynamic positioning to maintain location, but anchors may be used when working in shallow water. Because these vessels tend to pitch and roll more than semisubmersibles, there is greater wear and tear on the drilling equipment. This generally means more work for divers.

Diver's tasks on drill ships include inspection, maintenance, and repair of the ship's primary equipment such as sea chests and thrusters, keeping them clear of fouling, as well as the accessory structures such as moon pool doors, and drilling machine water intakes. Divers will also be used to assist in the recovery of any lost or damaged equipment and other tasks that may occur while drilling.

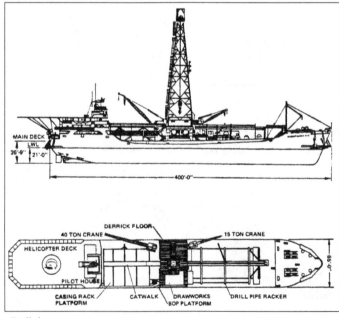

Drill ship

13.1.3 Diving from Drilling Rigs or Drill Ships

The following list provides a minimum outline of the work expected on a drilling rig. Prior to drilling, divers usually are required to do the following:

- Inspect the bottom for junk or obstructions before ballasting a submersible or lowering legs or mat of a jack-up.
- Fill voids under a jack-up or submersible mat with sandbags when the bottom is uneven.
- Inspect cementing operation of the conductor.
- Guide the blowout preventer into place, often under conditions of poor visibility when a TV monitor cannot be relied on.
- Stab the marine riser into the BOP when the drilling rig is slightly off-center over the hole (and the TV monitor is inoperative).
- Guide choke and kill lines through guide arms and funnels attached to each side of the marine riser, and stab them into the BOP.
- Stab the Koomey pod to the manifold on top of the BOP.
- Make various inspections, as needed, throughout the operation.
- Clean marine growth from conductor piles and guides.
- Stab the drilling assembly into the conductor pile.

During drilling operations, there is little for the diver to do unless trouble develops. The diver may be asked to replace the BOP Ax-ring (gasket) as necessary and change BOP hydraulic hoses because of leakage or damage. Subsequent to drilling, the duties of the diver may include the following:

- Actuate the manual override in cases where a BOP hydraulic connector fails to release when the BOP has to be lifted off the wellhead.
- Install a corrosion cap on top of the wellhead along with a pinger and recall buoy.
- Install a "Christmas tree" (a collection of valves, tees and elbows that route the crude oil or gas in the proper directions once the production phase starts).

NOTE: Manufacturer's drawings should always be consulted before attempting any work on a BOP or wellhead. Damage to the conductor can mean the destruction of the entire well.

13.1.4 Safety Precautions for Drilling Work

The diving supervisor is responsible to do the following:

- Hook up and test all deck equipment (compressors, chamber, etc.) that the diving crew will depend on and which might have been left untended between diving jobs. Idle equipment deteriorates rapidly.
- Ensure all equipment is safe and will perform to specs before the job begins.
- Inspect all winch cables and terminations that will be used on the diver's stage. Worn or rusted components must be replaced and not used.
- Perform job hazard analysis (JHA or HSA) and toolbox safety meeting with the diving crew.
- Prepare a detailed dive plan. The dive plan is approved by the oil company diving representative before any work is performed.
- Obtain all permits to work (PTW) required prior to any diving being performed.

The diver is responsible for the following:

- Before making a dive, always study the plans and prints of the system carefully and make certain to understand exactly what is expected on the dive.

- Always step with caution when near the edge of the moon pool.

- Use caution when passing through the air gap during both ascent and descent. Turbulence can be dangerous to the dressed diver.

- Avoid rubbing the diving suit against guide cables, which are heavily greased.

- Be careful of strong currents in deep water.

13.2 BLOWOUT PREVENTERS (BOPs)

A blowout is what happens when the drill reaches an area of pressure higher than the hydraulic head of pressure exerted by the drilling mud inside the drill hole. The result is the uncontrolled blowout of this mud, followed by the oil or gas. This situation is very dangerous, as shown by the blowout and subsequent explosion and fire on the Deepwater Horizon rig in the Gulf of Mexico (April 2010). The blowout preventer (BOP) is responsible for preventing these incidents and for bringing the well back under control by allowing heavier mud to be pumped down. The blowout is first prevented by the closing of one or more pairs of hydraulic rams in the BOP. These rams are pistons made of steel or tough rubber and are usually placed horizontally, one on top of each other.

There are two types of rams: kill (also called shear) and choke rams. When kill rams close, they cut through the drill pipe and seal off the BOP stack bore. Choke rams close and seal around the drill pipe. Both types of rams have locks that keep them hydraulically closed once they have been activated.

Once the rams are closed, heavy mud is pumped down two pipes called the kill and choke lines. These are connected to the drill below the rams and can circulate the heavier mud while drilling operations and the BOP are shut down.

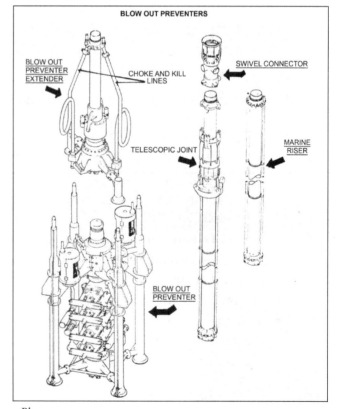

13.2.1 Diving Tasks on the BOP

Diving tasks related to the blowout preventer are mainly inspection of connections and troubleshooting any electrical, hydraulic, or mechanical malfunction. Installations vary; therefore, the diver should study the manufacturer's drawings. In addition, divers are frequently used to do the following:

- Check and replace guideline cables, which are attached to the top of the guide post and run up to the drilling platform.

- Check and verify the BOP's orientation using a "bullseye" level or compass.

- Change the gasket between the BOP and connector housing. This may need to be replaced if a leak is discovered when pressure testing the conductor housing by pumping fluid through the drill pipe.

Blowout preventers

- Manually override the hydraulic connector for raising the BOP. The hydraulic connector may not release when the BOP has to be lifted off the guide-base, in which case a diver attaches a tugger line to the release mechanism.
- Deploy or replace transponders.
- Inspect connections, including the riser kill and choke connectors, the production control pods on the riser, and various hoses.

Blowout preventer removed by divers and being loaded on a supply boat

13.3 OIL PRODUCTION

Once drilling the hole is completed, the production phase of offshore operations begins. Production of oil requires a stable and safe platform. Production platforms come in a variety of designs. They provide a drilling base (for occasional work overs), production and processing facilities, personnel accommodations, communications and logistics storage, and transportation facilities. The final design will be based on several factors such as water depth, field size, typical sea state, seabed, cost, etc. The production facility will remain on-site for the entire life of the field. Production platforms are either bottom supported (jacket and gravity-based platforms) or floating (FSOs, FPSOs, tension leg and single buoy moorings {SBMs}).

13.3.1 Bottom-Supported Production Platforms

There are two types of bottom-supported structurse commonly seen used for long-term oil production: jacket platforms and gravity-based platforms.

13.3.1.1 Jackets (Jacket Platforms)

Jackets are built with a square or rectangular framework of large diameter steel pipe (the lower module)

4-legged jacket completed and ready for painting before going offshore in the Black Sea

supporting a platform deck (the topside module), and often a helideck. Production jackets are typically 4-, 6- or 8-legged structures. Outlying or satellite platforms are often single legged. All of these structures are built onshore, inspected and painted, then brought offshore for installation. The structure is carried on a barge on its side, then it is stood up in the water, using a massive crane barge. The legs of these platforms are hollow caissons, which have steel piling driven down through them into the seabed. Then the space

Topside module for the jacket above

253

(annulus) between the caisson and the piling is filled with concrete, locking the caisson and the piling solidly together. Finally, the topside module is set into place and welded solid. The maximum depth at which jacket-type construction is used is usually about 150 – 200 feet.

Jacket with Christmas tree, GOM

Satellite platform, GOM

Production platform, West Africa

13.3.1.2 Gravity-Based Structures

A fairly recent development in bottom-supported structures, the gravity-based structure is the most stable offshore structure of all and the least vulnerable to damage due to weather or corrosion. These gravity-based structures have a base module, cast with concrete (but sometimes made of steel) that sits on a rock mattress on the seabed. The name gravity base stems from the sheer weight of the structure that holds it in place. The base module has several compartments, some of which contain ballast rock, the others used for product storage. Once the base structure is in place, the topside module is set on top and secured down. The largest of these structures, the Hibernia Platform offshore of Newfoundland, Canada, has a combined weight (base, topside and ballast) of 1,200,000 tons. This platform was designed to withstand enormous ice pressures and heavy seas. It had to be because it sits close to the same place where the *Titanic* sank due to iceberg contact, and in the exact location where the semisubmersible Ocean Ranger sank in over 100-foot seas in the early 1980s, taking the crew of 88 with her to bottom.

Hibernia platform, Newfoundland, Canada
Source: Government of Canada

Gravity-based platform in the U.S. Gulf of Mexico

The Hibernia platform sits in 250 feet of water, and it is currently thought that between 250 and 300 feet is the deepest practical depth to install one of these gravity-based structures.

13.3.2 Floating Production Platforms
There are three types of floating production facilities seen: floating production storage and offloading units made from tankers, tension leg platforms, and single buoy moorings, which, though not technically a production facility, allows the product to be move to one without it going ashore.

13.3.2.1 Floating Production Storage and Offloading (FPSO)
In water too deep to practically install a gravity-based or jacket platform, the oil companies have started using old oil tankers. These tankers are attached to a swivel turret, which in turn is held in position by a series of eight anchors. Subsea flex hose runs from subsea pipelines up through the swivel turret,and into the tanker, allowing crude from several producing wells to flow onboard the tanker, which now is considered an FPSO or in some cases an FSO (storage only – no production). The FPSO trails a float hose out behind it, which allows other tankers to pull up and load cargo.

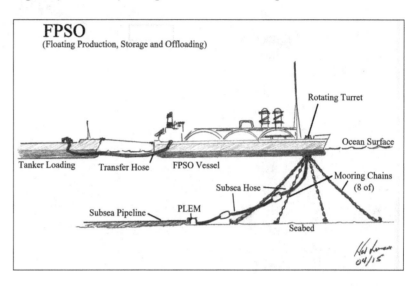

FPSO vessels have production facilities onboard. They do not refine the crude oil, but they remove excess gas and condensate from the oil so that a better quality product may be shipped. FSO vessels, on the other hand, have no production facilities on board. They simply collect crude oil from feeder pipelines and store it on board the vessel until other tankers come along to collect it. FSO vessels are most often used in fields where the crude is not VGO (very gassy oil) and has little condensate in it.

FSO YOHO, offshore West Africa 2014

Float hose trailing out behind FSO for loading other tankers

These FPSO vessels require regular maintenance and inspection by divers. The float hose has to be changed whenever there is damage done to it, and it must be closely inspected on a regular basis. In addition, the vessel itself often has a requirement for divers, for inspections, and sea-chest cleaning.

13.3.2.2 Tension Leg Platforms

First used in the North Sea in the early 1980s, the tension leg platform is most often used in deeper water, between 500- and 1,500-foot depths. These rigs are used some for exploration but are most commonly used in the production phase and are used extensively in the North Sea and the U.S. Gulf of Mexico oil fields.

Mars tension leg platform, U.S. Gulf of Mexico
Source: U.S. Coast Guard

Although the rig itself is floating, it is secured by steel cable tethers to a bottom-mounted framework that is typically secured by pilings or very heavy ballast. These tethers are kept under great tension (hence the name tension leg) and have very little vertical movement. The lateral movement is also limited enough that pipelines or drill strings are easily able to flex enough to overcome the movement.

Although they are very stable and will withstand the sea states most often encountered far offshore, these tension leg rigs are not indestructible. The Mars platform was heavily damaged during Hurricane Katrina.

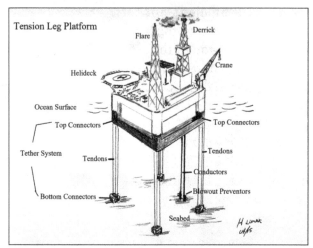

Diagram of tension leg platform

13.3.2.3 Single Buoy Moorings (SBM)

The single buoy mooring, or SBM, is a system that allows tankers to load or unload without ever having to enter a harbor and tie up to a dock. The system was first used during World War II on Guam by the U.S. Navy. It allowed them to bring tankers in to unload aviation fuel without having to build a sheltered harbor and unloading facility. Although SBM systems differ in size, they are all similar in construction and layout.

They usually have an eight-anchor pattern, with the anchors consisting of either piling driven into the seabed and cut off just above the seabed, or occasionally heavy delta-flipper style anchors. Heavy chain runs from the anchors to the buoy's fixed base. Subsea pipelines (2 or more) run to a pipeline end module (PLEM) situated on the seabed below the buoy. Subsea flex hoses then run from the PLEM up to the underside of the buoy.

Arial view of VLCC tanker loading at an SBM buoy
Source: Canadian Coast Guard

There is a swivel between the base of the buoy and the top of the buoy that allows tankers hooked up to it to "weathervane" or swing with the wind and current. A float hose then runs from the buoy to the tanker to transfer the crude oil, and there are huge mooring hooks on the top of the buoy to hold the large hawsers that secure the bow of the tankers to the buoy.

SBM buoys are most often used in the 120- to 180-foot range of water depth. SBM buoys provide a lot of work for divers. In fact,

A typical small SBM offshore West Africa, 2014

most SBMs have their own dedicated diving crews to perform all of the IRM work involved. SBMs come in different sizes for different applications. They can vary from a basic no frills SBM to one equipped with a surface-supplied diving station, complete with chamber.

13.3.3 Diving on Production Facilities

Diving crews perform many different underwater tasks on production platforms, FSPOs and buoys. Most of these facilities have seawater intakes and discharges that must be shut down and locked out prior to starting diving operations. Others, such as SBM buoys, must have the swivels locked to protect the divers. The following lists typical underwater tasks performed by diving crews:

- Floating hose changes and inspections on SBM, FPSO, and FSO units
- Subsea hose changes and inspections on SBM, FPSO and FSO units
- Scheduled structural inspections on all facilities, including NDT, still photos, and video
- Cathodic protection monitoring and replacement on facilities
- Maintenance and cleaning of seawater intakes and discharges on jacket platforms and facilities
- Leak detection, pipeline repair, and replacement
- Anchor system inspection, maintenance, and replacement on SBM, FSPO, and FSO units

13.4 OFFSHORE PIPE-LAY AND CONSTRUCTION

Offshore pipe laying and construction takes place before, during, and after the production phase in oil-field work. Before production, pipelines are laid by pipe-lay barges to connect the oil wells with the production facilities. The pipelines are buried by trenching barges, and jackets are installed by derrick (crane) barges. During production, as pipelines wear out (and they often do), they are replaced with new ones laid by lay barges; new wells are brought online by laying new pipelines, and valve skids are replaced by derrick barges. In recent years, as oil fields grow older, it is becoming very common to have high pressure seawater injection systems installed to get every last barrel of oil from a deposit. This process involves new pipelines installed from pumping stations to the well locations. Then after the field is no longer producing, all of the infrastructure must be removed, a process known as oil-field abandonment. Each and every one of these operations listed above involves underwater work by divers.

13.4.1 Derrick Barge

A derrick barge is basically a huge floating crane used to lift the massive structures offshore and set them into place. Usually the cranes on these derrick barges exceed 1,000-ton capacity with "small" 300-ton cranes used to lift the rigging for the main crane. Occasionally these barges are dual purpose, as in a "derrick/lay barge" used for both heavy lifting as well as pipe-lay. Although most derrick and lay barges are anchor barges, some of them are equipped with DP systems and thrusters to make them more versatile.

DLB Hercules with its 3,500-ton crane offshore Congo, 2007

When installing a jacket platform, the derrick barge sets the legs of the structure or "jacket" upon which the topside module of the platform will be mounted. When installing new valve skids or valve manifolds, the derrick barge is used to lift them from a cargo barge and set them on the seafloor. Divers will perform the following tasks when working from a derrick barge:

- Inspect ocean bottom before setting jacket legs, valve manifolds, or valve skids.
- Place sandbags under the mud mats of subsea structures to fill in an uneven ocean bottom.
- Line up timber saddles of a jacket structure with any existing pipelines.
- Line up valve manifolds or valve skids with any existing pipelines.
- In very deep water, stab skirt piles into tops of jacket legs that do not reach the surface.
- During operations to fill the annulus between the pile and leg of a jacket structure, inspect and, if necessary, operate the grout valves.
- Measure and take metrology between valves and pipelines for fabrication of spool pieces.
- Subsea tie-ins between valves, risers, and pipelines using spool pieces.

On platform installation, once the jacket is in place, the derrick barge is used to install the topside module of the platform on top of the jacket. The diving crew is often de-mobilized during this phase. The following safety precautions must be observed when performing diving operations from a derrick barge:

- Never get under a suspended load, in or out of the water.
- Never perform subsea lifting operations with less than clear communications.
- Never perform subsea lifting operations if the sea state is causing the cable to "snatch".
- Never swing the crane or boom up or down when the load is on bottom.
- Always look for the load when you hear the "swing alarm" on the barge crane.
- Never allow the deck crew to swing a load above dive control or the dive station.

13.4.2 Lay Barge

A pipe-lay barge, sometimes called a lay barge, handles pipeline of single or double sections which are welded together onboard. The pipe sections are covered in concrete "weight coat" and are taken offshore on cargo barges to the lay barge. In the past, the welding used to be all done manually, but in recent years it is increasingly done by automatic welding systems. The finished welds are X-ray inspected and the joints are covered with bitumen, a heavy protective coating. Finally, the pipe is lowered down the stinger (an articulated support frame made of large steel pipe) to the seabed as the barge pulls itself forward on its anchors. On a typical pipe-lay, the "start-up head" or starting end of the pipeline is attached to a massive dead-man or gravity anchor by what is known as an AR (abandonment and recovery) cable, and when the pipe-lay is finished, the "lay-down head" or finish end is lowered to bottom. The pipelines are usually empty when laid, creating a dangerous pressure differential and divers must take precautions. Pipe-lay barges are also used for construction tasks such as subsea tie-ins and subsea valve and piling installations.

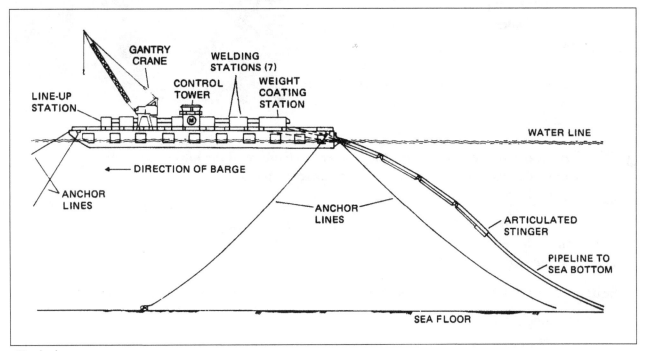

Pipe-lay barge

Diving from a lay barge requires that the diver be familiar with many different diving skills, from diving on the stinger to take measurements to installing a riser to be welded or flanged to the pipeline. It helps to have a good construction background and familiarity with all the tools required to make tie-ins, such as bolt tensioning equipment. The work on lay barges can be of two different types:

- Shallow diving on the stinger to check stinger and pipeline attitude
- Deeper diving to the seabed for start-up and lay-down heads, subsea tie-ins, and touchdown monitoring during the pipe-lay

When diving on articulated stingers performing stinger checks, divers must have good communications and a good working helmet camera. Divers have to be careful to keep hands, feet, and umbilical clear of the pipe rollers on the stinger. Calm weather is particularly important when diving on stingers because stinger movements in rough weather can make the job considerably more hazardous. In any case, as in all diving operations, dive control must have clear communications to the barge control tower, and the standby diver must remain ready to deploy at all times. Dive control is located above and just to one side of the stinger-hitch (point where the stinger attaches to the lay barge). In addition to actual diving, the following work is usually performed by the diving crew on a pipe-lay barge:

- Maintaining accurate records of all diving equipment and keeping them securely stowed in the diving locker or sea containers when not in use
- Regularly scheduled maintenance and testing of all parts of the diving spread
- Maintaining an adequate supply of spare parts and consumable supplies for the diving spread so as to remain independent of the shore once construction of the pipeline is underway
- Attaching the stinger to the stinger hitch on the barge and detaching it when pipe-lay operations have been completed
- Placing marker buoys on existing pipelines along the pipeline route using inflatable boats
- Installing dummy spools, start-up and lay-down heads on the pipeline, and tightening the flanges with a hydraulic bolt tensioning system (this is usually done in the pipe alley)

Stinger on pipe-lay barge in Saudi Arabia. Note the field joint number painted on the pipe.

WARNING: During rough weather, the stinger hitch area and the lower end of the pipe ramp are the most dangerous areas to work on the entire lay barge.

NOTE: If it is not possible to inspect a stinger on the dock before beginning an operation, always study the blueprints carefully before working on it. Stingers vary in design and in construction. The diver must have a thorough grasp of the mechanics of operation of the stinger in order to carry out duties efficiently and safely.

The underwater work typically performed by the diving crew on a pipe-lay barge includes the following:

- Flooding the stinger compartments according to a predetermined schedule
- Stinger checks as the pipeline is being moved out
- Installing riser clamps on the platforms
- Preparing jacket-leg clamps and installing
- Measuring the distance between the jacket leg or the riser and the end of the pipeline
- Guiding the riser to the bottom, lining up with all the clamps
- Securing the bottom clamps
- Checking that water is being forced out of the end of pipeline by use of a sizing pig
- Following the pipeline to locate possible buckles or free-span areas
- Performing free-span corrections as required (filling in under pipeline with grout or sand bags)
- Cutting the pipe, if necessary
- Removing dummy spools (temporary short sections of pipe inserted for pipe-lay process only)
- Accurately measuring the length of new pipe required as well as angles required on the pipe flanges (This process is known as pipeline metrology)
- Installation of spool pieces (known as subsea tie-ins) to join pipelines to risers or valves
- Installation of pipeline flange protectors (known as doghouses)

The following safety precautions must be observed by the diving crew and the diver when working on a pipe-lay barge:

- Never hook a davit sling directly over a field joint—move forward or aft at least 10 feet.
- Never get under a pipeline that is suspended in the davits.
- Strip off the diving suit before entering a decompression chamber because the suit may have grease on it from underwater work around davit chains or cables.
- Make certain a pipeline is flooded before attempting to burn into it.
- Make certain the pipeline is not in suspension or under tension where the cut is to be made when it is necessary to cut a pipeline.
- Keep clear of pipeline ends, holes, or open valves unless the line is completely flooded.
- Never work around a pipeline when there is a detectable flow into the pipeline.
- Never put fingers, hands, or any body part between two pipe flange faces, even when the pipeline appears to be lying firmly on the bottom.

WARNING: Diving from any barge can be hazardous. It is mandatory that the diver be thoroughly familiar with all aspects of the equipment to be used, including any barge equipment that poses a threat. This will include DP thrusters, anchor wires, and anchor winches.

13.4.3 Trenching Barge (Jet Barge)

Pipelines and cables are often buried in a trench on the sea bottom to protect them from damage caused by anchors or fishing gear and to stabilize them on the seabed. The trench is dug from a trenching barge, also known as a jet barge or bury barge. This process is normally performed after the pipe or cable has been laid on the bottom. The depth of the trench (burial depth) can range anywhere from 1 foot to 15 feet, depending on the area, such as shipping lanes and anchorage sites.

The trenching barge includes a sled that does the actual excavating on the sea bottom. Sleds differ in design, depending on the nature of the seabed and the objectives of the operator. Sleds may use high pressure water jets with air lifts, a water extruder, or a plowing system (most often used with cable). Undersea trenches are usually not filled in after the pipe or cable is laid; the natural movements of the seabed are normally relied upon to fill the trench.

Divers usually have to work in zero visibility on a trenching barge sled because of the nature of the work. It is therefore essential for the diver to become as familiar as possible with the sled on the surface so that the diver can safely find his/her way around it on the bottom. Because pipelines and cables are often laid in deep water, diving is sometimes done in saturation mode, employing a sat diving bell attached to the sled by a guide wire, known as a swim line. Even when diving is performed on surface mixed-gas or surface air, a wet bell or stage is used and a swim line is run from the sled to the bell clump weight.

Trenching sled (for subsea cable) being deployed in West Africa, 2015

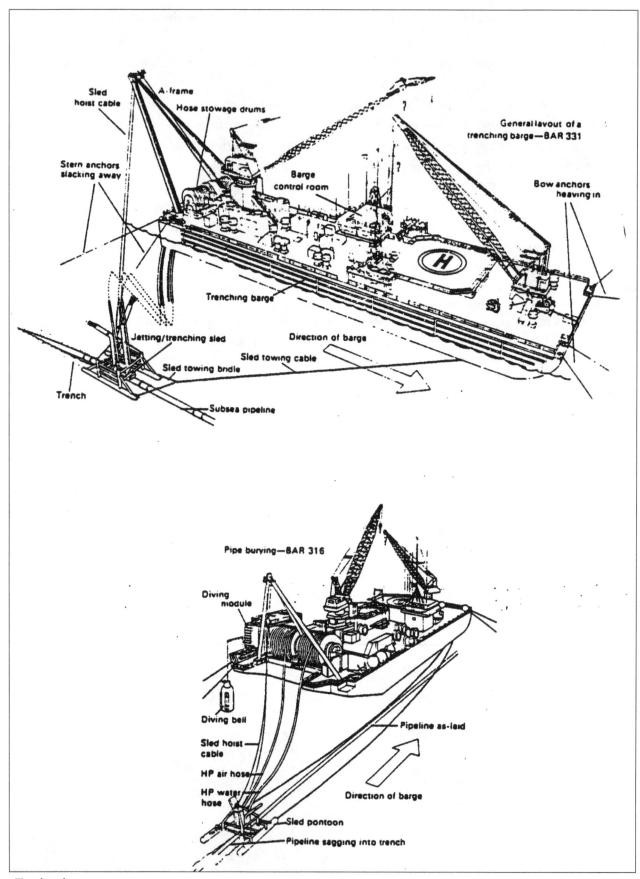

Trenching barge

The following are some of the underwater tasks the diving crew will perform when operating on a trenching barge, burying either pipeline or cable:

- Loosen all the bolts on riser clamp caps to allow the pipe to shift down through the clamps as the pipeline is jetted and settles to the bottom of the trench.
- Inspect the bottom in the vicinity of the riser to clear possible debris that might interfere with setting of the sled.
- Guide the sled over the pipeline and set it as close to the riser as possible.
- Blow a hole at the riser either with backward-pointing jets from the sled or by hand with a jetting nozzle.
- Inspect the first 200 feet of trench to determine if it is satisfactory (known as a ditch check dive).
- Inspect to determine no material remains under the pipeline if the riser does not settle into the trench.
- Inspect riser after tightening all riser clamp bolts.
- Periodically inspect the sled, hoses, and the trench during the excavating operation. The frequency of these checks depends on the type of bottom, equipment being used, and the degree of tidal movement in the area. (These dives are known as "ditch checks.").
- Mark valves, crossovers, or cables that interfere with the movement of the trenching barge along the pipeline.
- Guide the sled by any obstruction.
- Hand jet any material from under the pipeline whenever an obstruction prevents the sled from excavating the trench.

When working on a trenching barge and burying either a subsea cable or a pipeline, the divers must be careful to follow these safety precautions:

- Avoid getting under a jet or plow sled while it is being lowered.
- Learn to locate by touch alone, avoiding dangerous areas of the sled.
- Work in the lee of the sled if there is a current running.
- Pay special attention to the umbilical to prevent it from becoming entangled or damaged.
- Use down lines and swim lines whenever possible to provide orientation in poor visibility.
- Use the catwalk if the sled is equipped with one.
- Inform the supervisor if unsure of anything.
- Immediately terminate dive if communications fail.

WARNING: Never go directly under the riser or pipeline since either could settle suddenly and unexpectedly.

WARNING: Divers must not be near the sled while jetting and suction pumps are in operation. The potential for an accident is dangerously high. All systems must be locked out and tagged out prior to diver intervention.

13.5 OFFSHORE CABLE-LAY

Offshore facilities (platforms, jackets, and SBMs) require electrical power to operate. In addition, there are often requirements for remote monitoring and communications between various offshore facilities and also between offshore facilities and the shore. Subsea power and fiber-optic cables are laid to accomplish this. Prior to laying cable, a route survey is performed to identify any hazards or obstructions that threaten the cable during the cable-lay process or during its service life. Depending on the obstruction, it may be removed or the route may be altered. In the past, route surveys were performed by divers. Today, although divers are still used occasionally, these surveys are most often done with side-scan sonar.

These cables are typically 5 to 8 inches in diameter and often weigh 40 to 50 pounds per foot. A large cable reel, hydraulic under-roller and tensioning machine are installed onboard a barge or ship. The lay vessel gets into position, then pays out cable for the starting point. Once the start point of the cable has been secured, the vessel moves along, following the cable route, paying out cable as it goes. As with pipeline, cables are usually buried below the seabed with a trencher, and at pipeline crossings the cable is protected by a concrete mattress.

There are several tasks that are performed by the divers on a subsea cable-lay.

- Installation and subsequent removal of cable flotation for beach pulls
- Guiding cable ends into risers on platforms and offshore installations
- Removing small debris detected by the side-scan sonar
- Installation of the trenching sled on the cable
- Burial depth monitoring during the cable lay process
- Installation of grout bags and concrete mattresses at pipeline crossings
- Removal of the trenching sled at the completion of a cable run

Cable-lay projects that include beach pulls typically have severely restricted visibility, due to the shallow water involved. Also, since most subsea cables require burial and are trenched, most cable-lay diving is performed in limited or zero visibility, regardless of the depth.

Cable-lay projects that have beach pulls often require that the diving crew leave the vessel and travel by small craft to the beach. When these projects are performed in areas where there are security risks, the members of the diving crew must always ensure that security teams are in place before leaving the cable lay vessel to travel to the beach. Militants and pirates are always waiting for an opportunity to act.

Cable-lay barge on a project in West Africa, 2015

Jungle beach pull, West Africa, 2015

When working on a cable-lay project, these safety precautions must always be followed:

- Always ensure security is in place (where required) before leaving the lay vessel.
- Always practice good umbilical management. Know where your umbilical is at all times.
- Never dive unless the trencher and under-roller are locked out and tagged out.
- When lifting debris, always return to the stage or bell before lifting with the crane.
- Never approach a concrete mattress underwater unless it is setting firmly on bottom.
- After placing a concrete mattress, always count the hooks or shackles on the deployment frame to ensure all are clear from the mattress.
- After placing a concrete mattress, always return to the stage or bell before coming up on the crane.
- Offshore platforms are often surrounded with seabed debris – be careful in restricted visibility and always wear protective boots, gloves, and coveralls.

13.6 TRAVELING TO AND FROM THE OFFSHORE JOB SITE

There are two methods used to transfer crews to and from the offshore job site: by sea or by air. If the vessel or platform has a helideck, transfers will be performed by helicopter. Otherwise, it will be done by either supply vessel or crew boat. We will briefly examine the two methods of crew transfer.

13.6.1 Crew Boats and Supply Boats

Regardless where in the world the diver goes to work, the crew boats always seem to look the same. Almost all of them are the same: they are built off the same plans. The standard crew boat is powered by two GM diesels (also called Detroit diesels). They have a cruising speed of 20 knots (23.8 mph), and they roll like something possessed in a sea. They are loud enough to give you a headache, they move along quite well if the weather is calm, and they have a distinct smell of vomit when the water is rough. Crew boats have an open aft deck, and often there will be a few pallets of supplies on deck to be delivered offshore. The passenger cabin is amidships, just aft of the wheelhouse, and, unfortunately, sits directly above the two diesel engines. This means one thing for the passenger: If you do not have ear plugs, you will likely have a headache by the time you reach your destination. Every crew boat and supply boat is required to provide a safety orientation for the passengers, and this is usually done in the form of a video played in the passenger cabin. Many offshore workers do not pay attention to the orientation or even stay in the cabin while it is presented. Do not follow the crowd on this. Listen and pay attention to the orientation. In an emergency, it may save your life. Passengers are also required to print and sign their name for the POB (personnel on board list). This list is used to let the Coast Guard know how many persons they are searching for, if the crew boat sinks or burns, resulting in an abandon-ship event.

The aft deck is where the personnel being transferred are instructed to keep their seabags. There are two things that the diver should beware of: 1) the aft deck on a crew boat often will be washed by a sea, either due to bad weather or crossing another vessel's wake; 2) cargo on pallets has been known to shift, as often it is not well secured on the aft deck of crew boats. Place your seabag up above, on the open deck above the passenger cabin (behind the wheelhouse) if possible. If not, keep it well forward, close to the door to the passenger cabin. Regardless where you keep your bag, keep an eye on it.

Offshore supply boats are used less frequently to transfer passengers, but they are used. Much larger than a crew boat, the supply boat's primary mission is, as the name suggests, to ferry supplies. These vessels are much better to travel in because they are larger, they roll a lot less, and they are usually much quieter to the point you could sleep in the cabin. The aft decks on supply boats are usually wet, being a low freeboard vessel. Divers should always take their seabags and other personal belongings inside the cabin during the trip. Supply vessels have a cruising speed of 10 knots (just under 12 mph), so the diver will have a slightly longer cruise.

Offshore crew boat

Offshore supply boat

13.6.1.1 Embarking and Disembarking

At the dock, crew boats and supply boats usually put the stern against the dock and "pin" the vessel to the dock (power astern, squeezing the rubber fenders together). Most times a crew member or two will pass the bags onboard and set them on the aft deck, where it is the passenger's responsibility to stow them. The diver should use caution when boarding over the stern. Never board with hands full, and watch the footing.

Billy Pugh

Offshore, there are two ways of embarking and disembarking, and both can be dangerous. One method is by using a "Billy Pugh" man basket, and the other is over the stern. The method will usually depend upon the vessel or installation design. If there is a man-rated crane available, the Billy Pugh is the safest option.

When using a Billy Pugh, luggage is placed in the center (usually by the boat crew) and then the passengers stand on the base ring with their arms laced through the netting. The elbows are used to hold on, not the hands, and when the basket is about to land, one leg is extended slightly out behind with the other slightly bent at the knee to absorb the shock of landing on deck. When boarding the basket from a crew boat or a supply boat, do not board until instructed. When you do, do it quickly and hang on, as it will lift very quickly to get it clear of the boat.

When climbing over the stern offshore, first watch to see if the boat you are leaving is heaving up and down (usually it is). If so, wait until given the go-ahead, and then time your jump so you go on the top of a sea. This will ensure

Personnel transfer from supply boat to lift boat

the vessel will not come up and crush your feet. Do not carry bags or belongings with you. Pass them separately.

13.6.2 Helicopters

The quickest and easiest way to travel to the offshore job site is by helicopter. Larger installations, such as gravity-based platforms have more robust helidecks and often use larger helicopters, such as the Super Puma or Sikorsky S-92, but the most common choppers used are the Sikorsky S-76 or the Bell 412 (known to military vets as the HUEY or the Griffon). Most, if not all, of the pilots and maintenance personnel were in the military, and their professionalism makes air transport offshore a safe operation. However, there are times when helicopters crash or are forced to ditch. Due to their construction, and the fact that the turbines and gearboxes are very heavy and located high in the fuselage, helicopters tend to roll upside down as soon as they land in the water. Many choppers today have auto-inflating air bags attached to make them float in an upright attitude. There have been one or two cases where this has actually worked, but most times, the flotation bags hold the downed chopper upside down on the surface. In spite of how this sounds, it is good news for the passengers – the helicopter is floating, allowing them to get out underwater before it sinks.

Although exiting an upside-down helicopter underwater sounds easy and exciting, it is neither. All offshore personnel are required to have helicopter underwater escape training (HUET) when they are expected to be transferred by helicopter. This training is available in many locations worldwide and is often given along with the basic offshore safety induction and emergency training (BOSIET) and sea-survival training. HUET training teaches the offshore worker how to brace for impact, how to don underwater escape devices (if provided), how to knock out windows, how to safely exit the helicopter when it is inverted and underwater. Practical training is included in the courses.

Every facility that has helicopters landing and taking off, whether offshore or onshore, always has a person trained to supervise operations, known as the helicopter landing officer (HLO).

Bell 412 flying offshore. Note floatation bags mounted on the skids.

The HLO is the one who ensures that passengers are properly prepared to travel, supervises passenger and cargo loading, escorts the passengers to the aircraft, and then signals the helicopter that it is OK to leave.

Every helicopter landing area has at least one scale. The scale is used to weigh the passengers and the cargo they plan to take. Allowable cargo weights vary with the type of helicopter used, but with the

412, the weight in cargo each passenger is allowed to take is 40 kilos or 88 pounds. The diver would be well advised to find out in advance what the cargo weight limit is and pack his seabag accordingly.

Prior to boarding the helicopter, passengers are required to watch a safety video that outlines the various features of the particular model of helicopter traveled on. This will include seatbelt harness configuration, proper passenger loading, safety gear to be worn (survival suit or life jacket and hearing protection) brace position, fire extinguisher locations, how to knock the windows out, and if provided, the details on the underwater escape devices.

13.6.3 Safety Guidelines for Travel Offshore
The following are safety guidelines for travel offshore. Some apply to travel by air, some to travel by sea; and many will apply to both modes of travel.

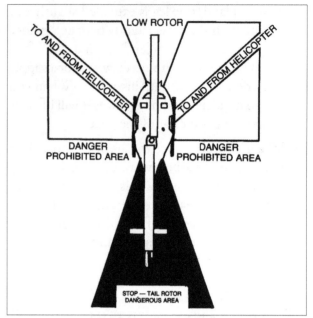

Danger zones and safe passage areas around a helicopter

- Ensure that your sea survival and HUET training are up-to-date before travel.
- Always wear a life jacket when embarking or disembarking crew boats.
- Never carry anything by hand when using a Billy Pugh for embarkation.
- Always pay attention to safety notices and videos provided.
- Never wear a hat or loose clothing on the helipad or helideck.
- Always wear safety glasses or wrap-around sunglasses on the helipad or helideck.
- Never go on the helipad or helideck unless instructed to by the HLO.
- Do not enter or exit a helicopter until instructed by the HLO.
- Do not remove ear protection while in flight.
- Do not go on deck alone on a crew boat in rough weather.
- Stay clear of any deck cargo on crew boats, particularly in rough weather.
- Only smoke in designated smoking areas on the beach or offshore.

13.7 OFFSHORE EMERGENCIES
In any heavy industrial work situation, there are inherent dangers, and offshore work is certainly no exception. The employee is responsible for knowing the dangers in the workplace, learning how to avoid them, and what to do in the event of an emergency. The inherent dangers in the offshore diving industry include immersion following an accident, sinking, fire, and exposure to hazardous materials. The offshore worker needs to know what measures to take to prevent as well as handle accidents, fires, or exposure to hazardous materials. Survival of such incidents depends on specialized training and practicing for emergencies with regular safety drills. The specialized training for offshore workers includes basic offshore safety induction and emergency training (BOSIET), which includes sea survival, fire fighting, and helicopter underwater escape; first aid training with CPR and AED, and workplace hazardous material information system (WHMIS) training. This section will only briefly introduce and summarize the subject matter.

13.7.1 Station Bills

All offshore employees need to be familiar with all of the information on the station bill, which includes: location of the muster station, escape routes, alarm sounds, location of alarms, fire-fighting equipment locations, location of lifeboats and rafts, and the lifeboat or raft designated for you. Station bills are posted in plain view in the platform control room (vessel bridge), common areas such as crew's mess and exercise room, and on the inside of every crew cabin door. Become familiar with the station bill.

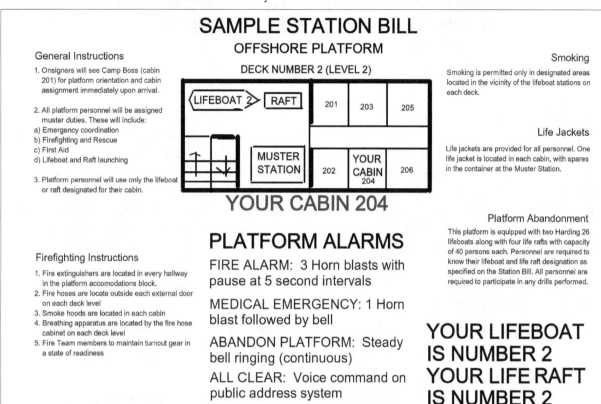

Sample station bill, as displayed on the inside of cabin doors on offshore structures and vessels

13.7.2 Fires

The majority of fires are caused by inattention to, or violation of, the simple rules of safety. Personnel on all offshore structures and vessels must adhere to all fire and safety instructions to avoid fire emergencies and to properly deal with emergencies. Every offshore fire poses a dire threat to offshore personnel and every offshore fire is preventable. The fires that do occur are usually caused by one of the following:

- Welding, cutting, and grinding
- Electrical equipment
- Fuel leaks
- Lagging fires
- Galley fires
- Scaffold boards, tarpaulins, etc.
- Equipment overheating
- Laundry
- Smoking in accommodations
- Oil or gas pipeline or valve leakage or failure
- Cutting abandoned oil or gas pipeline

13.7.2.1 Firefighting

Fire is the rapid chemical oxidation of one or more materials. Any fire requires four elements: fuel, oxygen, a source of heat, and a chemical chain reaction. If any one of these four elements is missing, a fire cannot start, nor can it continue to burn. How a fire is fought depends on what class of fire it is. All fires are classified according to the type of fuel involved as follows:

- Class A: ordinary combustible materials such as wood, paper, and fabrics
- Class B: flammable liquids such as oil, gasoline, and paint thinners
- Class C: electrical fires
- Class D: flammable metals such as magnesium
- Class K: kitchen oils or fats

13.7.2.2 Fire Extinguishers

Fire extinguishers may be large cart-mounted units or portable, handheld extinguishers. Fire extinguishers are designed to fight different classes of fires. Those designed to fight Class A fires either smother (remove oxygen) or quench (remove heat) the fire. Class B extinguishers smother the fire. Class C extinguishers must be charged with a non-conductive fire retardant. Class D fires must be smothered with a dry powder. Class D extinguishers may contain either sodium chloride powder or graphite powder. Class K fires are similar to Class B, and the extinguishers and method of use are similar as well. The proper extinguisher must always be used. An extinguisher designed to fight Class A fires must never be used on a Class B, C, or D fire. Class A extinguishers are usually charged mainly with water, and water will only cause a Class B, D, or K fire to spread. Being highly conductive is inappropriate for an electrical fire.

Every employee on an offshore installation or vessel needs to follow these basic fire safety rules:

- Be familiar with all of the information on the station bill in your cabin.
- Have up-to-date fire-fighting training (part of BOSIET).
- Be familiar with the fire alarm sound and code on your vessel or platform.
- Know how to activate the fire alarm system on your vessel or platform.
- Know where your nearest fire extinguisher is located at all times.
- Know where the nearest fire hose cabinet is located at all times.
- Know where the muster station is located and the quickest route to it.

13.7.3 Hazardous Materials

Hazardous materials are substances capable of posing a high risk to health, safety, and property. They may be explosives, flammable liquids and solids, poisons, toxic chemicals, radioactive materials, corrosives, or biological agents. Federal rules and regulations govern the shipment and handling of hazardous materials.

Hazardous materials are labeled according to federal law in most western nations. In the United States and Canada, all containers of hazardous materials are marked with diamond-shaped signs (placards), indicating the class of hazardous material inside. Placards from the Federal Hazardous Materials Table are shown on the following page.

Many types of hazardous materials are found on offshore installations. Handling of these materials is best left to qualified personnel, but the offshore diver also needs to be aware of the hazards. Divers should familiarize themselves with types of hazards found in the work environment and know what to do in the event of a hazardous material accident.

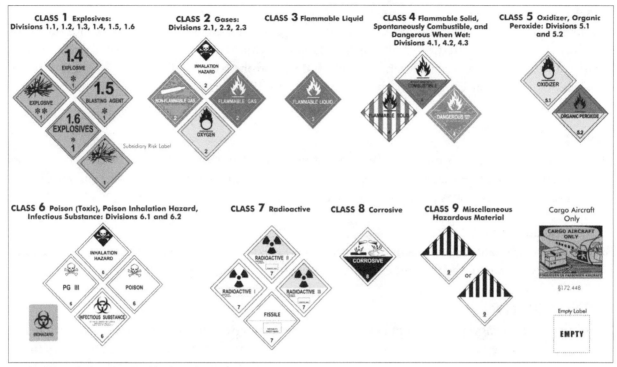

Federal hazardous materials table placards

For work in Canadian waters or on job sites in Canada, divers must obtain WHMIS training from an approved instructor. This training goes into great detail on the following: the routes of entry (inhalation, absorption, and ingestion) of toxins; immediate and long-term hazards, and how best to protect yourself and others. All diving personnel would be well advised to find a WHMIS training course and attend it.

13.8 SURVIVING OFFSHORE EMERGENCIES

In the event of an offshore emergency, survival can depend on certain survival techniques and equipment. It is imperative for offshore workers to become familiar with these techniques and equipment.

13.8.1 Survival Techniques

In an emergency, the chances of survival and rescue depend on the following important steps: preparation, protection, location, provision, and rescue.

13.8.2 Preparation

Employees need to be aware of the location of emergency equipment and know routes to assembly points. All personnel need to read any information on the use of such equipment and become familiar with any types they are likely to operate. Safety drills must be taken seriously. Familiarity with procedures and equipment will help workers remain calm and do what needs to be done in a real emergency. After drills, all equipment should be maintained in good condition and ready for use.

13.8.3 Protection

Protection is vital to survival in an offshore emergency. The degree of protection can vary from extra clothing to totally enclosed lifeboats. All protection works only if used correctly; therefore, the offshore worker needs to be totally familiar with all protection gear and know how to use it.

13.8.4 Location

It is important that others can find a person in an emergency. Again, familiarity with any location aids is the key. The proper use of devices such as strobes, smoke canisters, or pyrotechnic flares often makes rescue efforts more effective. However, keep in mind that strobe battery life is limited, and the supply of devices such as smoke canisters and flares is limited and, if used indiscriminately, will soon run out. Use strobes, flares, and smoke only when there is a definite chance of being spotted.

13.8.5 Provisions

Proper survival preparedness includes emergency stores of food and water. Rations in emergency packs tend toward carbohydrate-rich foods because carbohydrates require less water to digest and metabolize than proteins. Carbohydrates are a good source of readily available energy, as well.

13.8.6 Rescue

Rescue can be a hazardous and strenuous event that will require the survivor to exert himself/herself. He/she must be aware of the possible effects of this during and after any rescue attempt.

13.9 IMMERSION

In an offshore emergency, personnel may find themselves immersed in the water, either intentionally or accidentally. The biggest dangers of immersion are hypothermia and drowning. Hypothermia is defined as a significant decrease in body core temperature below the normal level of 98.6°F (37 C). It is caused when the body loses heat faster than it can produce it. Thirty minutes is considered long-term immersion, and at this point hypothermia is a serious threat. Continued immersion will lead to unconsciousness, and, without a life jacket, drowning. The best protection from hypothermia is to get out of the water; get dried off; and stay dry. A life jacket or personal flotation device is the best protection from drowning. A survival suit will protect the wearer from both hypothermia and drowning.

13.9.1 Life Jackets

There are many different types of life jackets, but whatever the type, there are rigorous requirements for life jackets to ensure adequate construction and performance. They must be easily donned, comfortable, hold the mouth and nose of an unconscious person clear out of the water, and be able to right the person from a face down position in not more than five seconds. Life jackets should also allow the wearer to jump from a height of at least 15 feet into the water without injury to the wearer or damage to the life jacket.

The user is responsible to know the type of life jacket available and how to use it effectively. There are three types of marine life jackets:

- Inherently buoyant
- Partially inherently buoyant
- Automatic gas inflatable

13.9.1.1 Inherently Buoyant

The simplest type of life jacket is constructed of synthetic foam material to provide buoyancy. It is covered in a durable material of a highly visible color such as international orange and has reflective tape strips on the upper part. They are made to be easily donned without getting them on the wrong way.

13.9.1.2 Partially Inherently Buoyant

This type of life jacket is less common in the maritime environment. It contains synthetic buoyancy material and is capable of being "topped off" with on oral inflation tube to provide extra buoyancy if required.

13.9.1.3 Automatic Gas Inflatable

This life jacket is constructed with at least two separate inflatable chambers. If there is loss of buoyancy in any one chamber, the remaining chambers are capable of compensating. There are three mechanisms for inflation: automatic inflation on immersion, single manual motion (pull one toggle to inflate all chambers), and oral inflation.

13.9.2 The Proper Use of Life Jackets

It is the responsibility of the individual to fully understand and know the instructions for use of the type of life jackets available. If it becomes necessary to enter the water once the life jacket has been donned, the following procedure should be followed:

- Remove any false teeth, glasses, and any sharp objects.
- Get down to a height of less than 30 feet above the water, if possible.
- Block off the nose and mouth with one hand; place the other on top of the life jacket and grip it securely. This positions and braces the life jacket for impact with the water.
- Look down and check that all is clear.
- Stand up straight, look directly ahead, and step off. Bring feet and knees together.

Once the person is in the water, the spray hood, if present, should be deployed. The person should move away from the danger area using arms as paddles while keeping the legs still. The survival position should be assumed, with the feet and knees together and hands placed under the life jacket. If there are a number of survivors in the water, they should form a "survival circle" or "huddle" in an effort to stay warmer, remain together, and be more easily seen by rescuers. Do not waste energy by swimming if no rescue craft is in sight. If one is close at hand, however, swim toward it on the back, using arms only, to conserve energy.

Survival position

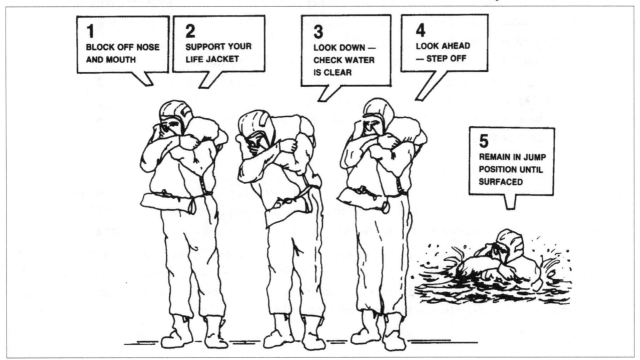

Steps for entering the water

Personal flotation devices such as floater coats will only work properly if zipped up with the belt securely fastened. The same holds true for life jackets. They must be properly worn in order to work properly. Although a life jacket or personal flotation device will protect you from drowning, remember you are still in grave danger from hypothermia. Attempt to locate life rafts or lifeboats, call out to the occupants, and try to get on board and out of the water as soon as possible.

13.10 RESCUE

Rescue itself can be hazardous if those being rescued are not aware of the proper rescue techniques and procedures. Ignorance of the proper procedures may actually hinder rescue efforts. Therefore, all personnel need to become familiar with the rescue procedures of their employer.

Rescue can come in many forms, but it will take place either from the water or from the air.

13.10.1 Rescue from the Air

Rescue from the air will always be performed by helicopter. A lift of one of the following types will be lowered to personnel in the water:

- Single lift. This method involves lowering a simple rescue sling, a rescue basket. The person being rescued has to know how to correctly put on the rescue sling or board the basket.
- Hi-line transfer. A rescue worker is lowered to a life raft or survival craft and assists with the loading of survivors. This person guides the rescue sling, basket, or Stokes litter (for severely injured survivors) with a line to ensure fast and safe recovery.
- Double lift. A rescue worker is lowered with a rescue sling and then accompanies the survivor back to the helicopter.

The following safety points must be remembered every time a water rescue is performed by helicopter:

- Do not touch the rescue sling, rescue basket, or Stokes litter until it has made contact with the water. Helicopters generate a deadly static charge that must be discharged by water contact.
- The rescue sling must be worn properly. It goes under the arms and across the back just below the shoulder blades. Do not have it in the small of the back.
- Keep your arms down at your sides while in a rescue sling. Do not raise your arms, even when being pulled into the helicopter. Raising the arms will result in falling out of the sling.
- When boarding a rescue basket, sit down on the bottom of the basket and hold the sides by hand. Do not kneel or stand while in a rescue basket.

Once inside the helicopter, the rescued individual will follow the directions of the helicopter crew chief or SAR Tech as they are given.

13.10.2 Rescue from the Water

Persons in the water should wait for the rescue craft to come to them. The captain or coxswain of a boat may have to avoid survivors that swim toward the boat, thus complicating the rescue effort. Survivors should approach the boat only after it has stopped alongside and when instructed to do so.

If the rescue is being made from a small craft such as a lifeboat or fast rescue craft, crew members will help lift survivors on board. If the rescue vessel is large, such as a supply ship, survivors may have to climb on board using scramble nets or ladders. In this case, the survivor should grab the rescue equipment while at the top of a swell so that as the water falls away, the person is free to continue to climb aboard.

13.11 EVACUATING AN OFFSHORE INSTALLATION OR VESSEL

Should it become necessary to abandon an offshore installation or vessel, it is imperative that personnel are familiar with the operator's evacuation procedures. This includes knowing the location muster stations, life rafts and lifeboat boarding stations and what the individual's responsibilities are in such a situation. Evacuation of offshore installations or vessels will be either be carried by air in a helicopter, by sea in a life raft or motor boat, or in some emergencies using a combination of both. The installation manager or vessel's captain will typically keep personnel informed of why an evacuation is necessary and exactly how the evacuation will be performed.

13.11.1 Helicopter Evacuation

Helicopter evacuation will differ from helicopter crew transfers in that there will be larger numbers of personnel around the Ready Room, waiting to move to the helideck, and if it is an emergency evacuation, there will be no luggage or cargo transported. There are some general procedures that should be followed:

- Listen closely to the preflight briefing or video.
- Don survival suit or life jacket properly
- Don hearing protection when approaching the helideck and during flight.
- Remove hats and loose items of clothing.
- Do not carry anything by hand.
- Closely follow the instructions given by the HLO.
- Stay in the safe areas when approaching the helicopter.
- If there are high winds, walk in a crouch to avoid "rotor dip".
- Board the helicopter only when instructed to do so.
- Properly fasten the harness and keep it fastened during the flight.

13.11.2 Motor Boat Evacuation

If evacuation is going to be performed by water, it will most likely be in a totally enclosed lifeboat known as a Totally Enclosed Motor Propelled Survival Craft (TEMPSC). These crafts are designed to be impact resistant, fire retardant, and inherently buoyant. They are also fitted with self-contained air support systems. There are various types, but the operational procedures of all these craft are similar.

Designated personnel, often called coxswains, are in charge of the TEMPSC, and all passengers must follow their directions. Once on board the survival craft, all personnel must be seated, get strapped in, and remain seated. It is vital to the safety of all aboard to stay put unless the coxswain gives permission to move.

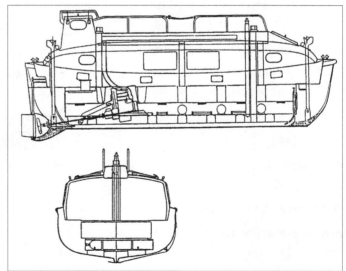

In the event of a transfer to either a helicopter or rescue ship, it is important that the occupants avoid panic and exit the craft in an orderly manner. Remain seated and strapped in until ready to disembark. Do not attempt to leave the craft until secured in a helicopter rescue sling or until attached to a lifeline. When transferring to a ship, attempt to leave the TEMPSC at the top of a swell.

Harding 26' covered lifeboat

13.11.3 Life Raft Evacuation

Life rafts on offshore installations vary in the ways they are launched: conventional, hydrostatic, and davit launched. In all cases, there a number of checks that should be performed prior to launch.

- The painter (bow line or tow line) must be secured to a strong point.
- The length of the painter must be sufficient.
- The number of people the raft can hold should be checked.
- Someone must check for obstructions in the water below before throwing the raft over the side.

Once all survivors are on board the life raft, the following vital actions must then be taken:

- The painter should be cut using the safety knife provided, and the raft should be immediately paddled away from any danger (usually downwind on an angle).
- Once clear of the area, the sea anchor should be attached to a strong point on the outside of the raft and thrown overboard. This will help stabilize the raft and slow the rate of drift.
- Entrances should be closed for protection from the weather.
- Seaworthiness of the raft should be maintained by bailing, inflating the side and floor chambers, and looking for leaks.
- Lookouts should be posted.

Transfer to a rescue vessel or helicopter from a life raft will happen in the same manner as for evacuation from a TEMPSC (see above).

13.12 SUMMARY

The offshore oil industry provides many jobs for commercial divers. Work is available in the exploration, drilling, and production phases of fossil fuel recovery. Each type of oil-field job requires a specific skillset and knowledge. This chapter provides only an introduction to these requirements. Safety is the primary consideration, and the offshore worker must be familiar with all safety regulations as well as the procedures for emergencies and evacuation.

13.13 GLOSSARY OF TERMS RELATED TO OFFSHORE OPERATIONS

-A-

A frame: A steel framework used for lifting or lowering heavy items; the gantry on a diving LARS; the gantry for the launch and recovery of a saturation bell.

Air tugger: A pneumatically operated winch.

AR cable: Abandonment and Recovery Cable – a cable (or hawser) used to secure the start-up head of a pipeline or subsea cable to a dead-man anchor or used to set down the lay-down head of a pipe or cable.

AX ring: A soft stainless steel O-ring used in pipeline flanges to prevent leakage (see Flange skillet).

-B-

Ball joint: Universal joint at the bottom of a marine riser just above the blowout preventer stack, allowing for deflection.

Blind flange: A cap over a deadend flange on a pipeline.

Blowout preventer (BOP): A heavy piece of machinery attached to the top of the conductor (see below) to prevent blowouts. It contains a number of valves and rams that are designed to prevent pockets of gas, encountered during drilling, from escaping up around the outside of the drill pipe out of the well. All drilling operations are undertaken through the blowout preventer stack.

Bolt tensioning system: A system of hydraulic jacks used to tighten pipeline flange bolts to a preset value. The bolt tensioning systems stretch the steel bolts, using hydraulic jacks.

-C-

Casing string: Steel tube that lines a well, made up of sections of pipe screwed together.

Choke and kill lines: Two lines from the side outlets in a BOP stack equipped with fail-safe or hydraulically operated valves near the preventer.

Christmas tree: A system of pipes and valves on a submarine wellhead.

Conductor: Heavy-walled pipe that provides a stable opening into the seafloor. Its length (between 100 feet and 200 feet) is determined by the surface geology of the drill site. Stability is partly achieved by binding the conductor to the soil it penetrates with cement. It must not only withstand the tremendous lifting pressures of natural gas pockets encountered during drilling, but it must also support the considerable weight of the well casings, the wellhead, and the blowout preventer stack.

Control pod: See Koomey Pod.

-D-

Davit: A hydraulic side boom used for adjustments of pipeline position. Also used for swinging boats, diving bells, or other equipment over the side.

Dead man anchor: An anchor used to restrain a pipeline or cable as it is laid across the seabed. Also used by vessels on hard bottom where a traditional anchor will not "bite." DMAs work by virtue of their weight as opposed to digging into bottom, as in the case of the traditional anchor.

Delta flipper anchor: An anchor designed to "bite" into the bottom, known as a delta flipper because of the distinctive delta shape of their flukes, and the fact that the anchor stock "flips" on a hinge toward the strain.

Dope coat: Corrosion-resistant dielectric coating on pipe to be used in a pipeline.

Drill string: Column of drill pipe made up of singles and drill collars that extends from the surface to the bottom of the hole.

Dummy spool: A temporary spool piece installed in a pipeline as it is laid, to permit the installation of a T piece or valve skid after laying.

-F-

Fail-safe valve: Valve held open by remotely-maintained hydraulic pressure.

Field joint: The joint that completes the mating of two lengths of pipe in a pipeline (40 feet apart).

Fish: Any tool or other object lost in a hole, requiring a "fishing job" before normal operations can continue.

Flange: The flat-faced bolt-together end section of a length of pipe.

Flange protectors: A small doghouse-style structure of plate steel, placed over pipeline flanges to provide protection against damage by fishing gear.

Flange skillet: A light sheet metal ring and handle assembly installed on the outer circumference of an AX ring that provides a handle and maintains proper alignment during flange bolt-up.

Flange series: The series number (e.g. 3000 Series) determines the size, thickness, number of bolts, diameter, and length of bolts in a given flange.

Flange-up: Term used to describe the process of mating two flanges, including alignment, bolting, and the hydraulic tensioning of flange bolts.

Floating hose: Rubber hose made specifically for transferring hydrocarbon products, designed to be positively buoyant, empty or full. These are used on FPSOs, FSOs, and SBMs to transfer product.

Free span: Unsupported pipe running over a depression in the seafloor.

Free span correction: The process of filling in under a free span, using sandbags or grout bags.

-G-

Guillotine saw: A hydraulic-powered hacksaw designed to cut pipelines off square underwater.

-H-

H₂S: Hydrogen sulfide, a highly poisonous gas found in many oil fields; has distinctive rotten-egg smell.

Hot tap: A process by which a hole may be drilled into a live pipeline to "tap" into it with another line.

-J-

J tube: J-shaped section of pipe that provides the transition from horizontal to vertical pipe, as in from a subsea pipeline into a jacket riser.

Jacket: Underwater lower section of an offshore platform that is fastened by pilings driven through the legs into the seabed.

Jack-up rig: Offshore drilling rig with a floating hull and retractable legs, which can be lowered to the seabed to elevate the hull above wave level.

Jet sled: Device on a jet (or dredge) barge used to blast a pipeline ditch into the ocean bottom with high-pressure water jets, and then suck up the loosened mud or sand.

-K-

Koomey pod: Also called control pod. A control link (attached to the BOP stack) between the hydraulic cables from the platform and the hoses that operate the valves of the BOP stack. For safety reasons, two independently functioning pods are always attached to each BOP stack.

-L-

Lay-down head: Flanged cap bolted onto the final end of a pipeline, used to lower the pipe to bottom. It has a pad-eye built in to accept the AR cable.

Live: In use. A live pipeline is a pipeline that is in use.

-M-

Manifold: A valve assembly (skid-mounted) that allows flow to be directed down different pipelines.

Marine riser: A thin-walled pipe of about 18–24 inches in diameter that extends from the top of the BOP stack to just under the drilling floor (at the surface of the ocean).

Marine breakaway connection: A short section of pipe with a specific break strength inserted in the middle of float hoses to save the subsea hose from damage in a mooring line breakaway.

Mast or derrick: A structure towering above the drill floor (usually tall enough to accommodate three joints of made-up drill pipe) that holds the blocks, winches, and cables that not only move drill pipe in and out of the hole, but also handle the heavy equipment required in a subsea system.

Moon pool: A large opening in the center of a drill ship through which all drilling operations are conducted; a large opening in the center of a diving support vessel through which the bell is deployed.

-O-

Oil string: Casing string that is run to keep the well open.

-P-

Pad eye: Welded to the dome cap of the first piece of pipe in the pipeline, it is used to hold the end of the pipeline in place as the barge pulls away laying pipe. Also a u-shaped piece of steel welded to something to provide a lift point or pulling point.

PIG: A plug-like object used to test a pipeline for leaks and correct sizing or to clear a line that is flooded or otherwise blocked. Acronym for pipeline internal gear.

Pig trap: A deadend in a pipeline to trap the pig out of the main pipeline itself.

Pinger: A sonic device used for location of a well or any other item underwater.

Pipe alley: The area (usually down the starboard side) of a lay barge where the pipe joints are laid out, welded together and x-rayed.

Pipeline ramp: The sloped area aft of the pipe alley and the tensioning machine that leads down toward the stinger.

Pipeline tensioning machine: Hydraulic machine with "shoes" made of tire treads that squeezes against the pipeline and holds the correct tension on the pipe to avoid sags, kinks, and bows during pipe-lay process.

PLEM: Acronym for pipeline end module. Formerly known as a sled, it is the offshore termination point of supply pipelines used for FPSO, FSO, or SBMs, where the subsea hose connects.

Plidco clamp: Two-piece cast steel assembly with rubber gaskets that bolts together around a pipeline to repair leaks.

-R-

Recall buoy: A marker used to visually identify the location of a well.

Riser: Vertical section of pipeline that extends from the bottom up to the platform deck above the waterline. Any section of pipe that runs vertically.

Riser clamp: A bolt-together clamp to affix a riser to a jacket leg.

-S-

SAR Tech: Search and Rescue Technician. Occasionally private contractors, these are usually Coast Guard members, often former military special forces personnel.

Shoes: Rubber roller used to support and control the movement of pipe at the line-up station and along the length of the pipeline ramp.

Sleeper: A concrete block placed on the seabed to hold a newly laid pipeline up, so as not to touch an existing pipeline or submarine cable at an intersection.

Smart flange: A steel compression fitting installed over a cut-off end of a pipeline to provide a flange for the installation of spool pieces.

Smart PIG: A pipeline pig fitted with sensors to measure wall thickness, detect leaks, and establish position.

Spool piece: A section of pipe installed after pipe-lay to connect a pipeline with a valve, riser, or other pipe.

Start-up head: Cap with pad-eye built in, bolted to start end of a pipeline to accept the AR cable.

Stinger: An articulated, variable buoyancy device constructed of steel pipe that supports the pipeline between the lay barge and the ocean bottom.

Stinger hitch: A massive steel block that locks the end of the stinger assembly to the lay barge.

Subsea drilling system: Conductor, casing strings, guide base, blowout preventer, and the marine riser.

Subsea hose: Non-floating rubber hose made specifically for transferring hydrocarbon products. These are used on the bottom on FPSO, FSO, and SBM facilities, as well as on the occasional platform.

-T-

T piece: A pipeline section in the shape of a T that permits two pipelines to connect.

Tensioning shoes: Rows of tires or treads on the pipeline tensioning machine that grip the pipe to relieve sag in the pipeline as it is being laid.

Topside module: The upper section of an offshore platform with decks that sets on top of the jacket section.

-V-

Valve skid: A steel skid with protective steel frame that contains a pipeline shut-off or control valve.

-W-

Weight coat: A shell of concrete that forms the outer protective covering of large-diameter subsea pipe and eliminates any buoyancy in the pipeline.

14.0 POWER PLANTS AND PUMP HOUSES

One of the most common jobs that the inland diver will perform is servicing either electric power plants or industrial pump houses. The vast majority of electricity used in the world today is produced using water; either by way of hydroelectric dams or with thermal power plants. Many manufacturing facilities also use water, whether a paper mill, a food processing plant, or a manufacturing plant. And then, of course, there are the potable water supplies that supply our drinking water. Each of these facilities requires intervention by divers on a regular basis in order to remain operational.

14.1 SAFETY LOCKOUT PROCEDURES

The expression "an ounce of prevention is worth a pound of cure" is never more true than when a diver is working in, on, or around equipment that has moving parts, is energized, has suction, or has differential pressure. It is critical to take the time to ensure all lockouts are in place on the job—it saves lives.

14.1.1 Standard Lockout Procedures

Most power plants or mills have a lockout system. Paperwork is filled out, detailing all protections in place, the operation to be performed, and who holds the work authorization. Then locks are placed on the start switches of equipment to be worked on. Next, red tags with the words "**Do Not Operate**" are placed on the controls of the equipment. The paperwork and the keys to the locks go with the diving supervisor; the lockout cannot be terminated until the lockout paperwork and keys are surrendered.

A standard equipment lockout has the diving supervisor and the plant operator both filling out and signing a work authorization permit. Then the locks and tags are installed to physically prevent the equipment from operating. This process ensures the diving crew is protected from accidental start-up.

14.1.2 Lockouts During Shut-downs

Power plants and mills require periodic shut-downs for maintenance and repair. During these shut-downs, outside contractors are brought in to reduce down time. There may be several of these contractors involved, with most of their employees unfamiliar with the day-to-day operation of the systems. Some of these contractors have the authority to operate the systems, and this requires special lockout procedures during shut-downs.

During a shut-down, the diving supervisor places his/her own locks and tags on all equipment and systems that will affect the crew; this is in addition to the operator's locks and tags. The paperwork connected with the work authorization permit paperwork must reflect these changes.

14.2 HYDROELECTRIC DAMS

To produce electricity with hydropower, a dam is constructed on a stream, forming a headpond. The water in the headpond travels down a huge pipe known as a penstock. At the bottom end of the penstock the water passes through the blades of the turbine, causing it to spin. The turbine is attached to a generator, which produces the electricity. After it has passed through the turbine, the water passes out through the draft tube into the tailrace and continues downstream. The stream levels can fluctuate dramatically below these hydro dams, depending on the amount of electricity generated and the headpond height.

Diver entering the headpond of a hydro dam

14.2.1 Hydro Dam Features

To allow for maintenance and repair of the turbines, the penstock and draft tube must have gates or stop logs to allow de-watering. The gates at the top of the penstock are known as head gates; those below the draft tube are called tailrace gates. These gates are basically huge steel doors that are lowered and raised in slotted tracks, called gains. The gates rest on steel plates set into the concrete on bottom, known as sills.

Debris traveling down through the penstock can cause serious damage to the turbine or its flow control assembly (wicket gates). To prevent debris from entering the penstock, a screen of rugged steel bars (the trash rack) is installed on the intake portion of the hydro dam. Most trash racks are designed to be removable and are set in gains.

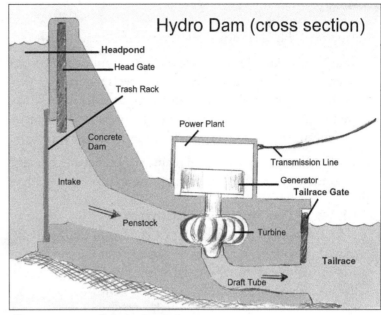

Key components of a hydroelectric dam

Every dam has a spillway to dispose of excess water. These spillways use gates similar to the head gates. Because of the volume of water that moves through the spillways, most dams have a concrete sluiceway and apron below to prevent erosion. Many dams also have concrete baffle blocks below the spillway to diffuse the flow of water, which also helps prevent erosion.

14.2.2 Typical Diving Operations at Hydro Dams

Because dams restrain large bodies of water, a sudden and catastrophic failure of a dam would cause death and destruction in communities in the flood plain. To avoid this, hydro dams are subject to bi-annual inspections. These inspections are performed by structural engineers, using divers and surface-monitored video systems.

Usually when hydro dam gates are closed, it is for maintenance on the turbines or wicket gates. When performing maintenance tasks, it is best to have the penstock and turbine areas as dry as possible. To achieve this, divers are often necessary for de-watering.

14.2.2.1 Gate-Sealing Methods

Occasionally the head gates do not seal completely, which permits more water to pass than is acceptable for the maintenance tasks at hand. When this occurs, the gates must be sealed and divers are often used to accomplish this job. There are several materials used to seal gates: oakum, cotton cord, polyethylene film, peat moss, coal cinders, and even manure. The principle is simple. The weight of all of the water in the reservoir creates an enormous amount of pressure on the upstream side of a dam, including on the closed but leaking head gate. This pressure differential will force anything into the crack that a diver places near the leak on the upstream side. This technique is usually successful in sealing the leak, at least temporarily, which is all that is necessary.

As useful as the head pressure is in sealing, it can also be deadly to the diver. The higher the head (water weight), the greater the pressure and the greater the risk to the diver. The pressure could trap the diver against the bottom of the gate or even in the crack the diver is trying to seal. This phenomenon is known in the industry as differential pressure, or Delta P. It is imperative that the flow be checked after the gates are placed and before the diver enters the water. The flow is checked by looking behind the head gates. A flow with the volume of a garden hose is workable; if it has the volume of a fire hose, it will be dangerous for the diver and the head gate should be reset. Only experienced hands should seal the bottom of head gates.

Tailrace gates are installed below the draft tubes, which carry water from the turbines back into the river. They are installed at the same time as the head gates to allow de-watering of the draft tubes. If the tailrace gates leak, divers can attempt to seal them with the method described above. These gates are less dangerous because there is less pressure differential. But the decreased pressure differential also means they are more difficult to seal because sealing material doesn't jam into the crack as well.

Trash racks require occasional maintenance, usually cleaning to remove debris, but most of this work is done by surface crew while gates are in place and trash racks are removed.

14.2.2.2 Alkali Aggregate Reactivity

Hydro dams are often subject to a condition known as alkali aggregate reactivity (AAR), which is caused when the sand and stone aggregate in the concrete react to the cement. The concrete expands and virtually tries to self-destruct. Various methods of preventive maintenance and repair are used to lessen these effects on structures. Saw cuts remove material, allowing room for expansion. These saw cuts extend below water, and divers install tracks for diamond wire saws. Often huge cofferdams are installed by divers to allow the work to be done in the dry. Areas that have been damaged are often repaired by divers by chipping to sound concrete, installing form work, and pumping concrete.

14.3 THERMAL PLANTS AND INDUSTRIAL PUMP HOUSES

14.3.1 How Thermal Plants Work

Thermal power plants use steam energy rather than water pressure to generate electricity. The steam is produced by boilers fired by wood, oil, coal, or natural gas. The steam travels at high pressure through pipelines to the turbines, which are in turn connected to generators. After the steam passes through the turbines, it enters a condenser, which cools and condenses it back into water to be reused again for steam.

There are two separate water systems in a thermal plant. The water that is used in the production of steam is usually de-mineralized and treated to remove any material that will cause harm to the boilers, turbines, and condensers. The other water system is the cooling water, used in the condensers. Cooling water is pumped in through an intake, used only once, and then returned to its source. Usually the discharged cooling water travels through a lengthy underwater pipeline to help cool it and, thus, minimize environmental impact.

The intakes for the cooling water always have trash racks on the outside to keep large debris from fouling the pumps. Inside the pump house, traveling trash screens remove smaller debris and marine organisms that will foul the pumps. The intakes also have stop logs to allow de-watering to take place. These stop logs are set in gains similar to head gate gains at hydro plants.

Oil-fired 1,000 megawatt thermal generating plant

Diver working at thermal plant

Diver working on hydro dam head gates

Cooling water pump house intake, with trash racks visible

The discharge for cooling water usually has a diffuser assembly, which helps to spread out, or diffuse, the heated water. Discharge structures usually have provisions built in to allow the pipe itself to be de-watered.

14.3.2 Typical Diving Operations in Thermal Plants

The outer trash racks on a cooling water pump house are usually designed so they may be removed, but they seldom are. Periodically, divers are brought in to clear debris away from the trash racks or to clean the racks themselves.

The fore bay area, located between the outer trash racks and the stop log gains, is a favorable breeding ground for mussels and other marine growth. Divers are required, on a regular basis, to keep the marine growth in check so that it does not impede the water flow.

Trash racks on a new hydro dam before flooding

Periodically, the stop logs on the cooling water intakes must be closed for maintenance of equipment such as cooling water pumps. Like the head gates in a hydro dam, the stop logs often leak and must be sealed. The stop logs used to de-water cooling water pump houses at thermal plants are the same as most others; they usually require divers to create a seal. But the cooling water intakes do not have the same head pressure as at a hydro dam, so pressure differential is provided by large submersible pumps set up on the inside of the stop logs. The same methods and materials are used to seal pump house stop logs as are used in hydro dams to seal the head gates.

Traveling trash screens are designed to allow the debris that is picked up to be dumped into a pit. They do not, however, always work as intended. Sticks and small logs occasionally jam these screens, and divers are required

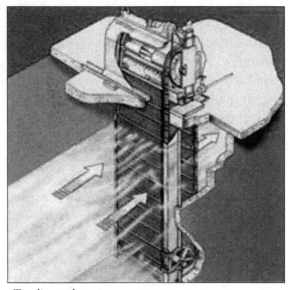
Traveling trash screen
Graphic Courtesy of Equova Water Technologies

to clear them. Occasionally, one screen will jump the track and become bent. This usually means a diver will be required to remove that section of screen.

14.3.3 Typical Diving Operations in Industrial Pump Houses

As a rule, industrial pump houses are put together with less forethought than the pump houses at thermal power plants. Few, if any, have provisions for de-watering, short of actually plugging the intake pipeline. Usually, minor maintenance of the pumps is performed by divers, including cleaning and impeller replacement. Most are designed to have the pumps lifted out by crane for major overhauls. Silt, sediment,

Thermal plant pump house, with pumps on the left, screens on the right.

and marine growth removal is probably the most common operation that divers are required to perform in industrial pump houses.

14.4 NUCLEAR POWER PLANTS

In spite of all of the negative publicity generated by incidents at three different plants over the past 40 years—3 Mile Island, Chernobyl, and Fukushima—the world is coming to see that one of the best and safest methods of power generation is nuclear. Like all other power generation operations, nuclear plants require divers on a regular basis to continue to operate.

14.4.1 How Nuclear Plants Work

Nuclear power plants are thermal power plants with one major difference: The steam is generated

by a nuclear reaction using radioactive fuel and producing radioactive spent fuel. Once the steam has been produced, operations happen in much the same way as in conventional thermal plants. The nuclear reaction takes place in a lead-shielded concrete containment building called the reactor building. This building has a domed roof with an inner and outer dome. The space between these domes is filled with water for emergency dousing. The reactor building has an airlock door and is always maintained at several pounds below atmospheric pressure to help prevent leaks from the inside outward.

Nuclear Plant: reactor on left, turbine hall on right

The pump houses at nuclear plants are the same as those at other plants except that there are radiation monitors at all exits. The pumps, stop logs, trash racks, and traveling screens are all the same.

14.4.2 Typical Diving Operations in Nuclear Plants

As stated earlier, cooling water pump houses at nuclear plants are similar to those found at conventional plants, except it is necessary to pass through radiation monitors when entering or leaving the area.

Because the pump houses are similar, the same problems are usually encountered. Divers are required, when placing stop logs, to clean the sill and seal the stop logs. The traveling screens also require periodic cleaning by divers. The only difference in these operations is that the diver must wear a radiation badge on his/her underwear under the drysuit.

Nuclear plants use purified, de-mineralized water for steam. Freshwater is pumped, as needed, through a pipeline to a treatment plant. Upstream of the treatment plant, all diving operations are carried out as they would be elsewhere. In the treatment plant and downstream of the plant, all diving equipment that will, or possibly may, enter the water must be decontaminated, even new equipment. This mode of diving, like the diving done in potable water, is known as "reverse hazmat."

Inside the turbine hall, the cooling water valves at the steam condensers are serviced by divers. This involves adjusting and replacing the seats on large wafer valves. Divers are used to allow an "in-service" repair, reducing the downtime for the plant. The work on these valves involves confined space entry and, of course, radiation work.

In the reactor building, divers are occasionally used to perform work in the dousing tank, which is located up between the inner and outer domes. The dousing water is mildly radioactive and contains hydrazine, a known carcinogen. This work is to be performed as **hazmat.** The diver must wear both a badge and radiation pad under his/her suit.

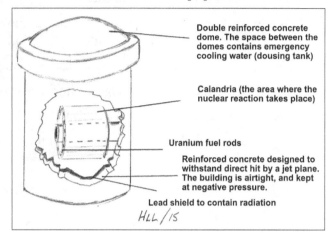

Drawing of reactor building (CANDU Reactor)

In the spent-fuel handling area, the spent-fuel bay occasionally requires divers for various tasks. All spent fuel will be removed prior to the operation, but this work is performed as radioactive **hazmat.** Even though the fuel is gone, the bay and the water in the pool remains contaminated.

Regardless of the diving operation to be performed at a nuclear plant, the diving supervisor must have a pre-job meeting with radiation control to discuss the operation and exposures.

14.5 SAFETY GUIDELINES FOR POWER PLANTS AND PUMP HOUSES

- Every member of the diving crew should attend the safety/orientation course for the plant or mill the crew is working in.

- A plant-specific JSA should be performed before every individual diving operation

- The diving supervisor must always read the work authorization permit, paying close attention to the isolated equipment, before he/she signs it.

- If the diver is working outside the trash racks, the unit on each side of the diver must also be included in the lockout.

- When working on dams, the diver should always take into consideration the head or differential pressure. When sealing head gates, the diver should look at the flow downstream. If the flow is excessive, plant operations should lift and reset the gate to reduce flow before putting a diver in.

- When using a man basket to lower the diver into the water, the basket should be brought back on deck as soon as the diver is in place. This allows for a quick response by the standby diver.

- When large ice floes are present, it is critical to station a person with a pick pole or a motorboat to keep the floes away from the diver's umbilical.

- Divers must be on the lookout, especially during shut-downs, for radiography and stay well clear. They should not enter areas that are taped off, roped off, or barricaded.

- When working in pump houses, plant operations must make sure both the primary and standby diver will fit through the access hatches.

- Handrails in a pump house always have a damp, salt atmosphere, and handrails corrode. Divers should never lean or climb on them.

- When working in a nuclear plant, no one is allowed to leave an escort unless wearing an orange or green badge. Without a green badge, it is forbidden to enter a green door without an escort.

- Divers must never leave a radiation area without using a radiation monitor.

- Always leave the radiation badge in the rack at the end of the shift.

- Never wear street clothes into a radiation area.

- Never take food, drink, or snacks into a radiation area.

15.0 UNDERWATER INSPECTION

Since the early 1980s, there has been a dramatic increase in the worldwide understanding that underwater structures need to be inspected and maintained. Considering the costs of construction and operation, operators recognize that they can no longer afford to ignore the structures' subsea condition. This trend includes offshore platforms and pipelines, as well as dams, power plants, bridges, outfalls, piers, and dry docks in harbors and inland. These areas need to be monitored and maintained in the same way as the topside areas.

Generally speaking, the purpose of an underwater inspection program is to determine the integrity of an underwater structure and to provide assurance that all reasonable precautions have been taken to verify its integrity. Verifying the integrity of a structure includes confirming that the installation was performed correctly, that the foundation is secure and that physical damage is detected. More specific to the inspection diver, the basic objective of an inspection is to locate, identify and clearly describe problems or potential problem areas. In addition to having clearly defined inspection objectives, a large part of the success of an underwater inspection depends of the qualifications of the diver. Therefore, it has become increasingly important for divers to increase their skill level beyond diving itself and comprehensive programs have been developed specifically to train and qualify underwater inspectors.

15.1 DIVER QUALIFICATIONS

It has been estimated that inspection, repair, and maintenance activities comprise 80–90% of the contracts in a diving contractor's business. Owners and insurers of inshore and offshore marine infrastructure are increasingly requiring that contractors provide divers with specialized inspection training.

In the United States and South America, the qualification required most often for diver inspectors is ASNT (American Society of Nondestructive Testing), which identifies levels of qualification as I, II or III. ASNT addresses the diver's non-destructive testing (NDT) skills only. The ASNT certified diver also needs to acquire skills in other vitally important areas of underwater inspection.

Internationally, the inspection certification required most often is CSWIP. This originally stood for Certification Scheme for Welding Inspection Personnel. The welding inspection program has since been expanded to include all types of underwater inspection. CSWIP has various levels of certification for divers: 3.1U – general visual and video inspection underwater; 3.2U – close visual, video and NDT underwater; and 3.4U – inspection coordinator for underwater inspections. The inspection diver must be capable of recognizing, accurately describing and identifying weld defects, concrete defects, timber defects, and damage observed on various types of structure. Inspection diving also requires skills in documentation of conditions observed, corrosion assessment and monitoring and the ability to produce understandable narrative commentaries during video inspections. A more detailed explanation of the principles and requirements of NDT are described in Chapter 16: Non-Destructive Testing.

15.2 INSHORE STRUCTURES

Divers who inspect inshore structures need skills that sometimes differ from offshore inspections and sometimes are quite similar. The sections below describe some of the more common inshore areas that divers are asked to inspect. The primary types of inshore underwater structures that require inspection are piling and pilework structures, trestle posts and structures, cribs, seawater intakes and outfalls, bridges, power plants, and hydro dams.

15.2.1 Piling and Pilework Structures

There are four principle types of piling found in pilework structures: bearing piles, batter piles, fender piles, and sheathing piles.

15.2.1.1 Bearing Piles

Bearing piles get their name from the fact that they bear the weight of the structure and the loads placed on the structure (live load). Bearing piles are always driven vertically to the point where they cannot be driven any further (refusal). These piles may be of wood, steel, or concrete. Bearing piles always have a horizontal member (pile cap) above them. This pile

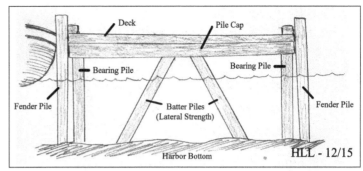

Cross-section of a pilework dock

cap distributes the load of the structure on all of the piles. The piles are always driven in groups, usually in straight rows called pile bents.

Wood-bearing piles are constructed from machine turned straight trees, usually softwood. Typically, they are pressure treated with a wood preservative to protect against decay and marine borers. Timber piles quite often have diagonal braces and horizontal wales, also of timber, bolted to them. These braces and wales reduce deflection between the pile cap and the mud line. When timber piles are inspected, the diver looks for the following: signs of decay, evidence of marine borer activity, stress failures (cracks, breaks), and corrosion of steel fasteners.

Steel-bearing piles will be either H beam piles or pipe piles (constructed of pipe). Pipe piles are often rock socketed, which is performed by sending a drill string down the inside of the pipe pile after driving, drilling a socket into the rock, and pumping grout or concrete down the pile to lock it into the bedrock. Even when they are not rock socketed, pipe piles are frequently filled with reinforced concrete. Steel piles are usually covered with a protective coating to prevent corrosion and often have cathodic protection that may consist of sacrificial anodes or an impressed current system. Cathodic protection and impressed current systems are discussed in Chapter 16: Non-Destructive Testing. When inspecting steel piles, the diver must look for the following: signs of corrosion, damage to protective coatings, and condition of cathodic protection system.

Concrete-bearing piles may be any shape, depending on the formwork the manufacturer uses to cast them. Concrete piles are always precast. They are poured off-site, then brought to the site and driven. Concrete piles are very durable but are subject to a few problems: stress fractures, freeze thaw, and alkali aggregate reactivity (AAR). Stress fractures can occur when the piles are being driven or from live load and often are not visible until there is a serious crack in the pile. Freeze thaw, as the name suggests, is caused by the constant cycles of hot and cold that piles are exposed to in colder climates. AAR occurs when the alkalinity of the cement in the concrete reacts with the aggregate (sand and stone) causing the concrete to virtually self-destruct. When inspecting concrete piles, the diver looks for the following: cracks (regardless of size), spalling (pitting and chipping), and reduction of cross-section size (called necking in).

15.2.1.2 Batter Piles

Batter piles get their name because they are driven on an angle or batter. Batter piles are used to stop lateral deflection or movement in a pilework structure. This deflection or movement may be caused by movements of loads on the structure or by other forces, as in the case of a ship contacting a wharf. Batter piles are always connected to a pile cap. Quite often in a bent of bearing piles, there will be two or more batter piles. Batter piles are usually constructed of the same material as the bearing pile. When inspecting them, the diver looks for the same conditions. The diver should also look for signs of stress because batter piles take lateral strain.

15.2.1.3 Fender Piles

Fender piles, as their name implies, protect a structure from wear and damage, usually caused by ship traffic. Most fender piles are wood or steel. Concrete is seldom used. The fender piles are not necessarily driven to refusal because they protect the structure and do not bear weight. Plastic piles are now being used extensively as fender piles. They are made of recycled U/V-protected plastic. Fender piles may be individual units or part of a group, as in a "fender unit" or "pile cluster." A fender unit usually has two or more fender piles tied together with horizontal wales to take the stress as a unit and as individual piles. A pile cluster (usually wood) consists of several piles driven in a cluster and bound together with cable to act as a fender unit. Fender piles and units are often designed to be expendable, and, therefore, it is not uncommon to see untreated wood and unprotected steel used. When inspecting fendering systems, the diver should expect to see impact, crush, and chafe damage to the systems. All of this damage must be documented because the condition of the system will determine the effective life.

15.2.1.4 Sheathing Piles

Sheathing piles may serve any of the following purposes: seawall, wave break, diffusion of water flow, or the containment of backfill. Concrete is seldom used in sheathing piles because of the cost, but occasionally rectangular concrete sheathing is used. Wood and steel are used most commonly. Wood is used both "in the round" and square sawn. Steel piles are either H piles with panels slid in the H channels or steel sheet piling. Sheet piling is constructed using prefabricated W-shaped panels with interlocking edges. These sheets are locked together as they are driven, forming a solid steel wall. Most sheathing pile walls are tied together with at least one horizontal wale. When inspecting a sheathing pile wall, the diver looks for the same conditions that are found in other pile applications. When inspecting sheet pile, the locks should also be examined.

15.2.2 Trestle Posts and Trestlework Structures

Trestle posts are similar to bearing piles in that they are installed vertically, with a horizontal member (trestle cap) above them to distribute the load. Trestle posts are used when building a structure on rock, usually when there is no silt (overburden) to support driven piling. Trestlework structures are usually constructed of wood (typically square sawn), with the trestle post bents supported by diagonal braces. Because wood floats, trestlework always contains ballast. This ballast (usually rock) is contained in pens (ballast boxes) affixed to the structure. When inspecting trestlework, the diver looks for evidence of decay in the timbers and for signs of corrosion in the fastenings.

15.2.3 Timber Cribwork

At one time, timber cribwork was the most common marine structure found in many areas. Although used less often today, timber cribwork structures are still being built. Basically, a timber crib is a rugged wooden box, filled with weight and sunk with the upper portion extending above the water to form a support pier. These piers form wharves, support buildings, and in many cases support road and rail bridges. Some timber cribs are built to fit a rock bottom, but most are built with a flat bottom and sit on a rock mattress of stone of uniform size, compacted and spread level as a bed for the crib to rest upon. When inspecting timber cribwork, the diver needs to look for scour between the bottom of the crib and the rock mattress, as well as, signs of corrosion in fastenings and evidence of decay in timbers. The diver must also observe the ballast rock, looking for evidence that any has spilled out of the crib.

Timber crib dock

15.2.4 Concrete Cribs

Concrete cribs are now used extensively in the construction of marine structures, replacing nearly all timber cribwork. Concrete cribs are huge concrete boxes, built with valves in the floor for sinking. They are placed on a rock mattress and filled with ballast. When these cribs are placed, there is usually an 18"-24" gap between the cribs. This gap is known as a keyway. When there is backfill placed behind the cribs, for example to create a parking area, a concrete panel, known as a key, is slid down into the keyway to retain the backfill. Many concrete cribs today have scour protection installed at the time of construction to prevent rock mattress scour caused by propeller wash. This scour protection may be large rock (armor stone), precast concrete panels or concrete filled fabric mats. When inspecting concrete cribs, the diver looks first for damage to the crib boxes and checks the bottoms of the keyways for evidence of escaping backfill. If there is silt on the bottom, the diver must feel under the silt at the bottom of each keyway for piles of gravel. If there is scour protection, the diver should check all along the bottom of each crib for scour. If there is silt on bottom, that does not mean that there is no scour. The diver should feel underneath the silt with his/her hand or with a probe to check for scour.

Concrete crib dock

15.2.5 Seawater Intakes and Outfalls

Many power plants and heavy industries use seawater for cooling. To avoid sucking marine life and debris into the intake pipeline, most make use of an intake structure, which may be a screen over the end of the pipeline. Usually there is a box made of wood, concrete or steel with multiple openings covered with grates called trash racks. When seawater is used for industrial purposes, it must be returned to the sea in an outfall pipeline. Before the diver inspects an intake or outfall, it is critical to make certain that the system is locked out. If the structure is wood, the diver looks for signs of decay. If steel, the diver looks for corrosion; if concrete, the diver looks for cracks or spalling. Most trash racks are steel, so the diver must look for corrosion on the trash racks. If screens are covered in marine growth or if any condition exists that will reduce or restrict water flow, this must be documented.

Special Precautions

Typically, when problems are obvious on a marine structure above the surface, there are usually much more severe problems below the water line. For this reason, the diver must be very careful when performing inspections on marine structures. The notes below will help the diver to be safe, but if the inspection cannot be done safely, it should not be done at all. The diver and diving crew must be sure to take the following precautions:

- Always check the condition of ladders before climbing. Ladders with loose, missing or severely corroded rungs must not be used.
- Look up and around before mooring alongside any marine structure. Broken fenders, loose timbers or large pieces of loose concrete must be avoided. They may fall on the vessel or in the water. Either situation can be dangerous for the diver and surface crew.
- Keep a lookout for vessel traffic. Flags, lights and Coast Guard notification are not a guarantee that vessels will not approach. It is important for the operations crew to remain alert at all times.

- Watch out for yourself and your umbilical while working around wharves because wharves and docks are dumping grounds. Rusted steel, cables and broken glass are hard on an umbilical. If there is a lot of debris with sharp edges, the diving supervisor should consider a canvas shroud on the umbilical. If the bottom is littered with debris, it may be necessary to use a floating hose.

- Make sure ballast floors, armor stone, and scour pads are secure before moving around them. An avalanche of ballast can injure or trap a diver on the surface as well as beneath the water. Average armor stone is 5 to 7 tons but may be over 10 tons. Scour pads often weigh 25 tons.

- Be aware that industrial structures such as pulp and paper mills often have several small intakes in addition to the main intake. Because different departments control different machines and many machines use water to operate, it is critical to make sure that all equipment is locked out in the area that will be inspected. The diving crew should not assume one lockout will be sufficient for all equipment.

- Be extra careful around corroded areas when inspecting steel piling, whether pipe piles, H piles or sheet piles. A diver can grab what looks like the edge of the steel, but it may be soft scale masking a razor-sharp corroded edge. Consider kevlar or leather gloves when working around corroded steel.

15.2.6 Bridge Piers and Abutments

Many road and rail bridges are constructed on bodies of water that are so wide that the support structure of the bridge must actually be in the water. Some bridges utilize a structural retaining wall (abutment) on each shore with a central span; others have support piers in the water or a combination of both. Occasionally, bridges are built on piling only, but the most common method is the concrete pier.

There are two methods commonly used to construct concrete piers. The first method, seldom used, involves a rock mattress and a concrete crib. The second method involves driving sheet pile in the shape of the pier and dewatering the inside area. This sheet pile structure is called a cofferdam. Steel H piles are driven to refusal on the inside and the entire cofferdam is poured with reinforced concrete. In the past, once the concrete was poured, divers cut the cofferdam away. Today, a pile extractor usually does the work. Many bridge piers have steel plates on the rounded upstream and downstream ends. The rounded ends are called bullnoses. The plates are called ice shields and their purpose is to protect the underlying concrete from ice floes or other debris moving with the current.

Concrete bridge pier

15.2.6.1 Inspection Tasks on Bridges

When inspecting pile work bridges, the diver uses the same methods as on a pile work marine structure with some exceptions. The diver must look carefully for scour due to current on the downstream side of the structure. If the structure is in freshwater, the diver must also look for ice damage. If the piles are steel, the diver should look for corrosion.

When inspecting concrete piers, the diver should observe the condition of the concrete and check closely for ice damage, looking where the ice shield ends for spalling or cavities behind the shield. The diver should check at the base of each pier, particularly on the downstream side, for scour. If there is silt and debris, this is not an indication that there is no scour. The exact same methods should be used when inspecting bridge abutments.

15.2.7 Hydroelectric and Storage Dams

Hydroelectric dams are built in the dry, but from the day they start operation until they are decommissioned, they are primarily covered in water. For this reason, divers are required every few years to inspect them. Hydro dams are usually concrete and some have an earthen dam adjoining them. Every dam, regardless of whether it is simply a storage dam for a water supply or a power plant dam has at least one intake, and also a spillway. The spillway is a relief gate system to dump excess water in flood conditions.

Hydroelectric dam

When inspecting a dam, the diver should perform the following inspections:

- Look closely at the condition of the concrete and watch for ice damage at the winter water line. Pay close attention to the concrete at gate and stoplog seals. Spalling here can cause serious problems dewatering.
- Look closely at the seals themselves. Corrosion will also prevent a tight seal, again causing problems with dewatering.
- Carefully inspect at the concrete by the gate and stoplog gains. Spalling near the gains should be noted. Cracks, especially if they extend behind the gains, can cause dewatering problems.
- Check the gains for corrosion and for misalignment that may cause problems with gates or stoplogs.
- Examine the trash racks for bent or missing bars.

Special Precautions

The following is a list of special precautions the diver should take when inspecting either a storage dam or a hydro dam.

- Make certain the unit being worked on is locked out, as well as the unit on each side. More on this type of diving may be found in Chapter 14: Power Plants and Pump Houses.
- Get drawings of the dam. These will show exactly what will be inspected, and what the owner calls each section. Terminology is usually the same, but not always.
- When inspecting near intake and spillway gates, make certain there is no differential pressure suction before the diver enters the area.

15.2.8 Thermal Power Plants

Thermal power plants, whether oil, coal, natural gas or nuclear, have one thing in common; they require cooling water to operate. Some are built on the water with direct intake and outfalls while others are set back, requiring intake and outfall pipelines or tunnels.

Cooling water pump houses always have interior screens to catch debris before the pumps. These may be removable rigid screens or the more common traveling trash screens. These screens, mounted on an oval track assembly, constantly travel while the pumps are operating dumping the trash they collect in a pit. Outside of the screens are gains and seals for stop-logs used for dewatering. When inspecting a power plant pump house, the diver needs to do the following:

- Check the frame assembly for the traveling screen. The operator can easily see the screens by rotating them but relies on the diver to check the framework.
- Look for signs of corrosion, loose or missing braces, bolts, or anchors.
- Check the bearing surfaces that the wheels run on.
- Look closely at the stoplog seals for corrosion. Look for spalling or cracks in the concrete by the seals.
- Check the stoplog gains for corrosion. Look for concrete problems near the stoplog gains.

Special Precautions

Before diving at any power plant, the diver must make certain that lockouts are in place. When entering a pipeline or tunnel, the diver must use the proper procedures for a penetration dive.

15.2.9 Industrial Pump Houses

Many industrial pump houses do not have provisions for dewatering. To service the pumps, they must be removed. These pump houses quite often require divers for inspection. Before a dive is made in a pump house, the pumps must be locked out and all systems de-energized. Some systems have an automatic and manual mode. The system must be locked out in the manual mode. Before inspecting pumps, the diver and the diving supervisor must first look at the drawings to determine where the steadying brackets, lubrication lines, bell and trunk flanges and the cathodic protection are located. While looking at the drawings, it is important to note the client's terminology. The diver inspecting pump houses should do the following:

- Look closely at the steadying brackets for evidence of stress from torque and vibration.
- Look at the fittings on the lube lines and the lines themselves.
- Check the fit of the bell and trunk flanges and make sure the bolts have not loosened from vibration.
- Check the floor of the pump pit for siltation and debris. The presence of such debris may indicate a problem with the trash rack at the intake structure.

15.2.10 Freshwater Intakes and Outfalls

Removing screens or trash racks to inspect the interior of the structure or the pipeline or tunnel is considered a penetration dive and has to be performed properly according to the requirements of that type of diving. With outfall structures, the most common problem encountered is flow restriction caused by interior buildup of suspended or semi-suspended solids. Examples of this are human waste in sewage outfalls and salt in brine pipelines. Diving on any sewage outfall is considered a HAZMAT dive and all of the appropriate precautions must be taken. Whether it is for a power plant, factory, municipal water supply or fish farm, a freshwater intake always requires an unrestricted flow of water. To ensure an unrestricted flow, divers are used to inspect intakes. Before diving on an intake, the diver must make sure all systems are locked out and all flow stopped. When inspecting an intake, the diver should do the following:

- Look closely at the screen or trash racks for damage and for blockage.
- Check the silt level around the intake structure.
- Look for evidence of scour in the silt. This may indicate that the intake is picking up silt while in operation.

15.3 SAFETY PRECAUTIONS FOR DAMS, PUMP HOUSES, BRIDGES AND INTAKES

15.3.1 Hydroelectric Dams

Before putting a diver in the water, it is critical to always make sure lockout procedures have been followed. When the diver is on the upstream side, the (differential) pressure is a potential threat to the diver. To gauge flow, look at the downstream side of the gate. If it is impossible to look at the downstream side, a weighted plastic jug can be hung on a line to gauge the flow. If the flow is strong, a diver should not enter until it has been slowed or stopped. Almost every year there are divers needlessly killed due to differential pressure (Delta P). As this text is being written, there is an investigation ongoing into the death of a young diver on a tidal power plant in Nova Scotia, Canada. His body was sucked under the tidal gate, leaving his helmet and bailout bottle on the upstream side. With Delta P, it happens very fast, is very violent, and once it starts, there is no second chance for the diver. The pressure exerted may be calculated using the following formula:

A × DW × psi/ft (water) = DP, where A = area of the hole, DW = difference in water depth on the two sides of the structure, and DP = the differential pressure exerted.

Example: You have been asked to inspect the bottom of a head gate at a hydro dam. There is a crack 10 inches long and 3 inches high. The water depth is 78 ft., with no water on the back side. In this case, A= 30 sq. in., DW= 78 ft., and the psi/ft of water is 0.432. We calculate it as 30 × 78 × .432 = 1011 lbs. Should the diver get sucked against this crack, there will be 1011 lbs.of force exerted by the water on the diver's body.

15.3.2 Pump Houses

Before dressing the diver, measure the size of all manholes and access hatches to ensure that both the diver and standby will fit through easily.

Make certain all lockout procedures have been followed before putting the diver in the water.

If the diver must use a fixed-in-place ladder, send a crew member down first with a life jacket to check the condition of the ladder. If in doubt, do not allow the diver to climb the ladder.

15.3.3 Bridges

When operating in current, always tend the diver downstream (the diver should be downstream of the support vessel).

Watch out for ice floes around the diver's umbilical. If ice is present, use a sinking hose. If an ice floe catches the umbilical, it may pull the diver off the bottom or it may crush or sever the umbilical.

15.3.4 Intakes

Before diving on an intake, it is critical to make sure it is locked out.

Divers should not be sent into an intake unless it is treated as a penetration dive. Any dive more than 6 feet inside the intake screen or trash rack is a penetration dive.

15.4 PIPELINES

For many centuries, humans have been building pipelines to transfer everything from irrigation water to natural gas. For the most part, pipelines today are cast iron, steel, concrete, fiberglass or plastic. Different methods of connection include bolted flange, Victaulic coupling, bell flange (also called bell and spigot), glued joint, and welded joint.

15.4.1 Pipeline Types and Materials

Cast iron, concrete, fiberglass, PVC, and steel are all materials used for pipelines, but the most common types of pipe in new pipelines is steel for oil pipeline and PVC plastic for low pressure water pipeline. With the exception of oil, gas, and natural gas, which use concrete coated steel, most fluids can be transferred through plastic, and plastic is cheaper and easier to handle. Plastic pipeline has many advantages over cast iron, steel, and concrete. Cast iron and steel both corrode over time due to electrolysis and plastic does not. Concrete is subject to freeze-thaw and will crack with lateral strain; plastic will bend more easily and is totally resistant to freeze-thaw damage.

The drawback to plastic pipe, however, is that it floats. Therefore, when plastic pipeline is laid, it must have ballast weights attached to it. These weights are constructed of concrete and are bolted together over the pipe at regular intervals.

Steel pipe, used in the petroleum industry, also requires ballast weights or concrete weight coat as most petroleum products are lighter than seawater, and therefore will cause the pipeline to float when in use.

15.4.2 Internal Pipeline Inspection

Internal pipeline inspections may be performed using one of four methods: diver inspection, sled-mounted camera, remotely operated vehicle (ROV) or a smart pig. Regardless of the method used, the objectives are the same: to determine the interior condition of the pipeline and identify and locate problem areas. Internal pipeline inspection by a diver is always considered a penetration dive. See Chapter 21: Diving Under Exceptional Conditions

A pipeline pig is a device slightly smaller than the inside diameter (ID) of the pipe that is forced by pressure or pulled through a pipeline. A smart pig is a pipe pig that has the capability to determine the condition of the pipeline wall, find holes or cracks and locate them for repair. These units are very expensive, quite rare and used only when absolutely necessary. Recently, production was drastically reduced in the oilfield in Prudhoe Bay, Alaska, due to pipeline corrosion. This happened at a time when oil prices were at an all-time high and could have been avoided by using a smart pig.

The ROVs used in pipeline inspections are basically a motorized camera sled. Some travel on tracks or wheels, but most use thrusters. They tow their tether (control cable) behind them as they go. The tether carries commands to the thrusters and cameras (pan and tilt, still photo) and carries video signal back to the surface control unit.

Sled-mounted cameras are simply underwater video cameras strapped on a sled that is slightly smaller than the ID of the pipeline. The sled is pulled through the pipeline while shooting video. Location is determined by the amount of camera umbilical (tether) that is out.

Most clients prefer to have a diver look at their pipelines when possible, and with good reason. An observant and alert diver will pick up details that no camera will see. Not all pipelines are large enough to accommodate a diver, however, and divers are restricted in the length of penetration. A good rule of thumb is if the diver cannot turn and reverse direction in the pipe, a sled should be used. That means that any pipe less than 40-inch ID should not have a diver in it.

Specialized contractors, not diving contractors, usually perform internal pipeline inspections by ROV and smart pig. The other two methods are often used by diving contractors. Whether using a diver or a sled-mounted camera, lockout procedures must be followed and all flow must be stopped.

When inspecting an intake pipe (or tunnel), inconsistencies should be noted. If there is growth on the walls and suddenly it stops, it needs to be investigated. Interrupted or diverted water flow will cause changes in the interior condition.

If there are signs that silt is being picked up at the intake, the diver should look for a buildup in the pipeline. Typically, silt buildups are found toward the midpoint of an intake, providing that it is a straight run. If not, the diver should look a few feet beyond each bend and always measure the depth and length of the buildup so the flow restriction may be calculated.

The following are also duties of a pipeline diver:

- Look closely at the joints in the pipeline. If it is welded steel, the welds need to be examined, and any cracks in the welds should be documented.
- Watch for any indication that there has been flow in through the flange, indicating a gasket failure, if the joints are flanged.
- Look for spalling, cracks, or breaks in concrete pipe.
- Look for corrosion in steel or cast and makes note of the depth of any corrosion found.

15.4.3 External Pipeline Inspections

When conducting an external pipeline inspection, it is the job of the diver to look for scour under the pipeline (known as free-span), regardless of the type of pipe. Free span on any pipeline means an unsupported pipeline, and must be documented by measuring the depth and length of the scour area and locating it accurately in the reports. Other duties of the diver include the following:

- Check all pipeline joints. If bolted flange, random bolts should be tried with a wrench. If any are found to be loose, check all. If welded steel or welded plastic, the welds are closely inspected. For plastic pipe, the diver checks the weights to ensure that fastenings are sound.
- Look at the silt at each joint. If there is leakage at the joint, quite often the silt will have been sucked into intake joints or blown away from outfall joints.
- Look for ice damage to the pipe or the weights near shore if the pipeline runs up on shore.
- Ensure that pipelines in navigable waterways that are not buried have not sustained any damage from vessels or anchors.
- Make certain any flaws or damage found in the inspection is located accurately, not approximated.

15.4.4 Pipeline Route Survey

Diving crews often assist in pipeline installation. Prior to the installation of any pipeline, the bottom must be checked for obstructions in the area where the pipe will lay. This inspection is called a route survey. When performing a route survey, the following tasks should be performed:

- Mark the proposed route with a weighted line.
- Follow with a diver or ROV, looking for any obstruction that will hold the pipeline off the bottom and therefore place stress on the pipe.
- Take pneumo readings every couple of feet, in case electronic gear cannot accurately map the seafloor.
- After the pipe has been laid and the post-lay inspection is being performed, any spots where the weights (or the pipe itself) do not rest on the seafloor should be noted.
- Look for rock or hard objects against the pipe that may cause problems.

15.5 SUBMARINE CABLES

In today's world, in spite of wireless technology, cables are still required to connect communities, countries, and continents. Any cable that crosses the bottom of a body of water is known as a submarine cable. Inspections are required both before laying (route survey) and after (post-lay). Also, divers are used to install cable protection after installation. One type of cable protection is cast iron or steel plates (armadillo plates) that overlap and are bolted together. Grout-filled mats, precast concrete mattresses, and sand and grout bags are also used.

Concrete mattresses for pipeline and cable protection

15.5.1 Cable Route Survey

- A weighted line is first laid in the proposed cable track by a diver. Cables are very heavy and a rock ridge, abandoned pipeline, sunken vessel or scrap steel can cut through the casing.
- Potential hazards to the cable must be moved, corrected (cushion mats) or the route must be altered.
- A diver then follows the line looking closely for obstructions.

15.5.2 Post-installation Inspections

- The diver checks the underside of the cable for anything missed on the route survey. If obstructions are found, the diver marks it with a buoy. The cable can be slung and lifted to place cushions.
- If the cable has unsupported areas, as in crossing a deep hole, the proper procedure is to mark both ends. The engineers may decide to support it with sand bags or grout bags and knowing the exact location will save time later.

15.5.3 In-use Inspections

- The diver looks at the cable protection.
- The diver determines if it has moved, whether it is protecting the cable, and if it is showing signs of wear or ice or vessel damage. The diver also looks at the cable where it enters shoreline conduits (ducts), checking for signs of chafing.
- Out beyond the cable protection, the diver looks for possible damage caused by anchors or fishing gear. Warning signs on shore do not mean that there will be no damage. Any damage found must be accurately located by either GPS or buoy.

15.6 VESSEL INSPECTIONS

The underwater portions of vessels also need to have regular inspections to ensure their integrity and safety. Divers are most often used for this purpose. Therefore, it is critical that divers understand how ships are constructed and the terminology used to describe the various areas and parts of vessels.

15.6.1 Common Features of Vessels

Regardless of the type of vessel, when an inspection is performed, the diver must use the proper terminology. There are general terms common to all vessels and specific terms for different hull designs.

15.6.1.1 General Terms

The front of a vessel is called the bow and the back is called the stern. Any fixture toward the bow is considered fore, or forward (as in forward hatch or forepeak). Likewise, any fixture toward the stern is considered aft or after (as in after deck or aft-most crane). The left side (facing forward) is called port and the right side is called starboard. Floors are called decks, ceilings are overheads or deckheads, and walls are called bulkheads.

15.6.1.2 Specific Terms

The outside skin of the vessel that displaces the water and the structure inside of that skin are the hull. The deck found at the top of the hull is known as the main deck. The area below the main deck is called below or below deck. Any portion of the ship above the main deck is referred to as superstructure. The lowest portion of the hull, usually well below the waterline, is known as the bilge. Quite often, the hull is extended slightly above the main deck, about waist high. This extension is known as the bullworks (pronounced as bullarks). Holes through the bullworks at deck level (for drainage) are called scuppers. The top edge of the bullworks is called the gunwale (pronounced gunnel).

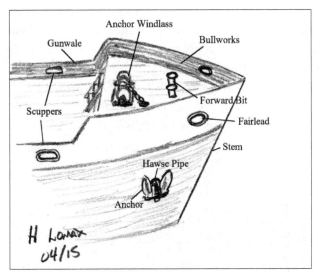

Sketch of forepeak of seagoing vessel

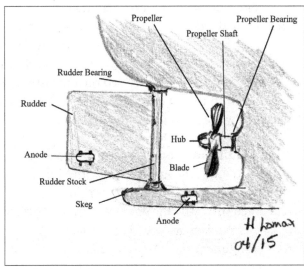

Sketch of stern of seagoing vessel

The foremost edge of the bow is called the stem. Slightly aft of the stem are holes through which the anchors are lowered and raised. These are the hawse-pipes. Under the stern, just aft of the propeller(s) is the rudder. The rudder is mounted on a shaft called the rudder stock. The rudder stock comes through the hull skin in a sealed watertight fitting known as the rudder bearing. Occasionally the rudder stock is unsupported, but most times it has a bearing below the rudder on the skeg. The skeg is an extension of the main fore and aft frame member that is called the keel.

In the past, the construction of every vessel started with the keel. The keel was a solid piece of steel (timber in wooden ships) that ran from the base of the stem to the base of the stern post on the outside of the hull. Today most vessels are built in modules or sections. The keel is often on the inside of the hull, with only a short section outside at the after end of the ship. Often ships now have two bilge keels, found at the center of the curved area where the side of the hull meets the bottom. This area is known as the "turn of the bilge."

The propellers are mounted on a shaft, the propeller shaft, which runs from the main engine out through the hull at the sternpost. A watertight seal (the stuffing box), or an oil filled bearing (the cutlass bearing), allow the shaft to spin while keeping water out. Usually the bearing is on the inner end of a pipe called the stern tube. The stern tube often has a steel ridge around the outer end, the rope guard.

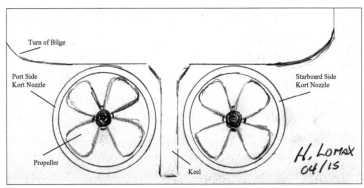

Kort Nozzles under a tugboat

Some propeller shafts extend quite far beyond the stern tube and require braces to steady the shaft. These braces are known as struts. Some vessels (particularly tugs) have a beveled pipe installed around the propeller, known as a Kort Nozzle. The Kort Nozzle directs the thrust of the propellers and increases the thrust by as much as 30%.Marine engines are usually at least partially water-cooled. Cooling water is collected below the waterline through hull intake fittings. When more than one intake is in the same area of the hull, they often have one large, grated opening, the sea chest. Cooling water is usually pumped back overboard above the waterline.

Many larger ships and barges have lateral thrusters. Lateral thrusters are propellers set in a pipe that runs from one side of the hull to the other. These thrusters are powered separately from the main engines and are used when docking the vessel or by the Dynamic Positioning System for maintaining position during surface support of subsea operations. Typically, these thrusters are located at either or both ends of the vessel (bow thruster and stern thruster). Thrusters sometimes have a grating over the ends of the pipe. Usually, the propeller used on a thruster is a variable pitch propeller. Also, there is what is known as an azimuth thruster, one that rotates 360°, or very close to it. Typically, these thrusters are set up so that they will extend below the hull when in use and withdraw inside the hull when not in use.

15.6.2 Hull and Propulsion Unit Inspections

Typically, hull and propulsion unit inspections are carried out for one of two reasons: a regularly scheduled survey by the vessel's insurance company or suspected damage after a collision or grounding incident. Either case warrants a careful and thorough inspection.

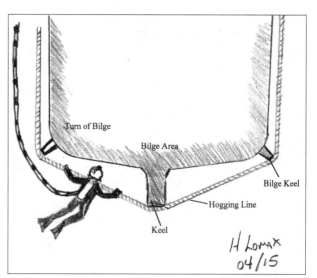

Inspecting hull of a ship

When performing hull or propulsion unit inspections, the diver should use a hog line. A hog line is a length of rope that runs from the gunwale on one side of the ship, under the hull and up the other side to the gunwale. A hog line serves as a down line for the diver, gives him a reference point, and allows the surface crew to know exactly where the diver is under the hull. When the hog line is moved, the surface ends are moved simultaneously, with the bottom (hog) following. In this way, a methodical grid inspection can be easily carried out. If the vessel being inspected has bilge keels, the hog line may catch on the keels when moved. The hog line should be cleared so it hangs vertically.

The diver needs to take the time to look over drawings before starting the inspection. Every vessel is different, and the drawings will show what to expect. For example, if the surveyor wants to inspect the plates around frame S-5, the drawing will show where the hog line should be set up, how the plates are laid out, and whether there are any fixtures such as bilge keels, anodes, etc.

As far as possible, without leaving the hog line, the diver should try to follow the welds and look around at the surrounding plates. Dents, cracks, cracked welds, missing or chipped coatings should all be noted in the diver's report. The diver must look through the grates into the sea chests and make note of any observed build-up of marine growth. Every intake is checked to ensure that it will allow an unrestricted flow of water. The condition of anodes is noted. A clean, shiny anode is not a working anode. If possible, the diver should get measurements of the anodes so engineers can determine the remaining life.

When inspecting propulsion units, the diver should look at the drawings first to see how the ship is constructed so that when inspecting the unit, it will make sense. The edges of propellers, both leading and trailing, must be examined for nicks. The diver will look closely at the ends of the blades and report any bends or deviation noticed, as these will cause vibration in the propeller shaft and damage the

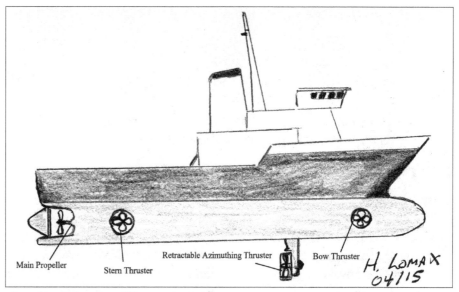

Propulsion units on an offshore service vessel

bearings. It is also essential to check the rope guard, if applicable, on the stern tube. If the propeller is variable pitch, the diver checks where the blades bolt on. Loose or missing bolts must be reported. If the propeller has struts, the diver must closely inspect the bearing on the shaft and the point on the hull where the struts are welded. If the propeller has an exposed nut at the end of the shaft, the diver looks for evidence that it is loose. Any scraps of cable or rope in or around the propeller should be reported and removed as well, because rope on the shaft will wind up into the stern tube, create additional drag, increase manifold temperatures and can cause engines to shut down.

Rudder inspections are usually quite simple. Damage to the rudder should be easily seen. The rudder bearings on the hull and the skeg should be closely inspected. Any damage observed on the rudder or the bearings should be noted.

15.6.3 Special Safety Precautions
It is critical to adhere to the following steps to ensure the diver's safety when working on or around ships:

- Before a diver is put in the water on a ship's hull, the diving supervisor should first meet with the master (or mate) and the chief engineer and lock out all machinery with intakes, including the main engines. It is his responsibility to make sure the lockout procedures have been followed. The lockout key should always stay with the diving supervisor until the job is done.

- The main engines and all lateral thrusters must be locked out. If needed, the engineer should be requested to restrain the main shaft from turning if there is a strong current. Flowing water will cause the propellers to rotate slowly. On smaller vessels, a pipe wrench on the shaft works well.

- It is important to make certain that no auxiliary equipment on board the vessel is set on automatic start if that equipment has intakes outside the hull.

- The ship's draft, depth below the hull and the time of low tide should be checked. Make sure that the diver will not be trapped or crushed under the hull as the tide drops if the vessel to be inspected is in waters with an extreme tidal range.

- Ensure that the diver does not enter a crush hazard area. These areas include between the ship's hull and the dive boat, between the ship's hull and a fender, between the ship's hull and the dock and between the ship's hull and the bottom on a falling tide.

Divers and diving supervisors must do the following:

- Use a hog line to avoid dropping to the bottom and jumping several tables. A hog line will make any job under a vessel's hull easier.
- Make certain that the local Coast Guard traffic center and the harbor master have been notified of any diving operations. Keep a close eye on vessel traffic.
- Use the alpha flag by day and the red/white/red lights by night. Make sure the flag or lights are visible and not hidden by the hull of the vessel being inspected.

15.7 OFFSHORE PLATFORM INSPECTIONS

Offshore platforms all have one thing in common: once they are placed, they become high-end real estate for marine life. Regardless what oilfield or ocean they are in, they attract marine growth and dozens of species of fish. Fishermen realize this and virtually every offshore structure is covered in lost or abandoned fishing gear. This fishing gear presents a hazard to divers and makes a proper inspection nearly impossible to perform. Removal of fishing gear first removes entrapment hazards and allows a proper inspection. Most offshore platforms can be grouped into fixed or floating structures. Fixed structures include jack-up rigs, jackets and gravity base types. Floating structures include single buoy moorings, anchored and tension leg platforms. Divers are employed to inspect offshore platforms for structural damage, debris on the seabed, corrosion, marine growth, cathodic protection system condition and condition of the base of the structure.

The reasons for inspection during the operational life of an offshore structure include the following:

- Certification or maintenance of a Certificate of Fitness.
- Operator's assurance of reliability and safety.
- Work associated with accidents, repairs after accidents or other modifications.
- Identification of preventive maintenance measures to eliminate or reduce future repair requirements.

15.7.1 Fixed Structures

Jack-up structures are actually a jack-up rig that is positioned in one fixed location and used as a permanent platform. Jack-ups have usually 3 or 4 steel lattice legs that rest on bottom and hold the rig steady. Usually the rig is jacked up until the main deck is 30 to 40 feet or more above the water.

Fixed steel or jacket structures are typically made of tubular steelwork welded into a framework with near vertical legs. The piles are tubular steel and are driven through the main legs. This fixes the platform onto the sea floor. Once piles are driven, the annulus (space between), the piles and the legs are concrete filled.

Gravity base type fixed structures are usually constructed of reinforced concrete. They consist of a cluster of concrete ballast tanks supporting a concrete box type structure on which the deck section is fabricated.

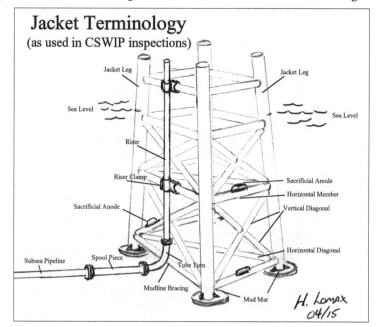

Jacket Terminology
(as used in CSWIP inspections)

Jacket Leg · Jacket Leg · Sea Level · Sea Level · Riser · Riser Clamp · Sacrificial Anode · Horizontal Member · Vertical Diagonal · Sacrificial Anode · Horizontal Diagonal · Subsea Pipeline · Spool Piece · Tube Turn · Mudline Bracing · Mud Mat

H. Lomax
04/15

Fixed leg (jacket) structure with topside module not shown for clarity

15.7.2 Floating Structures

Floating structures vary in design and size. They include semisubmersibles, drilling vessels, single buoy moorings, and catenary anchor leg mooring buoys, all of which are anchored to the sea floor. They are used in the exploration or production phases of offshore work.

Single buoy mooring systems are a type of offshore structure that can be a piled, gravity or anchored structure, depending on the design. The above-water part of the structure incorporates a turntable so that a tanker can load at any orientation.

15.8 INSPECTION METHODS

Underwater inspections often rely on the eyes of the diver. In addition to being able to recognize problem areas, the diver must also be skilled at orientation, taking measurements and recording his findings. The inspection diver also needs to be familiar with the terminology used in underwater inspection work. Unless the diver is a structural engineer, he should never describe a structural deficiency without using the word "appears" or "apparent" in the sentence. For example, if there is decay in a timber, or freeze-thaw damage in concrete, the diver would have seen what "appears" to be decay, or what "appears" to be freeze-thaw damage. Divers are hired as objective observers, not as interpreters of their observations. Inspection methods most often used are: visual, video, still photography and non-destructive testing (NDT). More information on non-destructive testing may be found in Chapter 16: Non-Destructive Testing.

15.8.1 Visual Inspections

The diver is the client's eyes. The client wants to know the condition of his/her property—that is why the diver was hired. Therefore, the diver must take the time to do the inspection properly.

Every time an inspection is performed, whether on a structure, vessel or pipeline, it is important to look at the drawings first. Divers should not attempt to inspect a structure where nothing is known. Both the diver and the supervisor should be familiar with all of the features to be encountered and with the client's terminology for those features.

When inspecting mid-water, the diver uses a drop line and a clump weight unless there are sufficient handholds for the diver to steady himself/herself. When performing an inspection on a vessel, the diver uses a hog line. If the diver is fighting to maintain the proper position, the diver cannot be as observant as he/she should be.

Two distinct underwater visual inspection procedures are commonly performed. These are termed general visual inspection and close visual inspection. The primary objective of a general visual inspection is to observe and document the general or overall condition of the structure. Close visual inspection is the detailed inspection of components of a structure or of a defective condition such as physical damage, weld cracking or corrosion damage.

In a visual inspection, the client is relying on the diver's observations and the supervisor or inspection coordinator's notes. The diver's observations should always be written as notes or recorded, either on tape or digitally. The topside crew should use a note pad or loose-leaf for inspection notes; inspection notes are not made on the dive sheet. The diver should check the notes when he is back on deck.

Prior to the dive, provisions should be made for locating any deficiencies by having stations pre-marked and shot lines and tape measures ready.

15.8.2 Video Inspections

There have been many advances in video technology in the past few years and all proper inspections performed today use surface-monitored video. Thirty years ago, underwater video cameras were very large, black and white, and very expensive. Now, cameras are available that are less than one inch in diameter and less than three inches long. Black and white is still used for some structural inspections, but most systems use color. Helmet mounted cameras are often used to help the diver in diving operations. They are not as efficient as handheld cameras when performing inspections but they are the most commonly used. Regardless whether a hand-held or helmet mounted video camera is used, a proper video inspection is always surface-monitored.

This chapter provides only the basics on video inspection. Refer to Chapter 20: Underwater Photography and Video for more detail.

The most important thing to remember for video inspection is to move the camera slowly and steadily. The best videographers are not fast. They are careful and accurate.

When the diver is in the water with a camera, the diver should take the time to find out where the camera's field of view is. Often, to avoid picture washout, the camera is not exactly aligned with the lights.

The following information will help ensure an effective video inspection is performed:

- When setting up to shoot video, set the monitor up in a dark area. If the sun is on the screen, the picture will be washed out. Cover the windows in the dive control van.
- Shoot every dive on a new tape, disk, or hard drive segment. Be certain to have enough tape or space available on the disk, or hard drive for the job.
- Allow topside to do a brief intro before commencing a dive. This will include the date, location, diving company name, supervisor's name, diver's name, and the client's name.
- If there is a lens cap for the camera, use it when the camera is out of the water. Do not allow the camera lens to point toward the sun.
- Be careful when using video gear. The video lights run hot. When the lights are on, the filaments are very fragile. A slight bump will usually shut down the operation.
- Treat the videotapes, or disks gently. Each one represents money to the employer. Do not place tapes or memory cards near magnets, electric motors, or generators. Do not leave disks in sunlight or out of protective cases.

When running the dive, perform the following:

- Always test the video gear before the dive. Bottom time is too precious to waste waiting for an electronic glitch to be ironed out.
- If using tape, remember that every tape has a short section at the beginning and end that is non-magnetic. Advance the tape five seconds to get beyond the dead tape before starting recording.
- Watch the monitor. If the situation or circumstance the diver is describing do not appear on the monitor, it will not be on the recording. Direct the diver to get the best video of the structure or vessel being inspected.
- Repeat every description that the diver provides. Often when a video is recorded, phantom current will block one side of the communications from the recording. It is better to repeat descriptions than to have to reshoot.
- When the diver is back on deck, check to make sure that the video is useable. If using tape, remove the tape, break the lock tab, and label the tape with the date and location. If using disks, remove and label the disk. If using hard drive, electronically label the recording, save it and back it up on a CD.

The diver must do the following:

- Make certain to know the correct terminology for the structure or vessel being inspected.

- From the moment the video inspection begins, describe verbally everything being shot with the camera. The recording will probably be shown in a boardroom, so watch your language.

- When shooting video, ask for the recording to be paused before hauling slack on the umbilical or camera cable. When the recording is restarted and the topside crew says, "recording," wait five seconds or so before proceeding. This will allow for lag.

- When shooting video of structural defects, it helps to get a hand, ruler or tape measure in the picture to give the viewer a size reference. Do not use a knife as a size reference because the blade will reflect light and wash out the picture.

- When shooting video with a handheld camera, the diver should hook the camera tether to his dive harness in such a way that it can be released if necessary. The diver should keep the camera in the crook of the arm so that wherever his arm is pointed, the camera points. Remember, slow and steady movement is always the answer for top quality video.

- Kill the camera lights before the camera reaches the surface. Underwater video lights are water-cooled and will burn out on surface. They also present a danger to the tender or surface crew. If shooting in the splash zone, be careful with the lights.

15.8.3 Still Photography

Underwater still photography has advanced considerably over the years. In the past, the diver had to carry the camera and a mesh bag full of flash bulbs. There are now digital 35mm cameras with power strobes that cut the diver's work in half. With new digital video capture technology, still photography is not often required but there are still some cases where stills are used. In some structural inspections, stills are specified and captured video will not suffice. On extremely long pipeline penetrations, there may not be sufficient video tether and stills may be the only option available.

Housing for digital 35mm still camera
Photo courtesy of Sea and Sea

Strobe used with the housing showna
Photo courtesy of Sea and Sea

It should be noted that video cameras will quite often give a usable image even when the diver cannot see, but still photography requires clear water (at least four feet of visibility). In order to reduce backscatter, the strobe should be mounted on an arm at least 4 inches from the camera body.

The following recommendations will help ensure that effective still photography is performed.

If running the dive, do the following:

- Use fresh batteries for the camera on every dive.
- Check strobe or flash unit before entering the water.
- Make notes of every still taken and the subject of each photo.

The diver must do the following:

- Before entering the water, check to make sure there is room on the memory card in the camera.
- If possible and the diver knows the required distance from the subject, preset manual settings on the camera before the dive. Manual settings are usually the best choice for inspection stills.
- If possible, the diver should lean against a solid object to steady the camera when shooting stills.
- Rinse the camera with freshwater as soon as it gets back on deck and dry the camera thoroughly before attempting to upload images to a computer.

15.8.4 Weld Inspection

Electric arc welding is the primary bonding process used to fabricate offshore steel structures and vessels but welds are never completely defect free. Often these defects, considered superficial at the time of fabrication, become "stress risers" once the structure has been in service for a period of time. These "stress risers" become small, hairline cracks. If they are not discovered in an early stage, they often result in the complete failure of the weld. The only repair solutions possible underwater, either welding or clamping, can be extremely expensive.

Weld inspection concentrates on fatigue-sensitive welds, especially where the risk of failure cannot be tolerated. It usually involves detailed, close inspection procedures, with a high standard of surface finish required through the use of power brushes or sandblasting. This is true particularly if magnetic particle inspection is to follow.

As stated earlier, weld inspection requires that the diver be familiar with underwater arc welding techniques and terminology.

15.8.5 Corrosion Inspection

Corrosion of underwater structures is most often defined as the electrochemical destruction of metals in the marine environment. Corrosion is the major mode of deterioration, particularly in older structures, and leads to loss of wall thickness, pitting and weld decay.

When two dissimilar metals are connected in an electrolyte such as seawater, a reaction occurs that causes a loss of metal on one or both metals. This is commonly known as "galvanic corrosion." It is a major concern of the inspection diver.

15.8.5.1 Inspection Objectives

Identifying problem areas or demonstrating that there are no problem areas, are the reason that underwater inspections are performed. When the client looks at test results, video or stills, he must know exactly from where on the structure or vessel these results were obtained.

As stated previously, structures and vessels all have terms to describe their features and different clients have their own preferences in terminology. Most terms are the same, but to be safe, the diver must make careful note of specific terminology on drawings.

There are two major objectives in corrosion inspection: locate and describe existing corrosion damage in critical locations such as risers, conductors and welds; and determine if the cathodic potential levels are sufficient to provide effective cathodic protection.

In visual inspection, the diver reports the overall condition of coatings, locates the presence of corrosion on bare metal, and describes percent cover, maximum and average depth, and maximum diameter of pitting. The diver should use a pit gauge for such measurements. He/she is often required to document his findings with still photography.

The inspection diver reports on the condition of anodes, including percentage consumed, whether the method of attachment is sound, whether it is active, and the extent of marine growth cover. The diver may be required to take cathodic potential (CP) readings in the area as well as take an overview or "stand-off" photograph for the topside engineer. An active anode will never look like new, and often tiny bubbles will be seen being emitted by the anode.

15.8.5.2 Cathodic Protection Systems

Marine structures are protected from galvanic corrosion in a number of ways. In addition to paint and concrete coatings, which physically insulate the structure from sea-water (the electrolyte), there are two cathodic protection systems commonly used underwater.

The first is called sacrificial anode cathodic protection because the material used is anodic relative to steel is preferentially consumed and is sacrificed. Most sacrificial anodes are zinc and aluminum. Larger platforms typically have many hundreds, even thousands, of zinc blocks often weighing 1000 pounds or more, with the largest number of anodes found on critical components of the structure.

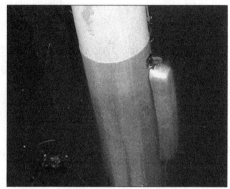

Sacrificial anode on steel pipe pile

The second type of cathodic protection is the impressed current system, which is common on platforms, in harbors and on ships. This system is different from sacrificial systems in that the voltage potential is produced by a topside power source. Commonly, a series of electrodes are selectively installed within the structure to insure an even potential distribution.

The advantages of impressed current systems are that they are inexpensive to install, their weight is insignificant and the power output may be varied as required. The major disadvantage is that it requires continuous monitoring over the lifetime of the structure. Divers may be typically involved in the repair and maintenance of the cables and conduits, particularly after storms.

15.9 HELPFUL TIPS FOR UNDERWATER INSPECTIONS

- When inspecting a structure, the diver should consult "as built" drawings, if possible, and lay out stations prior to starting the inspection. If as built drawings are not available, he will orientate the structure by assigning a north, east, south and west side, if applicable, and lay out station marks on each side with a survey tape. A shot line and station marks will locate deficiencies both laterally and vertically.

- When inspecting a vessel, the diver should consult the builder's drawings to identify frames and transverse bulkheads before starting. By using the hog line and welds, any deficiencies in the hull can be accurately located.

- When inspecting a pipeline internally, the diver's hose should be tightened and marked when he is at the entrance. This procedure should be repeated at deficiency locations. A measurement between the marks will give the distance within the pipeline. For external pipe inspections, a shot line should be used. Note: interior pipeline inspections are considered penetration dives (see Chapter 21: Diving Under Exceptional Conditions.)

- Accurate measurements are important. The same system (metric or standard) should be used that was used during the construction of the structure or vessel being inspected.

15.10 GLOSSARY OF TERMS FOR UNDERWATER INSPECTIONS

Descriptive terms and phrases used to describe conditions encountered or features of the various structures or vessels to be inspected are as follows:

15.10.1 Terms Used for Concrete Inspection

Alkali aggregate reactivity (AAR): A condition caused when the aggregate in the concrete reacts with the cementatious material in the concrete causing expansion and unsound concrete.

Cracks: A hairline is considered small; ¼ inch wide is large. They usually do not run straight.

Construction joint: A planned joint between concrete pours. They usually run straight.

Cold joint: A joint caused by a delay between different layers of the same pour. Cold joints usually do not run straight.

Delamination: This occurs when the outside face of the concrete separates from the structure. This condition is sometimes caused by corrosion in the reinforcing steel.

Exposed rebar: Reinforcing steel (rebar) is intended to have a minimum of three inches of concrete covering it. Delamination, spalling, or cracks may expose the rebar.

Freeze-thaw damage: It is seen in colder climates. This condition occurs when concrete is wet and alternately covered with water and exposed to extremely cold air.

Honeycombing: This is when aggregate (stone) is exposed with voids around aggregate. In honeycombing, the aggregate is not fractured. The condition is caused by improper consolidation during concrete pour.

Laitance: White, sometimes chalky, substance on the concrete surface, caused by failure to screed concrete between pours; often seen on cold joints.

Spalling: Pits in the concrete, usually with fractured aggregate that may or may not have exposed rebar. They are caused by freeze-thaw, corrosion of reinforcing or AAR (alkali aggregate reactivity). Usually, if spalling is caused by AAR, the concrete around the spalled area is unsound and very soft.

15.10.2 Terms Used for Metal Inspection

Corrosion: This may consist of scaling or pitting. There will be loss of original metal due to electrolysis.

Cracks: Typically found on welds, adjacent to welds and in stress areas. They may be caused by metal fatigue or stress due to vibration, overloading, or impact.

Pitting: Dimples, pits, or holes in the steel caused by corrosion.

Scaling: Large flakes of corroded metal that cause the item to appear to be larger than it is. When scale is removed, usually there is a black, powdery layer (easily brushed off) with shiny white metal underneath.

Weld defects: Pores, undercut or foreign material trapped in a weld.

15.10.3 Terms Used for Timber Inspection

Cracks: Any breakage of the timber members that run across the grain of the wood. These are caused by deflection due to impact or overloading.

Crush damage: Timber fibers actually crushed due to impact or overloading. Collapsed timbers due to decay often appear crushed but are not.

Decay: Irregular holes and cavities that are often seen at the unprotected ends of treated timbers. Decay is caused by fungal organisms. Typically, these organisms prefer softer food and they often leave the knots untouched.

Marine borer activity: This is typically found on untreated timber at the mud line that looks exactly like what it is, worm-eaten wood.

Splits: Any breakage of the timber members that run with the grain. They are usually caused by twisting or deflection due to impact or other stress but may be caused in piling by excessive force in driving.

15.10.4 General Inspection Terminology

Anode: A zinc, aluminum or alloy ingot affixed to a metal structure or vessel to prevent corrosion.

Bent: A group of piling all connected to the same pile cap.

Bulkhead (structural, marine): A retaining wall built between two piers or docks to create a slip berth for vessels to moor in.

Bulkhead (nautical): A wall on a vessel that may be lateral (called transverse) or longitudinal (fore and aft).

Cantilever: A structure that is overhanging (may also be by design).

Condition: How the structure appears. A structure may be in either good or poor condition, but the shape remains the same. Do not use the term "shape" for condition.

Deflection: A condition in which the two ends of a structural member remain in the original location, but the center of the member is moved.

Deviation: When a structural member is not plumb, that member has a deviation from the vertical.

Fastener: A bolt, spike, rivet or screw used to join members of a structure or vessel.

Free span: An unsupported area under subsea pipeline or cable caused by scour or uneven bottom during the pipe or cable laying process.

Gains: Metal or concrete track on a dam or intake that a stop-log, gate or trash rack sets in.

Horizontal diagonal: Diagonal braces running in a horizontal direction between legs on offshore structures.

Lateral: Running perpendicular to the long dimension of a structure.

Leg: Vertical support on a bottom affixed offshore structure.

Longitudinal: Running parallel to the long dimension of a structure.

Mud mat: Wide plate at the base of a jacket platform leg. These are installed to help keep the jacket from sinking in the seabed until piles are driven through the legs during initial installation.

Orientate: To assign the four main points of the compass to sides of a structure.

Scour: Cavities around or beneath structures caused by natural water flow or propeller wash.

Skeg: The stern of the keel of a ship, especially the part connecting the keel with the rudderpost.

Vertical diagonal: Diagonal braces running vertically between legs on an offshore structure.

Z Drive: An azimuth thruster unit, often retractable, that serves as the main propulsion on some tugs.

16.0 NON-DESTRUCTIVE TESTING

When you consider the offshore, inshore, and inland marine structures and installations in all of the various countries in the world, they may well number in the millions. These include oil-field structures and facilities, offshore wind farm installations, dock and wharf structures in harbors, highway and rail bridge structures, and the many thousands of miles of pipeline running across the seabed in virtually every ocean.

The marine environment is extremely harsh and causes damage to marine structures both above and below the water surface. This considerably shortens the life span of the structures unless remedial work is performed, even when preventative measures are taken. Owners, users and insurers of the marine structures monitor this damage with structural inspections to enable them to take the appropriate measures to reduce damage and allow them to plan repair operations to extend the life span of the structure.

The inspection diver is a critical component in the process of monitoring the condition of marine structures. The information he collects during his inspection will be analyzed by engineers and ultimately will determine what preventative measures will be used or what repairs will be performed. ROV use is quite common in subsea inspection today, but there is still a great need for inspection divers that will not likely change in the foreseeable future.

Every vessel and offshore structure, most inshore marine structures and every road and rail bridge structure requires a regular structural inspection program. The reasons for the inspections are as follows:

- To obtain or renew certificates of seaworthiness or fitness from regulatory agencies.
- To accurately track ongoing damage, such as corrosion or ice damage.
- To ensure soundness or safety of installations for owners and insurers.
- To plan maintenance or structural repair programs.
- To assess structural condition following damage due to ship collision or extreme weather events.

16.1 INSPECTION AND TESTING OF MATERIALS

All materials used in the manufacture of engineered products (vessels, structures and pipelines) are tested, particularly those to be used in the marine environment and those to be used in the oil or transportation industries. Every length of pipe, every sheet of steel, every weld, every bolt and every load of concrete is subject to close inspection during construction. Certain elements are selected for closer inspection when there is reason to believe that there is a possibility of flaws or defects. Once the manufactured item is in use, the condition is monitored over its effective life span by an inspection program. There are two different methods of testing used to determine integrity of structures or structural components: destructive testing and non-destructive testing.

16.1.1 Destructive Testing
As the name suggests, this method of materials testing actually destroys a small sample of the material that is tested. This method is used primarily in the manufacturing stage but may also be used on in-service structures. Steel slugs are taken on occasion from in-service structures and a patch is welded over the hole. These slugs are then tested to give a representative sample of condition. Chain samples are taken from SBM moorings for testing. Structural bolts are taken for testing and core samples are taken from concrete. The bolts and are typically pulled to test tensile strength and tweaked laterally to test shear strength. The chain samples are pulled until they break to test break-strength. The concrete cores are crushed to test compressive strength. If destructive testing was the only method, eventually every structure would be poked and prodded full of holes, and it would come to a point where the testing was in fact harming the integrity of the structure.

16.1.2 Non-Destructive Testing (NDT)

The non-destructive method of testing materials and the physical properties of structures is the preferred method for in-use structures, as it does not alter the structure nor does it affect the structural integrity. However, NDT does allow the engineer to closely examine the structure's condition and make evaluations on effective life span, soundness and safety.

16.2 DEFECTS AND DAMAGE ON MARINE STRUCTURES

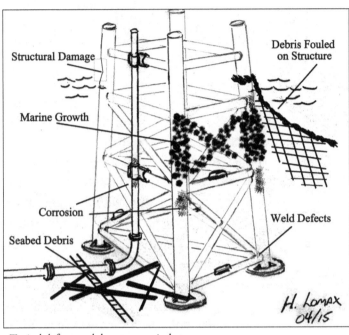

Typical defects and damage on a jacket

All underwater structural inspections performed are very similar regardless of the structure involved. The engineers all have one thing in common: they wish to evaluate the condition of the structure. A structural inspection, if performed properly, will always examine the following:

• Structural damage due to outside forces (ship impact, storm damage, ice damage)

• Marine growth on the structure

• Debris fouled on the structure

• Seabed debris accumulation

• Corrosion (steel structures or components)

• Concrete condition (concrete structures)

• Defects related to original construction (weld defects or concrete defects)

16.2.1 Structural Damage

Structural damage is the term used to indicate obvious defects to the structure (broken concrete, flattened or buckled steel members) typically caused by outside forces while the structure is in service. These outside forces include ship impact, storm damage, damage caused by ice, damage due to currents or tides. The structural damage is typically noticed during the visual or video portion of the inspection and may include:

• Dents, buckled, or flattened areas of steel members
• Broken or missing structural members
• Cracked, spalled, or broken concrete
• Paint or epoxy coatings chipped or scraped off
• Damage to boat landings, ladders, stairs, or handrails
• Damaged power or control cables or cable-ducts
• Scouring at the base of the structure
• Damaged or broken anodes or anode brackets
• Damage to risers or riser clamps
• Damage to fire water lines
• Damage to instrumentation (tide sensors, wave monitors, transducers, etc.)

All structural damage is carefully documented, usually with both video and stills. Damage is located using sketches of the structure and the damaged areas are carefully measured, with the measurements noted. The presence of damage (particularly impact damage) will cause the inspection diver to look closely at adjacent areas for stress damage (such as, cracks in concrete or in welds) which are also carefully documented.

16.2.2 Marine Growth

Virtually every marine structure is, to some extent, fouled with marine growth. The longer any given structure is in service, the larger the volume of marine growth, up to the point where it becomes one 100% covered to maximum sustainable thickness. At that point any marine growth that cannot be supported will be dropped to the seabed. Marine growth poses a problem for marine structures for the following reasons:

- The profile area of the structure or components of the structure is increased causing water flow and wave action to exert more force on the structure. Due to the nature of marine growth colonization, this condition is worst near the surface where wave action is greatest.
- Marine growth changes the cross-sectional profile of the structural members causing greater drag in the currents. This causes, among other things, scouring at the seabed elevation.
- Marine growth encasement makes it difficult to properly inspect a structure without removal.
- Marine growth blocks seawater intakes and discharges for cooling water pumps, fire-fighting pumps, desalination systems, and other systems.
- Marine growth affects the rates of corrosion on steel structures. In some instances, biological corrosion of the structure caused by the presence of marine growth takes place.

Marine growth is generally classified as being one of two types: soft fouling or hard fouling. Soft fouling, the first type to attach to a new installation, includes algae, bacteria, sponges, sea squirts, anemones, and sea grasses. Hard-fouling marine growth includes barnacles and mussels.

Soft-fouling marine growth: sea grass, coral, and rockweed

Hard-fouling marine growth: barnacles and mussels.

The marine growth on structures is noted during the inspection, with the percentage of cover (0 – 100%) noted. Marine growth will have to be removed to some extent on all inspections; the least of which would be to examine cathodic protection system elements such as sacrificial anodes and to take measurements. In some cases, a more detailed inspection is required, and all marine growth is removed from the structure.

16.2.3 Debris Fouled on the Structure

At first glance, the significance of debris fouled on the structure may seem totally irrelevant to a structural inspection. However, the debris most commonly found fouled is rope and commercial fishing nets. These items become caught on features such as anodes, ladders, instrumentation lines and intakes. They then pose a threat to surface craft that regularly approach the structures. The threat is not only to the water craft but to the structural features as well. Countless anodes are broken off when fouled with rope or fishing net that becomes wound in propellers of service vessels. The debris itself also becomes a home for marine growth, which increases the problems that marine growth poses. In addition, fouled debris poses a risk of fouling to the divers performing inspection and maintenance work on the structure. Fouled debris removal is often specified in inspection contracts, but when it is not, the amount, nature and location of debris is reported.

16.2.4 Seabed Debris Accumulation

To anyone who has never actually seen the seabed surrounding a marine structure, the presence of seabed debris might seem a strange concept. But bridges, docks and offshore structures all require both the initial construction and constant repair and these operations generate huge amounts of debris. Scrap steel, cable ends, dropped tools and scaffolding, pieces of chain, ladders, even steel toolboxes dropped overboard all contribute to the seabed debris. Like fouled debris, this seabed debris may not seem relevant to a structural inspection, other than as a hazard to the inspection diver. However, seabed debris often is steel or other ferrous metal and the presence of this debris may cause the following problems to a marine structure:

- Inhibit the ability of the cathodic protection system to properly protect the structure
- Galvanic (dissimilar metals) corrosion where debris is in contact with the structure
- Fretting corrosion due to vibration or movement of debris caused by underwater currents
- Foul control cables for seabed level equipment or systems
- Impact damage to the structure or other features while debris is falling to the seabed
- Increased seabed scouring around the base of the structure

Seabed debris removal is not usually part of the inspection contract. The type, amount and exact location of all seabed debris must be recorded in the inspection report to allow the client to have it removed later.

16.2.5 Corrosion of Steel Structure or its Components

Whenever a piece of metal is placed in water, the process of corrosion occurs. When that same metal is placed in seawater, corrosion occurs at a greatly accelerated rate. Due to the superior strength, flexibility, low cost and ease of workability of mild steel, it is the material of choice for most marine structures. Steel does have a downside, as far as the marine environment goes: it is an active metal. This means that when immersed, it gives off electrons readily: unless it is protected, steel corrodes fast underwater. There are several types of corrosion that occur on steel structures:

- General corrosion
- Pitting and scaling corrosion
- Galvanic corrosion
- Fretting corrosion
- Crevice corrosion
- Flow corrosion
- Biological corrosion
- Metal fatigue

16.2.5.1 General Corrosion

General corrosion is the term used when a steel structure or element has corroded over much of the surface area in a uniform manner. That is, all areas appear to be corroding at an equal rate with no significant loss of metal in any one area.

16.2.5.2 Pitting and Scaling Corrosion

Pitting and Scaling Corrosion are different from general corrosion in that they tend to be more localized and the surface corrosion is not uniform. Pitting is the term used when the metal surface is marked with dimples or pits of varying depth. Pitting tends to occur with multiple pits in one pitted area with adjacent areas seemingly free of pitting. Scaling is the term used when the metal surface is covered in heavy corrosion buildup (called scale). This often appears as if the surface of the metal has swollen outward. When scaling is removed, there is often a jet-black soft layer underneath (manganese compounds) that may be brushed away easily by hand, to expose shiny white metal beneath.

16.2.5.3 Galvanic Corrosion

Galvanic Corrosion also called dissimilar metals corrosion occurs when two metals both come in contact with an electrolyte, in this case, salt water. The more active metal will act as an anode and sacrifice itself to save the more noble metal that acts as a cathode. (See Section 16.4: Cathodic Protection.)

16.2.5.4 Fretting Corrosion

Fretting Corrosion occurs when there are two pieces of metal pressed hard against one another and one or both of them has regular movement. This movement cleans corrosion off the metal, much like a grinder, which then allows fresh corrosion to take place. Chain links suffer from fretting corrosion, as do riser clamps on offshore platforms.

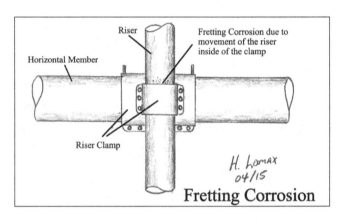

Fretting Corrosion

16.2.5.5 Crevice Corrosion

Crevice Corrosion is a condition in which the metal actually dissolves and forms a metallic ion solution inside a crevice in the metal. Outside the crevice, there is a lower concentration of metal ions than inside. The metal outside the crevice will start going into solution at a faster rate trying to reach a state of equilibrium. Moving seawater outside the crevice carries this ion solution away, causing the need for more metal to go into solution.

16.2.5.6 Flow Corrosion

Flow Corrosion sometimes called "erosion corrosion," is typically seen in pipelines and risers both subsea and surface. It most often occurs at elbows, reducers, bends and valves, where the flow is interrupted and particles contained in the fluid impact the interior pipeline wall. Flow corrosion also is occasionally seen on steel structures exposed to very strong subsea currents.

16.2.5.7 Biological Corrosion

Biological Corrosion is the name given to corrosion caused by marine biological action. This is often the result of marine growth on the structure and can happen in one of the following ways:

- By producing corrosive substances such as hydrogen sulfide or ammonia, which chemically attack the metal
- By producing or actually being a catalyst in the corrosive action
- By the reaction of sulfate-reducing bacteria (SRB) under anaerobic conditions (indications are that since oxygen cannot diffuse through heavy marine growth, this bacteria substitutes itself for the oxygen in the usual cathodic reaction)
- By the formation of concentration cells around and under the organisms

16.2.5.8 Metal Fatigue

Metal Fatigue is the failure of metals due to repetitive stress (bending, flexing). Although metal fatigue is not really corrosion, when this occurs in a severely corrosive environment, the damage is usually exponentially worse. Typically, the failure will begin with one single, large fatigue crack that leads to sudden, catastrophic failure. Marine structures are subject to this type of stress and corrosion due to the following conditions: exposure to seawater, current and wave action; and live and static loads and vibration.

16.2.6 Concrete Condition

Although there are not as many methods of non-destructive testing for concrete marine structures or concrete components of marine structures, it is none-the-less very important to monitor their condition. The NDT methods available for concrete structures include ultrasound testing and cathode potential readings on the rebar steel. The inspector will want to examine the structure for the following in-service damage: spalling, de-lamination, exposed rebar and cracks. As with any other structural defects or damage observed in an underwater inspection, these need to be carefully recorded, sized, and located in the inspection report.

16.2.7 Defects Related to Original Construction

Often during a structural inspection, defects will be identified that are related to the original construction of the structure. On a concrete structure, the following construction related flaws might be seen: honeycombing, laitance, cold joints and marks from form removal. On a steel structure, weld deformities might be seen, including: pitting, porosity, slag inclusion, insufficient penetration and undercut. Any construction related defects should be noted along with the measurements and location of each defect in the inspection report.

16.3 NON-DESTRUCTIVE TESTING METHODS

The typical in-situ structural inspection utilizes a few, but not all of the NDT methods. Most regularly scheduled inspections consist of the following: close visual inspection; video inspection; confirming measurements; still photographs; ultra-sonic thickness testing and cathode potential readings. Another commonly used NDT method is flooded member detection, but it is performed less often than the UT and CP readings. The non-destructive testing methods used underwater are:

- Visual, video and still photography
- Ultrasonic thickness testing
- Cathode potential testing
- Flooded member detection
- Magnetic particle inspection
- Magnetographic flaw detection
- Radiography
- Electromagnetic detection
- Alternating current field measurement
- Alternating current potential drop

16.3.1 Visual, Video and Still Photography

Typically, when one thinks of non-destructive testing, visual, video and still photography would not come to mind, but for the overall picture of a structure's condition, there is no better method. The human eye sees in 3 dimensions and catches many items and conditions that would otherwise go unnoticed. Once the diver has seen it, he can measure it and then video it or obtain a still photograph. There is more information on video and stills in Chapter 20: Underwater -Photography and Video.

16.3.2 Ultrasonic Thickness Testing

Ultrasonic Thickness (UT) testing is used most often to confirm the thickness of steel on the various members of a structure, but it may also be used to detect internal flaws. A transducer is held firmly against the steel and high frequency sound waves are sent through the steel. There are two types of UT devices: the A-scan unit, which is surface monitored on a CRT monitor, with umbilical cables that run

to the diver and the digital handheld type, which the diver reads out. The A-scan units must be calibrated prior to each use. The digital units are pre-calibrated but a reference block reading is taken before use to confirm calibration. Marine growth is scraped away to expose the steel surface prior to taking readings to allow the transducer to be held firmly against the steel. In order to use these devices on the surface, a couplant such as petroleum jelly or grease must be smeared on the steel to carry the sound waves. The handheld units on the market today will read through most protective coatings, including epoxies. Lower frequency UT is sometimes used to obtain thickness measurements and detect internal flaws in concrete.

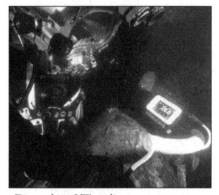
Diver taking UT readings
Photo courtesy of Cygnus Instruments

16.3.3 Cathode Potential Testing

Cathode Potential (CP) readings do not detect defects or damage. They confirm that the steel structure (or steel within a concrete structure) is acting as a cathode, as opposed to acting as an anode. CP readings are taken with a handheld unit (CP Meter) with a digital readout on one end and a probe on the other. The probe is stabbed (pushed hard into) the steel and a reading of the DC current present (usually just under 0.8V) in the structure is taken. CP meter calibration is tested before each use by using a steel block and a zinc block in a clean bucket of seawater.

Diver taking CP readings on a jacket
Photo courtesy of Simon Jarrold

16.3.4 Flooded Member Detection

Tubular steel marine structures are typically designed to have all tubular members (except those that have piling driven down through them) remain dry inside for the life of the structure. This serves two purposes: it reduces the load on the structure and it eliminates internal corrosion. For this reason, each member of the structure is separated from the adjacent ones by a bulkhead or the wall of the adjacent member. A member will become flooded only when there is some sort of structural failure. Flooded member detection (FMD) may be performed using two methods: radiography or ultrasound. Radiography FMD is always performed using an ROV. Ultrasound FMD is performed using a diver and an A-scan UT unit with a stand-off bracket attached to the unit. FMD readings are always taken at the 6 o'clock position on horizontal or horizontal-diagonal members and at the lowest possible set-up location on vertical or vertical-diagonal members. The readings are taken on surface, usually by an engineer or engineering technician.

16.3.5 Magnetic Particle Inspection

A process that can only be used on ferrous metal structures or objects, magnetic particle inspection (MPI) is a method of detecting surface or near surface cracks in steel or iron. A strong magnet is used to magnetize the area to be inspected and ink (an oil-like substance with suspended metallic particles) is spread on the same area. Excess ink is wiped off and an ultraviolet light (eg. Blackbirn) is shone on the area to reveal the cracks for video or

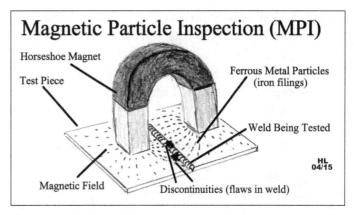

still photos. This process is often done at the nodes on jacket legs (the point where the horizontals and diagonals meet the vertical legs) as these are high stress areas.

16.3.6 Magnetographic Flaw Detection

Using the same principles as MPI, a magnetic tape is laid on the surface to be tested by divers. The tape makes a magnetic "impression" of the area including cracks and flaws. The tape is then brought to surface and analyzed by a magnetographic flaw detector that translates the information on the tape into a digital image. All surfaces to be tested using this method must be cleaned to bare metal. This process works only on ferrous metal structures or ferrous metal structural components.

16.3.7 Radiography

Radiography is photography that uses x-ray or gamma-ray (γ-ray) radiation instead of visible light rays to leave an image on film. The production of x-rays requires very bulky equipment (think hospital x-ray machines) and very high voltage, therefore it is not used underwater. Gamma (γ-ray) radiation requires a source (Iridium 192) in a radiation proof housing and film cassettes. The diver places the film cassettes and the housing (usually held in place by ratchet strap), and moves away (usually 25 feet) from the target area. The housing has a surface controlled remote aperture that opens for a pre-set time period to fully

Radiography unit

expose the film to the radiation. Once the aperture has been closed, the diver recovers the film and sets up the next shot. Typically, three shots are taken at different points for each deployment. These operations are most often performed with both a diver and ROV working together. All personnel on radiography work require specialized training and dosimeters (badges) are worn to measure radiation exposure.

The photo above shows a radiography unit, mounted on a short section of pipe. The two lines in the foreground are air lines to open and close the aperture. The canister contains the radioactive isotope, and the entire set up is held in place by ratchet straps.

16.3.8 Electromagnetic Detection

Used to locate stress cracks in both ferrous and non-ferrous metals, electromagnetic detection (also called eddy current testing) is a method that can be used on structures with protective coatings. It can also be used to check the thickness of the protective coatings. This system is surface monitored. An electromagnetic probe is brought into close proximity to the metal to be tested, inducing a circular AC current pattern (eddy current) on the surface of the metal. Interruptions in the pattern (caused by cracks) show up on a CRT display topside. Electromagnetic Detection (EMD) is widely used offshore for weld inspection.

16.3.9 Alternating Current Field Measurement

Alternating current field measurement (ACFM) has all but replaced MPI in offshore NDT inspections. It is a combination of the EMD and ACPD methods, and obtains results on almost all metals, ferrous and non-ferrous, through protective coatings up to 5mm thick. Another surface-monitored and surface-interpreted method, ACFM measures both the length and depth of cracks and the results can be recorded and stored.

16.3.10 Alternating Current Potential Drop

ACPD is not used to locate cracks or defects in metals. It is used to measure the depth of cracks or flaws. Two probes, called field probes, are brought in contact with the metal surface and a mild AC current is generated between them. Another probe with two contacts is placed straddling the crack or defect and measures the resistance caused by the crack or flaw, which is then recorded on surface by a technician.

ACPD field probes and measurement probe

16.4 CATHODIC PROTECTION

Whenever a piece of metal is placed in water, the process of corrosion occurs. When that same metal is placed in seawater, corrosion occurs at a greatly accelerated rate. The salt in seawater makes it a better electrolyte, allowing the metal to give off electrons at a higher rate. Different metals give off electrons at different rates. Active metals give off more electron and noble metals give off fewer electrons in this process known as electrolysis. The chart below illustrates noble and active metals.

There are different methods of protecting metallic structures from corrosion. The following methods are used either individually or with more than one method on a given structure, with varying degrees of success.

Noble Metals
- Stainless Steel
- Titanium
- Copper
- Copper / Nickel
- Brass
- Lead
- Tin
- Iron
- Steel
- Aluminum
- Zinc

In seawater, a more active metal will always act as a sacrificial anode and protect the more noble metal, provided there is good electrical contact. For example, tin will protect brass and aluminum and zinc will protect steel.

Active Metals

- Protective coatings (paints, epoxies)
- Encasement with concrete
- Cathodic protection systems

In order to provide cathodic protection for a metallic item or structure, we must set up what has become known as a corrosion cell. In a corrosion cell, there are four components that are absolutely essential:

- A cathode (the item that requires protection from corrosion)
- An anode (the item that corrodes)
- An electrolyte (a fluid that allows a mild DC current to flow via chemical ions)
- Good electrical contact between the cathode and the anode

Cathodic protection may be provided for a metallic vessel or structure using one of two methods: sacrificial anodes or impressed current anodes. The difference between the two methods is explained below.

16.4.1 Sacrificial Anodes

Looking at the chart of metals above, we see the more noble metals are toward the top and more active metals are toward the bottom. Since stainless steel is at the top of the list, any metal below that point will act as an anode to protect stainless steel because it will give off electrons (corrode) at a faster rate than the stainless steel. Notice also that below iron and steel are aluminum and zinc. Both of these metals may then be used as an anode for iron or steel. Based on the chart, we can understand that we require an anode of a more active metal to sacrifice itself to protect a cathode metal, hence the term "sacrificial anode."

Ship anodes are typically zinc because ships are steel, and when they are in for scheduled dry-dock visits, the anodes can be easily replaced. But since zinc is more active than aluminum (and therefore is consumed faster), most of the sacrificial anodes installed on marine structures are aluminum or an aluminum/zinc alloy. The aluminum is still more active than steel, but is not consumed (by electrolysis) as quickly as zinc is, thus reducing the frequency of anode replacement.

Sacrificial anodes are typically cast of molten aluminum, zinc or an alloy, with a steel rod or bar inserted into the molten metal. This allows the anode to be welded onto the steel of the ship or structure that the anode will be protecting. Installation by welding ensures good electrical contact, which is

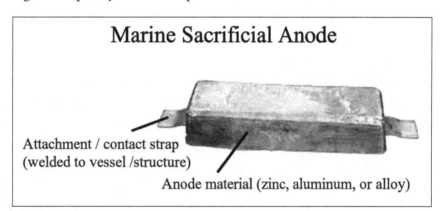

essential in order for the anode to work properly and protect the cathode (ship or structure).

In recent years, several anode manufacturers have begun supplying anodes for marine structures with bolt on brackets. There is a bracket that is welded to the structure, and the anode then bolts to the bracket with a sharpened "contact screw" that is tightened to ensure a good connection. This saves time and cost when the anodes require replacement every few years.

Another method of installing sacrificial anodes is to use an "anode sled" attached by an electrical wire to the structure to be protected. The use of sleds is recommended any time that there is a danger of stand-off anodes being fouled or broken off by ships, ice, floating debris or other hazards. First electrical

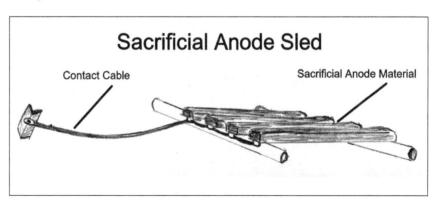

contact brackets are welded to the structure. Then the anode sleds (pictured above) are placed in a safe location on the seabed. Heavy wire (welding cable) is then run to connect the contact brackets and the anode sleds.

16.4.2 Impressed Current Cathodic Protection

The other method of providing cathodic protection to marine structures is by way of an impressed current system. The impressed current system also uses anodes, but the anodes are not constructed of more active metals than the structure. This is because instead of letting natural current occur, a transformer is used to "impress" a mild DC current (with the anode negative) that then protects the structure by making it the cathode in the system. The anodes are either isolated stand-off anodes attached to the structure or remote anodes located on the seabed as anode sleds or anode blocks.

16.5 CERTIFICATION FOR NON-DESTRUCTIVE TESTING

Most often, when a client requires non-destructive testing on a vessel or structure, they will insist on having divers who carry a recognized certification to perform the inspection or at least the NDT portion of the inspection. There are a couple of different NDT certifications available.

16.5.1 ASNT

On inland and coastal marine structures within the United States the accepted and recommended certification is the American Society for Non-Destructive Testing (ASNT) certification. The ASNT certifies inspectors at one of the following levels:

- The level I inspector may perform NDT inspections and perform field calibrations on the test equipment used.
- Level II inspectors may do all of the above plus interpret and evaluate the inspection results.
- Level III inspectors may perform any or all of the above plus establish new techniques, designate the methodology for any given inspection and interpret standards or codes that have been previously established.

16.5.2 CSWIP

Offshore structures and any other structures directly related to the oil-patch are normally regulated by OGP (Oil and Gas Producers International), and OGP insists on CSWIP inspections of all oil production facilities. CSWIP, a certification scheme originally started by The Welding Institute in the UK, originally was an acronym for Certification Scheme for Welding Inspection Personnel and was meant for surface welding inspectors only. Since that time, the scope has broadened to include diving and ROV inspectors and certification training is provided in many locations around the world. There are four levels of underwater certification:

- 3.1U is for inspection divers, including visual, video, stills, UT and CP readings
- 3.2U is for inspection divers as above but includes all of the NDT welding inspection methods
- 3.3U is the 3.2U equivalent for ROV pilot inspectors
- 3.4U is for inspection coordinators

16.6 GLOSSARY OF TERMS

-A-

Anode: Negatively charged metallic object in the corrosion cell that gives off electrons, thereby protecting the positively charged object (the cathode)

ACFM: Alternating Current Field Measurement

ACPD: Alternating Current Potential Drop

ASNT: American Society for Non-Destructive Testing

-C-

Corrosion: The process by which metals degrade by giving off electrons through an electrochemical reaction. It is typically greatly accelerated when the process occurs in seawater.

CP: Cathodic potential is a value measured to predict the rate of corrosion on a given item.

Crack: A distinct gap or opening in a material that is not always visible to the naked eye.

CRT: Cathode-ray tube is often used in surface monitors for various NDT units.

-D-

Debris: Any materials that do not belong in their present location which includes but is not limited to construction or renovation refuse, scrap material, and abandoned fishing lines or nets.

Destructive testing: The process of testing materials using various methods, whereby a representative (often random) sample is cut from the material in order to be tested and a patch is installed to make good.

-E-

Eddy Current: The circular current set up by the electromagnetic detection technique.

Electrolysis: An electrochemical process having measureable DC electrical activity (natural or induced) that occurs when metals corrode.

Erosion corrosion: More commonly known as flow corrosion

-F-

Ferrous metals: Iron or metals containing iron, such as steel.

Ferromagnetic: Strongly attracted to either pole of a magnet. Ferromagnetic materials such as iron or steel contain unpaired electrons that align when exposed to external magnetic fields.

Flow corrosion: Corrosion caused either by the rapid movement of a fluid against a metal (inside a pipe) or the rapid movement of a metal object through a stationary fluid (ship's propeller).

Fouling: Encrustation or entanglement such as marine growth encrustation, known as fouling, and fishing net entanglement, known as fowling.

-G-

Galvanic corrosion: Also known as dissimilar metals corrosion, galvanic corrosion occurs when dissimilar metals are both immersed in an electrolyte and the more active metals give off electrons (corrode), thereby becoming the anode and making the more noble metal the cathode.

Gamma rays: Gamma rays have the shortest wavelength and contain the most energy. This is the only type of radiation used in underwater radiography.

-I-

Iridium 192: The radioactive element used in underwater radiography to produce Gamma or γ-rays. This element is extremely hazardous, must be kept in shielded containers and must only be handled by properly trained personnel.

-M-

Magnetic flux leakage: A phenomenon where a magnetic field is interrupted and identifies cracks, pits and corrosion on steel structures and is used in various NDT techniques

Marine growth: This term is used for all of the various marine plants and animals that attach themselves to marine structures due to the shelter they provide.

Magnetographic tape: Tape used in the magnetic flaw detection method that is placed on a steel structure to detect flux leakage that indicates flaws.

MPI: Magnetic Particle Inspection

-N-

NDT: Non-destructive testing

Non-destructive testing: The process of testing materials using various methods where the material is left undamaged by the testing process.

Non-ferrous metals: Metals or alloys that contain no iron or very little iron (such as stainless steel). Non-ferrous metals are highly conductive, non-magnetic and lighter than ferrous metals.

-R-

Radiography: The process of producing a photographic image using radiation rays (x-rays or γ-rays) instead of light rays to activate the film emulsion.

-T-

Transducer: A device that transmits and receives a signal (usually sonic, or ultra-sonic). Transducers are always connected to an interpretation device (ultrasound unit or depth sounder) usually by coaxial cable.

-U-

UT: Ultrasonic testing

Ultrasound: Extremely high frequency sound waves (above hearing range) used to measure thickness.

17.0 TOOLS USED UNDERWATER

The commercial diver is expected to be a carpenter, a pipe fitter, a ditch digger, a concrete mason, an iron-worker, an electrician, a photographer, and a ship builder, depending upon the underwater project the diver happens to be working on. Since the diver is expected to perform the duties of these various trades, the diver also should have at least a basic knowledge of the tools required and be aware of the safety requirements to avoid injury.

17.1 HAND TOOLS

Few, if any, underwater operations will be performed without the use of at least some tools. The tools most often used are hand tools. The diver never carries tools with him on his descent or ascent. Hand tools are always lowered either individually on tool lines (messengers), lowered several at a time in a bucket or lowered in a large steel toolbox that is set on bottom close to the work site. The canvas tool buckets used underwater are

Two different types of canvas tool bucket. Photos courtesy of Klein Tools

the same as those used by linesmen but with two differences: They have drainage holes with brass grommets around the bottom and usually there is a lead weight inside.

Almost any item immersed underwater becomes a home for marine growth and, in order to perform any work, usually some or all of the marine growth has to be removed. For small areas, this is accomplished with a hand scraper or the diver's knife. The scraper is the most used hand tool. Other hand tools used by the diver, in order of frequency used are: the measuring tape, the adjustable wrench and the sledgehammer. Most often, the sledgehammer is 6 – 8 pound, with a short handle.

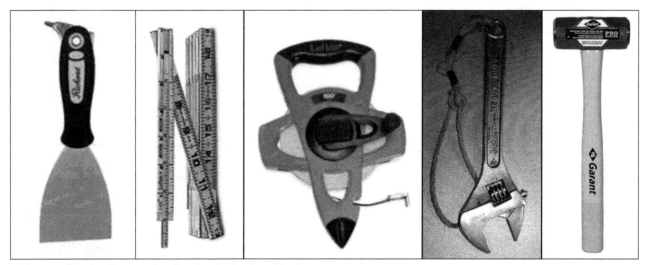

Selection of hand tools most often found in the diver's tool bucket
Photos courtesy of A. Richard Tools, Lufkin Tools, Lufkin Tools, Author, and Garant Tools respectively

Any number of other hand tools are used, including wood chisels, crowbars, ratchets, open and box end wrenches, screwdrivers, and many others. Some tools hold up to repeated underwater use while some fall apart after one single use. Any tool used in salt water should be rinsed off with freshwater after use. Usually hand tools have a short rope lanyard attached, made of ¼ inch rope, to allow for easy location and attachment.

17.2 EXCAVATION TOOLS

Silt, which consists of topsoil, plant matter and fine sand, runs off the land and into brooks, streams and rivers, where it is then carried toward the ocean. At the same time, sand from the ocean is carried around by wave action and ocean currents. Usually, this moving silt is deposited exactly where you least want it to be: exactly where you need to work. Most underwater jobsites require at least some silt removal and others require extensive excavation. The tool used depends on the amount of material to move and the distance it needs to move. A water jet will move silt short distances and is good for burying a subsea pipeline. If, however, you must remove three feet of silt to expose a pipeline flange, an airlift is the best choice. Airlifts suck up material (silt, sand, gravel) and deposit it much farther away. The airlift works on the Venturi principle. Air is injected into the pipe close to the nozzle. As the air rises up the pipe, a venturi creates suction, which draws anything in front of it up through the tube: silt, sand, or gravel.

There are other methods of excavation, including air lances, trash pumps and gravel pumps, but the most often seen methods on underwater projects are the airlift and the water jet.

 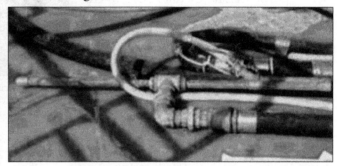

Intake end of 10-inch airlift   Underwater nozzle for water jet

17.3 TOOLS FOR TIMBER WORK

When working with timber underwater, the requirements are similar to those used on the surface. You must have a method to cut the timber, and in order to fasten pieces together, you must have methods to drill the timber and to tighten the bolts that fasten the timber together.

If there are very few cuts, a normal bucksaw might be used, but most often a pneumatic or hydraulic powered chainsaw is utilized for cutting timber underwater. Pneumatic and hydraulic saws, drills and impacts operate the same as your own electric ones, however, they are powered differently.

Diver cutting timber cribwork with hydraulic chainsaw
Photo: Stanley Hydraulics

Pneumatic tools are fine for shallow water but are ineffective beyond 60 fsw while hydraulic tools (ROV mounted) have been used at close to 4000 fsw.

Hydraulic drill   Hydraulic impact wrench

Hydraulic chainsaw
Photos courtesy of Stanley Hydraulics

Each hydraulic or pneumatic tool has specific operating pressures and flow rates. If insufficient pressure and flow is supplied to the tool, it will not have enough speed or torque. If the pressure and flow are too great, damage will be done to the tools. Pressure and flow must be monitored and adjusted for each tool used. As with woodworking on the surface, a sharp tool makes a good carpenter. A sharp tool is also a safer tool for the diver to use. It is imperative that the auger bitts used with the drill and the chainsaw chains be kept sharp. Spare chains and bitts allow sharpening to be performed while the work is ongoing.

17.4 TOOLS FOR CONCRETE WORK

Specialized tools are used for working with concrete. Circular cut-off saws with diamond blades are used for making straight cuts, breakers are used to chip out concrete and drilling is done by two different types of drill: rotary hammer drill and diamond core drill. The rotary hammer is used for smaller diameter holes, such as those used for wedge anchors. The diamond core drill is used for larger diameter holes, such as those used for installing epoxy rock anchors. Usually these tools are hydraulically driven.

Both types of drills have a third hose, where most hydraulic tools have two hoses. The hammer drill has an air hose, to allow the cuttings to be blown out of the hole. If this is not done on a regular basis, the bit will become hopelessly jammed in the concrete. These hammer drill bits are carbide tipped and are quite expensive. The diamond core drill has a water hose. The water flows through the drill string and bit for lubrication and cooling during the drilling and cannot be stopped without stopping the drill, or damage will be done to the diamond bit. These bits are very expensive. Often a core drill is used with a bolt-on drill press assembly to maintain drill alignment.

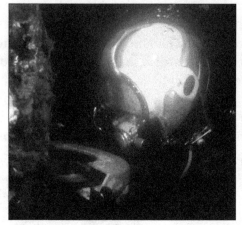

Diver using cut-off saw
Photos courtesy of Stanley Hydraulics

Diver using breaker

Cut-off saw
Photos courtesy of Stanley
Hydraulics

Jack-hammer
(breaker)

Hammer drill

17.5 TOOLS FOR STEEL WORK

Many of the same tools seen in your neighborhood welding shop are used underwater on steelwork. The differences are that they are air or hydraulic powered instead of electric powered when used underwater. They typically have sealed, watertight bearings. The most commonly used drill for steel work underwater is the hydraulic/magnetic drill. This is a drill press held in place magnetically that has a slug cutter bit. The grinders used are very similar and the exact same grinding disks are used as are used on surface. For more information on the welding and cutting of steel, see Chapter 12: Marine Construction.

The hand tools used in steel work such as wire brushes, chipping hammers, ball-peen hammers, coal chisels, C-clamps and punches are identical to those used in surface steelwork.

Diver using hydraulic grinder
Photo courtesy of Stanley Hydraulics

Hydraulic angle grinder

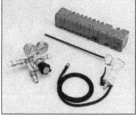
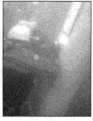

Hydraulic
magnetic drill
Photo courtesy of
MagDrill

Broco underwater cutting
torch
Photo courtesy of Broco
Underwater

Diver welding
anode on pipe pile

17.6 TOOLS FOR REMOVING MARINE GROWTH, CORROSION, AND DEFECTIVE CONCRETE

As stated earlier, every underwater structure becomes, to some extent, covered in marine growth. In order to perform work, regardless if it is a detailed inspection or a repair, the diver first has to remove the marine growth. If it is a large area that must be cleaned, a hand scraper will obviously not suffice. In addition to marine growth, often there are areas of corroded steel or defective concrete that must be removed in order to perform a repair on a marine structure. The tool that divers use most often to cover a large area is the high-pressure water blaster. These are not your basic backyard high-pressure washer, nor are they the commercial car wash unit. Typically, these machines have a 6- or 8-cylinder diesel driving a very high volume, high pressure pump, that puts out nozzle pressures in between 6,000 and 20,000 pounds per square inch at the tip. These units will cut through a 2 × 4 quicker than a chainsaw, and, if passed over the toe of a rubber boot, they will cut it (and the toes inside) off, so they must be used carefully at all times.

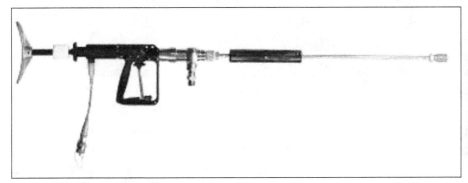

A typical high-pressure water blast gun
Photo courtesy of Woma

Barnacle buster on a hydraulic grinde
Photo courtesy of Darin Baumann

Smaller areas of extremely heavy growth, corroded steel or defective concrete are often cleaned with a "barnacle buster." This is an aggressive rotary brush device mounted on a hydraulic grinder. It is just as effective as the name suggests for barnacles. These units are used on offshore jacket structure legs to clean locations to install riser clamps and they will clean off all coatings to white metal.

17.7 PIPELINE CONSTRUCTION AND REPAIR TOOLS

There are many different tools used in offshore pipeline work. We will look primarily at the tools unique to these particular operations, in order to familiarize you with these tools.

In order to join two pipeline ends together, short sections of pipe (spool pieces) are used. When installing a spool piece, it is critical that the length is correct (usually within ¼ inch) and that the angle of the bolting flange on each end is correct. Metrology is the term used for measuring and angle calculation for spool piece fabrication. In order to get exact measurements and angles, metrology tables are used.

Pipeline metrology table (master unit
Photos courtesy of Darin Baumann

Protractors on metrology table

One table is installed on each pipeline flange. The tables are adjusted so that they are perfectly level and plumb. The measuring cable is stretched between the master unit (with cable spool) and the slave unit. The cable clamps are installed to mark the length of the spool piece and the vertical and horizontal angles are read off of the protractors. It is critical to have the metrology tables set up exactly level and plumb and securely clamped down before any measurements and angles are taken. These measurements and angles allow the field engineers to draw an accurate blueprint of the spool piece, which is then fabricated on the surface. Once fabrication is complete and the welds are x-rayed, the spool piece is installed by the divers.

Subsea pipelines vary in size from 2 inch to 48 inch in diameter. The typical flange connection is made by bolting. On smaller diameter pipelines (less than 12 inch), the engineers quite often will accept bolt tightening using a hydraulic impact gun. On the larger pipelines, a hydraulic bolt tensioning system is usually used. With a bolt tensioning system, specially designed hydraulic

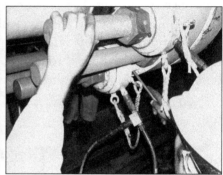

Bolt tensioning jack before installation   Bolt tensioning a flange on the surface

jacks are used to actually stretch the flange bolts. As the bolts are stretched, the nuts are tightened up against the flange, maintaining the tension. The pressures on the bolt tensioning system start out low and are increased on successive passes. The final pass pressure can go above 20,000 psi, depending on the size of the pipeline and the series of the flange. These bolt tensioning systems are often called "hydra-tight" units, which is also one of the manufacturers. Divers are typically used to tension any bolts on the surface, as well; startup heads, lay-down heads, and dummy spools.

Before hydraulic bolt tensioning systems were available for pipeline work, divers used a tool known as a hammer wrench (flogging spanner) in order to tension the pipeline bolts. These wrenches come in all of the common flange bolt sizes, from very small, to large enough that two men are required to lift them. Hammer wrenches are still used on every project to test the bolts. After the bolts have been tensioned, the divers go over every bolt with the hammer wrench to double check. As the name suggests, the hammer wrench is operated by hitting it with a sledgehammer that is usually an 8- or 10-pound hammer.

A typical hammer wrench
Photo courtesy of Darin Baumann

Even though hydraulic impact wrenches are not used for the final tensioning on pipeline flanges, they are quite often used to initially draw the flanges together. Barnacle busters are often used to clean marine growth off the flanges. In addition, hand tools such as calipers, tape measures, sledgehammers, scrapers, spud wrenches, and pry bars are used on pipeline work.

Quite often on offshore pipeline projects, an existing pipeline must be cut in order perform a subsea tie-in to a new line. Since most offshore pipelines carry petroleum products, this effectively rules out using ultrathermic cutting gear unless the pipeline can be thoroughly flushed out. The tool used to safely cut petroleum pipelines is the guillotine saw. This tool is basically a hydraulically powered industrial hacksaw and it makes short work of a pipeline.

Hydraulic guillotine saw with power pack

17.8 INSPECTION TOOLS

When performing structural inspections on marine structures, often water blasters, scrapers or barnacle busters are used, depending on the level of inspection. Standard measuring devices such as tapes, rulers, pit gauges and vernier calipers are used for sizing structural members and measuring damage, corrosion or defects. Specific inspection tools are used as well. These include cathode potential (CP) meters and ultrasound (UT) thickness gauges as shown in the following photographs.

CP meter on lying deck and being used underwater by a diver
Photos courtesy of Deepwater Corrosion Services

CP meters are calibrated on site before any readings are taken during the inspection. One small block of steel and one of zinc are placed into a bucket of seawater (or fresh, depending on the inspection location) and the probe is pushed against each one in turn and the readings recorded. The CP meter gives a digital readout of the cathode potential, which indicates to the engineers the degree to which the cathodic protection system is actually working on the structure being tested or will indicate the need for further protection on the structure.

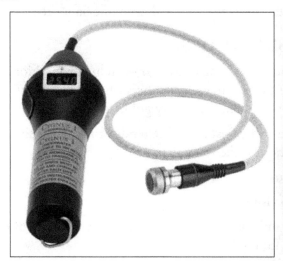

UT thickness gauge and diver using UT gauge to measure wall thickness of pipe piling
Photos courtesy of Cygnus Instruments

UT thickness gauges are also calibrated before every use on an inspection. Typically, there are two small blocks of steel, ¼ inch and ½ inch that are held against the probe in order to calibrate the tool before each use. The UT thickness gauge measures the wall thickness of steel structural members.

17.9 TIPS FOR USAGE, MAINTENANCE AND CARE OF TOOLS

If the diver's tools are not maintained and become unusable, it may take a week to get a replacement tool offshore. Diving contractors will not usually rehire any diver who abuses or fails to maintain the tools. The following tips will help with tool usage, care, and maintenance:

- When airlifting, open the valve slowly at first, to avoid a runaway machine. Extra weight always helps on the business end of an airlift as well.

- Try floatation on heavy power tools if you are working mid-water or on a wall.

- Syntactic foam strips taped to hydraulic lines or welding cables make them easier to manage.

- When water blasting, tie the wand off so the tip is the right distance from the surface you are blast cleaning if possible. This saves having any retro action on the diver.

- A dull blade or chain on a saw will cause excessive wear on the tool, prevents the diver from making straight cuts and waste time. Change dull blades or chains immediately.

- Chisels, bits, blades and chains that can be sharpened should be sharpened as soon as they are dulled and not when the diver is waiting for them.

- Sharp tools should either have blade guards or have duct tape placed on the blade tip before they are placed into the tool basket to protect the edge and the diver.

- Every tool used underwater should be rinsed off. Check the manufacturer's usage manual for each tool for special cleaning or lubrication instructions.

- Pneumatic and hydraulic hoses should be coiled and kept clear of foot traffic.

- White or yellow paint on tools will make them much easier for the diver to see underwater.

- Small hand tools should have a short rope lanyard to make them easier to locate.

- Hand tools with moving parts (adjustable wrenches) require lubrication. Normal cooking oil will provide the lubrication without harming the environment.

- When using an ultrasonic thickness tester, attach a short lanyard to the handle, with a hand scraper on the other end. This will allow you to clean spots to shoot and keep one hand free.

17.10 SAFETY GUIDELINES FOR USING TOOLS

When using tools, both hand tools and power tools, what you don't know can hurt you. Prior to using any power tool for the first time, read the user's guide and talk to crewmembers who are familiar with that tool. The diver should, as a minimum, always abide by the following safety guidelines:

- Always practice good umbilical management when using surface tended tools. If possible, tend the tool hose the same distance from the dive hose as the water depth.

- Never use an airlift unless it has diffuser bars on the intake end.

- Never use high pressure water blast in zero visibility.

- Never use a tool for anything other than its intended purpose. A significant percentage of workplace injuries occur due to using the wrong tool for the job.

- Always use "whip checks" on pneumatic and hydraulic lines.

- Never use a power tool on the surface or underwater unless it has a "dead-man" switch or trigger.

- Never use a power tool on surface or underwater unless it has all protective guards in place.

- When using power or hand tools on surface, wear all PPE.

- Keep hands and feet clear of water blaster and water jet nozzles.

- Always think before you cut. Stored energy in steel, timber, rope or chain is capable of causing injury or death to the diver or his surface crew.

- Always start saws and grinders away from the target surface. Starting torque causes tools to skip across the surface being cut or ground.

- Never tie or tape a trigger in the "on" position.

- Never use a grinding disk on surface that has been underwater as they will fly apart every time.

18.0 SALVAGE

In simple terms, salvage is the process of wreck removal, cargo or equipment retrieval, vessel flotation, and/or rescue work. Salvage operations usually become necessary as the result of the stranding or sinking of a vessel, the crash of an aircraft or the need to rescue or recover personnel or property adrift at sea or lost underwater. Salvage in any one of these situations involves a thorough knowledge of the construction of the item to be salvaged (vessel, aircraft, vehicle) in order to minimize further damage during the salvage process. Often, knowledge in search methods, rigging, underwater welding and cutting, various diving modes and many types of mechanical skills may be required as well.

18.1 SHIP SALVAGE

The most common type of vessel salvage situation is stranding, which almost always demands prompt and correct action. In most cases, the stranded vessel retains most of its original value. It is the salvor's job to minimize any further loss of value, while at the same time minimizing any environmental impact caused by the loss of the vessel's fuel (bunkers) or her cargo. There are three general categories of ship salvage performed: rescue salvage, harbor salvage, and offshore salvage.

18.1.1 Rescue Salvage
Rescue salvage is the term used for helping vessels damaged at sea by towing, fire-fighting, minor patching, and pumping. Eighty-six percent of all salvage operations performed today are rescue salvage and the most important service involves preparing and towing damaged vessels to a safe harbor.

18.1.2 Harbor Salvage
Harbor salvage is the salvage of wrecks in harbors. Methods of clearance include dewatering by pumping or by use of air pressure, crane lifts and lifting devices such as pontoons and air bags. It often requires mud and sand removal under the stranded vessel to break the suction. Because most marine traffic is coastwise and a large number of underwater hazards exist along the coasts, the most frequent casualty is the stranding of vessels on coastal shoals or reefs.

18.1.3 Offshore Salvage
Offshore salvage is the salvage of vessels stranded or sunk in exposed locations along the coast and vessels sunk out in deeper water. This salvage involves the most difficult problems, specifically those due to weather conditions and to the distance to logistically needed supplies. Stranded vessels are exposed to the damaging effects of weather of increasing intensity, consequently increasing the risk of further damage due to the actions of the sea. Offshore salvage most often is a race against time.

18.2 SALVAGE SURVEYS

Because of the hazards inherent in any salvage operation, the first step after locating the casualty is to perform a survey. The purpose of a survey is to determine the nature and extent of the damage; the best method of salvage and the amount of work, equipment and personnel needed to make the vessel water or airtight or to salvage the missing item. The salvage survey is the basis of a sound salvage plan.,. It should be thorough and well documented. Thoroughness in all aspects of preparation and execution may not be the fastest way of completing the task, but in the long run, it is usually the most efficient and effective. Thorough preparation will help to avoid causing further damage and will also minimize the hazards faced by the crews involved. There are two types of surveys: external and internal.

18.2.1 External Surveys

External surveys are conducted to assess any damage to the hull, determine how the vessel is aground, and the vessels' orientation (upright, inverted, or on its side). This external survey will also determine the condition of any cargo and equipment on deck.

Caution should be exercised when conducting external surveys. Possible hazards include falling through holes in the deck, missing ladders, injury from falling objects or machinery and loose plating, jagged plates, loose rigging, and loose cargo.

The external survey should include the name and registry, size and cargo of the vessel. The diver's duties include the following:

- Determine the position of the vessel in relation to the ground and water line (upright, bottom up and other positioning marks).
- Survey the bottom around the vessel, taking note of depth and any obstructions.
- Assess the extent of the damage.
- Determine number of holes in hull, location and size.
- Determine what preparation is necessary for patching.
- Determine if there is wreckage or cargo that needs to be removed.
- Determine if securing points for patches are available.

Operations personnel duties include the following:

- Prior to beginning the undersea part of the operation, confirm with the ship's master that all intakes are shut down and that the propeller shaft is locked.
- Obtain information on tides and swells.
- Determine if there is any equipment on board the vessel to be salvaged that will be usable in the salvage, such as steam pumps, winches and booms, wire rope, line, or anchor chain.

18.2.2 Internal Surveys

The internal survey is used to determine if the damage can be repaired or if the vessel can be salvaged. It will determine any specific cargo problems and the location of pipelines and valves, and sources of potential danger. Internal surveys should be especially well planned and divers should always use an in-water standby and a shrouded umbilical when penetrating interior areas. The divers should study the ship's plans, and, if possible, even visit a sister ship. If the vessel is aground, the divers will check for rock and/or coral heads protruding through the hull.

Hazards of internal surveys include holes, jagged plates, fouling on floating gear and possible contact with toxic materials. Divers must also realize that any gear and crew's personal effects that will float, if not secured prior to sinking, will be floating in passageways and compartments of the casualty. If there was loss of life, this may include the bodies of crew and passengers. Dives under these conditions should be performed as hazmat dives.

The internal survey should determine the following:

- If damage can be repaired on-site
- If cargo can be salvaged and by what method
- The location of pipes and valves
- If the vessel is aground, search for any coral or other objects penetrating the hull

Operations personnel duties include the following:

- Study plans of the ship.
- Devise a survey plan.
- Maintain communication with divers.
- Keep an accurate record of the survey.

18.3 MARINE DAMAGE CONTROL

The larger part of salvage work is rescue salvage: helping ships in peril and getting them to shore, not refloating sunken ships. What typically happens in cases like this is a diving crew will mobilize aboard an offshore salvage tug, steam offshore, locate the casualty, do an assessment, patch the hole, board and monitor the casualty while the salvage tug tows her in to a safe harbor. In the case of a simple fix, such as a hull penetrator, the diving crew often will stay aboard the salvage tug to return to port.

18.3.1 Casualty Assessment

Threats to the vessel must be identified and dealt with in order of highest priority. Highest priorities are conditions that, if not corrected immediately, will cause the ship to founder. Lower priority would be damage to propulsion or steering systems or loss of cargo. The only time these priorities change is when the cargo is extremely flammable (refined petroleum products or crude oil), explosive (munitions or industrial explosives) or otherwise deadly (radioactive materials or toxic chemicals). In these cases, the safety of the crew must always be considered before any action is taken. Only one thing takes priority over saving the casualty—the safety of divers and the support crew. Threats to the environment must also be considered and dealt with to the extent possible. Whether it is through pumping off fuel, containment booms or other measures, environmental protection is always a high priority.

Upon arrival, a survey must be conducted to find answers to the following questions:

- Is the ship in danger of sinking or grounding?
- Is there a threat to the ship's crew?
- Is there a threat to the salvage crew?
- Is there a threat to the environment?
- Is the cargo in danger?
- What can be done to get the ship to shore?
- What, if any, measures have the ship's crew taken to correct the problem?

Before a diver is put in the water, the following steps must be taken:

- Pumps, intakes and propulsion must be locked out.
- Drawings should be closely checked and the options considered.
- The diver will be briefed for a quick inspection of the problem area and to take any measurements required for temporary patches.

Once all of the immediate threats to the vessel have been handled secondary problems, if any, will be handled. Divers must remain alert. If a breach in the hull has been patched, it is critical to watch water levels constantly and "babysit" the pumps until the casualty is ashore. Temporary hull patches are just that—temporary. The divers and crew must never assume that if the pumps will handle the water that everything is now contained, and all hands can hit the rack. A second patch needs to be ready as well as a back-up plan and a constant watch must be maintained until the casualty is delivered safely ashore.

18.4 TEMPORARY HULL PATCHES

Depending on the conditions encountered, a diver may be required to patch anything from a three-inch pipe fitting to a huge gash in the hull caused by a collision. Every breach in a ship's hull, whether a broken interior sea water cooling pipe or torn hull plating caused by grounding or collision, poses a threat to the vessel and must be sealed. Each situation is unique and there is no "one size fits all" patch. Hull penetrators, cracked plates and torn plates are all conditions that divers may encounter. Regardless of the patch method used, it should be secured in such a way that the drag created when the casualty is underway will not tear it off. If a long tow or steam is required to get the casualty ashore, it is imperative to consider patching from inside the hull. Interior patches require strong backs and bracing to hold the patch in place.

Disabled freighter

18.4.1 Hull Penetrators

Hull penetrators are the single most common problem encountered at sea, and they are usually the simplest to correct. Marine engines, main and auxiliary, require seawater for cooling and every power source on board ship has at least one seawater intake and one discharge. That means there are at least two through-hull fittings per engine, unless they feed from and discharge to common sea chests.

Deep-sea salvage tug

Undetected corrosion and excessive vibration are two causes of sudden and catastrophic failure of interior piping. This changes the penetrators from being a functional part of the ship to being a serious threat to her survival. Small, round penetrators, like those used for wastewater discharge and auxiliary engine cooling, are the easiest to seal. A wooden plug slightly larger than the diameter of the penetrator with a tapered end, can be installed with a short sledgehammer.

Larger openings, such as sea chests, usually have a grate on the outside. For these openings, a Tucker patch is used. These patches consist of a piece of plywood larger than the opening, with neoprene foam rubber glued to the inside face. The patch is held in place by hook or tee bolts that catch behind the grating on the sea chest and are tightened by a diver from the outside.

18.4.2 Torn Hull Plates

Collisions, grounding, shifting cargo and ice damage are some of the causes of torn hull plating. Torn hull plates usually result in a hole, as opposed to a crack. Holes are more difficult to patch than cracks. Some holes may be patched with a Tucker patch, but the Tucker patch must be constructed differently than for a sea chest. Before a temporary patch can be installed, the damaged area must be completely cleared. If cutting is required, any existing gas pockets must be ventilated from compartments and vent holes must be burned or drilled to stop further accumulation of gas. Burning to remove large pieces must be done from the bottom up. In that way, the diver stays above the cut, thereby avoiding having pieces fall on him. Marine growth such as barnacles must be cleaned away from the hole and securing points must be prepared for the patch.

18.4.3 Cracked Hull Plates

In severe winter storms in the North Atlantic, it is not uncommon to see seas in excess of 60 feet and on rare occasions seas will reach 80 to 100 hundred feet. The hulls of ships caught in these storms are constantly flexing. Normally, flexing is a good thing compared to the alternative—breaking. When exposed to prolonged storm conditions, however, hull plates occasionally crack due to metal fatigue. Ships have been saved and brought ashore simply by hanging a tarpaulin over a hull crack and letting the hydraulic pressure hold it in place. A rain jacket hung over a crack and secured with rope has saved smaller fishing vessels. Salvage patches, however, are a much better solution.

18.4.4 Types of Patches

Factors that help determine the type of patch include size of the patch, lifting equipment, list of the vessel, position of the patch, material on hand and the method of dewatering. The rule of thumb is: use a pump if the patch is on the outside; use air if the patch is on the inside. In addition to the Tucker patch, there are three other types of patches: American, British standard, and plank by plank.

18.4.4.1 Tucker Patch

To build a Tucker patch for a hole, use planks instead of plywood because more strength is required. For large holes, multiple layers of planks running in the opposite direction give even more strength. Hook bolts or tee bolts are then used to secure the patch to the plate around the edges of the hole. For holes on the curved parts of the hull (the bilge turn), a flexible cable patch may be used. These are constructed by nailing fire hose between timbers, attaching canvas or neoprene to the inside face and attaching cables to the outside face of the timbers. The patch is positioned over the hole and the cables are warped tight and secured.

Installing a Tucker Patch in the dry

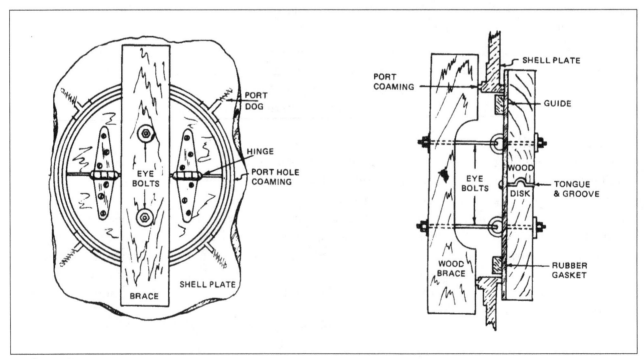

Tucker Patch

18.4.4.2 The American Patch

The American, or box patch, is usually made of white pine or Douglas fir. The wood is normally tongue and groove diagonal planking that uses canvas or some other appropriate material between the layers. It is secured over good frames with hogging lines, tackle or turnbuckles. The divers first make a template of the hole so that the patch can be constructed topside. It is important that the template be accurate so that the framework of the patch can be properly trimmed to fit the contour of the hull. If the

patch is large, a door can be installed to allow access for divers through the patch. The leading edge should be beveled. The gasket for the patch must be a minimum of four inches thick. It can be made of canvas-covered cotton, oakum, rags, kapok, felt, greased manila, rubber, or stuffed fire hose. When installing the patch, it must be

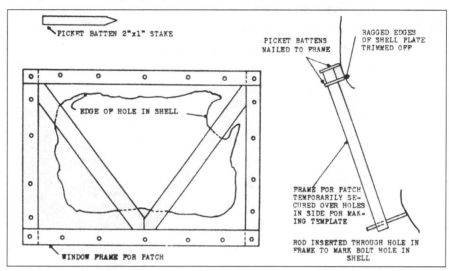

American Patch

weighed to compensate for the positive buoyancy of the timber. This is done by multiplying the total cubic feet of wood by 32 (the buoyancy of white pine or Douglas fir) to determine the amount of metal, in pounds, needed to give the patch neutral buoyancy. Pumps are used to help seal the patch. Check the integrity of the seal by observing the water level. If there are leaks, they can be sealed with bagged sawdust, oakum, kapok or plastic packing and secured with channel iron or angle clips. Using the American patch presents the least work for the divers. Even though it can weigh up to 50 tons, the American patch is best for underwater holes. It makes good backing for concrete patches and should be strong enough to allow the vessel to make a safe journey to harbor for repairs.

18.4.4.3 The British Standard Patch

The British Standard patch involves more work for the divers, but it is also a good backing for concrete patches. The process is much the same as for the American patch. The divers will make a template so the patch may be constructed topside. The planks are beveled and secured with straps of metal or wire.

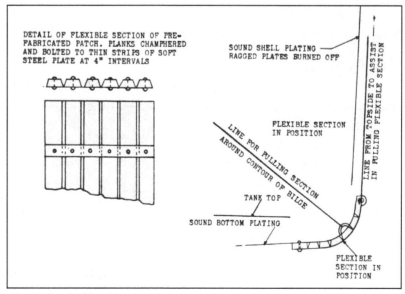

British Standard Patch

18.4.4.4 Plank-by-Plank Patch

A plank-by-plank patch is used as a last resort when the patch will have to go through a small opening. It is made of tongue and groove planking. Planks are secured from top to bottom and, as with the American patch, planks must be weighted to overcome buoyancy. Leaks are sealed by pumping and adding caulking in the cracks.

18.4.4.5 Other Types of Patches

In addition to the above patches, there is a combination of damage control patches that include concrete patches, bucket patches, welded patches, plugs, wedges and collision and salvage mats. Wooden hulled vessels can be patches by simply nailing marine plywood over white leaded canvas. Welded patches are only good for flat surfaces. Wedges and plugs reduce flow of air or water. Bucket patches are used only for small holes.

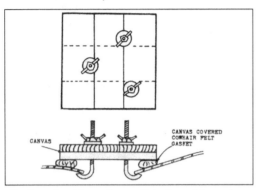

Patch made with two layers of planks at right angles

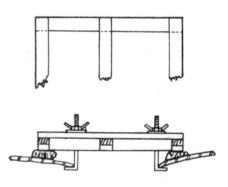

Patch made of tongue and groove on 4" × 4" timber frame

18.5 COFFERDAMS

Cofferdams are used to gain freeboard for a partially sunken vessel. The ship should be in an upright position or have no more than a 15-degree list. As a rule of thumb, large cofferdams should have a maximum depth of fifty feet. Beyond this depth it is difficult to seal and work with cofferdams. When considering construction of a cofferdam, the salvor should take into account tides, condition of the main deck, stability when the vessel becomes lively, amount of structure to be removed and the time available.

18.5.1 Types of Cofferdams

There are three types of cofferdams: fence, hatch, and makeshift.

18.5.1.1 The Fence

The fence (or complete) cofferdam extends completely around the deck of the ship. The strength and damage of the deck must be taken into consideration. This type of cofferdam presents more work, because the entire deck must be cleared of all fittings. Because of its large size, currents and seas have a greater effect on the structure and it is more difficult to make watertight. Stability will be much greater once the ship becomes lively because of the larger water plane area. In preparation for construction, all obstructions will have to be removed using cutting torches and possibly explosives. Once this is completed, accurate measurements will have to be taken of the entire deck area. The frame is usually constructed of 12 × 12 wooden timbers, steel stiffeners and half lap wooden timbers. The sheathing and gasket are usually of the same type as the American patch. When installing the cofferdam, the positive buoyancy of the timbers will need to be overcome. The cofferdam will be secured to the deck by turnbuckles, chain falls and hook bolts. After the last section is in place, it will be necessary to test for leaks by pumping. Leaks can be stopped by the same methods previously described for patches.

18.5.1.2 The Hatch

The hatch (or partial) cofferdam has less trouble with currents and seas, requires less pumping capacity, is easy to fit and can be made as one section. It also allows the upper part of the ship to be left intact. However, stability will be a problem because of high weight in the ship and the deck must be made watertight. The cofferdam will require internal shoring. Measurements will be needed of the hatch opening and securing points prepared. The frame is made of bolted wood timbers, steel stiffeners and braces. The sheathing and gasket are the same as for American patches.

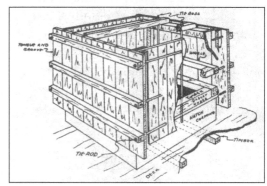

Wooden cofferdam for small hatches

18.5.1.3 Makeshift

Makeshift or miscellaneous type cofferdams can be made from oil drums, barrels, boxes, smokestacks or any other appropriate items at hand. When using such items, they normally have to be strengthened to overcome pressure or require valves to allow pressure equalization. They are usually secured with C- clamps, turnbuckles, and hook bolts.

18.6 CONCRETE IN SALVAGE

Concrete is used in salvage operations to reinforce and make watertight seals on bulkheads, cofferdams, plugging valves and pipes, sealing cracks and patches. Drains must be installed in concrete patches to allow for the relief of water pressure. If at all possible, concrete should be poured out of the water. It will set up in about 45 minutes underwater, but it will continue to be weak for several days. Forms used to pour concrete must be watertight. Because concrete is heavy, it is important to try for strength in the concrete without bulk. It is recommended that high early Portland cement (Type III) be used for concrete salvage work. This cement is used where high concrete strength is required after a short curing period. Concrete made with Type III cement reaches its design strength after seven days, whereas Type I requires 28 days. Before committing to a big expense, a concrete test sample should be mixed. It is best to make a one or two cubic foot form and pour the sample in the same way the batch will be used.

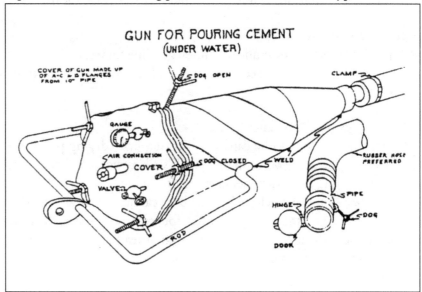

18.6.1 Pouring Concrete

Concrete must be poured in forms that are able to contain the load until the concrete has set up. Braces, studs and reinforcing wales may be necessary to add strength and rigidity to the form. Forms must be as watertight as possible. Tongue and groove sheathing will give the concrete a smooth, watertight surface. Plywood may also be used. A concrete gun should be used for pouring into inaccessible areas such as pipelines, sea chests or valves. The pressure need only just exceed bottom pressure.

18.7 GAS HAZARDS AND CONFINED SPACE

Gases can present serious problems in salvage operations. Gases can be found in any closed compartment, where one compartment opens into another, in compartments adjacent to flooded compartments, where fuels and oil have been stowed and where cargo has been exposed to seawater. Gases may come through broken pipelines and holes as well. Gases lie in layers. Heavy gases settle toward the bottom, while lighter gases rise. The elimination of gas hazards is critical. If elimination of the gas hazard in its entirety is not possible, breathing apparatus must be used (see Chapter 21: Diving Under Exceptional Conditions for more safety guidelines in confined-space diving). There are three main types of gas hazards that salvors must be aware of: toxic gases, explosive gases, and oxygen deficiency.

18.7.1 Toxic Gases

Hydrogen sulfide (H_2S) is the most toxic gas found in salvage operations. The gas is extremely dangerous, causes unconsciousness and is rapidly fatal. It is produced by the decay of organic materials and smells like rotten eggs when in low concentrations. It can be tested with an H_2S detector. Treatment is the immediate administration of pure oxygen, artificial respiration and immediate notification of a doctor.

Carbon monoxide (CO) is produced by incomplete combustion. It is colorless and odorless and can be found in painted voids and closed spaces. It can be tested with a CO detector. CO gas can be fatal in less than an hour at sea level and at depth its effects will be accelerated. Symptoms include headache, vomiting, weakness or dizziness. Treatment is the immediate administration of pure oxygen, fresh air and artificial respiration.

Chlorine gas is another toxic gas danger and is caused when wet cell storage batteries come in contact with salt water. Chlorine has a very strong smell (like bleach) and is often visible as a yellowish haze. The initial symptoms in low concentrations are eye and throat irritation. Heavier concentrations will cause skin irritation, severe cough, vomiting and unconsciousness. Exposure to light concentration may be treated with saline irrigation of the eyes and inhaled corticosteroids for throat and lungs. Exposure to heavier concentrations will require rapid medical evacuation.

18.7.2 Explosive Gases

Explosive gases include crude oil fumes, gasoline fumes, fuel oil fumes, hydrogen gas (which is produced by underwater cutting), acetylene and naphtha fumes. They can be detected by odor or explosive gas meters.

18.7.3 Oxygen Deficiency

Oxygen deficiency can be caused by rusting iron, drying paint, fire and refrigerants. Carbon dioxide (CO_2) is produced by burning fossil fuels such as wood and coal. Carbon dioxide replaces the oxygen in the air, creating an oxygen deficient environment. A CO_2 indicator can be used to test its presence and intensity. Symptoms include headaches, weakness or dizziness. Treatment is administration of oxygen or fresh air. The other method to test for oxygen deficiency is to use an oxygen monitor. These units display the oxygen percentage with a digital readout. Salvage crews must never enter an area with an oxygen level approaching or below 16%.

18.8 UNDERWATER SALVAGE OPERATIONS

The salvage of any item from underwater involves two distinct phases of operation: the search phase and the recovery phase. Some salvage operations are simplified because the casualty (the item to be recovered) is partially out of the water or has left a marker such as an oil slick. However, a search must often be performed to locate the item before recovery can be affected. All searches, regardless of the method used, must be performed in a methodical, orderly fashion to ensure that all portions of the search area are covered completely and so that a minimum amount of time is expended on the search.

18.9 SEARCH METHODS

Various search methods are employed, depending on several factors: size of the item, water depth, the resources available, underwater conditions (thermocline layers, tide shear) and on the size of the search area involved.

18.9.1 Sonar and Electronic Imaging

Sonar is the term used for devices that emit sound pulses and record the echoes sent back to the device after striking submerged objects on the sea bottom. Sonar was developed for military applications, but today sonar use is more widespread. Originally used on submarines to detect other submarines and vessels and on surface vessels to detect submarines, the operator would direct his beam in a particular direction manually, listening in earphones for a return (reflected pulse). Modern sonar units are automatic, and the operator sees the results on a screen. The two types of sonar used are pulse sonar, and side scan sonar.

Sonar systems emit a sound wave, sometimes called a "ping." This wave will be reflected off any objects in its path. The time that it takes the reflected wave to return to the sonar device indicates the distance to the object. Bearing can also be measured using two or more hydrophones to receive sonar waves.

Research vessels use towed arrays for sea floor mapping. These arrays consist of several sending units (called transducers) that scan the bottom from several angles. The data from these side-scan transducers is fed into a computer system that provides a three-dimensional model of the sea floor. This technology is now being used in salvage, construction and oil field operations.

Whenever possible, salvage ships utilize electronics to initially locate the item to be salvaged. This initial location may be carried out by a magnetometer, side scan sonar or a combination of the two methods. Magnetometers will identify disturbances in the earth's magnetic field caused by ferrous metals, such as iron or steel. Large targets cause large disturbances, and are more easily located, even if covered in bottom silt.

Clive Cussler (author of the Dirk Pitt novels) used a magnetometer to locate the civil war submarine CSS *Hunley* and the ironclad civil war vessel *Monitor*. Once initially located, side-scan sonar often will be able to

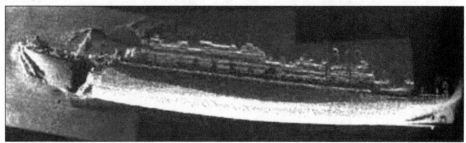

Side-scan sonar image of sunken ship (notice collision damage on port bow)
Photo: NOAA

accurately detail the position, attitude and even (to some extent) the condition of the submerged casualty. In some locations, where iron ore is naturally present on the seabed, the magnetometer has more difficulty and the side-scan sonar is the only option.

Properly used by an operator who knows the system, these devices will put the salvage operation into the recovery phase very quickly. Electronic fish finders (pulse sonars) are the least effective of the options, but if they are all that is available, it will save bottom time. The printout Fathometer has been used successfully on many searches in the past, even finding items that side scan sonar had missed. Certain conditions, however, will limit the effectiveness of electronic imaging. Extreme tide shear caused where opposing strong currents collide may eliminate the use of sonar. Another condition that sometimes eliminates sonar is sharp thermocline layers. As previously mentioned, iron ore in the surrounding rock can eliminate the magnetometer. In these cases, alternative search methods may have to be considered.

18.9.2 Direct Contact Searching

In the absence of electronic imaging equipment, a method to be considered is direct contact. One type of direct contact search involves towing a cable behind two vessels with the bight of the cable dragging across the bottom. The other type of direct contact search involves dragging a grappling hook, or a series of them, behind one or two vessels. In both methods, it is necessary to keep the speed of the towing vessels dead slow to keep the drags on the bottom. This method should not be considered for any item that may be damaged by the cable (aircraft, for example). Although used successfully in the past (as with the recovery of the sunken submarine USS *Squalus* in 1939), this is not a very effective search method for two reasons: any protrusion above the seafloor will snag the bight of the cable or the hook and divers must be deployed to check every contact.

18.9.3 Manual Searching with a Diver

If electronic imaging cannot be used and direct contact searching is not an option, divers will be used for the search. Obviously if the search is being performed by diver, the size of the area to be searched will be limited. The three types of manual search most often performed are the umbilical sweep, grid wire searches and snag line searches. The umbilical sweep, in which the diver uses his umbilical for a radius, works well in low visibility, but the search area is not nearly as large and is not covered nearly as well. The

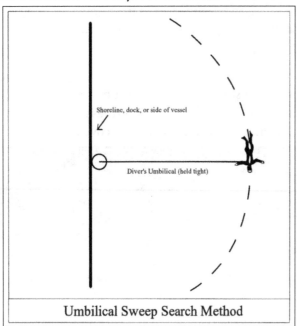

Umbilical Sweep Search Method

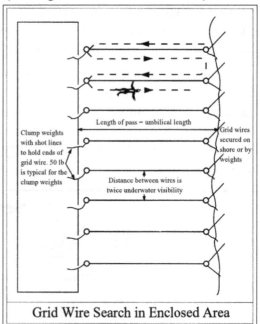

Grid Wire Search in Enclosed Area

grid wire (also called the jackstay) search is the most effective method, although it takes more time to set up and requires more rigging. A variation of the jackstay search is the snag line and it works very well.

To perform the umbilical sweep, the tender holds the diver's umbilical tight and the diver swims or walks in an arc keeping tension on the umbilical. The diver starts in close then consecutive sweeps are made with the tender slacking out a little more umbilical between sweeps, then holding it. This method is not nearly as effective as the grid wire (jackstay) and only works in relatively shallow water.

The grid wire search may be performed in enclosed areas, such as a river bed, canal or a ship's berth, or it may be performed out in open water, whether in the center of a harbor, or offshore. This method is usually performed with two or more wires, and as a pass is completed, the first wire is relocated as the

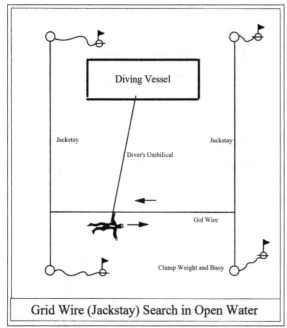

Grid Wire (Jackstay) Search in Open Water

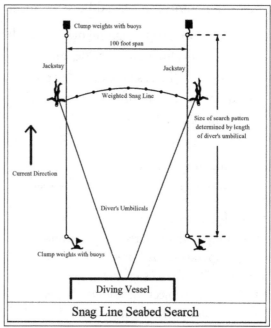

Snag Line Seabed Search

diver is following the second wire. This method almost always gets results, as the entire pattern is searched.

The grid wire (jackstay) search works best when there is a little underwater visibility, but will work in zero visibility as well. A modification often used is to have the diver use a "search line" as he/she traverses the grid wire. The diver holds a line (usually 6 feet long) that slides along the grid wire with a shackle. This allows the grid wire to be moved a little farther each time it is repositioned, thereby speeding up the search.

The snag line version of the jackstay search uses two divers. The divers each hold one end of the weighted snag line and move in the same direction along the jackstay wires. Providing the search location is correct, this method will find the object. The clump weights are at least 50 pound, when there is only manpower to handle them, but heavier clump weights hold the wires in location better.

18.10 RECOVERY METHODS

After the item to be salvaged has been located and a survey performed, the recovery phase of the operation begins. Usually, when a salvage operation takes place, the main requirement is to recover the item as quickly as possible without doing further damage to it. There are four recovery methods used for salvage underwater: direct lifting, flotation devices, pumping, and internal flotation.

18.10.1 Direct Lifting
Direct lifting is the best option and is accomplished by slinging the object to be salvaged and attaching the

A drilling machine being recovered by direct lift

slings to a crane, which is usually mounted on a barge or a structure. In areas with extreme tidal ranges, the slings can be made fast to a vessel at low tide and the rising tide will lift the object. The object is then taken to shallower water on the high tide and the process is repeated on the next tide cycle. Before slings are placed on an object, drawings should be consulted. The lift capacity of the crane or the vessel must be known, as well as the weight of the object and the amount of bottom suction.

The following points must be addressed prior to starting a direct lift operation:

- Always use proper rigging practice in direct lift operations.
- Ensure all slings and shackles are tested and certified for 150% anticipated loading.
- Check all slings, shackles and spreaders after installation before lifting begins.
- Know the weight of the lift, both below and above the water.
- Do not exceed the safe working load of the crane.
- Ensure clear communications between the diver, diving supervisor, and crane operator.

When performing a controlled lift with a crane, a diver or divers should follow the lift to the surface but be sure to keep out from under the load.

18.10.2 Flotation Devices

The most frequently used recovery method on salvage operations is flotation devices. These may be "hard" or "soft" devices which are attached to the object with slings. Proper placement of flotation devices is critical to this type of salvage operation. When used in a "cradle" configuration, flotation devices have been known to crush the wheelhouse structure on salvaged vessels. Therefore it is necessary to consult drawings to determine the proper placement. Also critical to the operation is the inflation sequence.

Salvage Pontoons on USS *Squalus* salvage operation (1939)
Photo: U.S. Navy

18.10.2.1 Hard Flotation Devices

Hard flotation devices are usually steel tanks (called pontoons) with air inlet valves, exhaust valves, and flood valves. These are used to refloat larger vessels and were successfully used to salvage vessels such as the submarine USS *Squalus* (1939) and the cruise ship *Costa Concordia* (2014).

JW Automarine enclosed vertical lift bags

SUBSALVE USA parachute lift bags

18.10.2.2 Soft Flotation Devices

In most applications, soft devices (called lift bags) have all but replaced pontoons. These bags are available from several manufacturers around the world, the most notable being SUBSALVE USA. They come rated to lift anything from 50 to 50,000 pounds, in either vertical or horizontal configurations. These bags may be open or closed bottom design, with the heavier bags usually closed bottom. They have built-in overpressure relief valves, inlet and dump valves. The soft devices have two main advantages over the hard: they are much lighter and easier to handle and, being softer, there is less potential to cause damage to the object being salvaged. Even delicate items such as aircraft can be successfully lifted with soft flotation devices.

Refloating a sunken fishing vessel using soft flotation (2004)   Vessel refloated with soft flotation being towed ashore (2004)

Usually, the best method is to gradually fill all devices simultaneously. If the flotation devices are only inflated on one end or one side, there is a risk of lifting one end of the object and dropping it or placing too much stress on the object. To avoid this, a manifold is used to allow simultaneous inflation. Before adding air to the devices, surface support units (boats and barges) must be moved well out of the way. Once an object leaves the bottom with flotation, it cannot be stopped, unless it is a staged lift. There is more information on various types of lift, as well as lift bag safety in Chapter 23: Underwater Lift Bags. As with any lift, all shackles, knots and slings must be carefully examined before lifting. Divers must be kept out of the water during inflation and be kept out from under the lift once it is suspended above the seafloor.

A sunken river ferry being pumped out   Sunken river ferry re-floated

18.10.3 Pumping

Restricted to vessels, pumping is an option when a portion of the hull remains above the water and the hull can be patched. In order to refloat a casualty by pumping, every opening below water must be sealed or be extended up above the waterline (with a cofferdam). Hatches, ventilators, portholes and man ways must be made watertight as well as any holes caused by collision or grounding. Large salvage pumps are used for refloating casualties; therefore, the salvage vessel must be large enough to carry several salvage pumps and have a crane to load them on the casualty. Water contaminated with oil or other environmental hazards must be pumped into tanks or a containment barge. Pumping is not usually an option if there is bulk cargo in the holds, because bulk cargo such as grain, potash, salt, ore and aggregates will almost always render salvage pumps useless, even when using intake strainers.

Vessels that are salvaged by pumping are patched on the outside of the hull. Then as the water level inside drops, hydraulic pressure presses the patches into place. The river ferry in the photos above had several cracks (from ice pressure) in the hull, which was made of timber. The divers simply stretched poly tarpaulins along the hull, and fastened them with nailed boards. This allowed the ferry to be pumped dry and be towed at a later date 50 miles down the river for repairs. Occasionally a vessel may be resting at too great an angle and must be parbuckled (rolled upright) in order to be pumped. This process is carried out by means of heavy ground tackle, anchors and winches. Often the casualty will require reinforcing of the hull in order to withstand the forces of the parbuckling and not break apart.

18.10.4 Internal Floatation

Occasionally, a vessel will sink with no damage to the hull. In some cases, it may be raised by means of internal flotation. If the design of the vessel will allow air to be pumped in, and the water depth is not too great, this option may be considered. Any compartment that is to be filled with air must be at least partially open at the bottom to allow for expansion of the air on ascent. Great care must be taken when using internal flotation to avoid hull rupture. Vessels on their side or those completely upside down are usually the best candidates for internal flotation.

18.11 ENVIRONMENTAL PROTECTION

On most marine salvage jobs, environmental protection is now second only to saving the casualty's passengers and crew. With the vast cargoes of petroleum products and other toxins that have been spilled over the years, one thing has been learned: there is a limit to what can be allowed to spill into the water and that limit has been reached.

The following steps should be taken when dealing with any suspected hazardous cargo:

- Determine what the cargo is and the properties of the cargo (without assuming anything). Crude oil looks like tar, but it is 100 times more flammable than gasoline. Radioactive material can also appear harmless when it is unmarked, but can be lethal.

- Contact the proper authorities for spill response and contain any active spills, if possible, until the spill response teams arrive.

- Take the proper action to stop or prevent a spill before it happens. Usually patching the hole is not an option when tanks are full, but off-loading cargo onto other vessels may be. Ballasting the casualty heavily on the undamaged side may also work.

18.11.1 Petroleum Spills

Most spills at sea are petroleum products. Since there have been so many incidents, management of these spills has been tried and tested. There are three ways of dealing with petroleum spills.

1. Dispersal is a method used with lighter oils (gasoline, kerosene, diesel fuel) that are not heavy enough to be collected effectively. A dispersal agent (such as dish detergent) is usually spread by boat or aircraft. This causes the oil to spread out into a microscopically thin layer that will evaporate much more quickly.

2. Collection is the method used for heavier oils and large spills of light oil. Containment booms are floated on the water and special "slick licker" vessels are used. These vessels are equipped with holding tanks and a conveyor that actually picks the oil up off the water's surface. Final cleanup is then performed by using absorbent mats and pads.

3. Although usually reserved for uncontrollable and potentially disastrous spills, some experts argue that incineration is an option that is not used often enough. An incendiary device is fired or dropped from an aircraft to ignite the slick and burn it off. The downside of this method is that in some cases, tar balls form and drop to the seafloor. Environmental scientists now believe that if the incineration method had been used initially in the Exxon *Valdez* disaster, the environmental impact would have been drastically reduced. After that incident, areas of the Alaskan coastline took nearly 25 years to recover.

18.12 CRIME AND ACCIDENT SCENES

Crime and accident scenes contain all of the necessary information required for the forensic investigators to piece together the events leading up to the incident. Although somewhat more difficult for an investigator to work, an underwater scene is no different than an on-land scene.

18.12.1 Preservation of the Scene

The preservation of the scene underwater is difficult, but important. Whenever possible, the salvage should be delayed until police divers have finished working. If there are no police divers available, the entire scene should be recorded on videotape with police investigators present. A detailed grid should be laid out to locate any and all items in the debris field, because investigators may require detailed measurements and still photographs. Do not remove or even relocate items before the investigators give approval.

When proceeding with the salvage, it is important to make certain to protect the items recovered. It is the job of the diver, when slinging for lifts, to not further damage the items. Secure or remove any loose items that may go adrift. The topside crew should keep the curiosity seekers away from the salvaged items.

18.12.2 Recovery of Evidence

When recovering evidence, the primary goal is to maintain the condition of the evidence until it can be processed at a laboratory. It is important that the items not be damaged during the recovery. Small items should be placed in a container of water for transport to the lab. This will help reduce oxidation and preserve the evidence.

18.12.3 Recovery of Remains

When recovering human remains, the rescue team must treat every victim with the respect and dignity that would be expected for a family member. A body should not be brought on deck uncovered. Have a body bag or tarp ready and get the body covered, if possible, at the water's surface. If the body is trapped in a vehicle or an aircraft, tarp the cabin area just as it reaches the surface.

Almost every human body recovered from the water will be autopsied to determine the cause of death and the contributing factors. Divers must not cause further damage to the body during the recovery. Bodies that have been immersed for long periods or immersed in warmer water are easily damaged. A Stokes litter is usually the best recovery tool, with the body bagged and strapped in before recovery.

18.13 FORMULAS USED IN SALVAGE WORK

Area formulas

1. Area of a rectangle = L × W

    L = Length

    W = Width

2. Area of a circle = ¼(Pi) × D²

    ¼(Pi)=.7854

    D = Diameter

3. Area of a sphere = Pi × D²

    Pi = 3.1416

    D = Diameter

4. Area of a cylinder = [(¼ × Pi × D²) × 2] +

                    [(Pi × D) × L]

    ¼(Pi) = .7854

D = Diameter

L = Length

Pi = 3.1416

Volume formulas

1. Volume of a sphere = D³ × ⅙(Pi)

    ⅙(Pi) = .5236

2. Volume of a cylinder = D² × ¼(Pi) × L [Pi × R² × L]

3. Volume of a square prism = L × H × W

    L = Length

    H = Height

    W = Width

> **NOTE**: Freshwater weighs 62.4 pounds per cubic foot, and 8.33 per gallon. Salt water weighs 64 pounds per cubic foot, and is 8.54 pounds per gallon. If volume is in gallons, substitute 8.54 or 8.33 pounds.

Buoyancy formulas

1. Displacement = V × W

    V = Volume of submerged body

    W = Weight of liquid displaced

2. Buoyancy = D – W

    D = Displacement in pounds

    W = Weight of object in pounds

3. Lifting capacity in salt water = V × 64 – W

    V = Volume in cubic feet

    64 = Weight of one cubic foot of salt water

    W = Weight of object

Costa Concordia in port, 2005.
Photo: Wikipedia

Costa Concordia sinks, Jan. 13, 2012.
Photo: Wikipedia

18.14 CASE STUDY: THE SALVAGE OF THE *COSTA CONCORDIA*

The massive cruise ship *Costa Concordia*, over 120 feet longer than *Titanic*, sank in early 2012 near a resort island in Italy's Tuscan Archipelago. At the time of her sinking, she was, if not the largest, certainly one of the largest cruise ships afloat. She had been built 8 years before, in 2004, and launched in 2005.

During the evening of January 13, 2012, the vessel was passing Isola del Giglio, Italy, when she struck an underwater rock with her port stern, tearing a one-hundred ten-foot gash in the hull. Her engine room immediately flooded, making her a dead ship. She then drifted without propulsion in a wide circle, took on an increasing list to starboard and then came to rest on the rocks at the mouth of Giglio Harbor.

The government of Italy was determined to protect the sensitive environment of Isola del Giglio, a very high end tourist and diving destination. Oil containment booms were placed, and the fuel and lube oil were removed from the casualty.

The *Costa Concordia* salvage project was the largest civilian salvage project ever performed and only one other project, the post-attack salvage of warships in Pearl Harbor (US Navy, 1942–45), exceeded it in time expended, diving hours performed and tonnage salvaged. The *Costa Concordia* project was the most difficult and expensive salvage project performed to date.

There were several reasons for this level of difficulty: Isola del Giglio has several species of sea plants and shellfish not found anywhere else in the world that had to be carefully relocated and preserved; the casualty had to be removed in one piece and towed away; the casualty was resting on rocks that sloped down into very deep water; the casualty was in an exposed area where wave action due to storms threatened it; much of the work was in depths of over 120 fsw and the entire wreck site had to be returned to its original condition after the salvage operations were completed.

Titan Salvage formed a joint venture company with Micoperi, an Italian marine construction firm, to compete for and execute the contract. The salvage plan, greatly simplified, was to secure the wreck from sliding down the slope; support the wreck to keep it from breaking up; attach port-side sponsons (square steel salvage pontoons); parbuckle (roll in place) the wreck so that it was upright; attach starboard side sponsons to the wreck and de-ballast and refloat the wreck for towing to a shipyard to be dismantled.

Securing the *Costa Concordia* in place with cable bundles, summer 2012.

This work involved a lot of diving, and divers were mobilized from every continent on earth to form the dive teams. These divers worked thousands of hours underwater on the project, most of it in the deep air range, as the seafloor directly below the bottom of the wreck varied between 120 and 140 fsw.

Barge on left has one dive crew installing cable bundles. Barge on right (moored in cruise ship's swimming pool) has 2 dive crews, both installing grout bags to support the wreck prior to parbuckling.

Securing the wreck from sliding down the rock slope was a priority task to hold the casualty in place for the future parbuckling operations. Dive teams installed anchor blocks towards the landward side of the ship. Tensioning devices attached to the anchor blocks were connected to several cable bundles (each larger in diameter than a basketball) running underneath the hull to 5" chain. As the bundles were connected they were tensioned to hold the wreck in place under monitored load. While Titan was in the process of doing this, other divers were busy removing and relocating the sea grass and shellfish.

Once the sea life was relocated and the installation of the anchor blocks was nearly half way completed, additional diving crews simultaneously began the work of supporting the wreck from underneath. This was deemed necessary because the entire wreck was suspended off bottom, with a freespan between two pinnacles of rock, one near the bow and one just ahead of the stern.

Costa Concordia support platform being completed in Italian shipyard. Photo courtesy of Shelby Harris, Titan Salvage

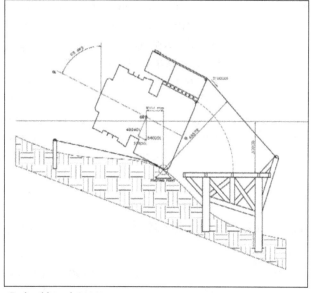

Wreck ready to parbuckle
Image courtesy of Titan Salvage

Parbuckling drawing
Image courtesy of Titan Salvage

Although the wreck had to be supported, the supports had to meet two criteria: they had to be robust enough to hold the weight and they had to be easily removed afterward, leaving no trace left behind. Titan had a brilliant idea for this: pump grout bags in place, with lifting straps on the grout bags for removal after the fact. Several hundred grout bags, many specially built to conform to the sea floor, were pumped in place until the wreck was firmly supported over its entire length. At the height of these operations there were over 150 divers on the job on 10 separate crews. Six of those crews were performing deep air dives day and night using surface decompression (*USN Rev 6*). Titan-Micoperi took no chances and had a total of 9 deck decompression chambers available for the crews and had at least one hyperbaric physician on site 24 hours per day, 7 days per week. In addition to the grout supports, there were large steel platforms installed for the wreck to rest on after the parbuckling was completed. These were installed in much the same manner that offshore structures are installed in the oilfield and firmly anchored into the rock seabed.

Once the wreck was held in place, supported and the platforms were in place, chains and cables were put around the wreck to parbuckle it. Square steel pontoons (sponsons) were installed on the port (upper)

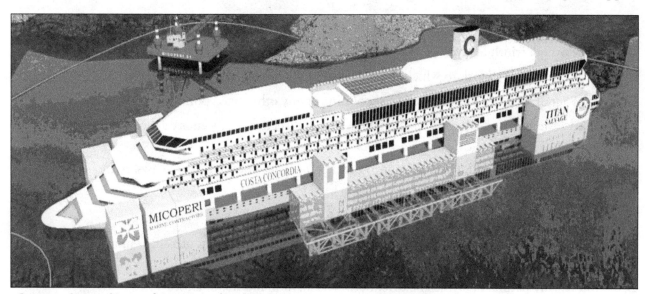

Computer Generated Image of *Costa Concordia* refloated, 2012. Image courtesy of Titan Salvage

side, to allow for dry installation and to use their weight to assist in the parbuckling of the wreck. As in the case of most of the operations involved, the parbuckling was difficult to prepare for, with extremely heavy rigging used, since the strains exerted on the rigging were very great in order to roll a ship of that size. The parbuckling, like any extremely heavy lift or pull, was not a fast operation: it took nearly two days. Once the wreck was righted and sitting on the platforms, steel pontoons were installed on the starboard side. The final step in the procedure was to pump the ballast water out of all of the pontoons, providing enough lift to float the wreck, and allow it to be towed to dry dock. Although this project utilized many common techniques, many aspects of these were revolutionary due to both the magnitude and unprecedented scope of the work. Titan-Micoperi completed the refloating and delivered the wreck to a shipyard in Genoa, Italy in late July, 2014: a very remarkable feat. The site cleanup at Isola del Giglio, Italy, continues at the time this case study is being written in January 2016.

18.15 GLOSSARY OF SALVAGE TERMINOLOGY

Divers should be familiar with the specialized terminology of the sea, ships, and salvage. Only by knowing and understanding the correct terminology will the diver be able to properly communicate with the salvage master and fully understand what is required.

-A-

A-frame: A support used for hoisting, formed by two legs in the form of an inverted "V", sometimes known as a shear leg.

Abaft the beam: Any direction between the beam and the stern.

Abeam: Bearing 90° or 270° relative to one's own ship.

Anchor windlass: The engine used to heave in the anchor.

Anemometer: Instrument used to measure wind velocity.

Aperture: Space provided for the propeller between the stern frame and the stern post.

Appendages: Fittings and structures which extend beyond the outline of the hull, such as bilge keels, rudder post, strainers, struts, skegs, etc.

Awash: The state of being level with or just below the water.

-B-

Backstay: A piece of standing rigging leading aft.

Beam: The overall width of a vessel.

Becket: The fitting on a block to which the dead end of the fall is attached.

Belay: The act of securing a line to a cleat, set of bitts or any other fixed point.

Bight: The middle part of a line, wire or chain as distinguished from its ends or the middle part of a rope forming a loop.

Bitt: One pair of strong cylindrical uprights on which mooring lines or towing hawsers are belayed.

Bitter end: The final or ultimate end of a line or wire.

Boat falls: General term applied to tackle used to hoist one end of a boat in davits.

Bollard: Strong cylindrical upright on a pier around which the eye or bight of a ship's mooring line is made fast.

Breakwater: Any natural or artificial barrier between a harbor and the open sea.

Bulwark: Solid, fence-like barrier along the edges of weather decks.

Bunker: A storage space for fuel of any type.

Bunkers: Originally referring to coal, now used for any type of ship's fuel.

Buoyancy: An upward force that is equal to the weight of the water displaced by an object.

By the head: Short for "down by the head," when a vessel's draft forward is deeper than her draft aft.

By the stern: Short for "down by the stern," when a vessel's draft aft is deeper than her draft forward.

-C-

Caisson: The gate at the end of a dry dock.

Camber: Athwartships arch in the deck, designed to cause water to flow outboard toward the scuppers.

Camel: Floating spar or other timber used to fend a ship off a pier.

Capstan: Hoisting device consisting of a capstan head on a shaft.

Careen: The act of a grounded ship in rolling over her beam-ends.

Carpenter stopper: A device used for gripping and holding wire under a load.

Carry away: The act of breaking loose.

Casualty: Term used to describe the object of the salvage operation. Typically referring to a ship, but may refer to an aircraft, locomotive or motor vehicle requiring salvage or rescue.

Catenary: The downward dip in a line, wire, or chain.

Cathead: Cylindrical devices at the end of the shaft on a winch or horizontal shaft windlass on which the turns of a line or wire are taken for heaving. Also called a gypsy.

Center of buoyancy: The geometric center of the underwater body.

Center of gravity: Point where the whole weight of the ship and contents is acting vertically downward.

Chafing gear: Hoisting apparatus consisting essentially of an endless chain, two or more sheaves and a set of gears that multiplies the applied power.

Chain stopper: A stopper for a chain cable consisting of a pelican hook that engages the chain, a turnbuckle and an eye that shackles to a padeye on deck. Also, any stopper for wire that is made of chain.

Cheek: One of the sides of a block.

Chock: Metal fairlead for mooring line, located on the gunwale.

Cleat: A device for belaying line or wire, consisting essentially of a pair of projecting horns.

Coaming: Bulwark around a hatch opening.

Coefficient of friction: Friction loss due to the contact of a vessel's bottom with various types of ground (sand, mud, rock, etc.).

Cofferdam: A watertight structure temporarily installed on a submerged vessel to obtain freeboard in order to pump out the water and raise the vessel.

Companionway: Deck opening giving access to a ladder.

-D-

Davit: One of a pair of strong booms, by which a boat (lifeboat or tender) is hoisted in or out; the pair is called a set of davits. Also a small fixed boom used for raising and lowering objects over the vessel's side.

Dead light: A metal cover for a porthole.

Deck load: Cargo stowed on the weather decks.

Derelict: A wreck floating awash.

Displacement tonnage: The entire weight of a vessel and her contents, expressed in long tons.

Deviation: A magnetic compass error caused by magnetic properties of a vessel, expressed in east or west.

Discharge head: Vertical distance from where water enters a pump to the point of discharge.

Dog: Small bent lever that is turned to wedge tight a watertight door.

Dolphin: A piling or nest of piles off a pier or beach or off the entrance to a dock, which is used for mooring.

Drogue: A sea anchor.

Dunnage: Any materials used to separate cargo, create space for cargo ventilation or insulate cargo against chafing or damage.

-F-

Fairlead: Any device used to lead a line, wire or chain around an angle or obstruction so that it will "lead fair" to a desired point.

Fall: Term applied to a line, wire or chain that is reeved on a purchase.

Fantail: The after end of the main deck.

Fast: To make secure.

Fathom: Unit of length equal to six feet (one arm-span).

Fender: Any device used to act as a shock absorber for vessels and craft, usually located against bridges, piers or other structures.

Flake: Act of disposing a line, wire or chain by laying it out in long, flat bights, one beside the other.

Flotsam: Floating debris left on the surface by a sunken ship.

Fluke: Part of an anchor that bites or digs when a strain comes on the chain or line.

Forestay: A piece of standing rigging leading forward.

Freeboard: Distance from the waterline to the main deck.

Free communication: Water allowed to come in and go out to the open sea through a hole or damage.

-G-

Gangway: Opening in a bulwark or life rail that gives access to a gangplank of accommodation ladder; the accommodation ladder and its rigging.

Gross tonnage: Interior capacity of a cargo vessel in units of 100 cubic feet.

Ground tackle: Collective term for the equipment used in anchoring or in mooring with anchors, whether to keep vessel on station, or to use as a hold point for winching off of a casualty.

Gunwale: Upper edge of the bulwark (pronounced "gunnel").

Guy: Any line, wire, or tackle which provides athwartships support for a boom.

-H-

Hawse pipe: Large pipe through which cable or chain runs from the deck out through the side.

Hawser: Any wire or large line used for towing or mooring.

Heaving line: A line with a weight at one end.

Heel: The act of a vessel rolling or listing temporarily out of perpendicular.

High line: Line stretched between ships or ship and the beach on which a trolley block travels back and forth to transfer cargo or persons.

Hogging line: Line dropped in a bight either fore or aft under the keel, often to allow a diver to follow it.

-I-

Inboard: Expresses the idea of "toward the centerline."

Irish pennant: A loose end of line carelessly left dangling.

-J-

Jacob's ladder: A rope or wire ladder.

Jetsam: Goods cast overboard to lighten a vessel in distress.

-L-

Lanyard: Any short line used as a handle or as a means for operating a piece of equipment. Also, any line used to attach an article of equipment to a person, such as a knife or weapon.

Lash: To secure by turns of line or wire.

Left-laid: Refers to line or wire in which the strands spiral along in a counterclockwise direction as one looks along the line.

Life line: Safety line bent to a man going over the side, boarding a wreck or engaging in similar hazardous duty.

Lift: Term applied to any load to be hoisted.

Light displacement: The weight of a vessel when she is nearly as empty as she ever gets. Light draft.

Lightening hole: A hole cut in a structure to reduce weight.

Lloyd's Open Form: a formal contract between the casualty's owners and the salvor, giving him the right to salvage the stricken vessel and recover his expenses, plus a "salvage award" as determined by the courts.

Load displacement: The weight of a vessel when she is loaded as heavily as possible.

Load line marks: Marks on the side of a vessel that indicates the limits to which she may be loaded. Also called a Plimsoll mark.

Longitudinal: A part of the framing running in a fore and aft direction.

Long ton: Maritime unit of weight equal to 2,240 pounds.

Luff tackle: A purchase containing one single and one double block.

-M-

Manway: Doorway or hatchway designed for the passage of personnel.

Marlinspike: Tapered steel tool used to open the strands in wire rope for splicing.

Messenger: A line or wire used to heave another line or wire across an intervening space.

Metacenter: The point where a perpendicular from a ship's center of buoyancy intersects her centerline.

Monkey fist: A complicated knot, with or without a weight enclosed, worked into the end of a heaving line.

-N-

Net tonnage: The gross tonnage minus the deducted spaces.

-O-

Oakum: Tarred hemp fiber used to caulk seams in wooden decks and hulls.

Outboard: Away from the centerline.

Overboard discharge: Any opening in the side of a ship through which wastewater is discharged.

Overhead: The underside of a deck which forms that overhead of compartments on the next deck below.

-P-

Padeye: A metal pad, containing an eye and welded, bolted or riveted to the deck or some strong point.

Parbuckle: (Salvage) To roll a vessel in order to right it by means of rigging, winches and anchors.

Pawl: Metal tongue on a hinge, engaged to a chain, cable or ratchet to arrest motion in a single direction.

Pelican hook: A hook that can be opened while under a strain by knocking away a locking ring that holds it closed; used to provide instantaneous release.

Pontoon: A hard floatation device, usually made of steel, used for refloating sunken objects.

Porthole: The small, round windows often located between the gunwale of a ship and the waterline.

Position buoy: Towing spar used to mark the location of an object towing astern, as the end of a magnetic sweep cable.

Preventer: Refers to any line, wire or chain whose general purpose is to act as a safeguard in case something else carries away.

Pudding: Bulky fender attached to a strongback or to the stem or gunwales of a boat. Usually found on harbor tugs.

-R-

Reeve: To thread, as when threading a needle, but refers to the process of threading the fall on a purchase. The act of a line or wire in threading through an opening, as a line reeves through a snatch block.

Rigging: General term used for the line and/or wire which support a ship's masts, stack, etc. (called standing rigging), and the lines, wires and tackle which hoist, lower and otherwise control the motion of movable deck gear (called running rigging).

Right-laid: The clockwise spiraling of strands along a rope or wire.

-S-

Salvage Master: The person (often the Captain of a salvage tug) in charge of a salvage operation.

Sampson post: A king post: the single bitts in a small boat.

Sea anchor: Any device streamed from the bow or stern of a vessel for the purpose of creating a drag to hold the vessel's end into the sea.

Sea chest: A structure fitted to the internal shell plating for supplying water to condensers, engines, etc.

Secure: Expresses the idea of to fix, attach, make fast, to knock off, to cease.

Seizing stuff: Three-strand, right laid, American hemp.

Shaft alley: A long compartment in the after part of the ship where the propeller shaft operates.

Shear leg: Hoisting rig consisting of two spars joined together at the head and set up so as to resemble an inverted "V", also known as an A Frame.

Short stay: When the anchor cable has been hove in just short of causing the anchor to break ground.

Shot: A unit of measure (usually for chain) equal to fifteen fathoms.

Skeg: The lower extension of the stern frame of a vessel that extends aft of the sternpost and is used to support the rudderpost.

Skid: Long, heavy timbers used in construction to cradle.

Slush: The act of applying a protective coating to line or wire.

Spar: Long, cylindrical timber or metal pipe.

Spar buoy: A floating spar, often of metal.

Spring line: A mooring line that leads forward or aft.

Stage: The hanging platform on which men stand or sit when working over the side.

Stanchion: Any vertical post of column acting as a support for the overhead.

Stave: To crush inward.

Stay: A piece of standing rigging providing support.

Stem: The most forward part of a vessel or the vertical or nearly vertical forward extension of the keel.

Stop off: The act of attaching a stopper to a line, wire or chain that is under strain, usually to hold the strain temporarily while the slack above the stopper is being shifted for belaying.

Stopper: Any apparatus for stopping off a line, wire or chain, but usually consisting of a length of line, wire or chain, with one end bent to a solid support.

Strake: A continuous row of plating from the bow to the stern, identified by letters beginning with "A" strake, which is the garboard strake, and continuing outward and upward to the sheer strake.

Structural bulkhead: A bulkhead that is a strength member of the framing as well as a partition.

Stud: A metal piece in a link of anchor chain that keeps the link from kinking.

Stuffing box: A watertight fitting that allows a rotating shaft (propeller or rudder) to pass through the hull

Stuffing tube: A device that makes watertight the aperture in a bulkhead that a pipe passes through.

Suction head: Vertical distance from water level to point where water enters the pump.

-T-

Thimble: Circular or heart shaped, grooved metal buffer fitted snugly into an eye splice.

Top up: To raise the boom to its working angle by means of its topping lift.

Topping lift: A line, wire or tackle used to hoist, lower and support the head of a cargo boom or the outboard end of a sailing boom or boat boom.

Total head: Vertical distance from waterline to the point of discharge.

Towing bitts: Strong bitts on a tug, aft, especially designed for sustaining the strain of the towing hawser.

Transom: A square stern.

Transverse frame: Frame running athwartships and supporting a deck: also called a deck beam.

Turn of the bilge: The line along which the side meets the bottom.

-U-

Unlay: The act of untwisting and so separating the strands of a line or wire.

-V-

Variation: Magnetic compass error caused by the difference between the magnetic pole and true north (toward the geographic pole), expressed in degrees east or west.

-W-

Warp: To move one end of a vessel broadside by heaving on a line secured on the dock.

Watertight: Capable of resisting flooding or containing no leaks.

Watertight integrity: Quality of watertightness.

Weather deck: Any deck or portion of a deck that is exposed to the elements.

Wildcat: Circular steel disc on the shaft of a windlass. Its edge contains depressions that engage the links of a chain cable.

Winch: A hoisting engine containing one or two cylindrical gypsies or catheads on a horizontal shaft.

19.0 RIGGING

The use of lifting devices, ropes, cables, chains, and slings to move material, equipment or cargo from one location to another is known as rigging. On most construction projects, there is usually at least one crew of riggers who perform the rigging work for all trades. Divers, however, often must perform their own surface rigging and always must perform the underwater rigging themselves. Divers are frequently required to rig heavy steel, concrete, or equipment underwater, without help or advice, while fighting against a current, often in poor or no visibility, with only the tools that they have brought with them. Furthermore, they must not only do this safely, but they must do it right the first time. Underwater rigging requires good sense, proper planning, skillful execution, and the right gear.

After safe diving operations, rigging is the most important skill the commercial diver has to learn. Almost every job the commercial diver performs will involve rigging. A mistake can lead to damage to goods or equipment, injury or even death. This section will be only the beginning of an education about rigging. A competent diver must practice what is presented here to begin to develop critical rigging skills.

SPECIAL CAUTION

Stored energy is one of the most common causes of injury or death to riggers. It is absolutely imperative that all personnel stay clear of any rope, wire rope or chain that is under heavy strain. Natural fiber, synthetic and wire rope all whip violently to one side or the other when they part. A parting rope or cable can hit with enough force to easily cut a person in half. Chain, on the other hand, will fly straight back on itself when it parts, also with enough force to cause fatal injury.

19.1 ROPE

There are two types of natural fiber ropes and several synthetic fiber ropes commonly used in rigging and offshore diving operations.

19.1.1 Natural Fiber Rope

The two types of natural fiber rope are both made from hemp. Sisal, which is made from sisal hemp (produced in Mexico and the West Indies), is a cheaper and lower strength rope often used for tarp tie-downs, lashing, and quite often as a "breakaway link" to secure a diving umbilical in strong current. Manila rope is made from abaca, or Manila hemp, which comes from the leaf stalk of a banana plant native to the Philippines. It is a very strong rope that weathers better than many synthetic ropes. In the past, all sailing vessels used Manila rope. Today it is mainly used in rope tackle, cargo nets and scrambling nets.

19.1.2 Synthetic Rope

The most commonly used types of synthetic rope are nylon and polypropylene. Nylon rope is the strongest commonly used rope. Nylon ropes are either twisted or braided, usually white, soft to the touch, and are heavier than water. Nylon rope will stretch to nearly twice its length. It is durable and weathers well, even when exposed to direct sunlight. Because it is synthetic, nylon rope is susceptible to damage from chemicals and petroleum products. Nylon is used when strength is important but stretching and floatation are not. Nylon rope is often used for lifting slings, although cutting and abrasion hazards must be avoided. Polypropylene is the most commonly used rope type. It comes in a variety of colors, and is either twisted or braided with twisted being the most common. Polypropylene is not as strong as nylon, does not stretch as much and is cheaper. Poly is lighter than water and is often the rope of choice for marine work. Because poly is also synthetic, it, too, is susceptible to chemical and petroleum product damage. It does not weather as well as nylon and will break down from direct sunlight but it withstands abrasion and cutting hazards better than nylon. Polypropylene is often used for moorings and for lifting slings.

19.1.3 Properties of Rope

Most rope construction is spun, or "hawser laid" and is composed of a number of thin yarns spun into thicker strands, which are laid up together to form the rope. Most rope is three stranded, with the strands laid up right-handed. As the rope is laid up, its length contracts like a coil spring, giving the rope some elasticity. The illustration details the construction of typical fiber rope.

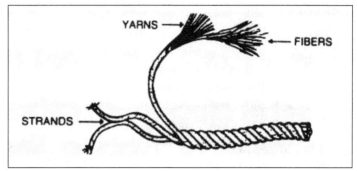

Construction of fiber rope

Fiber rope is strained to its breaking point, which is recorded, and then a percentage of that breaking strength is used as the "safe working load" for that particular rope. This safe working load should never be exceeded, because it provides a safety factor that is absolutely essential in rigging. The safe working load of all fiber rope is ⅕ of its breaking strain when used for hoisting loads and ⅒ of its breaking strain when supporting personnel.

To compute the strength of manila rope, convert the diameter of the rope into eighths of an inch, then square the numerator and multiply the squared numerator by 20. The answer is in pounds. The formula for ½" manila is applied as follows: ½ = ⁴⁄₈; 4 × 4 × 20 = 320 lbs. Thus, the maximum safe working load for this size of manila rope is 320 lbs.

19.1.4 Care of Rope

Countless new coils of rope have been hopelessly tangled when some well-meaning soul without a clue grabs the wrong end of the coil. This may not sound like a serious problem, but when you consider that the safety line on a diving umbilical is ⅜" and a coil of ⅜" rope is typically 1,200 feet in length, you can see that a screw-up opening a new coil can ruin a lot of rope in a hurry. The illustration below will help:

Whenever a length of rope is measured out for a specific purpose and cut, both sides of the cut must be protected against unraveling. This is done most initially by taping the ends. To properly tape a rope end, wind the tape in the exact same direction as the rope twist and give it three tight wraps, pressed down. Tape will only last

New rope is always uncoiled from the center of the coil.

A basket or drum that is slightly larger in diameter than the coil is perfect for storage.

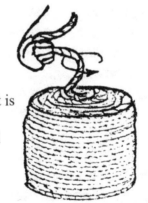

Right-lay rope (most rope is right lay) is uncoiled from the center of the coil in a counter-clockwise direction.

Always secure the end when you are finished.

Uncoiling a new coil of rope

for a short while, so all rope ends should be whipped (or melted if synthetic) as soon as the diver has the time. The proper technique for whipping rope ends is found later in this chapter

Proper maintenance and handling are important for keeping rope safe and serviceable. Rope must be kept clean and free of mud or grease. It should not be stored in a damp or wet place or thrown into a corner where it can tangle and kink. Rope should always be stored coiled. Synthetic ropes should never be stored in direct sunlight. Caution must be taken to avoid abrasion from dirt, grit, or sharp edges. It is important not to walk on ropes as this grinds in contaminants.

Rope should be neatly coiled so that it will pay out smoothly when needed. To coil rope, first shake it out in a straight line so there will be no kinks. Hold the end with the left hand. With the right hand, pull in enough rope to make a loop about eighteen inches long. Roll the rope a half turn toward the body with the right thumb and forefinger while placing the loop in the left hand. This will counteract the twist put in the rope as the loop is made, and will help to eliminate kinks. To make a flat coil, lay the outer circle first and coil in toward the center in a clockwise direction. Give a half turn to each coil to eliminate kinks. If the coil is too loose, tighten it by twisting the center with the palm of the hand. To uncoil it, start in the center.

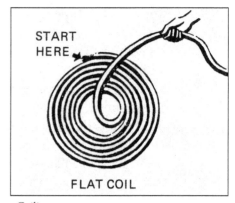

Coiling rope

The ends of every rope should be "whipped" to keep them from unraveling. There are several methods of doing this. The simplest method is American whipping. For ropes of synthetic fibers like nylon, whipping may be done by applying a hot iron or flame to the ends. This fuses the strands. For a more permanent and satisfactory whipping on a natural-fiber rope, use a back splice, although this makes a small lump on the rope end that may be undesirable for some specific uses.

19.1.5 American Whipping Technique

Waxed sail twine or electrician's twine is the best to use for whipping. Another good twine that is commonly used for whipping is tarred marlin. Tarred marlin is often used to whip steel cable. American Whipping is illustrated in the drawing below. The steps are as follows:

1. Lay a loop of the twine on the end of the rope as shown above. End A should be fairly short.
2. Turn the loop Cover the end A and take several turns around the end of the rope, spiraling away from the end and drawing each turn tight.
3. When the whipping is as wide as the diameter of the rope, pull on end A until the loop has disappeared.
4. Trim off ends A and B.

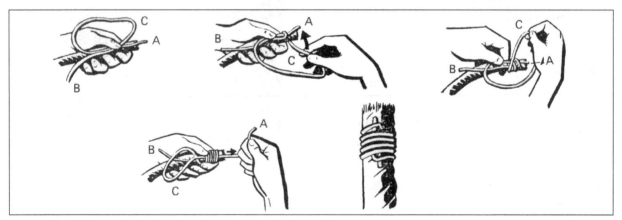

American whipping illustration

19.2 KNOTS, BENDS, AND HITCHES

By definition, a knot is a method of attaching or joining rope that may be tied without great difficulty, will hold secure under strain and then may be easily untied after the strain is taken off. Every knot, bend, or hitch reduces the strength of the rope it is tied in: knots and bends by half and hitches by one quarter. All knots are formed by using 3 simple turns: the bight, the loop, and the overhand.

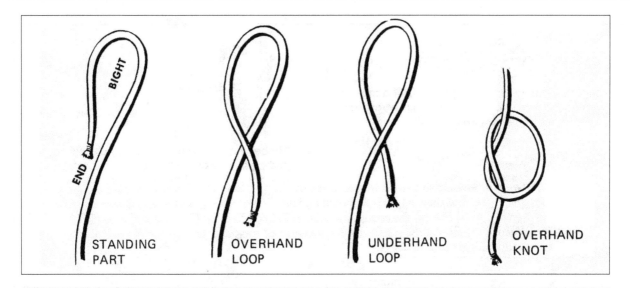

STANDING PART   OVERHAND LOOP   UNDERHAND LOOP   OVERHAND KNOT

1. **Bowline:** a universal knot that is easily tied and untied. It is commonly used wherever a hitch is needed that will not slip or jam. **The "King of Knots."**

2. **French bowline:** used to form two nonslip loops.

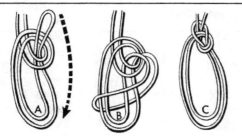

3. **Bowline on a bight:** used to tie a bowline in the middle of a line or to make up a set of double leg spreaders.

4. **Triple bowline (rescue bowline):** effective for lifting injured persons because it has three loops available to support both legs and back.

5. **Running bowline:** makes an excellent slipknot or noose. It runs freely on the standing part, is easily untied, and is strong.

6. **Carrick bend:** a knot used for joining together large ropes. It is generally easy to untie after being subjected to strain.

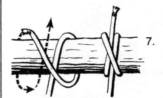

7. **Clove hitch:** a quick, simple hitch for fastening a rope around a post or pipe.

Common knots

8. **Figure eight knot:** used at the end of a rope to temporarily prevent the strands from unraveling, or to prevent the end from running through a block.

9. **Reef or square knot:** used to join two ropes or lines of the same size; holds firmly and is easily untied.

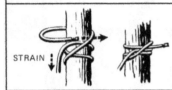

10. **Rolling hitch:** used for lifting round loads such as pipe or for securing a line to a post.

11. **Two half hitches:** used to secure rope to a post.

12. **Sheet bend:** used for joining together the ends of two free lines, especially light or medium ropes of different sizes.

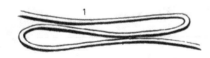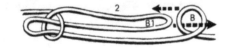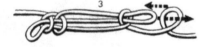

13. **Sheepshank:** used for temporarily shortening a rope or to eliminate a weak point in the line.

14. **Timber hitch:** useful for hoisting planks, timber, and pipe. Use only when load is steady. Do **not** use to lower a load to a diver. Do **not** use in the water.

15. **Butterfly knot:** used to put a tied bight in the middle of a line. Most useful to divers. Does not require access to either end of the rope to tie it. Easily untied.

16. **Catspaw:** used to attach a rope to a hook and is particularly useful when securing the middle of a rope to a hook. It is tied by forming two loops in the rope and twisting them away from you (at least three twists). The two twisted loops are then brought together and placed over the hook. Use instead of Blackwall, which should not be used for lifting operations.

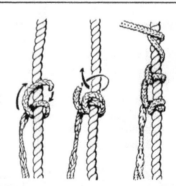

17. **Stopper hitch:** used to secure a line under load to prevent its accidental release while the line is slacked at the bitter end. Ensure the stopper is tied against the lay of the load line.

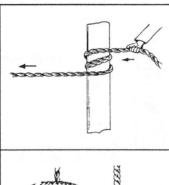

18. **Snubber:** for holding or slowly lowering a heavy load. The load on the hand line is only a fraction of the load on the live line. Three or four turns should be taken.

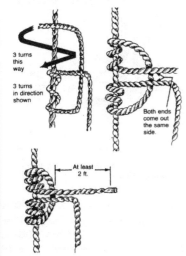

3 turns this way

3 turns in direction shown

Both ends come out the same side.

At least 2 ft.

19. **Triple sliding hitch:** generally used to secure a safety belt lanyard to a life line. The sliding hitch can also be used as a stopper or jam to secure or snub another running line. Used to climb another line: when slack, it slides; when a load is applied downward, it locks.

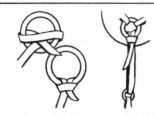

20. **Girth hitch:** used extensively in connecting primacord in explosive work and in general hitching applications.

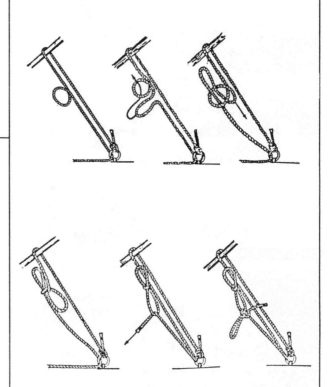

21. **Trucker's hitch:** used to take excess slack out of a standing line and to maintain tension in the line without slipping. The Trucker's Hitch, also known as a Baker Bowline, gives a simple mechanical advantage of three to one less a great amount of friction determined by the coarseness of the line or rope used. The hitch can be secured with a simple slip half-hitch.

19.3 SPLICING FIBER ROPE

A rope splice is the joining of the ends of two ropes or the end of a rope with the body of a rope, by the weaving of strands. A splice reduces the load-carrying capacity of a rope by 10 to 15%, regardless of the type or age of the rope. Care must be taken during the splicing operation to avoid loss of twist and to maintain the form and lay of yarns and strands.

19.3.1 The short splice

The short splice is the strongest of all splices, but it is not suitable if the rope runs over sheaves or through blocks because the diameter of the rope is about doubled at the joint. For example, short splices are suitable for endless slings. The steps to make a short splice are as follows:

1. Begin by unlaying (untwisting) the ropes a few turns. If the rope is large, make temporary whippings on the ends of the strands.
2. Alternate the strands of the two ropes.
3. Tie strands down to prevent more unlaying.
4. Tuck strand 1 (below) over an opposing strand and under the next strand.
5. The tuck of strand 2 goes over strand 5, under the second, and out between the second and third.

6. Repeat operation with strands 1 and 3 from same rope end.
7. Remove tie and repeat operation on other rope end. Make two or more tucks for each strand.
8. Then roll the tucks and cut off ends.
9. Smooth the splice by rolling between the hands or on the floor under a foot.

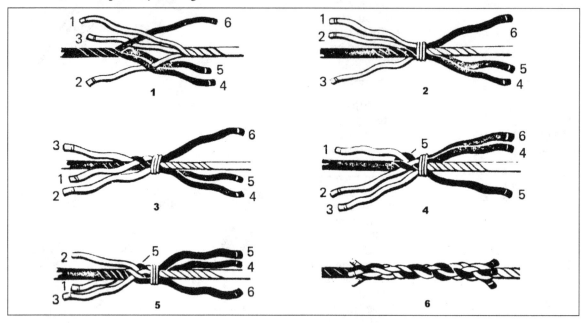

19.3.2 The long splice

The long splice is slightly weaker than the short splice, but it increases the rope diameter only slightly, allowing it to run through sheaves and blocks without catching. A long splice should be made only with two ropes of the same size. The steps to make a long splice are as follows:

1. Unlay each rope end about 15 turns. Place the two rope together, alternating strands of each end.
2. Using opposite pairs, unlay one end (4) and fill its place with the "partner" strand (2). Repeat operation exactly with another pair of strands (1 and 6) in opposite direction.
3. Trim the longer strand (4) and tie each pair of opposing strands (2 and 4) with an overhand knot, tucking each strand twice. The tuck goes over the first strand, under the second, and out between the second and third.
4. Strands 3 and 5 are simply tied with an overhand knot.
5. Strands 1 and 6 are halved and opposite strands tied with an overhand before tucking.
6. Roll and pound all tucks into the rope and then clip the individual strand ends.

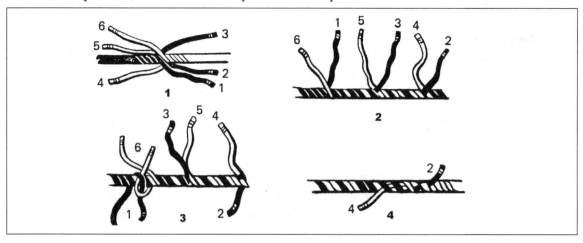

19.3.3 The eye splice

The eye splice is used to form an eye in the end of a rope. It is the strongest type of rope loop, stronger than any knot that forms an eye. This splice is made like the short splice, except only one rope is used. Metal or nylon thimbles should be fitted to all eye splices used for heavy lifting or when the possibility of chafing of the eye exists. The steps to make an eye splice are as follows:

1. Begin by unlaying the end four or five turns.
2. Tuck strand 2 over strand c, under b, and then out between strands a and b.
3. Tuck strand 1 once over strand b and under a.
4. Tuck strands twice, as shown for strand 2.

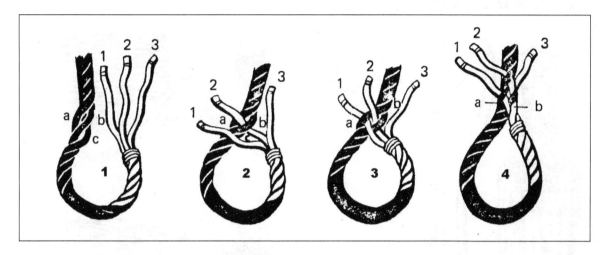

19.4 WIRE ROPE

Wire rope consists, in general, of a number of wire strands formed in a spiral about a center axis. Most ropes have six or eight strands, supported by a central element known as the core. Each strand is composed of a number of individual wires that have been formed spirally about an axis. The core is usually made from hemp, jute, or man-made fiber that cushions the strands and absorbs lubricant. When manufactured, wire rope is lubricated inside and out, but this original lubrication will not last the life of the rope. If it is not kept lubricated inside and out, wire rope will quickly rust. Cable must be lubricated internally and externally while in service as well. Wire rope is manufactured either right-lay or left-lay. The standard (most commonly used) is right-lay and left-lay often must be special ordered. For this reason, right-lay wire rope is often referred to as "standard lay" or "regular lay" rope. See illustration below:

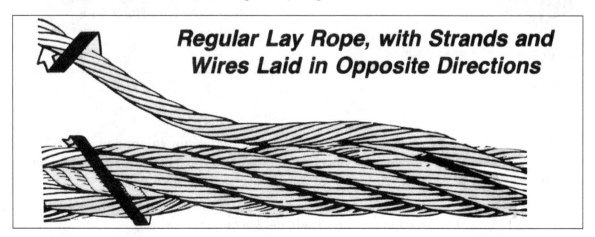

Regular Lay Rope, with Strands and Wires Laid in Opposite Directions

As previously stated, wire rope is constructed of a great many individual wires. These wires are laid into strands by a spinning process. Then the strands are laid (also by spinning) around a central core that may be either a fiber or a separate steel wire rope. Wire rope is typed by the number of wires and strands in the construction. A 6 × 19 wire rope is constructed with 6 strands of 19 wires each.

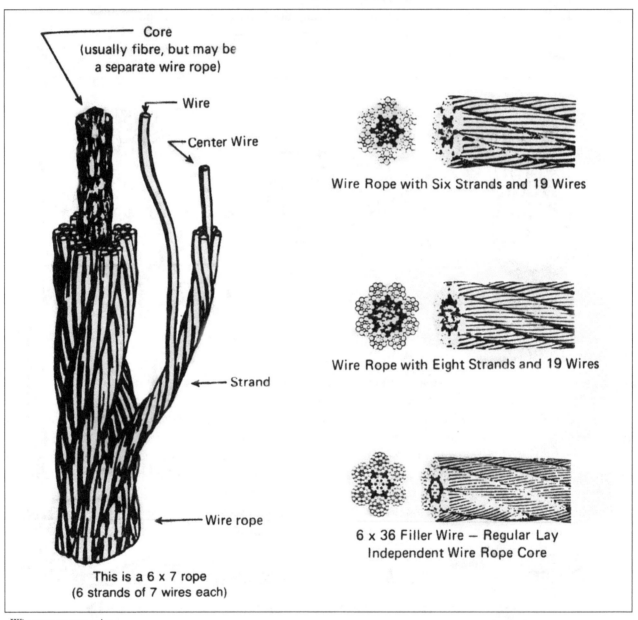

Wire rope construction

Wire rope, like fiber rope, has a safe working load (SWL). The formula for computing the SWL of wire rope is SWL = 8D² (diameter of the wire rope squared and multiplied by eight). The answer is in tons. For example, to find the SWL of half inch wire rope, we would calculate it in this way: 0.5 × 0.5 × 8 = 2 tons.

The actual load on the wire rope should only be a fraction of the breaking load. Like fiber rope, the safe working load (SWL) is ⅕ of its breaking strain for loads and ⅒ for personnel.

19.4.1 Rotating Cable

Wire rope, also called cable, is classified as either rotating or non-rotating. Standard cable is rotating cable, right-lay. This means that the strands twist right, like screw threads. When a strain is placed on the cable, the strands attempt to straighten, thereby causing the load, if suspended, to rotate. Rotating cable is used for tuggers and winches, as stay or guide wires, barge towlines, and for wire slings and spreaders. Wire rope, like natural fiber and synthetic fiber, is available in either right- or left-hand lay. Unless otherwise specified, it will always be supplied in right hand lay, since right hand lay is considered "standard."

19.4.2 Non-rotating Cable

Non-rotating cable is manufactured with inner and outer layers that have opposing twists, which cancel one another when a strain is placed on the cable. Non-rotating cable is much more expensive. Cranes of all types should only be rigged with non-rotating cable. Non-rotating cable is the type often used on the LARS for diver's stages and clump-weights. Non-rotating cable is also available in right or left hand lay. It is important to ensure the required lay prior to ordering the cable. Many double drum cranes use right-hand on one winch and left-hand on the other winch.

19.4.3 Care of Wire Rope

Some riggers are of the opinion that wire rope is steel, and it requires no special care. Nothing could be further from the truth. If it is not properly cared for, wire rope often will not last as long as fiber rope. In order to avoid failure due to metal fatigue, sharp bends and chaffing must be avoided in wire rope.

As with fiber ropes, it should be kept free of sand, grit and other abrasives. Wire rope must be regularly lubricated with grease or cable dressing both inside and out. A non-lubricated wire rope is actually destroying itself every time a strain is taken: the individual wires and strands drag and chafe against each other without the proper internal lubrication.

As with fiber rope, new wire rope must be properly taken off the spool or it will kink. A kink in a wire rope destroys the rope, so this must be avoided at all cost. To avoid kinks, set the wire spool up on a stand so that it will rotate freely.

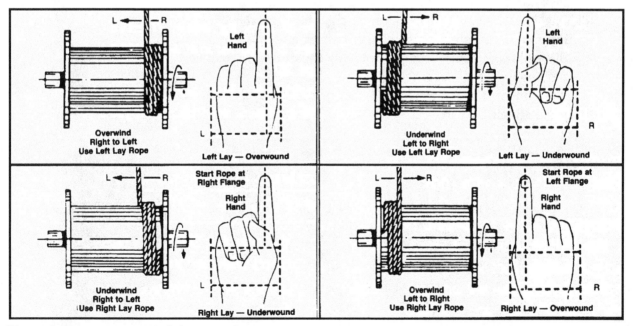

How to wind wire rope onto a winch drum correctly

If installing the wire rope on a winch, there must be some method of "braking" to keep tension on the wire rope as it is wound onto the winch drum. Wire rope must be attached to the proper anchorage point on a winch drum. The lay of the wire rope and whether it is over-wound or under-wound determines which side of the drum is used for the anchorage point as the illustration below shows.

19.5 SPLICING WIRE ROPE

Wire rope is spliced in roughly the same way as fiber rope, but because wire is much less pliable, greater skill is required and particular care must be taken with whippings and seizings. Splicing reduces the strength of wire rope by approximately one-eighth but a badly made splice will obviously reduce it appreciably more. The less the strands are distorted and disturbed when tucked, the less the loss of strength to the wire rope. When preparing wire for splicing, the ends of the strands must always be firmly whipped before they are unlaid from the rope. The only wire rope splice seen offshore is the eye splice. The steps to make an eye splice in wire rope are as follows:

19.5.1 Wire Eye Splice

1. To make an eye splice, put a stout whipping on the rope and unlay the strands to the whipping.
2. Cut out the heart (core) of the rope.
3. Form the eye required and stop the 2 parts of the wire firmly together to prevent movement during the tucking of the strands. This may be done using a vice or vice-grips.
4. Place 3 strands on 1 side of the wire and the remaining 3 on the opposite side of the wire.
5. Place the eye so that the tucking end lies to the left of the standing part thus enabling strand number 1 to be inserted from the right-hand side and against the lay.
6. Tuck strand number 1 under the strand immediately below it.
7. Tuck numbers 2, 3, and 4 under successive strands of the standing part. Tuck number 6 under the remaining 2 strands of the standing part.
8. Finally, tuck number 5 so that it emerges between the 2 strands under which number 6 lies and after passing under 1 strand only. This will result in the 6 strands emerging equidistantly around the standing part.
9. Now pull the strands down towards the crown of the eye, taking care not to cripple the wire.

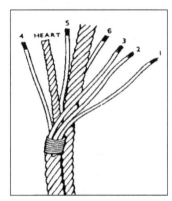

Steps 1 through 5

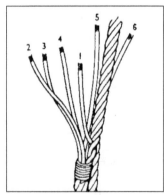

Step 6

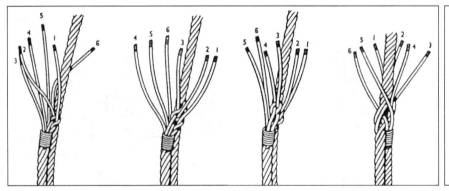

Step 7   Step 8

10. Place a seizing outside the tucks to prevent them easing back during subsequent stages. If the strand cores are jute or hemp, remove the whippings at the end of the strands, cut out the cores and then replace the whippings.

11. Tuck these coreless strands in regular sequence again, placing a seizing outside each series of tucks.

12. Take ⅓ of the wires out of each strand and stop them back toward the crown of the eye.

13. Tuck the remaining ⅔ once, and then stop back half the wires in each strand again.

14. Tuck each of the ⅓ strands once, remove the seizing from each tuck and then tap down all tucks with a mallet, starting from the first tuck and finishing at the tail to remove any slack and round up the splice.

15. Break off all ends, including those stopped back, by bending each separate wire to and fro. A small hook is thus formed in the end of each wire that will prevent it from drawing through the holding strand.

19.5.2 Saddle Clamps

When you need to make an eye in a wire rope and you do not have the time to splice, the saddle clamp is the only other option. When installed properly, these saddle clamps will provide an eye with 80% of the original wire rope strength. These clamps are often called Crosby Clamps or Crosby Clips because the best manufacturer, Crosby, tests and guarantees every clamp. To determine the number of saddle clamps to install on a given wire, use the following formula: D × 3 + 1 = number. That is diameter of wire rope times three, plus one equals the number of clamps. For a 1-inch wire, that is 1 × 3 + 1, or 4 saddle clamps. Never use less than 3, regardless of wire size. To determine the spacing between the clamps, use the following formula: D × 6 = Distance. That means the wire diameter × 6 is the spacing between the saddle clamps. For a ½-inch wire rope, that is ½ × 6 or 3 inches between the clamps.

Photo courtesy of Crosby

There is a right and a wrong way to install a saddle clamp, and if installed the wrong way, they will not hold. Remember the following statement: "**Never saddle a dead horse.**" The saddle portion of the clamp has to be on the "live" part of the wire and never on the "deadend" of the wire. The "U" bolt goes over the dead end and the saddle goes on the live end – EVERY TIME.

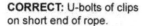

CORRECT: U-bolts of clips on short end of rope.

WRONG: U-bolts on live end of rope.

WRONG: Staggered clips; two correct and one wrong

CORRECT: (With clips removed) no distortion on live end of rope.

All saddle clamps must be installed in the same manner. Often some backyard engineer will say "alternate the clamps, one each way," but don't listen to that. When installing the clamps, tighten the nuts as you would lug nuts on a wheel: a little tension on each one, alternating until they are tight. Once all of the clamps are installed, put a slight strain on the wire and re-tighten. If the wire will be taking a large strain, put a large strain on the wire, wait half an hour and re-tighten the clamps again.

19.5.3 Wire Rope Terminations

Often a wire rope must have a "permanent" end or termination installed. Examples of this are on the ends of crane or tugger cables and hoist cables for diving bells, diver's stages or diver's tool baskets. Often it falls to the diving crew to install these terminations. There are three common types of termination: the swaged (crimped) eye splice, the wedge socket and the spelter socket.

Swaged (crimped) eye and thimble

The swaged eye, when it has a thimble installed, is as strong as the wire rope itself. However, one big drawback to this termination is that it requires a special hydraulic press to install and is typically done at a wire rope dealership or crane dealership. On a rare occasion, a large crane barge will be set up to do them. The other drawback is that if this type termination is in a position where it constantly flexes, it will fail.

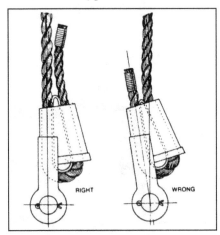

Wedge socket

The wedge socket is the termination used on virtually every bell lift wire and stage wire in the commercial diving industry. The sketch above shows the right and wrong way to install wedge sockets, but in the "right" sketch, there is something missing. When a wedge socket is installed, the "tail" or dead end of the wire is left at least 8 inches long and the dead end has another short piece of wire attached to it with a saddle clamp. This is done just to ensure that there is absolutely no way of the wire rope pulling out of the socket. Wedge sockets, although they reduce the strength of the wire rope to 70%, are an excellent termination, able to take all of the movement and strain a diving bell can subject them to. As with any rigging, they require regular inspection for wear, or damage to the wire rope.

The spelter socket is a termination that is often used for restraining wires on such things as crane booms, LARS A Frames and the like. These are installed by pushing the cable end into the small end of the socket, loosening up the cable strands and pouring molten zinc or epoxy resin into the wide end of the socket. Spelter sockets are a very strong termination, but the zinc and the steel in the cable create dissimilar metals corrosion when this type of wire rope termination is used underwater. That is the reason epoxy resin is seeing increased use in spelter sockets.

Spelter sprocket
Photo courtesy of Crosby

19.6 CHAIN

Chain is most often seen in more permanent applications, such as on anchors, moorings and to restrain items such as floating fenders. Chain is not seen as often as rope and wire rope in rigging applications, but occasionally it is used. Chain size is measured by taking the diameter of the side of one link. Because there are so many different types and grades of chain, there is no simple formula for establishing the breaking strength or the safe working load. It is left to the rigger to determine the size and grade of the chain, then to consult a chain capacity chart (provided by chain suppliers).

There are two basic types of chain commonly seen: standard link chain and stud-link chain. Standard link chain has oval shaped links and is used for lifting, binding loads and to secure items on or to a vessel. Stud link chain is extremely strong chain, very heavy, and most often used for anchor chain or mooring chain. Stud-link may be recognized by the steel stud that runs across from side to side in each link. Anchor and mooring chain has the length measured by "shots." One shot is 90 feet or 15 fathoms.

Stud-link chain

Standard chain supplied by a reputable manufacturer will have the grade stamped on the side of links, as is shown in the photo on the right. Standard chain is available in several grades, but the most common are grade 30, grade 80, and grade 100. The higher grades are very strong. In ⅜-inch chain, grade 80 has a safe working load of 7,100 pounds. The same size chain in grade 100 has a SWL of 8,800 pounds. Typically, grade 30 is used for binding cargo and grade 80 and 100 are used for lifting.

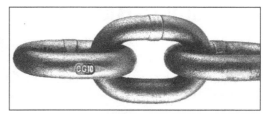

Standard chain with the grade marked on the side of the links.
Photo courtesy of Crosby

Chain is very robust and will withstand a lot, but it does wear, and it can be damaged. Once damaged or worn, it should not be used. There are signs to look for when inspecting chain for suitability for use.

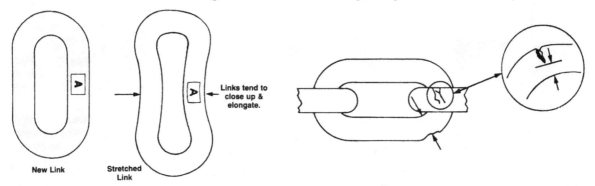

New Link

Stretched Link

Links tend to close up & elongate.

If put under too great a strain chain will, in fact, stretch. A chain that has been stretched will have links that appear to be crushed inward on the flat side of the oval. Any chain that shows evidence of stretching has been subject to strain that far exceeds the safe working load and should not be re-used. When a chain has been subjected to a shock load, it often will have stress cracks near the ends of the links. These may be seen in addition to signs of stretching. Visible stress cracks will eliminate a chain from being used.

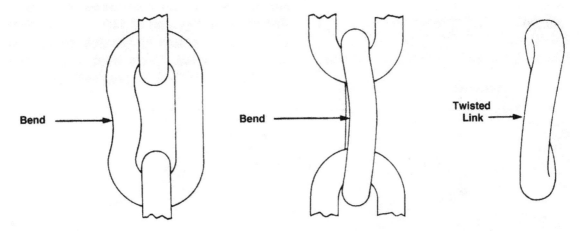

Bend

Bend

Twisted Link

Chain must be laid out reasonably straight prior to putting it under strain. If a chain has a knot in it when it comes under strain or if it makes too tight a bend around a fixed object, bent links will result. If a chain has a twist in it when it comes under strain, the links will twist. Evidence of bent or twisted links will require that the chain not be used for rigging. Long-term use typically produces wear on the inside of the end of the links of a chain. If the wear is to the state that the cross-sectional diameter is reduced, don't use the chain.

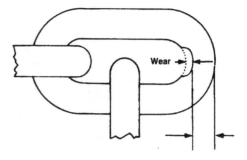

Wear

19.7 RIGGING HARDWARE

The one piece of rigging hardware used more than any other is the shackle. On most commercial diving operations, there will be literally hundreds of shackles, ranging from 2-ton to as high as 300-ton or larger, depending on the operation. There are a few different types of shackles available.

Screw-pin shackle
Photo courtesy of Crosby

Screw pin D shackle
Photo courtesy of Crosby

Anchor or 3-part shackle
Photo courtesy of Crosby

Screw-pin shackles are fast and easy to use, and they are still used for surface rigging by some contractors. But for underwater work, screw-pin shackles are no longer accepted as being safe. The anchor shackle, or 3 part safety shackle, is now required on virtually every jobsite for underwater use and most diving contractors now use them for surface rigging as well. With the nut and cotter key on the shackle pin, they never come apart unless you take them apart deliberately. Many diving contractors change out the cotter keys for a split pin made from a welding rod with the flux broken off. They are far easier for the diver to use underwater than a cotter key. The D shackles are designed to be used with chain. One serious safety issue has been "knock-off" foreign made shackles. Always confirm the source of shackles and rigging hardware with certification paperwork. The safe working load of a shackle is always in raised letters on the side of the bell.

Another commonly used piece of rigging hardware is the turnbuckle. Turnbuckles are used to tighten cable and are often used on guy-wires, stay-wires and temporary rails. There are several configurations of turnbuckle: hook and eye, eye and eye, eye and jaw, and jaw and jaw. The best turnbuckle to use is the jaw and jaw, since it has a pin with a cotter key that will not come loose inadvertently.

Jaw-and-eye turnbuckle
Photo courtesy of Crosby

Eye-and-eye turnbuckle
Photo courtesy of Crosby

Turnbuckles are built with one end having a right hand thread and the other having a left hand thread. They are built this way so that when both ends are attached to a cable or chain, twisting the turnbuckle one way will lengthen it, and turning it the opposite way will shorten it.

Most rigging work performed involves lifting objects from one location to another. The hook of the lifting device, whether that device is a crane or a chain fall, is never attached directly to the object lifted, even if there is an engineered lifting eye or ring on the object. In offshore rigging operations involving a crane, the hook is further away from the load than in onshore rigging, but we will get into that later. To connect the load to the lifting hook, we use slings or straps, made of fiber rope, wire rope, chain, nylon or polyester.

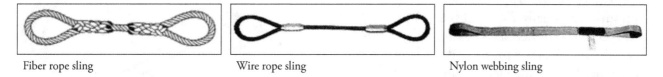

Fiber rope sling   Wire rope sling   Nylon webbing sling

Fiber rope slings are typically used for lighter lifts, and are often made up on the job. Wire rope, nylon or polyester webbing and chain slings are purchased from a rigging supplier. Wire rope slings are available from ⅜ inch up to 2 inch in diameter. Webbing slings are available from 1-inch wide to 10-inches wide or more. These slings are always supplied with an attached tag, which specifies the safe working load in different configurations. There are four basic configurations used with lifting slings: straight, choker, basket and legged. Always consult the specification tag to confirm the sling capacity in the configuration that you plan to use. The basic sling configurations are illustrated below.

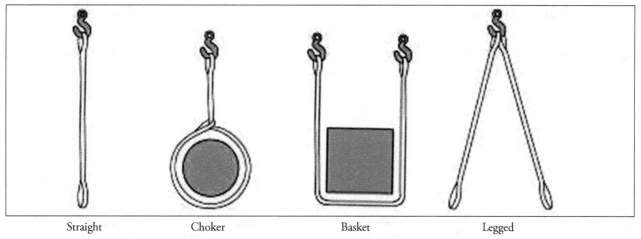

Straight   Choker   Basket   Legged

On the tag provided with the slings, the safe working load for each configuration and each sling angle is specified, because they are not all the same. The angle of the sling greatly affects the load on the sling. The illustration below indicates the load on slings at various angles when making a 1000-pound lift.

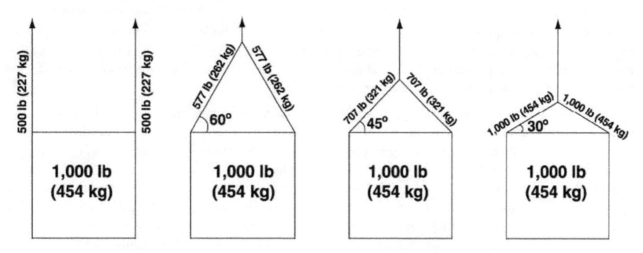

A spreader is used for several reasons: to maintain balance on a lift, the slings available will not reach either side of a wider lift or the slings are on too shallow an angle due to the width of the lift. In any of these cases, we use a spreader. A spreader consists of a top ring, known as a master link, and two or more legs, which may be constructed of wire rope or chain. Spreaders are usually 2 or 4 legged, but specialty spreaders are built for special lifts. A standard spreader always has legs of equal length, and the legs may have safety hooks, or eye and thimble to permit attachment to the load with shackles.

2-part spreader with hooks

4-part spreader with safety shackles

In the illustrations above, a specification tag can be plainly seen, up near the master link. We check safe working load and test information on these spreaders by reading the tag information the exact same way we do for slings. When using spreaders and slings, we always ensure that there are no twists, kinks or sharp bends (on corners) before taking a strain with the lifting device, to avoid damage to the sling or spreader.

Not all loads are perfectly shaped for easy lifting. Lifts do not come pre-packaged and sometimes there are pipes, fittings or other projections that must not be damaged by slings. Sometimes slings and spreaders cannot be used without the slings passing over a sharp edge that presents a chafing hazard to the slings. In these cases, we use what is known as a spreader beam. If the load is extremely awkward and hard to balance, or if we are performing a "tandem lift" with two lifting devices, we use an equalizer beam.

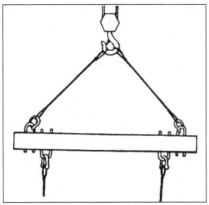

Spreader beam

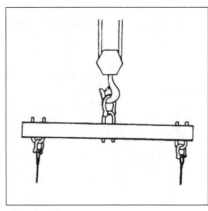
Equalizer beam

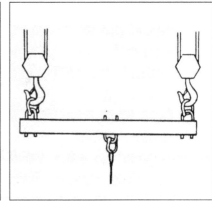
Equalizer beam on a tandem lift

Spreader beams and equalizer beams may be made of steel I-beam, hollow steel tubing or steel pipe, but regardless how they are constructed, they must always be tested and rated. They always have the safe working load stamped and often painted on the side of the beam. Spreaders and equalizers must always be inspected before use, and the safe working load must never be exceeded.

In order to safely lift any object, the rigger must have four pieces of information: the weight of the object to be lifted; the capacity of the rigging hardware; the weight of the rigging hardware and the capacity of the lifting device. The capacity of the rigging hardware is always stamped or marked on a tag. If using a crane with a load sensor, it is easy enough to find the weight of the rigging hardware. The capacity of the crane is always plainly marked on a chart. But the unknown is always the weight of the object. In offshore operations, every item taken offshore has the weight plainly marked, as required by IMCA and IMO. But on an inland diving project, it may not be that easy. Always establish the weight of any lift prior to the start of lifting operations. Do not be that person who upset the crane and got his/her picture on TV.

Occasionally, the rigger may need to change the angle of a rope or wire. Examples of this would be when a load must be skidded across the deck of a barge or when using a winch mounted on deck to take a strain up on an object on the seabed. If a rope or wire is pulled around any solid object, friction results and damage is done to the rope or wire. In order to avoid this, we use a wheel or, more specifically, a block to allow the wire or rope to change direction without friction causing breakage or chafing damage. The size of the pulley (sheave) in the block is determined by the size of the rope or wire used. The minimum size of the sheave is the rope or wire diameter times 8. For example, a 1-inch wire would require an 8-inch sheave. The block normally used in this case is a snatch block. The bight of the wire or rope can be inserted into the snatch block without feeding the end through, and considerable time can be saved on the job.

The illustrations at right show a snatch block in the closed (working) position, in the open (loading) position and possible mechanical advantage. If the wire or rope leading into and out of the block is close to being parallel, there is a 2:1 mechanical advantage. This is a good thing if you are using the snatch block as a moving block, but if it is being used to redirect a wire, this same force must be reckoned with on the anchoring point that the block is attached to.

Closed snatch block
Photo courtesy of Crosby

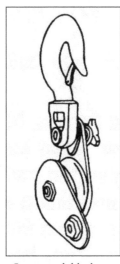
Open snatch block

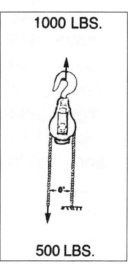
1000 LBS.

500 LBS.

Mechanical advantage

19.8 LIFTING DEVICES

Each lift performed by the rigger is unique, so different techniques and different lifting devices are used for different lifts. The items lifted are not necessarily the same, nor are the conditions or the area. A container holding a deck decompression chamber uses different lifting techniques than a pallet of pipeline bolts. The two types of lifting devices used in marine and diving operations are manual lifting devices and cranes. All lifting devices used, however small the lift, must be in good working order and inspected and proper rigging practice must be used at all times.

19.8.1 Manual Lifting Devices

There are three different manual lifting devices commonly used in diving operations: block and tackle, chain falls and lever hoists. Each of these devices has operations that it is well suited for.

19.8.1.1 Block and Tackle

Block and tackle is the name given to a system of wooden blocks and natural fiber rope commonly used for lifting. This system has actually been used since at least the first century and works on the same principles that modern crane hoists use. A triple (three sheave) block is seen in the illustration.

The sides (cheeks) of the blocks are constructed of hardwood, as are the spacers in between them. The pins, pulleys (sheaves), the beckets, and the hooks are made of hardened steel. The rope

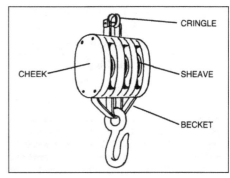
A triple block

used (tackle) is always natural fiber manila rope. This is the same type of system that was used for the rigging on the old sailing ships and block and tackle is still produced and used today. Using the triple sheave block and tackle shown below (called a 3-part block), one small diver could easily lift a 500-pound weight by himself/herself.

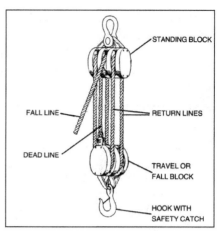
Rigged block

The block and tackle shown is what is known as a "simple" system, consisting of one set of blocks and one length of rope and uses mechanical advantage to enable a strain applied to the fall line to be multiplied on the travel block. To calculate the mechanical advantage of a simple block system, count the number of return lines and the dead line. Do not count the fall line. Not including the fall line, the system shown above has 5 lines (called parts), so the mechanical advantage is 5:1. In other words, pulling downward with a 100-pound force on the fall line will create a lift force of 500 pounds on the travel block.

The illustration at right shows various configurations of blocks, with the mechanical advantage of each shown below it. Notice that the number of lines (excluding the fall line) always equals the mechanical advantage of the block system. With a 2:1 advantage, the strain exerted on the fall will lift twice that amount of weight; 3:1 will lift three times. This method of calculating mechanical advantage is the same for any block system, including crane blocks.

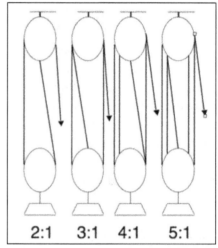
Block configurations

Block and tackle systems usually do not come with a designated safe working load but the following formula may be used to establish SWL:

$$\frac{\text{SWL of rope} \times \text{number of sheaves} \times 10}{\text{Number of sheaves} + 10} = \text{SWL of block and tackle system}$$

Block and tackle may be used either vertically or horizontally. When using block and tackle, always ensure that the attachment point and any supporting framework used is strong enough to support the weight of the lift, or the horizontal strain, with a 5 to 1 ratio. When using, always ensure that the ropes all run straight and are not twisted. If the lift must be suspended, ensure that there is a sturdy cleat handy to make the fall line fast, or you may end up standing holding the fall line for a long time. Always store the block and tackle gear by hanging it up. Do not lay it on the deck or the ground. Rinse well when used underwater.

19.8.1.2 The Lever Hoist (come-along)

The lever hoist, like the shackle, will be found on at least 90% of diving operations. The lever hoist, also called a come-along, is produced in a cable or chain configuration. A chain come-along (the type that is most often used in diving operations) is shown in the illustration below. These units work equally well when used in the vertical or in the horizontal position.

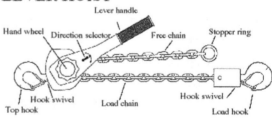
LEVER HOIST

The lever hoist works by using the mechanical advantage of a lever, with a system of ratchets and pawls that grip the chain or cable. The upward (toward the main hook) stroke does not take a strain, but the downward stroke (toward the chain) does take a strain. A switch on the handle reverses the direction of the pull and has a "free chain" position that allows the chain to be rapidly pulled through the unit. Available in capacities from 1 ton to 10 tons, they are a great lifting device when used properly. Every time a lever hoist is used underwater, it must be inspected and serviced by a qualified person before it is used again.

19.8.1.3 The Chain fall (endless chain)

Chain falls, also called chain hoists, or endless chains, are another manual lifting device often found on the commercial diving job-site. Chain falls operate by pulling on the endless chain (hand chain) that turns a system of gears inside the head of the device. The chain fall is usually used in the vertical position, with chains hanging straight down. Although they will operate horizontally, it is very difficult to keep the chains from becoming crossed over and jamming up. Chain falls are available in 1-ton to 30-ton capacity.

On crane lifts, chain falls are occasionally used between the slings and the lift to allow manipulation of the load in cases where the load has to be precision placed. One example of this would be placing a very heavy gearbox against a marine diesel and aligning the shaft. Chain falls may be used underwater, but there is one major drawback: they are assembled with clutches (very much like the one in your pickup), and these clutches degrade when they are immersed in water. Any time that a chain fall is used underwater, it must be totally stripped down, re-built and tested before being used again. If this is not done, there is a very good chance that the unit will bind up under strain on the next use. Chain falls should be stored hanging.

Chain-falls (endless chain)
Photo courtesy of John McElligott

19.8.2 Cranes

There are many types of land-based and marine cranes, but we will only discuss those normally used in conjunction with diving operations. The major difference between land-based and marine cranes is land-based cranes are usually mobile and marine cranes are usually (not always) fixed in position.

19.8.2.1 Land-Based Cranes

The two types of land-based crane most often used in diving operations are the hydraulic mobile crane and the conventional crawler crane. The designation land-based means that these machines were designed to be used on land, but occasionally they are mounted on barges for inshore use. They are most often used purely in the land-based mode on coastal and inland diving operations.

Conventional crawler

Hydraulic mobile

The hydraulic mobile cranes vary from hydraulic booms mounted on flat-bed trucks (called boom trucks) to purpose built crane carriers and off-road rough terrain crane carriers. All hydraulic cranes have a few things in common: they may be driven on the road, they have telescopic booms, they all use out-rigger legs for stability, and they all have hydraulic gear winches that do not have free-fall capability. The telescopic booms are constructed with rectangular or oval sections, the base section being the largest and each successive section being slightly smaller and all fitting in each other. The boom sections are extended and retracted with hydraulic pistons, so the crane can be used with different boom lengths and the boom length may be easily adjusted while the crane has a load off the ground.

The conventional crawler crane crawls on bulldozer style tracks. Although they can move on the job-site, they have to be transported by float trailer on the roads. They have a fixed length lattice boom, the heavy-duty booms made of steel beam or angle, the lightweight booms made of pipe. Although they are called a fixed length boom sections may be added or subtracted, but not while operating. Conventional cranes, also known as friction cranes, use a series of gears and clutches to turn the winches and most have free-fall capability. This is the type of crane that is used for pile driving and dredging since both require free-fall.

19.8.2.2 Marine Cranes

Marine cranes are those that have been designed specifically to be used in the marine environment, be that on board a ship, barge or mounted on an offshore platform. The four types of marine crane typically used in diving operations are as follows: the davit, the A-frame, the hydraulic crane and the conventional crane.

The typical davit is a fixed length, fixed elevation boom that may have swing capability (usually not), with a sheave or series of sheaves at the end of the boom to handle the lift wires. Davits vary in size from small ones (1 ton) used to launch a mini-ROV, to ship's lifeboat davits (20 ton), right up to the pipeline davits (40 ton) used to lift long lengths of pipeline from the seabed when performing subsea pipeline repair.

Pipeline davits

A frame cranes get their name from their shape: two rugged H-beams in an inverted V shape that are affixed to one end of a heavy lift barge. There are diagonal braces (H-beam or cable) run from the far end of the barge or from a secondary A-frame to hold the primary A-frame aloft and a large deck-mounted winch has its wire run up through sheaves at the top of the frame. Some of these A-frame cranes are capable of enormous lifting capacity, up in the tens of thousands of tons, but they are only capable of a vertical lift. If the load needs to move ahead, back or side to side, the entire barge must be moved.

A frame barge

Although there are dozens of styles of marine hydraulic cranes, they can be classified in one of two ways: telescopic boom cranes and articulated boom cranes. The telescopic boom cranes are very similar to their land-based counterparts but usually have a few variations to make them more suitable for the marine environment. These variations typically include non-corrosive fittings, more wire capacity on the winch drums and heave compensation to avoid dynamic shock loading from wave action. The articulated booms have hinged joints, much like the human elbow, that are articulated with hydraulic rams. These booms also are built with non-corrosive fittings and heave compensation. The hydraulic booms vary in capacity, but the larger cranes are typically rated up to 300-ton.

Most derrick barges or offshore crane barges are fitted with a conventional crane. The capacity of these cranes varies, but most offshore crane barges have between a 2,500-ton and a 5,000-ton crane, in order to have the ability to place topside modules on platforms and other heavy lift projects. These cranes usually have a boom that is constructed of very heavy steel I-beam. Like their land-based counterparts, most of the marine conventional

200 t hydraulic articulated crane on DSV   3500 t conventional crane on barge

cranes have two lines, the main block and the whip line. The whip line only has a fraction of the main block's capacity. Usually they have free-fall capability on the whip line but not on the main block. The main block on these cranes is often rigged 24 parts, so heavy lifting and lowering movements take time. On most crane barges, there is a smaller, secondary crane on board to move the rigging components for the larger crane. Typically, this is a 200- or 300-ton crawler crane.

19.8.3 Safety in Crane Operations

Regardless the type of crane being used or whether it is on an inland job or offshore job, there are two top priorities: the safety of all personnel on the job and not damaging the item being lifted. The methods used to ensure that both of those priorities are met are as follows:

1. **Safe cranes**: Land based cranes must be certified annually by the Occupational Safety and Health Administration (US) and the Crane Certification Bureau (Canada). Marine cranes must be certified annually by either Det Norske Veritas (DNV) or the American Bureau of Shipping (ABS), depending on the type of vessel and crane. Certified cranes are required to display a sticker, usually near the crane cab, with the date of certification clearly marked. This inspection covers everything from the crane turn-table, winches and boom to the hooks on the crane wires.

2. **Safe rigging**: All rigging components used in a lift must be certified, and depending on jurisdiction, this is usually a six-month certification. All components must be inspected before every lift, and lifts are never performed with worn, damaged or defective rigging.

3. **Safe rigging practice**: All lifts must be properly rigged with the correct slings and hardware used in the proper manner. This author recommends *Bill Newberry's Handbook for Riggers* as a pocket guide. His book is recognized and accepted worldwide. Safe rigging practice includes not only installing slings or spreaders but also signaling the crane. Offshore, this is usually done with radios, but hand signals are used on those occasions when radios will not work or there is interference. The rigger must know all of the hand signals for hydraulic and conventional cranes. These are included in this chapter, along with rigging safety guidelines.

4. **Safe operating conditions**: There are certain conditions required in order to safely perform a lift with a crane. These include: the crane properly set up to lift, favorable weather, adequate lighting, an unobstructed view of the lift and bystanders kept back a safe distance. Favorable weather on an inland project means wind below 30 knots, and never in electrical storms. On an offshore project, it means seas less than 12 feet, wind below 30 knots, and never in an electrical storm. Depending on the location of the project frost or extreme cold may prevent lifting.

In land-based lifting, the positioning of the crane is critical. The crane must be set up on a secure base, able to safely reach to perform the lift and have clearance for the boom to operate without striking obstructions or coming too close to power lines. Ensuring that the crane is set up on a secure base is often the crane operator's responsibility and if he fails to do so properly, the rigger can be injured or killed. Always examine the base of the outriggers or the tracks. They must be on a firm, hard surface. An outrigger sinking into the ground means an upset crane and that quite often leads to an injury or death. Use large timber or steel pads under outrigger pads whenever the ground does not appear firm to distribute the weight over a larger area.

Always look up and all around for power lines. A crane boom does not have to come in contact with a power line in order for an accident to happen. This author witnessed the death of a rigger in 1975, when a hydraulic boom came within 10 feet of a high-tension wire. There was a bright flash as the electricity arced across the space, then travelled down the crane wire to the load. Unfortunately, the rigger had one hand on the load at that moment and lost his life. A crane to power line clearance chart is provided in this chapter but check the recommended clearances in the jurisdiction where you are working. Not all are the same.

Power Line Voltage in KV (x 1000 volts)	Clearance Between Boom or Crane Cables and Lines
50 KV and below	10 feet (3 meters)
50 to 200 KV	15 feet (4.6 meters)
200 to 350 KV	20 feet (6.2 meters)
350 to 500 KV	25 feet (7.6 meters)
500 to 750 KV	35 feet (10.7 meters)
750 to 1000 KV	45 feet (13.7 meters)
NOTE: THE ABOVE ARE CONSIDERED MINIMUM CLEARANCES	

The crane should be set up in an area without any obstructions in the range of the boom, if possible. Buildings, signs, flagpoles or overhead structures will all impact crane operations. It is not only the boom that must be clear, however. The counterweight of the crane must also be able to move without being obstructed when the crane swings.

In offshore crane operations, setup is not usually a consideration. That is usually addressed by the vessel positioning. There are seldom, if ever, overhead wires to consider, but there certainly are obstructions when working in close proximity to offshore structures. However, the weather conditions are a definite safety consideration. The following is a "stop lift" chart, typical of those used offshore:

Weather Conditions	Operations Stopped
Seas meeting or exceeding 12 feet (4 meters). Seas are considered to be wind wave plus swell height.	All dynamic crane operations
Seas meeting or exceeding 15 feet (5 meters)	All dynamic and static crane operations
Wind speeds (gusts) 30 knots or above	All dynamic and static crane operations
Electrical storm or visible lightning approaching	All crane operations (lower boom if possible)

Although land-based and offshore rigging are essentially the same, there are a few important differences that should be pointed out. The illustrations below show an identical lift rigged for both applications.

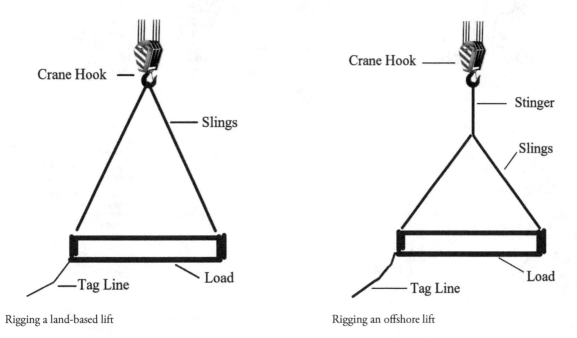

Rigging a land-based lift   Rigging an offshore lift

While both of these applications use slings, notice that the slings on the land-based lift attach directly to the crane hook. Offshore lifts always use a stinger between the slings and the hook. The stinger is usually a wire rope sling with a master link at the top and a safety hook at the bottom to attach the slings. The reason a stinger is used is to keep the crane hook well above the deck to eliminate the possibility of anyone being hit by a swinging hook caused by the vessel movement in the seas. Stingers vary in length, but most contractors use a 12- or 15-foot stinger for every lift. Both applications use a tag line. Shackles are another matter. Most land-based operations will accept a screw pin shackle, but most offshore operations use 3 part shackles.

19.8.4 Hand Signals

Most crane operators will not move a load unless they receive a signal. Most crane operators will stop if they are given improper signals and insist on a new signalman. Crane signals are a sign language and the language is the same, no matter where you are working. Crane operators use a signalman because he is up in the crane cab and cannot see the load close up nor can he see the back side of the load. In blind lifting operations he cannot see the load at all. The following chart contains the internationally used crane signals.

Although radios are usually used in offshore lifting operations, it is imperative to know crane signals, because a radio failure is possible, radio interference can and does happen and you likely will perform land-based lifts as well. There are a few things to remember about signaling cranes: make sure the operator can see your hands at all times; make sure you can see the load at all times; if performing underwater lifting, make sure you can hear the dive radio; never have more than one person signaling at one time and make sure the sun is not behind you when signaling a crane. The signalman should always wear a bright safety vest in order to stand out to the crane operator, particularly if there are a lot of personnel on deck.

STOP

Arm extended, palm down, move hand horizontal.

USE MAIN HOIST

Tap fist on head; then use regular signals.

USE WHIPLINE (Auxiliary)

Tap elbow; then use regular signals.

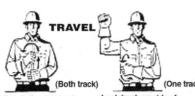

TRAVEL

(Both track)

Both fists in front of body, making a circular motion about each other indicating direction of travel; forward or backward.

(One track)

Lock track on side of raised fist, rotate other fist in direction of opposite track.

LOWER BOOM

Arm extended, fingers closed, thumb pointing downward.

RAISE BOOM

Arm extended, fingers closed, thumb pointing upward.

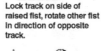

HOIST

With forearm vertical, finger pointing up, move hand in small horizontal circles.

LOWER

With arm extended down, move forefinger pointing down, move hand in circles.

LOWER THE BOOM AND RAISE THE LOAD

With arm extended, thumb down, flex fingers in and out as long as load movement is desired.

Arm extended, fingers closed, thumb down, other arm vertical, forefinger upward and rotate hand.

RAISE THE BOOM AND LOWER THE LOAD

With arm extended, thumb pointing up, flex fingers in and out as long as load movement desired.

Arm extended, fingers closed, thumb pointing upward, other arm bent slightly with forefinger pointing down and rotate hand.

SWING

Arm extended, point in direction of swing of boom.

MOVE SLOWLY

Use one hand to give any motion signal and place other hand motionles in front of hand giving the motion signal (Hoist slowly shown as example.)

EXTEND BOOM

Both fists in front of body with thumbs pointing outward.

RETRACT BOOM

Both fists in front of body with thumbs pointing toward each other.

OPEN CLAM BUCKET

Arm extended, palm down, open hand,

CLOSE CLAM BUCKET

Arm extended, palm down, close hand,

EXTEND BOOM

RETRACT BOOM

DOG EVERYTHING

Clasp hands in front of boy.

19.8.5 Radio Signals

When signaling a crane with a radio, first ensure that a clear channel is available. Perform a radio check with the crane operator. Speak clearly, without shouting into the radio. If the crane has more than one line, indicate the line (main hoist or whip) to be used prior to lifting. When directing a crane by radio, always indicate the operation before the direction, as in "boom up" or "swing left." The only exceptions to this rule are the hoist cables. When moving the hoist cables, you always indicate the direction first, as in "up on the wire," or "down on the main block." Always indicate the direction of swing by the operator's orientation (swing left is always to the operator's left). The terms used are "swing left" or "swing right." If powering up or down fast, slow the movement before stopping to avoid putting an excessive dynamic load on the crane. When moving, try to give the operator an idea how far (up three feet, swing left two feet). When swinging, always stop the movement slightly before the load is where you want it to stop. Loads always lag slightly on the swing. When you stop a movement, the term is "all stop"; never use "that's good" or "that's OK." When there is a load on the hook, the term used is "up on the load" or "down on the load." When the crane is free, use the terms "up on the wire" or "down on the wire." When finished with the crane, always inform the crane operator so he can take his hook up and away. For more detail on crane signals using radio, see Appendix III: International Crane Signals.

19.9 RIGGING SAFETY GUIDELINES

Since such a large part of diving work involves rigging, it is very important that the rigging be performed safely and correctly: every single time. A knot that comes loose may be very embarrassing in front of a large diving crew. An improperly lifted load, if dropped, can cause injury or death. Do not be the diver that got fired that everyone talks about. Practice your rigging skills and follow these guidelines.

Guidelines for general rigging:

- Learn to properly coil rope and always do it properly. Remember: it coils clockwise.
- Learn to tie knots correctly and what knots work best in different applications.
- Learn to splice rope and learn to recognize an improperly spliced rope.
- Learn how to do whipping (seizing) and whip rope ends in your spare time.
- Always have a sharp knife on your belt whenever you're on the job.
- Never cut a rope without taping up or whipping both cut ends.
- Always carry a roll of electrical tape when on the job.
- Stay away from rope, cable or chain that are under heavy strain.
- Never use lever hoists or chain falls without safety latches on the hooks.
- Never use a cheater on a lever hoist handle. Get a bigger come along.
- Never overload a chain fall. Get a bigger one or use a crane.
- Never saddle a dead horse. If you don't understand, read up on saddle clamps again.
- Always tighten both sides of a saddle clamp evenly.
- Always re-tighten saddle clamps after putting a strain on the wire.

Guidelines for crane lift rigging:

- Only the designated signalman can start a lift.

- Anyone on the crew can stop a lift if he sees an unsafe condition.

- Always make sure you are seen by the operator when signaling, even when using radios for crane signals. If it is not possible, use the relay system (another signalman passes signals on).

- When signaling, ensure you do not have the sun (or bright deck lights) behind you.

- Do not allow yourself to get distracted when signaling a crane

- Always remove bystanders from the area where the lift is being performed.

- Never, under any circumstances, get beneath a suspended load.

- Never allow a suspended load to pass over anyone else.

- When weather is obviously deteriorating, do not start lifting operations if close to the cut-off.

- Never pull on the side of a shackle, only on the top of the bell or the pin.

- Only use shackles that are rated above the weight you are lifting: check the SWL.

- Always inspect slings, straps and spreaders before using.

- Never use rigging hardware that shows signs of excessive wear or damage.

- Always use a stinger in marine lifting operations.

- Never lift a load when slings are twisted or tangled.

- Never pass a sling over a sharp edge. Use a softener to protect it.

- Never lift a load without at least one tag line attached.

- Never use a tag line made of two lines joined together: single line only.

- Never wrap a tag line around your hand or wrist.

- Never have an eye or loop in the end of a tag line.

- Always use slow crane movements when a load is suspended.

- Never take a side pull on a crane boom. They are not designed to pull sideways.

- Never leave unused spreader hooks swinging free. Hook them in the master link.

- Between lifts, take the stinger hook well up above head height until you need it.

- Always center the block above the load before starting a lift. Never start a lift unless the crane wires are vertical. Take the time, stand back and look before lifting.

- Always know the weight of the load before you rig a lift. Never do a "mystery lift."

- Never let a crane wire go slack by letting the block touch the ground.

20.0 UNDERWATER PHOTOGRAPHY AND VIDEO

Underwater inspections most generally require images in order to provide the client or engineer with a clear understanding of the physical condition of the item or structure being inspected and the conditions that the item is exposed to. An image allows the client to see the structure (and any defects or damage) instead of simply hearing the inspector describe it. Images are obtained by using one of two methods: still photography or video. In this chapter, we will discuss the underwater conditions that have an effect on images, the equipment, the methods used to obtain both types of image and the best ways to ensure top quality results.

20.1 STILL PHOTOGRAPHY

Most underwater inspections require a video record of the inspection accompanied by a written report. The written report will typically include still photographs of the item inspected with detailed photos of any defect or damage encountered during the inspection. There are two methods of obtaining these still photographs: using an underwater still camera and "capturing" a still from a video. The capture method very rarely will produce a good quality photo due to the rapid movement of the camera. Professionals produce professional quality results. This chapter will deal with dedicated still cameras. Still photos have several advantages over video: a permanent record exists; still photos may be enlarged and cropped and very high resolution can be achieved. However, there are critical elements to still photography. They are as follows:

- Subject matter must be in frame and in focus and this cannot be surface monitored.
- The quality of the image is dependent on the pixel density of the camera used.
- Lighting has to be correct in order to obtain a quality photograph.

20.1.1 Subject Matter and Focus

The viewfinder screen on the digital underwater camera shows a digital picture of exactly what image will be stored on the memory card once the shutter is activated. The user must look carefully at the subject and how it is "bracketed" within the viewfinder screen. If the left side or the top of the subject is cut off, that is precisely how the subject will appear in the image. Camera manufacturers like to use the term "point and shoot" in their advertising, but "point and shoot" is for amateurs and produces amateur photos. Framing subject matter comes down to this: what the camera sees is only what you see when you're looking at the viewfinder screen. Never more and never less. The diver must be constantly aware of exactly what is in frame and constantly aware of the focus when shooting still photos.

Some digital cameras have either automatic or fixed focus, but good quality single lens reflex (SLR) cameras have automatic focus with a manual over-ride option. Sharp focus may be seen on the viewfinder screen in clear water, but in turbid water, the diver will want to use a pre-set focal distance and a measured prod attached to the camera to measure the camera standoff. The pre-set focal distance should never exceed ⅓ of the actual visibility underwater.

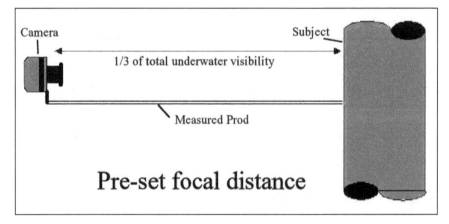

In surface photography different length lenses may be used, but in underwater photography, shorter length, wide-angle lenses are always used. The reason for this is that the diver must get close to the subject due to poorer visibility, low light and poor contrast. Depth of field is another consideration in photography. In short, depth of field means the depth of foreground between the camera and subject and the depth of background beyond the subject that is in sharp focus when the subject itself is in focus. In order to get the maximum depth of field, we require a shorter length lens, a smaller aperture setting and the maximum distance possible between the lens and the subject. We use shorter lenses underwater already, due to light, visibility and contrast. Keep in mind to use a higher f-stop number, which means a smaller aperture setting. Then we know we are getting the maximum depth of field possible.

20.1.2 Image Quality

The quality of the image obtained is directly related to the quality of the camera. In digital cameras, when the shutter opens, light falls onto a light sensitive computer chip. This chip will be either a Complimentary Metal Oxide Semiconductor (CMOS) or a Charged-Coupled Device (CCD). Both take in light and give off electrical impulses. The digital image produced by the camera depends on both the quality of the lens and the quality of the camera. Digital camera quality is measured by the number of pixels per unit of screen, the numbers should be high enough that ratings are in "mega-pixels". For underwater inspection, no less than a 12 mega-pixel camera should be used. DSLR cameras with manual settings for aperture (f-stop), shutter speed and focus are preferred. In addition, a true "underwater" camera, that is one with a depth-rated waterproof body, is the best option, rather than a "surface" camera in a waterproof housing.

20.1.3 Lighting

In the past, when film cameras were used, there were different "film speeds" provided by the film manufacturers. The "film speed" indicated how fast that particular film would react to light. There were originally two grading systems, the ASA (North American) and DIN (European) systems. In the 1970s, a standardized international system was set up, known as ISO. The table below illustrates the differences:

Standard	Slow			Medium		Fast	
ASA	25	50	100	200	400	800	1600
DIN	15	18	21	24	27	30	33
ISO	25/15	50/18	100/21	200/24	400/27	800/30	1600/33

In film cameras, the aperture (diameter of the opening inside the shutter) had to be adjusted to suit the speed of the film being used for the photograph. The digital camera reacts to the light allowed to make contact with the CMOS or CCD chip and the amount and quality of light determines the quality of the image in much the same way that the film in the film camera reacted and determined the quality. Digital SLR cameras have an aperture adjustment, some with a control identical to the film cameras, others with a menu item on the screen with "f-stop" designations to indicate the aperture diameter. Either way, the camera pixels' electronic sensitivity to light is adjusted using the ISO numbering system. Adjustment of this control by one f-stop will either double the aperture size, or cut it in half: the lower the f-stop, the wider the aperture and the more light exposure. Often, a process known as "bracketing" is used. One photograph is taken at what is thought to be the "correct" aperture setting, one below, and one above, to ensure that one quality photo is shot.

As we learned in underwater physics, light loses its intensity as the depth of water increases, due to reflection and attenuation. Colors are absorbed the further one moves below the water surface. In order to overcome this loss of light and color, the photographer must use artificial light in order for a camera to obtain a quality photograph. This is done with an electronic strobe. The strobe is synchronized with the camera and it flashes at the exact millisecond that the camera shutter opens. Strobe manufacturers give the user a Guide Number (GN) based on the ISO numbers that allows the selection of the proper f-stop, but this will depend on the distance from the strobe to the subject. To calculate the proper f-stop, the following formula is used: f-stop used is equal to the Guide Number, divided by the distance. For example:

$$\text{f-stop used} = \frac{\text{Guide Number}}{\text{Distance to subject}}$$

$$\text{f-stop used} = \frac{22}{2} = 11 \quad \text{f-stop used is 11}$$

Underwater DSLR camera with strobe lights.
Photo courtesy of Nauticam

The shutter speed selected for flash photography underwater is usually the same as that used on the surface, so the shutter speed is set at $\frac{1}{60}^{\text{th}}$ sec, the correct f-stop is selected using the formula above and we are then ready to take the photograph: except for one more little problem that we will now discuss.

In surface photography, the biggest concerns when using a strobe are "red eye" and "shadow" but in underwater photography, the concern is reflection. Every single cubic foot of seawater has many suspended particles caused by conditions such as suspended silt and small marine organisms. These particles reflect the light back toward the camera causing a condition known as "backscatter". This backscatter will ruin an otherwise perfect photograph. The sketches below illustrate the problem of backscatter.

We know that light travels in a straight line. It also tends to reflect back toward the light source in a straight line when it hits perpendicularly. But when it hits on an angle, it tends to reflect off on the same angle, much like a pool ball bouncing off another ball (or the table bank). Because light acts in this way, the greater the angle between the light source and the camera, the less that backscatter creates a problem.

As in surface photography, holding the camera still will always produce a better photograph. This sometimes will involve something as simple as the diver wrapping his legs around something solid, such as a vertical diagonal member or an anode. Other times it may involve the diver being more creative, such as installing a temporary down line or hogging line to hold him steady to "get the shot." The diver is advised to take whatever measures are necessary to get the best photo possible every time.

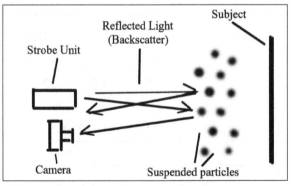

Not enough angle between camera and strobe unit

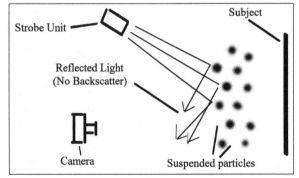

Good angle between camera and strobe unit

20.2 CARE AND MAINTENANCE OF THE STILL CAMERA

Being on vacation with a camera with no free storage space is annoying. Arriving at 140 fsw to take still photographs with no free space can get somebody fired. Here are a few tips for underwater photography:

- Make sure that the memory card has sufficient space before inspections.
- Download images off memory cards after each dive and back them up.
- Rinse the camera with fresh water after each use in seawater.
- Make sure the camera lens is cleaned before each dive.
- Make sure the camera has fresh batteries or a fully charged battery before each dive.
- Make sure the flash unit has fresh batteries or a fully charged battery.

20.3 UNDERWATER VIDEO

There are two types of underwater video: self-contained and surface-monitored. Self-contained underwater video is never used in commercial diving operations for two reasons: the video image remains unseen until the dive is finished and it does not contain real-time audio. Surface-monitored video is the only type examined in this chapter since it is the only type acceptable in the commercial diving field.

Underwater video, once used only for inspection purposes, is now recorded on most commercial diving operations (and every offshore operation) today as a required part of the "black box" record maintained of every dive performed. The "black box" videos basically see what the diver sees, record what the diver does, and are stored for a 24-hour period unless an incident occurs during the dive. In these instances, the video is stored until any required investigations have been completed. This chapter will be concerned with those videos recorded as part of an inspection, whether the video is recorded with the "black box" camera or with another separate unit.

20.3.1 Types of Video Camera

The original underwater video cameras that first appeared offshore in the late 1960s were cathode tube cameras, with a photo-cathode positioned behind the lens and a cathode tube positioned at the back of the camera. These units, still seen occasionally, are very large (the size of a 6 cup coffee thermos), quite heavy and very sensitive to light. In fact, they are so sensitive to light, that the lens must be covered at all times when the camera is on the surface. Because they are constructed with vacuum tubes, these cameras require extreme care in handling. A solid whack and tubes can loosen or break, shutting down the video.

Silicone Intensified Target (SIT) cameras first appeared offshore in the late 1970s and are still very widely used by both divers and ROVs. The SIT camera is monochrome (black and white) and does not have high resolution, but they are an extremely low light camera, requiring only the equivalent of starlight in order to produce an image. Although they are not usually used for inspections, every ROV has at least one of the SIT cameras and many diving contractors use them for the helmet-mounted black box cameras.

The Charged Coupled Device (CCD) camera is the most commonly used camera offshore today. Virtually every inspection performed now and many black box systems use the CCD camera. CCD cameras are solid-state construction, as opposed to tube construction and will withstand a lot of rough handling. They are not as sensitive to very bright light so lens covering is not usually necessary on surface. These cameras are available both in monochrome and color and produce a very high resolution image. These units are not affected by magnetic fields as other cameras are, therefore they are usable in conjunction with MPI and other NDT methods. The only drawback is that CCD cameras have a limited depth of field.

20.3.2 Shooting Underwater Video

There are two modes of underwater video used with divers: helmet-mounted and handheld video. There are distinct advantages and disadvantages to each mode as shown in the table below.

Helmet-Mounted Camera	Handheld Camera
Diver has both hands free	Diver has one hand occupied at all times
Difficult to maneuver into tight places	Easy to fit into tight spaces
Camera tether is part of diver's umbilical	Extra tether to keep clear of obstructions
Difficult for close inspection due to parallax	Excellent for close inspection
Diver often cannot see items videoed (parallax)	Parallax very seldom an issue with hand-held video
Enhances diver safety when used	Additional fouling hazard for diver when used
Diver neck fatigue on longer inspections	Diver arm fatigue on longer inspections

Parallax is the term used to describe the discrepancy between the line of sight of the person using the video camera, and the line of sight of the camera itself. This actually occurs using both the hand-held mode and the helmet-mounted mode, but is much more pronounced when using a helmet-mounted video camera.

In the sketch on the right, the diver is unable to see the area to be inspected and show it on video at the same time. In the sketch on the right, the same thing happens. Many divers are unable to grasp this concept of parallax, and many who do, mysteriously forget all about it as soon as they leave the surface.

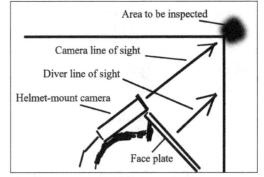
Parallax (scenario 1)

You will most likely have helmet-mounted video wherever you work. You may be required to use this to perform video inspections or you may be given a surface monitored hand-held camera to use in addition to your hat cam. Regardless which mode is utilized for an inspection, there are a few things that don't change that the diver must keep in mind in order to shoot good quality video. They are as follows:

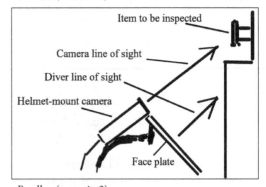
Parallax (scenario 2)

- Always test the video system, including record capability, before inspections.
- Before you perform a video inspection brush up on the structure's terminology.
- Before the inspection, find out where the light hits as opposed to the camera's field of view: they often are not perfectly aligned.
- Before you start the inspection, wait for topside to do an introduction.
- Provide a running commentary while shooting video: you are the tour guide.
- If you have stopped for any reason, pause a few seconds before re-starting commentary.
- Use slow and steady movements in video inspection. The tortoise always beats the hare.
- Listen to topside comments. If they say they can't see something, they probably can't (parallax).
- As you are reaching surface, remind topside to shut down the lights.

20.3.3 Video Recording and Storage

The original video recording machines were reel-to-reel machines, roughly the size of a microwave oven, and took up a lot of space in Dive Control. As technology advanced, there were videocassettes, then disks, and now there are computer hard drives. Although some of the systems seen on the job today are straight DVD, most are combination DVD/HD or straight hard drive. Before starting a video inspection, there must be ample storage for the videos that will be shot. If you are using a DVD machine, you will require a separate DVD for each dive and the DVD must be empty. If using a hard drive, there must be sufficient space available to record each dive separately. After the inspection, the important thing to remember is to protect the video footage so that it cannot be erased, recorded over or otherwise lost. If the machine has DVD capability, burn the video onto a DVD as soon as each dive has been completed and ensure that the disk is labeled correctly. If the machine is a hard drive, ensure that the video is protected and in a separate, protected file after each dive. At the end of the day, transfer the video files onto a portable thumb drive or portable hard drive. Each video must be labeled (digitally or with label and pen) as follows:

- Date and time of inspection
- Location of inspection
- Structure (vessel) inspected
- Diving Company performing the inspection
- Client (who the inspection was performed for)
- Duration (in minutes) of the recording

20.3.4 Commentary

The commentary always starts with topside: either the diving supervisor or inspection coordinator provides an introduction. The following information is always included: the diving contractor, the supervisor and diver, the client, the item or structure inspected (sometimes the part as well), the geographic location and the date of the inspection. If you are performing this task, write it down. That almost makes it idiot proof.

When providing commentary for a video, you speak in your normal voice, speak slowly, speak clearly, do not cuss and try your best to remember the correct terminology. "What in the heck did they call that thingy" is probably not going to cut it during a video inspection. A favorite trick of mine when I forgot terminology, is to show the mystery item on the screen and pause for a half second. My supervisor would say "stuffing box" whereupon I would say "exactly, sir, the stuffing box." Now I do the exact same thing, and it makes my divers look good. If you have to stop and haul some slack on your umbilical, ask topside to "pause the recording." Pull the slack umbilical you need and then tell them to "start the recording" again. It is also a good idea when you are showing a particular feature, to ask topside if they have a good image of the item or not. That allows you to re-position yourself if they cannot see the item. Just keep in mind that movements and speech are both better if slower when it comes to video inspection.

20.3.5 Terms Used for Camera Movements

Regardless where you work, diving crews (and ROV crews) always use the exact same terminology for the camera movements. The camera movement terminology is as follows:

- Pan left or right: without changing location, pivot the camera slowly left or right
- Tilt up or down: without changing elevation, pivot the camera slowly up or down
- Move left or right: keeping the camera pointed the way it is, move it to left or right
- Move up or down: keeping the camera pointed the way it is, move it up or down
- Come in or out: move the camera closer to or further from the subject
- Rotate clockwise or counterclockwise: rotate as if you were looking out through the lens

The sketch below illustrates the camera movement terminology commonly used in video inspections.

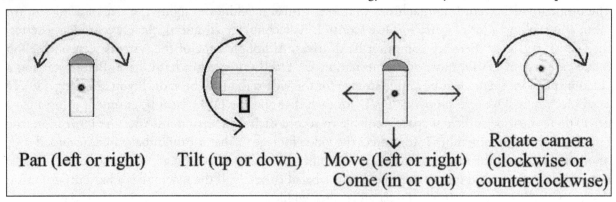

Pan (left or right) Tilt (up or down) Move (left or right) Rotate camera
                                        Come (in or out)   (clockwise or
                                                              counterclockwise)

20.4 CARE AND MAINTENANCE OF VIDEO EQUIPMENT

To properly maintain and care for an underwater video system, the diver should do the following:

- Ensure good ventilation for the video system hard-drive to avoid overheating.
- Regularly inspect the video tether, looking for chafing, splits or cracks.
- Regularly inspect the camera, lights and waterproof connectors.
- Rinse the camera, lights and waterproof connectors after every use in seawater.
- Clean the camera lens before video inspection dives.
- Clean the light lens before video inspection dives.
- Never run the lights when out of water as they are water cooled.
- Never allow people to walk or step on the video tether.
- Always use a strain reliever on the video tether (Chinese fingers type).

21.0 DIVING UNDER EXCEPTIONAL CONDITIONS

A surface-supplied diving operation under normal conditions has the diver and diving crew working to perform underwater tasks and the primary concerns are safe usage of tools and equipment and proper usage of the diving tables. There are some diving operations performed under what are known as exceptional conditions. These include contaminated water diving, confined-space diving, and penetration diving. These types of operation have an increased threat posed to the diver and diving crew by contaminated water, contaminated air, and restricted ability to recover the diver in the event of an emergency. Each of these operations has a proper procedure and safety guidelines that must be followed.

21.1 CONTAMINATED WATER DIVING

In Chapter 4: Diving and Support Equipment, we learned one of the purposes of the diver's suit is to offer protection from contaminants in the water. Some types of suit protect better than others. The level of protection required by the diver depends on two things: the type of contaminants in the water and the level of contamination in the water.

21.1.1 Types of Contaminants

There are almost as many types of contaminants found in water as there are sources of contaminants. Not all contaminants are hazardous to human health. Some are hazardous without immediate effects; others are hazardous with immediate effects. Some contaminants encountered have deadly effects while others do not. One of the biggest problems with water-borne contaminants is that often they cannot be seen, smelled or otherwise detected without water and sediment sampling and chemical testing. There are three categories of water contamination that pose a real threat to the diver:

- Biological contamination (human and animal waste; fish offal; medical waste)
- Chemical contamination (petroleum products; industrial chemicals; fertilizers)
- Radioactive contamination (leaks and spills from nuclear power plants or research facilities)

21.1.1.1 Biological Contamination

Most often found in inland lakes, rivers and coastal harbors, biological contamination is the most common form of water pollution. This contamination may be naturally occurring, or it may be the result of dumping human or other biological waste. Biological contamination falls into one of three categories: bacterial, protozoan or viral. Depending on the type and the concentration, exposure to biological contamination can have very grave consequences for the unprotected diver.

The largest source of bacterial contaminants is human and animal waste, commonly called sewage. Sewage contains *fecal coliform* bacteria, which is present in the intestines of every warm-blooded animal. Several life-threatening diseases and conditions are directly linked to fecal coliform contamination, including: gastroenteritis, dysentery, Crohn's Disease, and typhoid fever. Some of the ways that sewage enters the water are: untreated sewer outfalls, malfunctioning waste treatment plants, farmland runoff, high water levels during flood seasons and poorly designed residential septic systems. Another bacterium found in human waste is *Vibrio cholerae*. This bacterium is the one that cause cholera, a disease than if untreated, leads to the death of those infected. Other bacteria typically found in water polluted with waste are *Vibrio vulnificus* and *Aeromonas hydrophillia*, both of which can lead to death in humans. These bacteria enter the human body either through ingestion or absorption.

Protozoan contamination is often found in water contaminated with bacteria. Protozoa are single-cell organisms, several species of which feed on bacteria. Acanthamoeba, one protozoan that feeds on bacteria, is often found in water contaminated with fecal coliform. This protozoan can enter the bloodstream through an open wound and causes Granulomatous amoebic encephalitis, a brain disorder which is fatal in nearly 55% of cases. Survivors are usually left with severe and permanent neurological deficits. The other protozoans found in wastewater are not usually deadly, but one, Giardia lamblia, will make the diver wish he/she were dead. It causes severe intestinal cramping, diarrhea, and a very high fever.

The Hepatitis A virus is almost always found in water contaminated with human waste. Though it is seldom fatal, Hepatitis A can cause permanent liver damage and the infected person is often very sick with diarrhea and vomiting. There are Hepatitis vaccinations available commercially.

The dinoflagelate pfiesteria piscicida, which was responsible for the "Toxic Bloom" that spread from Florida up the East Coast to Virginia a few years ago, is also a contaminant to avoid. That particular algae bloom was responsible for the deaths of several dolphins and manatee in Florida and many commercial fishermen and divers experienced skin disorders, neurological symptoms, and balance problems after coming in contact with it.

21.1.1.2 Chemical Contamination

At one time, chemical contamination was found only in industrial areas, but unfortunately this is no longer the case. Due to the prolonged use of chemical fertilizers by farmers and homeowners, very few rivers or lakes do not have at least some degree of contamination. Regulation and enforcement by the environmental watchdogs of various governments is making a difference, but there is a long way to go.

The first chemicals most think of, when considering water contamination, are petroleum products. This is a possible result of media bias, since when the volume of chemicals in the water is calculated, petroleum products only contribute about 25% of the pollution, far outweighed by both agricultural fertilizers and household products. Regardless, petroleum products in the water pose a threat to the diver that has to work in that water. Crude oil contains some very nasty chemicals as shown the charts below.

Chemical	What is being done to monitor exposures?	Routes of exposure and absorption	Acute (immediate) health risks	Chronic (long-term) health risks	Comparison Values: safe level for humans [1,2,3]	How to protect against exposure
Benzene Colorless, sweet-smelling liquid and vapor. Evaporates very quickly and dissolves slightly in water.	Local Poison Control Centers and Health Departments are tracking calls related to potential exposures to this chemical, and several federal agencies, including the EPA, are taking frequent air and water samples.	Benzene vapors, (or fumes) can be inhaled and benzene can be consumed in contaminated food or water. It can also be absorbed through the skin. Benzene does not accumulate in significant amounts in the body.	Eating or drinking highly-contaminated food or water can cause vomiting, stomach irritation, dizziness, sleepiness, convulsions, rapid heart rate, and death. Inhaling low levels of benzene can irritate eyes, nose, throat and skin. People with chronic diseases such as asthma may be more sensitive to fumes.	Long-term exposure can adversely affect bone marrow and cause anemia, leukemia and death.	In Air: 10 ug/m3 Chronic; 0.1 ug/m3 Cancer. In liquids: 5 ug/l Chronic; 0.6 ug/l Cancer. In Soil: 30 mg/kg Chronic; 10 mg/kg Cancer.	If benzene is released into the air, leave the area. Avoid contact with contaminated water, soil or sediment.
Hydrogen sulfide Hydrogen sulfide is a poisonous, flammable, colorless gas that smells like rotten eggs. People usually can smell hydrogen sulfide at very low concentrations in air.	Local Poison Control Centers and Health Departments are tracking calls related to potential exposures to this chemical, and several federal agencies, including the EPA, are taking frequent air and water samples.	Hydrogen sulfide can be inhaled or absorbed through the skin. In the body, hydrogen sulfide is primarily converted to sulfate and is excreted in the urine. Hydrogen sulfide is rapidly removed from the body.	Inhaling low levels concentrations of hydrogen sulfide can irritate the eyes, nose, or throat. People with chronic diseases such as asthma may have trouble breathing. Brief exposure to concentrations of hydrogen sulfide greater than 500 ppm can cause loss of consciousness. In many cases where people are removed from the exposure immediately, they regain consciousness without any other effects.	Chronic exposure to high levels may cause long-term or permanent effects including headaches, impaired attention span, memory, or motor function.	In Air: No health effects have been found in humans exposed to typical environmental concentrations of hydrogen sulfide 0.2 -0.5 ug/m3).	If hydrogen sulfide is released into the air, leave the area. Avoid contact with contaminated water, soil or sediment. Because the gas is heavier than oxygen, it hangs at low levels in the air, closer to the ground.

Courtesy of Centers for Disease Control and Prevention (CDC)

Chemical	What is being done to monitor exposures?	Routes of exposure and absorption	Acute (immediate) health risks	Chronic (long-term) health risks	Comparison Values: safe level for humans [1,2,3]	How to protect against exposure
Ethyl benzene Ethyl benzene is a colorless liquid. It is highly flammable and smells like gasoline. It is naturally found in coal tar and petroleum.	Local Poison Control Centers and Health Departments are tracking calls related to potential exposures to this chemical, and several federal agencies, including the EPA, are taking frequent air and water samples.	Ethyl benzene can be inhaled, absorbed through the skin, or ingested in contaminated water.	Exposure to high levels of ethyl benzene in air for short periods can irritate eyes and throat. Exposure to higher levels can cause dizziness or vertigo.	Long term exposure has not been studied in humans.	In air: 3,000 ug/m3 In water: 1,000 ug/l In soil: 5,000 ug/kg	If ethyl benzene is released into the air, leave the area. Avoid contact with contaminated water.
Toluene aka Methylbenzene Toluene is a clear, colorless liquid and vapor that smells like gasoline. Toluene occurs naturally in crude oil.	Local Poison Control Centers and Health Departments are tracking calls related to potential exposures to this chemical, and several federal agencies, including the EPA, are taking frequent air and water samples.	Toluene can be inhaled, absorbed through the skin, or ingested in contaminated water.	Short term exposure to low to moderate levels can cause tiredness, confusion, weakness, impaired memory or motor control, nausea, loss of appetite, loss of hearing and color vision. Inhaling high levels of toluene in a short time can make you feel light-headed, dizzy, or sleepy. It can also cause unconsciousness and may be fatal.	Long term exposure to toluene may affect the nervous system or kidneys.	In air: 300 ug/m3 In water: 200 ug/l In soil: 1,000 mg/kg	If toluene is released into the air, leave the area. Avoid contact with contaminated water, soil, or sediment.
Xylene Xylene is a colorless, sweet-smelling liquid and vapor. It is highly flammable and evaporates easily. It occurs naturally in petroleum and coal tar.	Local Poison Control Centers and Health Departments are tracking calls related to potential exposures to this chemical, and several federal agencies, including the EPA, are taking frequent air and water samples.	Xylene can be inhaled, ingested in contaminated water and absorbed through the skin.	Short term exposure to high levels can cause headaches, lack of coordination, dizziness, confusion, and impaired balance. Such exposure can also irritate skin, eyes, nose, throat and stomach. Other symptoms may include breathing difficulties, especially in those with chronic lung problems. At very high levels, exposure may cause unconsciousness and death.	Symptoms may include impaired reaction time, concentration and memory, and changes in the liver and kidneys.	In air: 3,000 ug/m3 In water: 2,000 ug/l In soil: 10,000 mg/kg	If xylene is released into the air, leave the area. Avoid skin contact with tar, gasoline, paint varnish, shellac and contaminated water.
Naphthalene and Methylnaphthalene Naphthalene is a colorless to white or brown solid or vapor that smells like mothballs. It evaporates quickly and dissolves in water. 1-Methylnaphthalene is a clear liquid and 2-Methylnaphthalene is a solid.	Local Poison Control Centers and Health Departments are tracking calls related to potential exposures to this chemical, and several federal agencies, including the EPA, are taking frequent air and water samples.	Naphthalene can be inhaled, absorbed through the skin, or ingested through contaminated water.	Exposure to high levels of naphthalene can cause nausea, vomiting, diarrhea, blood in urine, rash and yellow skin. Exposure to extremely elevated levels (500 ppm) of airborne naphthalene can be fatal.	Long term exposure has been linked to hemolytic anemia, a disorder of red blood cells. Symptoms of this anemia include fatigue, lack of appetite, restlessness, and pale skin.	In air: 3 ug/m3 In water: 700 ug/l In soil: 700 ug/kg	If the concentration rises above (~1300 mg/m3) in the air, leave the area. Avoid contact with contaminated water, soil and sediment.
Generic alkanes (including octane, hexane, nonane) Alkanes are colorless liquids or vapors that smell like gasoline. They are present in crude oil and petroleum products. They are highly flammable and evaporate easily.	Local Poison Control Centers and Health Departments are tracking calls related to potential exposures to this chemical, and several federal agencies, including the EPA, are taking frequent air and water samples.	Alkanes can be inhaled, absorbed through the skin, or ingested in contaminated water.	Inhaling high levels of n-hexane (a specific type of medium-sized alkane), can cause numbness in the feet and hands and muscle weakness in the feet and lower legs. Inhaling high levels of some alkanes can cause asphyxiation.	Toxicity is dependent on type of alkane as well as route and duration of exposure. Long term exposure to n-hexane can causes weakness and loss of feeling in the arms and legs. In one study, exposed workers removed from the exposure site recovered in 6 months to a year.	In air: 31,000 ug/m3* In water: 120,000 ug/l* In soil: 600 mg/kg* *Decane and white oil	If generic alkanes are released into the air, leave the area. Avoid contact with contaminated water, soil or sediment.

Courtesy of Centers for Disease Control and Prevention (CDC)

The list above contains the most dangerous chemicals found in most crude oil. It is not a list of all of the chemicals found in crude. Refined petroleum products sound much safer, but refined products such as gasoline, aviation fuel and heating oil contain many chemical additives that are not listed here.

Exposure to the chemicals found in petroleum products can also occur when performing diving operations in an area where there has been a spill in the recent past. Some crude oil, due to clean-up attempts and/or wave action will form "tar balls." These are huge clumps of heavy crude that settle to the seabed and spread out in the bottom sediment. These tar balls contain all of the chemical properties of the crude and will pose a toxicity threat, particularly if the sediment is disturbed. In addition, the dispersant chemicals used in oil spill clean up are often more hazardous to the diver than the crude itself would be. For example, after the Deepwater Horizon incident in the Gulf of Mexico in 2010, British Petroleum aerial sprayed Corexit® on the ensuing oil spill to disperse it. Corexit contains 2-butoxyethanol, organic sulfonate and propylene glycol. The 2-butoxyethanol is a known carcinogen and the dispersant is thought to cause neurological damage, spontaneous internal bleeding, decreased sperm counts and extremely elevated cancer risks in humans exposed to it. Corexit is absorbed through exposed skin before it can be wiped off. And that is only one of many chemicals used to disperse and clean up oil spills. Any diving operations performed in areas where oil spill clean-ups have recently occurred should be performed using hazmat diving procedures and equipment, and only after water and seabed sediment samples have been tested.

Industrial chemicals are a whole different story. Depending on the industry and the chemicals used, there are some that are far worse than those found in petroleum products. The National Oceanic and Atmospheric Administration (NOAA) lists several chemicals that are so dangerous and toxic that no diver should ever be exposed to them under any circumstances. These chemicals are as follows:

- Acetic anhydride
- Acrylonitrile
- Carbon tetrachloride
- Cresol
- Chlordane
- Dichloropropane
- Epichlorohydrin
- Ethylbenzine
- Methyl chloride
- Methyl parathion
- Perchloroethylene
- Styrene
- Trichloroethylene
- Xylene

The chemicals listed are only the most toxic that must be avoided, but there are many other chemicals found in the harbors and rivers where divers work. These include polychlorinated biphenyl (PCB), a chemical found in electrical transformers and a known carcinogen (cancer-causing agent) and tributyltin (TBT), an anti-fouling agent (now partially banned) used in marine paint. The PCBs and TBTs tend to accumulate in the sediment on river and harbor bottoms, the TBTs being most often found near ship yards. Working dives on bottom in or around shipyards should be considered hazmat operations.

In order to list the toxic chemicals and chemical compounds found in the fertilizers and pesticides that our farms, municipalities, and homeowners are using (and are entering our watersheds) it would take several pages. But the fact that pesticide chemicals are specifically designed to kill living organisms as fast as possible should make one take pause and think. These same pesticides that the Environmental Protection Agency (EPA) is trying to keep from the watershed areas are now being used by fish farms in the aquaculture industry. Salmon farms in Eastern Maine and New Brunswick, Canada, have been charged with killing wild lobster with a pesticide (Round-up) that they were using to try to control an infestation of sea lice in their salmon stocks. Any dive performed on bottom near a salmon farm site should be treated as a hazmat dive.

21.1.1.3 Radioactive Contamination

Due to strict regulatory controls, radioactive contamination in water is something that most divers will not have to encounter, unless working at a nuclear plant. There have been very few documented spills of radioactive heavy water at nuclear plants and the dumping of radioactive waste is something that is rarely encountered due to strict controls on radioactive materials at the national and international levels.

21.1.2 Levels of Contamination

Often, substances that are toxic to humans can be tolerated in small concentrations without any noticeable health effects for many years. Unfortunately, some toxins are stored in the human body, and once these stored toxins reach a level that the body cannot tolerate, there are usually serious, sometimes fatal medical problems. Regulatory bodies such as the EPA in the United States and their counterparts in other countries usually have "acceptable levels" of various toxins present in air, ground and water. These are the levels at which the toxins can be present but not do immediate harm to humans.

In some areas, natural phenomenon will help keep contamination levels low. For example, swift running rivers often have lower levels of contamination, since any contaminants are rapidly washed downstream to the ocean. Harbors in areas with extreme tidal ranges (Cook Inlet, Bay of Fundy) see a continual and large flushing action and contaminants are removed or rapidly diluted.

There are certain areas where one might expect to see higher levels of contamination: downstream from an industrial area; containment ponds; treatment ponds; harbors where untreated sewage is dumped and harbors or bays that have large rivers emptying into them. These areas have even higher levels of contamination in the bottom sediment than in the water. If there is any doubt as to the levels of contamination and water and sediment samples cannot be taken and tested, all dives should be performed as if they were hazmat operations.

21.1.3 Routes of Entry

There are three routes of entry by which toxins can enter the human body: inspiration (breathing), ingestion (through the mouth), and absorption (through the skin). The quickest way to get a toxin into the body is the absorption route, as the toxin enters the capillaries in the skin and is immediately in the bloodstream. The most sensitive areas (quickest for absorption) are the eyes, lips, genital areas and any cuts, lesions or skin abrasions. Because absorption is the most efficient route of entry, it is absolutely imperative that diving crewmembers wear the proper protective suits, gloves and eye protection when working near any toxic substances. Toxic substances that give off fumes will require the proper protection as well. Some will call for respirators, others require breathing air systems. Because ingestion is also a route of entry, eating is not allowed anywhere in the vicinity of toxic substances and good personal hygiene is always required.

NOTE: IT IS STRONGLY RECOMMENDED THAT WORKPLACE HAZARDOUS MATERIALS (WHMIS) TRAINING BE TAKEN PRIOR TO WORKING AROUND TOXIC SUBSTANCES

21.1.4 Hazmat Diving

Whenever diving operations are performed in water with a known high concentration of contaminants, whether it is biological, chemical or radioactive, these operations are considered hazardous-materials diving (hazmat diving). Hazmat-diving work always requires special protection for the diver and, depending on the contaminants and the conditions, often requires special protection for the surface crew, particularly the tenders who are exposed to the contaminants through tending the diver's hose, performing the decontamination wash-downs and dressing the diver down.

21.1.4.1 Hazmat-Diving Equipment

When performing hazmat-diving operations, it is imperative that no part of the diver's body is exposed to the contaminated water. The first step in totally isolating the diver from the water is to use a drysuit. A typical drysuit has seals at the wrists and the neck. To eliminate the exposure area at the wrist seal, we use ring cuffs and hazmat gloves. To eliminate the exposure at the neck, we use a helmet-specific yoke that is attached to the suit. These yokes are available to adapt to almost any diving helmet. When a suit-mounted yoke is used, the helmet is used without the neoprene part of the neck-dam.

When a helmet-specific yoke is used, the diving helmet is basically joined to the suit, forming a watertight joint between the two. The ring cuffs also form a watertight joint at the wrists. Kirby Morgan, Desco, and other helmet manufacturers also have hazmat exhaust kits available for the helmets, which places three or four additional mushroom valves between the helmet exhaust and the water, guaranteeing a dry head during the dive. The important thing to realize here is that they are called helmet-specific yokes for a reason: every helmet will require the yoke designed to fit it. The suits used for hazmat are usually Viking, Whites or Gates. Suits used for hazmat

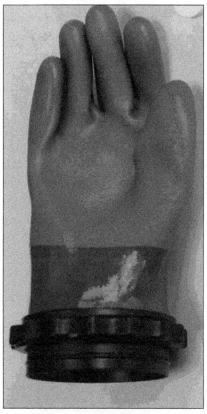

Aqualung hazmat gloves

Aqualung suit with KM37 yoke

must be vulcanized rubber suits. Before performing any hazmat dive, it is recommended that a list of all chemicals and compounds in the water be obtained along with their concentrations. This information is then given to the suit manufacturer and they will provide the "break through time", which is the time in minutes that it will take for the chemical(s) to penetrate the suit material. This step **must not ever** be skipped, because some suits cannot be used with some contaminants. Often, if several dives must be made, several suits must be on hand for the job, due to permeation of the chemicals into the suit material.

It is absolutely imperative that a leak test be performed on the hazmat gear before every dive. The suit is connected to the helmet and the gloves are attached. Then the suit is fully inflated with air. Once this has been done, the entire system is leak tested, using snoop or a detergent/water solution. The test is done as follows: front of diving helmet; front of yoke; front of suit (including valves); wrists; gloves; back of suit (including shoulder zipper); back of yoke; back of diving helmet. Leaks show as expanding bubbles. Any leakage requires a repair or replacement. Leaks are not acceptable, period. Once the diver dresses in, a leak test is done on the gloves, zipper and yoke only, since all other areas have been tested.

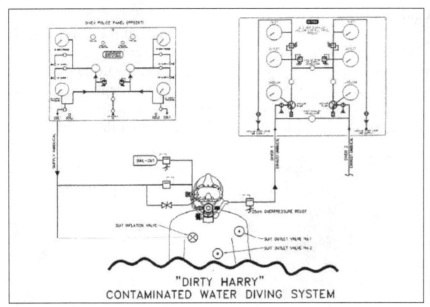

Dirty Harry System in use

Photos and illustration courtesy of Divex

17C with Ultra-Jewel regulator

One of the best hazmat systems available is the "Dirty Harry" system, produced by Divex. This system utilizes a Viking suit and a Kirby Morgan helmet with a Divex Ultra-Jewel reclaim regulator. The system comes complete with a reclaim unit allowing the diver's exhaust to be returned to the surface. This not only avoids one more possible spot for a leak but also eliminates exhaust bubbles, which will often improve the air quality on the surface because it avoids agitation of the contaminated water. This agitation often creates more fumes.

21.1.4.2 The "Hot Zone" System

Every safely run hazmat operation uses the "Hot Zone" system. The example shown below is the one that is used for extremely toxic contaminants. With less toxic contaminants, as few as 3 zones may be used.

HOT ZONE	Full hazmat gear worn by diver and any personnel in this area
DECON 1	Initial wash-down with de-greasers or antiseptic cleaners – diver remains fully dressed in
DECON 2	Secondary wash-down with strong detergent – diver remains fully dressed in
DECON 3	Final wash-down with potable water – diver dresses down in this location; after wash-down
COLD ZONE	Dive Control located in this location; no protective equipment required

Depending on the toxicity of the contaminants and the "routes of entry", tenders near the "Hot Zone" may be required to wear various levels of protection. These include: rain suit, boots, gloves and goggles; full- surface hazmat suit with respirator; or full-surface hazmat suit with breathing air supply.

Surface hazmat suit with breathing air supply
Photo courtesy Saint-Gobain

Hazmat diver preparing to dive
Photo courtesy Richard Johnson

The diver is never dressed down until after the final decontamination wash-down, regardless how many zones are used. The decontamination process must be thorough, but it must also be performed as quickly as possible, as this is a period of high thermal stress for the diver. The decontamination wash-downs are performed with hot water and it can get very hot inside the suit. Having the diver open the steady-flow valve (vent) and leave it cracked open will definitely help in this case, as will intermittent rinses with cold water. It is very important that the diver remain fully dressed in (helmet on) in any area that the surface personnel require respirators or breathing air systems.

21.1.4.3 Decontamination

Whenever a diver performs hazmat work, there is a decontamination process involved. The methods used will depend on the contaminants encountered. Dives in petroleum products (refinery biox ponds or oil spill incidents) typically will require a de-greaser in the initial wash-downs. Dives in wastewater treatment lagoons typically will require antiseptic soaps in the initial wash-downs. The wash-downs are done with a pressure wash system that allows the injection of these de-greasers and soaps, with enough pressure to clean the gear properly but without enough pressure to harm the diver. This is usually in the range of 100 – 150psi. In most cases, the wash-downs are performed with hand-held pressure wands, but in some cases (many nuclear plants) there are wash-down stands, pipe frameworks with nozzles built in that spray the wash-down fluid over the diver. The diver's umbilical is decontaminated in the exact same manner as it is being recovered at the end of the dive.

Initial wash-down with degreaser
Photo courtesy Richard Johnson

Detergent and water wash
Photo courtesy U.S.Navy

Diver's final dress down
Photo courtesy Richard Johnson

21.1.4.4 Radioactive Hazmat

Radioactive hazmat dives are performed in the same manner as all other hazmat dives but with one exception: the diver wears a badge (dosimeter) on his underwear beneath his suit and all of the diving crew members wear them inside their protective suits. Typically, all divers attend a several day long radiation work course at the nuclear facility prior to commencing any diving operations and particularly diving operations

Diver in Belgian nuclear plant, dressing in with Gates suit and an Aquadyne
Photos courtesy of Francis Hermans

where radiation exposure is a possibility.

As in other hazmat operations, radioactive hazmat requires a series of wash-downs before the diver can actually finish dressing down. Typically, the diving equipment used is then left at the nuclear facility for a period of time to allow decontamination to be completed. This decontamination is closely monitored from the time that the diver climbs out of the water until the equipment is released back to the contractor.

Diver returning to surface, then being decontaminated at nuclear plant.
Photos courtesy of Francis Hermans

21.1.5 Summary

As we have seen in this section, there are contaminants found in some water that can seriously harm or even kill the diver if he is exposed to them. We also learned that some of these contaminants will sicken the diver at the time of exposure and others won't show up until time has passed, perhaps years. The absolute last thing that any diver needs is to be exposed to a toxic contaminant. Sometimes it is hard to find out if there are contaminants, and if so, what they are and what effect they will have (short- and long-term). It is strongly recommended all of the proper precautions be used any time the diver is aware of any contaminants in the water. On some jobs, that may mean simply wearing a drysuit and on others, full hazmat. Regardless of the circumstances, the diver must do all that he can to protect himself from contaminants. In hazmat operations, the following safety measures must be taken:

- Positively identify contaminants (water and sediment samples recommended)
- Obtain MSDS information for all contaminants identified
- Indentify level of protection required for both diver and surface crew
- Determine the effects contaminants will have on suit (include break-through time)
- If possible, use only WHMIS trained personnel on diving crew

21.2 CONFINED-SPACE DIVING

A confined-space dive is any dive where the air on surface is of questionable or poor quality and does not have free exchange with the atmosphere. The poor air quality may be the result of contaminants in the water, oxygen depletion due to corrosion or from decaying marine growth. Regardless of the source of air contamination, the surface crew most certainly cannot perform their jobs nor can they help the diver in an emergency unless they are safe. Most industrial work sites require a Confined Space Entry Permit be issued prior to any confined space entry.

We learned in Chapter 3: Underwater Physiology that the oxygen level in air must be above 16% to retain consciousness. The oxygen levels must be tested in confined spaces prior to any personnel entering and oxygen monitors must be used with a low-level alarm any time that breathing apparatus are not worn.

Contaminant levels must also be measured. The oxygen levels may be in the acceptable range but contaminants (methane, hydrogen sulfide, carbon monoxide and other gases) may still be in the range where they are toxic to humans. Contaminants must be identified by detection devices and never by your sense of smell. For example, hydrogen sulfide (H_2S) is a threat in concentrations over 5ppm. H_2S has a distinctive rotten egg smell, but when it is in concentrations close to 10ppm, it kills the sense of smell almost immediately. Entering an area contaminated with H_2S you may or may not notice the smell and you may think (just before you collapse) that it has cleared up.

When oxygen is low, or other contaminants are present, positive pressure breathing apparatus must be worn by all personnel entering the confined space. For every person working in a confined space, a rescue person is required to be present (with breathing apparatus and safety harness) at the opening.

Breathing apparatus is not always required. Depending on the level of contaminants and the oxygen level, blower fans and exhaust fans may be all that is required in order to work safely in the confined space. However, if fans are used to keep the environment safe, all personnel must evacuate immediately if power is lost to the fans. In this example the diver would be left in the water where he is safe until the power is restored, or until temporary lighting and breathing apparatus are brought online.

Confined space diving is most often performed on inshore or inland diving operations and includes any area below deck in a pump house, water, or sewage treatment plant and also in potable water towers. In offshore operations, confined space dives may be performed in tanks, cargo holds or other compartments of vessels, both floating and sunken.

21.2.1 Safety Precautions for Confined-Space Diving

When diving in confined space, the following safety measures must be taken:

- A full risk assessment must be performed, including a JSA with crew participation.
- All diving crew entering the confined space must wear a tethered retrieval harness.
- Positive pressure breathing apparatus must be worn if air quality is poor.
- The diver dress-in area must be located in an area with good air quality.
- The diver's helmet must be in free-flow mode (vent open) any time the diver is above the water surface and inside the confined space. This includes during water entry and exit.

21.3 PENETRATION DIVING

A penetration dive is defined as any dive where the diver is required to work under an overhang below surface greater than six feet or where the diver is inside any enclosed area underwater that extends more than six feet horizontally or diagonally. The reason these penetration dives are considered exceptional conditions is due to the diver being under an overhang or inside a pipe, tunnel or chamber, and the umbilical no longer leads directly to the surface. The farther the diver moves under the overhang (or into the tunnel), the more drag is placed on his umbilical. As drag increases, the diver can no longer pull slack hose and the surface crew cannot pick up slack on the hose. There is another, more serious problem. If the diver loses communications, line-pull signals will not work when the umbilical does not lead directly to surface.

Penetration dives, when performed properly, use in-water tenders. In-water tenders are divers whose sole mission is to tend the hose of the diver performing the penetration. The in-water tender is placed at the opening of the pipeline, tunnel or chamber where the diver is working. As the diver moves, the in-water tender slacks the hose or picks up on the slack. In-water tenders are used for the standby diver's hose, as well. A penetration dive will often require more than twice the number of diving crew that would be required on a normal surface-supplied dive to the same depth.

Penetration work must be carefully risk assessed. During the risk assessment several important points must be considered, including the following:

- The time it will take the diver to cover the penetration distance and return.
- How the time in the point above will impact bottom time and decompression.
- The size of bailout required for both primary and standby diver considering the time it takes to return and surface.
- The amount of time required for the standby diver to reach the diver in an emergency.

Inshore, penetration dives are performed at some hydro dam or pump house intakes, all pipelines and tunnels, and under some dock structures. Offshore, in salvage operations, penetration dives are performed on the interior portions of sunken vessels or aircraft.

21.3.1 Safety Precautions for Penetration Diving
The following safety measures must be taken when performing penetration dives:

- A full risk assessment must be performed, including a JSA with crew participation.
- The primary and standby divers will require bailout capability to allow them to return the full length of the penetration and ascend to surface, including any decompression commitment.
- The standby diver umbilical must be at least ten feet (3 meters) longer than the primary umbilical.
- Splices in the umbilical should be avoided. Joiners restrict gas flow and communication wire splices are potential problem areas. The pneumo hose must never be spliced.
- Each diver requires an in-water tender at the mouth of the penetration. Long penetrations will require an in-water tender for the primary diver and one for the standby diver.
- An additional in-water tender is required any time the umbilical is required to make a sharp turn.
- Lock out / tag out must be performed on any and all equipment in the immediate area prior to the dive (see Chapter 14: Power Plants and Pump Houses).
- All flow must be stopped prior to a diver entering any pipeline, tunnel, or chamber.

22.0 REMOTELY OPERATED VEHICLES

Remotely Operated Vehicle (ROV) is the term used for the tethered, unmanned submersibles used by many subsea contractors, navies, research bodies and government departments world-wide today. These machines are controlled entirely by the operator (called the pilot), with the exception of some auto depth and station keeping features that are enabled by the pilot. They are definitely not to be confused with the un-tethered autonomous underwater vehicles, which are a free-swimming unit, used for survey, seafloor mapping, seismic work and environmental monitoring. This chapter provides only a brief introduction to the ROV. Divers wishing to work as ROV pilots or technicians will require specialized training. Previous training in electronics, mechanics, fluid mechanics or engineering is usually required for trainees and a background in the diving industry (oil-field diving) is a definite advantage.

22.1 DEVELOPMENT OF ROV TECHNOLOGY

The first basic units were known as Cable-Controlled Underwater Recovery Vehicles (CURVs). They were developed by the United States Navy and the British Royal Navy. Both navies financed extensive research through the late 1950s and the 1960s. At this time, both navies were using underwater video cameras as "drop cameras" and on towed sleds. The next logical step was a camera that could be propelled in different directions, or "fly" through the water. The original requirement was for a remote controlled salvage, recovery and rescue device that could assist in the rescue of trapped submariners, recover items such as practice torpedoes and salvage downed aircraft. The U.S. Navy used one (CURV III) in 1965 to help recover a hydrogen bomb lost in the Mediterranean Sea, and the Royal Navy used one (the Cutlet) on a regular basis to recover practice torpedoes. Many still classified missions were performed during this time as well.

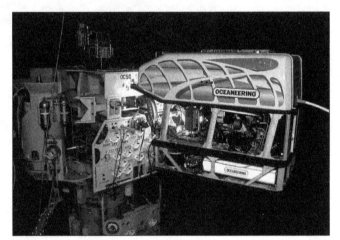

ROV using a torque tool to manipulate a valve on a subsea manifold. Photo courtesy of Oceaneering International

Once remote vehicle technology became common knowledge, private tech corporations built on what the two navies had created and developed the first of the "observation class" vehicles. They appeared in the late 1970s and were by then known as ROVs. The research continued with the observation vehicles soon being followed by work-class vehicles and then by mini-ROVs. The research continues today on improved propulsion systems, navigation and control systems and advanced tooling for different applications. The driving force behind most of the ROV innovation then and now are the requirements of the oil industry.

22.2 TYPICAL ROV USAGE

Remote Operated Vehicles are used extensively today to perform a vast multitude of tasks. They are used by the customs inspectors of various countries to perform inspections of foreign cargo vessels; police forces to recover evidence; oceanographic and environmental organizations to obtain water and sediment samples; diving contractors to perform inspections on hydro dams and nuclear plants where the conditions are unsafe for divers; to perform structural inspections offshore; to perform tasks that divers usually perform in oil installations too deep for divers; and to perform trenching and burial operations on subsea pipelines and cables. Often they are used offshore to assist divers at their tasks, by providing high intensity underwater lighting and video monitoring, as well as other tasks. There are several reasons that an ROV is selected instead of using divers: severely contaminated water will not sicken or kill an ROV; these machines do not require decompression; they are able to work at depths a diver cannot work and in high risk areas they can be utilized without endangering a life. On the negative side, the ROV is limited in the operations it can perform and the pilot is limited in his spatial awareness to what he can see on the video.

22.3 HOW ROVS WORK

With the exception of the very few ROVs that are deployed from and tethered to submarines (navy and scientific machines), all ROVs have one thing in common: they are tethered to and controlled from the surface. The ROV tether, like the diver's umbilical, is the machine's lifeline and it will not operate without the tether. Tethers are either the old style (hard wire) or new style (fiber optic). The newer tethers are less than half the size of the old ones and create far less drag due to current and vehicle movement. The tether is used to carry electric power and data from surface to the ROV and carry video signal and data back from the ROV to the surface. The electric power is used to run lights, hydraulic pumps, cameras and other items onboard the machine. The data carried consists of the control of physical movement of the ROV, navigation and positioning information, control of manipulators and tools and control of cameras on board the machine. The video signal is what the various cameras on the ROV see.

Work class ROV being deployed – cylinder on top is the TMS
Photo courtesy of Marine Technological Society

Most machines in use today use a Tether Management System (TMS) to tend the ROV tether. A TMS is a winch that winds up or pays out the tether as the ROV requires. This winch has an electrical and electronic slip ring, a device that allows the winch to continue rotating while maintaining electrical power and electronic signal. The ROV is launched by the LARS or crane and the TMS pays out tether as the ROV descends. The TMS slacks the tether as the ROV requires, then recovers it as the ROV returns to surface, where the LARS or crane then recovers the machine and the TMS.

Every single ROV uses multiple thrusters (some electric, some hydraulic) to provide vertical movement, fore and aft movement, roll, pitch and trim. The amount of thrust on the machine depends on the size of the machine and the intended purpose of the machine, but it varies from 5 hp to over 200 hp.

All machines have cameras. Small observation machines may just have one video camera, large machines often have several cameras, both video and still. Video cameras onboard an ROV are most often equipped with a "pan and tilt" feature, remote focus and remote zoom, to allow for the best video possible. Most high end ROVs are equipped with several different types of video camera, including special low-light SIT cameras, ultra high-resolution cameras and high-resolution digital still cameras.

Every single ROV uses floatation to enable them to "fly" with as little effort as possible. Even the large, tracked machines fly to the job, set down on bottom and then travel on their tracks. Some ROV pilots prefer a positively buoyant machine, some prefer a negatively buoyant machine, but most companies specify the buoyancy in their procedures. Buoyancy is controlled by the adding or removing of syntactic foam floatation and the adding or removing of lead ballast. The buoyancy must be adjusted to compensate for tools and manipulators. All tools do not weigh the same, so each time a new tool is introduced, the ROV crew must calculate the weight and displacement, then make buoyancy adjustments.

Smaller ROVs usually are all electric. Thrusters are electric, and if any manipulators or tools are onboard, they are electric. The larger units have onboard hydraulics. This allows them to have hydraulic thrusters as well as hydraulically powered tools and manipulators.

The instrumentation on ROVs varies with the size of the machine and the operations they perform, but the typical machine used offshore carries as a minimum: a SONAR unit (pulse or side-scan), auto depth control and a navigation package that usually interfaces with shipboard survey.

The tools used on any given ROV depend on the machine. Smaller machines are only able to use electric tools, since they do not have onboard hydraulic systems. The larger machines can utilize a full range of tools, including modified versions of the hydraulic tools, high-pressure water jets, water-blasters, inspection tools and NDT equipment that a diver uses offshore.

22.4 TYPES OF ROV

Although they vary in size from a 13-pound, hand-launched, mini-ROV to a 100-ton-tracked trenching ROV, there are just 3 recognized classes of vehicle: observation class, light-work class, and work class.

22.4.1 Observation-Class Vehicles

Observation-class machines are equipped with cameras only. They do not carry tools. These units usually are much smaller than the work-class ROVs

A propeller being inspected by a small observation class ROV (Fisher Sea Otter) Photo courtesy of JW Fisher, Inc

and are launched either by hand or with a small davit. The camera packages vary from a single-video camera to multiple-video and still cameras. Due to the limited thrust available in these units, they are never utilized in areas prone to any current or flow.

22.4.2 Light-Work Class Vehicles

The light-work class ROV is equipped with a single 4-function manipulator, small electric tools and, of course, cameras. These machines are occasionally hand launched but usually a davit is used for launch and recovery.

22.4.3 Work-Class Vehicles

Work-class vehicles are larger units (some up to 100 tons), have greater thrust (up to 200 hp) and most often have sophisticated navigation systems with features such as auto depth and auto heading to assist the pilots in

Various sizes of work-class vehicle. Left-to-right: Tiger, Surveyor, Cougar, and Panther. Photo courtesy of Bluestream

operation. Many are equipped with side-scan SONAR. The typical work class unit has 2 or 3 multi-function manipulators and a large hydraulic tool package. These units usually have a dedicated LARS and are outfitted with a tether management system. This is the vehicle used in deepwater oil work.

22.5 ROV SAFETY

As with most other machines, the ROV is completely safe when operated and maintained properly and when all safety precautions are followed. There is potential, however, for injury when working with or working on ROVs. The thrusters (particularly on the larger machines) are capable of causing serious injury or death. When ROV systems are being tested on deck, only trained, qualified personnel should approach the machine. The electrical systems on the ROV are capable of causing electrocution. All work performed on the tether, connections and electrical systems must be performed by skilled, trained technicians. Many of the systems (thrusters, manipulators, tools) on larger units are powered by onboard hydraulics. These hydraulic systems operate at very high pressure. A pinhole leak on a hydraulic line has the potential to cause serious injury or death to anyone who passes too close. Prior to servicing any of the systems on the ROV, the systems need to be de-energized, lockouts need to be put in place and only personnel with the proper training should perform ROV maintenance.

22.5.1 Safety in Combined Diving and ROV Operations

It is not uncommon for diving operations to include having an ROV on the site and deployed at the same time that divers are in the water. The following precautions should be followed for combined operations:

- Maintain clear communications between Dive Control and ROV Control at all times.
- When operating an ROV in the vicinity of a working diver, there must be a guard placed over the thrusters to avoid fouling the diver's umbilical and to prevent hands or feet from coming in contact with the thrusters.
- Both crews need to practice good umbilical management and care must be taken so that neither one crosses over the other.
- Except in the case of a trapped or damaged ROV, the diver should always be recovered first.
- The diving supervisor and ROV supervisor should agree on an exclusion zone for the machine (a safe distance to be kept between the ROV and the diver while working).

23.0 UNDERWATER LIFTBAGS

When working underwater, situations constantly arise where the tools or materials being used are too heavy to be easily handled. Often, a little ingenuity will solve the problem. This author used a heavy one-inch impact for a few months that was made neutrally buoyant with a Styrofoam commercial lobster fishing buoy attached. Soda-sorb cans (filled by pneumo) are used to carry 160-pound pipeline flange bolts and jury-rigged lube oil cans filled with air can lighten hydraulic hoses and welding cables. But when there are heavy items that must be lifted properly and a crane is not an option, the best method to use is lift bags.

23.1 TYPES OF LIFT BAG

The lift bag is one device that is commonly used in nearly every underwater operation. Lift bags come in several configurations: enclosed "pillow" bags, open "parachute" bag, and specialty bags that have a job-specific design, such as vehicle recovery or EOD recovery systems. Provided the right type of lift bag is used and the bags are configured properly for the lift, the lifting operations can be performed safely.

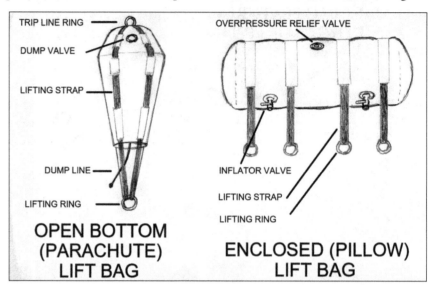

Drawings of the two most common types of lift bag: the parachute bag and the pillow bag.

23.2 LIFT BAG FEATURES

There are several manufacturers of lift bags, but the most common bags used are those produced by SUBSALVE USA, JW Automarine, Canflex, and Carter. It is strongly recommended that any lift bags used are from a recognized supplier and an approved manufacturer. All lift bags, be they 500 pound or 50 tons, have similar construction. Every properly designed lift bag will have the following features:

- Integral lifting straps that pass over the top of the device
- Attachment ring (master link) on the lifting straps
- A "dump valve" to release air from the bag
- A D-ring on the top (parachute bags) for an inverter (trip) line
- An "over pressure" valve (pillow bags) to prevent bursting the bag
- An "inflator valve" (pillow bags) to allow air line attachment
- A specifications tag on one lift strap that provides the rated capacity and test information

23.3 METHODS OF LIFTING

The method of lifting chosen obviously depends on the operation being performed. The method used in a salvage operation, for example, would differ greatly from the method used to move a pipeline spool across the seabed. Regardless of which lifting method is used, the diver must use proper rigging practice as on every lift. There are three basic methods of performing a lifting operation with lift bags.

- Lifting to the surface
- Staged lifting to the surface
- Restrained lifting

23.3.1 Lifting to the Surface

This method of using lift bags is usually only used in salvage operations and it involves bringing the object to be lifted the entire way to the surface in one lift. There are two serious drawbacks to this method: the lift is uncontrolled once it starts and the lift bags quite often dump once they reach surface sending the lift back down to the seabed. To avoid dumping air, parachute bags are seldom used with this method.

The "to surface" method of lifting is most often used in shallow water only. The lift bags are attached to the item to be salvaged, fill lines are attached and the diver is removed from the water before the bag inflation begins. This avoids any chance of the diver being caught in the rigging and having an uncontrolled ascent.

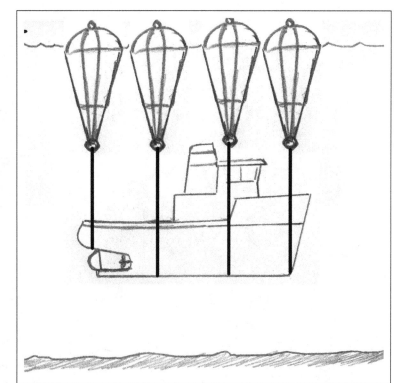

Lift bags in a "to surface" arrangement

23.3.2 Staged Lifting to Surface

Another method primarily used in salvage operations, "the staged lift" method has the lift bags positioned so that they are staged at different heights above the item being salvaged. This allows the lift to be brought off the seabed, but the higher rigged bags, known as "control bags" cause it to stop before all of the bags reach the surface, controlling the ascent and keeping the item a short distance below the surface.

The "staged lift" method is often used in deeper water. As with the "to surface" method, the diver is brought out prior to the inflation of the lift bags to avoid accidents and usually enclosed bags are used.

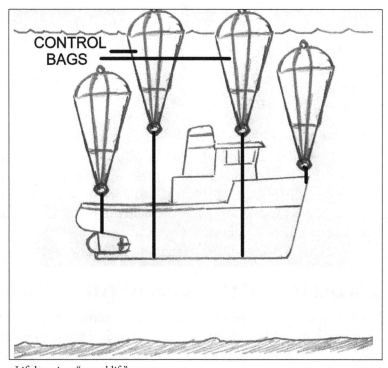

Lift bags in a "staged lift" arrangement

23.3.3 Restrained Lifting

The lifting method used most often on construction projects and subsea pipeline tie-ins is the "restrained lift". This method gets its name because there are restraining lines run from the item being lifted to heavy dead-man anchors to avoid an uncontrolled ascent. Primarily, restrained lifting is used when an item has been "wet stored" on the seabed and requires repositioning prior to installation.

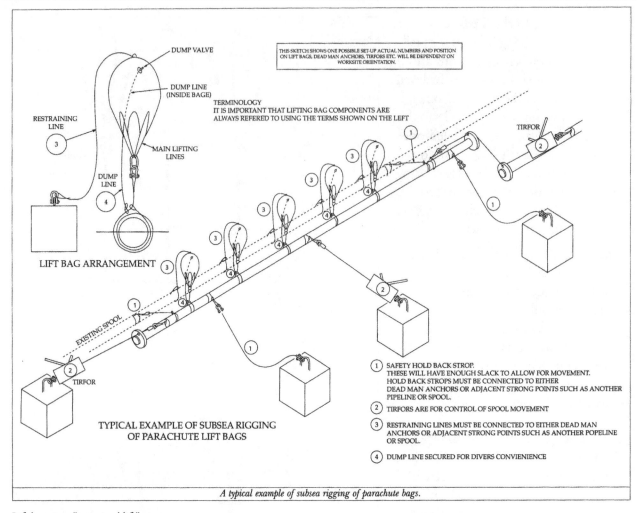

DUMP VALVE

THIS SKETCH SHOWS ONE POSSIBLE SET-UP ACTUAL NUMBERS AND POSITION ON LIFT BAGS, DEAD MAN ANCHORS, TIRFORS ETC. WILL BE DEPENDENT ON WORKSITE ORIENTATION.

DUMP LINE (INSIDE BAGE)

RESTRAINING LINE

TERMINOLOGY
IT IS IMPORTANT THAT LIFTING BAG COMPONENTS ARE ALWAYS REFERED TO USING THE TERMS SHOWN ON THE LEFT

TIRFOR

MAIN LIFTING LINES

DUMP LINE

LIFT BAG ARRANGEMENT

EXISTING SPOOL

TIRFOR

TYPICAL EXAMPLE OF SUBSEA RIGGING OF PARACHUTE LIFT BAGS

① SAFETY HOLD BACK STROP.
THESE WILL HAVE ENOUGH SLACK TO ALLOW FOR MOVEMENT. HOLD BACK STROPS MUST BE CONNECTED TO EITHER DEAD MAN ANCHORS OR ADJACENT STRONG POINTS SUCH AS ANOTHER PIPELINE OR SPOOL.

② TIRFORS ARE FOR CONTROL OF SPOOL MOVEMENT

③ RESTRAINING LINES MUST BE CONNECTED TO EITHER DEAD MAN ANCHORS OR ADJACENT STRONG POINTS SUCH AS ANOTHER POPELINE OR SPOOL.

④ DUMP LINE SECURED FOR DIVERS CONVIENIENCE

A typical example of subsea rigging of parachute bags.

Lift bags in a "restrained lift" arrangement.
Diagram: *IMCA Supervisor's Manual* courtesy of IMCA

The sketch above illustrates the proper way to utilize this method when performing a subsea tie-in. The spool piece is restrained by five steel cables, with tirfors attached to the existing pipeline and to dead-man anchor (DMA) blocks. This type of work most often uses the open "parachute" type bags. Notice also that each lift bag in the sketch has an inverter line attached to the top of the bag. In the event that the lift bag becomes detached from the lift this line causes the bag to invert and dump all of the air from the bag. It is actually mislabeled as a "restraining line" (3) on the sketch, however these lines are actually called an "inverter" or "trip" line and the holdback lines to the load itself are called restraining lines.

23.4 DEPLOYING LIFT BAGS TO THE DIVER

Since they are a lifting device, lift bags should never be deployed unless they are first inspected carefully, are found to be in good condition and have an in date test certificate. Lift bags, like all other subsea equipment used, are to be inspected prior to use (*IMCA D016, Rev.3*). Lift bags are never sent or carried down loose because exhaust from the diver's helmet can cause a parachute bag to inflate, pulling the diver off bottom and leading to a blow up incident. The "wrap and strap" method is used to deploy the parachute bag. Once the bag has been visually inspected, the "dump line" is confirmed to be attached where the diver can easily get at it. Then the bag is tightly rolled up and tied or strapped in a tight roll to be sent down to the diver. When the diver receives the bag, he attaches the lifting shackle to the load and readies the inverter line before he unties and unrolls the lift bag. **Lift bags must never be sent down loose.**

23.5 CARE AND MAINTENANCE OF LIFT BAGS

Lift bags, like all other subsea equipment, require proper care and maintenance. This will not only extend the working life of the lift bag, but most importantly, it will help to ensure that the lift bag will not fail while in use. Proper care includes the following:

- Do not store lift bags in direct sunlight.
- Do not store lift bags where they may be exposed to chemicals or petroleum products.
- Do not store lift bags in close proximity to electric motors or welding machines.
- Clean lift bags (especially of oil, grease or chemicals) after each use.

Since they are considered a lifting device, lift bags must be carefully inspected before each use and if there are deficiencies with the lift bags, they must not be used until the deficiencies are remedied. The following components are inspected on each lift bag:

- Bag skin: inspected for punctures or chafing
- Welded seams: seams in the bag skin are inspected for defects
- Strop panels: the panels that hold the strops in place outside the bag skin must be secure
- Webbing top ring: the ring that ties all of the webbing strops together must be without defect
- Webbing side strops: on parachute bags, the side strops must be free of defect or chafing
- Webbing leg strops: on enclosed bags, the leg strops must be free of defect or chafing
- Inverter line D ring: on parachute bags, the inverter D ring must be secure and without defect
- Leg strop D rings: on enclosed bags, the leg strop D rings must all be without defect
- Master link: on parachute or enclosed bags, the master link must be secure and without defect
- Dump valve: the dump valve must work easily and be free of defect or damage
- Dump valve lanyard: on parachute bags, the dump lanyard must be clear and secured near the master link to allow the diver to easily access it
- Inlet valve: on enclosed bags, the inlet valve must work easily and be free of damage or defect
- Relief valve: on enclosed bags, the over-pressure relief valve must work easily and be free of defect or damage

When inspecting lift bags, the manufacturer's name, model number, capacity, bag serial number and date of inspection is recorded, along with the inspection results. The diving supervisor or systems technician typically signs the inspection checklist. Unused lift bags are always tested at six month intervals according to *IMCA D016, Revision 3*. This does not eliminate the need for the inspection prior to usage.

Tears, cuts, or chafing to the bag skin may be repaired on site, using a patching kit and instructions provided by the lift bag manufacturer. Damage, wear, or chafing to the actual rigging (webbing strops, top ring or master link) must be repaired by the manufacturer at the factory. Valves may be lubricated but only as directed by the lift bag manufacturer in the lift bag user's manual.

23.6 SAFETY GUIDELINES FOR LIFT BAG USE

Lift bags are classified as "soft-lifting devices" as opposed to "hard-lifting devices" such as steel salvage pontoons or steel floatation units. Unfortunately, the classification term "soft" causes many to think that lift bags do not pose any safety risks to the diver. This is definitely not so, as illustrated in the following two case studies.

23.6.1 Case Study Number 1

In 2004, a diving contractor was attempting to refloat a small tug in the port of Long Beach, California, with enclosed lift bags. One diver observing the bag inflation became trapped between one bag and the vessel's hull. The diving supervisor was unable to hear the diver's screams over the background noise from the compressors and the diver was crushed to death.

23.6.2 Case Study Number 2

In 2006, a diving contractor was performing subsea pipeline tie-ins as a part of the Hurricane Katrina repair work in the Gulf of Mexico. A saturation diver had his umbilical over the spool piece when the lift bag inflation hose became fouled in the propeller of a DP thruster. The lift bag, spool piece and diver were rapidly pulled toward the surface. The diver subsequently died due to severe crush injuries, but he probably would have perished due to arterial gas embolism without the crushing as a factor..

23.6.3 Safety Guidelines

We can see by the two case studies above that lift bags can indeed be dangerous to the diver when they are not used properly. There have been many other incidents with lift bags and divers: every last one due to unsafe practices. The following safety guidelines must always be adhered to when using lift bags:

- Always perform a risk analysis and JSA before commencing any lifting operations.
- Always perform an inspection of every lift bag before use.
- Never use lift bags with damaged or defective lifting straps.
- Pre-plan lift bag positioning and attachment, then stick to the plan.
- Always inspect all rigging hardware, including spreader beams, before every lift.
- Never used damaged or defective rigging hardware (shackles, D-rings, straps or slings).
- Never allow a diver to pass underneath any item suspended by lift bags or cranes.
- Never attempt to overcome bottom suction on an item to be salvaged by using additional floatation. Use jetting or other methods to "break suction" prior to lifting.
- Always deploy parachute bags using the "wrap and strap" method. Never deploy open bags.
- Avoid having divers deployed when inflating lift bags, unless performing a "restrained lift".
- When performing a "restrained lift", ensure restraint weights exceed lift capacity by at least 3:1 ratio.
- Always ensure lift bag inflation lines are kept clear of DP thrusters or other moving equipment.
- Do not leave lift bag inflation lines untended in the water.
- Always practice proper umbilical management when divers are in the water.

24.0 UNDERWATER DEMOLITION

Every structure, land-based or marine, will last only as long as the material that was used to construct it. Many structures undergo extensive repairs or refits, replacing material that has corroded or otherwise become unserviceable. However, every structure has a point at which it is no longer feasible to perform repairs. The period of time from the structure's entering service until it reaches the point where some aspect of demolition is required is known as the effective life span of the structure. When a structure requires major repairs, demolition of part or all of the structure often becomes necessary. Also, new construction often requires bedrock excavation, which is another type of demolition. Underwater demolition can be divided into two categories: explosive and non-explosive.

24.1 NON-EXPLOSIVE DEMOLITION

In many cases, explosives are not an option when structures must be demolished because of the danger to nearby structures or facilities. Likewise, when bedrock must be removed, proximity to surrounding structures or facilities may dictate the exclusion of explosives. In these cases, non-explosive demolition techniques are employed, including mechanical methods of demolition and expanding grouts.

24.1.1 Mechanical Demolition

There are almost as many forms of mechanical demolition as there are types of marine structures. Every material used has its own properties and requires particular tools or methods to remove or demolish it.

24.1.1.1 Timber Structure Demolition

Timber structures may be demolished in one of three ways: hydraulic saw (effective), hydraulic grapple (less effective), or cable cutting (least effective). When cutting on a timber structure, it is important that loads and stored energy are considered, not only to prevent binding the chain or circular saw but to prevent injury to the diver. Timber structures are usually fastened with steel which will require cutting gear. There are several standard practices to remember when demolishing timber structures:

- As a rule, saws cut timber members one at a time, nd timbers are removed as they are cut.
- When using hydraulic circular or chainsaws, even with diamond blades, it is best to avoid steel fastenings and rock whenever possible.
- Grapples and cable cutters,require the location and recovery of multiple timbers after the fact. Often these timbers are buried or partially buried under rock ballast.
- The removal of timber and ballast, depending on the quantity and site conditions, may be more effectively performed with a crane and clam bucket.

24.1.1.2 Steel Structure Demolition

Steel structures may be demolished in one of four ways: hydraulic saw, ultra-thermic cutting, hydraulic shear, or diamond wire. The effectiveness of each method depends on the type of structure, the condition of the material, and access to the structure.

- Hydraulic saws work well, but on steel thinner than one-half inch, cutting rods are faster. Hydraulic saws are harder to handle and often require tracks and special rigging.
- On thicker steel or when there is severe corrosion, saws are often the best choice.
- If the structure is pile work, then the best choice is usually a shear. These tools resemble an oversized cable cutter and will crush almost anything.
- To avoid safety problems associated with gas pockets and cutting rods, steel structures with concrete infill are best cut with a saw, shear, or diamond wire.

24.1.1.3 Concrete Structure Demolition

Concrete structures may be mechanically demolished using one of the following methods: diamond wire saw, hydraulic demolition hammer, hydraulic circular saw, or a jackhammer. The choice of method depends on the size of the structure, access, and the amount of concrete to be removed.

- Diamond wire cutting involves considerable set-up. It is used primarily when large pieces of concrete are to be removed and it usually involves the use of large cranes and easy access.

- Demolition hammers are always attached to the boom of an excavator or backhoe. They require land or barge access. These units work on the same principle as a jackhammer, so rebar will have to be cut during the operation. Since the hammer will be chipping the concrete into pieces, removal of the rubble must be considered.

- Hydraulic circular saws, with blades available up to six feet in diameter, will cut concrete to a depth of over two feet.

- Many concrete structures can be cut into small pieces and disassembled with only a small crane and a saw. The effective depth of the saw limits the structures on which it can be used.

- When using a jackhammer, the concrete is broken into small pieces and rebar must be cut, either with shears or cutting gear. Smaller jobs will justify a jackhammer, but it is not an efficient option for a large project because as much time will be spent removing rubble as is spent on the jackhammer. If demolition hammers can reach the job, they are much more efficient.

24.1.1.4 Bedrock Removal

Bedrock removal may be performed mechanically by demolition hammer, hydraulic rock splitter or jackhammer.

- The most efficient method is the demolition hammer, but even when mounted on a long reach excavator, the machine will only reach thirty-odd feet below the barge.

- A hydraulic rock splitter is the best method for depths exceeding the reach of a demolition hammer and excavator. This tool is basically a wedge that is spread by a hydraulic ram, causing the rock to break. Unless the rock has large cracks running through it, a drill or chipper will be required to provide a place to start the rock splitter.

- The least effective option for mechanical bedrock removal is the jackhammer. Jackhammers are used on small jobs or when no other option is available.

24.1.2 Expanding Grouts

Expanding grouts are a very effective method of demolishing rock and concrete. In fact, they are almost as effective as explosives. This product works well in the marine environment and is effective underwater. As with explosives, holes are drilled in the rock or concrete and the grout is then mixed. The grout is bagged in poly plastic tubes for underwater work. The holes are then loaded. The grout expands as the curing process takes place, creating several tons of outward pressure on the sides of the holes which breaks the concrete or rock into pieces. The method is basically the same as blasting, with the exception that the reaction happens slowly, so shock, sound and flying debris are not a problem.

24.1.3 Safety Tips for Non-Explosive Demolition

When performing non-explosive demolition, the following safety guidelines will apply:

- When performing non-explosive demolition, start at the top of the structure. The demolition process should be the reverse of the construction process.
- Check for utilities (power, gas, water) before proceeding with demolition. Unless there is proof it has been turned off, assume it is still on.
- If the structure had oil or gas lines, make sure they have been flushed. "Empty" lines are the ones that always explode.
- Leave the hydraulic saw "cold" when lowering it to a diver. Make the saw "hot" only when the diver is ready to cut.
- Unload timber cribs as the cutting progresses. <u>Never</u> cut timbers on a fully ballasted crib unless the diver is above the ballast.
- When ultra-thermic cutting, always cut "cold." Make the gear "cold" as soon as the rod starts burning. Gear that is "hot" without oxygen running is producing hydrogen and may explode when an arc is struck. Gear that is left "hot" while cutting is destroying the diving gear.
- Be careful when cutting severely corroded steel. Make sure heavy scale has been knocked off and will not be blown off by "gas pops."
- When cutting piles or panels, always have restraints on the member being cut or have it hooked up to a crane.
- When working with expanding grout, always wear safety glasses, gloves and a mask.
- When using expanding grout above water, always keep all personnel away in case of blowout.
- If the diver is not sure what will happen, the cut should not be made. Loads, stresses, and stored energy must always be considered when cutting or otherwise removing structural members.
- **Never** allow a diver in the water while using a clam bucket, grapple, or while cable cutting.
- When using cutting gear, do not cut steel with concrete infill unless ventilation holes have been burned to avoid gas pockets. Likewise, make sure all tanks or compartments have been ventilated.
- Never dive with demolition going on overhead.
- Do not dive in or under any structure unless everyone is positive that it is safe to do so.

24.2 EXPLOSIVE DEMOLITION

Modern explosives technology is highly developed and both the variety of explosives and application techniques make explosives a very useful tool underwater. They can be used for removing subsurface structures and wrecks. Explosives can also be used for trenching through rock or coral, widening channels, cutting steel, timber or concrete piling and steel cables. These underwater explosions differ from those on land because the surrounding water serves to completely confine or tamp, the detonation much more efficiently than could be accomplished on land eliminating the need for blasting mats. Also, because of the confining and cooling characteristics of the surrounding water, an underwater explosion will undergo an oscillation process that is not seen in surface explosions.

The commercial use of explosives, called blasting, is a highly regulated industry involving licensing, permits and other restrictions. Blasting should be left to technically qualified and licensed personnel. It is unlikely that a diver without specialized training will be required to do blasting design and installation but divers may be called upon to do some blasting-related work., Because of this, divers need to have a basic understanding of explosives, the way they are used and to have an appreciation of the dangers involved in explosive demolition. If handled **safely** and according **to all specifications**, explosives are as safe as any other tool in the diver's toolbox. This section is designed to provide an understanding and appreciation of explosives: it will not make the diver a blaster or qualify him to use explosives, but it will assist in safe operations on diving sites where demolition is going on.

24.2.1 Types of Explosion
There are four basic kinds of explosion: mechanical, such as an over-pressurized scuba bottle; geothermal, such as volcanoes; nuclear; and chemical.

Demolition involves chemical explosions. A chemical explosion is the violent, sudden expansion of gases released by a chemical reaction in a gaseous, solid or liquid mix. The mix expands extremely rapidly to a volume much greater than the original volume. The rate of expansion is known as velocity and it is the velocity of an explosion that determines its power to do work.

The essential properties of an explosion are as follows:

• Reaction does not take place until a suitable impulse, such as a priming detonation is provided.
• Reaction is extremely fast.
• Reaction causes a complete or nearly complete conversion into gaseous products.
• Reaction is exothermic (heat releasing).

24.2.2 Classification of Explosives
Explosives are classified according to the way in which their energy is released and the manner in which they produce an explosion. Explosions are considered either low order or high order based on their speed of expansion. Expansion is measured in feet per second (fps). Low order explosions expand at less than 6500 fps while high order explosions expand at more than 6500 fps.

Explosives are further classified according to their sensitivity. This is a measure of the strength of the impulse required to start an explosive reaction. The higher the sensitivity, the more dangerous the explosive, and the more carefully it must be handled. Low sensitivity explosives may be difficult to detonate directly.

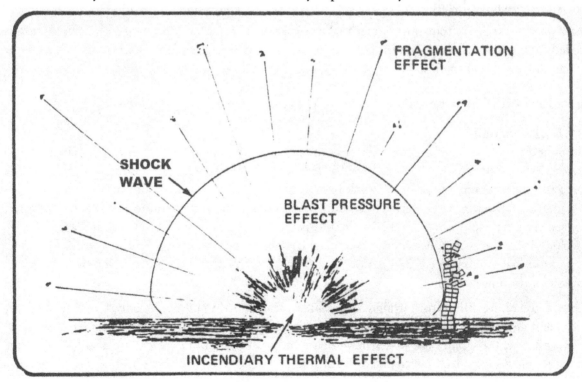

Effects of an Explosion

24.2.3 Types of Explosives

24.2.3.1 Low explosives
Low explosives transform from their basic form to gas by a burning process known as deflagration, rather than by detonation. Low explosives are slower and less powerful than high explosives, completing the deflagration process at less than 6500 fps. Low explosives include black powder, smokeless powder, blasting powder, and rocket propellant.

24.2.3.2 Primary explosives
are the most sensitive explosives. They do not burn but explode from spark, flame or percussion. Their detonation is violent and produces a considerable localized shock. The sensitivity of these initiating explosives is used to start deflagration or detonation in other explosives. Mercury fulminate, lead azide, lead picrate, lead styphnate, and diazodinitrophenol are in this category.

24.2.3.3 High explosives
High explosives expand from their initial form so quickly that they are said to detonate. The complete process occurs throughout the entire mass at a velocity faster than sound and results in a cutting or shattering effect. For example, dynamites detonate at a velocity of 19,000 fps, TNT at 22,500. (To obtain good results underwater, the detonation rate should be at least 14,000 fps.) High explosives include nitroglycerin, nitrocellulose, nitroguanidine, TNT, picric acid, PETN, cyclonite and dynamite.

Some high explosives burn, some decompose from heat without burning others are very inflammable. Some explode easily from shock while others do not. The main characteristic of high explosives is that they are made to detonate by the shock of another explosion, usually that of a primary explosive. However, there are those that explode easily and are themselves so powerful that they are used to initiate the explosion of less-sensitive high explosives. These are known as secondary high explosives, primers or boosters and include TNT, Tetryl and PETN. An example of this are TNT boosters which are often used with Tovex.

Anytime an explosive transmits enough force to set off another charge, the second detonation is called a sympathetic detonation. Initiators or boosters are powerful enough to set off the main charge in a sympathetic detonation.

24.2.4 Explosive Characteristics of Various Types of Explosive

24.2.4.1 Dynamite
Straight dynamite contains nitroglycerine as the only explosive material. Dynamite is manufactured in a series of grades ranging from 30 to 60%. The percentage represents the amount of nitroglycerine present, with the remainder of the stick being composed of cellulose wood pulp by weight. This percentage is also sometimes referred to as the dynamite's strength. Dynamite is relatively expensive, extremely sensitive to shock and friction and is very highly flammable. Dynamite has a velocity of 20,000 fps and is highly water resistant, which makes it good for underwater work. However, dynamite that is submerged for a period exceeding 24 hours must be waterproofed by sealing it in plastic or dipping it in pitch.

"Extra" dynamite differs from straight dynamite in that a portion of the nitroglycerin is replaced by sufficient amounts of ammonium nitrate to maintain grade strength. When compared to straight dynamite, "extra" grades are lower in velocity and water resistance. They are also less sensitive to shock or friction, less flammable and considerably less expensive. Dynamite is used primarily for quarrying, stumping and ditching. Dynamite, for the most part, is being replaced by newer compositions such as Tovex.

24.2.4.2 Tovex

Tovex, also known as Trenchrite, Siesmogel, and Seismopac, is a water-gel explosive compound made of ammonium nitrate and methylammonium nitrate. This product is safer to manufacture, store, and transport than traditional dynamite, and it is far less toxic. For these reasons, Tovex has almost entirely replaced dynamite. Tovex is a silver, metallic looking gel that comes packed in sausage tubes of various sizes. This product can be loaded in underwater patterns and left for 24 hours or more before use.

24.2.4.3 TNT (Trinitrotoluene)

TNT is relatively insensitive to shock and reasonably stable in any climate. It is insoluble in water. TNT has a velocity of 23,000 fps and is widely used in military and civilian construction operations. The fumes are poisonous, therefore it should not be used in confined spaces. TNT may be detonated by electric or non-electric caps or with prima cord (det-cord).

24.2.4.4 Composition-4 (C-4)

C-4 is white, putty-like and has no distinct odor. C-4 has a velocity of 26,000 fps and remains pliable in temperatures ranging from -70°F to +170°F, while maintaining its explosive properties. It is extremely stable, very resistant to shock and will burn. The fumes are poisonous. C-4 is used primarily for cutting and breaching, but it is so versatile that it can be adapted to many special tasks such as specialized charges to minimize the quantity and maximize effect of the shockwave. If used underwater, it must be kept in packages to prevent erosion.

24.2.4.5 PETN

PETN is white in color and has a velocity of 26,000 fps. It is used as the explosive core in prima cord (det-cord) and as the base charge (initiator) in electric and non-electric firing caps.

24.2.4.6 Multi-Component Explosives (Liquid Binary Systems)

These systems come as a kit that consists of specified amounts of liquid and solids that come in separate containers and pouches. As long as they remain separated they are not explosive and unmixed components may be transported by any means. However, once mixed they become highly explosive and all caution must be exercised. They can be detonated with electric or non-electric caps or detonating cord and they have a velocity of around 22,000 fps, depending on the particular product. Normally used for metal cutting, multi-component explosives include Quadrex, Astropac, Astrolite, Tri-ex, and Tovex.

24.2.4.7 Nitro-Carbonitrates

These are commercial blasting agents that are insensitive chemical compositions or mixtures containing no nitroglycerin. The main advantage to these explosives is their safety in handling. They are packed in sealed metal cans so their water resistance is practically unlimited, providing they are properly handled. They will not freeze and are very economical. Their unconfined velocity is about 7,000 fps, while their confined velocity is 13,000 to 22,000 fps.

24.2.5 Shaped Charges (Munroe Effect)

These are high-density, high strength explosives formed in a metal or glass cone-shaped liner. The shape concentrates the effects of the blast by focusing a greater than normal amount of the heat and energy into a very small area. When detonation occurs, the cone is collapsed and transformed into a molten slug which is followed by a small, high temperature jet of particles traveling at velocities of 10,000 fps to 30,000 fps. The slug strikes the target with such heat and force that the target flows radically from the point of impact, leaving a smooth, deep hole. Shaped charges are very economical because a great deal of force can be generated by a small amount of explosive.

The principle factors that control the performance of shaped charges are: the type and weight of explosive; the diameter, material and shape of the cone and the "stand-off," or distance, from the target. Shaped charges are used to cut holes, pipelines, pilings, well casing, precision cutting of metals and to breach steel, earth, or concrete.

24.2.6 Prima Cord (Det-cord)

Used for priming or detonating single or multiple explosive charges, prima cord looks like heavy-duty plastic-covered laundry line. It may be white or colored. Detonating cord contains six pounds of PETN per 1,000 feet and detonates at a velocity of 27,000 fps. It is very versatile and can be used to enlarge holes, cut trees or underwater timber piles (one wrap per inch of diameter for wood), wrap around other explosives, tie off with, prime and detonate. Prima cord can be detonated by the shock of electric or non-electric blasting caps and can be used as a booster to explode larger charges.

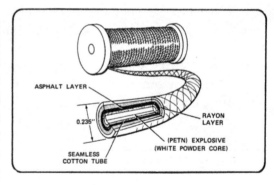

Detonating cord

24.2.7 Safety or Time Fuse

Safety or time fuses are used to initiate non-electric blasting caps. They may be orange, green or tan in color and should not be confused with Prima cord. The fuse normally comes in fifty-foot rolls wrapped in paper, is about ¼ inch in diameter and contains a core of black powder (Prima Cord comes in 1000' lengths on a spool). Special-application time fuses come in a variety of colors, denoting their burning time and special usage. The burning rate is normally around forty seconds per foot, but it should be tested. It is important

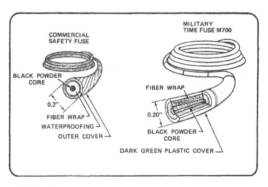

Safety fuses

to test a minimum of six feet at a time under the same conditions in which the fuse is to be used. Use a fuse lighter to light the safety fuse and time it as it burns. The minimum time fuse length should never be shorter than 3 feet. When using safety fuse, the first 6 inches must be cut off due to moisture absorption when the fuse is left to sit for longer than 6 hours.

24.2.8 Non-electric Blasting Cap

This cap has a recess on one end into which the time fuse is inserted. The cap contains three charges: a flash charge, priming charge and a base charge that is 13.5 grains of PETN. The priming charge will either be lead azide or fulminate of mercury. Fulminate of mercury is the most sensitive explosive used in demolition work.

24.2.9 Electric Blasting Cap

These consist of a PETN base charge, a priming charge, bridge wire and leg wires sealed into the end of either an aluminum or copper shell. If the shell is aluminum, the priming charge is lead azide. If it is copper, the priming charge is fulminate of mercury.

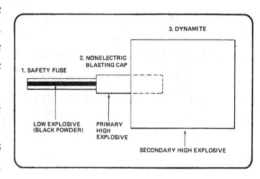

When the proper current is applied to the leg wires, it heats the bridge wire sufficiently to detonate the priming charge, which, in turn, detonates the base charge. Electric caps should always be tested prior to placing charges. When working underwater, the caps should be kept as close to the surface as possible.

Blasting cap used as an initiator

24.3 SELECTING AN EXPLOSIVE

The selection of an explosive for specific operations requires careful consideration of the principal properties of explosives. The following qualities should be considered:

- Strength: The measure of the amount of energy released by an explosive on detonation.
- Velocity of detonation: The rate at which a detonation wave travels through a column of explosive.
- Density: This depends on the explosive's ingredients. With a high-density explosive, the energy of the shot will be concentrated.
- Sensitivity: Explosives must be sensitive enough for initiation by a standard detonator.
- Stability: All brands of explosives are rigorously tested for stability before they leave the factory.
- Water resistance: When blasting in wet conditions, an explosive of suitable resistance should be chosen. Explosives of a lower water resistance can be coated to improve this quality.
- Resistance to low temperatures: Explosives containing nitroglycerin tend to freeze below -8 C.

24.4 FIRING SYSTEMS

A firing system is a complete means of detonating a charge from a remote position and includes a primer. A firing system may be electric, non-electric or a combination of both. In the air, the system can be as simple as a fuse leading to a blasting cap, with a match to light it. Underwater, the system is more likely to be a complex arrangement of electric wiring, blasting caps, detonating cord, prima cord primers and a blasting machine. The most common firing system in underwater blasting is as follows: high explosive; TNT primer; prima cord; blasting cap; electric wire; blasting machine. The prima cord is run to surface and attached to an inflatable buoy. The blasting cap is attached to the prima cord and then a wire is run from the blasting cap a safe distance away to a blasting machine.

24.4.1 Detonating Cord System

The detonating cord firing system enables personnel to detonate one or more charges simultaneously through the use of an explosive-filled trunk line. This system requires an electric or non-electric cap, det-cord trunk lines and det-cord branch lines. Trunk lines are laid out, and then branch lines are connected to the trunk lines. Finally, the cap is attached to the trunk line. Care must be taken to avoid a break or kink in the cord when laying it.

24.4.2 Non-electric System

The non-electric firing system is designed to enable personnel to initiate the detonation of a charge with a small flame. It may be used to fire either single or multiple charges simultaneously or in sequence. Non-electric systems are generally not as safe as electric firing because of the problem of someone entering the firing area after the fuse has been ignited and possible "hang fires."

The non-electric system consists of a non-electric cap, time fuse and a fuse igniter. The time fuse must first be tested using the "burn test" and measured. The cap must be inspected. Once it is determined to be safe, the fuse is inserted into the open end of the cap and the cap is crimped around the fuse. The cap is then attached to the charge. Finally, the fuse igniter is attached to the other end of the fuse.

If the charge does not function, all personnel should remain at a safe distance for at least 30 minutes before attempting to determine the malfunction cause. No attempt should be made to remove the misfired fuse cap assembly. It is necessary to assemble a new initiating charge and place it below the original unit on the same trunk line or in contact with the bulk charge, if it is accessible.

24.4.3 Electric System

An electric firing system is one in which an electric power source is attached at the instant of firing. This system can be used to fire a group of charges simultaneously or in succession. The electric system consists of an electric cap, firing wire (two-conductor, 18-gauge) and an appropriate blasting machine. To lay out an electric firing system, the firing wire and caps are first tested. Then the caps are connected to the circuit and inserted into the charges. From a safe site, the entire circuit is tested. Finally, the blasting machine is connected. When firing charges in succession, the charges must be fitted with delay caps. Regular delay caps are manufactured in ten standard periods of delay ranging from one second to two seconds. Millisecond delay caps range from 25 milliseconds to 1000 milliseconds. As the number of detonators and the power supply dictate, connections of the firing and connecting wires of an electrical system may be in common series, parallel or in series parallel. Parallel or series parallel circuits should be used only when the number of caps exceeds the capacity of the blasting machine. These circuits require the attention of personnel thoroughly familiar with the electrical problems involved. The circuits must be balanced to ensure detonation of all charges because inaccurate balancing in a parallel circuit may cause a misfire of one or more charges, with consequent delay and danger. Detection and investigation of a misfire from a parallel circuit is usually difficult because most of the charges will be detonated.

It is necessary to use a series circuit when the number of detonators is within the rated capacity of the blasting machine. The best series circuit is the common series. The prime advantage of a series circuit is that it can be checked in its entirety (assuming all caps have the same resistance) and does not require electric balancing. The series circuit is safest because if one cap fires, they all fire.

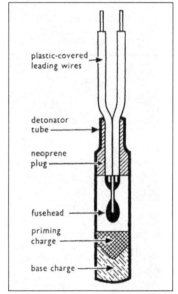

plastic-covered leading wires

detonator tube

neoprene plug

fusehead

priming charge

base charge

Section of an electric detonator

24.5 BLASTING ACCESSORIES

24.5.1 Crimpers
These are used to crimp the open end of non-electric blasting caps to the time fuse. Crimpers are made of a non-sparking material. They are also used as a screwdriver, punch and to make a square cut across time fuse and prima cord. The front notch is used for crimping, the rear notch for cutting. A stop prevents the crimpers from cutting blasting caps.

24.5.2 Blaster's Galvanometer
This is an instrument that enables the blaster to test individual electric caps to determine whether or not a blasting circuit is closed. It can be used to locate faulty connections, grounds, and short circuits, and determine the approximate resistance of a circuit.

A silver chloride battery powers the galvanometer because it supplies a constant, weak current over a long period of time. The available current is less than $\frac{1}{10}^{th}$ of what is required to explode blasting cap. When the silver chloride cell is exhausted, the same type of battery must replace it. Anything else could cause caps to detonate when tested.

24.5.3 Blasting Machines
Blasting machines are small impulse-type generators designed so that no current flows from them until the twist handle or plunger reaches the end of travel. Current is then released to the firing line at peak power.

There are two main types of blasting machines, rated by the number of instantaneous electric blasting caps they will fire in series. The first type is the ten-cap machine, which will fire ten caps in a common series circuit. A parallel series circuit should only be used when the number of caps exceeds the capacity of the machine on hand. The second type is the fifty-cap machine. The detonator requires .6 amps to fire in a parallel or series parallel circuit. It requires 1.5 amps to fire in a series circuit.

24.5.4 Extraneous Electricity in Electric Blasting
Extraneous electricity is any unwanted electrical energy that may be present in an area of electric blasting operations. It is a hazard if it is able to enter an electric blasting circuit. There are four principal types of extraneous electricity: stray current, lightning, static electricity and radio frequency energy.

Stray current is defined as a flow of electricity outside of a conductor that normally carries it. With few exceptions, it is caused by leakage from defective electrical systems. These defects can be either eliminated or controlled with proper installation and an effective preventive maintenance program. Other sources of stray current can include galvanic action, cathodic protection systems, induced current from high voltage lines and other electrical equipment. Tests to detect the presence of stray current should be made by using a voltmeter capable of accurate readings as low as 0.05 volts on both AC and DC scales.

To protect against stray currents, lead wires should be fully insulated and installed well away from pipelines, lighting wire and similar conductors. Safety disconnects should be used on the line.

Lightning can be a hazard to any operation where explosive materials are used. Atmospheric disturbances can initiate electric caps by inducing a current into the blasting circuit. If hazardous atmospheric conditions exist, operations should be stopped and the area cleared until the danger is past.

Static electricity can present a potential hazard. After it is generated, if it is stored or accumulated on some person or object and then discharged into an electric cap or other static electricity-sensitive explosive, it is dangerous. Static electricity generators include moving conveyor belts, dust storms, snowstorms, thunderstorms and clothing. The accumulation of static electricity can be prevented by grounding to earth all persons or objects on which a static charge might accumulate. The electrical resistance of the ground connection should be high enough to prevent the possibility of appreciable stray current flow, but low enough to dissipate the static electricity.

Radio frequency energy from radio transmitters can cause electric cap detonation under some conditions. Blast sites in the vicinity of transmitting facilities should be evaluated by contacting the technical authorities at the installation. Best practice is to ban the use of radio transmitters in the area while blasting.

24.6 EXPLOSIVES UNDERWATER

24.6.1 Characteristics of Underwater Explosions

Underwater explosions create a series of waves that are transmitted through the water as hydraulic shock waves (water hammer) and through the seabed in the form of seismic waves. The hydraulic shock wave consists of an initial high intensity wave that is followed by pressure waves of diminishing strength.

In the photo above, a rock plug is blasted from the end of a tunnel. The charge is 30 cases of 3" Tovex placed between 30 and 50 feet below the surface. Even in this fast-running water, the initial shock wave turned the water white for a long distance, both upstream and downstream.

The intensity of the shock and pressure waves will be directly contingent upon the size and type of charge, bottom condition, charge placement, depth and distance from explosion. Bottom conditions can amplify or dampen the shock or pressure waves. A hard, rocky bottom tends to amplify the effect, while a soft bottom may dampen the waves. The contour of the bottom can also affect the direction of shock and pressure waves, as well as cause secondary reflecting waves. The magnitude of shock and pressure waves generated by charges freely suspended in the water is considerably greater than that of charges placed in drill holes in rock or coral.

The initial wave is the most dangerous. The pressure waves are less severe, but follow very closely to the initial shock wave. Turbulence in the area of the explosion will continue for an extended time after the detonation.

An underwater detonation produces a rapidly expanding bubble of gas, which in effect does the actual work. This gas bubble expands to its maximum diameter, after which the surrounding water will cause the bubble to cool as it collapses. But as it collapses, the increasing pressure causes the temperature to rise, which will, in turn, cause the bubble to expand again until the same processes described above cause another collapse. This oscillation continues until the gas is entirely dissipated through heat loss. This means that the target is subjected to repeated "blows," and causes more work done by one underwater explosion than would be accomplished by a similar explosion on land.

While the shock and pressure waves are tamped by the water at depth, this effect is greatly reduced in shallow water. The first expansion of gas can break the surface and no oscillation process will occur. Smaller charges may need to be considered in shallow water.

24.6.2 Underwater Explosives Operations for Divers

Divers who are not blasters are sometimes trained to perform certain tasks involved in explosive underwater demolitions. These tasks usually involve job site preparation, assisting with drilling, placement of charges and primers, installation of detonator cord and post-detonation inspection of the job.

When drilling holes to hold charges, divers usually will line up the diamond-drill for the blaster. This is known as "collaring the hole." After the hole is drilled, the diver will inspect the hole with a rod, ensuring that the hole is clear and measuring for depth at the same time. If it is clear and the depth is correct, the top will be plugged to keep dirt out until the charges are loaded with "powder."

The diver will also be tasked with loading the holes with explosive (blasters call it powder). There are two ways this may be done: prima-cord (charge lead) taped along the side of sausages (tubes of explosive) or a TNT primer with wire attached lowered into the hole and the sausages dropped in behind. Once the explosive is in the hole, the top few inches is filled with crushed stone (known as stemming the hole). The diver must be very careful not to load powder into relief holes.

Once the holes are loaded, a "trunk line" of prima-cord is run. When using TNT primers, the cords from the primers are attached to the trunk line. When using straight prima-cord, the charge leads are attached to the trunk line. The diver must not allow the prima-cord to become fouled: a cross over, twist or knot will cut off charges and lead to a misfire. Once all of this is completed, divers are removed from the water and the end of the trunk line is attached to a float or buoy. An electric blasting cap is then attached to the prima-cord and affixed to the buoy. The firing wire is then run from the cap to the blasting machine to finish the circuit. The blasting machine is set up at a safe distance (never less than 300 yards) from the blast.

In the following photo series, a diamond drill is seen drilling beside a dock. A diver is seen running the prima-cord trunk line to the charges. Finally, the blast (100 sticks of 3"

Diamond drill rig on barge drilling holes for explosives adjacent to dock.

Tovex) is set off under 45 feet of water. A total of 14 feet of bedrock was removed with no damage done to the dock.

Inserting detonators in explosives is very dangerous and should never be done in underwater blasting. The blasting cap should never be inserted until all diving operations are complete. In underwater blasting today, prima cord is always run between the subsurface charges and the blasting cap which stays on surface.

Placing a shaped charge is a relatively safe job that involves clamping an explosive-filled container at a prescribed spot in a certain way. Such shaped charges are relatively insensitive to any blows or bumps normally encountered in diving. The diver is essentially performing a non-technical task.

Post-blast inspection of underwater work sites has peculiar dangers and should be carefully planned and executed. With modern job-fitted explosives, direct blast effects are confined to a predictable area, but indirect effects are not predictable. Previously safe structures may be rendered unsafe. Divers must enter underwater post-blast areas with extreme caution and a wary eye for objects that may have become dangerous because of blast waves. The post blast inspection must never be performed until the blaster gives the "all clear," which is usually 30 to 60 minutes after the blast has gone off.

Diver running prima cord trunk line from surface to explosives.

24.6.3 Effects of an Underwater Blast on the Human Body

The so-called "safe" distance from a blast is calculated by multiplying the TNT equivalent weight of the explosives, in pounds, by 40. For example, if a charge of 50 pounds of TNT were detonated underwater, the "safe" distance would be 40 × 50 = 2000 feet.

Detonation: 100 tubes of 3 inch Tovex under 45 fsw.

In truth, **there is no "safe" distance from an underwater explosion.** (See Chapter 2: Underwater Physics.) The only safe place for the diver is out of the water. A diver in the water when an underwater blast occurs could be injured or even killed, depending on several factors. These include the size of the blast, its distance, velocity and the character and depth of the bottom. A pressure of 500 psi is sufficient to cause injury. Internal organs that contain air spaces, including the lungs, intestinal tract, stomach and head, are subject to shredding or perforation damage due to blast pressure. Symptoms of injury to these organs are vomiting blood, unconsciousness, shock (a sign of internal bleeding), loss of hearing, and vertigo.

If a diver expects an underwater blast and has time to take action, the diver should get out of the water and out of range of the blast. If the diver cannot get out of the water in time, the diver should get as far away as possible and float on his/her back with his/her head and upper section of the body out of the water.

24.6.4 Responsibility

It is the responsibility of the diving supervisor to ensure no lives are placed at risk. Planning of blasting operations is essential and must include consultation with local authorities. The safety and welfare of the public as well as divers is the prime consideration. If in doubt, underwater blasts should be delayed until all safety measures have been double-checked. In addition to safety, the supervisor is responsible for the protection of marine life. Marine life may be chased from the area using noisemakers, or by surrounding the blast site with an air curtain.

DISCLAIMER

The use of explosives on surface or underwater is inherently dangerous. Only specially trained, licensed, and competent individuals should attempt to use explosives. When using explosives, all local, state, and federal regulations for procurement, transport, safe storage, and use of explosives must be followed. The information contained in the "explosive demolition" portion of this chapter is in no way intended to be a substitute for explosives training.

24.7 UNEXPLODED ORDINANCE (UXO)

Ordinance is the term commonly used for military munitions. This includes mortar rounds, land mines, artillery rounds, airdropped bombs, missiles, torpedoes, anti-ship mines, and naval shells. Unexploded ordinance (UXO) is the term used when these military explosives misfire when used, when they are left in an abandoned ammunition dump or when they are otherwise lost or misplaced without detonating. There are many locations offshore where unused WWI and WWII ordinance was dumped. Some of these dump sites were not even accurately mapped. In WWII, the allied forces dropped on average, 27,700 tons of aerial bombs per day, every day, between 1939 and 1945. That was three freighter loads of bombs every day just in the European Theatre. And that was only the weight of the aerial bombs and did not include artillery or naval ordinance. This should give the reader some idea of the volume of munitions shipped overseas during that period. Virtually all of those munitions were manufactured in the United States and Canada. They were loaded on ships primarily in New York, Boston, Saint John and Halifax. In those days, all cargo was handled with cranes and wooden pallets. A great deal of cargo was lost overboard both during loading and unloading. When working in any harbors where munitions were handled, particularly when excavating or dredging, it is advisable to watch out for UXO. Whenever UXO is encountered, it must not be handled: ordinance becomes very unstable over time and even more unstable when immersed in seawater. Any time that UXO is encountered all diving operations in the surrounding area must be terminated until military Explosive Ordinance Disposal (EOD) personnel have cleared the area. When the commercial diver encounters any type of UXO, he **MUST NOT** disturb the items but call in the military EOD divers.

24.8 EXPLOSIVE DEMOLITION SAFETY

All safety precautions must be followed to the letter when handling explosive material. The lives of divers, other workers and bystanders depend on following these precautions. With explosives, there is no such thing as bad luck. In addition to the manufacturer's recommendations, the following guidelines apply:

ALWAYS:

- Follow the specific guidelines that pertain to each explosive.
- Handle packages of explosives with extreme caution.
- Keep explosives in dry places.
- Use non-steel tools to open cases of explosives.
- Leave cases of explosives in magazines unopened.
- Keep explosives away from open lights, flame or sparks.
- Keep packages of explosives or blasting caps covered.
- Keep high explosives or blasting caps out of direct sunlight.
- Keep blasting caps in a different box from explosives.
- Keep blasting caps or explosives away from wires carrying electricity.
- Use proper tools to crimp blasting cap to fuse.
- Handle fuses carefully in cold weather.
- Use at least six feet of safety fuse in any charge.
- Use wooden sticks with no exposed metal parts for tamping.
- Make certain that no diving operations are being carried out within 2,000 yards of the blast site.
- Make certain all persons are safely under cover before firing a blast.
- Keep non-essential personnel away from the danger area of the blast.
- Remember that the galvanometer is a delicate instrument. Pass it hand-to-hand and don't throw it. Place in a fixing wire box when secured.
- Stack boxes of explosives so that the roll of the ship or boat will not cause them to fall.
- If using safety fuse, test by timing a six-foot section of fuse well away from the charge and by itself to find out time of burning.
- Secure the stationary end of the firing wire loose in the firing wire box to reel clips when cranking so that it will not beat against itself.
- Leave 12 inches of overhang on detonator cord for moisture absorption.
- Perform a "burn test" on time fuse.
- Cut the first 6 inches of time fuse off the end of the roll to be used to account for moisture absorption.
- Ground for a 10-second count prior to picking up a detonator. (Holding a knife blade or crimper in your hand, insert the other end in the ground and count to 10.)
- Wear gloves when handling C-4 or conventional dynamite on the surface. Failure to do so will give you a headache that is second to none!
- Use a non-sparking rod (preferably wood) for tamping holes.

NEVER:

- Store explosives so that cartridges stand on end.
- Smoke while handling explosives.
- Have matches nearby while handling explosives.
- Use frozen high explosives as they become very sensitive.
- Shoot into explosives with any firearms or allow shooting in their vicinity.
- Overcharge or waste explosives.
- Force explosives into a hole or past any obstructions in a hole.
- Use explosives that are obviously deteriorated.
- Leave explosives uncared for.
- Expose any explosive not being used for the charge being prepared.
- Use damaged lead wire or connecting wire in blasting circuits.
- Connect electrical wires during the approach of thunderstorms.
- Try to pull the wires out of an electric blasting cap.
- Store fuses in hot places.
- Cut fuse on a slant.
- Try to light a fuse with burning paper.
- Use safety fuse and non-electrical blasting caps in wet work without having a thoroughly waterproof joint between fuse and cap.
- Cut safety fuse until you are ready to insert it in cap.
- Hold the primed cartridge or block in hand when lighting safety fuse or splicing electric detonator wires.
- Attempt to investigate the contents of blasting caps.
- Carry blasting caps in clothing pockets.
- Half-heartedly spare force or energy in operating blasting machines.
- Install blasting caps on the detonator cord until all diving work is completed.
- Use blasting caps made by more than one manufacturer in the same circuit because resistance in the bridge wires will differ.
- Attempt to reclaim or use blasting caps, fuses, prima cord or any other types of explosive that have been water soaked, even if they are dried out.
- Insert wire nails or any other implements into the open end of a non-electric blasting cap to remove it from a box. Always use the fingers.
- Tamper with or change the circuit of a blasting machine.
- Store any metallic tools or implements in explosive magazine.
- Attempt to investigate a misfire too soon. Follow misfire procedure and wait at least 30 minutes if electrical or at least 60 minutes if cap and fuse.
- Allow VHF, UHF or FM transmitter radios or marine radar to be used within a quarter-mile radius from the time loading begins until after the blast.
- Use empty dynamite boxes for kindling.
- Attempt to fight an explosives fire.

24.9 GLOSSARY OF TERMS

-A-

Air curtain: Hose or pipe with perforations, laid on bottom and pressurized with air to create a wall of air bubbles. This "air curtain" stops or greatly dampens the effect of the blast shock wave.

Ammonium nitrate: The primary ingredient in dynamite and a major ingredient in blasting agents.

ANFO: A blasting agent containing ammonium nitrate fertilizer and diesel fuel.

-B-

Blast log: Record of shots, showing significant details of blasts.

Blasting agent: A non-cap sensitive blasting product containing no high explosive ingredients.

Booster: Generally a "cast primer" that boosts the detonation of a cap or cord to a level that fires blasting agents and is often produced with TNT.

Brisance: The shattering power in the immediate area of an explosion. It is a measure of the kind of work an explosion will do and is dependent on velocity.

-C-

Cast primer: A priming charger consisting of a cylinder of military-type explosive. It's used with a cap or detonating cord to prime ANFO or water-gel slurry main charges.

Charge: This is the explosives load in a hole.

Cratering: Blasting an indentation.

Crimpers: This is a tool used for crimping blasting caps to a safety fuse.

-D-

Deflagration: This is the result of low-order explosive detonation.

Detonator: Caps or detonating cord.

-E-

EOD: Explosive Ordinance Disposal.

Extraneous electricity: Any unwanted electrical energy that may enter blasting circuits from any source.

-F-

Fire: To detonate the charge.

Fumes: Toxic gases (NO_2, CO) produced by all explosives.

-G-

Galvanometer: A device used for checking electrical continuity in a blasting circuit.

Ground: Electrical connection to earth.

-I-

Initiator: An intermediate charge used to initiate the main charge.

Insensitive: An explosive not easily detonated.

-L-

Lead wire: Main blasting line; shooting cable.

-N-

Nitramon: A high explosive.

NG: Nitroglycerin, the highly explosive oil that is a sensitizing and energy ingredient in most dynamites.

-P-

Powder: General term used by blasters for all explosives and blasting agents.

Primer: A cartridge of explosive with a cap or detonating cord in place, usually TNT.

Pulp dopes: Carbonaceous combustibles (wood, meal, rice hulls, nut shells, etc.) in dynamites to provide fuel source and control of density, fumes and other properties.

-R-

Relief holes: Holes drilled at the perimeter of the blast area to stop the rock breakage at that point.

Resistance: The difficulty in causing current to flow in an electrical circuit and is measured in ohms.

R.O.D.: Rate of detonation.

-S-

Sensitive: An explosive very easily detonated.

Silver chloride: A type of battery used in a blaster's galvanometer.

Shoot: To detonate a charge.

Shunt: Shorting device on cap wires. To shunt is to short or connect together the wires from a cap or circuit.

Spit: The flame produced by the safety fuse inside the fuse cap.

Stemming: Material (often crushed stone) used to fill the hole above the explosive charge. The stemming helps to direct the explosive force, and keep it from blowing out of the hole.

Strength: The energy content of an explosive.

-T-

Tovex: water gel ammonium nitrate based high explosive that is the replacement for dynamite.

-U-

UXO: Unexploded Ordinance.

-W-

Water gel: A type of explosive containing no NG.

25.0 DIESEL ENGINES AND COMPRESSORS

25.1 INTRODUCTION

The most important consideration in surface-supplied air diving is to provide the diver with an adequate supply of air suitable for breathing. The diver's air supply may either be an air compressor, a bank of high-pressure air cylinders, or a combination of the two. Regardless of the source, the air must meet certain established standards of purity, be supplied in an adequate volume for breathing, and at a rate of flow which will properly ventilate the helmet or mask. Air supply requirements depend upon specific factors for each dive, such as depth, duration, level of work, number of divers being supported and the type of diving system being used. The formula we use for calculating supply volume of LP compressors is found in both Chapter 2: Underwater Physics and Chapter 6: Surface-Supplied Diving.

To meet air purity standards required for diving, air supplied by a standard compressor is exhausted into a volume tank (receiver), where, as a result of expansion, it is cooled and some of the moisture is eliminated. There is a potential in all oil-lubricated compressors for the compressed air to pick up a quantity of lubricating oil and vapor and to carry them into the diver's air hose. To prevent this condition, the air is passed from the receiver through a highly efficient filtration system where any oil vapors are removed from the air. It is essential that this system be serviced regularly, otherwise, the breathing air will become contaminated with oil vapor and will be noxious to the diver. Air taken from any machinery space or downwind from the exhaust of an engine or boiler must be thought of as contaminated. To avoid such a condition, care must be exercised in the placement and operation of diving air compressors and diesel engines. For more on air purity, see Chapter 6: Surface-Supplied Diving, Section 6.10 Breathing Gas Requirements and Chapter 2: Underwater Physics, Section 2.8.1 Components of Dry Atmospheric Air.

The diesel engine, rather than the gasoline engine, is the common source of power for compressors on most commercial dive sites. Gasoline, because of its high volatility, is not allowed in offshore operations. Diving air compressors can also be powered by electric motors, but a source of electricity must be available. The diesel engine, on the other hand, is self-contained and is, more appropriate for offshore operations. As one of the most vital components of surface-supplied diving equipment, the compressor and the diesel engine that drives it must be maintained in proper operating condition at all times.

25.2 DIESEL ENGINES

Diesel engines differ from other internal combustion engines in several ways. Some of these differences are important to the diver. Diesel engines are the most efficient internal combustion engines. The primary difference in this type of engine is the fuel that diesels burn. It is the characteristics of the fuel that give diesel engines their high efficiency. Fuel in a diesel is not ignited by spark, as in a gasoline engine, but rather by compression. Because diesel engines operate at higher compression than gasoline engines (20:1 as opposed to 8:1), they are more strongly built. That is why diesels are generally larger and heavier than gasoline engines of comparable power. Diesel engines are often noisier than gas engines as well.

The following factors are of significant interest to a diver who must work with diesel engines:

- They are allowed in locations such as oil rigs, barges, wooden pier areas, or other industrial areas where gasoline engines may not be permitted.

- The greater strength and weight of these engines mean heavier rigging and lifting devices are required on mobilization and demobilization day.

- Diesel engines are the engines of choice for providing power to compressors, hot water heaters, water/grit blasting machines, and for virtually all other mechanized power requirements on most commercial diving jobs.

- Diesel engines located near dive operations produce enough noise to be distracting.

A diesel engine is composed of five distinct mechanical systems. These systems all work together to produce rotational motion on a shaft that can be directed to turn parts of another machine, such as an air compressor. The five systems of a diesel engine are the fuel system, lubrication system, cooling system, intake system, and exhaust system. Each system has its role to perform, and each must work in order for the engine to run. This requires attention to each system. Allow one system to fail and the entire diesel engine will fail.

25.2.1 The Fuel System
The fuel system functions to deliver clean air and water-free oil to the engine. Several components make up the fuel system in a diesel engine, starting with the fuel tank.

25.2.1.1 Fuel Tank
Though simple in mechanical terms, the fuel tank is critical to the effective operation of the diesel engine. Fuel must be delivered to the engine unadulterated by contaminants, especially water. Most tanks are fitted with water condensation drains. Before a diesel engine is started, the tank needs to be drained of any accumulated water. Water can leak into the tank and be included with the fuel, but most commonly, water can condense out of the air in the fuel tank during down time. For this reason, the fuel tank should be topped off soon after the engine is shut down in order to fill the tank space with fuel rather than air. Water in the fuel is one of the most common causes of engine malfunction and a situation easier to prevent than to fix.

25.2.1.2 Pump
On larger diesel engines, a low-pressure diaphragm pump is part of the fuel system. Located in line between the tank and the filters, it supplies a steady volume of fuel through the filters to the injector devices.

25.2.1.3 Filters
Filters form another important part of the fuel system and deserve frequent attention. Fuel filters are usually metal canisters with cotton or treated paper forming the core. Their function is to filter water and particulates from the fuel. Fuel filters have vent screws on top or at a high point to bleed air (which cannot be allowed in the fuel system) and should be fitted with sediment drains at a low point for draining off collected water. Care must be taken when draining fuel filters to ensure that air is not allowed into the system. Fuel filters should be changed periodically according to the manufacturer's specifications.

25.2.1.4 Injectors
On the downstream end of the fuel system, fuel is sprayed into superheated air in the cylinders by means of extremely high-pressure pumps and injectors. The injectors are sometimes made a part of the injector pumps or sometimes are separate. Injector pumps will also have vents at high points for bleeding air.

Diesel engines commonly use a fuel injection system called mechanical injection. Because injectors are part of the fuel system, and the fuel system is the most likely cause of malfunctions that the diver must fix, divers must be familiar with mechanical fuel injection systems. Many types of mechanical fuel injection systems have been developed for small diesel engines. Two types are of particular interest to divers. The "common rail" uses a single, low-pressure fuel header that delivers fuel to unit injectors. The unit injector has a high-pressure pump built into it that is operated by a rocker arm from the camshaft. Pump-controlled fuel injection is controlled by high-pressure fuel lines leading to separate injectors. The three different types of pump-controlled systems most commonly encountered by divers are as follows:

- The distributor type has one high-pressure injection pump, with a rotating distributor head and directs fuel to the appropriate injector. The fuel lines to the injectors must be of equal length to ensure proper injection timing.
- The individual pump type uses injection pumps for each cylinder. They are mounted inside the engine and are driven off a lobe on the engine cam. This type of injection pump is controlled by the control rack linkage.
- The multipump type is similar to the individual pump system except that injection pumps are mounted in a separate casing outside the engine block. Pumps operate off a separate camshaft geared into the main engine cam.

25.2.1.5 Fuel System Maintenance

The following maintenance tasks are often the responsibility of the dive crew.

If water or sediment are present in the fuel system and corrective action is not taken, the engine will eventually cease to run or fail to start. This is a high price to pay for failing to keep the fuel clean. The fuel system must be drained of water, filters must be replaced, air must be vented from the system and the system must be primed. These tasks are within the ability of the dive crew to perform and do not require the services of a diesel technician.

Fuel system maintenance begins with draining the fuel tank until clean diesel fuel comes out. (NOTE: fuel oil spilled on steel decks is a significant safety hazard. If a spill occurs, excess oil must be removed with rags. Then degreaser is applied and the deck thoroughly flushed with water. The degreasing should be repeated if necessary.) Next, both fuel lines and filters, starting at the tank, should be drained until clean fuel is coming through the entire system. The engine needs to be turned over to operate the supply pump.

Once all the fuel throughout the system is determined to be clean, the entire system must be purged of air. Any air in the system will block the flow of fuel.

The dive crew can bleed air out of the supply pump by loosening the vent screw or discharge line pipe nut, turning the engine over and watching for clean fuel with no bubbles. The vent screw needs to be retightened. The next tasks are to vent air from the filters and then from the high-pressure injection pump(s).

With multiple injection pumps, the pumps should be vented in sequence, moving downstream from the filter. On engines with a unit injector, it is necessary to bleed the fuel line to the supply header. It is critical to retighten all vent screws and fuel connections. Where necessary, two wrenches should be used, being careful not to stress the fuel lines. Finally, connections should be wiped dry, the engine turned over and everything checked for leaks. The engine should now start in the usual manner.

25.2.2 The Lubrication System

The lubricating system of a diesel engine is relatively simple. Oil is supplied under pressure from a rotary gear pump to all crankshaft bearings, the camshaft locating brush, the gear train and valve rocker gear. The oil is drawn through a strainer to the suction side of the pump and discharged through an oil gallery to the relief valve and to the main bearings. The crankshaft is drilled to supply oil to the bearings.

Reduction of engine wear is the goal of the lubrication system. The primary purposes of the lubrication system in an engine are to reduce friction and to carry contaminants away from moving parts. Because friction is reduced and heat is reduced. Lubricating oil must be kept clean, must be of the type of oil specified by the manufacturer and must be changed when change is due. The dive crew should smell lubricating oil when checking it and if it smells like fuel oil it's contaminated and service is needed.

Some common terms used when referring to lubricating oil:

- SAE: Society of Automobile Engineers. SAE sets the viscosity grades of motor oil.
- API: American Petroleum Institute. API sets the code for oil's work capacity. "C" is commercial grade, "CC" or "CD" are for all climate conditions in diving-use diesels.
- "Series" refers to the number of additives. "1" is non-detergent, "2" is for passenger cars and "3" is for industrial use.

25.2.2.1 Choosing the Right Oil

Straight mineral oils are not suitable to lubricate diesel engines and neither are oils of less detergency than specified. Multigrade oils must be SAE 10/30 and must have a degree of detergency equivalent to MIL-L-2104B or Type B. Multigrade oils must not be used in heavy-duty applications.

Starting temperatures should determine lubricant viscosity, as follows:

- Up to 32°F (0 C)   SAE 10 W
- Between 32° F and 85°F (0 C and 30 C)   SAE 20/20 W
- Above 85°F (30 C)   SAE 30

25.2.2.2 Lubrication System Maintenance

The lube oil and filter should be changed every 250 hours or more frequently if warranted by dusty conditions or an internal fuel oil leak or any contaminating condition. Series 3 oils must be used when oil changes are made at periods longer than 25 hours.

25.2.3 The Cooling System

The cooling system on diesel engines used on dive locations is normally an air-cooled type, which requires little attention. Fins or ribs built into the casings of various parts of the engine should be kept clean and free of obstructions and the engines must be placed so there is clearance for circulation of air.

Water-cooled diesel engines are less common in diving applications. If one is used, it is necessary to ensure water levels are kept adequate, radiators are kept clean, and fans are working properly.

25.2.3.1 Overheating

Overheating in a diesel engine, especially in an air-cooled engine, may indicate problems with the lubrication system, which also functions to keep temperatures down. If overheating occurs, shut down the engine immediately and begin investigating the oil lubrication system. Clean the engine block off as well.

25.2.4 The Intake System

The intake system consists of the filters and piping through which air is drawn into the engine. Because of the nature of diesel compression combustion air is drawn directly into the cylinder and the quality of that air is important. The valves which allow air into the cylinders, the cylinder walls and the piston heads all suffer if dirty air is permitted into the engine.

Diesels use standard type air filters, either dry filter or oil bath type. Dry filters will filter out only about 60–70% of air contaminants and oil bath filters will catch up to about 85% of contaminants.

25.2.4.1 Intake System Maintenance

Diesel engines use great quantities of air, so care must be taken to place them where both quantity and quality of fresh air is adequate. Filters on the intake side should be checked frequently and every day in dusty or dirty conditions.

25.2.5 The Exhaust System

The exhaust system of a diesel engine is of special concern to divers because the byproducts of internal combustion include carbon monoxide, which is fatal to divers. **Care must be exercised at all times to ensure that engine exhaust systems are placed in such a position that compressors will not intake the engine's exhaust fumes.**

In the event exhaust is being directed by placement, ship's motion or wind into compressor intakes, **immediate corrective action is mandatory**, including switching air sources without delay. This is a common event in diving locations and immediate action must **always** be taken. Do not allow rain to get into exhaust ports.

25.3 DIESEL FUEL

Diesel engines require clean, water-free fuel oil in order to perform reliably. Diesel fuel is high-energy fuel and the diesel system of combustion is highly efficient. Nevertheless, it requires about 35% of the fuel consumed to keep the engine in motion, leaving 65% of the fuel's energy to be used for doing the work that is required. There are four kinds of diesel fuel:

- No.1 diesel is clear to yellow in color, has a flash point (lowest ignition temperature) of about 100°F (gasoline flashes at about 40°F) and is used in variable speed, high-rpm engines.

- No.2 diesel is light amber to dark brown in color, has a flash point of 125°F and is used in uniform speed, high load applications. This kind of diesel fuel is used in diving operations.

- No.3 diesel is obsolete and no longer produced.

- No.4 diesel is dark brown to black in color, has a flash point of about 130°F and is used for slow, constant speed engines (e.g. ocean-going ship's main engines).

25.4 POWER TAKE-OFFS AND CLUTCHES

Starting a diesel engine requires a great deal of energy. If a diesel engine were permanently connected to a load, such as a compressor, it would be virtually impossible to start. In fact, it is necessary, for many reasons, to be able to separate the running engine from its load. This is accomplished with power take-offs or clutches.

25.4.1 Power Take-offs

There are many different kinds of power take-offs. Some are designed and manufactured on site to fit special applications while others are built into the engine system or added on as a manufacturer's option. Power take-offs usually involve some kind of lever and wheel-and-belt arrangement allowing a belt to be tightened or loosened at will whether or not the engine is running.

Power take-off maintenance is simply a matter of keeping wheel bearings greased and belts in good shape. Slack in a belt should be between ⅞ inch and 1 inch while 1½ inch is too much. To adjust the tightness of a belt in a power take-off, either move the engine or the machine it is driving, depending on which is easier. Alignment needs to be within ⅛-inch or excessive belt and bearing wear will occur.

25.4.2 Clutches

Clutches generally work by friction between two plates: one spins at the engine speed and the other is mounted on the shaft of the machine being driven. Levered springs keep the driven plate in the engaged or disengaged position. When the lever is manipulated in one direction, the driven plate is pushed up against the spinning plate, gradually but quickly gaining speed and momentum through friction alone. If the lever is moved in the opposite direction, the clutch disengages. This separates the engine from the driven unit. Clutches require greasing through several grease fittings. It is critical not to over-grease. Oil or grease on a clutch plate itself will reduce friction and cause a loss of power to the driven unit.

25.5 STARTING AND STOPPING DIESEL ENGINES

To start a hand-cranked diesel engine, the operator should do the following:

- Visually inspect the unit for loose fittings and other inconsistencies then check the fuel and lubricating oil levels.

- Fill the oil container with engine oil to the level marked on the air cleaner if an oil bath air cleaner is fitted.

- Ensure fuel and lubricating oil systems are primed.

- Prime fuel filter by using the priming lever on the lift pump if the engine is fitted with a fuel lift pump.

- Move decompressor levers away from the flywheel.

- In cold weather, lift overload trip knob on "H" series Lister engines. Turn engine control lever counter-clockwise on "S" series Listers to the vertical position (excess fuel position). Return the lever on the "S" series to the horizontal (run) position.

- Check the crank handle to ensure the ratchet tooth is free, Failure to do this may cause injury.

- Lightly oil the end of the crankshaft extension and fit the starting handle.

- Ensure that the engine is not starting against a load. Do not stop engine against a load.

- Crank the Lister "H" series clockwise, the "S" series counterclockwise. Turn the engine slowly from three to ten turns, depending on the ambient temperature and the length of time the engine has stood unused.

- Crank the handle vigorously. Release the decompression levers to start the engine.

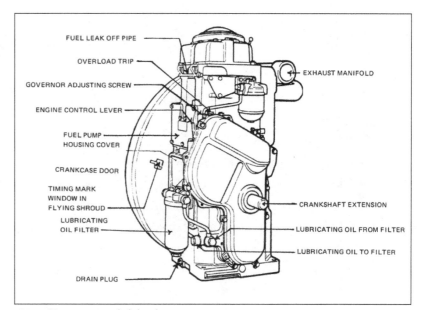

Lister H series air cooled diesel engine

- Decompression levers are not required for electric or pneumatic starting.

- Variable speed control can be fitted on all engines and has a range of 650 rpm to maximum.

NOTE: On engines fitted with speed control, the control lever should be set to half speed. When the engine starts, speed may be reduced as required. Small speed adjustments may be made on engines without speed control by loosening the locknuts on the governor spring adjusting screw and turning the screw in to reduce speed and out to increase speed. After adjusting, tighten the locknuts. Do not increase speed above 2½%.

To stop a hand-cranked diesel engine, the operator should do the following:

- Turn the engine control lever clockwise and hold until engine stops on "S" series engines. On an "H" series, it is necessary to pull the engine control lever toward the flywheel and hold until the engine stops. Decompression levers are never used for stopping.

- Remote stopping control is available if required. It consists of a hand lever and Bowden cable.

25.6 MAINTENANCE OF DIESEL ENGINES

Diesel engines are generally rugged machines engineered and constructed for use in industrial situations, but they still require regular maintenance. This is important to divers because most often it is the divers themselves who perform most of the maintenance on the diesel engines that serve their dive location. Divers are not required to be diesel mechanics, although this is a good combination of skills, but every diver must be able to conduct preventive maintenance, do pre- and post-use checks and troubleshoot. Fortunately, diesels are reliable engines and maintenance is straight forward. The first rule of diesel engine maintenance is: "If it isn't broke, don't fix it." The second rule of maintenance is, "Prevent breakdowns by proper preventive maintenance." The third rule is, "If it doesn't work, look for dirty or watery fuel."

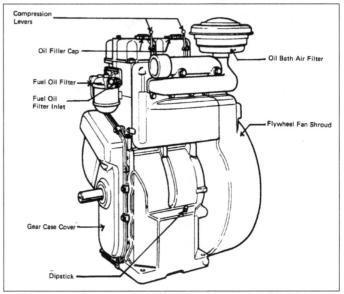

Lister H series diesel engine, end view

25.6.1 Scheduled Maintenance Items

Daily Maintenance

- Check the supply of fuel oil.
- Check the level and condition of lubricating oil.
- Clean the air cleaner in very dusty conditions.
- Drain the moisture trap in exhaust pipe if fitted.
- Clean the rotary cooling air fan screen if fitted.
- Check the tightness of all fastenings and the sealing of joints in the air cleaner system.

100-Hour Maintenance

- Clean the air cleaner under moderately dusty conditions.
- Check for fuel and lubrication oil leaks and tighten nuts and fittings as necessary.
- Wipe the engine and base plate clean.
- Clean the cylinder and cylinder head cooling fins under very dusty conditions.
- Check the level of electrolyte in the battery if electric starting is used.

250-Hour Maintenance

- Drain the lubricating oil and refill with the correct grade and type. Also renew the lubricating filter element.
- Clean the fuel injector nozzles if the exhaust is dirty.

500-Hour Maintenance

- De-carbonize if the engine shows loss of compression or blow-by past the piston but otherwise do not disturb*.
- Adjust the valve tappet clearance.
- Clean the cooling fins if necessary.
- Wash the engine down with paraffin or fuel oil.
- Clean the cylinder and cylinder head cooling fins under dusty conditions.

1500-Hour Maintenance:

- De-carbonize* the engine.
- Clean the inlet manifold and exhaust system*.
- Clean the fins on the cylinder head and cylinder.
- Examine and clean the fan blades.
- Check the free working of the governor linkage.
- Drain and clean the fuel tank.
- Renew the fuel filter element.
- Clean the fuel injector nozzle and adjust the pressure settings*.
- Adjust the injector pressure setting*.
- Check the fuel pump timing and balancing*.

6000 Hour Maintenance:

- Check the big end and main bearings*.
- Inspect the camshaft bearings and tappets*.
- Renew the valve springs*.

*Denotes job items to be handled by a trained shop mechanic.

25.7 TROUBLESHOOTING THE DIESEL ENGINE

Any time you are "troubleshooting" a machine, it means identifying the cause of malfunctions so that proper repairs can be made. Troubleshooting a diesel engine requires knowledge of the construction of the unit and the principles of its operation. With such understanding any diver can start at the beginning and follow through all steps in the functioning of each part until the cause of the trouble is found.

25.7.1 Steps in Trouble Shooting

Think before taking action. Study the problem thoroughly. Ask these questions:

- Were there warning signs preceding the trouble and what were they?
- What previous repair and maintenance work has been done?
- Has similar trouble occurred before?
- If the unit still operates, is it safe to continue to run it while making further checks?

Always check the simplest and most obvious things first to save time and trouble. Typical problems that are easily remedied include: lower power caused by loose throttle linkage or dirty fuel filter and excessive lube oil consumption caused by leaking gaskets or connections.

25.7.1.1 Difficulty in Starting the Engine

- No fuel in the tank: Fill the tank then prime or bleed the fuel system.
- Clogged fuel filter: Replace or clean the filter and prime the fuel system.
- Air blockage in the lines: Bleed and prime the system.
- Bad injector: Replace the injector and prime the system.
- Sticking fuel pump rack: Check the rack for binding and replace or align bent control rods.
- Fuel lift pump fails to pump fuel to the injection pump: Replace or repair the fuel lift pump.

25.7.1.2 Problems with the Engine Stopping or Dying

- No fuel in the tank: Fill the fuel tank and prime/bleed the system as required.
- Dirt or water in the fuel tank or fuel lines: Drain the fuel filter and prime the system.
- Clogged fuel filter or fuel line: Replace or clean the filter then flush and clean the fuel line.
- Overloading engine:.Reduce the load on the engine; and turn the engine over to ensure freedom of movement and allow the engine to cool down.

25.8 AIR COMPRESSORS

There is no item of equipment on a dive site more important than the compressor that provides divers with their breathing air. Compressors are so necessary to the daily work that every diver must be familiar with basic functioning and operation of compressors.

The quality of compressed air made available to divers is determined in large part by the quality of the air going into the compressor. Aside from assuring that compressors are properly maintained and oiled, placement of the compressor in a location where there is ample amounts of fresh, clean air is most important. If contaminated air reaches the intake, contaminated air in the storage tanks will result.

There are the acceptable parameters for compressed breathing air, as found in both the OSHA and CSA standards. The same purity standards are used by regulatory agencies world-wide and are as follows:

- Oxygen level: 20 – 22% by volume
- Nitrogen and Rare Gases levels: 78 – 80% by volume
- Carbon monoxide level: not more than 5 ppm
- Carbon dioxide level: not more than 500 ppm
- Methane level: not more than 10 ppm
- Volatile non-methane hydrocarbons levels: not more than 5 ppm (as methane equivalent)
- Volatile halogenated hydrocarbons levels: not more than 5 ppm
- Oil, particulates and condensates: not more than 1 mg/m³
- Pressure < 15.3 MPa: at a dew point 5°C under the lowest temperature its exposed to during the year
- Pressure > 15.3 MPa: at a dew point not more than –53°C or water vapour level not more than 27 ppm (by volume)
- Odour: any noticeable odour must be analyzed

25.8.1 Types of Compressors

There are two types of compressors used in diving. They are designated by the amount of compression they attain: low pressure (LP) and high pressure (HP). Low pressure compressors (below 500 psi) supply breathing air directly to the volume tanks that supply the divers with air. High pressure compressors fill the storage bottles that store large quantities of air as backup (HP quads) and fill the tanks in which divers carry their emergency air supply (bailout bottles). HP and LP Compressors are not interchangeable as to function.

25.8.2 Compressors Used in Diving

An air compression system for a diving operation should ideally consist of a main LP compressor, backup LP compressor, an HP compressor and a backup HP compressor. It should also include sufficient stored HP air to supply air for a rescue operation and conduct all required decompressions in the water or in chamber plus enough to blow the chamber down to 165fsw and ventilate as required.

If the main compressor should stop running during dive operations (that is a diver is breathing on it), the stored LP air in the volume tank will provide a few minutes breathing time, enough for one of the dive team members to start the backup LP compressor. The dive supervisor has the responsibility to watch the gauges and has the option to switch to HP air if the standby LP compressor fails to function as it should. Once the immediate situation is resolved, the main compressor should be checked out.

Compressors need to be placed where the noise they produce will not interfere with the diving operation (diver and deck communications). Weld the frame to the deck or otherwise secure compressors so they do not move in heavy weather. Make sure there are adequate whips to carry the air to where it is needed. Place HP compressors close to the location of HP storage bottles so HP whips can be kept short. All HP whips must be secured with whip checks and clamps. Ensure all the fittings needed to make connections between compressors and bottles, quads, rack boxes or other end uses are readily available.

25.9 TERMS RELATED TO COMPRESSORS

Aftercooler: A device for lowering the temperature of compressed air after the final stage of compression.

CFM: This stands for cubic feet / minute (the total volume of air drawn into a cylinder in one minute, before compression).

Compression stage: The actual pressurizing of air in one or more steps.

Cushion chamber: A small tank between the compressor and volume tank that dampens pressure oscillation

Differential pressure: The pressure range between compressor loading and unloading.

Free air: CFM of air discharged from the compressor at 1.0 ATM of back pressure.

Intercooler: A device for lowering the temperature of compressed air between compression stages.

Loaded: The state in which the cylinder contains pressurized air when the compressor is at rest.

Receiver tank: A volume tank mounted on the compressor unit.

SCFM: Standard cubic feet per minute at rated working pressure.

Unloaded: The condition of a compressor when it pumps air back out the suction side with no compression taking place (the cylinder contains no pressurized air when the compressor is a rest).

25.10 LOW-PRESSURE (LP) COMPRESSORS

LP compressors are found on virtually every commercial surface-supplied job. In diving applications, they are either diesel driven with the engine and compressor connected by a belt or electrically driven. Diesel driven compressors are probably more prevalent because they are self-contained units requiring only diesel fuel. Electric driven compressors are quieter to operate and produce no exhaust, but they do require wiring up at either 220 or 440v. In both cases, the power supply and the compressor itself can be mounted in a steel "skid" that protects the machinery and provides lift points for mobilization and demobilization.

LP compressors used in commercial diving are total displacement piston type compressors. Reciprocating pistons move back and forth during opening and closing cycles of various valves and air is compressed and pushed out of the cylinders on the compression stroke of the pistons. Springs and ambient air pressure interrelate at the appropriate moment in the piston's travel to open and shut the inlet/exhaust valves.

A Lister diesel powered Quincy 350

A pair of 5120 Quincy compressors

LP compressors can be single stage or multiple stages. In commercial diving operations, multiple stage compressors are the norm. The first stage of compression exhausts its compressed air into the inlet of the second compression stage, where it is further compressed then passed on to the volume tank. Multiple stage compressors are more efficient than single stage and. by slight cooling of the air between stages, allow for lower temperatures. Lower temperatures mean less wear and less maintenance.

An LP compressor quickly compresses large volumes of air to a relatively low pressure. A compressor must deliver air to the diver at a sufficient pressure to overcome the ambient water pressure, with sufficient additional pressure to overcome friction in the umbilical. There must be sufficient "over-bottom" pressure to make the regulator on demand helmets work and to provide vigorous free-flow capability as well. The diving helmet manufacturers specify the required over-bottom pressure required at various depths. See Section 6.10.3 of Chapter 6: Surface-Supplied Diving for the over-bottom pressures required.

In addition to sufficient air pressure, the diver has to be delivered sufficient volume of air as well. As a rule of

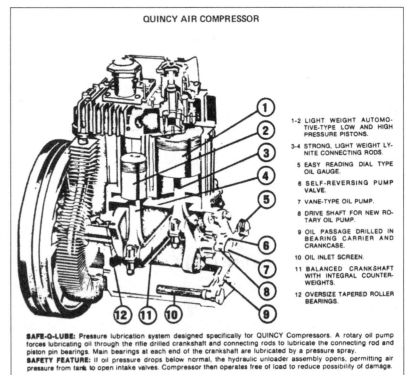

456

thumb, a demand type mask or hat requires about 1.5 cubic feet of air per minute (cfm) on the surface. A free-flow type of hat requires three times as much or about 4.5cfm on the surface. Because the diver will be working at depth, the effect of the pressure at that depth must be considered. The formula for calculating volume requirements is found in the Chapter 6: Surface-Supplied Diving.

25.10.1 VD Pilot Valve

In order to permit the compressor to rest, and to provide a quantity of stored air in case of compressor malfunction, compressed LP air is stored in volume tanks. A dive spread can have numerous volume tanks and compressors all joined together with whips and valves to provide alternatives and backups. The compressor has a device that senses the stored air pressure and causes the compressor to load or unload as necessary. This sensing device, called a variable differential un-loader or VD pilot valve, is pneumatically and spring operated and is adjustable. By an adjustment to the VD pilot valve, the compressor can be set to begin compressing air (loading) when the pressure in the volume tank reaches a low of, for example, 120 psi. The VD pilot assembly can be set to unload the compressor at, for example, 150 psi. Although the diesel engine and compressor are both turning over, the compressor is only working to keep the pressure between 120 and 150 psi. With this arrangement, the diver has a continuous supply of air from the volume tanks, which the compressor automatically refills as pressure reaches a preset level.

"Short cycling" is the condition where a compressor loads and unloads quickly, within two or three minutes per cycle. Short cycling is hard on the compressor and indicates the need for an adjustment of some sort. Short cycling might be caused by a number of conditions. If a compressor is short cycling, it needs attention (See Section 25.14: Troubleshooting Compressors in this chapter.)

LP compressors can and will suffer significant damage if they are operated without sufficient lubricating oil pressure. To prevent damage in the event of a loss of oil pressure, compressors are fitted with a system called the hydraulic un-loader. A compressor should never be operated if the hydraulic un-loader or any other component is malfunctioning.

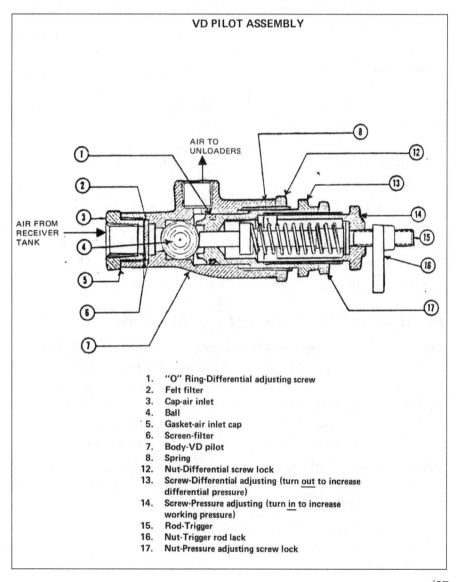

VD PILOT ASSEMBLY

1. "O" Ring-Differential adjusting screw
2. Felt filter
3. Cap-air inlet
4. Ball
5. Gasket-air inlet cap
6. Screen-filter
7. Body-VD pilot
8. Spring
12. Nut-Differential screw lock
13. Screw-Differential adjusting (turn out to increase differential pressure)
14. Screw-Pressure adjusting (turn in to increase working pressure)
15. Rod-Trigger
16. Nut-Trigger rod lack
17. Nut-Pressure adjusting screw lock

25.10.2 Filtration

Air used by divers must be safe to breathe and following compression it must be filtered before being sent to the diver. Various types of filters are commercially available. Filters should be placed between the compressor outlet and the volume tank so only filtered air gets into the storage system.

A Deltech filter is commonly found in diving operations. It is a clear-walled cylinder containing a mesh of chemical materials that filter out oil, oil mist, water and dirt. As the absorption and filtering qualities of the filter are expended, the filter gradually turns red from the bottom up. The filter interior is replaced when it is solid red. The filter has a drain cock on the bottom for draining off accumulated water. It should be drained often enough to prevent the visible collection of water in the bottom of the filter.

CAUTION: If it is necessary to replace a filter unit, it should not be re-pressurized suddenly by popping open an upstream valve. The sudden impact of air will crush the fine structure of the filter and destroy its usefulness. Air pressure should be added to a new filter slowly. The use of multiple filters is prudent: several filters should be put in line.

Compressed air is vapor laden. As it sits in storage tanks and cools, the water condenses and collects at the bottom of the volume tank. Volume tanks all have moisture drains, and they should be opened about every half hour during diving operations. Moist air is bad for both the diver's lungs and for diving equipment.

25.10.3 Compressor Lubricating Oil

Lubricating oil for compressors must be of special type. Any oil in a diver's lungs is too much oil, but some oils are worse than others. Oil for breathing-air compressors should be high flash (400°F) and it must be what is considered "food safe" oil. If synthetic oil is used, it should be non-detergent and oxidation inhibiting. Heavy-duty mineral oil can be used but it does not have the qualities of the specially formulated synthetics such as Monolec and will lose its lubricating qualities very quickly. Do not use unapproved oil in breathing air compressors. Oil should be changed in a diving compressor every 200 hours.

The use of filters, frequent draining of water traps and proper compressor operation and maintenance should all add up to pure air for the diver. To ensure the purity of the air, quality checks must be run periodically. Law requires independent 3rd party air quality tests every six months or whenever there is an indication that the air might be polluted. Air test kits are sent out by the 3rd party laboratories that perform the testing. Interim air tests may be performed using Dräger test equipment.

25.11 HIGH PRESSURE (HP) COMPRESSORS

Commercial diving operations have considerable need for high pressure air: bailout bottles must be kept full and reserve banks of HP air must be kept topped up for use when LP air delivery to divers or chambers is stopped for any reason. High pressure compressors trade volume and time for pressure. HP compressors are slow and they compress small amounts of air at a time. Whereas a standard size LP compressor could be expected to compress 93 cubic feet per minute, an HP compressor as found on a commercial diving site will function more in the range of 5 - 8 cubic feet per minute.

HP compressors require the same type of care as LPs. They must be lubricated with approved oils and typically it is different from the oil used for LP compressors. HP compressors are subjected to greater heat so care must be taken to keep them clean so cooling surfaces can function.

HP compressors use high pressure fittings and whips, which must be checked during operation for leaks. A leak in an HP system is always a serious condition requiring attention, because the high pressures involved can easily act to change a small leak into a burst fitting. Check for leaks with a soap and water mixture ("snoop"). If a leak is found, the system must be depressurized and the problem fixed. Then it is necessary to re-pressurize and snoop again. **Never attempt to tighten any fitting while it is under pressure**.

As with any breathing air compressor, the air going into an HP compressor must be pure and free of contaminants. Intakes must be in a position to be supplied with fresh air, unadulterated by engine exhaust, smoke or dust. Filters need to be inspected, replaced as necessary and drained frequently.

25.12 STARTING AND STOPPING COMPRESSORS

Most HP compressor manufacturers recommend starting the unit without a load on it (all drains wide open) and running it that way for a minute to circulate the lube oil before putting a load on (closing drains). They recommend doing the same for one minute prior to stopping. Read the starting and stopping instructions in the owner's manual of the machine you are using. They built it: they ought to know it. Prior to starting a compressor unit, perform checks to ensure conditions are correct. Failure to do so may harm the machinery. The following represent the minimum checks that should be performed:

25.12.1 Checks Done Prior to Starting

- Check the lubrication oil in both the engine and the compressor. Add oil as necessary. Remember that the compressor takes food-safe oil. Do not use the same oil for both. Do not overfill.
- Check the fuel level if using a diesel-driven unit. Always top it off if necessary before and after operations to prevent air spaces in the fuel tank where condensation can form. Drain any water from the bottom of the fuel tank.
- Check the liquid coolant level.
- Drain all water traps and filters.
- Visually inspect the unit for any obvious malfunctions.
- If the power unit is diesel, disengage the clutch between the drive unit and compressor.

25.12.2 Starting the Compressor

- If the power unit is electric, ensure the "manual-off-auto" switch is in the "off" position. Then turn on the main power and push "auto" or "manual" to start the unit.
- If the power source is diesel, and there is an "air start," which uses compressed air from the receiver to turn over the engine, open the air start valve and start the engine. Close the air start valve when the engine fires.
- Start a diesel engine by hand if there is no air start or if the receiver contains insufficient air to start the engine. Move the decompression levers on top of the engine to the position that allows the engine to crank over slowly. The right position will be obvious because the engine will not crank over at all if the levers are in the wrong position. (Move them away from the flywheel to start.) Also ensure that the "engine stop" device is not in the "stop" position.
- Set the throttle about ⅓ of the way up.
- Crank over the engine with the hand crank until maximum speed has built up and, while continuing to crank, throw the decompression levers to their other position, one by one.
- Once the diesel has started, adjust to about ½ throttle as necessary to give it a good, even warm-up. Once it has had an opportunity to warm up at about ½ throttle, engage the clutch and throttle up to operating speed.
- Stopping an electric compressor is easy. Push the "stop" button.

- Stop a diesel-driven compressor by throttling the unit down to ⅓, disengaging the clutch and then pushing the engine stop device.
- Top off with diesel fuel and do a general visual inspection to make sure the compressor is ready for the next day's operations.

25.13 COMPRESSOR MAINTENANCE AND CARE

Breathing air compressors are critical for the diving operation. These units operate continuously and they require proper maintenance to continue operating.

CRITICAL SAFETY NOTE:

BEFORE MAINTAINING OR REPAIRING ANY COMPRESSOR, MAKE ABSOLUTELY SURE THAT THE UNIT CANNOT AUTOMATICALLY START OR BE STARTED REMOTELY.

All breathing air compressors must be kept clean. If greasy particulate matter is allowed to accumulate, cooling fins will be less effective, leading to overheating and eventually some of that dirt may find its way into the air system. These units should be wiped down daily, with a thorough cleaning being regularly scheduled. The following schedule outlines maintenance tasks common to all compressors. Individual compressors may have additional maintenance tasks outlined in the operating manual:

25.13.1 Daily Maintenance
- Check oil pressure and maintain it at approximately 15 lbs.
- Check the level and condition of lubricating oil.
- Drain the drop legs and traps in the air distribution system.
- Give the compressor an overall visual check.
- Drain the moisture accumulations from the air receiver.

25.13.2 Weekly
- Check the air distribution system for air leaks.
- Clean the cooling surfaces of the compressor intercooler and aftercooler.
- Operate the safety valves.

25.13.3 Monthly
- Replace or clean the intake filter element: more often in dirty working conditions.
- Inspect the oil for contamination and change if necessary.
- Check the belts for correct tension.
- Check the pulley clamp bolts and set screws for tightness.
- Inspect the filter felts on the VD pilot.
- Inspect the filter felts on the hydraulic un-loader, 3-way valve or VD pilot, whichever is applicable.

25.13.4 Semi-annually
- Inspect the valve assemblies.

25.13.5 Annually
- Inspect the cushion chamber and discharge line for excessive carbon accumulations.
- Inspect the pressure switch diaphragm and contact points.
- Inspect the contact points in the motor starter.
- Lubricate the electric motor or engine in accordance with the manufacturer's recommendations.

NOTE: Always rotate the compressor by hand after long periods of storage.

25.14 TROUBLESHOOTING COMPRESSORS

When a compressor fails to function properly, a diver or tender is usually sent to determine the nature of the problem and to make a quick decision about whether the problem can be easily and immediately fixed, or whether the problem will require more extensive diagnosis and repair. The essence of troubleshooting is to look for any simple and obvious causes of the trouble first and eliminate them. Eventually, each diver will reach his maximum level of expertise. At that point, if the troubleshooting has been done correctly and it has been determined that a quick, easy solution is not to be found, the unit needs more extensive diagnosis and repair by a more qualified mechanic. Following are the most common causes of compressor malfunction:

25.14.1 Low discharge pressure

- Air leaks: Listen for escaping air, and "snoop" for leaks. After bleeding off pressure, tighten or replace as necessary.
- Restricted air intake: (Clean the air filter in a non-flammable, non-toxic solvent or detergent. Check for obstructions to smooth air intake.
- Slipping belts: Tighten the belts.
- Various internal mechanical malfunctions will require the attention of a qualified mechanic. These include leaking head valves, malfunctioning hydraulic un-loader, blown gaskets, worn connecting rod inserts, worn piston pin bushings, loose valve assemblies or pistons and pistons hitting the head.

25.14.2 Knocking

- Loose motor or compressor pulley: Tighten the pulley clamp bolts and set screws.
- Lack of oil in the crankcase: Check for proper oil level. If low, suspect possible damage to bearings.
- Malfunctioning oil pump: Check the oil pump and pressure gauge by unscrewing the pressure gauge until oil seeps around the threads while the compressor is running. If oil leaks out at the threads, do not unscrew the gauge all the way.as the oil pressure is reaching the gauge. If no oil seeps at the loosened threads, the oil pump may be malfunctioning. If oil is seeping but the gauge does not register pressure, the gauge may be faulty.
- Various other internal malfunctions, specifically worn connecting rod inserts, worn piston pin bushings, loose valve assemblies or pistons or pistons hitting the head, require the attention of a qualified mechanic.

25.14.3 Overheating

- Poor ventilation: Relocate the compressor to an area where an ample supply of cool fresh air is available.
- Dirty cooling surfaces: Clean the cooling surfaces.
- Incorrect pulley location: Check the arrow on the pulley for the correct direction. The motor may need to be reversed.

25.14.4 Stalling

- If the power is diesel, check the throttle setting and linkages.
- If the power is electric, have a competent electrician check the motor and wiring.

25.14.5 Excessive belt wear

- Pulley out of alignment: Realign.
- Belt too loose or too tight: Adjust.

- Slipping belt: Adjust tension.
- Pulley-wobble: Check for worn crankshaft, keyway or pulley bore. Check for bent pulleys or crankshaft.

25.14.6 Oil in the discharge air
- Wrong oil viscosity: Change to correct viscosity using compressor specification documents.
- Restricted air intake: Check for restriction.
- Oil in the air intake filter system: Remove, clean and replace.
- Restricted breather valve: Check for free operation.
- Excessive oil in compressor: Check and drain if necessary.
- Worn piston rings, misaligned connecting rods or other internal malfunctions require the attention of a mechanic.

25.14.7 The compressor stops
- If the diesel power supply stops, troubleshoot it.
- If electric and the motor stops, check appropriate breaker or fuse boxes.

25.15 SAFETY GUIDELINES

Diesel engines and compressors, like most machines, are completely safe to work near or work on provided that personnel follow the proper safety precautions. The following guidelines should be observed:

- Never run diesel engines or compressors without the proper belt guards.
- Always wear ear protection when working near compressors to avoid long-term injury.
- Never work on any machinery unless it has been locked out and cannot start.
- Never work on automatic start machinery unless the unit is on "manual start" and locked out.
- Many fuel injectors operate on high pressure. Wear leather gloves and eye protection when working near or on running diesel engines. A leak in an injector line can spray a jet-like stream.
- Air lines between stages on the HP compressor are under high pressure. Wear leather gloves and eye protection whenever working near or on running compressors.
- Never attempt to tighten any fitting (liquid or gas) that is under pressure.

APPENDIX I

U.S. NAVY DECOMPRESSION TABLES
FOR AIR-DIVING OPERATIONS

U.S. Navy Diving Manual Revision 6

Table 9-7. *No-Decompression Limits and Repetitive Group Designators for No-Decompression Air Dives.*

Depth (fsw)	No-Stop Limit	Repetitive Group Designation															
		A	B	C	D	E	F	G	H	I	J	K	L	M	N	O	Z
10	Unlimited	57	101	158	245	426	*										
15	Unlimited	36	60	88	121	163	217	297	449	*							
20	Unlimited	26	43	61	82	106	133	165	205	256	330	461	*				
25	595	20	33	47	62	78	97	117	140	166	198	236	285	354	469	595	
30	371	17	27	38	50	62	76	91	107	125	145	167	193	223	260	307	371
35	232	14	23	32	42	52	63	74	87	100	115	131	148	168	190	215	232
40	163	12	20	27	36	44	53	63	73	84	95	108	121	135	151	163	
45	125	11	17	24	31	39	46	55	63	72	82	92	102	114	125		
50	92	9	15	21	28	34	41	48	56	63	71	80	89	92			
55	74	8	14	19	25	31	37	43	50	56	63	71	74				
60	60	7	12	17	22	28	33	39	45	51	57	60					
70	48	6	10	14	19	23	28	32	37	42	47	48					
80	39	5	9	12	16	20	24	28	32	36	39						
90	30	4	7	11	14	17	21	24	28	30							
100	25	4	6	9	12	15	18	21	25								
110	20	3	6	8	11	14	16	19	20								
120	15	3	5	7	10	12	15										
130	10	2	4	6	9	10											
140	10	2	4	6	8	10											
150	5	2	3	5													
160	5		3	5													
170	5				4	5											
180	5				4	5											
190	5			3	5												

* Highest repetitive group that can be achieved at this depth regardless of bottom time.

Source: *U.S. Navy Diving Manual, Revision 6*

Table 9-8. *Residual Nitrogen Time Table for Repetitive Air Dives.*

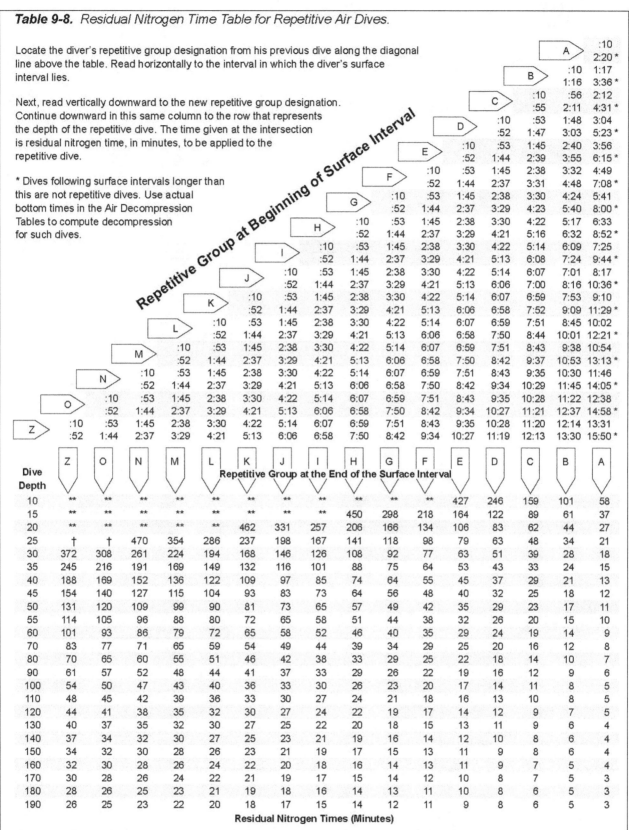

Locate the diver's repetitive group designation from his previous dive along the diagonal line above the table. Read horizontally to the interval in which the diver's surface interval lies.

Next, read vertically downward to the new repetitive group designation. Continue downward in this same column to the row that represents the depth of the repetitive dive. The time given at the intersection is residual nitrogen time, in minutes, to be applied to the repetitive dive.

* Dives following surface intervals longer than this are not repetitive dives. Use actual bottom times in the Air Decompression Tables to compute decompression for such dives.

Repetitive Group at Beginning of Surface Interval

		:10	
A		2:20 *	
B		:10	1:17
		1:16	3:36 *
C		:10	:56	2:12
		:55	2:11	4:31 *
D		:10	:53	1:48	3:04
		:52	1:47	3:03	5:23 *
E		:10	:53	1:45	2:40	3:56
		:52	1:44	2:39	3:55	6:15 *
F		:10	:53	1:45	2:38	3:32	4:49
		:52	1:44	2:37	3:31	4:48	7:08 *
G		:10	:53	1:45	2:38	3:30	4:24	5:41
		:52	1:44	2:37	3:29	4:23	5:40	8:00 *
H		:10	:53	1:45	2:38	3:30	4:22	5:17	6:33
		:52	1:44	2:37	3:29	4:21	5:16	6:32	8:52 *
I		:10	:53	1:45	2:38	3:30	4:22	5:14	6:09	7:25
		:52	1:44	2:37	3:29	4:21	5:13	6:08	7:24	9:44 *
J		:10	:53	1:45	2:38	3:30	4:22	5:14	6:07	7:01	8:17
		:52	1:44	2:37	3:29	4:21	5:13	6:06	7:00	8:16	10:36 *
K		:10	:53	1:45	2:38	3:30	4:22	5:14	6:07	6:59	7:53	9:10
		:52	1:44	2:37	3:29	4:21	5:13	6:06	6:58	7:52	9:09	11:29 *
L		:10	:53	1:45	2:38	3:30	4:22	5:14	6:07	6:59	7:51	8:45	10:02
		:52	1:44	2:37	3:29	4:21	5:13	6:06	6:58	7:50	8:44	10:01	12:21 *
M		:10	:53	1:45	2:38	3:30	4:22	5:14	6:07	6:59	7:51	8:43	9:38	10:54
		:52	1:44	2:37	3:29	4:21	5:13	6:06	6:58	7:50	8:42	9:37	10:53	13:13 *
N		:10	:53	1:45	2:38	3:30	4:22	5:14	6:07	6:59	7:51	8:43	9:35	10:30	11:46
		:52	1:44	2:37	3:29	4:21	5:13	6:06	6:58	7:50	8:42	9:34	10:29	11:45	14:05 *
O		:10	:53	1:45	2:38	3:30	4:22	5:14	6:07	6:59	7:51	8:43	9:35	10:28	11:22	12:38
		:52	1:44	2:37	3:29	4:21	5:13	6:06	6:58	7:50	8:42	9:34	10:27	11:21	12:37	14:58 *
Z		:10	:53	1:45	2:38	3:30	4:22	5:14	6:07	6:59	7:51	8:43	9:35	10:28	11:20	12:14	13:31
		:52	1:44	2:37	3:29	4:21	5:13	6:06	6:58	7:50	8:42	9:34	10:27	11:19	12:13	13:30	15:50 *

Repetitive Group at the End of the Surface Interval

Dive Depth	Z	O	N	M	L	K	J	I	H	G	F	E	D	C	B	A
10	**	**	**	**	**	**	**	**	**	**	**	427	246	159	101	58
15	**	**	**	**	**	**	**	**	450	298	218	164	122	89	61	37
20	**	**	**	**	**	462	331	257	206	166	134	106	83	62	44	27
25	†	†	470	354	286	237	198	167	141	118	98	79	63	48	34	21
30	372	308	261	224	194	168	146	126	108	92	77	63	51	39	28	18
35	245	216	191	169	149	132	116	101	88	75	64	53	43	33	24	15
40	188	169	152	136	122	109	97	85	74	64	55	45	37	29	21	13
45	154	140	127	115	104	93	83	73	64	56	48	40	32	25	18	12
50	131	120	109	99	90	81	73	65	57	49	42	35	29	23	17	11
55	114	105	96	88	80	72	65	58	51	44	38	32	26	20	15	10
60	101	93	86	79	72	65	58	52	46	40	35	29	24	19	14	9
70	83	77	71	65	59	54	49	44	39	34	29	25	20	16	12	8
80	70	65	60	55	51	46	42	38	33	29	25	22	18	14	10	7
90	61	57	52	48	44	41	37	33	29	26	22	19	16	12	9	6
100	54	50	47	43	40	36	33	30	26	23	20	17	14	11	8	5
110	48	45	42	39	36	33	30	27	24	21	18	16	13	10	8	5
120	44	41	38	35	32	30	27	24	22	19	17	14	12	9	7	5
130	40	37	35	32	30	27	25	22	20	18	15	13	11	9	6	4
140	37	34	32	30	27	25	23	21	19	16	14	12	10	8	6	4
150	34	32	30	28	26	23	21	19	17	15	13	11	9	8	6	4
160	32	30	28	26	24	22	20	18	16	14	13	11	9	7	5	4
170	30	28	26	24	22	21	19	17	15	14	12	10	8	7	5	3
180	28	26	25	23	21	19	18	16	14	13	11	10	8	6	5	3
190	26	25	23	22	20	18	17	15	14	12	11	9	8	6	5	3

Residual Nitrogen Times (Minutes)

** Residual Nitrogen Time cannot be determined using this table (see paragraph 9-9.1 subparagraph 8 for instructions).

† Read vertically downward to the 30 fsw repetitive dive depth. Use the corresponding residual nitrogen times to compute the equivalent single dive time. Decompress using the 30 fsw air decompression table.

Source: *U.S. Navy Diving Manual, Revision 6*

Table 9-9. *Air Decompression Table.*
(DESCENT RATE 75 FPM—ASCENT RATE 30 FPM)

Bottom Time (min)	Time to First Stop (M:S)	Gas Mix	100	90	80	70	60	50	40	30	20	Total Ascent Time (M:S)	Chamber O$_2$ Periods	Repet Group
30 FSW														
371	1:00	AIR									0	1:00	0	Z
		AIR/O$_2$									0	1:00		
380	0:20	AIR									5	6:00	0.5	Z
		AIR/O$_2$									1	2:00		
In-Water Air/O$_2$ Decompression or SurDO$_2$ Recommended														
420	0:20	AIR									22	23:00	0.5	Z
		AIR/O$_2$									5	6:00		
480	0:20	AIR									42	43:00	0.5	
		AIR/O$_2$									9	10:00		
540	0:20	AIR									71	72:00	1	
		AIR/O$_2$									14	15:00		
Exceptional Exposure: In-Water Air Decompression — In-Water Air/O$_2$ Decompression or SurDO$_2$ Required														
600	0:20	AIR									92	93:00	1	
		AIR/O$_2$									19	20:00		
660	0:20	AIR									120	121:00	1	
		AIR/O$_2$									22	23:00		
720	0:20	AIR									158	159:00	1	
		AIR/O$_2$									27	28:00		
35 FSW														
232	1:10	AIR									0	1:10	0	Z
		AIR/O$_2$									0	1:10		
240	0:30	AIR									4	5:10	0.5	Z
		AIR/O$_2$									2	3:10		
In-Water Air/O$_2$ Decompression or SurDO$_2$ Recommended														
270	0:30	AIR									28	29:10	0.5	Z
		AIR/O$_2$									7	8:10		
300	0:30	AIR									53	54:10	0.5	Z
		AIR/O$_2$									13	14:10		
330	0:30	AIR									71	72:10	1	Z
		AIR/O$_2$									18	19:10		
360	0:30	AIR									88	89:10	1	
		AIR/O$_2$									22	23:10		
Exceptional Exposure: In-Water Air Decompression — In-Water Air/O$_2$ Decompression or SurDO$_2$ Required														
420	0:30	AIR									134	135:10	1.5	
		AIR/O$_2$									29	30:10		
480	0:30	AIR									173	174:10	1.5	
		AIR/O$_2$									38	44:10		
540	0:30	AIR									228	229:10	2	
		AIR/O$_2$									45	51:10		
600	0:30	AIR									277	278:10	2	
		AIR/O$_2$									53	59:10		
660	0:30	AIR									314	315:10	2.5	
		AIR/O$_2$									63	69:10		
720	0:30	AIR									342	343:10	3	
		AIR/O$_2$									71	82:10		

Table 9-9. *Air Decompression Table (Continued).*
(DESCENT RATE 75 FPM—ASCENT RATE 30 FPM)

Bottom Time (min)	Time to First Stop (M:S)	Gas Mix	100	90	80	70	60	50	40	30	20	Total Ascent Time (M:S)	Chamber O₂ Periods	Repet Group
40 FSW														
163	1:20	AIR									0	1:20	0	O
		AIR/O₂									0	1:20		
170	0:40	AIR									6	7:20	0.5	O
		AIR/O₂									2	3:20		
180	0:40	AIR									14	15:20	0.5	Z
		AIR/O₂									5	6:20		
In-Water Air/O₂ Decompression or SurDO₂ Recommended ---														
190	0:40	AIR									21	22:20	0.5	Z
		AIR/O₂									7	8:20		
200	0:40	AIR									27	28:20	0.5	Z
		AIR/O₂									9	10:20		
210	0:40	AIR									39	40:20	0.5	Z
		AIR/O₂									11	12:20		
220	0:40	AIR									52	53:20	0.5	Z
		AIR/O₂									12	13:20		
230	0:40	AIR									64	65:20	1	Z
		AIR/O₂									16	17:20		
240	0:40	AIR									75	76:20	1	Z
		AIR/O₂									19	20:20		
Exceptional Exposure: In-Water Air Decompression ------------ In-Water Air/O₂ Decompression or SurDO₂ Required ----------														
270	0:40	AIR									101	102:20	1	Z
		AIR/O₂									26	27:20		
300	0:40	AIR									128	129:20	1.5	
		AIR/O₂									33	34:20		
330	0:40	AIR									160	161:20	1.5	
		AIR/O₂									38	44:20		
360	0:40	AIR									184	185:20	2	
		AIR/O₂									44	50:20		
420	0:40	AIR									248	249:20	2.5	
		AIR/O₂									56	62:20		
480	0:40	AIR									321	322:20	2.5	
		AIR/O₂									68	79:20		
Exceptional Exposure: In-Water Air/0₂ Decompression ------------ SurDO₂ Required-----------------------------------														
540	0:40	AIR									372	373:20	3	
		AIR/O₂									80	91:20		
600	0:40	AIR									410	411:20	3.5	
		AIR/O₂									93	104:20		
660	0:40	AIR									439	440:20	4	
		AIR/O₂									103	119:20		
Exceptional Exposure: SurDO₂ --														
720	0:40	AIR									461	462:20	4.5	
		AIR/O₂									112	128:20		

Source: *U.S. Navy Diving Manual, Revision 6*

Table 9-9. *Air Decompression Table (Continued).*
(DESCENT RATE 75 FPM—ASCENT RATE 30 FPM)

Bottom Time (min)	Time to First Stop (M:S)	Gas Mix	DECOMPRESSION STOPS (FSW) Stop times (min) include travel time, except first air and first O₂ stop									Total Ascent Time (M:S)	Chamber O₂ Periods	Repet Group
			100	90	80	70	60	50	40	30	20			
45 FSW														
125	1:30	AIR									0	1:30	0	N
		AIR/O₂									0	1:30		
130	0:50	AIR									2	3:30	0.5	O
		AIR/O₂									1	2:30		
140	0:50	AIR									14	15:30	0.5	O
		AIR/O₂									5	6:30		
In-Water Air/O₂ Decompression or SurDO₂ Recommended --														
150	0:50	AIR									25	26:30	0.5	Z
		AIR/O₂									8	9:30		
160	0:50	AIR									34	35:30	0.5	Z
		AIR/O₂									11	12:30		
170	0:50	AIR									41	42:30	1	Z
		AIR/O₂									14	15:30		
180	0:50	AIR									59	60:30	1	Z
		AIR/O₂									17	18:30		
190	0:50	AIR									75	76:30	1	Z
		AIR/O₂									19	20:30		
Exceptional Exposure: In-Water Air Decompression ------------- In-Water Air/O₂ Decompression or SurDO₂ Required ----------														
200	0:50	AIR									89	90:30	1	Z
		AIR/O₂									23	24:30		
210	0:50	AIR									101	102:30	1	Z
		AIR/O₂									27	28:30		
220	0:50	AIR									112	113:30	1.5	Z
		AIR/O₂									30	31:30		
230	0:50	AIR									121	122:30	1.5	Z
		AIR/O₂									33	34:30		
240	0:50	AIR									130	131:30	1.5	Z
		AIR/O₂									37	43:30		
270	0:50	AIR									173	174:30	2	
		AIR/O₂									45	51:30		
300	0:50	AIR									206	207:30	2	
		AIR/O₂									51	57:30		
330	0:50	AIR									243	244:30	2.5	
		AIR/O₂									61	67:30		
360	0:50	AIR									288	289:30	3	
		AIR/O₂									69	80:30		
Exceptional Exposure: In-Water Air/O₂ Decompression ------------- SurDO₂ Required--														
420	0:50	AIR									373	374:30	3.5	
		AIR/O₂									84	95:30		
480	0:50	AIR									431	432:30	4	
		AIR/O₂									101	117:30		
Exceptional Exposure: SurDO₂ ---														
540	0:50	AIR									473	474:30	4.5	
		AIR/O₂									117	133:30		

Source: *U.S. Navy Diving Manual, Revision 6*

Table 9-9. *Air Decompression Table (Continued).*
(DESCENT RATE 75 FPM—ASCENT RATE 30 FPM)

Bottom Time (min)	Time to First Stop (M:S)	Gas Mix	DECOMPRESSION STOPS (FSW) Stop times (min) include travel time, except first air and first O₂ stop								Total Ascent Time (M:S)	Chamber O₂ Periods	Repet Group
			100	90	80	70	60	50	40	30	20			

50 FSW

Bottom Time (min)	Time to First Stop (M:S)	Gas Mix	100	90	80	70	60	50	40	30	20	Total Ascent Time (M:S)	Chamber O₂ Periods	Repet Group
92	1:40	AIR									0	1:40	0	M
		AIR/O₂									0	1:40		
95	1:00	AIR									2	3:40	0.5	M
		AIR/O₂									1	2:40		
100	1:00	AIR									4	5:40	0.5	N
		AIR/O₂									2	3:40		
110	1:00	AIR									8	9:40	0.5	O
		AIR/O₂									4	5:40		
In-Water Air/O₂ Decompression or SurDO₂ Recommended ---														
120	1:00	AIR									21	22:40	0.5	O
		AIR/O₂									7	8:40		
130	1:00	AIR									34	35:40	0.5	Z
		AIR/O₂									12	13:40		
140	1:00	AIR									45	46:40	1	Z
		AIR/O₂									16	17:40		
150	1:00	AIR									56	57:40	1	Z
		AIR/O₂									19	20:40		
160	1:00	AIR									78	79:40	1	Z
		AIR/O₂									23	24:40		
Exceptional Exposure: In-Water Air Decompression ------------ In-Water Air/O₂ Decompression or SurDO₂ Required ----------														
170	1:00	AIR									96	97:40	1	Z
		AIR/O₂									26	27:40		
180	1:00	AIR									111	112:40	1.5	Z
		AIR/O₂									30	31:40		
190	1:00	AIR									125	126:40	1.5	Z
		AIR/O₂									35	36:40		
200	1:00	AIR									136	137:40	1.5	Z
		AIR/O₂									39	45:40		
210	1:00	AIR									147	148:40	2	
		AIR/O₂									43	49:40		
220	1:00	AIR									166	167:40	2	
		AIR/O₂									47	53:40		
230	1:00	AIR									183	184:40	2	
		AIR/O₂									50	56:40		
240	1:00	AIR									198	199:40	2	
		AIR/O₂									53	59:40		
270	1:00	AIR									236	237:40	2.5	
		AIR/O₂									62	68:40		
300	1:00	AIR									285	286:40	3	
		AIR/O₂									74	85:40		
Exceptional Exposure: In-Water Air/O₂ Decompression ------------ SurDO₂ Required-------------------------------														
330	1:00	AIR									345	346:40	3.5	
		AIR/O₂									83	94:40		
360	1:00	AIR									393	394:40	3.5	
		AIR/O₂									92	103:40		
Exceptional Exposure: SurDO₂ --														
420	1:00	AIR									464	465:40	4.5	
		AIR/O₂									113	129:40		

Source: *U.S. Navy Diving Manual, Revision 6*

Table 9-9. *Air Decompression Table (Continued).*
(DESCENT RATE 75 FPM—ASCENT RATE 30 FPM)

Bottom Time (min)	Time to First Stop (M:S)	Gas Mix	DECOMPRESSION STOPS (FSW) Stop times (min) include travel time, except first air and first O₂ stop									Total Ascent Time (M:S)	Chamber O₂ Periods	Repet Group
			100	90	80	70	60	50	40	30	20			
55 FSW														
74	1:50	AIR									0	1:50	0	L
		AIR/O₂									0	1:50		
75	1:10	AIR									1	2:50	0.5	L
		AIR/O₂									1	2:50		
80	1:10	AIR									4	5:50	0.5	M
		AIR/O₂									2	3:50		
90	1:10	AIR									10	11:50	0.5	N
		AIR/O₂									5	6:50		
In-Water Air/O₂ Decompression or SurDO₂ Recommended --														
100	1:10	AIR									17	18:50	0.5	O
		AIR/O₂									8	9:50		
110	1:10	AIR									34	35:50	0.5	O
		AIR/O₂									12	13:50		
120	1:10	AIR									48	49:50	1	Z
		AIR/O₂									17	18:50		
130	1:10	AIR									59	60:50	1	Z
		AIR/O₂									22	23:50		
140	1:10	AIR									84	85:50	1	Z
		AIR/O₂									26	27:50		
Exceptional Exposure: In-Water Air Decompression ------------- In-Water Air/O₂ Decompression or SurDO₂ Required ----------														
150	1:10	AIR									105	106:50	1.5	Z
		AIR/O₂									30	31:50		
160	1:10	AIR									123	124:50	1.5	Z
		AIR/O₂									34	35:50		
170	1:10	AIR									138	139:50	1.5	Z
		AIR/O₂									40	46:50		
180	1:10	AIR									151	152:50	2	Z
		AIR/O₂									45	51:50		
190	1:10	AIR									169	170:50	2	
		AIR/O₂									50	56:50		
200	1:10	AIR									190	191:50	2	
		AIR/O₂									54	60:50		
210	1:10	AIR									208	209:50	2.5	
		AIR/O₂									58	64:50		
220	1:10	AIR									224	225:50	2.5	
		AIR/O₂									62	68:50		
230	1:10	AIR									239	240:50	2.5	
		AIR/O₂									66	77:50		
240	1:10	AIR									254	255:50	3	
		AIR/O₂									69	80:50		
Exceptional Exposure: In-Water Air/0₂ Decompression ------------ SurDO₂ Required---														
270	1:10	AIR									313	314:50	3.5	
		AIR/O₂									83	94:50		
300	1:10	AIR									380	381:50	3.5	
		AIR/O₂									94	105:50		
330	1:10	AIR									432	433:50	4	
		AIR/O₂									106	122:50		
Exceptional Exposure: SurDO₂ ---														
360	1:10	AIR									474	475:50	4.5	
		AIR/O₂									118	134:50		

Source: *U.S. Navy Diving Manual, Revision 6*

Table 9-9. *Air Decompression Table (Continued).*
(DESCENT RATE 75 FPM—ASCENT RATE 30 FPM)

Bottom Time (min)	Time to First Stop (M:S)	Gas Mix	100	90	80	70	60	50	40	30	20	Total Ascent Time (M:S)	Chamber O₂ Periods	Repet Group
60 FSW														
60	2:00	AIR									0	2:00	0	K
		AIR/O₂									0	2:00		
65	1:20	AIR									2	4:00	0.5	L
		AIR/O₂									1	3:00		
70	1:20	AIR									7	9:00	0.5	L
		AIR/O₂									4	6:00		
80	1:20	AIR									14	16:00	0.5	N
		AIR/O₂									7	9:00		

In-Water Air/O₂ Decompression or SurDO₂ Recommended --

90	1:20	AIR									23	25:00	0.5	O
		AIR/O₂									10	12:00		
100	1:20	AIR									42	44:00	1	Z
		AIR/O₂									15	17:00		
110	1:20	AIR									57	59:00	1	Z
		AIR/O₂									21	23:00		
120	1:20	AIR									75	77:00	1	Z
		AIR/O₂									26	28:00		

Exceptional Exposure: In-Water Air Decompression ------------ In-Water Air/O₂ Decompression or SurDO₂ Required ----------

130	1:20	AIR									102	104:00	1.5	Z
		AIR/O₂									31	33:00		
140	1:20	AIR									124	126:00	1.5	Z
		AIR/O₂									35	37:00		
150	1:20	AIR									143	145:00	2	Z
		AIR/O₂									41	48:00		
160	1:20	AIR									158	160:00	2	Z
		AIR/O₂									48	55:00		
170	1:20	AIR									178	180:00	2	
		AIR/O₂									53	60:00		
180	1:20	AIR									201	203:00	2.5	
		AIR/O₂									59	66:00		
190	1:20	AIR									222	224:00	2.5	
		AIR/O₂									64	71:00		
200	1:20	AIR									240	242:00	2.5	
		AIR/O₂									68	80:00		
210	1:20	AIR									256	258:00	3	
		AIR/O₂									73	85:00		
220	1:20	AIR									278	280:00	3	
		AIR/O₂									77	89:00		

Exceptional Exposure: In-Water Air/O₂ Decompression ------------ SurDO₂ Required-------------------------------

230	1:20	AIR									300	302:00	3.5	
		AIR/O₂									82	94:00		
240	1:20	AIR									321	323:00	3.5	
		AIR/O₂									88	100:00		
270	1:20	AIR									398	400:00	4	
		AIR/O₂									102	119:00		

Exceptional Exposure: SurDO₂ ---

300	1:20	AIR									456	458:00	4.5	
		AIR/O₂									115	132:00		

Source: *U.S. Navy Diving Manual, Revision 6*

Table 9-9. *Air Decompression Table (Continued).*
(DESCENT RATE 75 FPM—ASCENT RATE 30 FPM)

Bottom Time (min)	Time to First Stop (M:S)	Gas Mix	100	90	80	70	60	50	40	30	20	Total Ascent Time (M:S)	Chamber O₂ Periods	Repet Group
70 FSW														
48	2:20	AIR									0	2:20	0	K
		AIR/O₂									0	2:20		
50	1:40	AIR									2	4:20	0.5	K
		AIR/O₂									1	3:20		
55	1:40	AIR									9	11:20	0.5	L
		AIR/O₂									5	7:20		
60	1:40	AIR									14	16:20	0.5	M
		AIR/O₂									8	10:20		

In-Water Air/O₂ Decompression or SurDO₂ Recommended --

Bottom Time (min)	Time to First Stop (M:S)	Gas Mix	100	90	80	70	60	50	40	30	20	Total Ascent Time (M:S)	Chamber O₂ Periods	Repet Group
70	1:40	AIR									24	26:20	0.5	N
		AIR/O₂									13	15:20		
80	1:40	AIR									44	46:20	1	O
		AIR/O₂									17	19:20		
90	1:40	AIR									64	66:20	1	Z
		AIR/O₂									24	26:20		
100	1:40	AIR									88	90:20	1.5	Z
		AIR/O₂									31	33:20		

Exceptional Exposure: In-Water Air Decompression ------------- In-Water Air/O₂ Decompression or SurDO₂ Required ----------

Bottom Time (min)	Time to First Stop (M:S)	Gas Mix	100	90	80	70	60	50	40	30	20	Total Ascent Time (M:S)	Chamber O₂ Periods	Repet Group
110	1:40	AIR									120	122:20	1.5	Z
		AIR/O₂									38	45:20		
120	1:40	AIR									145	147:20	2	Z
		AIR/O₂									44	51:20		
130	1:40	AIR									167	169:20	2	Z
		AIR/O₂									51	58:20		
140	1:40	AIR									189	191:20	2.5	
		AIR/O₂									59	66:20		
150	1:40	AIR									219	221:20	2.5	
		AIR/O₂									66	78:20		
160	1:20	AIR								1	244	247:00	3	
		AIR/O₂								1	72	85:00		

Exceptional Exposure: In-Water Air/O₂ Decompression ------------- SurDO₂ Required--

Bottom Time (min)	Time to First Stop (M:S)	Gas Mix	100	90	80	70	60	50	40	30	20	Total Ascent Time (M:S)	Chamber O₂ Periods	Repet Group
170	1:20	AIR								2	265	269:00	3	
		AIR/O₂								1	78	91:00		
180	1:20	AIR								4	289	295:00	3.5	
		AIR/O₂								2	83	97:00		
190	1:20	AIR								5	316	323:00	3.5	
		AIR/O₂								3	88	103:00		
200	1:20	AIR								9	345	356:00	4	
		AIR/O₂								5	93	115:00		
210	1:20	AIR								13	378	393:00	4	
		AIR/O₂								7	98	122:00		

Exceptional Exposure: SurDO₂ --

Bottom Time (min)	Time to First Stop (M:S)	Gas Mix	100	90	80	70	60	50	40	30	20	Total Ascent Time (M:S)	Chamber O₂ Periods	Repet Group
240	1:20	AIR								25	454	481:00	5	
		AIR/O₂								13	110	140:00		

Source: *U.S. Navy Diving Manual, Revision 6*

Table 9-9. *Air Decompression Table (Continued).*
(DESCENT RATE 75 FPM—ASCENT RATE 30 FPM)

Bottom Time (min)	Time to First Stop (M:S)	Gas Mix	DECOMPRESSION STOPS (FSW) Stop times (min) include travel time, except first air and first O₂ stop									Total Ascent Time (M:S)	Chamber O₂ Periods	Repet Group
			100	90	80	70	60	50	40	30	20			
80 FSW														
39	2:40	AIR									0	2:40	0	J
		AIR/O₂									0	2:40		
40	2:00	AIR									1	3:40	0.5	J
		AIR/O₂									1	3:40		
45	2:00	AIR									10	12:40	0.5	K
		AIR/O₂									5	7:40		
In-Water Air/O₂ Decompression or SurDO₂ Recommended --														
50	2:00	AIR									17	19:40	0.5	M
		AIR/O₂									9	11:40		
55	2:00	AIR									24	26:40	0.5	M
		AIR/O₂									13	15:40		
60	2:00	AIR									30	32:40	1	N
		AIR/O₂									16	18:40		
70	2:00	AIR									54	56:40	1	O
		AIR/O₂									22	24:40		
80	2:00	AIR									77	79:40	1.5	Z
		AIR/O₂									30	32:40		
Exceptional Exposure: In-Water Air Decompression ------------ In-Water Air/O₂ Decompression or SurDO₂ Required ----------														
90	2:00	AIR									114	116:40	1.5	Z
		AIR/O₂									39	46:40		
100	1:40	AIR								1	147	150:20	2	Z
		AIR/O₂								1	46	54:20		
110	1:40	AIR								6	171	179:20	2	Z
		AIR/O₂								3	51	61:20		
120	1:40	AIR								10	200	212:20	2.5	
		AIR/O₂								5	59	71:20		
130	1:40	AIR								14	232	248:20	3	
		AIR/O₂								7	67	86:20		
Exceptional Exposure: In-Water Air/O₂ Decompression ------------ SurDO₂ Required--														
140	1:40	AIR								17	258	277:20	3.5	
		AIR/O₂								9	73	94:20		
150	1:40	AIR								19	285	306:20	3.5	
		AIR/O₂								10	80	102:20		
160	1:40	AIR								21	318	341:20	4	
		AIR/O₂								11	86	114:20		
170	1:40	AIR								27	354	383:20	4	
		AIR/O₂								14	90	121:20		
Exceptional Exposure: SurDO₂ ---														
180	1:40	AIR								33	391	426:20	4.5	
		AIR/O₂								17	96	130:20		
210	1:40	AIR								50	474	526:20	5	
		AIR/O₂								26	110	158:20		

Source: *U.S.Navy Diving Manual, Revision 6*

Table 9-9. *Air Decompression Table (Continued).*
(DESCENT RATE 75 FPM—ASCENT RATE 30 FPM)

Bottom Time (min)	Time to First Stop (M:S)	Gas Mix	DECOMPRESSION STOPS (FSW) Stop times (min) include travel time, except first air and first O₂ stop									Total Ascent Time (M:S)	Chamber O₂ Periods	Repet Group
			100	90	80	70	60	50	40	30	20			
90 FSW														
30	3:00	AIR									0	3:00	0	I
		AIR/O₂									0	3:00		
35	2:20	AIR									4	7:00	0.5	J
		AIR/O₂									2	5:00		
40	2:20	AIR									14	17:00	0.5	L
		AIR/O₂									7	10:00		
In-Water Air/O₂ Decompression or SurDO₂ Recommended ---														
45	2:20	AIR									23	26:00	0.5	M
		AIR/O₂									12	15:00		
50	2:20	AIR									31	34:00	1	N
		AIR/O₂									17	20:00		
55	2:20	AIR									39	42:00	1	O
		AIR/O₂									21	24:00		
60	2:20	AIR									56	59:00	1	O
		AIR/O₂									24	27:00		
70	2:20	AIR									83	86:00	1.5	Z
		AIR/O₂									32	35:00		
Exceptional Exposure: In-Water Air Decompression ------------- In-Water Air/O₂ Decompression or SurDO₂ Required -----------														
80	2:00	AIR								5	125	132:40	2	Z
		AIR/O₂								3	40	50:40		
90	2:00	AIR								13	158	173:40	2	Z
		AIR/O₂								7	46	60:40		
100	2:00	AIR								19	185	206:40	2.5	
		AIR/O₂								10	53	70:40		
110	2:00	AIR								25	224	251:40	3	
		AIR/O₂								13	61	86:40		
Exceptional Exposure: In-Water Air/O₂ Decompression ------------- SurDO₂ Required-----------------------------------														
120	1:40	AIR							1	29	256	288:20	3.5	
		AIR/O₂							1	15	70	98:40		
130	1:40	AIR							5	28	291	326:20	3.5	
		AIR/O₂							5	15	78	110:40		
140	1:40	AIR							8	28	330	368:20	4	
		AIR/O₂							8	15	86	126:40		
Exceptional Exposure: SurDO₂ ---														
150	1:40	AIR							11	34	378	425:20	4.5	
		AIR/O₂							11	17	94	139:40		
160	1:40	AIR							13	40	418	473:20	4.5	
		AIR/O₂							13	21	100	151:40		
170	1:40	AIR							15	45	451	513:20	5	
		AIR/O₂							15	23	106	166:40		
180	1:40	AIR							16	51	479	548:20	5.5	
		AIR/O₂							16	26	112	176:40		
240	1:40	AIR							42	68	592	704:20	7.5	
		AIR/O₂							42	34	159	267:00		

Source: *U.S. Navy Diving Manual, Revision 6*

Table 9-9. *Air Decompression Table (Continued).*
(DESCENT RATE 75 FPM—ASCENT RATE 30 FPM)

Bottom Time (min)	Time to First Stop (M:S)	Gas Mix	100	90	80	70	60	50	40	30	20	Total Ascent Time (M:S)	Chamber O$_2$ Periods	Repet Group
100 FSW														
25	3:20	AIR									0	3:20	0	H
		AIR/O$_2$									0	3:20		
30	2:40	AIR									3	6:20	0.5	J
		AIR/O$_2$									2	5:20		
35	2:40	AIR									15	18:20	0.5	L
		AIR/O$_2$									8	11:20		
In-Water Air/O$_2$ Decompression or SurDO$_2$ Recommended ---														
40	2:40	AIR									26	29:20	1	M
		AIR/O$_2$									14	17:20		
45	2:40	AIR									36	39:20	1	N
		AIR/O$_2$									19	22:20		
50	2:40	AIR									47	50:20	1	O
		AIR/O$_2$									24	27:20		
55	2:40	AIR									65	68:20	1.5	Z
		AIR/O$_2$									28	31:20		
60	2:40	AIR									81	84:20	1.5	Z
		AIR/O$_2$									33	35:20		
Exceptional Exposure: In-Water Air Decompression ------------- In-Water Air/O$_2$ Decompression or SurDO$_2$ Required ----------														
70	2:20	AIR								11	124	138:00	2	Z
		AIR/O$_2$								6	39	53:00		
80	2:20	AIR								21	160	184:00	2.5	Z
		AIR/O$_2$								11	45	64:00		
90	2:00	AIR							2	28	196	228:40	2.5	
		AIR/O$_2$							2	15	52	82:00		
Exceptional Exposure: In-Water Air/O$_2$ Decompression ------------- SurDO$_2$ Required------------------------------------														
100	2:00	AIR							9	28	241	280:40	3	
		AIR/O$_2$							9	14	66	102:00		
110	2:00	AIR							14	28	278	322:40	3.5	
		AIR/O$_2$							14	15	75	117:00		
120	2:00	AIR							19	28	324	373:40	4	
		AIR/O$_2$							19	15	84	136:00		
Exceptional Exposure: SurDO$_2$ --														
150	1:40	AIR						3	26	46	461	538:20	5	
		AIR/O$_2$						3	26	24	108	183:40		

Source: *U.S. Navy Diving Manual, Revision 6*

Table 9-9. *Air Decompression Table (Continued).*
(DESCENT RATE 75 FPM—ASCENT RATE 30 FPM)

Bottom Time (min)	Time to First Stop (M:S)	Gas Mix	DECOMPRESSION STOPS (FSW) — Stop times (min) include travel time, except first air and first O$_2$ stop									Total Ascent Time (M:S)	Chamber O$_2$ Periods	Repet Group
			100	90	80	70	60	50	40	30	20			
110 FSW														
20	3:40	AIR									0	3:40	0	H
		AIR/O$_2$									0	3:40		
25	3:00	AIR									3	6:40	0.5	I
		AIR/O$_2$									2	5:40		
30	3:00	AIR									14	17:40	0.5	K
		AIR/O$_2$									7	10:40		
In-Water Air/O$_2$ Decompression or SurDO$_2$ Recommended														
35	3:00	AIR									27	30:40	1	M
		AIR/O$_2$									14	17:40		
40	3:00	AIR									39	42:40	1	N
		AIR/O$_2$									20	23:40		
45	3:00	AIR									50	53:40	1	O
		AIR/O$_2$									26	29:40		
50	3:00	AIR									71	74:40	1.5	Z
		AIR/O$_2$									31	34:40		
Exceptional Exposure: In-Water Air Decompression ------------ In-Water Air/O$_2$ Decompression or SurDO$_2$ Required ----------														
55	2:40	AIR								5	85	93:20	1.5	Z
		AIR/O$_2$								3	**33**	44:20		
60	2:40	AIR								13	111	127:20	2	Z
		AIR/O$_2$								7	**36**	51:20		
70	2:40	AIR								26	155	184:20	2.5	Z
		AIR/O$_2$								13	**43**	64:20		
80	2:20	AIR							9	28	200	240:00	2.5	
		AIR/O$_2$							9	15	**53**	90:20		
Exceptional Exposure: In-Water Air/O$_2$ Decompression ------------ SurDO$_2$ Required------------------------------------														
90	2:20	AIR							17	29	248	297:00	3.5	
		AIR/O$_2$							17	**15**	67	112:20		
100	2:20	AIR							25	28	295	351:00	3.5	
		AIR/O$_2$							25	**15**	78	131:20		
110	2:00	AIR						5	26	28	353	414:40	4	
		AIR/O$_2$						5	26	**15**	90	154:00		
Exceptional Exposure: SurDO$_2$ --														
120	2:00	AIR						10	26	35	413	486:40	4.5	
		AIR/O$_2$						10	26	**18**	101	173:00		
180	1:40	AIR					3	23	47	68	593	736:20	7.5	
		AIR/O$_2$					3	23	47	**34**	159	298:00		

Source: *U.S. Navy Diving Manual, Revision 6*

Table 9-9. *Air Decompression Table (Continued).*
(DESCENT RATE 75 FPM—ASCENT RATE 30 FPM)

Bottom Time (min)	Time to First Stop (M:S)	Gas Mix	DECOMPRESSION STOPS (FSW) Stop times (min) include travel time, except first air and first O₂ stop									Total Ascent Time (M:S)	Chamber O₂ Periods	Repet Group
			100	90	80	70	60	50	40	30	20			
120 FSW														
15	4:00	AIR									0	4:00	0	F
		AIR/O₂									**0**	4:00		
20	3:20	AIR									2	6:00	0.5	H
		AIR/O₂									**1**	5:00		
25	3:20	AIR									8	12:00	0.5	J
		AIR/O₂									**4**	8:00		
In-Water Air/O₂ Decompression or SurDO₂ Recommended --														
30	3:20	AIR									24	28:00	0.5	L
		AIR/O₂									**13**	17:00		
35	3:20	AIR									38	42:00	1	N
		AIR/O₂									**20**	24:00		
40	3:20	AIR									51	55:00	1	O
		AIR/O₂									**27**	31:00		
45	3:20	AIR									72	76:00	1.5	Z
		AIR/O₂									**33**	37:00		
Exceptional Exposure: In-Water Air Decompression ------------- In-Water Air/O₂ Decompression or SurDO₂ Required ----------														
50	3:00	AIR								9	86	98:40	1.5	Z
		AIR/O₂								5	33	46:40		
55	3:00	AIR								19	116	138:40	2	Z
		AIR/O₂								10	35	53:40		
60	3:00	AIR								27	142	172:40	2	Z
		AIR/O₂								14	39	61:40		
70	2:40	AIR							12	29	189	233:20	2.5	
		AIR/O₂							12	15	50	85:40		
Exceptional Exposure: In-Water Air/O₂ Decompression ------------- SurDO₂ Required--														
80	2:40	AIR						24	28	246		301:20	3	
		AIR/O₂						24	14	67		118:40		
90	2:20	AIR					7	26	28	303		367:00	3.5	
		AIR/O₂					7	26	15	79		140:20		
100	2:20	AIR					14	26	28	372		443:00	4	
		AIR/O₂					14	26	15	94		167:20		
Exceptional Exposure: SurDO₂ --														
110	2:20	AIR					21	25	38	433		520:00	5	
		AIR/O₂					21	25	20	104		188:20		
120	2:00	AIR				3	23	25	47	480		580:40	5.5	
		AIR/O₂				3	23	25	24	113		211:00		

Source: *U.S. Navy Diving Manual, Revision 6*

Table 9-9. *Air Decompression Table (Continued).*
(DESCENT RATE 75 FPM—ASCENT RATE 30 FPM)

Bottom Time (min)	Time to First Stop (M:S)	Gas Mix	DECOMPRESSION STOPS (FSW) Stop times (min) include travel time, except first air and first O_2 stop									Total Ascent Time (M:S)	Chamber O_2 Periods	Repet Group
			100	90	80	70	60	50	40	30	20			
130 FSW														
10	4:20	AIR									0	4:20	0	E
		AIR/O_2									0	4:20		
15	3:40	AIR									1	5:20	0.5	G
		AIR/O_2									1	5:20		
20	3:40	AIR									4	8:20	0.5	I
		AIR/O_2									2	6:20		
In-Water Air/O_2 Decompression or SurDO$_2$ Recommended ---------														
25	3:40	AIR									17	21:20	0.5	K
		AIR/O_2									9	13:20		
30	3:40	AIR									34	38:20	1	M
		AIR/O_2									18	22:20		
35	3:40	AIR									49	53:20	1	N
		AIR/O_2									26	30:20		
40	3:20	AIR								3	67	74:00	1.5	Z
		AIR/O_2								2	31	37:00		
Exceptional Exposure: In-Water Air Decompression ------------- In-Water Air/O_2 Decompression or SurDO$_2$ Required ----------														
45	3:20	AIR								12	84	100:00	1.5	Z
		AIR/O_2								6	33	48:00		
50	3:20	AIR								22	116	142:00	2	Z
		AIR/O_2								11	35	55:00		
55	3:00	AIR							4	28	145	180:40	2	Z
		AIR/O_2							4	15	39	67:00		
60	3:00	AIR							12	28	170	213:40	2.5	Z
		AIR/O_2							12	15	45	81:00		
Exceptional Exposure: In-Water Air/O_2 Decompression ------------- SurDO$_2$ Required-------------------------														
70	2:40	AIR						1	26	28	235	293:20	3	
		AIR/O_2						1	26	14	63	117:40		
80	2:40	AIR						12	26	28	297	366:20	3.5	
		AIR/O_2						12	26	15	78	144:40		
90	2:40	AIR						21	26	28	374	452:20	4	
		AIR/O_2						21	26	15	94	174:40		
Exceptional Exposure: SurDO$_2$ ----														
100	2:20	AIR					6	23	26	38	444	540:00	5	
		AIR/O_2					6	23	26	20	106	204:20		
120	2:20	AIR					17	23	28	57	533	661:00	6	
		AIR/O_2					17	23	28	29	130	255:20		
180	2:00	AIR				13	21	45	57	94	658	890:40	9	
		AIR/O_2				13	21	45	57	46	198	417:20		

Source: *U.S. Navy Diving Manual, Revision 6*

Table 9-9. *Air Decompression Table (Continued).*
(DESCENT RATE 75 FPM—ASCENT RATE 30 FPM)

Bottom Time (min)	Time to First Stop (M:S)	Gas Mix	100	90	80	70	60	50	40	30	20	Total Ascent Time (M:S)	Chamber O₂ Periods	Repet Group
140 FSW														
10	4:40	AIR									0	4:40	0	E
		AIR/O₂									0	4:40		
15	4:00	AIR									2	6:40	0.5	H
		AIR/O₂									1	5:40		
20	4:00	AIR									7	11:40	0.5	J
		AIR/O₂									4	8:40		
In-Water Air/O₂ Decompression or SurDO₂ Recommended --														
25	4:00	AIR									26	30:40	1	L
		AIR/O₂									14	18:40		
30	4:00	AIR									44	48:40	1	N
		AIR/O₂									23	27:40		
35	3:40	AIR								4	59	67:20	1.5	O
		AIR/O₂								2	30	36:20		
Exceptional Exposure: In-Water Air Decompression ------------ In-Water Air/O₂ Decompression or SurDO₂ Required ----------														
40	3:40	AIR								11	80	95:20	1.5	Z
		AIR/O₂								6	33	48:20		
45	3:20	AIR							3	21	113	141:00	2	Z
		AIR/O₂							3	11	34	57:20		
50	3:20	AIR							7	28	145	184:00	2	Z
		AIR/O₂							7	14	40	70:20		
55	3:20	AIR							16	28	171	219:00	2.5	Z
		AIR/O₂							16	15	45	85:20		
Exceptional Exposure: In-Water Air/O₂ Decompression ------------ SurDO₂ Required--------------------------------------														
60	3:00	AIR						2	23	28	209	265:40	3	
		AIR/O₂						2	23	15	55	109:00		
70	3:00	AIR						14	25	28	276	346:40	3.5	
		AIR/O₂						14	25	15	74	142:00		
80	2:40	AIR					2	24	25	29	362	445:20	4	
		AIR/O₂					2	24	25	15	91	175:40		
Exceptional Exposure: SurDO₂ ---														
90	2:40	AIR				12	23	26	38	443	545:20	5		
		AIR/O₂				12	23	26	19	107	210:40			

Source: *U.S. Navy Diving Manual, Revision 6*

Table 9-9. *Air Decompression Table (Continued).*
(DESCENT RATE 75 FPM—ASCENT RATE 30 FPM)

Bottom Time (min)	Time to First Stop (M:S)	Gas Mix	DECOMPRESSION STOPS (FSW) Stop times (min) include travel time, except first air and first O₂ stop									Total Ascent Time (M:S)	Chamber O₂ Periods	Repet Group
			100	90	80	70	60	50	40	30	20			
150 FSW														
5	5:00	AIR									0	5:00	0	C
		AIR/O₂									0	5:00		
10	4:20	AIR									1	6:00	0.5	F
		AIR/O₂									1	6:00		
15	4:20	AIR									3	8:00	0.5	H
		AIR/O₂									2	7:00		
20	4:20	AIR									14	19:00	0.5	K
		AIR/O₂									8	13:00		
In-Water Air/O₂ Decompression or SurDO₂ Recommended --														
25	4:20	AIR									35	40:00	1	M
		AIR/O₂									19	24:00		
30	4:00	AIR								3	51	58:40	1.5	O
		AIR/O₂								2	26	32:40		
35	4:00	AIR								11	72	87:40	1.5	Z
		AIR/O₂								6	31	46:40		
Exceptional Exposure: In-Water Air Decompression ------------- In-Water Air/O₂ Decompression or SurDO₂ Required ----------														
40	3:40	AIR							4	18	102	128:20	2	Z
		AIR/O₂							4	9	34	56:40		
45	3:40	AIR							10	25	140	179:20	2	Z
		AIR/O₂							10	13	39	71:40		
50	3:20	AIR						3	15	28	170	220:00	2.5	Z
		AIR/O₂						3	15	15	45	87:20		
Exceptional Exposure: In-Water Air/O₂ Decompression ----------- SurDO₂ Required-------------------------------------														
55	3:20	AIR						6	22	28	211	271:00	3	
		AIR/O₂						6	22	15	56	113:20		
60	3:20	AIR						11	26	28	248	317:00	3	
		AIR/O₂						11	26	15	66	132:20		
70	3:00	AIR					3	24	25	28	330	413:40	4	
		AIR/O₂					3	24	25	15	84	170:00		
Exceptional Exposure: SurDO₂ ---														
80	3:00	AIR					15	23	26	35	430	532:40	4.5	
		AIR/O₂					15	23	26	18	104	205:00		
90	2:40	AIR				3	22	23	26	47	496	620:20	5.5	
		AIR/O₂				3	22	23	26	24	118	239:40		
120	2:20	AIR			3	20	22	23	50	75	608	804:00	8	
		AIR/O₂			3	20	22	23	50	37	168	355:40		
180	2:00	AIR		2	19	20	42	48	79	121	694	1027:40	10.5	
		AIR/O₂		2	19	20	42	48	79	58	222	537:20		

Source: *U.S. Navy Diving Manual, Revision 6*

Table 9-9. *Air Decompression Table (Continued).*
(DESCENT RATE 75 FPM—ASCENT RATE 30 FPM)

Bottom Time (min)	Time to First Stop (M:S)	Gas Mix	DECOMPRESSION STOPS (FSW) Stop times (min) include travel time, except first air and first O₂ stop									Total Ascent Time (M:S)	Chamber O₂ Periods	Repet Group
			100	90	80	70	60	50	40	30	20			
160 FSW														
5	5:20	AIR									0	5:20	0	C
		AIR/O₂									0	5:20		
10	4:40	AIR									1	6:20	0.5	F
		AIR/O₂									1	6:20		
15	4:40	AIR									5	10:20	0.5	I
		AIR/O₂									3	8:00		
In-Water Air/O₂ Decompression or SurDO₂ Recommended --														
20	4:40	AIR									22	27:20	0.5	L
		AIR/O₂									12	17:20		
25	4:20	AIR								3	41	49:00	1	N
		AIR/O₂								2	21	28:00		
30	4:00	AIR							1	8	60	73:40	1.5	O
		AIR/O₂							1	5	28	39:00		
Exceptional Exposure: In-Water Air Decompression ------------ In-Water Air/O₂ Decompression or SurDO₂ Required ----------														
35	4:00	AIR							4	14	84	106:40	1.5	Z
		AIR/O₂							4	8	32	54:00		
40	4:00	AIR							12	20	130	166:40	2	Z
		AIR/O₂							12	11	37	70:00		
45	3:40	AIR						5	13	28	164	214:20	2.5	Z
		AIR/O₂						5	13	14	44	85:40		
Exceptional Exposure: In-Water Air/O₂ Decompression ------------ SurDO₂ Required---														
50	3:40	AIR						10	19	28	207	268:20	3	
		AIR/O₂						10	19	15	54	112:40		
55	3:20	AIR					2	12	26	28	248	320:00	3	
		AIR/O₂					2	12	26	14	67	135:20		
60	3:20	AIR					5	18	25	29	290	371:00	3.5	
		AIR/O₂					5	18	25	15	77	154:20		
Exceptional Exposure: SurDO₂ --														
70	3:20	AIR				15	23	26	29	399	496:00		4.5	
		AIR/O₂				15	23	26	15	99	197:20			
80	3:00	AIR		6	21	24	25	44	482	605:40		5.5		
		AIR/O₂		6	21	24	25	23	114	237:00				

Source: *U.S. Navy Diving Manual, Revision 6*

Table 9-9. *Air Decompression Table (Continued).*
(DESCENT RATE 75 FPM—ASCENT RATE 30 FPM)

Bottom Time (min)	Time to First Stop (M:S)	Gas Mix	DECOMPRESSION STOPS (FSW) Stop times (min) include travel time, except first air and first O₂ stop									Total Ascent Time (M:S)	Chamber O₂ Periods	Repet Group
			100	90	80	70	60	50	40	30	20			
170 FSW														
5	5:40	AIR									0	5:40	0	D
		AIR/O₂									0	5:40		
10	5:00	AIR									2	7:40	0.5	G
		AIR/O₂									1	6:40		
15	5:00	AIR									7	12:40	0.5	J
		AIR/O₂									4	9:40		
In-Water Air/O₂ Decompression or SurDO₂ Recommended --														
20	4:40	AIR								1	29	35:20	1	L
		AIR/O₂								1	15	21:20		
25	4:20	AIR							1	6	46	58:00	1	N
		AIR/O₂							1	4	23	33:20		
Exceptional Exposure: In-Water Air Decompression ------------- In-Water Air/O₂ Decompression or SurDO₂ Required ----------														
30	4:20	AIR							5	11	72	93:00	1.5	Z
		AIR/O₂							5	6	29	45:20		
35	4:00	AIR						2	9	17	113	145:40	2	Z
		AIR/O₂						2	9	9	35	65:00		
40	4:00	AIR						6	13	23	155	201:40	2.5	Z
		AIR/O₂						6	13	12	43	84:00		
Exceptional Exposure: In-Water Air/O₂ Decompression ------------ SurDO₂ Required--														
45	4:00	AIR						12	16	28	194	254:40	2.5	
		AIR/O₂						12	16	15	51	109:00		
50	3:40	AIR					5	12	23	28	243	315:20	3	
		AIR/O₂					5	12	23	15	65	134:40		
55	3:40	AIR					9	16	25	28	287	369:20	3.5	
		AIR/O₂					9	16	25	15	76	155:40		
60	3:20	AIR				2	11	21	26	28	344	436:00	4	
		AIR/O₂				2	11	21	26	15	87	181:20		
Exceptional Exposure: SurDO₂ --														
70	3:20	AIR				7	19	24	25	39	454	572:00	5	
		AIR/O₂				7	19	24	25	20	109	228:20		
80	3:20	AIR			17	22	23	26	53	525	670:00	6	
		AIR/O₂			17	22	23	26	27	128	267:20		
90	3:00	AIR		7	20	22	23	37	66	574	752:40	7	
		AIR/O₂		7	20	22	23	37	33	148	318:20		
120	2:40	AIR	9	19	20	22	42	60	94	659	928:20	9	
		AIR/O₂	9	19	20	22	42	60	46	198	454:00		
180	2:20	AIR	10	18	19	40	43	70	97	156	703	1159:00	11.5	
		AIR/O₂	10	18	19	40	43	70	97	75	228	648:00		

Source: *U.S.Navy Diving Manual, Revision 6*

Table 9-9. *Air Decompression Table (Continued).*
(DESCENT RATE 75 FPM—ASCENT RATE 30 FPM)

Bottom Time (min)	Time to First Stop (M:S)	Gas Mix	DECOMPRESSION STOPS (FSW) Stop times (min) include travel time, except first air and first O$_2$ stop									Total Ascent Time (M:S)	Chamber O$_2$ Periods	Repet Group
			100	90	80	70	60	50	40	30	20			
180 FSW															
5	6:00	AIR									0	6:00	0	D
		AIR/O$_2$									0	6:00		
10	5:20	AIR									3	9:00	0.5	G
		AIR/O$_2$									2	8:00		
15	5:20	AIR									11	17:00	0.5	J
		AIR/O$_2$									6	12:00		
In-Water Air/O$_2$ Decompression or SurDO$_2$ Recommended --														
20	5:00	AIR								4	34	43:40	1	M
		AIR/O$_2$								2	18	25:40		
25	4:40	AIR							4	7	54	70:20	1.5	O
		AIR/O$_2$							4	4	26	39:40		
Exceptional Exposure: In-Water Air Decompression ------------ In-Water Air/O$_2$ Decompression or SurDO$_2$ Required ----------														
30	4:20	AIR						2	7	14	83	111:00	1.5	Z
		AIR/O$_2$						2	7	7	31	57:20		
35	4:20	AIR						5	13	19	138	180:00	2	Z
		AIR/O$_2$						5	13	10	40	78:20		
Exceptional Exposure: In-Water Air/O$_2$ Decompression ------------ SurDO$_2$ Required--														
40	4:00	AIR					2	11	12	28	175	232:40	2.5	Z
		AIR/O$_2$					2	11	12	14	47	96:00		
45	4:00	AIR					7	11	20	28	231	301:40	3	
		AIR/O$_2$					7	11	20	15	61	129:00		
50	3:40	AIR				1	11	13	25	28	276	358:20	3.5	
		AIR/O$_2$				1	11	13	25	15	74	153:40		
55	3:40	AIR				5	11	19	26	28	336	429:20	4	
		AIR/O$_2$				5	11	19	26	14	87	181:40		
Exceptional Exposure: SurDO$_2$ --														
60	3:40	AIR				8	13	24	25	31	405	510:20	4.5	
		AIR/O$_2$				8	13	24	25	16	100	205:40		
70	3:20	AIR			3	13	21	24	25	48	498	636:00	5.5	
		AIR/O$_2$			3	13	21	24	25	25	118	253:20		

Source: *U.S. Navy Diving Manual, Revision 6*

Table 9-9. *Air Decompression Table (Continued).*
(DESCENT RATE 75 FPM—ASCENT RATE 30 FPM)

Bottom Time (min)	Time to First Stop (M:S)	Gas Mix	DECOMPRESSION STOPS (FSW) Stop times (min) include travel time, except first air and first O₂ stop									Total Ascent Time (M:S)	Chamber O₂ Periods	Repet Group
			100	90	80	70	60	50	40	30	20			
190 FSW														
5	6:20	AIR									0	6:20	0	D
		AIR/O₂									0	6:20		
10	5:40	AIR									4	10:20	0.5	H
		AIR/O₂									2	8:20		
In-Water Air/O₂ Decompression or SurDO₂ Recommended ---														
15	5:40	AIR									17	23:20	0.5	K
		AIR/O₂									9	15:20		
20	5:00	AIR							1	7	37	50:40	1	N
		AIR/O₂							1	4	19	30:00		
25	4:40	AIR					2	6	9	67	89:20	1.5	Z
		AIR/O₂					2	6	5	28	46:40		
Exceptional Exposure: In-Water Air Decompression ------------- In-Water Air/O₂ Decompression or SurDO₂ Required ----------														
30	4:40	AIR					6	8	14	111	144:20	2	Z
		AIR/O₂					6	8	8	35	67:40		
35	4:20	AIR				3	8	13	22	160	211:00	2.5	Z
		AIR/O₂				3	8	13	12	44	90:20		
Exceptional Exposure: In-Water Air/0₂ Decompression ------------ SurDO₂ Required---														
40	4:20	AIR				7	12	14	29	210	277:00	3	
		AIR/O₂				7	12	14	15	56	119:20		
45	4:00	AIR			2	11	12	23	28	262	342:40	3.5	
		AIR/O₂			2	11	12	23	15	70	148:00		
50	4:00	AIR			7	11	16	26	28	321	413:40	4	
		AIR/O₂			7	11	16	26	15	83	178:00		
Exceptional Exposure: SurDO2 ---														
55	3:40	AIR			2	10	10	24	25	30	396	501:20	4.5	
		AIR/O₂			2	10	10	24	25	16	98	204:40		
60	3:40	AIR			5	10	16	24	25	40	454	578:20	5	
		AIR/O₂			5	10	16	24	25	21	108	233:40		
90	3:20	AIR		11	19	20	21	28	51	83	626	863:00	8.5	
		AIR/O₂		11	19	20	21	28	51	42	177	408:40		
120	3:00	AIR	15	17	19	20	37	46	79	113	691	1040:40	10.5	
		AIR/O₂	15	17	19	20	37	46	79	55	219	550:20		

Source: *U.S. Navy Diving Manual, Revision 6*

Table 9-9. *Air Decompression Table (Continued).*
(DESCENT RATE 75 FPM—ASCENT RATE 30 FPM)

Bottom Time (min)	Time to First Stop (M:S)	Gas Mix	DECOMPRESSION STOPS (FSW) Stop times (min) include travel time, except first air and first O₂ stop									Total Ascent Time (M:S)	Chamber O₂ Periods	Repet Group
			100	90	80	70	60	50	40	30	20			
200 FSW														
Exceptional Exposure														
5	6:00	AIR									1	7:40	0.5	
		AIR/O₂									1	7:40		
10	6:00	AIR									2	8:40	0.5	
		AIR/O₂									1	7:40		
15	5:40	AIR								2	22	30:20	0.5	
		AIR/O₂								1	11	18:20		
20	5:20	AIR							5	6	43	60:00	1	
		AIR/O₂							5	4	21	36:20		
25	5:00	AIR						5	6	11	78	105:40	1.5	
		AIR/O₂						5	6	6	29	52:00		
30	4:40	AIR					4	5	11	18	136	179:20	2	
		AIR/O₂					4	5	11	9	40	79:40		
35	4:20	AIR				1	6	10	13	26	179	240:00	2.5	
		AIR/O₂				1	6	10	13	13	49	102:20		
40	4:20	AIR				3	10	12	18	28	243	319:00	3	
		AIR/O₂				3	10	12	18	15	65	138:20		
45	4:20	AIR				8	11	12	26	28	300	390:00	3.5	
		AIR/O₂				8	11	12	26	15	79	166:20		
50	4:00	AIR			3	10	11	20	26	28	377	479:40	4.5	
		AIR/O₂			3	10	11	20	26	15	95	200:00		
210 FSW														
Exceptional Exposure														
5	6:20	AIR									1	8:00	0.5	
		AIR/O₂									1	8:00		
10	6:20	AIR									5	12:00	0.5	
		AIR/O₂									3	10:00		
15	6:00	AIR								5	26	37:40	1	
		AIR/O₂								3	13	22:40		
20	5:20	AIR						2	6	7	50	71:00	1.5	
		AIR/O₂						2	6	4	24	42:20		
25	5:00	AIR					2	6	7	13	94	127:40	1.5	
		AIR/O₂					2	6	7	7	32	65:00		
30	4:40	AIR				2	5	6	13	21	156	208:20	2	
		AIR/O₂				2	5	6	13	11	43	90:40		
35	4:40	AIR				5	6	12	14	28	214	284:20	3	
		AIR/O₂				5	6	12	14	14	58	124:40		
40	4:20	AIR			2	6	11	12	22	28	271	357:00	3.5	
		AIR/O₂			2	6	11	12	22	15	74	157:20		
45	4:20	AIR			4	10	11	16	25	29	347	447:00	4	
		AIR/O₂			4	10	11	16	25	15	89	190:20		
50	4:20	AIR			9	10	11	23	26	35	426	545:00	4.5	
		AIR/O₂			9	10	11	23	26	18	104	221:20		

Source: *U.S. Navy Diving Manual, Revision 6*

Table 9-9. *Air Decompression Table (Continued).*
(DESCENT RATE 75 FPM—ASCENT RATE 30 FPM)

220 FSW

Exceptional Exposure

Bottom Time (min)	Time to First Stop (M:S)	Gas Mix	100	90	80	70	60	50	40	30	20	Total Ascent Time (M:S)	Chamber O2 Periods	Repet Group
5	6:40	AIR									2	9:20	0.5	
		AIR/O2									1	8:20		
10	6:40	AIR									8	15:20	0.5	
		AIR/O2									4	11:20		
15	6:00	AIR							1	7	30	44:40	1	
		AIR/O2							1	4	15	27:00		
20	5:40	AIR						5	6	7	63	87:20	1.5	
		AIR/O2						5	6	4	27	48:40		
25	5:20	AIR					5	6	8	14	119	158:00	2	
		AIR/O2					5	6	8	7	38	75:20		
30	5:00	AIR				5	5	8	13	24	174	234:40	2.5	
		AIR/O2				5	5	8	13	13	47	102:00		
35	4:40	AIR			3	5	9	11	18	28	244	323:20	3	
		AIR/O2			3	5	9	11	18	15	66	142:40		
40	4:20	AIR		1	4	9	11	11	26	28	312	407:00	4	
		AIR/O2		1	4	9	11	11	26	15	82	179:20		

250 FSW

Exceptional Exposure

Bottom Time (min)	Time to First Stop (M:S)	Gas Mix	100	90	80	70	60	50	40	30	20	Total Ascent Time (M:S)	Chamber O2 Periods	Repet Group
5	7:40	AIR									3	11:20	0.5	
		AIR/O2									2	10:20		
10	7:20	AIR								2	15	25:00	0.5	
		AIR/O2								1	8	17:00		
15	6:40	AIR						3	7	7	41	65:20	1	
		AIR/O2						3	7	4	21	42:40		
20	6:00	AIR				2	6	5	7	12	106	144:40	2	
		AIR/O2				2	6	5	7	6	35	73:00		
25	5:40	AIR			4	5	5	7	13	24	175	239:20	2.5	
		AIR/O2			4	5	5	7	13	13	47	105:40		
30	5:20	AIR		4	4	5	9	11	20	28	257	344:00	3.5	
		AIR/O2		4	4	5	9	11	20	14	70	153:20		
35	5:00	AIR	2	5	4	10	11	14	25	29	347	452:40	4	
		AIR/O2	2	5	4	10	11	14	25	15	89	196:00		

300 FSW

Exceptional Exposure

Bottom Time (min)	Time to First Stop (M:S)	Gas Mix	100	90	80	70	60	50	40	30	20	Total Ascent Time (M:S)	Chamber O2 Periods	Repet Group
5	9:20	AIR									6	16:00	0.5	
		AIR/O2									3	13:00		
10	8:20	AIR						2	5	7	32	55:00	1	
		AIR/O2						2	5	4	16	36:20		
15	7:20	AIR			1	4	5	6	6	10	102	142:00	1.5	
		AIR/O2			1	4	5	6	6	5	35	75:20		
20	6:40	AIR	1	4	5	5	5	6	14	28	196	271:20	2.5	
		AIR/O2	1	4	5	5	5	6	14	15	52	124:40		
25	6:40	AIR	7	4	5	5	10	12	25	29	305	409:00	3.5	
		AIR/O2	7	4	5	5	10	12	25	15	80	180:20		

DECOMPRESSION STOPS (FSW) — Stop times (min) include travel time, except first air and first O2 stop.

Source: *U.S. Navy Diving Manual, Revision 6*

Table 2A-1. No-Decompression Limits and Repetitive Group Designators for Shallow Water Air No-Decompression Dives.

Depth (fsw)	No-Stop Limit (min)	Repetitive Group Designation															
		A	B	C	D	E	F	G	H	I	J	K	L	M	N	O	Z
30	371	17	27	38	50	62	76	91	107	125	145	167	193	223	260	307	371
31	334	16	26	37	48	60	73	87	102	119	138	158	182	209	242	282	334
32	304	15	25	35	46	58	70	83	98	114	131	150	172	197	226	261	304
33	281	15	24	34	45	56	67	80	94	109	125	143	163	186	212	243	281
34	256	14	23	33	43	54	65	77	90	104	120	137	155	176	200	228	256
35	232	14	23	32	42	52	63	74	87	100	115	131	148	168	190	215	232
36	212	14	22	31	40	50	61	72	84	97	110	125	142	160	180	204	212
37	197	13	21	30	39	49	59	69	81	93	106	120	136	153	172	193	197
38	184	13	21	29	38	47	57	67	78	90	102	116	131	147	164	184	
39	173	12	20	28	37	46	55	65	76	87	99	112	126	141	157	173	
40	163	12	20	27	36	44	53	63	73	84	95	108	121	135	151	163	
41	155	12	19	27	35	43	52	61	71	81	92	104	117	130	145	155	
42	147	11	19	26	34	42	50	59	69	79	89	101	113	126	140	147	
43	140	11	18	25	33	41	49	58	67	76	87	98	109	122	135	140	
44	134	11	18	25	32	40	48	56	65	74	84	95	106	118	130	134	
45	125	11	17	24	31	39	46	55	63	72	82	92	102	114	125		
46	116	10	17	23	30	38	45	53	61	70	79	89	99	110	116		
47	109	10	16	23	30	37	44	52	60	68	77	87	97	107	109		
48	102	10	16	22	29	36	43	51	58	67	75	84	94	102			
49	97	10	16	22	28	35	42	49	57	65	73	82	91	97			
50	92	9	15	21	28	34	41	48	56	63	71	80	89	92			

Source: *U.S. Navy Diving Manual, Revision 6*

Table 2A-2. *Residual Nitrogen Time Table for Repetitive Shallow Water Air Dives.*

Locate the diver's repetitive group designation from his previous dive along the diagonal line above the table. Read horizontally to the interval in which the diver's surface interval lies.

Next, read vertically downward to the new repetitive group designation. Continue downward in this same column to the row that represents the depth of the repetitive dive. The time given at the intersection is residual nitrogen time, in minutes, to be applied to the repetitive dive.

* Dives following surface intervals longer than this are not repetitive dives. Use actual bottom times in the Air Decompression Tables to compute decompression for such dives.

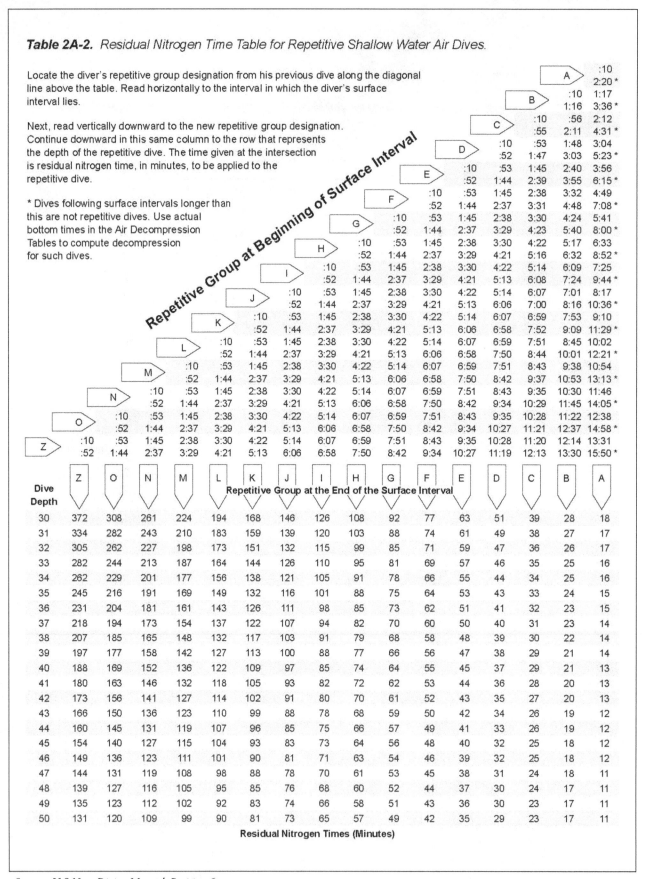

Dive Depth	Z	O	N	M	L	K	J	I	H	G	F	E	D	C	B	A
						Repetitive Group at the End of the Surface Interval										
30	372	308	261	224	194	168	146	126	108	92	77	63	51	39	28	18
31	334	282	243	210	183	159	139	120	103	88	74	61	49	38	27	17
32	305	262	227	198	173	151	132	115	99	85	71	59	47	36	26	17
33	282	244	213	187	164	144	126	110	95	81	69	57	46	35	25	16
34	262	229	201	177	156	138	121	105	91	78	66	55	44	34	25	16
35	245	216	191	169	149	132	116	101	88	75	64	53	43	33	24	15
36	231	204	181	161	143	126	111	98	85	73	62	51	41	32	23	15
37	218	194	173	154	137	122	107	94	82	70	60	50	40	31	23	14
38	207	185	165	148	132	117	103	91	79	68	58	48	39	30	22	14
39	197	177	158	142	127	113	100	88	77	66	56	47	38	29	21	14
40	188	169	152	136	122	109	97	85	74	64	55	45	37	29	21	13
41	180	163	146	132	118	105	93	82	72	62	53	44	36	28	20	13
42	173	156	141	127	114	102	91	80	70	61	52	43	35	27	20	13
43	166	150	136	123	110	99	88	78	68	59	50	42	34	26	19	12
44	160	145	131	119	107	96	85	75	66	57	49	41	33	26	19	12
45	154	140	127	115	104	93	83	73	64	56	48	40	32	25	18	12
46	149	136	123	111	101	90	81	71	63	54	46	39	32	25	18	12
47	144	131	119	108	98	88	78	70	61	53	45	38	31	24	18	11
48	139	127	116	105	95	85	76	68	60	52	44	37	30	24	17	11
49	135	123	112	102	92	83	74	66	58	51	43	36	30	23	17	11
50	131	120	109	99	90	81	73	65	57	49	42	35	29	23	17	11

Residual Nitrogen Times (Minutes)

Source: *U.S. Navy Diving Manual, Revision 6*

APPENDIX II

FORMS AND CHECKLISTS USED IN SURFACE-SUPPLIED DIVING OPERATIONS

SYSTEM PREDIVE CHECKS

Checks performed by lead diver prior to dress-in

Chamber	Confirm inner lock blown down to stop depth	
Chamber	Check and confirm medical O_2 pressure (off at chamber)	
Chamber Gas	Confirm chamber main and B/U gas supply pressure	
Main Gas	Confirm volume/pressure of mains (or compressor function)	
Backup Supply	Confirm B/U volume/pressure (or compressor function)	
Diver Egress	Confirm ladder ready and LARS function tested	
Hydraulics	Confirm LARS HPU and backup HPU are operational	

STANDBY DIVER PREDIVE CHECKS

Internal checks performed by standby diver and supervisor

Communications	Clear two-way communications (function test)	
Bailout Function	Diver breathes on bailout to prove proper function	
Main Gas Function	Diver closes bailout at hat; bleed off; supervisor opens main	

External checks performed by standby and lead diver on deck

Helmet Ready	Confirm helmet is cleaned, soaped, function tested	
Helmet Light	Supervisor flashes helmet light to function test	
Main Gas Supply	Lead diver reads out standby diver's main gas pressure	
Backup Gas	Lead diver reads out standby diver's backup pressure	
Bailout Secured	Confirm bailout is on at the bottle, off at the hat	
Bailout Pressure	Lead diver reads out bailout pressure from gauge	
Harnesses Secured	Confirm harness (stab jacket) is on properly and is tight	
Umbilical Secured	Confirm that snap shackle (carabiner) is secure on D-ring	
Suit Functioning	Test inflator(dry); test dump (hot water); visually inspect suit	
Diver's Knife	Confirm diver has a sharp knife in sheath	
Fins (boots)	Confirm diver has fins, protective boots, or ankle weights	
Rescue Lanyard	Confirm standby diver has a rescue lanyard	
Ready to Deploy	Confirm standby has hat and is ready to deploy	

Note:

All predive checks are recorded on the black box. The internal diver's checks are called out by the diver over the communications system. The external lead diver's checks are called out over handheld radio and relayed by the supervisor to the diver via the communications system. Any failure during the predive checks will mean postponing the dive until the component has been repaired and tested.

PREDIVE CHECKS FOR PRIMARY DIVER

Internal checks performed by diver and supervisor

Communications	Clear two-way communications (function test)	
Black Box	Test record capability of black box unit	
Bailout Function	Diver breathes on bailout to prove proper function	
Main Gas Function	Diver closes bailout at hat; bleed off; supervisor opens main	

External Checks performed by lead diver on deck

Helmet Secured	Visually check seal and hinge; check locking cam or pins	
Bailout Secured	Confirm bailout is on at the bottle, off at the hat	
Helmet Light	Supervisor flashes light on and off to confirm function	
Harnesses Secured	Confirm stab jacket or harness is on properly and tight	
Umbilical Secured	Confirm snap shackle (carabiner) is secure on D-ring	
Suit Functioning	Test inflator(dry); test dump (hot water); visually inspect suit	
Diver's Knife	Confirm diver has a sharp knife in sheath	
Fins (boots)	Confirm diver has fins, protective boots, or ankle weights	
Tools for Job	Confirm diver has all tools required for the job at ready	
Lines	Confirm down lines, swim lines or tool lines are in place	

Note:

All predive checks are recorded on the black box. The internal diver's checks are called out by the diver over the communications system. The external lead diver's checks are called out over handheld radio and relayed by the supervisor to the diver via the communications system. Any failure during the predive checks will mean postponing the dive until the component has been repaired and tested.

SURFACE DECOMPRESSION DIVE SHEET

Dive No.	Project:	Location:	Date

Diver:	Standby:	Tender:
Bailout Pressure:	HP Backup Pressure:	Main Gas Delivery:

LS:	Max Depth:	LB:	BT:
Table/Schedule:	Pneumos:		

Water Stops

Stop Depth	Time(Duration):	On Stop:	Leave:
Stop Depth	Time:	On Stop:	Leave:
Stop Depth	Time:	On Stop:	Leave:
Stop Depth	Time:	On Stop:	Leave:
Stop Depth	Time:	On Stop:	Leave:

Chamber Stops

Depth: 0 – 50fsw	Time:	Gas:	XXXXXXXXXX	XXXXXXXXXX
Depth:	Time:	Gas:	On Stop:	Leave:
Depth:	Time:	Gas:	On Stop:	Leave:
Depth:	Time:	Gas:	On Stop:	Leave:
Depth:	Time:	Gas:	On Stop:	Leave:
Depth:	Time:	Gas:	On Stop:	Leave:
Depth:	Time:	Gas:	On Stop:	Leave:
Depth:	Time:	Gas:	On Stop:	Leave:
Depth:	Time:	Gas:	On Stop:	Leave:
Depth:	Time:	Gas:	On Stop:	Leave:

Surface interval (minutes)	Decompression completed at:

Work performed:
Comments:

Supervisor Name_____   **Signature**_____

Dive Sheet for Single and Repetitive Dives

Diver 1 Main Gas Pressure:	Diver 1 Backup Gas Pressure:	Diver 2 Main Gas Pressure:	Diver 2 Backup Gas Pressure:

Diver		Location	Date
Leave Surface		Surface Interval	
Leave Bottom		New Group Letter	
Arrive Surface		Leave Surface	
Bottom Time		Leave Bottom	
Depth Dive One: Pneumo Readings:		Depth Dive Two: Pneumo Readings:	
Table/Schedule Used		Table/Schedule Used	R.N. Time
Group Letter		Total Bottom Time	
Decompression		Bailout Pressure Readings Before dive one Before dive two After dive two	
Comments Dive One		Comments Dive Two	
Standby Diver		Supervisor	

Supervisor Signature: _____

Daily Toolbox Safety Meeting

Supervisor Name: **Vessel:**

Signature: **Date:**

Make sure you perform the JSA required for each operation. **IF IN DOUBT ASK**

Meeting Topic:

Items Discussed During Meeting:

No.	Name	Position	Signature
1.		Diving Supervisor	
2.		Lead Diver	
3.		Diver Medic	
4.		Life Support Tech	
5.		Diver	
6.		Diver	
7.		Diver	
8.		Diver	
9.		Diver	
10.		Diver	
11.		Diver	
12.		Diver	

All crew members are to make note of the location of the following prior to commencing work:

Nearest fire extinguisher/fire hose cabinet

Nearest first aid station

Nearest life ring

Lifeboat station

Muster station for general alarm

JOB SAFETY ANALYSIS

Job Description:		Date:
Vessel:	Location:	Block:
Supervisor:	Client:	Job No:

Sequence of basic job steps	Potential accident or hazard	Recommended safe job procedure	Personnel responsible

- Additional Safety Equipment Required for This Job -			
__Permit to Work	__Fall Protection	__Full Face Shield	__Leather Gloves
__Lockout/tagout	__Work Vest	__Hearing Protection	__Fire Extinguisher
__Barrier Tape	__Respirator	__Cutting Goggles	__Other Equipment

Attending Personnel		
Name	Position	Signature
	Client Representative	
	Crane Operator	
	Diving Supervisor	
	Lead Diver	
	Diver Medic	
	Life Support Tech	
	Diver	
	Diver	
	Diver	
	Diver	
	Diver	
	Diver	
	Diver	
	Diver	
	Diver	

RECORD OF SAFETY TRAINING DRILL

Vessel/Platform:	Date:
Location/Project:	Shift:
Type of Drill:	Time:

Comments/ Description:

Participants:

Supervisor/Superintendent:	Signature:

Note:

The primary goal of safety training drills is to familiarize the crew with emergency procedures. Emphasis should be placed more on technique than on response time.

SAMPLE LOST COMMUNICATIONS PROTOCOL

In the event of lost communications between dive control and the diver, the dive is to be terminated as soon as safely possible.

1. As soon as communications between diver and surface are lost, the supervisor flashes the helmet light several times.

2. When the diver sees the helmet light flashing, the diver responds by hand signal in the helmet camera.

3. If the diver does not notice the flashing helmet light, standby diver will be deployed immediately.

4. Surface crew comes up on diver's umbilical.

5. Diver follows umbilical and proceeds to the down line or stage.

6. Once on down line or stage, diver keeps pneumo mid-chest and waits for stage to stop or, if on down line, **STOP** signal. The diver adjusts water stop elevation as directed by signals. If no signal, the diver proceeds directly to the dive ladder for surface decompression.

LINE PULL SIGNALS FOR SURFACE DECOMPRESSION

1 pull STOP

2 pulls DOWN – You have come too far, drop down until you are told to stop.

3 pulls UP – You are below your stop, come up until you are told to stop.

4 pulls UP – Come up now, your water stop is completed.

DDC Predive Checklist

Interior DDC Valve checks

Inner lock – Blowdown = OPEN	
Inner Lock – Exhaust = OPEN	
Inner Lock - BIBS OBDs = OPEN × 2	
Inner Lock – BIBS O_2 = OPEN × 2	
Inner Lock – BIBS Regulators Dialed Out × 2	
Inner Lock – Relief Valve = OPEN (secure)	
Inner Lock - Crossover = OPEN	
Inner Lock - Medical Lock Blowdown = OPEN	
Inner Lock – Medical Lock Door Crossover = CLOSED	
Inner Lock – Medical Lock Door = CLOSED and LATCHED	
Inner Lock – Pneumo & Theraputic = OPEN	
Inner Lock – Sample = OPEN	
Chamber Blanket Inside	
Chamber Bucket Inside	
Outer Lock – Blowndown = OPEN	
Outer Lock – Exhaust = OPEN	
Outer Lock – BIBS OBDs # 1 = OPEN (#2 closed)	
Outer Lock – BIBS O_2 # 1 = OPEN (#2 closed)	
Outer Lock – Relief = OPEN	
Outer Lock – Pneumo = OPEN	
Outer Lock – Sample = OPEN	
Outer Lock – Crossover = CLOSED	
Outer Lock – BIBS Regulators Dialed Out	

DDC Exterior Panel Valve checks

Pneumos (inner & outer) and Therapeutic Gauges = OPEN	
O_2 on at QUAD - on at DDC Pressure = 105 PSI/Bottle psi =	
O_2 Supply – Main Supply and to BIBS (inner) = OPEN	
O_2 Supply - Outer lock = OPEN	
Blowdowns Inner/Outer = CLOSED	
Exhausts Inner/Outer = CLOSED	
Relief Valves Inner/Outer = OPEN	
Drains Inner/Outer = CLOSED	
Overboard Dumps (inner) = OPEN	
Overboard Dumps (outer) = OPEN	
Main Air on to DDC Gauge/Off at Blowdowns Supply psi =	
Standby Air on at QUAD/Off at DDC panel Quad Supply psi = Regulated psi =	
Inner Lock @ 50 fsw -Outer Lock @ Surface – Dogs Off	
O_2 Meter Calibrated @ 21%	

DDC Postdive Checklist

Ensure all air and O_2 supplies are off at source; dial out O_2 reg	
Bleed pressure from gauges	
Bleed oxygen off BIBS	
Ensure all valves interior and exterior (unsecured) are OFF	
Check sound-powered phones	
Ensure chamber blanket is dry	
Remove BIBS oral nasal and clean	
Empty chamber bucket if used	
Wipe down chamber as required	
Ensure all valves off at DDC panel	
Visual both O-rings	
Dog both doors as required	

DP VESSEL/DIVING OPERATIONS INTERFACE CHECKLIST

ITEM	DESCRIPTION	DPIC	√
1	Master informed	Dive Sup Master	
2	DPOs informed	Dive Sup DPOs	
3	Chief Engineer informed	Dive Sup Chief Eng	
4	All suctions near the LARS isolated	Chief Eng	
5	Impressed current system isolated	Chief Eng	
6	Echo sounders/sonars off	Chief Eng	
7	Sewage treatment discharges isolated	Chief Eng	
8	No biodegradable waste thrown overboard during dive	Master	
9	Manned thruster controls	DPO	
10	Unused thrusters locked out/tagged out	Chief Eng DPO	
11	PTW for DP diving operations issued	Client Dive Sup Master	
12	Alpha flag displayed	Master	
	Day shapes displayed		
	Night lights displayed		
13	Note ship broadcast on VHF and field operations radio	DPO Dive Sup	

BRIDGE/DIVE CONTROL COMMUNICATIONS CHECKLIST

1	Hard-wired telephone	DPO Dive Sup L Diver	
2	VHF radio on dedicated diving channel	DPO Dive Sup L Dive	
3	VHF radio backup	DPO Dive Sup L Dive	
4	DP status lights (bridge to dive control)	DPO Dive Sup	

DP VESSEL/DIVING OPERATIONS INTERFACE CHECKLIST
PAGE TWO

REFERENCE SYSTEM CHECKLIST

5	GPS1 working and online	
6	GPS2 working and online	
7	FAN beam working and online	
8	Accoustic buoy working and online	
9	Taut wire working and online	

MISCELLANEOUS CHECKS

1	Vessel services in support of diving operations on line	Master Chief Eng	
2	Zodiac ready to deploy	Master Dive Sup	
3	Vessel in position and holding station	DPO	
4	Permit to dive received from vessel @ HRS	Dive Sup	

Diving Supervisor Name	Signature/Date
Master (Chief Mate) Name	Signature/Date

LOCKOUT TAGOUT TO ISOLATE EQUIPMENT
FOR DIVING OPERATIONS

VESSEL NAME:		DATE:
Location:	Vessel Master: Signature	
Chief Eng: Signature	Diving Supervisor: Signature	

EQUIPMENT TO BE ISOLATED	RESPONSIBLE PARTY	√
Main Propulsion System	Master/Chief Engineer	
Bow/Stern Thrusters	Master/Chief Engineer	
Dynamic Positioning System	Master/Chief Engineer	
Rudder	Master/Chief Engineer	
Main Intake Sea Chest	Chief Engineer	
Secondary Intake Sea Chests	Chief Engineer	
Fire-Fighting Water Intake	Chief Engineer	
Waste/Sewage Discharge	Chief Engineer	
Impressed Current Cathodic Protection	Chief Engineer	
Depth Sounder/SONAR	Master	

Is the master of the vessel aware of any other hazards to the diver?

Is the chief engineer aware of any other hazards to the diver?

Time Lockout Tagout put in place	
Time Lockout Tagout removed	

ACCIDENT/NEAR MISS REPORT FORM

Date of Incident	Location/Project		Vessel
Type of Incident: Near Miss Property Damage Personal Injury Fatality	Severity of Incident: No Lost Time Lost Time Medical Evacuation Long Term	Employee Name	
		Position	Job Experience

Home Address

Hrs on shift	Date Reported	Time Reported	Reported to:

Supervisor Name:		Witness Name:

Personal Protective Equipment	Yes/No	Describe the Incident
Hard Hat		
Safety Glasses		
Coveralls		
Safety Boots		
Hearing Protection		
Fall Arrest Harness		
Diving Helmet		
Bailout Bottle		
AR Vest and Harness		
Diving Coveralls		
Diving Gloves		

Describe Injury or Damage	Mitigating Factors

Contributing Factors	Report Prepared By
	Employee (witness) Signature/Date
	Supervisor/Superintendent Signature/Date

APPENDIX III

INTERNATIONAL CRANE SIGNALS
MANUAL AND VERBAL

International Hand Crane Signals

Stop	Hoist Load Slowly	Hoist Load	Auxiliary Hoist
Emergency Stop	Lower Load Slowly	Lower Load	Raise Boom & Lower Load
Travel (mobile eqpt)	Swing Boom Slowly	Swing Boom	Lower Boom & Raise Load
Dog Everything	Extend Boom 1 hand	Extend Boom 2 hands	Retract Boom 1 hand
Main Hoist	Raise Boom	Lower Boom	Retract Boom 2 hands

INTERNATIONAL VERBAL CRANE SIGNALS

Proper Use of Signals

For signaling a crane using verbal commands (radio), there are internationally recognized signals used. The rules for the proper use of these verbal signals are as follows:

- Only one banksman or signalman will direct the crane at any time.

- Anyone seeing a problem or safety issue may direct "All Stop" to the crane.

- The crane operator will repeat each signal prior to execution to ensure the signal has been received and understood.

- When using the main hoist or auxiliary hoist, the direction is **always** indicated first before the operation. For example, to raise the wire it is UP ON THE WIRE and never "Wire up." In all other operations, the operation is indicated first. For example, to swing to the operator's left it is SWING LEFT and to raise the boom it is BOOM UP.

- When using both hoists, always indicate the hoist to be used. For example, to lift the wire on the main it is UP ON THE MAIN WIRE. This is only required when using both hoists.

- In the event of cross-traffic or excessive static on the radio, operations will be stopped immediately, once the load is safe.

Verbal Crane Signals

When the crane operator and the banksman (signalman) cannot maintain visual contact, the following internationally recognized verbal crane signals are used.

ALL STOP
Stop whatever operation the crane is performing *immediately*, regardless what it is.

UP ON THE WIRE
Raise the crane wire. Travel speed may be adjusted by the words "slowly" or "easy."

DOWN ON THE WIRE
Lower the crane wire. Travel speed adjusted by the words "slowly" or "easy."

BOOM UP
Raise the crane boom. This operation is normally done at only one speed.

BOOM UP AND MAINTAIN LOAD*
Raise the boom and lower the load simultaneously to bring the load close to the crane.

BOOM DOWN
Lower the crane boom.

BOOM DOWN AND MAINTAIN LOAD*
Lower the boom and raise the load simultaneously to take the load away from the crane.

SWING LEFT

Swing to the crane operator's left. Swing speed adjusted by "slowly" or "easy."

SWING RIGHT

Swing to the crane operator's right. Swing speed adjusted by "slowly" or "easy."

DOG EVERYTHING

On conventional cranes, dog the boom and winches and engage swing brake or cab lock. On hydraulic cranes, hands off the controls.

*Not all cranes are capable of performing two operations simultaneously, particularly when handling heavier loads.

APPENDIX IV

PARTS LIST AND BLOW-APART DRAWINGS FOR COMMONLY USED BAND MASKS AND DEEP-SEA DIVING HELMETS

(KIRBY MORGAN DIVE SYSTEMS)

KIRBY MORGAN® Genuine Parts

Kirby Morgan 18 A/B P/N 500-025 / 500-026 & 28 P/N 500-028 / 500-029 Band Masks

Location #	Part #	Description
1	510-509	Head Harness (Spider)
2	525-740	KMB Hood Assembly, Foam Seal
3	545-015	Nose Block Device
	510-575	Nose Block Pad
4	520-020	Valve Body
5	510-550	Valve, Oral Nasal
6	530-060	Screw (18 only)
7 *	510-490	O-ring
	510-211	O-ring (28 & pre '99 18)
8 *	550-081	Regulator Mount Nut (350)
	550-038	Regulator Mount Nut (pre '05 28 & pre '99 18)
9	510-747	Oral Nasal Mask
10	515-005	Earphone, Right, 9"
10a		For Earphone Cover Set Order 510-842
10b	515-102	Communication Wire 9"
10c	530-098	Screw
10d	515-090	Earphone
10e	520-015	Protector, Earphone
10f		For Earphone Cover Set Order 510-842
10g	510-542	Covers, Earphone, Pre-April 2011
11	515-006	Earphone, Left, 15.5"
11a	515-101	Communication Wire 15.5"
11b	520-038	Tie-Wrap
12	515-009	Microphone
13	515-030	Communications Set
14	520-051	Comfort Insert (18 only)
15	530-097	Screw
16	545-007	Top Band
17 *	520-056	Mask, Fiberglass 1" Hole (18 only)
	520-055	Mask, Fiberglass (18 only, pre '99)
	520-125	Mask, Frame (28,1')
	520-096	Mask, Frame (⅞") (28, pre 2005)
18	530-535	Washer
19	530-415	Washer
20	530-317	Nut
21	545-016	Air Train
21a	510-762	Air Train Gasket KMB 18 ONLY
22	530-317	Nut
23	530-535	Washer
24	545-066	Standoff (28 only)
25	530-050	Screw
26	510-260	O-ring, View Port
27	520-004	Face Port (18 only)
	520-128	Face Port (28 & pre 1979 18's only)
28	560-070	Port Retainer
28n	550-116	Nose Block Guide
29	530-052	Screw, Port Plug
30	530-035	Screw
31	510-010	O-ring
32	510-008	O-ring
33	555-180	Packing Nut, Nose Block
34	550-062	Knob, Nose Block
35	525-752	Tri-Valve Exhaust (35a-35i)

Location #	Part #	Description
35a	510-786	Starboard Whisker Wing
35b	510-787	Port Whisker Wing
35c	510-761	Tri-Valve Exhaust Main Body
35d	520-200	Whisker Exhaust Valve Insert
35e	510-776	Exhaust Valve
35f	520-042	Tie Wrap
35g	520-118	Tri/Quad Valve Whisker Clamp
35h	530-008	Brass Screw
35i	530-009	Brass Nut
36	550-061	Spacer
37	540-015	Kidney Plate
38	530-045	Screw
39 *	545-080	Reg. Body, SuperFlow 350
	545-022	Regulator Body (pre '05 28 & pre '99 18)
40	550-060	Piston
41	535-807	Spring Set
42	550-059	Spacer
43	550-057	Shaft
44	530-055	Washer
45	510-011	O-ring
46	550-055	Packing Nut
47	550-053	Knob, Adjustment
48	530-601	Retaining Pin
49	530-030	Screw
50	545-020	Clamp
51	545-018	Cover Assembly
51a	535-905	Retaining Clip
51b	540-065	Cover Only, Regulator, Metal
51c	535-810	Spring, Purge Button
51d	520-017	Purge Button
51e*	520-078	Purge Button Sticker
	520-077	Purge Button Sticker (pre '05 28 & pre '99 18)
52	510-553	Diaphragm
53	530-303	Nut, Lock
54	550-052	Spacer
55	545-038	Roller Lever Arm Assembly
56	530-506	Washer
57 *	530-505	Washer (pre '05 28 & pre '99 18)
58 *	535-804	Spring (pre '05 28 & pre '99 18)
59	545-026	Inlet Valve
60	510-014	O-ring
61a	550-046	Inlet Nipple, "A"
61b	550-048	Inlet Nipple, "B"
61c	550-050	Jam Nut, "B"
62	510-552	Exhaust Valve
62a	540-122	Exaust Flange, Chrome
62b	510-401	Gasket
62c	530-020	Screw
63a	505-026	SuperFlow Regulator Assembly ("A" ⅞") (Order P/N 525-777)
63b *	505-027	SuperFlow Regulator Assembly ("B" ⅞") (pre '05 28 & pre '99 18) (Order P/N 525-773)
	505-069	SuperFlow 350 Regulator Assembly

Location #	Part #	Description
63c	505-028	Adjustment Knob Assembly
64	530-021	Screw
65	545-024	Cover, Water Dump (18)
	545-041	Cover, Water Dump, KMB 28
66	510-561	Valve, Water Dump, Black
67	550-063	Body, Water Dump (18 only)
68	545-009	Bottom Band
69	530-035	Screw (18 only)
70	550-040	Nut
71	530-308	Hex Nut
72	530-525	Kidney Plate
73	515-035	Communications Post
74	510-481	O-ring
75	550-043	Plug
76	555-175	Packing Gland
77	520-113	Ferrule Set
78	555-178	Packing Nut
79	515-045	W.P. Connector, Male (4 pin)
79a	505-047	W.P. Connector Assem. complt.
80	515-049	Single Wire Terminal
81	515-061	Terminal Block
82	550-019	Locknut
83	535-802	Spring
84	520-534	Flex Knob, Steady Flow
85	520-030	Washer
86	550-020	Bonnet
87	510-015	O-ring
88	520-031	Washer
89	510-010	O-ring
90	550-022	Valve Stem
91	550-023	Seat Assembly
92	550-024	Stud - Side Block
93a	550-026	Side Block - "A" N/A
93b	550-029	Side Block - "B", Chrome
94	550-140	Emergency Valve Body
95	550-138	Valve Stem, Emergency
96	540-095	Packing Washer
97	520-024	Packing
98	550-091	Packing Nut
99	520-525	Flex Knob, Emergency
100	535-802	Spring
101	550-019	Locknut
102	505-070	Emergency Valve Assembly
103	555-195	One-Way Valve
104	555-117	Adapter, Brass, 1/4" NPT(0,
105		Seat
106		Wiper
107		O-ring
108		O-ring
109		Poppet
110	510-483	Spring / Body
112		O-ring
113	505-060	One-Way Valve Assembly

	For Replacement Parts Kit
Order Complete see Loc. # 103	#525-330

O-ring
One-Way Valve Assembly

Location #	Part #	Description
114	550-095	L.P. Plug, w/O-ring
114b	310-003	O-ring
115a	510-011	O-ring
115b	520-033	O-ring, Teflon
116	555-154	Bent tube Assembly
117a	510-010	O-ring
117b	510-012	O-ring
118a	555-152	Regulator Hose w/O-rings
118b	555-155	Bent Tube Assem. w/O-rings
119a	505-022	"A" Side Block Assem. Complt.- N/A
119b	505-024	"B" Side Block Assem. Complt.
120	540-175	Bottom BandKeeper® Attachment Plate
120a	540-182	Bottom BandKeeper® Mount
121	530-073	Screw
122a	540-171	Top BandKeeper® Mount
122b	540-179	Top BandKeeper® Attachment Plate
122c	530-073	Screw
123	530-040	Screw
124	525-620	Tool Kit (not shown)

* As of January 1, 1999, all KMB 18B's are manufactured with the large tube SuperFlow 350 Regulators, part number 505-069, and a new frame part number 520-056. The large tube regulator cannot be retrofitted into pre '99 KMB 18B's without the purchase of a new frame. Small tube fiberglass frames, Part number 520-055, are available as replacement parts (see 17)

* As of September 2004, all KMB 28Bs are manufactured with the large tube SuperFlow 350 Regulators, part number 505-069, and a new frame part number 520-125. The large tube regulator cannot be retrofitted into pre September '04 KMB 28s without the purchase of a new frame. Small tube KMB 28 frames, Part number 520-096, are available as replacement parts (see 17)

Product Changes

Following publication of this booklet, certain changes in standard equipment, options, prices and the like may have occurred which would not be included in these pages. Your Authorized KMDSI dealer is your best source for up-to-date information on any of these products. © Kirby Morgan Dive Systems, Inc. reserves the right to change product specifications at any time without incurring obligations.

⚠ CAUTION

Use only Kirby Morgan original replacement parts. The use of other manufacturers' parts will interfere with the performance characteristics of your life support equipment and may jeopardize your safety. Additionally, any substitutions will void any warranties offered by KMDSI. When ordering spares, always insist on Kirby Morgan original parts.

Kirby Morgan Dive Systems, Inc.® 1430 Jason Way, Santa Maria, CA 93455
Phone: 805/928-7772 Fax: 805/928-0342
www.KirbyMorgan.com e-mail: kmdsi@KirbyMorgan.com

© MMXV Kirby Morgan Dive Systems, Inc. All rights reserved. Document #15070101.0

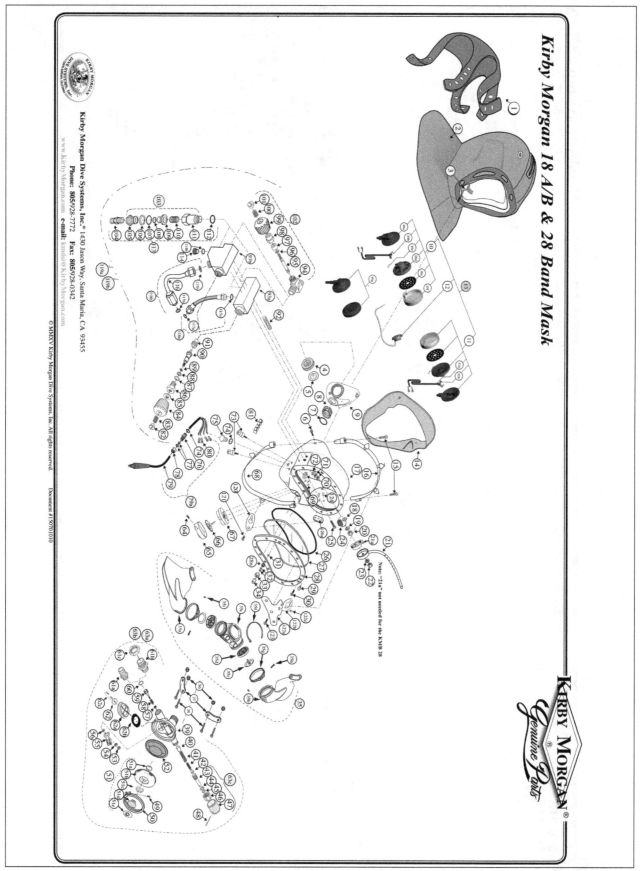

Kirby Morgan 18 A/B & 28 Band Mask

©MMXV Kirby Morgan Dive Systems, Inc. All rights reserved.   Document #150701010

Kirby Morgan Dive Systems, Inc.® 1430 Jason Way, Santa Maria, CA 93455
Phone: 805/928-7772   Fax: 805/928-0342
www.kirbymorgan.com   e-mail: kmdsi@kirbymorgan.com

Note: "21a" not needed for the KMB 28

©Kirby Morgan Dive Systems Inc, used with permission

KIRBY MORGAN® *Genuine Parts*

SuperLite® 17 A/B Helmet 500-010 / 500-011

Location #	Part #	Description
1	510-521	Head Cushion, SL 17A/B
	510-523	Replacement Foam
1a	525-745	Head Cushion Foam Spacer Kit (HCFS)
2	510-533	Drawstring Neck Dam
		Neck Clamp (Order Comp, see #7)
4	530-317	Nut
5	530-415	Washer
6	530-320	Nut, Lock
7	505-055	Neck Clamp Assembly
8-13		not used
14	505-008	Neck Clamp Yoke Assembly Comp.
15	530-066	Screw
16	530-601	Retaining Pin
17	550-255	Knob, Pull Pin
18	535-900	Safety Pin (Pull Pin)
19	560-051	Latch Catch Body
20	560-050	Latch Catch Body, Chrome
	535-808	Spring, Pull Pin
21	550-257	Plunger
22	505-010	Latch Catch Assem.. Pull Pin
23	530-034	17B Hinge Bolt, Electropolished
24	560-026	Hinge
	560-027	Hinge, Chrome
25	530-028	Lock Nut
26	540-157	Rear Hinge Tab, Electropolished
27	530-406	Washer
28	530-025	Screw
29	530-080	Screw
30	530-530	Washer
31	520-117	Urethane Yoke
	520-060	Fiberglass Yoke (Order 520-117)
32	550-019	Locknut
33	535-802	Spring
34	520-524	Flex Knob, Steady Flow
35	520-030	Washer
36	550-020	Bonnet
37	510-015	O-ring
38	520-031	Washer
39	510-010	O-ring
40	550-022	Valve Stem
41	550-023	Seat Assembly
42	550-024	Stud, Side Block
43a	550-026	A, Side Block Body (NOT AVAILABLE)
43b	550-029	B, Side Block Body
44a	510-011	O-ring
44b	520-033	O-ring (Teflon®)
45a	555-154	Bent Tube Assembly
45b	510-010	O-ring
46a	510-012	O-ring
46b	555-152	Reg. Hose Assem. w/O-rings
47a	555-155	Bent Tube Assem. w/O-rings
47b	550-095	L.P. Plug, w/O-ring
48	310-003	O-ring
49	550-140	Emergency Valve Body
50		
51	559-138	Valve Stem, Emergency
52	540-095	Packing Washer

Location #	Part #	Description
53	520-024	Packing
54	550-091	Packing Nut
55	520-525	Flex Knob, Emergency
56	535-802	Spring
57	550-019	Locknut
58	505-070	Emergency Valve Assembly
59	505-080	Emergency Valve Assembly, Brass
	510-483	O-ring
60		Body
61		Spring
62		Poppet [Order Complete see Loc. # 68]
63		O-ring [For Replacement Parts Order Kit #525-330]
64		Wiper
65		Seat
66	555-117	Adapter, Brass, ¼" NPT/02
67	555-195	One-Way Valve
68	505-060	One-Way Valve Assembly
70a	505-022	"A" Side Block Assembly (NOT AVAILABLE)
70b	505-024	"B" Side Block Assembly
	505-025	"B" Side Block Assembly, Brass
71	515-005	Earphone, Right, 9" [Order 510-842]
71a		For Earphone Cover Set [Order 510-842]
71b	515-102	Communication Wire 9"
71c	530-098	Screw
71d	515-090	Earphone Speaker
71e	520-015	Protector, Earphone
71f		Washer [For Earphone Cover Set Order 510-842]
71g	510-542	Covers, Earphone, Pre-April 2011
72	515-006	Earphone, Left, 15.5"
72a	515-101	Communication Wire 15.5"
72b	530-905	Tie-Wrap
73	515-009	Microphone
74	515-030	Communications Set
75	560-023	Starboard Weight, 17A/B
	560-022	Starboard Weight, 17A/B, Chrome
75a	560-070	Visor
76	530-070	Screw
77	530-540	Washer
78	545-027	Snap Tab
79	530-078	Screw
80	510-446	O-ring, SL 17A/B Bottom
81	510-211	O-ring
82	550-038	Nut, Regulator Mount
83	510-747	Oral Nasal Mask
84	510-550	Valve, Oral Nasal
85	520-020	Body, Valve
86	545-015	Nose Block device
	510-575	Nose Block Pad
87	530-090	Alignment Screw
88	550-339	Alignment Sleeve
89	560-006	Rear Weight, Chrome
	560-005	Rear Weight
90	530-070	Screw
91		Washer
92	520-065	Shell, Fiberglass
93	560-014	Handle, SL 17A/B
	560-015	Handle, SL 17A/B, Chrome

Location #	Part #	Description
94	530-040	Screw
95	560-019	Port Weight, SL 17A/B
96	530-535	Port Weight, SL 17A/B, Chrome
97	530-415	Washer
98	530-317	Nut
99	545-016	Air Train
99a	510-762	Air Train Gasket
100	510-535	Washer
101	530-317	Nut
102	530-050	Screw
103	530-052	Screw, Port Plug Screw
104	530-035	Screw
105	510-010	O-ring
106	510-008	O-ring
107	555-180	Packing Nut, Nose Block
	555-190	Packing Nut, Nose Block, Brass
108	550-062	Knob, Nose Block
	550-252	Knob, Nose Block, Brass
109	550-061	Spacer
110	540-015	Kidney Plate
111	550-116	Screw
112	545-022	Regulator Body
113	550-060	Piston
114	535-807	Spring Set
115	550-059	Spacer
116	550-057	Shaft
117	520-032	Washer
118	510-011	O-ring
119	550-055	Packing Nut
120	550-053	Knob, Adjustment
121	530-601	Retaining Pin
122	510-553	Diaphragm
123	545-018	Cover Assembly
123a	540-055	Retaining Clip
123b	535-810	Cover Only, Regulator, Metal
123c	520-017	Spring, Purge Button
123d	520-077	Purge Button
123e	530-030	Purge Button Sticker
124	545-020	Screw
125	530-303	Clamp
126	550-052	Nut, Lock
127	545-038	Spacer
128	530-506	Washer
129	550-046	Roller Lever Arm Assembly
130a	550-050	Inlet Nipple "A"
131a		Jam Nut "B"
131b	510-014	Inlet Nipple "B"
132a		O-ring
132b	545-026	O-ring
133	510-580	Inlet Valve
134	530-505	Inlet Valve Seat
134a	535-804	Washer
134b	510-552	Spring
135		Exhaust Valve
136	505-026	Demand Reg. Assem. "A" (spare part) [Purchase 525-777 Kit]
137		

Location #	Part #	Description
138a	505-027	Demand Reg. Assem. "B" (standard) [Purchase 525-773 Kit]
138b	505-028	Reg. Adjustment Knob Assem.
139	510-554	Whisker, Rubber (Pre 2004)
140	525-759	Quad-Valve Exhaust Kit
140a	510-786	Starboard Whisker Wing
140b	510-787	Port Whisker Wing
140c	510-760	Quad Valve Exhaust Main Body
140d	520-200	Whisker Exhaust Valve Insert
140e	510-776	Exhaust Valve
140f	520-042	Tie Wrap
140g	520-118	Tri/Quad Valve Whisker Clamp
140h	530-008	Brass Screw
140i	530-009	Brass Nut
141	550-116	Nose Block Guide
	550-249	Nose Block Guide, Brass
142	560-070	Port Retainer Assembly
	560-071	Port Retainer Assembly, Brass
143	520-004	Face Port
	520-128	Face Port, pre 1979
144	510-260	O-ring, View Port
145	550-040	Nut
146	530-308	Hex Nut
147	530-525	Washer
148	540-054	Earphone Retainer
149	530-032	Screw
150	530-035	Screw (Pre 2005)
151	550-063	Body, Water Dump
	510-561	Valve, Water Dump, Black
152	530-021	Screw
152a	545-024	Cover, Water Dump (Pre 2005)
152b	530-019	Screw, Quad Exhaust
152c	510-007	O-ring, Quad Exhaust Screw
153a	560-530	Cover, Water Dump Adapter
153b	520-042	Tie Wrap, Quad Exhaust
153c	510-033	O-ring, Quad Exhaust
154	515-061	Terminal Block
155	515-035	Communications Post
156	510-481	O-ring
157	550-043	Plug
158	515-049	Single Wire Terminal
159	515-045	Waterproof Connector, (Male) 4-Pin
160	510-481	O-ring
161	555-175	Packing Gland
162	520-113	Ferrule Set
163	555-178	Packing Nut
164	505-047	W.P. Connector Assembly
165	505-130	Chin Strap
166	505-134	Yoke Strap
167	505-138	Strap Guide
	525-620	Tool Kit (not shown)

Kirby Morgan Dive Systems, Inc.® 1430 Jason Way, Santa Maria, CA 93455
Phone: 805/928-7772 Fax: 805/928-0342 e-mail: kmdsi@KirbyMorgan.com
www.KirbyMorgan.com

© MMXV Kirby Morgan Dive Systems, Inc. All rights reserved.   Document #1507H1002

©Kirby Morgan Dive Systems Inc, used with permission

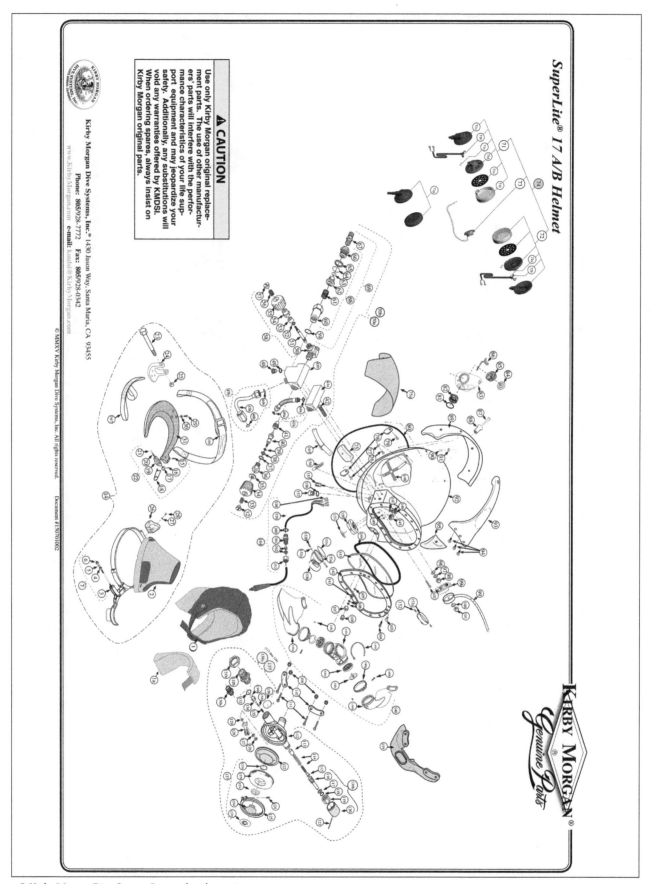

SuperLite® 17 A/B Helmet

⚠ CAUTION

Use only Kirby Morgan original replacement parts. The use of other manufacturers' parts will interfere with the performance characteristics of your life support equipment and may jeopardize your safety. Additionally, any substitutions will void any warranties offered by KMDSI. When ordering spares, always insist on Kirby Morgan original parts.

Kirby Morgan Dive Systems, Inc.® 1430 Jason Way, Santa Maria, CA 93455

Phone: 805/928-7772   **Fax:** 805/928-0342

www.KirbyMorgan.com   **e-mail:** kmdsi@KirbyMorgan.com

© MMXV Kirby Morgan Dive Systems, Inc. All rights reserved.   Document #150701002

©Kirby Morgan Dive Systems Inc, used with permission

Kirby Morgan 37 Helmet   500-050 / 500-051

Location #	Part #	Description
1	520-054	Visor
2	510-754	Head Cushion Assembly
	510-722	Head Cushion Bag
3	510-837	Head Cushion Foam Spacer Assembly
	510-836	Head Cushion Foam Spacer Bag
4	510-683	Chin Cushion Assembly
	510-639	Chin Cushion Bag
5	505-024	Side Block Assembly (B)
	505-025	Side Block Assembly (B), Brass
6	520-033	O-ring, Teflon®
7	555-154	Bent tube Assembly, No O-rings
8	510-012	O-ring
9	555-155	Bent Tube Assem w/O-rings
10	560-125	Weight, Top
	560-116	Weight, Top, Brass
11	530-070	Screw
12	530-032	Screw
13	530-070	Screw
14	530-540	Washer
15	505-107	Helmet Shell, 37 with Ring
16	530-078	Screw
17	530-540	Washer
18	530-527	Washer
19	530-078	Screw
20	560-133	Handle, 37
	560-136	Handle, Brass, 37
21	560-192	Plaque, 37
22	560-194	Handle with Plaque, 37
	560-195	Handle with Plaque, Brass 37
23	530-045	Screw
24	510-762	Air Train Gasket
25	530-050	Screw
26	530-535	Washer
27	530-415	Washer, Lock
28	530-317	Nut
29	545-016	Air Train
30	530-535	Washer
31	530-317	Nut
32	560-032	Weight, Port Side
	560-033	Weight, Port Side, Brass
33	530-062	Screw
34	530-052	Screw
35	530-035	Screw
36	550-062	Knob, Nose Block
	550-252	Knob, Nose Block, Brass
37	555-180	Packing Nut
	555-190	Packing Nut, Brass
38	510-008	O-ring
39	550-116	Nose Block Guide
	550-249	Nose Block Guide, Brass
40	560-070	Port Retainer, w/#39
	560-071	Port Retainer, Brass, w/#39 Brass
41	510-010	O-ring
42	520-004	Face Port
43	510-260	O-ring, View Port
44	530-015	Screw
45	505-110	Sealed Pull Pin
46	530-032	Screw
47	525-116	Screw
48	525-116	Front Stand Off
49	550-063	Body, Water Dump
50	550-561	Valve, Water Dump, Black
51	510-033	O-ring
52	520-042	Tie Wrap
53	530-019	Screw
54	510-007	O-ring
55	560-530	Cover, Water Dump Adapter
56	505-111	Chin Strap Assembly *Purchase 525-716 Kit*
57	510-786	Starboard Whisker Wing
58	510-760	Quad Valve Exhaust Main Body
59	520-042	Tie Wrap
60	520-200	Whisker Exhaust Valve Insert
61	510-776	Exhaust Valve
62	520-118	Tri/Quad Valve Whisker Clamp
63	530-008	Brass Screw
64	530-009	Brass Nut
65	510-787	Port Whisker Wing
66	505-730	Quad Valve Exhaust Assembly
67	530-045	Spacer
68	550-061	Spacer
69	540-015	Kidney Plate
70	505-069	SuperFlow® 350 Regulator Assembly *Purchase 525-771 Kit*
71	530-546	Washer for Swing Catch
72	530-035	Screw
73	550-061	Spacer
74	540-086	Swing Catch
75	520-167	Teflon® Washer for Swing Catch
76	535-825	Spring, Swing Catch
77	530-045	Screw
78	550-122	Spring Spacer
79	505-119	Neck Ring Assembly (neoprene) Med.
80	530-545	Washer
81	530-028	Lock Nut
82	560-111	Locking Collar
83	550-113	Adjustment Nut, Neck Pad
84	520-098	Neck Pad
85	530-064	Screw
86	550-045	T-Washer
87	530-027	Hinge Bolt
88	520-165	Washer
89	320-026	Comm. Mount Nut
90	515-029	Microphone Assembly
91	515-019	Earphone, Left, 15.5"
92	515-018	Earphone, Right, 9"
93	515-024	Comm. Assembly w/MWP
94	515-023	Comm. Assembly w/Posts
95	510-575	Nose Block Pad
96	545-015	Nose Block Device
97	520-020	Valve Body
98	510-550	Valve, Oral Nasal
99	510-747	Oral Nasal Mask
100	550-081	Nut, Regulator Mount
101	510-490	O-ring
102	540-054	Earphone Retainer
103	530-519	Washer
104	530-018	Screw
105	530-702	Snap
106	530-527	Washer
107	530-031	Screw

⚠ CAUTION

Use only Kirby Morgan original replacement parts. The use of other manufacturers' parts will interfere with the performance characteristics of your life support equipment and may jeopardize your safety. Additionally, any substitutions will void any warranties offered by KMDSI. When ordering spares, always insist on Kirby Morgan original parts.

Kirby Morgan Dive Systems, Inc.® 1430 Jason Way, Santa Maria, CA 93455
Phone: 805/928-7772   Fax: 805/928-0342   e-mail: kmdsi@KirbyMorgan.com
www.KirbyMorgan.com   Document #150701005

© MMXV Kirby Morgan Dive Systems, Inc. All rights reserved.

©Kirby Morgan Dive Systems Inc, used with permission

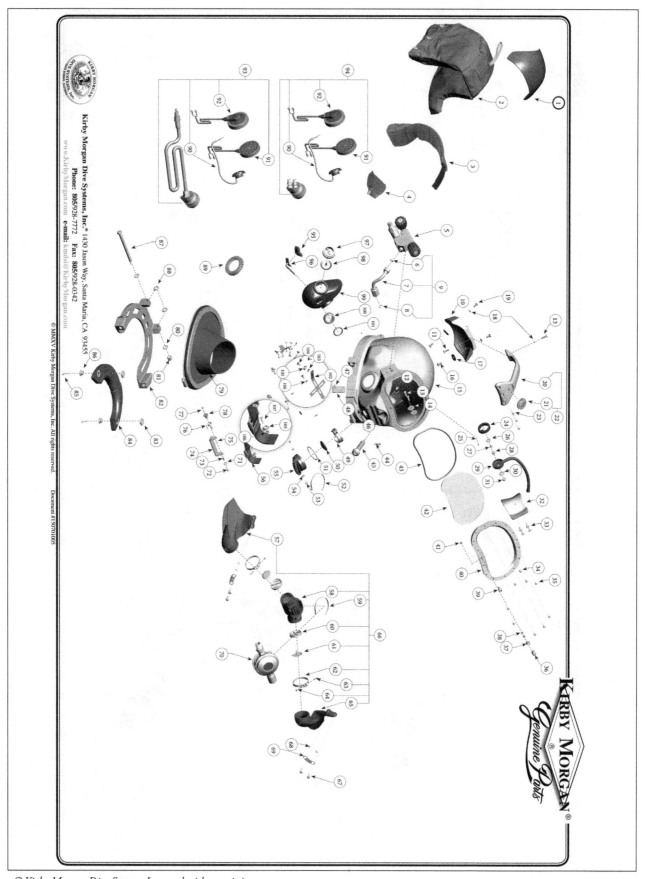

Kirby Morgan Dive Systems, Inc.® 1430 Jason Way, Santa Maria, CA 93455
Phone: 805/928-7772   Fax: 805/928-0342
www.KirbyMorgan.com   e-mail: kmdsi@KirbyMorgan.com
© MMXV Kirby Morgan Dive Systems, Inc. All rights reserved.   Document #150701005

©Kirby Morgan Dive Systems Inc, used with permission

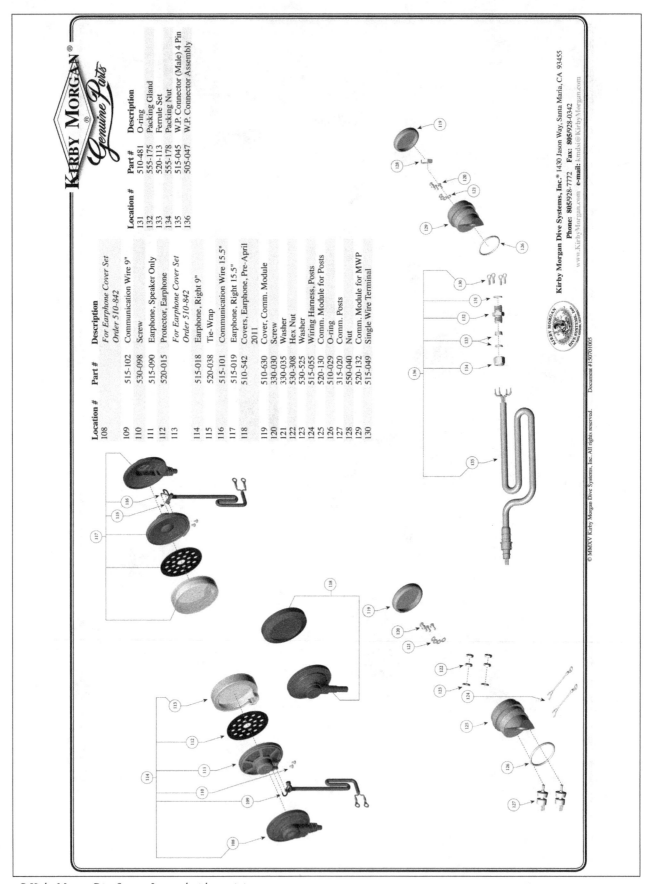

Location #	Part #	Description
108		For Earphone Cover Set Order 510-842
109	515-102	Communication Wire 9"
110	530-098	Screw
111	515-090	Earphone, Speaker Only
112	520-015	Protector, Earphone
113		For Earphone Cover Set Order 510-842
114	515-018	Earphone, Right 9"
115	520-038	Tie-Wrap
116	515-101	Communication Wire 15.5"
117	515-019	Earphone, Right 15.5"
118	510-542	Covers, Earphone, Pre-April 2011
119	510-630	Cover, Comm. Module
120	330-030	Screw
121	330-035	Washer
122	530-308	Hex Nut
123	530-525	Washer
124	515-055	Wiring Harness, Posts
125	520-130	Comm. Module for Posts
126	510-029	O-ring
127	315-020	Comm. Posts
128	550-040	Nut
129	520-132	Comm. Module for MWP
130	515-049	Single Wire Terminal

Location #	Part #	Description
131	510-481	O-ring
132	555-175	Packing Gland
133	520-113	Ferrule Set
134	555-178	Packing Nut
135	515-045	W.P. Connector (Male) 4 Pin
136	505-047	W.P. Connector Assembly

©Kirby Morgan Dive Systems Inc, used with permission

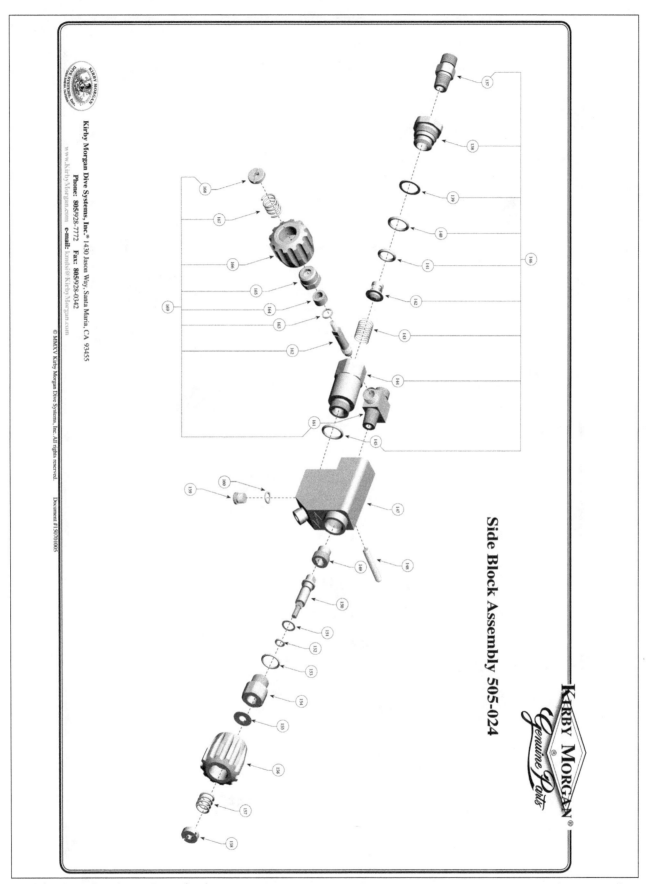

Side Block Assembly 505-024

Kirby Morgan Dive Systems, Inc.® 1430 Jason Way, Santa Maria, CA 93455
Phone: 805/928-7772 Fax: 805/928-0342
www.kirbymorgan.com e-mail: kmdsi@KirbyMorgan.com

© MMXV Kirby Morgan Dive Systems, Inc. All rights reserved.   Document # 150701005

©Kirby Morgan Dive Systems Inc, used with permission

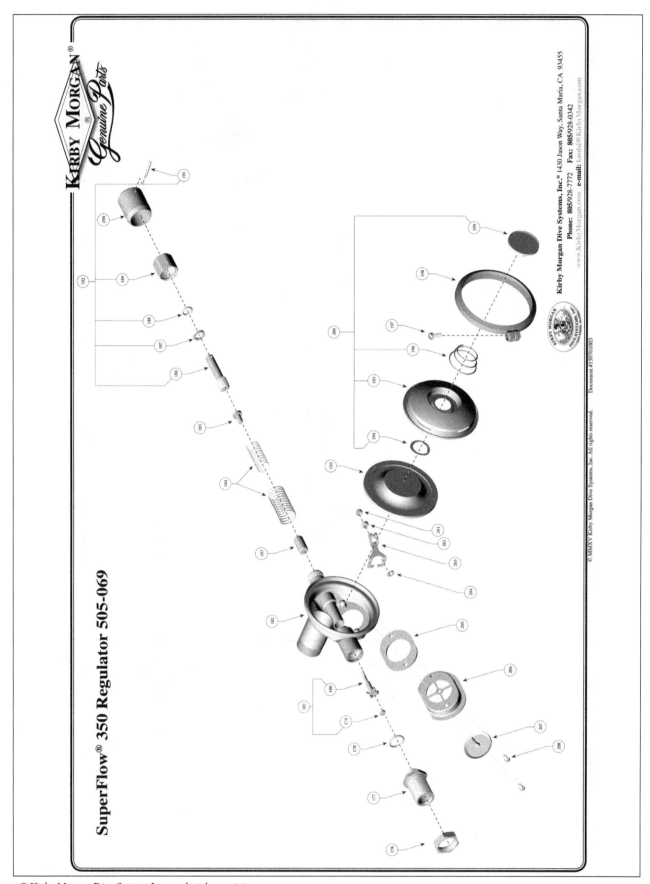

SuperFlow® 350 Regulator 505-069

©MMXV Kirby Morgan Dive Systems, Inc. All rights reserved.   Document #150701003

Kirby Morgan Dive Systems, Inc.® 1430 Jason Way, Santa Maria, CA 93455
Phone: 805/928-7772   Fax: 805/928-0342
www.KirbyMorgan.com   e-mail: kmdsi@KirbyMorgan.com

©Kirby Morgan Dive Systems Inc, used with permission

Side Block Assembly 505-024

Location #	Part #	Description
143	Order 555-117	Adapter
144	Order 555-195	Seat
145	Order 525-330	Wiper
146	Order 525-330	O-ring
147	Order 525-195	Poppet
148	Order 555-195	Spring
149	Order 525-330	Spring
150	Order 555-195	One-Way Valve
151	510-483	O-ring
152	505-060	One-Way Valve Assembly
153	550-029	Side Block, Body 'B'
154	550-024	Stud
155	550-023	Seat Assembly
156	550-022	Valve Stem
157	520-031	Washer
158	510-010	O-ring
159	510-015	O-ring
160	520-020	Bonnet
161	520-030	Washer
162	520-524	Flex Knob, Steady Flow
163	535-802	Spring
164	550-019	Lock Nut
165	550-095	Plug
166	310-003	O-ring
167	550-140	Emergency Valve Body
168	550-138	Valve Stem, Emergency
169	540-095	Packing Washer
170	520-024	Packing
171	550-091	Packing Nut
172	520-525	Flex Knob, Emergency Valve
173	535-802	Spring
174	550-019	Locknut
175	505-070	Emergency Valve Assembly

Location #	Part #	Description
178	510-014	O-ring
179	510-580	Inlet Valve
180	550-076	Inlet Valve Seat
181	545-026	Inlet Valve
182	545-080	Regulator Body
183	550-060	Piston
184	535-807	Spring Set
185	550-059	Spacer
186	550-057	Shaft
187	520-032	Washer
188	510-011	O-ring
189	550-055	Packing Nut
190	550-053	Knob, Adjustment
191	530-601	Retaining Pin
192	505-028	Regulator Adjustment Knob Assembly
193	510-553	Diaphragm
194	535-905	Retaining Clip
195	540-055	Cover Only, Regulator, Metal
196	535-810	Spring, Purge Button
197	530-030	Screw
198	545-020	Clamp
199	520-017	Purge Button
200	545-018	Cover Assembly
201	530-303	Nut, Lock
202	550-052	Spacer
203	545-038	Roller Lever Arm Assembly
204	530-506	Washer
205	510-401	Gasket
206	540-122	Exhaust Flange, Chrome Order P/N 525-027 Flange Kit
207	510-552	Exhaust Valve
208	530-020	Screw

SuperFlow® 350 Regulator Assembly 505-069 (Order P/N 525-771)

Location #	Part #	Description
176	550-050	Jam Nut
177	550-048	Inlet Nipple

Neck Ring Assembly, (Latex) Medium P/N 505-101

Location #	Part #	Description
209	540-105	Split Ring, (2 Required)
210	510-631	Latex Neck Dam, Medium
211	510-450	O-ring, Neck Ring
212	530-312	Clip, Hinge Pin
213	550-216	Front Yoke Hinge
214	530-018	Screw
215	530-024	Screw
216	530-022	Screw
217	530-220	Screw
218	540-115	Strap Plate
219	505-142	Pull Strap Assembly
220	530-311	Pin, Front Yoke Hinge
221	520-012	Front Yoke
222	540-056	Catch, Front Yoke
223	560-078	Stepped Neck Dam Ring

Kirby Morgan Dive Systems, Inc.® 1430 Jason Way, Santa Maria, CA 93455
www.kirbymorgan.com e-mail: kmdsi@kirbymorgan.com
Phone: 805/928-7772   Fax: 805/928-0342
© MMXV Kirby Morgan Dive Systems, Inc. All rights reserved.   Document #150701003

©Kirby Morgan Dive Systems Inc, used with permission

APPENDIX V

OMITTED DECOMPRESSION

Emergencies occurring during the dive may either interrupt decompression or cause one or more of the scheduled decompression stops to be missed altogether. Also, events may occur during the dive or during the decompression that cause the diving supervisor to choose to abandon the scheduled decompression in order to keep the diver or the diving crew safe. Omitted decompression events, therefore, may be planned or unplanned. These events or emergencies may include the following:

- Distraction affecting the diving supervisor or timekeeper, causing deviation from schedule
- Un-forecasted extreme weather event occurring very rapidly
- Inability to keep station (run-off of DP vessel, vessel anchor dragging)
- Unplanned movement of other vessels (vessel approaching the dive station)
- Uncontrolled ascent (diver losing grip on down-line, diver experiencing blow-up)
- Equipment malfunction (malfunctioning LARS, helmet or gas malfunction)
- Diver sustaining trauma injury in-water (prior to or during decompression)

Decompression schedules have been developed, tested and proven to safely eliminate inert gas. Failure to follow these decompression schedules puts the diver at risk of decompression sickness. Knowing this, we realize that omitted decompression is serious and must be dealt with properly. Divers who have omitted decompression may or may not present symptoms. If they do present symptoms, they are treated using flow charts and treatment tables according to the symptoms presented as they would be in any other case of pressure-related illness. However, if a diver has omitted decompression and is not presenting symptoms, there are procedures that must be followed to avoid pressure-related illness. See Table 9-3 from the *U.S. Navy Diving Manual (Rev 6)* below.

Table 9-3. *Management of Asymptomatic Omitted Decompression.*

Deepest Decompression Stop Omitted	Surface Interval (Note 1)	Action	
		Chamber Available (Note 2)	No Chamber Available
None	Any	Observe on surface for 1 hour	
20 or 30 fsw	Less than 1 min	Return to depth of stop. Increase stop time by 1 min. Resume decompression according to original schedule.	
	1 to 7 min	Use Surface Decompression Procedure (Note 3)	Return to depth of stop. Multiply 30 and/or 20 fsw air or O_2 stop times by 1.5.
	Greater than 7 min	Treatment Table 5 if 2 or fewer SurDO$_2$ periods Treatment Table 6 If more than 2 SurDO$_2$ periods	
Deeper than 30 fsw	Any	Treatment Table 6 (Note 4)	Descend to depth of first stop. Follow the schedule to 30 fsw. Switch to O_2 at 30 fsw if available. Multiply 30 and 20 fsw air or O_2 stops by 1.5.

Notes:
1. For surface decompression, surface interval is the time from leaving the stop to arriving at depth in the chamber.
2. Using a recompression chamber is strongly preferred over in-water recompression for returning a diver to pressure. Compress to depth as fast as possible not to exceed 100 fsw/min.
3. For surface intervals greater than 5 minutes but less than or equal to 7 minutes, increase the oxygen time at 50 fsw from 15 to 30 minutes.
4. If a diver missed a stop deeper than 50 fsw, compress to 165 fsw and start Treatment Table 6A.

US Navy Diving Manual, Revision 6

Uncontrolled Ascent on a No-Decompression Dive

If a diver makes an uncontrolled ascent to surface at a rate greater than 30 fsw per minute but the dive itself was a no-decompression dive, observe the diver on surface for one hour for signs and symptoms of either decompression sickness or arterial gas embolism. The chamber should be readied, but only treat the diver if symptoms present. If the dive location is remote from the nearest chamber, proceed to the nearest chamber location as soon as possible. In the event that symptoms do present, begin treatment immediately.

Omitted 30 and 20 Fsw Decompression Stops

If a diver fails to complete some or all of the scheduled time on the 30 or 20 fsw decompression stops, the following procedure is to be followed:

1. If the diver is on surface for less than one minute, return the diver to the stop he or she left, adding one minute to the stop time at that depth. Resume decompression following the original schedule.

2. If the diver is on surface for over one minute, but less than 5 minutes with a chamber available, complete the decompression using surface decompression. Immediately blow the diver down to 50 fsw on oxygen. If the diver was on an in-water oxygen stop at the time, compute chamber time by multiplying the remaining oxygen time on all stops by 1.1, then dividing that total by 30 minutes. Round up the result to the next higher half-period. If the diver was on an in-water air stop, first convert air time to oxygen time as follows: 1) obtain the air/oxygen trading ratio by dividing the total time shown in the table for this stop on air by the total time shown for this stop on oxygen. 2) Divide the remaining air time at this stop by the trading ratio to determine the equivalent oxygen time at this stop. 3) If the diver was on a 30 fsw stop, add the required oxygen time for the 20 fsw stop to the 30 fsw stop time. 4) Multiply this total by 1.1 and divide by 30 minutes. 5) Round the result up to the next higher half-period. In all instances, the minimum requirement is one half period (15 minutes @ 50 fsw on oxygen).

3. If the diver is on surface for more than 5 minutes but not more than 7 minutes, follow step 2 in the procedure above, but increase the time on oxygen at 50 fsw from 15 to 30 minutes.

4. If the diver is on surface for more than 7 minutes and the surface decompression schedule of the original dive required 2 oxygen periods or less, place the diver in the chamber and treat on a Treatment Table 5. If the original dive required 2.5 oxygen periods or more, treat on a Treatment Table 6.

5. If the diver is on surface for more than 1 minute and no chamber is available, return the diver to the depth of the omitted stop and continue in-water decompression by multiplying the length of all remaining air or oxygen stops by 1.5.

Omitted Decompression Stops Deeper than 30 fsw

If a diver fails to complete all or part of an in-water decompression stop at 40 fsw or deeper, immediately press the diver to 60 fsw in the chamber and begin a Treatment Table 6. If there is no chamber on site, return the diver to the first in-water decompression stop. Follow the original decompression schedule to the 30 fsw stop. If in-water oxygen is an option, switch to oxygen. Complete decompression from 30 fsw by multiplying all remaining air or oxygen stops required for this dive by 1.5.

Problem:

A diver has just finished working and has left bottom. His maximum depth was 44 fsw, and his bottom time was 121 minutes. His planned decompression was in-water air. He was 6 minutes into his 20 fsw water stop when he had to be brought to surface because a fishing vessel was approaching the LARS and would not respond to warnings. It takes exactly 3 minutes to dress this diver down and get him into the chamber for decompression. Describe how this situation is properly handled.

Solution:

According to step 2 in the procedure above, first we convert the air time to oxygen time by dividing his air stop time (34 min) by his oxygen stop time (12 min) resulting in a trading ratio of 2.83. Next, we divide his remaining air stop time (28 minutes) by the trading ratio, giving as a result of 10 minutes. Next, we multiply this result (10 min) by 1.1, giving us a result of 11. We then divide 11 by 30 minutes to obtain a result of 0.367. We then round this up to the next higher oxygen period which is 0.5 periods. This diver requires one-half oxygen breathing period (15 minutes) at 50 fsw in the chamber.

Problem:

A diver had to be recovered before she could start her decompression because an anchor cable broke. When the anchor cable broke, it destroyed the air supply regulators to the decompression chamber so there was now no chamber available. By the time everything is stabilized, the diver has been on deck for 3 minutes. She had required 14 minutes on an in-water air stop before things went bad, and you are not set up for in-water oxygen decompression. How do we handle this?

Solution:

When we look at step 5 in the procedure, we are told to return the diver to the depth of her omitted stop and to multiply any remaining air or oxygen stop time by 1.5. She originally required 14 minutes at 20 fsw, so we return her to 20 fsw for 21 minutes.

SELECTED BIBLIOGRAPHY

Bozanic J, Dinsmore D, editors. *NOAA Diving Manual 5th edition*. North Palm Beach, FL: Best Publishing Company; 2013.

Convention on the International Regulations for Preventing Collisions at Sea. International Maritime Organization; 2003.

Defence and Civil Institute of Environmental Medicine (DCIEM) Manual. DCIEM; 1982.

Edmonds C, Lowry C, Pennefather J. *Diving and Subaquatic Medicine 4th Edition*. Mosman, Australia: Diving Medical Centre; 1976.

IMCA D014 Rev. 2, International Code of Practice for Offshore Diving. London, UK: International Marine Contractors Association (IMCA); 2014

IMCA D023 Rev. 1, Guidance (DESIGN) for Surface Oriented Diving Systems. London, UK: IMCA; 2014.

IMCA D022 Rev. 1, Guidance for Diving Supervisors. London, UK: IMCA; May 2014.

IMCA D024 Rev. 2, Guidance (DESIGN) for Surface Oriented Diving Systems. London, UK: IMCA; 2014.

Lomax, H. *The Commercial Diver's Handbook*. North Palm Beach, FL: Best Publishing Company; 2013.

Maas, P. *The Terrible Hours*. New York: Harper Collins; 1999.

U.S. Navy Diving Manual Rev. 6. Washington, DC: Supervisor of Diving, U.S. Navy, U.S. Government Printing Office; 2008.

www.cdc.gov. Centers for Disease Control and Prevention. Atlanta, GA; 2016.

www.divingheritage.com. Diving Heritage; 2013.

www.kirbymorgan.com/company/history. Kirby Morgan Dive Systems, Inc.; 2016.

INDEX

CPSIA information can be obtained
at www.ICGtesting.com
Printed in the USA
BVHW021826190223
658796BV00007B/776